D1205791

The Papers of Robert Morris

E. JAMES FERGUSON, EDITOR

JOHN CATANZARITI, ASSOCIATE EDITOR

MARY A. GALLAGHER, ASSISTANT EDITOR

CLARENCE L. VER STEEG, EDITORIAL

ADVISOR ∽ UNIVERSITY OF

PITTSBURGH PRESS ∽ 1975

The Papers of

ROBERT MORRIS
1781–1784

VOLUME 2: AUGUST–SEPTEMBER 1781

The editing of THE PAPERS OF ROBERT MORRIS is sponsored by the National
Historical Publications Commission and the Graduate School and University Center and Queens College of The City University of New York, under
grants from the National Endowment for the Humanities and the Donaldson, Lufkin & Jenrette Foundation of New York City. Publication is assisted
by the National Historical Publications Commission.

LIBRARY OF CONGRESS CATALOGING
IN PUBLICATION DATA

Morris, Robert, 1734–1806.
  The papers of Robert Morris, 1781–1784.

  Includes bibliographical references.
  CONTENTS: v. 1. February 7–July 31, 1781.—
v. 2. August–September 1781.
    1. Morris, Robert, 1734–1806. 2. United States—
History—Revolution, 1775–1783—Sources. I. Ferguson,
Elmer James, ed. II. Title.
E302.6.M8A25 1973   973.3'092'4 [B]   72–91107
ISBN 0–8229–3297–0 (v. 2)

Title-page portrait of Robert Morris by Charles Willson Peale, ca. 1782

E
302
M82
1973

CONTENTS

ILLUSTRATIONS

EDITORIAL METHOD

Arrangement

This series will present the official Diary, correspondence, and other documents of Robert Morris during his administration as Superintendent of Finance and Agent of Marine, 1781–1784. The Diary, a daily record of transactions in the Office of Finance, provides the organizational basis of the series. Arranged in chronological sequence, Diary entries have been given a standardized form, each date appearing as a centered caption above the text of the entry. If the date of an entry is doubtful, it appears in square brackets. Following the Diary entry for each day are Morris's outgoing letters and other documents which he had a hand in or which originated in the Office of Finance, and incoming correspondence. However, when a letter received by Morris was answered the same day, it precedes the reply. Although this series is restricted to Morris's official papers, the editors may occasionally reproduce selections from his private and business correspondence which throw light on the management of the Office of Finance. Finally, enclosures other than letters to or from Morris are reproduced at the discretion of the editors.

Dating

The editors have placed the dateline at the head of each document, regardless of its place in the manuscript, and have supplied dates for documents in which they are partially or wholly missing. Such documents are placed according to the following rules:

1. When no day within a month can be assigned, the document is placed after all others in that month.

2. When no month is given, the document is placed at the end of the year.

3. When the year is missing and a probable one can be supplied,

---

This statement of editorial method has been revised in several details.

it is inserted in square brackets with a question mark and the document placed at the end of that year.

4. When a single year cannot be assigned, inclusive dates are conjectured within square brackets, and the document is placed following all others at the end of the first year.

5. Documents for which no date can be conjectured will be arranged under the heading "n.d." in the final volume of the series.

Punctuation

The editors have been guided by the following rules in rendering manuscript punctuation:

1. A period is placed at the end of every sentence. When the ending is uncertain, the original punctuation is retained.

2. When a precise mark of punctuation cannot be determined, modern usage is observed.

3. Passages made obscure or unintelligible by casual or incorrect punctuation are silently corrected. Where more than one meaning may be derived from such a passage, its original punctuation is retained and an explanatory note attached.

4. Passages lacking punctuation are supplied with minimum punctuation.

5. When used in place of periods, commas, semicolons, or question marks, dashes are replaced by the appropriate mark of punctuation. Dashes and commas randomly distributed in the manuscripts are silently removed.

Spelling

The original spelling in the manuscripts has been preserved, subject to the following exceptions:

1. Proper names are always left unchanged in the text of a document but are presented correctly in all editorial material.

2. When the misspelling of a proper name is so unclear as to be misleading, the correct spelling is placed in square brackets immediately following it or in a footnote. In all other cases the correct spelling is placed in the text and a note is subjoined.

3. Slips of the pen and typographical errors are silently corrected, but in doubtful cases the editors provide an explanatory note.

Capitalization

Manuscript capitalization is retained with the following exceptions:

1. The first word of every sentence is capitalized.

2. Names of persons, their titles, geographical places, and days of the week and names of the month are capitalized regardless of the usage in the manuscript.

3. In doubtful cases, modern usage is followed.

Abbreviations and Contractions

Abbreviations and contractions are normally expanded. The following textual marks deserve special note:

1. The ampersand is expanded to "and," but is retained in the forms "&c." and "&ca.," in the names of business firms, and in financial accounts.

2. The thorn is expanded to "th."

3. The tilde is replaced by the letter(s) it represents. Example: "recv̄d" is expanded to "received."

4. The 🜚 sign is expanded to the appropriate letters it depicts (e.g., per, pre, and pro) in correspondence and dairy entries, but is retained in tabular financial accounts.

5. Marks indicating repetition are replaced by "ditto," "do.," or the word(s) they represent.

In the following cases abbreviations and contractions are presented as they occur in the manuscript:

1. In the names of persons and titles, places, and days of the week and names of the months. If the abbreviated form of a proper noun is obscure, the expansion is entered in square brackets immediately following it.

2. In units of weight and measure, and monetary designations.

3. In words in which the apostrophe is used to indicate missing letters. Examples: "pray'd," "cou'd," and "tho'."

4. In any other abbreviations and contractions that remain in modern usage.

In all cases, superscript letters are brought down to the line.

Indecipherable Passages

In every case the editors have attempted to conjecture letters, words, and digits which are missing, illegible, or mutilated. Their procedure is as follows:

1. Where the conjectural material amounts to no more than four letters, it is inserted silently if there is no question what the word is.

2. Where such material amounts to more than four letters, and the letters are conjecturable, it is inserted in the text in square

brackets. Example: "[Penns]ylvania." If the editors' conjecture is uncertain, it is followed by a question mark enclosed within the brackets. Material supplied by the editors from a text other than the one printed is also inserted in square brackets.

3. Passages which are not conjecturable are indicated by the editorial insertion of an italicized explanatory phrase in square brackets, such as [*illegible*] or [*torn*].

4. Missing or illegible digits are indicated by suspension points, their number corresponding to the estimated number of such digits, as in "£[. .]0.10.2."

5. A blank left in the manuscript by the author is so depicted and the fact mentioned in a footnote.

Revisions in Manuscripts

1. Interlineations in the text and brief additions in the margin are incorporated silently in the text in the place indicated by the writer. Substantial marginal additions are also placed in the text at the appropriate point, either with the editorial insertion [*in the margin*] before and after them or with editorial comment suitable to the passage.

2. Scored-out passages, in general, are ignored. When an excision is significant, the deleted passage is either placed in the text in angle brackets ⟨⟩ before the words substituted or is presented in a footnote.

3. When their importance warrants it, variant readings derived from the collation of several texts of a document with the basic or master text are entered in footnotes.

Reproduction of Italicized Material

Proper names, nouns, and passages italicized in printed documents, as was the eighteenth-century fashion, are reproduced in roman type. This rule does not apply to words or passages which, in the judgment of the editors, the writer wished to emphasize by using italics.

Ciphers and Translations

Ciphers, which Morris sometimes employed in correspondence with American representatives abroad and on rare occasions in domestic communications, are discussed in editorial notes to the documents written in that medium. When presenting documents written in a foreign language, the editors have supplied translations in editorial notes.

A Note on the Text of the Diary

The text of the Diary kept in the Office of Finance by Morris and, on occasion, by Gouverneur Morris consists of three manuscript volumes in the writing of clerks. To deal with the special problems it poses, the editors have adopted the following procedures.

1. When listing Morris's outgoing correspondence, the Diary very often gives the volume and page of the Official Letterbook in which the letters were copied. Such references have been silently deleted.

2. The manuscript of the Diary is also characterized by the extensive use of "ditto," "do.," and appropriate marks to represent these abbreviations. For the sake of readability the editors have in many instances substituted for such abbreviations the words they were intended to replace. In doubtful cases, either the manuscript usage is retained or a note is subjoined.

EDITORIAL APPARATUS

Classification of Manuscripts

When a document is represented by two or more manuscripts, the editors have selected the most authoritative for publication and listed each in the order of descending authority in the source identification note which, with the exception of Diary entries, follows each document.

Descriptive Symbols for Manuscripts

AD	Autograph Document
ADS	Autograph Document Signed
ADft	Autograph Draft
ADftS	Autograph Draft Signed
AL	Autograph Letter
ALS	Autograph Letter Signed
AM LbC	Agent of Marine Letterbook Copy
D	Document
DS	Document Signed
Dft	Draft
DftS	Draft Signed
Diary	Diary in the Office of Finance, Robert Morris Papers, Library of Congress
LS	Letter Signed
LbC	Letterbook Copy
MS, MSS	Manuscript, Manuscripts
Ofcl LbC	Official Letterbook Copy of the Office of Finance, Robert Morris Papers, Library of Congress

Other Abbreviations

PCC	Papers of the Continental Congress, 1774–1789, Record Group 360, National Archives
RG	Record Group

WDC   War Department Collection of Revolutionary War Records, Record Group 93, National Archives

Location Symbols

These symbols, used in the National Union Catalog of the Library of Congress, and derived from a list published by the Library, denote institutions in which manuscripts described in this volume have been found. Each volume of this series will contain a revised table.

CSmH	Henry E. Huntington Library, San Marino, California
Ct	Connecticut State Library, Hartford
CtHi	Connecticut Historical Society, Hartford
DLC	Library of Congress, Washington, D. C.
DNA	National Archives, Washington, D. C.
De-Ar	Delaware Public Archives Commission, Dover
InU	Indiana University Library, Bloomington
M-Ar	Massachusetts Archives, Office of the Secretary of State, Boston
MB	Boston Public Library
MH	Harvard University Library, Cambridge, Massachusetts
MHi	Massachusetts Historical Society, Boston
MdAA	Maryland Hall of Records, Annapolis
MdAN	United States Naval Academy Museum, Annapolis
MdBJ-G	John Work Garrett Library, Johns Hopkins University, Baltimore
MdHi	Maryland Historical Society, Baltimore
MiU-C	William L. Clements Library, University of Michigan, Ann Arbor
N	New York State Library, Albany
NHi	New-York Historical Society, New York City
NHpR	Franklin D. Roosevelt Library, Hyde Park, New York
NN	New York Public Library, New York City
NNC	Columbia University Library, New York City
Nc-Ar	North Carolina Department of Archives and History, Raleigh
Nh-Ar	New Hampshire Division of Records Management and Archives, Concord
NjP	Princeton University Library, Princeton, New Jersey
PHarH	Pennsylvania Historical and Museum Commission, Harrisburg

PHi   Historical Society of Pennsylvania, Philadelphia
PPAmP   American Philosophical Society, Philadelphia
PU   University of Pennsylvania Library, Philadelphia
RNHi   Newport Historical Society, Newport, Rhode Island
RPJCB   John Carter Brown Library, Providence, Rhode Island
Vi   Virginia State Library, Richmond

The following symbols are used to identify repositories outside of the United States:

AGI   Archivo General de Indias, Seville
AMAE   Archives du Ministère des Affaires Étrangères, Paris

Annotation

While the editors believe that no purpose would be served by an extended discussion of the nature and extent of this form of editorial contribution, they wish to comment on three procedures followed in this series:

1. Individuals mentioned in the text of documents who are of sufficient historical importance to be listed in standard reference works usually have been sparingly identified in footnotes, except insofar as their activities are relevant to the exposition of the text. Obscure individuals have been described, when possible, at greater length.

2. Whenever the date of a resolution, order, ordinance, report, or other action of Congress is stated in the text of a footnote, the editors have not supplied a citation to the *Journals of the Continental Congress,* which is cited fully in the table of Short Titles below.

3. In cross-references to dates of other documents published in this series, the year is omitted when those documents appear in the same volume and belong in the same year.

Short Titles

This list of frequently cited titles will be revised as future volumes in the series appear.

Acts and Laws of Massachusetts
    Acts and Laws of the Commonwealth of Massachusetts [1780–1805] (Boston, 1890–1898)
Balch, *French in America*
    Thomas Balch, *The French in America during the War of Independence*

of the United States, 1777–1783, trans. Thomas Willing Balch, Edwin Swift Balch, and Elise Willing Balch (Philadelphia, 1891–1895)

Biog. Dir. Cong.
   Biographical Directory of the American Congress, 1774–1961 (Washington, 1961)

Bosher, *French Finances*
   J. F. Bosher, *French Finances, 1770–1795: From Business to Bureaucracy* (Cambridge, 1970)

Boyd, ed., *Jefferson Papers*
   Julian P. Boyd *et al.,* eds., *The Papers of Thomas Jefferson* (Princeton, 1950–)

Brunhouse, *Counter-Revolution in Pennsylvania*
   Robert L. Brunhouse, *The Counter-Revolution in Pennsylvania, 1776–1790* (Harrisburg, 1942)

Burnett, ed., *Letters*
   Edmund Cody Burnett, ed., *Letters of Members of the Continental Congress* (Washington, 1921–1936)

Butterfield, ed., *Adams Diary and Autobiography*
   Lyman H. Butterfield *et al.,* eds., *Diary and Autobiography of John Adams* (Cambridge, Mass., 1961)

Butterfield, ed., *Rush Letters*
   Lyman H. Butterfield, ed., *Letters of Benjamin Rush* (Princeton, 1951)

Campbell, *Sons of St. Patrick*
   John H. Campbell, *History of the Friendly Sons of St. Patrick and of the Hibernian Society for the Relief of Emigrants from Ireland* (Philadelphia, 1892)

Clark and Morgan, eds., *Naval Documents*
   William Bell Clark and William James Morgan, eds., *Naval Documents of the American Revolution* (Washington, 1964–)

Clowes, *Royal Navy*
   William Laird Clowes, *The Royal Navy: A History from the Earliest Times to the Present* (London, 1897–1903)

Colonial Records of Pennsylvania
   Colonial Records of Pennsylvania, 1683–1790 (Harrisburg, 1851–1853)

Contenson, *Société des Cincinnati*
   Ludovic de Contenson, *La Société des Cincinnati de France et la guerre d'Amérique, 1778–1783* (Paris, 1934)

DAB
   Allen Johnson, Dumas Malone *et al.,* eds., *Dictionary of American Biography* (New York, 1928–1958)

Deane Papers
   The Deane Papers (New-York Historical Society, *Collections,*
   XIX–XXIII [New York, 1887–1891])
Dict. Amer. Naval Ships
   Dictionary of American Naval Fighting Ships (Washington, 1959–)
DNB
   Leslie Stephen, Sidney Lee *et al.,* eds., *The Dictionary of National
   Biography* (London, 1885–1959)
East, *Business Enterprise*
   Robert A. East, *Business Enterprise in the American Revolutionary
   Era* (New York, 1938)
Ferguson, *Power of the Purse*
   E. James Ferguson, *The Power of the Purse: A History of American
   Public Finance, 1776–1790* (Chapel Hill, N. C., 1961)
Fitzpatrick, ed., *Washington Diaries*
   John C. Fitzpatrick, ed., *The Diaries of George Washington, 1748–
   1799* (Boston and New York, 1925)
Fitzpatrick, ed., *Writings of Washington*
   John C. Fitzpatrick, ed., *The Writings of George Washington from
   the Original Manuscript Sources, 1745–1799* (Washington, 1931–
   1944)
Freeman, *Washington*
   Douglas Southall Freeman *et al., George Washington: A Biography*
   (New York, 1948–1957)
Gardiner, *Order of the Cincinnati*
   Asa Bird Gardiner, *The Order of the Cincinnati in France* ([New-
   port, R. I.?], 1905)
Hastings and Holden, eds., *Clinton Papers*
   Hugh Hastings and J. A. Holden, eds., *Public Papers of George
   Clinton, First Governor of New York, 1775–1795, 1801–1804* (New
   York and Albany, 1899–1914)
Heath Papers
   The Heath Papers (Massachusetts Historical Society, *Collections,*
   5th ser., IV, 7th ser., IV–V [Boston, 1878, 1904–1905])
Heitman, *Register*
   Francis B. Heitman, *Historical Register of Officers of the Continental
   Army during the War of the Revolution, April, 1775, to December,
   1783,* new ed. (Washington, 1914)
Hoefer, ed., *Nouvelle biographie générale*
   J. C. F. Hoefer, ed., *Nouvelle biographie générale depuis les temps les
   plus reculés jusqu'à nos jours* (Paris, 1852–1866)
Hutchinson and Rutland, eds., *Madison Papers*
   William T. Hutchinson, Robert A. Rutland, William M. E. Ra-

chal *et al.*, eds., *The Papers of James Madison* (Chicago, 1962–)

JCC; Journals
   Worthington C. Ford *et al.*, eds., *Journals of the Continental Congress, 1774–1789* (Washington, 1904–1937)

Journals of the House of Representatives of Pennsylvania, 1776–1781
   Journals of the House of Representatives of the Commonwealth of Pennsylvania. Beginning the twenty-eighth Day of November, 1776, and Ending the Second Day of October, 1781 (Philadelphia, 1782)

Lewis, *Bank of North America*
   Lawrence Lewis, *A History of the Bank of North America* (Philadelphia, 1882)

Maryland Archives
   W. H. Browne *et al.*, eds., *Archives of Maryland* (Baltimore, 1883–1956)

Mitchell and Flanders, eds., *Statutes of Pennsylvania*
   James T. Mitchell and Henry Flanders, eds., *The Statutes at Large of Pennsylvania from 1682 to 1801* (Harrisburg, 1896–1911)

Morison, *John Paul Jones*
   Samuel Eliot Morison, *John Paul Jones: A Sailor's Biography* (Boston, 1959)

N.-Y. Hist. Soc., *Colls.*
   New-York Historical Society, *Collections*

Oberholtzer, *Morris*
   Ellis Paxson Oberholtzer, *Robert Morris, Patriot and Financier* (New York, 1903)

OED
   The Oxford English Dictionary (Oxford, 1933)

Paullin, *Navy of the American Revolution*
   Charles Oscar Paullin, *The Navy of the American Revolution: Its Administration, Its Policy, and Its Achievements* (Chicago, 1906)

Paullin, ed., *Out-Letters*
   Charles Oscar Paullin, ed., *Out-Letters of the Continental Marine Committee and Board of Admiralty, August, 1776–September, 1780* (New York, 1914)

Pennsylvania Archives
   Samuel Hazard *et al.*, eds., *Pennsylvania Archives: Selected and Arranged from Original Documents in the Office of the Secretary of the Commonwealth* (Philadelphia and Harrisburg, 1852–1935)

PMHB
   Pennsylvania Magazine of History and Biography

Reynolds and Faunt, comps., *Biog. Dir. S. C. Senate*
   Emily B. Reynolds and Joan R. Faunt, comps., *Biographical Directory of the Senate of the State of South Carolina, 1776–1964* (Columbia, 1964)

Sanders, *Executive Departments*
> Jennings B. Sanders, *Evolution of Executive Departments of the Continental Congress, 1774–1789* (Chapel Hill, N. C., 1935)

Saunders and Clark, eds., *State Records of North Carolina*
> William L. Saunders and Walter L. Clark, eds., *The State Records of North Carolina* (Raleigh, Winston, and Goldsboro, 1886–1906)

S. C. Hist. and Gen. Mag.
> *South Carolina Historical and Genealogical Magazine*

Sibley-Shipton, *Harvard Graduates*
> John Langdon Sibley and Clifford K. Shipton, *Biographical Sketches of Graduates of Harvard University, in Cambridge, Massachusetts* (Cambridge, Mass., and Boston, 1873–)

Syrett and Cooke, eds., *Hamilton Papers*
> Harold C. Syrett, Jacob E. Cooke *et al.*, eds., *The Papers of Alexander Hamilton* (New York, 1961–)

Ver Steeg, *Morris*
> Clarence L. Ver Steeg, *Robert Morris, Revolutionary Financier, with an Analysis of his Earlier Career* (Philadelphia, 1954)

Ward, *War of the Revolution*
> Christopher Ward, *The War of the Revolution,* ed. John R. Alden (New York, 1952)

Wharton, ed., *Rev. Dipl. Corr.*
> Francis Wharton, ed., *The Revolutionary Diplomatic Correspondence of the United States* (Washington, 1889)

EDITORS' ACKNOWLEDGMENTS

The editors welcome this opportunity to thank those who continue to make this series possible. They are grateful to the National Endowment for the Humanities, without whose support these volumes could not appear, for continuing and expanding its funding of the project. The foundation established by Donaldson, Lufkin & Jenrette, Inc., of New York City, which has contributed financial assistance since the project's inception, continues to be a benefactor of the Morris Papers. Thanks must go in particular to the firm's Executive Vice-President, Richard M. Hexter, for his dedication to the project. For its continuing sponsorship and encouragement the editors are indebted to the National Historical Publications Commission, especially its Executive Director, E. Berkeley Tompkins, and his staff, including Fred Shelley, Roger A. Bruns, and John D. Macoll.

The Graduate School and University Center of The City University of New York has provided the physical plant and services so necessary to the daily well-being of the project and its staff. Its past President, Mina Rees, and its current President, Harold M. Proshansky, have provided vital assistance to the operation of the project and lent encouragment at important times. Virginia P. White, Director of the Office of Sponsored Research and Program Funding, has been indispensable in securing the project's long-term financial support. Associate Dean of Administration J. Marilyn Mikulsky, her executive assistant, Janet Rogers, and their staff in the Office of Campus Planning always have been available to aid the Morris Papers. The editors also take pleasure in acknowledging the enthusiastic and knowledgeable services rendered by the staff of the Graduate School Library, especially Professors Margaret K. Rowell and Claire D. Bowie, and Carol B. Varela, Priscilla M. Pereira, and Helga Feder.

Other units of the City University have been generous in their support. The Queens College Office of Grants and Contracts has conferred supplementary financial sustenance essential to the project. The libraries of the senior colleges of the university, especially that of Queens College, have shared their resources with us. Finally, Gerald Graze, Executive Director of The Research Foundation of The City University of New York, which administers the project's funds, and his staff have helped to shoulder the day-to-day administrative details of the Morris Papers.

The appearance of this volume necessarily calls to mind the contributions of former and present members of the staff. In particular the editors have benefited from the assistance of Bernice Krader, former secretary and transcriber, Elizabeth M. Nuxoll, former assistant editor, Arthur E. Scherr and Henry Gabler, research assistants, and Francine A. Moskowitz and Nelson S. Dearmont, whose labors as assistant editors will be reflected more fully in future volumes. Professor Robert W. Hartle of the Department of Romance Languages, Queens College, has obligingly consented to review the foreign language documents and translations which appear in this volume.

Without the neighboring resources of the New York Public Library (Astor, Lenox and Tilden Foundations), one of the world's greatest libraries, the research on which these volumes are based could not have been carried out in any practical way. It is with special gratitude that we express our thanks to its staff of reference librarians, especially John Miller, Leon Weidman, and Serge Corvington of the American History Division; Maud D. Cole, Lewis M. Stark, and Peter Rainey of the Division of Rare Books; Paul Rugen, Jean McNiece, and John D. Stinson of the Manuscript Division; and John P. Baker, Faye Simkin, and Walter Zervas of the Administration Office.

Nothing the editors could say about the assistance they have received from libraries and manuscript repositories here and abroad would indicate the extent of their obligations to these institutions and their staffs. Sara Dunlap Jackson, Archivist of the National Historical Publications Commission, has readily shared her knowledge of the Revolutionary War manuscripts in the National Archives. At the Library of Congress Paul G. Sifton, Specialist in Early American History in the Manuscript Division, continues to answer the editors' many requests. Nicholas B. Wainwright, Director, James E. Mooney, Assistant Director, and Peter J. Parker, Chief of Manuscripts, at the Historical Society of Pennsylvania graciously assisted us whenever the need arose. For its attention to their many questions, the editors are also indebted to the staff of the Massachusetts Historical Society. The Society's Director, Stephen T. Riley, its Librarian, John D. Cushing, and his staff, Winifred Collins,

Gertrude Fischer, and Andrew D. Ash, Jr., and its Editor of Publications, Malcolm Freiberg, have extended every courtesy to the editors. At the State House in Boston, Leo Flaherty, curator of the Massachusetts Archives, pursued our inquiries with his usual expertise. Robert A. Lauze, Director of the New Hampshire Division of Records Management and Archives in Concord, offered extraordinary aid in making available the documents under his supervision. The editors gratefully acknowledge the cooperation of Thomas J. Dunnings, Jr., Assistant Curator of Manuscripts at the New-York Historical Society; Alden Jones at the Columbia University Library; Doris E. Cook of the Connecticut Historical Society; Gladys E. Bolhouse of the Newport Historical Society; Constance Hershey, Curator of Independence National Historical Park; Nancy G. Boles, former Curator of Manuscripts at the Maryland Historical Society; Phebe R. Jacobsen of the Maryland Hall of Records; Harriet Mc-Loone of the Henry E. Huntington Library; Carolyn B. Milligan of the American Philosophical Society; and the staffs of the Pennsylvania Historical and Museum Commission and the Yale University Library. Abroad, J. Laloy of the Archives du Ministère des Affaires Étrangères in Paris and Rosario Parra Cala, Director of the Archivo General de Indias in Seville, have contributed greatly to the project by facilitating the editors' quest for documents.

Finally, the editors wish to thank those who have discovered additional Morris letters and made them available to the project. Mrs. Robert M. Snyder of New Castle, Delaware, generously sent the editors items from her family collection of papers of the Financier and his descendants and subsequently donated them to appropriate repositories. Others who have contributed valuable unpublished material are Harry Ackerman of Burbank, California; Ellen B. Wells of Cornell University Library's Department of Rare Books; F. Garner Ranney, Archivist of the Diocese of Maryland at the Maryland Historical Society; and Paul H. Johnson, Curator of the library at the United States Coast Guard Academy in New London, Connecticut.

The Papers of Robert Morris

VOLUME 2: AUGUST–SEPTEMBER 1781

Diary: August 1, 1781

Sent The Letters of Ephraim Blaine and Alexr Blain enclosed in my Note to the Board of War requesting that the Contracts for York and Carlisle be drawn.[1]

Dismissed the Application of Messrs. Haryls and Richmond as inadmissable because I cannot dispose of the public Money but by Authority of Congress, but promised my interference in favour of the Prisoners.[2]

1. The letters from Commissary General of Purchases Ephraim Blaine, ca. July 31, and Alexander Blaine, ca. July 30, 1781, and RM's note to the Board of War have not been found. The Office of Finance's advertisement for York contract proposals, dated July 16, appeared in the *Pennsylvania Packet* on July 17. For the contract negotiations, see Diary, July 30 and August 24, and RM to William Scott, August 25, 1781. The advertisement for Carlisle contract proposals has not been found.

2. The letter to Congress from Abraham Haryls, not further identified, and Ebenezer Richmond of Rhode Island, who had been a surgeon's mate in the 11th Continental infantry in 1776 (Heitman, *Register*), has not been found, but it probably concerned American marine prisoners confined in British prison ships in New York harbor. The communication was read on July 28 and referred to the Board of War. Its report, which has not been found, was received in Congress on July 30 and, together with the letter of Haryls and Richmond, was referred to RM "to take order." No response by the Financier other than that recorded in the Diary printed here has been ascertained, but immediately following its action of July 30, Congress appointed a committee headed by Elias Boudinot of New Jersey, former commissary general of prisoners, to consider and report on the treatment of American prisoners in enemy hands. Adopting the committee's partial report on August 3, Congress condemned the conditions under which American marine prisoners were incarcerated, instructed Washington to remonstrate with the British and to supply the prisoners with such provisions and clothing as he could obtain, and extended the life of its committee.

The Americans who were held aboard prison ships at New York were merchant seamen from commercial vessels or privateers. According to information received by Washington, they were deliberately abused in order to force them to enlist in the British marine. Under rules accepted by both the British and American governments, the United States was liable for the expense of their keep. Congress had no money for this purpose, and the British refused to release or exchange the men until the charges were paid. Since British merchant seamen captured by American vessels were held in confinement by the states, rather than by Continental commissaries, Congress had no British seamen with which to effectuate an exchange. Hence, there

was little prospect that the American prisoners at New York would gain their freedom.

At Congress's direction, Washington, on August 21, 1781, wrote to the commanding officer of the British fleet citing complaints of overcrowded conditions aboard
the prison ships and proposing that the American commissary general of prisoners
or some other officer be allowed to visit the ships and report. The commanding
officer of the British marine at New York, Edmund Affleck, replied on August 30,
saying that although sudden accumulations of prisoners might cause overcrowding,
every effort was made to thin the prison population and that conditions aboard ships
matched European standards. He agreed to permit an American officer to visit the
ships if a British representative were allowed to inspect the "Jails and Dungeons,"
as well as the mines, where British prisoners were confined by American authorities.
Washington sent Affleck's letter to Congress on September 4, and Congress authorized him the same day to proceed in the matter at his own discretion. No arrangements were made, however, before Congress, on February 18, 1782, directed
Washington to negotiate a general cartel which would include all prisoners of war.
American captives continued to languish in prison ships at New York, although on
July 24, 1782, Congress vested RM, as Agent of Marine, with authority to carry out
exchanges. Washington to the Officer Commanding His Britannic Majesty's Ships
of War, August 21, to the President of Congress, September 4, to the Comte de
Grasse, October 23, to the President of Congress, December 27, 1781, and to Tench
Tilghman, July 10, 1782, Fitzpatrick, ed., *Writings of Washington*, XXIII, 24–25, 83–84,
255–256, 407–409, XXIV, 423; Edmund Affleck to Washington, August 30, 1781,
Washington Papers, DLC.

To the Board of War

[*Philadelphia, August 1, 1781.* On this date RM recorded in his
Diary a memorandum of a "Note to the Board of War requesting
that the Contracts for York and Carlisle be drawn." For the letters
enclosed in this communication, see the notes to Diary, August 1.
Letter not found.]

From John Jay

Madrid 1 Augt. 1781

Dear Sir

I thank you for your favor of the 5th. June which with the Duplicate, and Papers accompanying them I had the honor of receiving
from the Minister.[1] By the first good Opportunity I shall have the
Pleasure of replying to it particularly.

Be so obliging as to send the enclosed Letter for my Father [2] to
the Post Office, unless a good private Opportunity should offer.
Dont trouble Sr James [3] with it; I believe his Correspondence with
Fish Kill is not very regular.

Tell Caty [4] that my answer to her Letter will evidence my attention to it. Assure Mrs. Morris of our sincere Regard and Esteem.
I am Dear Sir with great Truth Your Friend and Servant

P.S. If Gour.[5] should be with you remember me affectionately to him. I have written to Congress.[6]

R. Morris

MS: ADft, Jay Papers, NNC.
1. Probably Conde de Floridablanca, Spanish Secretary of State for Foreign Affairs.
2. Jay to his father, August 1, 1781, Henry P. Johnston, ed., *The Correspondence and Public Papers of John Jay* (New York, 1890–1893), II, 59–60.
3. Sir James Jay, John's brother.
4. Catherine Livingston, Mrs. Sarah Jay's sister.
5. Gouverneur Morris.
6. Jay probably refers to his letters to Congress of April 25 and May 29, 1781; see Wharton, ed., *Rev. Dipl. Corr.*, IV, 384–389, 459–460.

Diary: August 2, 1781

Compleated the Contract with Mathias Slough Esqr. of Lancaster for Supplying the Post at Reading &Ca.[1]

Wrote Colo. Jacob Morgan respecting the delivery of Scales, Weights &Ca to Mr Slough.[2]

Wrote a Letter to His Excellency the Minister of France relative to Sale of Bills of Exchange, Supplies of the French Army, Navy &Ca.

A Letter from Capt. Jno. P. Jones to His Excelly. the President of Congress, having been referred to me to take order I agreed to advance him £400 hard Money for which he is to be accountable, rather than pay him that Sum, out of the Arrearages of his pay, for as I have no Funds that can properly be applied to the payment of Old Debts, I think it most consistent to let his Claims be settled as others of the same kind are to be settled.[3]

1. Contract not found. The Office of Finance's advertisement for Reading contract proposals, dated July 14, appeared in the *Pennsylvania Packet* on July 17. RM opened the bids on July 30, found Slough's to be "the lowest and most convenient," conferred with him, and then ordered the Board of War to draft the contract. See Diary, July 10, 16, and 30, 1781.
2. Letter not found. Morgan was superintendent of the Pennsylvania county commissioners of purchases.
3. While preparing to depart for Portsmouth, New Hampshire, to assume command of the Continental ship-of-the-line *America* under construction there, Jones had applied to RM for money to pay his debts in Philadelphia and to defray expenses of his journey. The Financier refused his request but suggested that Jones "exhibit his accounts to the Board of Admiralty for a Settlement previous to his Departure." Referred by the board to Congress, Jones thereupon petitioned for back pay and reimbursement for expenses incurred during prior service. Congress received his request on July 18 and on July 25 approved his statement of accounts and referred them to the Board of Treasury. Since Jones, like other claimants for payment of past debts, had to wait his turn until funds became available, he addressed Congress in

a letter of July 28, which has not been found, apparently requesting an advance of £400 chargeable against the sums credited to him. The letter was referred to RM, who (as this Diary entry indicates) was now willing to make the money available as an advance, although not as a partial payment of sums due on past accounts. It was not until December 9, 1782, that Jones collected $20,705 in full discharge of his claims. Jones's petition to Congress, July 17, 1781, PCC, no. 41, IV, 418; Morison, *John Paul Jones*, 316–317; Diary, August 3, and RM to Jones, August 4.

To Chevalier de La Luzerne

Philada. 2d. August 1781

Sir

Agreably to the intimations I made to your Excelly some days ago,[1] it was my intention to have gone to Camp yesterday, but an Act of Congress, of the   [2] day of July, rendered it necessary for me, to hold a Conference with a Committee of Congress and the Board of War. This was done and it was determined that a Member of the Board of War should go with me to Camp.[3] This circumstance has postponed my journey for a few days, but this is not all. The daily demands on me for Money are considerable, and beyond the utmost extent of any Funds I can command. The demands for past dues, in compensation for past services, and the like are rejected,[4] but those for the prosecution of the Campaigne must be attended to. If in my absence, and from that cause, there be any stoppage or considerable delay, the Consequences will be equally injurious to my reputation and to the Public Service. I have before mentioned to you that my dependance for immediate supplies of Money is on the produce of Bills of Exchange.[5] I am sorry, now, to observe that this dependance fails, and from a cause equally prejudicial to France and to the United States, considered in Collective Capacity, tho' perhaps advantageous to Individuals.

Your Excelly will remember, that when I was called to the Administration the Bills of your Army had been selling for two thirds, and even so low as for one half of their Value in Europe; what might have been the causes of this, it is not my business to enquire; the fact is incontestable. You observed it and endeavoured to remedy the evil by holding your own bills at five sixths; but the Merchants who had benefited by the former low rate, could not be brought at once to make so considerable an advance. They expected that the same causes which had reduced bills to one half, must again bring them down, and therefore were disposed to wait the event. I take the liberty here to observe, that the fluctuation of Exchange will naturally strengthen that expectation, and nothing but steady, firm perseverance on the part of Administration can, or indeed ought, to produce ready Sale on good terms. Bills of Exchange are remitted to France in payment for European Commodities. If the cost of this remittance is fixed, Commerce may so far be established on true commercial principles; otherwise it is a meer game of Hazard. Sensible of this, the Merchant will rather wait, his money in his Chest, the event of Public Necessity, than invest that Money in bills, which may shortly after be bought on better terms by his more cautious Neighbour. Hence it follows; that the Public will really command less Money than they otherwise might; nor is that all. While the Public can command the Money of the Merchants, as fast as it comes into their hands, the Servants of the Public can spend that Money to advantage and the very expenditure will increase the Circulation so as to bring it again sooner into the hands of the Merchant.

Your good Sense Sir, your experience and the unremitted attention which I have perceived you pay to every object which can relate to the Service of Your Sovereign, will render it unnecessary for me to prosecute any farther these observations.

It was from a knowledge of this subject, which many [6] years constant attention to this business had imparted that I saw the necessity of raising the Value of Bills by degrees and at the same time of opposing the most inflexible Firmness to every attempt at lowering their Price. The bills I drew on Messrs. Le Couteulx & Co [7] at sixty days sight were selling readily at four fifths until the Bills for your Army were offered at thirty days sight and at a lower rate. This Sir, has checked my sales and this induces me to mention to you another matter which will I foresee become of great importance. The Concurrence of many Venders of Bills cannot be more pernicious than the Concurrence of many purchasers of Supplies. The Merchant cannot reason more effectually on Public necessities which he must conjecture, than the Husbandman, on such wants as he has occular demonstration of. Melancholy experience has shewn, that the Contests between our purchasers has been extremely pernicious. What may have been the manner of conducting the business by the Agents of the King I do not positively know, but if I were to credit many Tales which I have heard about it, I should believe there had been errors at least, but I know too well the weakness and impropriety of listening to slanderous reports and I am very Confident that all possible care will be taken of His Majestys Interests. But Sir, if the supplies for the French Army and Navy are kept in a distinct channel I do not believe it will be possible to obtain them so cheap as they might otherwise be had.[8] The Ration consisting of one pound of bread, one pound of Beef or three quarters of a pound of Pork, one Gill of Country made Rum, and to every hundred Rations one quart of Salt and two Quarts of Vinegar, also to every 700 Rations Eight pound of Soap and three pound of Candles is now furnished at 9d with $1/_2$d allowed over for Issueing.[9] It may probably cost more to furnish Rations to the Army, perhaps as high as ten or Eleven pence Pensylva Currency.

You I suppose Sir can command the necessary Accounts to determine what the King now pays for the Subsistence of his Troops but as the French and American Ration differ I take the liberty for your further information to mention that the parts of a Ration are estimated as follows: for one pound of bread, two Ninetieths of a Dollar; for one pound of Beef or $3/_4$ lb. of Pork, four and one quarter Ninetieths; for one Gill of Rum, two Ninetieths; for Candles, Soap, Vinegar and Salt, one and a quarter Ninetieths of a Dollar for each Ration.[10] You will also observe that when Exchange is at four fifths, one Livre Tournois is equal to fourteen pence and two fifths of a penny Pensylvania Currency. I go into these details to enable your Excelly exactly to determine what is most for the interest of France, for I conceive it my Duty to give you a confidential State of our affairs whenever it can promote his Majestys Service which I beg leave to assure you, that I have every possible desire to assist being convinced that I can by no other means more fully comply with the wishes of the United States in Congress Assembled.

I beg leave further to observe that I have no personal wish to negotiate your Bills or to supply your Fleets and Armies; you must be very Sensible that I have already before me a Field of business sufficiently large. To extend it, will give me labor and Pain. I can derive no advantage from it nor will any thing induce me to engage in it except it be the prospect of rendering effectual Service to the Common Cause. I make this declaration not because I conceive it necessary to you, or from an ostentatious display of those Motives which actuate my Conduct, but there may be Persons to whom I am not so well known as I have the honor of being to your Excellency and who from Ignorance or interest might give to the purest intentions the foulest interpretation. I have been led much farther Sir than the occasion strictly required, but perhaps my observations may demand your attention; they certainly appear to me of Importance or I would not have given you the trouble of so long a letter.[11] I pray you to believe, that with every Sentiment of esteem and respect I have the honor to be Your Excellency's Most Obedient and Most humble Servant

Robt Morris

His Excelly The Chevr. De La Luzerne
Minister Plenipotentiary of France &c &c

MSS: ALS, Correspondance politique, supplément, Etats-Unis, AMAE; Ofcl LbC, DLC; copy, Bache Collection, PPAmP.

1. RM refers to his conference with La Luzerne on July 28, 1781. See Diary of that date.

2. Space left blank in manuscript.

3. On this conference and its results, see Diary, July 31, 1781, and notes. For RM's record of his visit to Washington's headquarters, see Diary, August 21.

4. As, for example, the claims of John Paul Jones. See Diary, August 2, and notes.

5. RM, like the officers of the French army in America, raised cash in the United States by selling bills of exchange on France. For his earlier comments on the sale of bills of exchange, see RM to Barbé-Marbois, July 4, 1781; for his subsequent efforts to arrange for the joint sale of bills with the French, see La Luzerne to RM, August 3, RM to La Luzerne, August 4 and September 25, Gouverneur Morris to RM, August 8, and Diary, August 3, 7, 8, 9, 10, 11, 21, and September 1–5.

6. PPAmP copy: "20."

7. RM's banker in Paris.

8. Here RM introduces his proposal for supplying the French as well as the American forces by contract. See Diary, August 21, and notes.

9. On the composition and money value of a ration, see the advertisements for Philadelphia and Lancaster contract proposals, June 30, for Reading and Fort Pitt, July 14, for York, July 16, and for Wyoming, September 12, Diary, July 16, RM to Washington, July 23, and RM's contract with Comfort, Richardson, and Joshua Sands, December 6, 1781, for West Point and its dependencies.

10. Most of these itemized money values varied slightly from those stated in RM's contract with Comfort, Richardson, and Joshua Sands, December 6, 1781, for West Point and its dependencies.

11. La Luzerne sent Rochambeau a copy of this letter and RM's letter of August 4 (see Diary, August 21). A copy of this letter was also enclosed in RM to Benjamin Franklin, November 27, 1781 (first letter).

To Jacob Morgan, Jr.

[*Philadelphia, August 2, 1781.* RM entered the following note in his Diary of this date: "Wrote Colo. Jacob Morgan respecting the delivery of Scales, Weights &Ca to Mr Slough." *Letter not found.*]

Contract with Mathias Slough

[*Philadelphia, August 2, 1781.* On this date RM made the following memorandum in his Diary: "Compleated the Contract with Mathias Slough Esqr. of Lancaster for Supplying the Post at Reading &Ca." *Contract not found.*]

From George Washington

Head Quarters Dobbs's Ferry [New York] 2d. Augt. 1781.[1]
Dear Sir

I have been honored with yours of the 23d. ultimo. I take the earliest opportunity of informing you that our whole dependence for Flour is upon you. The State of New York it is said has a considerable quantity yet within it, but so exhausted are the resources of the Legislature that they can command none of it. New Jersey has not either passed laws to draw forth the specific supplies demanded of her, or those laws are not executed, but the fact is, that we obtain nothing. I do not exactly know what Number of the three thousand Barrels which Mr. Lowrey is to purchase have been delivered.[2] I beleive not quite half. He has sent in none lately and the Army is this day without Bread. Expresses are gone to him requesting him to hurry forward the remainder which will not be more than 25 days supply at our present consumption which ought to increase considerably in a very short time; The militia and Levies being daily expected. Thus you see the absolute necessity which there will be of your immediately extending your orders.

I perfectly understood your letter in which you mentioned the good effects which would arise from disposing of provisions at a distance and purchasing near the Army.[3] I only meant to acquaint you of what I supposed you might be ignorant. That the provision actually provided by the States and deposited in Magazines was comparatively small. If the States will pay the Balance due from them into your hands, it is evident that there will be a vast saving, by expending the Money in the way of Contract.

I am much obliged by your remittance of the draft upon Richards and Company for 2500 dollars specie,[4] which I will have negotiated as early as possible, and by your undertaking to enable Genl. Schuyler to comply with his Contract for building Boats.[5]

MSS: Dft in the writing of Tench Tilghman, Washington Papers, DLC; Varick transcript, Washington Papers, DLC.

1. For the textual relationship of Washington's two communications to RM of this date, see notes to the second letter.

2. RM first authorized Thomas Lowrey to purchase 1,000 barrels of flour for Washington's army on May 29 and subsequently increased the total to 3,000 barrels. See RM to Washington, July 23, 1781.

3. RM's letter was dated July 5, 1781. See also Washington to RM, July 13, and RM to Washington, July 23, 1781.

4. This money was sent for Washington's personal subsistence. See RM to Washington, July 23 and September 13, 1781.

5. For RM's assistance to Major General Philip Schuyler, see RM to Schuyler, July 21, 1781.

From George Washington

[Headquarters, Dobbs Ferry, New York, August 2, 1781][1]

The expectation of the pleasure of seeing you has prevented me hitherto from making a communication of a most important and interesting nature.[2] But circumstances will not admit of further delay, and I must trust it to paper. It seems reduced almost to a certainty, that the enemy will reinforce New York with part of their troops from Virginia. In that case the attempt against the former must be laid aside, as it will not be in our power to draw together a force sufficient to justify the undertaking. The detachment which the enemy will probably leave in Virginia seems the next object which ought to engage our attention, and which will be a very practicable one, should we obtain a naval superiority, of which I am not without hopes, and be able to carry a Body of Men suddenly round by Water. The principal difficulty which occurs, is obtaining transports at the moment they may be wanted: for if they are taken up beforehand, the use for which they are designed cannot be concealed, and the enemy will make arrangements to defeat the plan. What I would therefore wish you to inform yourself of, without making a direct enquiry, is what number of Tons of shipping could be obtained in Philada. at any time between this and the 20th. of this month and whether there could also be obtained at the same time a few deep waisted sloops and schooners proper to carry Horses. The number of double decked Vessels which may be wanted, of 200 Tons and upwards, will not exceed thirty. I shall be glad of your answer as soon as possible, because if it is favorable, I can direct certain preparations to be made in Philada. and at other convenient places, without incurring any suspicions. There certainly can be no danger of not obtaining Flour in Philada. and as you seem to have doubts of procuring salt Meat there, I shall direct all that which is to the Eastward to be collected at points, from whence it may be shipped upon the shortest notice.

You will also oblige me by giving me your opinion of the number of Vessels which might be obtained at Baltimore or other places in Chesapeak in the time before mentioned or thereabouts.[3] I have the honor to be &c

Honbl. Robt Morris Esqr.

mss: Dft in the writing of Tench Tilghman, Washington Papers, DLC; Varick transcript, Washington Papers, DLC.

1. This and the preceding letter from Washington were originally drafted as a single communication. Because the last part of it (i.e. this second letter) contained intelligence about the intended movement of Washington's army southward, it was bracketed and marked thus by his aide, Tench Tilghman: "the following in a separate letter marked (private)."

2. Washington's mind was divided between pressing the allied attack on New York City with the possible help of de Grasse's fleet, recently arrived in the West Indies but its destination on the coast of North America still uncertain, and the possibility of transferring operations to Virginia, which was being harrassed almost at will by

the enemy. As this letter indicates, the latter alternative now held more promise because Washington believed that General Henry Clinton would summon part of Lord Cornwallis's forces to New York (an order actually issued but later rescinded) to assist in the defense of the city, thus rendering an American assault impracticable but leaving weakened British forces in Virginia. Besides the letter to RM printed here, Washington recorded in his diary on August 1 that he also "sent to make inquiry, indirectly," of New England merchants about the availability of transport vessels. Freeman, *Washington*, V, 302–307; Ward, *War of the Revolution*, II, 881; Fitzpatrick, ed., *Washington Diaries*, II, 247, 248–250; on Washington's subsequent decision to undertake operations in Virginia, see his letter to RM, August 17, and notes.

3. RM received this letter on August 6, after which he conferred with La Luzerne, and on August 7 departed for Washington's headquarters. See Diary, August 6, and RM to Washington, August 28.

Diary: August 3, 1781

Wrote Richard Harrison Esqr. Cadiz, enclosing sundry Important dispatches to Mr Jay.[1]

Issued a Warrant on Mr Swanwick in favor [of] S. Hodgdon, Commsy. General Mil: Stores, for £375, Specie, on account of purchasing Military Stores for the use of the Army this Campaign.

Issued a Warrant on Mr Swanwick in favour of Chevr Jones for 400£ Specie advanced on Account of Ship America.[2]

I Sold Mr. Peter Whitesides Twenty four Setts of Exchange drawn by Francis Hopkinson Esqr.[3] on the Minister Plenipotentiary at the Court of Versailles,[4] being part of those received from the Board of War, Viz. 9 Setts at 90 days Sight for 600 Ds. each, 15 Setts, at same sight a[t] 400 dollrs. each amounts to 11,400 dollrs. at Six shillings Pensylvania Currency in hard Money per dollr. of five Livrs. for which he is to pay the Delegates of Georgia, So. and No. Carolina the Monthly allowances made to them respectively, by the Act of Congress of the 30th Ultimo.[5] I consider this as a good Sale of the bills, as they could not at this time have been sold for more than 5/ ready Money, on Account of the number of French Army Bills now at Markett drawn at 30 days, and which are selling under the Price at which I hold my Drafts of 60 days, so that they check my Sales very much.[6]

This day compleated the Sundry letters in Cypher enclosed in mine of the 27th Last, to his Excellency John Jay Esqr. at Madrid.[7]

1. The enclosures were RM to John Jay, July 29, 1781, with an August 3 postscript, and to the Governor of Cuba and to Robert Smith, both July 17, 1781. See also the last entry in this Diary.
2. See Diary, August 2, and notes.
3. Former treasurer of loans.
4. Benjamin Franklin.
5. For the act of Congress of July 30, see notes to Diary, July 11; and Diary, July 25 and 26, 1781.

6. On competition with the French in the sale of bills of exchange and RM's efforts to arrange their joint negotiation, see RM to La Luzerne, August 2, and notes.

7. RM's letter to Jay is dated July 29, 1781. See note 1 above.

To Richard Harrison

[*Philadelphia, August 3, 1781*. On this date RM made the following entry in his Diary: "Wrote Richard Harrison Esqr. Cadiz, enclosing sundry Important dispatches to Mr Jay." For the enclosures, see notes to Diary, August 3. *Letter not found.*]

From Chevalier de La Luzerne[1]

Mr. Robert Morris   A Philadelphie le 3 août 1781
Mr.

J'ai lu avec la plus grande satisfaction la Lettre que vous m'avez fait l'honneur de m'écrire le 2. de ce mois. Il me paroit que les raisonnemens qu'elle contient emportent la plus entiere conviction quant à la negotiation de nos traittes:[2] J'en suis si persüadé que je vous prie de me permett[r]e de les faire parvenir au General de la Division françoise et de lui envoyer votre lettre afin qu'elle ne perde rien de sa force.[3] Il y a cependant un objet sur lequel je presume d'avance qu'il sera nécessaire d'avoir quelques termes certains; C'est 1°. le taux auquel vous croyez que vous pourrez tirer, 2°. quelle somme vous croyez pouvoir fournir par mois à l'armée.[4] Je conçois qu'il est difficile de repondre avec précision à ces questions: mais comme je ne doute pas qu'on ne les fasse et que j'ai extreme-ment à coeur le succes de l'opération que vous proposez, je desire d'éloigner d'avance autant que possible toutes les difficultés.

Quant à vos propositions pour les approvisionnemens et subsis-tances de nôtre armée, comme vous determinez les prix au[x]quels vous pouvez les faire, c'est une affaire de calcul et de comparaison qui me paroit devoir frapper le General et je vais le presser de prendre également ces propositions dans la plus serieuse considéra-tion.[5]

MSS: Copy, Correspondance politique, supplément, Etats-Unis, AMAE; copy in the writing of Gouverneur Morris, Bache Collection, PPAmP.

1. The following translation was prepared by the late Professor Beatrice Hyslop of Hunter College of the City University of New York and Mary A. Gallagher. It has been reviewed by Professor Robert W. Hartle of the Department of Romance Lan-guages, Queens College of the City University of New York.
"I have read with the greatest satisfaction the letter which you did me the honor of writing on the second of this month. It seems to me that the considerations which it contains as to the negotiation of our bills are completely convincing. I am so persuaded of this that I beg you to allow me to forward them to the General of the

French division and to send him your letter so that none of its force may be lost. There is, however, one matter on which I presume in advance that it will be necessary to have some firm commitments; that is 1st, the rate at which you believe that you will be able to draw; 2d, what sum you think you can furnish monthly to the army. I understand that it is difficult to answer these questions precisely, but as I do not doubt that they will be asked and since I have very much at heart the success of the operation which you propose, I wish to remove in advance insofar as possible all the difficulties.

"As for your propositions for the provisioning and subsistence of our army, since you determine the prices at which you are able to furnish them, it is a matter of calculation and of comparison which appears to me should be the General's responsibility and I am going to urge him to take these propositions also under the most serious consideration."

2. On RM's proposal for joint negotiation of bills of exchange with the French, see RM to La Luzerne, August 2, and notes.

3. No letter from La Luzerne to Comte de Rochambeau respecting RM's suggestions has been found, but see notes to RM to La Luzerne, August 2.

4. See RM to La Luzerne, August 4, for a reply to these questions.

5. On RM's proposals to supply the French army by contract, see Diary, August 21, and notes. A copy of this letter was enclosed in RM to Benjamin Franklin, November 27, 1781 (first letter).

From the Board of Treasury

[*Philadelphia, August 3, 1781.* On August 4 RM replied to the board's "Letter of Yesterday." *Letter not found.*]

Diary: August 4, 1781

Issued a Warrant on Mr Jno Swanwick in favour of Richard Peters[1] for £50 Specie for which he is to be accountable.

Wrote Messrs. Le Couteulx and Compy. advising of Bills drawn on them.[2]

Wrote a Letter to The President of New Hampshire respecting Ship America &Ca.

Wrote Capt Paul Jones on same Subject.

Wrote to The Governour of the State [of] Massachusetts, respecting do. &Ca.

Wrote to the Navy Board Boston relative to the equipment of the Continental Ships of War &Ca.

Wrote to John Langdon Esqr. respecting Money, Ship America &Ca.

Having Omitted in my Minutes to make mention of the Assistance I have received from Gouverneur Morris Esqr. I think it proper to declare that he has most chearfully afforded me every advice and Assistance which his Genius and Abilities enabled from my first Appointment to this time and that I found him so Capable and Usefull as to induce me to Solicit his Assistance in Official Character which having readily Consented to I made a Verbal Engagement with him, since Confirmed by my Letter of Appointment dated 6th July last being the date of the Acts of Congress which fixes a Salary for my Assistant,[3] and he is of course entitled to that Salary from that date, indeed it ought to have commencd much sooner as his Time and Attention were devoted to this Office long before.

I also employed Mr. Wm. Banks [4] as a Clerk in this Office where he first came to write on the 11th day of June and has continued to my satisfaction ever since. Consequently his Salary of five hundred hard Dollars per Annum Commences from that time.

I employed Mr James Finlay [5] in the same capacity for some days but finding himself unequal to the duties assigned him he declined in which I readily acquiesced.

Held sundry Conferences previous to my Departure for Camp and prepared Memorandums for that Purpose.[6]

1. The member of the Board of War who accompanied RM to Washington's headquarters later in the month.
2. Letter not found.
3. On this act, see notes to RM to Gouverneur Morris, July 6, 1781.
4. On William Banks, see Diary, June 11, 1781. The salary of clerks in the Office of Finance was determined by Congress on July 6, 1781.
5. Possibly James Finlay, who for a short time had been a clerk in the office of the commissary general of issues. Noting that "the situation of his Affairs in the West Indies" required him to leave the United States, Finlay applied to Congress later in the month for pay, but his petition was ultimately rejected by the Board of Treasury. Finlay's petition to Congress, August 27, 1781, PCC, no. 41, III, 252; *JCC,* XXI, 911.
6. In his Diary, August 21, RM reproduced one of the memorandums, a list of topics to be discussed with Washington.

To John Paul Jones

Office of Finance 4. Augt. 1781.

Sir

I am very sorry that your Detention in this City [1] has delayed so long the Letters which are to go by you to the Eastward relating to the Ship America,[2] And particularly so because I find by a Letter from the Navy Board [3] that the continental Share of the Prizes taken by the Alliance which had been intended for fitting the America have been otherwise applied so that the Order on the Agent at Boston [4] will probably produce but little or Nothing.

I have now written to the State of New Hampshire requesting they will supply Mr. Langdon with Money on Account of the United States.[5] As there is a considerable Balance due on the Requisitions of Congress I have every Hope and Expectation that this Request will be complied with and therefore it is not necessary to authorize the drawing of Bills on me. If on the contrary the State should not make the Advance to Mr. Langdon you will desire him to go on and you will write to me giving me Information on the Subject that I may take such further measures as shall appear to be necessary.

In consequence of the Reference made to me by Congress of your letter of the   6 I have advanced you four hundred Pounds on Account. You will remember that this Sum is to be accounted for hereafter and not to be considered as the Payment of any former Demands; you will therefore proceed accordingly.

I wish you Sir a speedy and safe arrival at the End of your Journey and all possible Success in the Object of it both for the sake of the Public and of yourself, being with real Esteem your most obedient and humble Servant

R.M.

MS: Ofcl LbC, DLC.
1. Congress elected Jones to command the *America* on June 26, but his departure for Portsmouth, New Hampshire, was delayed until August 12 "partly by sickness and partly by the Settlement of his Accounts." See Diary, August 2 and 3, and RM to John Langdon, August 4; Morison, *John Paul Jones,* 318.
2. Undoubtedly RM's letters of August 4 to John Langdon, the Governor of Massachusetts, the Navy Board of the Eastern Department, and the President of New Hampshire. Jones also carried RM's letters of July 2, 1781, to Langdon and the Navy Board of the Eastern Department, neither of which has been found. See RM to Langdon, August 4, and the Navy Board of the Eastern Department to RM, August 29.
3. Dated July 16, 1781. Proceeding in accord with an act of Congress of June 23, RM had advised the Navy Board in a letter of June 29 (not found) to retain the money from Captain John Barry's prizes for the order of Jones. See RM to the President of Congress, June 22 (second letter), and notes, and Diary, June 29, 1781.
4. For the order on John Bradford, see Diary, July 2, 1781.
5. See note 2 above.
6. Space left blank in manuscript. On Jones's letter to the President of Congress, July 28, 1781, which was referred by Congress to RM on July 30, see notes to Diary, August 2.

To Chevalier de La Luzerne

Philada. Augt. 4. 1781

Sir,

I was honored with your Letter of the 3d. yesterday Evening. I am happy that the Sentiments expressed in mine of the Second meet with your Excellency's Approbation, and shall readily Confide in your discretion, to make Such Use of it as you think proper.

The two Questions you ask, do not admit of a precise answer. The Rate of Exchange ought by no means to be under four fifths, indeed I could wish that it were higher, and am not without hopes of raising it, but that must depend on Circumstances, which I cannot Command.

John Paul Jones. Portrait by Charles Willson Peale, 1781.

The Sum which Can be furnished to the French Army, Monthly, by the Sale of Bills, admits Still less than the other of being precisely ascertained. Let me add, Sir, that the Sum which your Army may want, must greatly depend upon the Measures which may be taken to Supply it. Government ought to know its Expences precisely, if that were possible.

Upon this Principle, it will be of Use that your Stipulations Should be to pay a Certain Sum in France for every Ration. Consequently you will want no Money here for that purpose. I wish it were in my power to Reply more pointedly, for I am well Convinced of the Importance of Information on that Subject. Whenever I am in a Condition to know more I shall readily Communicate to you the Effect of my Enquiries. But, while it is my determination to Speak to you with that Confidence which your Ingenuous Conduct has Merited, I am equally determined, neither to Compromise myself, nor mislead you, by Relying on Unfounded Conjecture.[1]

I have the honour to be, very Respectfully, Your Excellencys Most Obedient and Humble Servant

Robt Morris

MSS: LS, Correspondance politique, supplément, Etats-Unis, AMAE; Ofcl LbC, DLC.

1. La Luzerne sent Rochambeau a copy of this letter and RM's letter of August 2. See La Luzerne to RM, August 3, and, for further discussion of RM's proposals for joint negotiation of bills of exchange, RM to La Luzerne, August 2, and notes, and for supplying the French army by contract, Diary, August 21, and notes.

To John Langdon

Office of Finance. August 4, 1781.

Sir

Captain Jones has been detained here partly by sickness and partly by the Settlement of his Accounts much longer than was expected and since my Letter to you of the second July [1] also sent by him I have advice from the Navy Board at Boston that they had appropriated before the Receipts of the Orders of Congress the Amount of the Continental share of the Alliances Prize money to the outfit of that Ship and the Dean.[2] Consequently nothing will be obtained for the America from that quarter. I have also since received your Letters of the sixth and ninth July [3] and thank you very much for the obliging Contents. I gather some hopes from these that the Subscriptions to the Bank will furnish you with Monies that may be employed in forwarding that Ship, and having also since that time had an opportunity of knowing the State of Accounts between the Continent and the several States I find considerable Sums are yet to be furnished by New Hampshire on the existing Requisitions of Congress wherefore I enclose herein a Letter to your Government [4] requesting them to supply what may be necessary for completing and sending to Sea the said Ship America with all possible Dispatch; the Amount of what they supply shall be credited against those existing Demands made by Congress on the State and as I am now calling on all the States for their respective Quota's of those Taxes I hope they will comply; [5] otherwise it is not possible to carry on the Public Service and those that fail must be answerable for the Consequences; this will render it unnecessary for you to draw upon me for any other Money than the Amount of what you receive for the Bank. You will keep exact Accounts of what you receive and expend and send me a State thereof in due time. I need not again recommend frugality for you know the Necessity of it as well as I do. I am Sir your most obedient and humble Servant

RM.

MS: Ofcl LbC, DLC.

1. Letter not found.
2. See the Navy Board of the Eastern Department to RM, July 16, 1781. The 34-gun frigate *Deane*, built at Nantes and brought to the United States in May 1778, was commanded by Captain Samuel Nicholson (1743–1811), who had been commissioned on December 10, 1776. Nicholson had been remarkably successful in capturing prizes in 1779 but cruised off South Carolina and the West Indies in 1780 and 1781 to little avail. He received sailing instructions from RM on September 21, but was relieved of his command in 1782 and tried by court-martial the following year and acquitted. In September 1782 his ship was renamed the *Hague* because of Silas Deane's apostasy. *DAB; Dict. Amer. Naval Ships*, II, 248; for the outfitting of the *Alliance* and *Deane*, see RM to the Governor of Massachusetts, August 4 and September 21, to the Navy Board of the Eastern Department, August 4 and September 21, and to John Brown, September 19.
3. Letters not found.
4. RM to the President of New Hampshire, August 4.
5. See RM's Circulars to the Governors of the States, July 6, 16, and 25, 1781.

To Le Couteulx and Company

[*Philadelphia, August 4, 1781.* On this date RM made the following entry in his Diary: "Wrote Messrs. Le Couteulx and Compy. advising of Bills drawn on them." *Letter not found.*]

To the Governor of Massachusetts (John Hancock)

Office of Finance 4. August 1781.

Sir,

On the twenty third of June last the United States in Congress Assembled directed me to take measures for the speedy launching and equipping the Ship America and directed the Board of Admiralty to assign to me the Share of the United States in the Prizes taken by Capt. Barry to enable me to carry their Orders into Effect.[1]

By a Letter from the Navy Board in the Eastern District dated the eighteenth of July at Boston [2] it appears that the greater Part of this money is already expended and that more is wanting to fit the Deane and Alliance for Sea. Congress have referred this Letter to me and in Consequence as I am convinced that Expence will constantly accrue while those Vessels continue in Port I request of your Excellency to furnish to the Navy Board such Monies as may be necessary to fit them out with all possible Expedition. I must further intreat to be favored with an Account of the Sums furnished that they may be carried to the Credit of your State on the late Requisitions of Congress and the Navy Board to be debited with them in the Treasury Books.[3]

I have the Honor to be with great Respect your Excellency's most obedient and humble Servant

RM.

ms: Ofcl LbC, DLC.
    1. Captain John Barry, commander of the frigate *Alliance*, had just returned from France with prizes he had taken in passage. For the application of the prize money to the completion of the *America*, see RM to the President of Congress, June 22, 1781 (second letter), and notes.
    2. This letter was addressed to the Board of Admiralty and is in the Letterbook of the Navy Board of the Eastern Department, DLC. Congress on July 30 referred part of it to RM, who had received similar advice from the Navy Board in a letter of July 16, 1781.
    3. This letter to the governor of Massachusetts was enclosed in RM to the Navy Board of the Eastern Department, August 4. For the outfitting of the *Alliance* and *Deane*, see also RM to John Brown, September 19, and to the Governor of Massachusetts and to the Navy Board of the Eastern Department, both September 21.

To the Navy Board of the Eastern Department[1]

Office of Finance 4 Aug. 1781.

Gentlemen

Your Letter of the sixteenth Ultimo came safe and since the receipt of it the Honble. Congress have referred to me your Letters of the eighteenth to the Commissioners of the Admiralty [2] for the Purpose (as I suppose) of taking Order with respect to the Continental Part of the Alliances Prizes which by a former Act [3] they had assigned as part of the Funds necessary to Compleat the America for Sea: but by both these Letters it appears you had not waited for Orders as to the Application of that Prize Money but had proceeded to expend the same on the outfits of the Alliance and Deane; this being already done renders it needless to form any Dependance on that Money, for the America. As I suppose the Agent will be under a Necessity of declining to Comply with the Order of the Admiralty Board in my favor for that Amount,[4] And as I think it highly proper that the Deane and Alliance should be sent to Sea with all possible Expedition, I take the Liberty to enclose herein a Letter to the Government of Massachusetts [5] requesting them to give you such Assistance and supply you with such Money as may be necessary to accomplish it. I have done this because the Admiralty Board are not in a Situation to give Orders or supply Funds, Mr. Lewis having resigned and Mr. Ellery being absent.[6] I am to request that you will transmit to me a regular and exact Account of the Monies you shall receive from the State of Massachusetts and of the Expenditure of them; and I expect that this will be sent as soon as the Ships are fitted for Sea. Congress have some Alterations in View respecting the Management of the Navy and when they take place you no doubt will be duly advised of them.[7] Shou'd you in the mean Time get the Ships ready before you receive any Orders I should think it would be well done to send them on a short Cruize together but of this you will be the best Judges. I can only recommend the utmost frugality in the outfits of expenditures on this Occasion as the State of our Finances require Oeconomy in every Department and I well know that in Naval Affairs particularly, dispatch always produces a great saving of Money.

You will receive this by Capt. Jno Paul Jones who is appointed to command the America; he has been detained much longer here by the Settlement of his Accounts than was expected. I hope you will readily afford him every Assistance you can in getting that Ship ready for Sea.

I observe you were preparing to Copper the Alliances Bottom but hope the Copper Ore mentioned in Mr. Bradfords Letters to Congress has not been used for that Purpose.[8] I have the Honor to be Gentlemen your most obedient humble Servant

R.M

MS: Ofcl LbC, DLC.

1. The commissioners of the Navy Board at this time were William Vernon and James Warren, who replied to this letter on August 29 and September 5.

2. "Letters" is probably a clerk's error, as only one communication of July 18 from the Navy Board to the Board of Admiralty has been found in the Navy Board Letterbook, DLC. See notes to RM to the Governor of Massachusetts, August 4.

3. Of June 23, 1781. See the reference cited in the preceding note.

4. For the order on John Bradford, Continental prize agent for Massachusetts, see Diary, July 2, 1781.

5. RM to the Governor of Massachusetts, August 4.

6. Congress had granted William Ellery a leave of absence from the board on July 9 and had accepted Francis Lewis's resignation on July 17.

7. As part of its reconstruction of executive departments, Congress discussed the reorganization of the Marine Department at intervals during the spring and summer of 1781. On September 7 it put marine affairs under the direction of RM in his capacity as Superintendent of Finance and disbanded existing naval agencies. See RM to the President of Congress, September 8.

8. See notes to Diary, July 16, 1781.

To the President of New Hampshire (Meshech Weare)[1]

Office of Finance
August 4th. 1781

Sir

The United States in Congress Assembled on the twenty third of June last directed me to take Measures for the Speedy launching and equipping for Sea the Ship America.[2] I am therefore to request that you will furnish to John Langdon Esqr. such Sums of Money as may be necessary for that Purpose which is to be On Account of the Requisitions of Congress on your State. I am also to request Sir that I may be favoured as soon as may be convenient with an Account of the Sums furnished so that they may in the Treasury Books be carried to the Credit of your State and Mr Langdon be debited for them. It is of the utmost Importance to many Public Objects that this Ship should soon be at Sea. I am therefore Confident that your Excellencys Efforts will be chearfully made for that Purpose. With the greatest Respect I have the honor to be Your Excellencys Most Obedient and Humble Servant.

Robt Morris

His Excellency The President of
The State of New Hampshire

MSS: LS, Weare Papers, Nh-Ar; Ofcl LbC, DLC; Force transcript, DLC.

1. This letter was enclosed in RM to John Langdon, August 4. Meshech Weare (1713–1786) was president of the New Hampshire Council, 1776–1784, and of the reorganized state government from 1784 until his retirement in early 1785. *DAB;* Sibley-Shipton, *Harvard Graduates,* IX, 590-605.

2. On this act, see RM to the President of Congress, June 22, 1781 (second letter), and notes.

To the Board of Treasury

Office of Finance 4th. Augt. 1781.[1]

Gentlemen

In reply to your Letter of Yesterday [2] I cannot give you an exact State of the Sum which will remain of the new Emission in the Hands of the Loan Officer in the State of Pennsylvania [3] when he shall have received in full the $^4/_{10}$ths. of that Emission agreable to the Resolutions of the eighteenth of March 1780,[4] but I think the Warrants already drawn on that Fund Amount to within about twenty to twenty five thousand Dollars of the whole. It is probable that the Loan Officer will be enabled to ascertain the exact balance in a few Days. I have the Honor to be Gentlemen your obedient humble Servant

R.M

MS: Ofcl LbC, DLC.
1. RM neglected to register this letter in the Diary of this date, but entered a note of its omission in the Diary of August 21.
2. Letter not found.
3. Thomas Smith.
4. On the act of March 18, 1780, see notes to John Morin Scott to RM, May 30, and the Secretary of Congress to RM, June 29, 1781.

From John Langdon

[*Portsmouth, New Hampshire, August 4, 1781.* On September 28 RM wrote to Langdon: "Your Letter of the fourth of August has been here some time." *Letter not found.*]

From the Governor of North Carolina (Thomas Burke)

WmsBorough [North Carolina]
August 4th. 1781

Robt. Morris Esqr
Dear Sir

I wrote you [1] some time [torn] very interesting to this State and no [torn] the United States, that is the procuring [torn] our defence and to enable us to make some [efforts?] against the common enemy. I then suggested that I wished to raise money in your City on Tobacco or other Produce of this State for repairing and bringing forward some Arms which I was informed had been ordered for us but which might be delayed for want of ready money for repairs and transportation; [2] what success my proposals might have been capable of, I know not; but the business of Providing Arms and Warlike Requisites is so necessary that I cannot forbear employing all my public and private Interest for the purpose. The Assembly has invested me with powers to procure them, and to pay for them with Tobacco or exportable produce, and also to permit the exportation of provisions for them.[3]

I have empowered Mr. Hawkins [4] to contract with Mr. Holker [5] for a certain quantity but that will not be sufficient. I have [an?] Idea that the private manufact[ories?] of [Penns]ylvania might furnish a good many and I [also?] think the Merchants of that State and this might be induced to import some to be paid for [by?] the articles above mentioned.

We shall furnish much to the Southern Army in the various articles of provision, [trans]portation and Cavalry Horses. We have now [*torn*] hundred men on their March to join Genl. Green [6] exclusive of our Regulars which are every day approaching to a completion.[7] Shall we, Sir be entitled to no money for all this from the United States? And can we rely on any credit to be used if necessary in aid of our own resources for so necessary a purpose as that of procuring Arms and Military requisites? I request you, Sir either in your public Character or as my private friend, a Title which I hope never will be brought in question, to give what assistance you can in making such a disposition as will enable me to procure arms and Stores in Exchange for the produce of this State. And you may rely on the engagements, for the delivery of them, being performed with liberal punctuality. You know me too well to doubt my promises in these matters. You know the value I set on the plain candid integrity of fair dealing and the Idea I have of its superlative efficacy in all political [*torn*]. You will therefore I hope rest a[ssured?] [*torn*] I have the power my engagement [*torn*] high. Mr. Hawkins who is [*torn*] and a man of merit will deliver [*torn*] has powers and instructions from [*torn*] contracts and he will take your [*torn*] assistance so far as you will favour him therewith.

In a letter from [*torn*] la Luzern is a French sentence [*torn*] [*illegible*] speaking of a Subsidy [*torn*] Superintendant of the Finances [*torn*] "to be [*illegible*] in the application of [*illegible*] from time to time of the necessities of the Southern Army." [8] Does this [intimate?] an appropriation in any degree or what is its full effect? I entreat you to write me on this Subject as early as it may be in your power [9] and be assured that I always am Dear Sir &c

MS: LbC, Governor's Papers, State Series, Nc-Ar.

1. This letter, probably dated July 11, has not been found.

2. Burke no doubt refers to Congress's order of April 26, 1781, directing the Board of War to repair muskets in its possession and forward not more than 2,000 each to the executives of Virginia and North Carolina. Lack of funds induced the Office of Finance to postpone their delivery, and on August 29 RM informed Governor Burke that Washington's decision in favor of military operations in Virginia no longer made the arms an urgent matter. See Diary, July 30, and notes, and August 15 and 22, 1781.

3. An act of assembly passed at a session which began in June and ended on July

14, 1781, authorized the governor, with the advice of the council, to purchase 2,000 stand of arms, 5,000 pounds of powder, a quantity of lead, and 3,000 blankets and "to purchase, borrow, or if absolutely necessary," impress tobacco or other exportable state produce sufficient to pay for the repair and transportation to North Carolina of the arms already procured in Philadelphia and for the purchase of any additional weapons delivered to North Carolina before April 2, 1782. Saunders and Clark, eds., *State Records of North Carolina,* XXIV, 407–408.

4. Benjamin Hawkins (1754–1816) of North Carolina had been Washington's French interpreter, 1776–1779, before being chosen by the North Carolina legislature in 1780 to procure arms for the defense of the state. Elected to Congress on July 14, 1781, Hawkins served from October following until 1784 and again in 1786–1787, and later became a United States Senator and Indian agent. *DAB; Biog. Dir. Cong.;* Burnett, ed., *Letters,* VI, xlix.

5. John Holker, French consul in Philadelphia and purchasing agent for the French fleet.

6. Major General Nathanael Greene, whose army at this time was encamped in the High Hills of Santee, South Carolina.

7. That is, completion of the state's quota of enlistments for the Continental army.

8. The source of Burke's information is doubtful, but his allusion may be to a distorted report of a letter from Chevalier de La Luzerne, French minister at Philadelphia, to Washington of June 1, 1781, in which La Luzerne disclosed that France had granted a subsidy of 6 million livres for 1781, of which a surplus of 1.5 million livres above commitments in France would be available for use in the United States. La Luzerne, however, said nothing about its application to the southern army. La Luzerne's letter and a contemporary translation are in the Washington Papers, DLC; see also notes to RM to the Secretary of Congress, May 28, 1781.

9. No acknowledgment of or reply to this letter has been found, but see note 2 above.

From George Washington

Head Quarters Dobbs's Ferry [New York] 5th: Augt. 1781.

Dear Sir

There are 311 Barrels of Salt Beef at Portsmouth in New Hampshire, which, to save land Carriage, I had directed to be sent to Providence by Water, but Mr. President Weare writes me that the risque is too great, as there are a number of privateers in that quarter. I have therefore informed him that you will dispose of it on the spot and procure a like quantity in Philada.[1] I shall be obliged to you for investing the Money which may arise from this sale in pork rather than in Beef. I have the honor to be &c

Honble. Robt. Morris Esqr

ENDORSED: 5th: August 1781/to/Robt. Morris Esq.
MSS: Dft in the writing of Tench Tilghman, Washington Papers, DLC; Varick transcript, Washington Papers, DLC.

1. For the correspondence on this subject, see Washington to President Meshech Weare of New Hampshire, July 8 and August 5, 1781, Fitzpatrick, ed., *Writings of Washington,* XXII, 339–340, 467, and Weare to Washington, July 23, 1781, Washington Papers, DLC.

Diary: August 6, 1781

Issued a Warrant on Mr Swanwick in favour Colo Saml Miles [1] for £17.10 Specie for Expence of a Team to Camp.

Received a Letter from the General,[2] which made it necessary to see the Minister of France [3] (wrote a Note to the Board of War postponing a Meeting with them untill 8 OClock), conferred with the Minister, and at 8 met the Board of War.

Had a Conference with the Board of War in the course of which agreed to pay for fifty Reams of Paper, for Transportation of 500 Stand of Arms and 2 field Pieces to Maryland and for Fifty Cords of Wood.[4]

1. Deputy quartermaster general for Pennsylvania.
2. No doubt Washington to RM, August 2 (second letter), requesting information about the availability of vessels at Philadelphia and Chesapeake Bay to transport his army at New York southward for operations in Virginia.
3. Chevalier de La Luzerne.
4. For an additional transaction on this day, see Diary, Minutes of Sundry Transactions for 1781, printed at the end of the year.

To the President of Congress
(Thomas McKean)

Office of Finance 6 Augt 1781.

Sir

I do myself the Honor to enclose to you, for the Inspection of Congress, the Papers No. 1, 2, and 3, being Copies of Letters dated the sixth, sixteenth, and twenty fifth of July, which I have written to the respective States in Consequence of the Act of Congress of the twenty eighth of June.[1] I also enclose a Paper, No 4, containing the Copy of a Letter, dated the twenty seventh of July, to those States who have not as yet passed the Law for laying a Duty of five Per Cent according to the Act of Congress of the third of Feby.[2] These Letters will sufficiently explain themselves; and, should they be approved of, I have only to add my Wish that the several Members of Congress will further the Applications to their respective States, and add the Weight of their Influence to my Intreaties, and the Authority of Congress.[3] I have the Honor to be, very respectfully your Excellency's most obedient and humble Servant.

Robt Morris

His Excelly The President of Congress

ENDORSED: Letter from the Supt of Finance/August 6th. 1781/Read Augt. 8th/Enclosing copies of letters he has written to the states./1. Pressing compliance with requisitions of C[ongress]/2. Stating accounts of States with the US/3. Obviating objection that the Account of States/with US will not be adjusted and giving assurance/to the Contrary, and desiring information/4. Urging a compliance with the act of/3 Feby for 5 per cent impost

MSS: LS, PCC, DNA; Ofcl LbC, DLC; copy, Bache Collection, PPAmP.

1. The resolution directed RM to urge the states to comply with requisitions. For further details, see notes to the Secretary of Congress to RM, June 29, and Diary, June 30, 1781.

2. On this act, see notes to Diary, July 2, 1781.

3. This letter, the text of which is in the writing of Gouverneur Morris, was read in Congress on August 8, and although no formal action was recorded, the Rhode Island delegates informed Governor William Greene on August 14 that Congress had approved the circulars. The Rhode Island and Connecticut delegates in Congress urged their states to comply (Burnett, ed., *Letters*, VI, 182–183, 184–185). A copy of this letter to the president of Congress was enclosed in RM to Benjamin Franklin, November 27, 1781 (first letter).

From the Board of War

[*Philadelphia, August 6, 1781*. On August 6 RM wrote to the Board of War: "I have just seen your Note of this Date." *Letter not found.*]

To the Board of War

Office of Finance 6. August 1781.

Gentlemen

I have just seen your Note of this Date [1] and should most readily have set aside my Engagement to the Chevr. De la Luzerne in Order to meet you at five O Clock this Afternoon but a Letter I have just received from his Excellency the Genl.[2] renders it absolutely necessary for me to see the Minister who is out of Town. Consequently I must request the Favor of You to postpone your hour until Eight this Evening by which Time I shall be returned and shall be happy to see you at my House, being Gentlemen your obedient humble Servant

RM.

MS: Ofcl LbC, DLC.

1. Letter not found.

2. See Diary, August 6, and notes.

From the Commissary General of Purchases (Ephraim Blaine)

Philadelphia 6th. August 1781

Sir

My going to Camp is the cause of this early application to you for supplying the Garrison at Fort Pitt and its dependencies.[1] [I] propose the following terms Vizt. To supply the Troops upon that station with the ration you have published from the first of September untill the 1st. of January, I shall expect Nine pence half penny per ration and if the time you mean to engage includes the Winter and Spring (or say for twelve Months), I shall expect Eleven pence half penny per ration. My reason for making so great a difference is, that Garrison ought never to have less than three months salt provision on hand, and no stall'd Cattle to be purchased in that Country and the salt to carry by land from this place; those expences will make the ration come very high. I have the Honor to be very respectfully Sir Your Most Obedient Servant

Eph: Blaine

Honl. Robert Morris Esqr.
Supt. of Finance

ms: LbC, Ephraim Blaine Papers, Peter Force Collection, DLC.
    1. This letter, written by Blaine in an unofficial capacity, undoubtedly was in response to RM's advertisement for Fort Pitt contract proposals, dated July 14, which appeared in the *Pennsylvania Packet* on July 17. For the negotiation of the contract, in which Blaine was joined by Michael Huffnagle, see Diary, September 7 and 12.

From John Holker

[*Philadelphia? August 6, 1781*. RM acknowledged Holker's "letter of Yesterday" in his reply of August 7. *Letter not found.*]

From Philip Schuyler

[*Albany, New York, August 6, 1781*. On August 29 RM wrote to Schuyler: "I was favored with your Letter, dated the sixth Instant at Albany, when I was at Camp." *Letter not found.*]

Diary: August 7, 1781

Held conference with Mr Chaloner[1] an Agent for the French Army. Complained of being undersold, pointed out the Consequences in a forcible Manner and Obtained his Promise not to sell Bills under Six Shillings.

Wrote Letters to The Governours of New Jersey, Delaware and Maryland informing of my departure and requesting them to pay Attention to the Letters of Mr. Gouverneur Morris my Assistant.

Signed Forty one Setts Blank Bills of Exchange and delivered to Mr Swanwick to be filled up and disposed of under Mr Morris's Direction.

Received a Letter from the Treasury Board just before my departure.[2]

Sett off for Camp at Eleven OClock.

After Mr. Morris's Departure [3] made up dispatches by the Southern and Eastern Posts; prepared Letter in Answer to the Treasury Board.[4] On Application of Mr Banks representing his Want of Money directed Mr Swanwick to pay him fifty Dollrs. on Account.[5]

Confered with Colo. Grayson [6] on the subject of sending Continental Schooners for Flour and Pork to Duck Creek.[7] Promised to pay the Men who might be hired for the Trip; recommended Oeconomy in making the Bargain.[8]

Mr. Marbois, in Conversation on the Sale of 1 of his Bills informs me that he expects large Numbers will be Offered for Sale very low by Persons coming from the Army.[9]

1. John Chaloner (1748–1793), a Philadelphia merchant and auctioneer, and his associate Charles White (not further identified) were employed by Commissary General of Purchases Jeremiah Wadsworth as assistant purchasing commissaries from 1778 until early in 1780. At the date of this Diary entry, Chaloner was the agent of Wadsworth and John Carter (John Barker Church) in their work as contractors for the French army. After the war, Chaloner continued his business association with White, managed the affairs of Wadsworth and Carter in Philadelphia for several years, and later served in the Pennsylvania legislature. Syrett and Cooke, eds., *Hamilton Papers*, III, 432n.–433n., IV, 624n.–625n.; Edward L. Clark, *A Record of the Inscriptions on the Tablets and Grave-Stones in the Burial Grounds of Christ Church* (Philadelphia, 1864), 208; East, *Business Enterprise*, 84–85, 94, 152–153; *JCC*, XIV, 570; "Notes and Queries," *PMHB*, VII (1883), 110. For assistance in the preparation of this sketch the editors are indebted to Mr. Ward J. Childs of the Philadelphia Department of Records.

2. Letter not found.

3. This and the following entries were made by Gouverneur Morris. RM resumed the Diary on August 21 after his return from Washington's headquarters at Dobbs Ferry, New York. For RM's account of his activities there, see Diary of that date.

4. Gouverneur Morris's reply is dated August 8.

5. William Banks, a clerk in the Office of Finance, received a salary warrant on August 11. See Diary of that date.

6. Colonel William Grayson, a member of the Board of War.

7. Duck Creek, in Delaware, empties into the lower Delaware River. United States Navy Department, Naval History Division, *The American Revolution, 1775–1783: An Atlas of 18th Century Maps and Charts* (Washington, 1972), map 12.

8. For complications in this plan, see Diary, and Gouverneur Morris to the Board of War, both August 10. Previously, RM had advised the Board of War to sell the Continental schooners. See Diary, July 24, 1781.

9. François, Marquis de Barbé-Marbois, was secretary to Chevalier de La Luzerne, French minister at Philadelphia. On the sale of bills of exchange, see the communications between RM and La Luzerne on August 2, 3, and 4.

Circular to the Governors of Delaware, Maryland, and New Jersey

Philada. 7th. August 1781

Sir

Being obliged to go to Camp on Public Business I shall set off this day. During my absence it is highly probable that the Service may require various applications to your Excellency. Should this be the case they will be made to you by Mr. Governeur Morris who is my official assistant. I am therefore to pray the same attention to his letters, as if they were written by me. I have the honor to be with great respect Your Excellencys most obedient and humble Servant

Robt Morris
S. I. of Finance

His Excy The Govr. and Commr in Chief
of the State of New Jersey[1]

ADDRESSED: His Excellency/The Govr. and Commr. in Chief/of the State of/New Jersey/R Morris ENDORSED: Letter from Robert/Morris 7 Augt 1781 MSS: ALS, to the Governor of New Jersey, William Livingston Papers, NN; LS, to the Governor of Delaware, Executive Papers, De-Ar; Ofcl LbC, DLC.

1. William Livingston.

To John Holker

Office of Finance
August 7th. 1781.

Sir

In consequence of your letter of Yesterday [1] and of the Conversation which has passed in the presence of His Excellency the Minister [2] I think it best for the Common Cause that I should return the four thousand Barrels of Flour He and You had so kindly agreed to assist me with.[3] It so happens that I had only applyed 610 Barrels thereof to the use of the United States as part of the Supplies of Pennsylvania therefore I have desired the Agents Messrs. Turnbull & Co. to hold the remainder 3390 at Your Order instead of mine, and the other 610 I shall cause to be replaced with all convenient expedition being ever desirous to Co-operate with you in promoting His Most Christian Majesty's Service.[4] I have the honor to be Your Obedient humble Servant

Robt Morris

The Honble. John Holker Esqr.
Consul General of France and
Agent of the Royal Marine

ADDRESSED: The Honble./John Holker Esqr./Consul General of France, and/Agent
of the Royal Marine
MSS: LS, Holker Papers, DLC; Ofcl LbC, DLC.
 1. Letter not found.
 2. Chevalier de La Luzerne, French minister at Philadelphia.
 3. RM recorded the agreement with Holker in his Diary, July 5, 1781. His reasons
for returning this flour are explained in RM to the President of Pennsylvania, August
23.
 4. This transaction, which was subsequently altered in some details, may be followed in Diary, August 8, Gouverneur Morris to the Governor of Maryland, and to
Matthew Ridley, both August 8, and RM to Ridley, August 21 and 27, and September
6 and 15, to John Davidson, August 27, to James Calhoun, August 28, and to Ridley
and Pringle, September 4, October 9, 16, and 30, and November 7, 1781.

Oath of Allegiance of Gouverneur Morris

[*Philadelphia*], *August 7, 1781*.[1] Except for Gouverneur Morris's
autograph description of his office as that of "Assistant to the Superintendt. of Finance," this oath is identical to RM's Oath of Allegiance, June 27, 1781. At the bottom of the manuscript the
following attestation appears: "Taken and subscribed before the
subscriber Chief Justice of Pennsylvania. August 7th. 1781. Tho
M:Kean."

ENDORSED: 1781/Gov. Morris
MS: DS, PCC, DNA.
 1. Gouverneur Morris actually took this backdated oath on August 8; see Diary
of that date. Another endorsement appears on the following document.

Oath of Office of Gouverneur Morris

[Philadelphia, August 7, 1781][1]

I, Gouverneur Morris,[2] do swear that I will faithfully, truly and
impartially execute the Office of Assistant to the Superintendt. of
Finance [3] to which I am appointed, and render a true account, when
thereunto required, of all public monies by me received or expended, and of all stores or other effects to me entrusted, which
belong to the United States; and will in all respects discharge the
trust reposed in me with justice and integrity, to the best of my skill
and understanding. So help me God.

Taken and subscribed
before the subscriber Chief Justice   Gouv Morris
of Pennsylvania August 7th. 1781.
        Tho M:Kean

ENDORSED: Oath of Office and Oath/of fidelity of Govr. Morris/Asst. to the Supt.
of Finance/filed Augt. 9th 1781.

Philad^a 7th August 1781

Sir

Being obliged to go to Camp on Public Business I shall set of this day, During my absence it is highly probable that the Service may require various applications to your Excellency. Should this be the case they will be made to you by Mr. Gouverneur Morris who is my official Assistant. I am therefore to pray the same attention to his letters, as if they were written by me. I have the honor to be with great respect

Your Excellencys
most obed^t and
hble Servant
Robt Morris
S.I. of Finance

His Exc^y
The Govr & Comm^r in chief
of the State of
New Jersey

Robert Morris to the Governor of New Jersey, August 7, 1781. ALS of the Circular to the Governors of Delaware, Maryland, and New Jersey.

MS: DS, PCC, DNA.

1. Gouverneur Morris took this backdated oath on August 8; see Diary of that date. On his appointment, see notes to RM to Washington, May 29 (first letter); and RM to Gouverneur Morris, July 6, and Gouverneur Morris to RM, July 7, 1781.

2. The words "Gouverneur Morris" are in signature.

3. The preceding six words are in Gouverneur Morris's writing.

From William Bingham

Philadelphia
August 7th 1781

Sir

On a late Application to Mr Lovell concerning the Settlement of my Accounts as political Agent in the West Indies,[1] he again referred me to you for a further Explanation on the Subject. As I know your Time is too much engaged to enter into a full Discussion of this Matter, I will only recapitulate the leading Points on which the Nature of my Claim is founded.

You may well remember that the Committee of Secret Correspondence engaged the Payment of my Expences during my Absence, and left any further compensation for my services, to be Settled at a future Day. These very Expences, (necessarily and indispensibly incurred) during a four Years Residence in the West Indies, amounted to upwards of Liv 161,000 Mque [Martinique] Currency. The Account I presented to the Committee for Salary and Expences inclusive, does not exceed Liv 110,000, which is Liv 51,000 less than my actual Expences only. A Scrupulous Attention to Motives of Delicacy would not permit me to charge the whole of my Expences to the Account of the Public, when Some profitable private Business that I was engaged in, enabled me to support a Part of them. But the Right of doing it was Still unquestioned.

As for my Commercial Transactions as Agent for the United States, if the public Benefits resulting from them were taken into Consideration, I am certain, that So far from having a Deduction from my other Accounts hinted at, by reason of private Advantages derived from my Agency, I should rather be entitled to *Compensation* for extra and important Services. Immediately on my Arrival in the West Indies, I risked my personal Credit to the Amount of Liv 250,000 for Arms, Ammunition and Cloathing, which by arriving at a critical Time, assisted in enabling our Army to Keep the Field, and give a Check to the Encroachments of the Enemy. Ever since that time, Congress has generally been indebted to me [for] a much larger Sum, which, if I had had the Use of, I might have efficiently converted to my own private Purposes, So as to have derived ten times the Advantage that the Advances to Congress will procure me. Even at this very Moment, I am obliged to draw on my own private Funds to discharge the public Debts.[2]

I will be much obliged to you (if you can afford a Leisure Moment) to make a few Remarks on this Business, as I find it will greatly facilitate the Settlement of it.[3] Indeed I should think myself inexcusable in troubling you on the Subject, if you was not the only Person, who is thoroughly acquainted with it.

I am with much Regard and Esteem Sir Your obedient humble servant

Wm Bingham

ADDRESSED: Robert Morris Esqr ENDORSED: Copy of my Letter to/Robert Morris Esqr./August 7th. 1781
MS: Copy, Bingham Papers, DLC.
   1. For a discussion of Bingham's accounts, see notes to James Lovell to RM, July 5, 1781.
   2. In his memorial to Congress, read September 18, 1780, Bingham claimed a balance of £34,000 specie and requested immediate payment of one-third in bills of exchange to enable him to meet the more pressing debts he had contracted on behalf of the United States. Congress on October 2 of that year responded generously by advancing him £7,000 sterling in bills on John Jay. Bingham's undated memorial is in PCC, no. 41, I, 319.
   3. RM addressed his remarks on Bingham's claims to Lovell on September 7.

From the Board of Treasury

[*Philadelphia, August 7, 1781.* On August 8 Gouverneur Morris wrote to the Board of Treasury: "Your Favor of the seventh Instant to the Superintendant of Finance was delivered yesterday just as he was setting off for Camp." *Letter not found.*]

Diary: August 8, 1781[1]

Attended the President of Congress and took the Oaths of Office as Assistant.[2]

Sent for Mr. Solomons the Broker,[3] informed him that Mr Chaloner had promised not to sell under six Shillings [4] and desired him to press the Sale of Bills. He informs of Sundry Persons selling French Bills. I desire him to gain Information of the Persons the Sums the Rates, to call on them and Urge them to keep up the Price, to threaten them, to give me Intelligence to Morrow Morning.[5]

Wrote Letters to the Governour of Maryland and to Mr Ridley [6] respecting Flour &Ca.

Wrote Letter to The Honorable Treasury Board.

Conferred with Mr Holker and agreed to deliver 1000 Barrells of Flour on the Navigable Waters of the Delaware and 2000 barrels on the Navigable Waters of the Chesipeak at Eighteen Livres per hundred the barrell included. Mr. Ridley is to get the latter 2000 Barrells and he is to hold them to Mr Holkers Use.[7]

Mr. Morse called on me and desired Payment of a Warrant for Specie on the Loan Officer.[8] Refused unless the Warrant were converted into Paper.

1. The Diary of this date was kept by Gouverneur Morris. See Diary, August 7 and 21.

2. Gouverneur Morris's oaths of allegiance and office, sworn before President of Congress Thomas McKean, were backdated to August 7, the day RM left Philadelphia for Washington's headquarters.

3. Haym Salomon.

4. On this rate of exchange, see notes to Gouverneur Morris to RM, August 8. For RM's attempts to arrange a collaboration with the French in selling bills of exchange, see his letter to Chevalier de La Luzerne, August 2, and notes, and the record of his conference with John Chaloner in Diary, August 7.

5. See Diary, August 9, for Salomon's report.

6. Matthew Ridley (1749–1789), a Baltimore merchant, had emigrated from England in 1770 as a factor for a London business firm. Returning to London in 1775, Ridley was active in behalf of American prisoners there, but removed to France in 1778 and back to Maryland in 1779. Ridley was associated with Mark Pringle (not further identified) in the firm of Ridley and Pringle, which did business with the state of Maryland, owned privateers, and was RM's purchasing agent in Maryland and Delaware. As Superintendent of Finance, RM turned to the firm for assistance during the Yorktown campaign. In March 1781 Maryland appointed Ridley its agent to negotiate loans and buy supplies in France, Holland, and Spain. It is a measure of RM's confidence in Ridley that when, in October 1781, he decided to educate his two eldest sons in Europe, he entrusted them to Ridley's care. In 1787, following the death of his first wife, Ridley married Catherine ("Kitty") Livingston, the daughter of Governor William Livingston of New Jersey. Herbert E. Klingelhofer, ed., "Matthew Ridley's Diary During the Peace Negotiations of 1782," *William and Mary Quarterly*, 3d ser., XX (1963), 95–98; Kathryn Sullivan, *Maryland and France, 1774–1789* (Philadelphia, 1936), 121, 129; *Maryland Archives*, XLV, 54, 236, 365; East, *Business Enterprise*, 147; RM to Ridley, February 6, 1781, Ridley Papers, MHi; RM to Ridley, October 14, 1781.

7. See RM to John Holker, August 7, and notes.

8. Charles Morse, a clerk in the office of the secretary of Congress until his death in 1782, had petitioned Congress for back pay of $232 specie. His letter was referred to the Board of Treasury on July 10, 1781, after which the board apparently issued a warrant on Thomas Smith, Continental loan officer of Pennsylvania. Morse accepted the rate of conversion to paper money demanded by Gouverneur Morris. *JCC*, XXIII, 723; Morse to the President of Congress, July 10, 1781, PCC, no. 78, XVI, 207–212; Diary, August 9.

Gouverneur Morris to the Governor of Maryland (Thomas Sim Lee)[1]

Office of Finance 8th. Augt. 1781.

Sir,

In the Absence of the Superintendant of the Finances of the United States it becomes my Duty as his official Assistant to take such Measures as the public Service may require.[2] This I trust will be my sufficient Apology for troubling your Excelly. at present.

An Abstract of the specific Supplies required by the Acts of Congress of the twenty fifth of February and fourth of November 1780 has already been transmitted [3] and altho there are not in this Office any proper Returns of the Deliveries made by your State to the Continent there is every Reason to say that considerable Ballances remain unsatisfied.

It is said that there are now in the public Magazines of Maryland considerable Quantities of Flour of which Article there is an immediate Demand for two thousand Barrels to be deposited on the navigable Waters of Chesapeak.[4] It is of Consequence that this Demand be complied with most speedily and punctually. I have therefore transmitted this by Express to Mathew Ridley Esqr. who will take your Excellency's Orders on the Subject and attend to the Execution of them.[5] Upon Receipt of the Invoices with the Charges thereon Credit will be given to your State for the Flour and Transportation agreably to the Terms prescribed by the Acts of Congress abovementioned.

It is I presume unnecessary to observe that this Flour must be good, sweet and pass the Inspection as merchantable. But it is my Duty to observe to your Excellency that the Supply is absolutely necessary by the twenty fourth of this Month. I persuade myself therefore of your Efforts to prevent any Disappointment.[6]

I have the Honor to be Sir your most obedient and humble Servant.

MS: Ofcl LbC, DLC.

1. Thomas Sim Lee (1745–1819) was governor of Maryland, 1779–1783 and 1792–1794, and a delegate to Congress for a short time in 1783. *DAB; Biog. Dir. Cong.;* Burnett, ed., *Letters,* VII, lxvii.

2. RM left Philadelphia for Washington's headquarters at Dobbs Ferry, New York, on August 7, leaving Gouverneur Morris in charge of the Office of Finance.

3. This abstract, enclosed in RM's Circular to the Governors of the States, July 25, 1781, has not been found. The specific supplies required of Maryland are listed in *JCC,* XVI, 197, XVIII, 1013, 1016.

4. RM had agreed to deliver these 2,000 barrels of flour to John Holker, agent

of the French navy, who was still at this time his business partner. See RM to Holker, August 7, and notes.

5. See Gouverneur Morris to Matthew Ridley, August 8.

6. In response to this letter and Gouverneur Morris's communication of the same date to Matthew Ridley, the Maryland Council instructed James Calhoun, its deputy quartermaster general for the Western Shore, to deliver the flour to Ridley at Baltimore, if possible; otherwise at Georgetown or elsewhere as Ridley directed. The Council also asked its agent at the Head of Elk, Henry Hollingsworth, whether he could "deliver any, and what part, where, and in what Time." Ridley to Governor Lee, August 18, and the Maryland Council to Calhoun, Ridley, and Hollingsworth, all August 19, 1781, *Maryland Archives*, XLVII, 428, XLV, 570–571; see also RM to the Governor of Maryland, August 21, 26, and 28, and the Governor of Maryland to RM, August 31.

Gouverneur Morris to Matthew Ridley

Office of Finance 8th. Augt. 1781.
Sir

I take the Liberty to enclose for your Perusal a Letter to his Excellency the Governor which you will Seal and deliver.[1] The two thousand Barrels of Flour mentioned in it are to be held by you at Mr. Holker's Order and you are to give him Notice of your Receipts of it as soon as received.[2] He will write you by this Opportunity.

If the Flour purchased by the State is not good or if you cannot get it of the Governor or within the Time the Deficiency arising from the Disappointment must be made up by Purchase. On this Subject I am to observe that the most desireable payment to the Superintendant and probably to the vender will be Bills of Exchange at six Shillings for five Livres which you may Promise and on Notice they shall immediately be transmitted. If the Flour cannot be purchased for Bills then purchase for hard Money and get as much Time for the Payment as possible. You will naturally take Care to make your Purchases on the lowest Terms and that the quality be good. By the rate of the Markets here and considering your Prospects of every Kind I should suppose Flour might be got with you at from twelve shillings to fifteen Shillings per Cwt.; the highest Price for the best here is from seventeen Shillings and sixpence to eighteen Shillings and it will be lower nothwithstanding all the Demands.

Whether you are under a Necessity of making any Purchases or not I beg you will learn in the easiest Manner at what Rate a Quantity of this Article may be had for Bills of Exchange as that Knowlege may be useful during the Course of the Campaign. I wish that the Flour now in question may be in as large Barrells as possible; and that the Invoices may be transmitted as soon as possible with the Names of the Places of deposit, and the quantity of each.

I will make no Apology for the Trouble I give nor will I doubt of your Exertions. My knowlege of you renders the one unnecessary and the other improper. You will avoid mentioning that you are impowered to Purchase as that may tend to relax the Efforts of your Government: but rely on it that you shall be enabled to fulfill any Engagements you enter into with the utmost Punctuality. I am convinced those Engagements will be made with all possible Oeconomy. And I pray you to beleive me very truly your Friend and Servant.

MS: Ofcl LbC, DLC.
1. See Gouverneur Morris to the Governor of Maryland, August 8.
2. On this transaction, see RM to John Holker, August 7, and notes.

Gouverneur Morris to the Board of Treasury[1]

Office of Finance 8 July [i.e. August] 1781.

Gentlemen

Your Favor of the seventh Instant to the Superintendant of Finance [2] was delivered yesterday just as he was setting off for Camp. He being absent I am in Answer to observe that the Propriety of allowing any Thing to Mr Wharton [3] or any other Public Officer in Consequence of the Acts of a Committee of Congress must be determined by these Acts and not by an Individual of the Committee. The Superintendant of Finance cannot properly take official Notice of such Things. But admitting the Propriety of Mr Wharton's Request you will recollect that the only Money subject to Mr Morris's Command was given for a particular Purpose and under express Engagements which cannot be violated. I have the Honor further to observe to you Gentlemen that the Propriety or Necessity of keeping one or more Clerks will be a proper Object of Enquiry at the Settlement of an Officers Account upon a Charge made for the Expence of it. With all possible Respect I have the Honor to be Gentlemen your most obedient and humble Servant.

R. [i.e. G.] M.

MS: Ofcl LbC, DLC.
1. Despite RM's initials at the bottom of this letter, the Diary of August 7 and 8 indicates that it was written by Gouverneur Morris. The letter's erroneous date undoubtedly was a clerk's error.
2. Letter not found.
3. Probably James Wharton (ca. 1732–1785), the son of John Wharton and Mary Dobbins and the brother of John Wharton, a former commissioner of the Navy Board of the Middle Department. The proprietor of a Philadelphia ropewalk, Wharton was appointed commissioner of naval stores by congressional commissioners assigned to build frigates in Philadelphia in January 1776. His primary function was to make purchases for outfitting Continental ships of war. He held this office until naval affairs

were reorganized under RM in September 1781. Before submitting his accounts, Wharton requested the services of a clerk, paid at Continental expense, to draw them up, and in the meantime, petitioned Congress for back pay for his years of service, unpaid except for £300. Congress rejected his demand for a clerk, ordered him to settle his accounts, and on July 28, 1781, referred his case to the Board of Treasury with instructions to confer with RM. According to a notation of August 6 on his letter to Congress, Wharton said in a conference with the board on August 4 that he wanted only money sufficient to hire clerks to complete his accounts, a request which the board doubtlessly reported in its August 7 letter to RM. *JCC*, XX, 649, 708–709; Wharton to the President of Congress and his memorial to Congress, both July 25, 1781, are in PCC, no. 78, XXIV, 327–330, 333–334; Commissioners for Building Philadelphia frigates to the Commissioners of Naval Stores, January 9, 1776, Clark and Morgan, eds., *Naval Documents*, III, 693–694, 696; Anne H. Wharton, *Genealogy of the Wharton Family of Philadelphia, 1664 to 1880* (Philadelphia, 1880), 9–11; Willard White Ellenwood, comp., *History of Ellenwood–Wharton and 20 Allied Families, 1620–1968* (New Carlisle, O., 1969), 773.

From John Paul Jones

[*Philadelphia, August 8, 1781.* On September 25 RM wrote to Jones: "On my Return from Camp to this City I found your Letter of the eighth of August with its Enclosures." *Letter not found.*]

From Gouverneur Morris[1]

Philadelphia 8th August 1781

Dear Sir

I enclose you two Letters, the one for Rhode Island and the other for New York,[2] which only want your Signature. You will have I suppose daily Oppertunities of forwarding them.

I am very sorry to inform you, that there is no Sale of Bills. There are now a great number of Persons in Philadelphia, Holders of Bills, who are all desirous of Selling, and I tremble for the Consequences. I have directed the Broker[3] to reason with them, intreat them, in short do every thing rather than lower the Rate of Exchange, but it is all in vain. Already they are selling at 5/6d, and I have no doubt but a few days will bring it to 5/ and probably to 4/6d.[4] These are the blessed Consequences of [po?]uring them out thro so many Channels.[5] It is really extraordinary that with the depreciation of Paper so directly before us, so little Care is taken to prevent the depreciation of Bills of Exchange. I am determined, notwithstanding the large line of discretion you have drawn, not to sell one Bill under 6/, unless in the last necessity: you will judge the Consequences.

I do assure you it gives me very great Pain to see the Interests of France so sacrificed; as to our Own whatever we may lose as a

Goverment, the Individuals will gain; of Consequence after the immediate Suffering no sting of Reflection remains. I must add, that Circumstances will not long permit the Restraints we now lie under, so that if no change happens with respect to this Matter, we must e'en enter the Lists, and run the race of depreciation with others.

MS: Copy, Correspondance politique, supplément, Etats-Unis, AMAE.

1. Internal evidence indicates clearly that this unsigned and unaddressed letter was intended for RM, who, on August 7, had left Philadelphia for Washington's headquarters at Dobbs Ferry, New York, where he may have received it. For RM's account of his activities at camp, see Diary, August 21.

2. Probably two of the six letters of RM's Circular to the Governors of Massachusetts, Rhode Island, New York, Delaware, Maryland, and North Carolina, July 27, 1781.

3. Haym Salomon, whose failure to heed the instructions mentioned in this letter and in the Diary of August 8 drew a sharp rebuke from Gouverneur Morris. See Gouverneur Morris to Salomon, August 10.

4. These sums are what government and commercial vendors of bills of exchange drawn on funds in France received in Pennsylvania pounds for five livres. At the nominal exchange generally accepted in the United States, five livres would bring nearly seven shillings Pennsylvania currency. But the highest rate at which Congress's drafts on its funds in France ever sold, according to RM, was five livres for six shillings, which was the rate Gouverneur Morris was trying to sustain. On rates of exchange, see RM's Circular to the Governors of the States, October 19, 1781.

5. On competition with French vendors of bills of exchange and RM's efforts to arrange a cooperative sale, see RM to La Luzerne, August 2, and notes.

Diary: August 9, 1781[1]

Issued a Warrant on Mr Swanwick for £71.5 Specie in favor Chevr Dubuyson [2] being a Balance due from the United States for the Baggage of the late Baron de Kalb.[3]

Mr Solomons [4] informs me of the venders of Bills. There are many of them all urgent for money; that he has represented to them the Propriety of keeping up the Prices but in vain. I determine to prevent their Sales, wait upon the Minister [5] and Propose a Plan of underselling them. He does not chuse to risque the Loss of selling Bills for 50,000 Livres at 4/6. I agree with him to give one Bill for 50,000 in Exchange of a number of small Bills to that amount. Gave Solomons order to press a Sale on Credit and explained to him Plan of preventing others from selling.[6]

Mr. Smith the Loan Officer call'd with Mr Morse.[7] Directed Acceptance of Morses Warrant as Paper which was done. Gave Orders to Mr Swanwick to pay it and make Entries &Ca as usual. Mr Smith states the Distresses of Public Clerks &Ca very forcibly. I express Concern but decline releiving them untill I know more of our Prospects as to Money. Promise to let him know on the Subject in a day or two.

Solomons informs me that he has Sold from Sixty to Eighty thousand Livres at 6/ on a Credit of eight Months. I refuse and direct it at four Months payable part in Hand the Remainder Monthly. Bills are this Day at 5/6 the highest.

1. The Diary of this date was kept by Gouverneur Morris. See Diary, August 7 and 21.

2. Chevalier Charles François Dubuysson des Hays (1752–1786), a French soldier of fortune recruited for the American service by Silas Deane, was commissioned major in the Continental army and aide to Major General Johann Kalb (see note 3 below) on October 4, 1777, and lieutenant colonel on February 11, 1778. While trying to save Kalb's life at the battle of Camden in August 1780, Dubuysson was badly wounded and captured; in recognition of his bravery, North Carolina appointed him brigadier general of its militia. Dubuysson was paroled by the British on account of his poor health, and Congress, on September 4, 1781, permitted him to return to France, where he died of his wounds. Heitman, *Register;* André Lasseray, *Les Français sous les treize étoiles (1775–1783)* (Paris, 1935), I, 191–194. For Dubuysson's subsequent dealings with RM, see Diary, September 7, and notes.

3. Johann Kalb (1721–1780), son of a Bavarian peasant, rose as a professional soldier in French service during the War of Austrian Succession and the Seven Years War, eventually attaining the rank of brigadier general in 1776. Engaged by Silas Deane to come to America with Lafayette, Kalb, who was known in the United States by his assumed title of "baron," was commissioned a major general in the Continental army on September 15, 1777, and served in Philadelphia, Valley Forge, and in the Southern Department before his death at the battle of Camden. *DAB.*

4. Haym Salomon.

5. Chevalier de La Luzerne, French minister at Philadelphia.

6. See Diary, August 10 and 11, and RM to La Luzerne, August 2, and notes. On the rates at which bills of exchange on France sold for Pennsylvania currency, see notes to Gouverneur Morris to RM, August 8.

7. For Charles Morse's warrant on Thomas Smith, Continental loan officer of Pennsylvania, see Diary, August 8, and notes.

From John Bradford

Boston August 9th 1781

Honored Sir,

Your kind and very obliging Favour of 27th June was duly receiv'd,[1] the Contents of which have made Impressions of Gratitude the latest Time will not be able to erase.

The justness of your Sentiments on the Impropriety of "your appointing" or even "recommending officers whose Conduct it is your Duty to inspect and controul" is evident, as it would be the same Solecism in Finance, as vesting the judicial and executive Powers in the same Person would be, in Government.

But tho this Arrangement may preclude me from an Appointment in this System, May I be indulged with the Liberty of requesting you to be mindful of Me in the Course of your Business? Would you be kind eno' to recommend me in any Department you might think me capable of filling? I know the Importance of your Influence, and am aware of your objecting, that it is the best Reason for great Caution in its Exertion, but sir, as I am sensible that a Man is in a Measure answerable for the Conduct of those he recommends, and that public Utility, rather than private Attachment, should be the motive of your Conduct, should an Opportunity of serving Me present, I would not ask to be prefer'd without the most authentic Testimonials of my Character from the most unexceptionable Characters. If I have any Ambition it is that of being true to my Trust and constant in my Engagements, but being of the wrong Side of Forty stand in need of being introduced on the Theater of the World.

I should not have thus dared to intrude on your precious Moments, nor added to the Multitude, who from your high Station must be continually humming their Concerns in your Ears, had not your kind assurance, that "you would attend to my requests" encouraged me, and permit me further to add, that I conceived you to be the most able to assist Me.

Having been so long in public Business it would be disagreeable to sink into private, and not knowing, but that in future the naval Department also might be subject to your Controul I thought it best to presume so far on your Candor as to be among the first Petitioners.

In any case I should think myself honourd by being in your Service, and should not be without hopes, if your friendly Hand would lead me to the Bottom of the Ladder of Promotion that I might rise in due Time.

I have the Honour to be with great Respect Your humble servant

J Bradford Junr

ADDRESSED: Honble. Robert Morris Esqr/Philadelphia ENDORSED: Boston 9 Augst. 1781/Jno Bradford junr Eqr.
MS: ALS, Robert Morris Papers, DLC.
1. RM's letter to John Bradford, Continental prize agent at Boston, has not been found, but it probably praised the latter's long service and discussed the pending reorganizations of the Treasury and Marine Departments, in which Bradford apparently desired employment. See notes to RM to Bradford, June 27, 1781, and the headnote to RM to the President of Congress, September 8. Acting as Agent of Marine, RM, on September 21, ordered Bradford to complete his accounts.

From James Tilton

Camp near White Plains [New York], 9 Augt. 1781.

Sir

The three Gentlemen to whom you referred me, did me the honor, before I left Philadelphia, to call me in at one of their meetings; they informed me, that they approved every principle which I had laid down, in my *observations;* [1] and that, in the advice they should give you, they should vary from me, in matter of *form,* only in two articles, viz. the number of Surgeons and the appointment of the Stewards of the hospitals; that the number of surgeons they should recommend would be eight and the appointment of the stewards to be in the surgeons, rather than the purveyor.

With regard to the number of the hospital Surgeons, they reasoned from the number of the regimental Surgeons, supposing it would, at all times, be convenient and easy to detach from the regiments to the hospitals, and that more or less of the regimental surgeons might always be employed, in hospitals. My Ideas are some what different as to this matter. I conceive, that the number of hospital Surgeons ought to be such, as to be equal to all the *ordinary* prescriptive duty of the hospitals; and that some emergency should require it, or an extraordinary reason be given, for detaching the regimental Surgeons from their regiments. After a severe battle, such a request from the hospitals would be thought reasonable; or upon a sudden march, leaving all the sick behind, a part of the surgeons could not be denied, by the officers, to take care of them. But I know, by repeated instances, that the officers of regiments part with their surgeons reluctantly, except in cases such as I have mentioned. With the least reflection, it must also appear very proper, that the regimental practice should be interrupted as little as possible. I am, therefore, of opinion, notwithstanding my deference and respect for these learned Gentlemen, that 8 surgeons is as much below the proper number as [2] 13 can be above it.

As to the appointment of Stewards, although, seemingly, a trivial matter, I am nevertheless solicitous, that it should be in the purveyor rather than the surgeons: for otherwise it might be objected to the plan proposed, *that there were no checks upon the surgeons.* When I formed the plan which I delivered to you, my intention was, that the purveying branch should be a check upon the prescriptive, and vice versa. I gave the Surgeons power to order every thing necessary for the sick, from the purveyor and Stewards, but endeavoured to put it out of their power to embezzle or riot on public stores, by depriving them, as much as possible, of any *tool* for that purpose. It may also be observed, that the purveyor cannot be responsible for Stewards, unless they are of his own appointment. And I must confess, that, as an honest man, without a wish or desire of a *dependent* amongst the public stores, I had rather be excused from the *previlege,* as well as the trouble of such appointments.

The hasty manner in which I left the city, put it out of my power to suggest my deliberate thoughts upon these subjects, to the Gentlemen, while sitting; and supposing them, by this time, to have made their report,[3] I am led to think, what I have now said, to be most pertinently addressed to you: and from the favourable reception you were pleased to give my former observations, I persuade myself, that these will meet with all the attention they deserve.

I am, Sir, with the greatest respect, your most obedient servant

James Tilton

R. Morris Esqr.

ADDRESSED: (public service)/Robert Morris Esqr:/Superintendant of Finance/ Philadelphia. ENDORSED: Letter from Doctor Tilton/on Hospital Arrangement/ No. 3
MS: ALS, PCC, DNA.
1. Tilton, a senior hospital physician and surgeon in the Continental hospital department, had submitted his Observations on Military Hospitals and Plan of Arrangement to RM on or about July 15. RM enclosed Tilton's essay in a letter of July 17, 1781, to Doctors Gerardus Clarkson, James Hutchinson, and John Jones, asking them to draw up a plan for reorganizing the Hospital Department. He also referred to them a copy of this letter from Tilton before they submitted their report to him on August 30 concerning Tilton's Observations. All the above-mentioned documents, together with a letter from the Director General of Military Hospitals to RM, July 26, 1781, and RM to Gerardus Clarkson, James Hutchinson, and John Jones, July 30, 1781, were enclosed in RM to the President of Congress, September 21. For further details on the Continental hospital department and its subsequent reorganization, see notes to RM to Clarkson, Hutchinson, and Jones, July 17, and the Director General of Military Hospitals to RM, July 26, 1781.
2. MS: "and."
3. See note 1 above.

From George Washington

Head Quarters Dobbs's Ferry [New York] 9th: Augt. 1781.
Dear Sir

Inclosed is the Copy of a letter which I have just received from Capt. Mitchell commanding the post at Wyoming, representing his distress for provision.[1] As this post was to have been supplied by Pennsylvania, and as you have now undertaken to furnish the supplies required of that state, I must request you to take the speediest means of giving relief to the Garrison.[2] The quantity of provision which I judged necessary was mentioned in the estimate which I transmitted to the Board of War,[3] and which you no doubt have seen. I have the honor to be &c

P.S. I have written to Capt. Mitchell to subsist his Men by collections from the Inhabitants untill a regular supply can be sent to him.[4]

ENDORSED: 9th: August 1781/to/Robt. Morris Esq:/supplying the Garrison of Wyoming.

MSS: Dft in the writing of Tench Tilghman, Washington Papers, DLC; Varick transcript, Washington Papers, DLC.

1. Alexander Mitchell of New Jersey, commissioned first lieutenant in the Continental army on November 23, 1776, and captain on November 1, 1777, in which rank he served until April 1783, had been placed in command of the garrison at Wyoming, Pennsylvania, on December 30, 1780. He informed Washington on August 1, 1781, that a shortage of provisions was arousing great disquiet among his men, that his applications to Pennsylvania for assistance had been rejected, and that he was appealing to him for supplies lest conditions at the post result in mutiny, desertion, or evacuation. Heitman, *Register;* Washington to Mitchell, December 30, 1780, Fitzpatrick, ed., *Writings of Washington,* XXI, 37–38; Mitchell to President Joseph Reed of Pennsylvania, May 25, 1781, *Pennsylvania Archives,* 1st ser., IX, 165; Mitchell to Washington, August 1, 1781, Washington Papers, DLC.

2. Although RM did not acknowledge this letter, a fact which suggests that Washington probably held it until the Financier's arrival at headquarters on the evening of August 10, he issued a warrant to Mitchell for supplies on September 29. See Diary, August 21 and September 29. RM's advertisement for Wyoming contract proposals, dated September 12, appeared in the *Pennsylvania Packet* on September 15.

3. Probably Washington to the Board of War, June 21, 1781, in Fitzpatrick, ed., *Writings of Washington,* XXII, 244–248.

4. See Washington to Mitchell, August 8, 1781, *ibid.,* 477–478.

Diary: August 10, 1781[1]

Conference with Broker [2] on Bills. Wrote him on that Subject, adjusted Plan to stop the Venders of Bills,[3] waited on the Minister [4] who informs he had not seen Mr Rochetrun,[5] will see him to day and write &Ca.[6]

Had Conferences with Colo Miles [7] about the Schooners.[8] He tells me Captains wont go without Payment of Arrearages. Will send them to me. Confered With Captains; they decline unless Arrearages are paid; peremptorily refuse. They are to consider and call again. Return and promise to go. Wrote the Board of War on the Subject; shewed and delivered it to the Captains.

1. The Diary of this date was kept by Gouverneur Morris. See Diary, August 7 and 21.

2. Haym Salomon.

3. See Diary, August 9.

4. Chevalier de La Luzerne, French minister at Philadelphia.

5. Probably de Roquebrune, head clerk of César Louis de Baulny, treasurer of the French army in America.

6. The allusions here are ambiguous, but see Gouverneur Morris to Haym Salomon, August 10. For other conferences on the sale of bills of exchange, see Diary, August 9 and 11.

7. Colonel Samuel Miles, deputy quartermaster general for Pennsylvania.

8. A reference to the plan, mentioned in the Diary of August 7, to send the Continental schooners to Duck Creek in Delaware to fetch flour and pork. For subsequent developments, see Diary, August 14.

Gouverneur Morris to Haym Salomon

Office of Finance 10th. Augt. 1781.

Sir

I am much surprized at the Information you gave me this morning of the Sales of Bills on such long Credit.[1] Before you ventured on any Thing of that Sort you should have given me notice of it. Tho I permitted a certain Sum to be sold on Credit I had no Idea of any Thing of that Sort being carried to such an Extent. However as you have done it I will not falsify your Promises but in future you must not Sell on Credit at all nor under six shillings for Cash. I will write to Mr. Morris [2] and should he think proper this Direction may be altered but not otherwise. I must insist on an Account immediately of what Bills you have sold and on what Rates of Credit. I mean as those disposed of within a Week past. If you have sold any under six Shillings as this was contrary to express Instructions it shall not be complied with.[3] I am yours &Ca.

MS: Ofcl LbC, DLC.
1. See Diary, August 10.
2. Letter not found. For a previous letter to the Financier on this subject, see Gouverneur Morris to RM, August 8.
3. For subsequent developments in the sale of bills of exchange, see Diary, August 11.

Gouverneur Morris to the Board of War

Office of Finance 10th. Augt. 1781.

Gentlemen

The Captains of the public Schooners wait upon you to fix the Terms on which they will go to Duck Creek with the Schooners and bring up the Flour and Pork lodged there.[1] Whatever Sum you agree for shall be paid and I am content that such Part as is essentially necessary shall be in Advance. You will know better than I can what Terms are most proper. I will however submit to your greater Information and Judgment whether a Sum in gross to include all Wages of Seamen, Provisions &ca. &ca. would not be most conducive both to their private Advantage and also to the public Interest. In promising Payment for the present Service all Idea of former Demands is excluded and so I have already informed them.[2]

With all possible Respect I have the Honor to be Gentlemen your most obedient and humble Servant.

MS: Ofcl LbC, DLC.
1. On this operation, see Diary, August 7 and 10.
2. See Gouverneur Morris to the Board of War, August 12, and for the outcome of the negotiations with the captains, see Diary, August 14.

From John Bondfield[1]

Philadelphia
The honble Robert Morris Esq   Bordeaux 10. Augt. 1781
Sir

Accept my unfeined congratulations for the honour conferrd on you by the unanimous voice of the United American States, an elevation superior to any in the gift of a Monarchy, where Cabal and intrigue influence almost all public places of Trust.

Monsieur Necker after having by unwearied application and unexampled marks of disinterested perseverance, raised the finances of this Kingdom to a state unknown for centuries, having reduced the Expenditure by many bold Strokes within the annual amount of the recette; [2] and at a period of extraordinary disbursements; in forming a navy totally annihilated defray'd the whole without the additional Impost of a livre on the subjects, by a cruel opposition from a branch of administration whose study ought to have Supported his existence, has been obliged to retire.[3] The effects of his resignation are already felt, Payments not being so strictly observed,[4] and the Farmers General [5] who were before in a humble State of Supplication and dependence have already obtained their former influence by a loan gratuite of Three millions, which the new Controlleur General [6] has received with apparent promises of gratitude. God grant the states of America ever independent, and their places of trust filt by men equally qualifyed for probity, abilities and application, as him who has the honour to be at the head of the american finances.

Wishing you every Satisfaction in the high office to which you are voted, permit me to assure you of my Sincere attachment. If at any time my Services on this Side can be to you useful permit me to crave the continuance of your friendship, and if at any time my interest should come to be canvast by the grand council or committee of the States (which the nature of my Station as agent at this city may occasion) of your Support.

With due respect I have the honour to be Sir Your most obedient Humble Servant [7]

MS: Copy, Robert Morris Papers, NN.
1. John Bondfield, a merchant sympathetic to the American cause residing at Montreal, procured supplies for the American forces retreating from Canada in May

1776. Later that year he resettled in Bordeaux, where he solicited the patronage of the American commissioners in France, forwarding their letters, and, apparently without success, seeking a major contract to supply clothing. Late in March 1778, William Lee, acting for the commissioners, appointed him commercial agent at Bordeaux, Bayonne, Rochefort, and La Rochelle. After the war he became consul at Bordeaux and handled American business there until at least 1789. His occasional correspondence with RM dates back to 1776, and the present communication, consisting of local information coupled with a reminder of his availability, is typical of his letters. Bondfield to RM, February 4, 1776, October 10, 1777, and March 4, April 4, and August 20, 1778, Robert Morris Papers, NN; Congressional Commissioners in Canada to Philip Schuyler, May 11, John Thomas to the Congressional Commissioners in Canada, May 15, and Benedict Arnold to the Congressional Commissioners in Canada, May 15 and 17, 1776, Clark and Morgan, eds., *Naval Documents*, V, 42, 97, 99, 133; William Lee to Richard Henry Lee, March 23, 1778, Worthington C. Ford, ed., *Letters of William Lee, . . . 1766–1783* (Brooklyn, N. Y., 1891), II, 407–408; Butterfield, ed., *Adams Diary and Autobiography*, II, 294n., IV, 51n.; Thomas Jefferson to Demoulin de Seille & Son, August 8, 1786, and to Dr. Lambert, November 13, 1787, Boyd, ed., *Jefferson Papers*, X, 200, XII, 353.

    2. That is, tax receipts.

    3. Jacques Necker resigned as French Director General of Finance on May 19, 1781.

    4. For a different view, see William Carmichael to RM, August 13.

    5. The Farmers General was a syndicate of 40 tax farmers incorporated in 1681 by Jean Baptiste Colbert (1619–1683), finance minister of Louis XIV, for the more systematic collection of various taxes on commodities. In 1726, during the reign of Louis XV, it became a quasi-monopoly. Private entrepreneurs, the Farmers General (who numbered 60 between 1756 and 1780) made profits by contracting to collect taxes for the crown and by performing a variety of banking services, including lending and transferring money for, and offering credit to, the government. As Director General of Finance from 1777 to 1781, Necker reduced the number of Farmers General to 40, curtailed their power and influence, and placed them under the careful supervision of his department. Bosher, *French Finances*, 8–9, 74–76, 156–161.

    6. The title *Contrôleur général des finances* was usually given to French ministers of finance, but neither Necker nor his successor, Jean François Joly de Fleury de la Valette (1718–1802), minister of state and finances, 1781–1783, held this title. *Ibid.*, 47, 172.

    7. Subjoined to the manuscript of this letter is Bondfield's letter of September 10.

From John Holker

[*Philadelphia, August 10, 1781.* On August 29 RM wrote to Holker: "Your Letter of the tenth Instant was delivered to me a few Days ago being after my return from Camp on the twenty first Instant." *Letter not found.*]

From Gouverneur Morris

[*Philadelphia, ca. August 10, 1781.* Writing on this date to Haym Salomon about the broker's dealings in bills of exchange for the Office of Finance, Gouverneur informed him that "I will write to

Mr. Morris" for further directions. For a previous letter to the Financier on this subject, see Gouverneur Morris to RM, August 8. *Letter not found.*]

Diary: August 11, 1781[1]

Various Applications for Money from Mr Hillegas [2] Clerks in the Office &Ca; declined answering untill some time next Week.[3] Mr. Holker is to let me have Bills of 1000 and 1500 Livres to the Amount of 50,000 Livres immediately.[4] Mr Rochetrun [5] calld on me about Exchange. Gave leave to sell at such Rate as he pleased. He mentions to me the Ideas I had communicated to the Minister.[6] Wishes that it may be a joint Operation and that he may have next Week to get as much Money in as he can. Says he could not venture at selling Bills under the Actual Exchange, for Fear of Blame from the Ministry without he did it in Concert with the Administration here. I decline any joint Operations, by Observing I am not attachd much to the Plan, but if it should be necessary I am content to bear the whole Loss and save him the Blame he apprehends. The Minister calls, and observes that the Effect of the Plan can only be momentary. The radical Cure of the Evil must be by putting all the Bills in the Hands of the Superintendant *or of an Agent to be subject to his Control.*[7] Agree with him in Opinion. He Observes that to lower the Exchange would be a certain Loss without any adequate advantage. Agree that the Advantage would be uncertain; assure him I am not attachd to the Plan.

Wrote The Board of Treasury, requesting Impression of 200 bills be taken from Plate, cut for this Office.

Issued Warrant in favour of Wm Banks [8] for £18.15 Specie on account of Salary due him.

Issued Warrant in favour of Wm. Woodhouse [9] for £6. Specie for 1 Ream large Paper.

1. The Diary of this date was kept by Gouverneur Morris. See Diary, August 7 and 21.
2. Michael Hillegas was Treasurer of the United States.
3. See Diary, August 16.
4. The bills of exchange were to be in Haym Salomon's favor. See Gouverneur Morris to John Holker, August 12; also Diary, August 9.
5. De Roquebrune.
6. Chevalier de La Luzerne, French minister at Philadelphia. For Gouverneur Morris's scheme to underbid competitors in the sale of bills of exchange, see Diary, August 9 and 10.
7. On RM's desire to avoid competition with the French in selling bills of exchange, see his letter to La Luzerne, August 2, and notes, in which he disclaimed any personal interest, but indicated his willingness to negotiate bills of exchange in

behalf of the French forces as well as the United States. He discussed the matter further with French officials during his visit to Washington's headquarters. See Diary, August 21.

8. William Banks was a clerk in the Office of Finance.

9. William Woodhouse (d. 1795), a Philadelphia bookbinder, bookseller, and stationer from 1765 until his death. In 1782 he established the only pencil manufactory in the United States. His son William Woodhouse, Jr., continued the business until 1814. H. Glenn Brown and Maude O. Brown, "A Directory of the Book-Arts and Book Trade in Philadelphia to 1820 Including Painters and Engravers," *Bulletin of the New York Public Library,* LIV (1950), 143.

Gouverneur Morris to the Governors of Delaware and Virginia

Office of Finance, August 11, 1781. "Having some Reason to beleive that the Letter of which the aforegoing is a Copy [1] has miscarried I take the Liberty in the Absence of the Superintendant to transmit this as his official Assistant." [2]

MSS: ALS, to the President of Delaware, Executive Papers, De-Ar; ALS, to the Governor of Virginia, Continental Congress Papers, Vi.

1. RM's Circular to the Governors of the States, July 25, 1781.

2. According to its manuscript endorsement, the letter addressed to Virginia, which is not clearly dated and possibly is of August 10, was received on August 23. See also the Governor of Virginia to RM, September 5.

Gouverneur Morris to the Board of Treasury

Office of Finance 11. Augt. 1781.

Gentlemen,

Mr Faulkner[1] informs me that the Inspectors are Subject to your Orders. He will bring with him a Plate cut under his Inspection for the Use of this Office. The Bills will be wanted immediately on the Arrival of the Superintendant. I am therefore as his official Assistant to request that you will direct two hundred of the Impressions to be made as soon as possible.

I have the Honor to be with all possible Respect Gentlemen yours &ca.

MS: Ofcl LbC, DLC.

1. Nathaniel Falconer was a Pennsylvania ship captain with a long record of transatlantic crossings for a decade prior to 1775. In that year his name appeared on a list of persons who were probably suggested for commands in the navy that Congress was then assembling. Falconer did not receive a command, but during the following year he served on the Pennsylvania Committee of Safety, performing a variety of duties relating to state naval affairs. In 1776 Continental agents employed him to supervise the construction of vessels at Philadelphia and Rhode Island. For a brief period he served the Board of War as supervisor of flour purchases undertaken by

Pennsylvania at Congress's direction, but was dismissed on February 17, 1778, for authorizing higher prices than those fixed by state law. This did not prevent his election on August 19, 1778, as one of the commissioners of the Navy Board of the Middle Department at Philadelphia, a position which he declined. On September 12 following, Congress named him a superintendent, or inspector, of the Continental press for striking bills of credit, bills of exchange, and loan office certificates, an office in which he was continued on December 4, 1780, and which he apparently retained until its discontinuation in June 1782. Falconer was a subscriber to the Bank of Pennsylvania, and in 1784 he became a shareholder in the Bank of North America. RM, as Agent of Marine, appointed him on November 21, 1781, one of three judges to inquire into the loss of the frigate *Trumbull.* Butterfield, ed., *Adams Diary and Autobiography,* II, 221 and n., 222n.; Minutes of the Pennsylvania Committee of Safety, December 30, 1775, June 13, 1776, and Commissioners for Building the Philadelphia Frigates to the Commissioners of Naval Stores, January 9, 1776, Clark and Morgan, eds., *Naval Documents,* II, 1162, 1163n., III, 304, 693–694, 696–697, V, 499; *Journals of the House of Representatives of Pennsylvania, 1776–1781,* 55; Marine Committee of Congress to Falconer, October 9 and 13, 1776, Paullin, ed., *Out-Letters,* I, 24–25, 31–32; *JCC,* XII, 887; Lewis, *Bank of North America,* 20, 137; Diary, and RM to the Inspectors of the Press, both November 13, RM to Samuel Nicholas, James Craig, and Nathaniel Falconer, November 21, 1781, and RM's Circular to the Inspectors of the Press, June 14, 1782.

To Gouverneur Morris

[*Dobbs Ferry, New York, ca. August 12, 1781.* Writing in his Diary in Philadelphia on August 21, RM described as follows a letter he had addressed to his official assistant while at Washington's head-quarters: "I wrote . . . to Gouverr. Morris Esqr. to give Orders for the purchase of 1000 barrels of flour at this City and have the same forwarded to Trenton and thence by land Carriage to the Army, but some intended movements of the Army and the other Measures I took at Camp rendering this unnecessary I wrote to countermand it." RM's initial letter, written in cipher, was received on August 16 and, judging by the fact that Washington's letter of August 2 took four days to reach RM, probably was dated August 12. See RM to Thomas Lowrey, August 14, and for the steps taken by Gouverneur Morris to implement RM's orders, see Diary, and Gouverneur Morris to John Hazelwood, both August 16. RM's letter of counter-mand, also not found, was probably dated August 15, the day after Washington received intelligence that de Grasse's fleet would be available for allied operations in the Chesapeake region. *Letter not found.*]

Gouverneur Morris to John Holker[1]

[*Philadelphia*], *Monday Morning, August 12, 1781.* "Mr. Gouvr. Morris's Compliments wait on Mr Holker. Mr. Morris neglected mentioning to Mr. Holker that the Bills should be filled up in Favor of

Mr Haym Solomon. Mr Morris wishes that there may be 20 Setts of 1.000 and 20 of 1500 Livres." [2]

MS: Ofcl LbC, DLC.
1. John Holker was a French consul and supply agent for the French navy in America.
2. The bills of exchange for Haym Salomon, broker for the Office of Finance, were those mentioned in Diary, August 11. See also Lists of Bills of Exchange Delivered to Haym Salomon, August 22, and RM to Le Couteulx and Company, August 26.

Gouverneur Morris to the Board of War

[*Philadelphia*], *Monday Morning, August 12, 1781.* "Mr. Gouvr. Morris's Compliments wait on the honorable the Board of War. When the Board shall have agreed with the Captains of the Continental Schooners on the Terms of fetching the Flour and Pork from Duck Creek, Mr Morris will be glad to know them and the Time of their Departure." [1]

MS: Ofcl LbC, DLC.
1. On this subject, see Diary, August 7 and 10, and for subsequent developments, Diary, August 14.

Diary: August 13, 1781[1]

Wrote Notes to Mr Holker, Mr Chaloner and Board of War and sent a Letter to Mr. Morris with Intelligence from Europe in Cypher.[2]

1. The Diary of this date was kept by Gouverneur Morris. See Diary, August 7 and 21.
2. The letters to John Holker and the Board of War probably are those dated August 12. The letters to John Chaloner and RM have not been found.

Robert Morris and Richard Peters to George Washington

Camp [Dobbs Ferry, New York] 13th. Augt. 1781

Sir

The Orders of Congress which we have the Honour to communicate directing us to confer with your Excellency on the Subject of the proposed Numbers and Arrangements of the Army for the next Campaign, not having pointed out the Reasons inducing the Measure, we have the Honour to lay before you our Ideas on the Subject so far as we are acquainted with the Matter from a Conference at which we were present in Philadelphia, had by a Comittee of Con-

Richard Peters. Portrait by Rembrandt Peale, 1806.

gress, the Subscriber as Superintendant of Finance and the Board
of War pursuant to a Resolution of Congress with a Copy of which
your Excellency has been furnished.[1] After the full Conversation
with which we were honoured the 12th. instant [2] it is unnecessary
to enter at large into those Reasons or to urge the pressing Necessity of oeconomizing our Affairs so as to make our Revenues in a
great Degree meet our Expences. Your Excellency must be equally
sensible with us of this Necessity and we are perfectly convinced you
are equally disposed to assist in every Measure tending to promote
so desirable an Object. You are also impressed with the Impolicy
of calling on the States for Men or Money in Numbers and Quantities so extensive as to alarm the timid and to excite among even the
zealous and considerate Ideas of the Impracticability of carrying on
the War upon such Terms. Demands of this Nature instead of ani-
mating to Exertions are only productive of hopeless Languor. Your
mortifying Experience of the inadequate Compliance heretofore
with former Demands [3] will explain the Motives inducing to the
Expediency of moderating those Demands so as to render them
productive and in Case of Failure to leave the delinquent State
without Excuse. Your Excellency has doubtlessly considered that
the Class of Men who are willing to become Soldiers is much diminished by the War and therefore the Difficulties of raising an Army
equal to former Establishments have encreased and will continue
to encrease and embarrass the States in their Measures for filling
up their Quotas should the Mode of recruiting the Army be continued in the present Line. You will also have considered that the
Enemy proportionably debilitated by the War are incapable of opposing to us the Force we originally had to encounter [4] and therefore the Necessity of such extensive Levies as we formerly raized
seems to be in some Measure superceded. In what Degree the
Forces of these States should be decreased we do not pretend to
determine; leaving this to your Excellency's better Judgment. But
from past Experience it should seem that the States are incapable
of bringing into the Field an Army equal to that called for by the
last Arrangement.[5] Or if all the Demands of Congress on the States
become merely pecuniary [6] it does not seem probable that they can
or will furnish Money for raizing, equipping and supporting such
an Army. We should be happy were we capable from any Information we are possessed of to assist your Excellency in the Investigation of the Subject with Respect to the probable Designs or Force
of the Enemy the next Campaign. This must in its Nature depend
upon Contingencies at present even beyond Conjecture. At this
Time therefore in our Apprehension the only solid Ground of

Procedure is to consider what Force these States under present Circumstances are capable of producing.

Having thus in general mentioned the Ideas which have arisen on the Subject we beg to leave the Matter to your Excellency's Consideration and take the Liberty of proposing the following Queries after further mentioning that it has been conceived it would be expedient in Case of a Reform to lessen the Numbers of Regiments so as to make fewer Commissioned Officers necessary and to encrease the Numbers of Non Comissioned Officers [7] and Privates in those Regiments.[8] It has been supposed that a considerable Saving would ensue from this Measure by not having so many Officers in full Pay with their Horses, Servants, Baggage and other consequential Expences in the Field; or if they remain in Quarters from Want of Commands they are in a Situation disagreeable to their own Feelings and uselessly expensive to the public. We presume that Gentlemen qualified for Staff Officers might be found among the retiring Officers and that Artificers and other Persons employed by the Staff Departments should not enter into the present Calculation as the Officers at the Heads of those Departments should be enabled to carry on their Business without taking Men from the Line,[9] a practice introduced from Necessity very prejudicial to Discipline and productive of pernicious Consequences by diminishing the effective Force of the Army.

Query 1. Is a Reduction of the Numbers of Officers and Men as fixed by the last Arrangement of the Army expedient or proper?

2. How can this Reduction be brought about consistent with the Good of the Service and what Arrangement should be made in Consequence of this Reduction?

The Answers to the above Queries will no Doubt include the Numbers of Men necessary for the next Campaign and the Organization of them so as to designate the Number of Regiments and the Numbers in those Regiments both of Commissioned and Non Commissioned Officers and Privates as well regimentally as by Companies. The Expediency of having fewer Regiments of Horse and Artillery and of consolidating the independent Corps will also we presume come under your Excellency's Consideration.

What Periods of Enlistment under present Circumstances are 3d. most proper to be adopted?

What Regulations can be made to modify the Practice of taking 4th. Soldiers from the Line as Servants to Officers? On this Head we beg Leave to submit to your Opinion a Copy of a Motion made in Congress on this Subject.[10]

What is to be done with Officers by Brevet or those who have no 5. particular Commands? Can they not be placed in the Regiments or retire on Half pay? [11]

Would it be practicable, consistent with Justice and the Good of 6. the Service to call into actual Service Officers who have retired on half Pay by the former Arrangement to fill Vacancies happening in the Lines to which they respectively belong?

We have the Honour to be with the greatest Respect and Esteem your very obedient Servants

Robt Morris

S. I. of Finance

Richard Peters

Member of the Board of War

Copy Genl Varnum's Motion [12]

"Resolved That no Officer be permitted to take with him on Furlough any Soldier without receiving the Permission of the Commander in Chief or commanding Officer of a Separate Department. And that the Board of War take Order that Soldiers now retained from the Army in either Department as Waiters to Officers immediately join their respective Corps."

His Excellency Genl Washington

ENDORSED: Camp 13th: Augt. 1781/from/Robt. Morris and Richd./Peters Esqr./answered 21st Augst.

MSS: LS in Peters' writing, Washington Papers, DLC; Dft in Peters' writing, Anthony Wayne Papers, PHi; Ofcl LbC, DLC.

1. On the resolution of Congress and the conference, see Diary, July 31, 1781, and notes.

2. RM and Richard Peters, representative of the Board of War, arrived at headquarters on August 11 and the following day, according to RM's Diary of August 21, "had a long Conference with the General relative to the Numbers of which the Army should Consist for the next Campaign and the means of reducing the Number of Officers and Augmenting those of the Privates. This Conference branched out into various other Articles respecting departments, Expenditures, Oeconomy &Ca &Ca and therefore was considered by Mr Peters and myself as a general Conversation, but in order to bring the substance of it to the Point on which it Originated we Wrote his Excellency an Official Letter on the Subject." The letter is printed here. Washington replied on August 21.

3. Dft and Ofcl LbC: "Requisitions." According to a statement published in 1791, congressional requisitions for the Continental army were 75,760 men for the campaign of 1777, 44,892 for 1778, 41,760 for 1779, and 41,760 for 1780. Men actually

inducted, excluding militia and a small number serving short enlistments in regiments not attached to any state line, were 34,820 in 1777, 32,899 in 1778, 27,699 in 1779, and 21,015 in 1780. Thereafter, Congress limited its call to 33,408 men for the remaining years of the war. Those actually in service numbered 13,292 in 1781, 14,256 in 1782, and 13,476 in 1783. *Statements of the Receipts and Expenditures of Public Monies, During the Administration of the Finances by Robert Morris, Esquire, Late Superintendant of Finances; with Other Extracts and Accounts from the Public Records, made out by the Register of the Treasury, by Direction of the Committee of the House of Representatives, appointed by an Order of the House of the 19th March 1790, upon the Memorial of the said Late Superintendant of Finance, August 30, 1790* [Philadelphia, 1791], 26–34; for further discussion of the army establishment, see note 5 below, and Washington to RM and Richard Peters, August 21, and notes.

4. British troops in North America declined from 50,156 (including those in Canada) in February 1778 to 30,531 in March 1781, but rose to 35,641 in September 1781. Piers Mackesy, *The War for America, 1775–1783* (Cambridge, Mass., 1964), 524–525.

5. The reference is to a sweeping reorganization of the Continental army establishment adopted on October 3, 1780, and revised on October 21 in accord with Washington's recommendation. All regiments hitherto not attached to state lines, except Hazen's regiment, were eliminated and incorporated into the lines of the various states. Without altering the status of Hazen's regiment, which was reserved for foreigners serving in the Continental army, Congress reduced the total number of regiments to 59 and the number of men in the army to approximately 33,000 in addition to commissioned officers and supportive personnel. At the request of Washington, who had promised the French a larger army, Congress on October 21 increased the size of the army by about 2,000 men. Washington's intervention also persuaded Congress to withdraw the option in its resolutions of October 3 permitting the states to enlist men for one year. Congress now required the states to fill their quotas only by enlistments for the duration of the war. Congress also yielded to Washington's importunities by granting half-pay pensions for life, not only to officers who served until the end of the war but to those dismissed as a result of the consolidation of regiments. Washington to the President of Congress, August 20, to John Mathews, and to James Duane, both October 4, to the President of Congress, October 11, and to John Sullivan, November 20, 1780, Fitzpatrick, ed., *Writings of Washington*, XIX, 402–413, XX, 113–116, 117–118, 157–167, 371–374; Ezekiel Cornell to the Governor of Rhode Island, October 24, and the President of Congress to the Several States, October 26, 1780, Burnett, ed., *Letters*, V, 425–426, 428. The number of men called for by the resolution of October 21, 1780, differs somewhat from the total entered in the 1791 *Statements* cited in note 3 above.

6. An allusion perhaps to Washington's often-expressed wish that the states be disassociated from any part in raising or providing for the Continental army. See Washington to the President of Congress, August 20, and to John Sullivan, December 17, 1780, Fitzpatrick, ed., *Writings of Washington*, XIX, 402–413, XX, 488–491.

7. Ofcl LbC: the preceding ten words omitted.

8. Commissioned officers multiplied as a result of the excessive number of regiments in the Continental army. In 1777 the various state lines comprised 107 regiments which, added to regiments unattached to any state and serving directly under Congress, brought the total to 116. Although officered, these regiments lacked rank and file. On August 5, 1777, a committee of Congress returning from Washington's camp reported 16,920 men fit for duty, including 14,089 privates, 1,247 commissioned officers, and 1,584 sergeants and corporals, a ratio of over 1 commissioned officer to every 11 privates or 1 officer, commissioned or noncommissioned, to every 5 privates. Privates were in short supply because states did not fill their enlistment quotas, and the rank and file were further depleted by being taken into noncombatant service.

The ranks were further reduced by desertion, sickness, and the expiration of enlistments. A committee of Congress reported from camp in May 1780 that some companies which, under the establishment of May 27, 1778, should have included 53 men, had only 4 rank and file and that most of the others had no more than 15. From the remarks of RM and Peters, it would appear that an excess of officers to enlisted men still persisted in 1781 although Washington had argued in 1780 that so many officers were resigning that not enough remained to staff the regiments in existence before the reduction of that year. *Statements of the Receipts and Expenditures of Public Monies, During the Administration of the Finances by Robert Morris,* 28, 30; Washington to the President of Congress, November 18, 1779, and October 11, 1780, Fitzpatrick, ed., *Writings of Washington,* XVII, 125–133, XX, 157–167; Committee at Headquarters to the President of Congress, May 16, 1780, Burnett, ed., *Letters,* V, 145–147; see also Washington to RM and Peters, August 21.

9. For lack of money to hire civilians, soldiers were employed in noncombatant service in the Quartermaster, Commissary, and other departments as well as at numerous military posts. Ferguson, *Power of the Purse,* 131; see also Washington to the President of Congress, November 18, 1779, Fitzpatrick, ed., *Writings of Washington,* XVII, 125–133.

10. See below and note 12.

11. Washington was extremely concerned about the treatment of officers who were deprived of command by the elimination of their regiments. It was at his insistence that officers made supernumerary by the reduction of the army on October 3 and 21, 1780, were granted half pay for life along with those who remained in service for the duration of the war. Washington to Elbridge Gerry, Robert R. Livingston, and John Mathews, January 23, 1780, and to the President of Congress, April 3, August 20, and October 11, 1780, Fitzpatrick, ed., *Writings of Washington,* XVII, 431–436, XVIII, 207–211, XIX, 402–413, XX, 157–167; the President of Congress to the Several States, October 26, 1780, Burnett, ed., *Letters,* V, 428.

12. Dft and Ofcl LbC: motion omitted. This motion of James Mitchell Varnum, a Rhode Island delegate to Congress, may have been the one made and committed on June 18, 1781.

Gouverneur Morris to John Chaloner

[*Philadelphia, August 13, 1781.* On this date Gouverneur Morris recorded a memorandum of this letter in the Diary of the Office of Finance. *Letter not found.*]

From William Carmichael[1]

Sn. Ildefonso Augt. 13th 1781

Dear Sir

I had the pleasure of receiving two copies of your obliging favor of the 5th of June last.[2] Governeur Morris had informed me of your appointment to the Superintendency of the Finances,[3] but at the same time gave me to understand that you had not determined to charge yourself with [the?] office. Your accepting it gives me a twofold satisfaction, the certainty of our money affairs being in a better train than they have been and the consolation of reflecting that you who know so much better than [we?] the Situation of Public Credit, do not think it [irreparable?]. I have always found that my anxiety for the Public weal, has increased in proportion to my distance from the Scene of Action, for it has usually been my misfortune to have little other information of what passes, than what I have been able to collect from the Public Prints. It is the general opinion here and I beleive in Europe that it will be impossible for the States during the war to retreive the Credit of their paper and of consequence that all their military operations must become more Languid every day, and Nothing will thoroughly eradicate this Idea but some brilliant success on our part. I hope before this Letter reaches you, that seconded by our Allies, we may be able to strike an Effective blow against the head Quarters of Loyalty in the Middle States and if we can once bring this nation [4] to act defensively for us to the Southward, a very short period may put an End to the Enemys hopes of Subjugation. For such they certainly entertained at the opening of this Campaign. The Taking of Pensacola [5] hath given great Joy here, and if the Expedition against Minorca should have as fortunate an Issue,[6] It will be an encouragement to persist in a War that must terminate happily, provided there is sufficient patience and activity. The affairs of England look badly. Those of the East seem to affect them most sensibly. The War which Hyder Ally [7] has carried sucessfully into the heart of their Important Possessions, The Superiority and early appearance of the French Marine on their Coasts, their Delay in sending the force, they had projected to send, all contribute to Disappoint their expectations of Riches and Triumph over the Defenceless Dutch Settlements and make them tremble for their own. The sense of their Critical Situation has awakened their attention to the Neutral Courts. Their representations have certainly had some weight. The Armed Neutrality is not like to do what was expected from it, and the Empress of Russia has like many a pretty woman shown herself a Backslider.[8] I do not find that Mr Neckar's Dismission has occasioned any great change in the Credit or system of the Finances of his Court.[9] I am told that this Court has funds to last them for two or three months in the next year and I hope they will find money enough without great Difficulty for the operations of the next Campaign. I am told that two or three of the Neutral Nations are borrowing at present. You know the Difficulties that a Competition of that Nature occasions and if we cannot obtain all that we desire in that way, we must rather impute our failure to the necessities of others, than their want of good will. I wrote you last month [10] that I began to have some hopes of [*one word illegible*] terminating a Business, that will help us greatly, when a general negotiation comes on the Carpet. To forward which I beleive there are many Engines at work at present, and possibly indeed probably, something will be done in it towards the Close of the Campaign.[11]

On These Subjects I write the Sentiments of a Friend to a Friend and I wish them to be reserved to himself, because I have heard that Letters which I have written to others have been criticised unmercifully and have given a pretext to some to blame my conduct. We are now at Sn Ildefonso, one of the pleasantest royal Residences in Spain, and indeed there are few Superior to it Elsewhere. Mr Jay has a pleasant house in the Midst of Kitchen and fruit gardens, and I occupy a pavillon of it, where I am as tranquil, altho not more than a quarter of a mile from the palace, as you can be on the banks of the Schuylkil.[12] Tho' not quite so Joyous as you sometimes are. We resemble the Israelites in one particular, For we long for the flesh pots of the Country which we have left behind us. The onions are out of Question for this you know is the promised land of onions. Every Nation has its particular modes and appetites and I should be injust, while I pine now and then for Mr Morris Society, Corn Beef and Madera If I did not also assure my Countrymen that there are many good things in Spain, that reconcile me every day more and more to the Country and make me desire ardently to see the union that at present subsists between us perfectly cemented. I beg you to mention me in the proper manner to Mrs Morris and to all the Circle of your friends who do me the honor to remember me. I am with much Esteem and respect Your Obliged and Humble Servant

Wm. Carmichael

ENDORSED: Il De Fonso/13 August 1781/Wm Carmichael
MS: ALS, Robert Morris Papers, DLC.

1. Carmichael was secretary to John Jay, the American minister to Spain.
2. Letter not found.
3. In a letter which has not been found.
4. That is, Spain.
5. Spanish forces led by Bernardo de Gálvez captured the British post at Pensacola in West Florida on May 9, 1781. Mark M. Boatner III, *Encyclopedia of the American Revolution* (New York, 1966), 853.
6. Following the successful relief of the British fortress on Gibraltar, under blockade by the Spanish navy since June 1779, a Franco-Spanish naval force in July 1781 attacked instead the British garrison at Minorca, which surrendered after a protracted siege on February 4, 1782. William M. James, *The British Navy in Adversity: A Study of the War of American Independence* (London, 1926), 306, 372.
7. In alliance with the French, the Indian prince Haidar (or Hyder) Ali (1722–1782), ruler of Mysore, fought and eventually suffered a series of defeats at the hands of the British in the Second Mysore War, 1780–1784. *Webster's Biographical Dictionary* (Springfield, Mass., 1972).
8. The League of Armed Neutrality, formed by Catherine II (1729–1796) of Russia in 1780 to protect the trade of neutrals, eventually included Denmark, Sweden, the Netherlands, Prussia, Portugal, Austria, and the Kingdom of the Two Sicilies. Although the League hampered British naval operations, it failed to protect the commerce of the Netherlands, on whom Britain declared war on December 20,

1780, and had no decisive influence on the outcome of the war, as Catherine recognized when she called it the "Armed Nullity." Samuel Flagg Bemis, *The Diplomacy of the American Revolution*, rev. ed. (Bloomington, Ind., 1957), 149–163.

9. For a different assessment, see John Bondfield to RM, August 10.

10. Letter not found.

11. Carmichael's allusion is obscure, but may refer to the possibility of concluding a treaty of alliance with Spain, which the Spanish foreign minister Floridablanca agreed to discuss in September 1781. See Richard B. Morris, *The Peacemakers: The Great Powers and American Independence* (New York, 1965), 241–243.

12. A reference to RM's country estate, a tract known as "The Hills," on the east bank of the Schuylkill River about three miles from Philadelphia. Oberholtzer, *Morris*, 291–292.

From Gouverneur Morris

[*Philadelphia, August 13, 1781.* On this date Gouverneur Morris wrote in the Office of Finance Diary that he "sent a Letter to Mr. Morris with Intelligence from Europe in Cypher." For the code probably employed, see notes to RM to John Jay, July 7, 1781. *Letter not found.*]

From the Paymaster General
(John Pierce)

[*August 13, 1781.* Writing to Pierce on April 19, 1782, RM acknowledged "your letters of the 13th. of August and 22d Jany. last." *Letter of August 13, 1781, not found.*]

Diary: August 14, 1781[1]

Issued a Warrant in favour of Robt Scott £9.4.4 for Engraving Plate, Bill and Seals for this Office.[2]

Various Applications for Money. Let Mr Geddes have Money on a Warrant.[3] Mr Thomson[4] called on that Subject; declined untill I can obtain a State from the Treasury. Mr. Hillegas[5] calls on the same Subject; postponed. Discounted a Warrant of 200 Ds. Specie for Mr Storey.[6] Received the Draft of a Letter from Mr Holker; sent Observations on it.[7] Am to have the Bills soon; four Setts received.[8]

Board of War call about the Schooners.[9] Captains ask to the Amount of £170. Think it too much. Agreed with them that Colo Miles[10] write to Duck Creek to have the Flour sent up upon the cheapest Terms, the Pork to continue there.

Mr. Gibson[11] calld to get Cash. Declined. I told him I was in Hopes that Money Might be Obtained six Weeks hence to pay the Civil List.

1. The Diary of this date was kept by Gouverneur Morris. See Diary, August 7 and 21.

2. See Diary, July 27, 1781, and notes.

3. Congress elected William Geddes (d. 1792), a collector at Chestertown, Maryland, before the Revolution, one of the commissioners of the chamber of accounts in the Treasury Department on November 3, 1778. Two years later, on November 22, 1780, it appointed him paymaster general, but retracted its vote the following day. Geddes was very likely still employed in the Treasury when he petitioned Congress on May 1, 1781, for a warrant on the Continental loan officer of Pennsylvania for an advance of salary. Observing that partial payments to its civilian personnel were "injurious and unjust," Congress on May 7 directed the Board of Treasury to pay the balances of salaries due to its employees on the civil list, and Geddes' application to the Office of Finance probably concerned this matter. On January 28, 1782, Congress elected him an auditor in the Treasury Department; in accepting his resignation on June 3, 1783, Congress expressed itself "well satisfied with his diligence and fidelity in the discharge of the duties of his late office." *Maryland Journal,* October 16, 1792; Burnett, ed., *Letters,* VI, 144n.; Geddes to the President of Congress, May 1, 1781, PCC, no. 78, X, 331; *JCC,* XX, 465.

4. Probably Charles Thomson, secretary of Congress. See Diary, August 15.

5. Michael Hillegas, Treasurer of the United States.

6. John Story (1754–1791) of Massachusetts, who volunteered for military service in May 1775 and rose to the rank of lieutenant colonel in the Continental army with his appointment as a deputy quartermaster in the northern army in October 1777. When Quartermaster General Nathanael Greene resigned in August 1780, he ordered Story to remain at camp to wind up unfinished business and settle Quartermaster Department accounts. On July 24, 1781, Congress ordered Story to continue with this business and, in response to his appeal for a promotion, awarded him the pay and rations, but not the rank, of a captain in the line. Dissatisfied, Story submitted his resignation, which Congress accepted on August 15. Not long afterwards, Story became an aide to Major General William Alexander, Lord Stirling. Heitman, *Register;* Perley Derby and Frank A. Gardner, comps., "Elisha Story of Boston and some of his descendants," *Essex Institute Historical Collections,* L (1914), 303; Story to the President of Congress, August 10, 1781, and his memorial to Congress, February 7, 1783, PCC, no. 78, XXI, 105–106, no. 41, IX, 219–221; *JCC,* XXIV, 183–184.

7. Neither the draft letter from John Holker, a French consul and agent of the French navy in America, to an unidentified correspondent nor Gouverneur Morris's observations on it has been found.

8. Probably a reference to the bills of exchange mentioned in Gouverneur Morris to John Holker, August 12.

9. For the background of this subject, see Diary, August 7 and 10, and Gouverneur Morris to the Board of War, August 10 and 12; for subsequent references to the Continental schooners, see Diary, August 28 and November 2, 1781.

10. Colonel Samuel Miles, deputy quartermaster general for Pennsylvania.

11. John Gibson, a member of the Board of Treasury.

To Thomas Lowrey

Camp: Dobbs's Ferry [New York] 14. Augt. 1781.

Sir,

I have ordered one thousand Barrels of Flour to be sent from Philadelphia to Trenton, to the Care of Colonel Neilson Quarter Master at that Post,[1] and in Order that no Duty may Happen in the Transportation I must request you will Aid Mr. Neilson in forwarding it to Camp. The Situation of the Army requires Attention to this

Matter. What Money you Pay for carting shall be repaid you on my Return to Philadelphia. I rely on your having it done on the best Terms you possibly can for the public Interest. I am Sir your most obedient and humble Servant.

RM.

MS: Ofcl LbC, DLC.
1. John Neilson, deputy quartermaster general for New Jersey. See Diary, August 21, for RM's orders, which he subsequently countermanded, regarding this flour.

Gouverneur Morris to John Holker

[*Philadelphia, August 14, 1781.* In the Diary of the Office of Finance for this date Gouverneur Morris wrote: "Received the Draft of a Letter from Mr Holker; sent Observations on it." The intended recipient of Holker's draft communication has not been identified. *Letter not found.*]

Account of John Holker

[*August 14, 1781*]. An account with RM for bills of exchange drawn in favor of Haym Salomon by Holker on "Monsieur Boutin trésorier de la marine à Paris." The first entry is for August 14, the last for November 28, 1781.

MS: AD, in French, Holker Papers, DLC.

Diary: August 15, 1781[1]

Discounted a Warrant of Chas. Thomson Esqr.[2] and one of Richd. Philips, Stewd. to the President of Congress.[3] Received advice of the Capture of the Trumbull Frigate. Wrote Letters in Consequence to Mr Jay and enclosed them to Superintendant to be Signed and forwarded.[4]

Conference with the Board of War about sending Arms to North Carolina. Declined engaging in it in the Absence of Superintendant.[5]

Issued Warrant on Swanwick for £113.2.6 in favour of Colonel Miles [6] being for Transportation of Arms to Baltimore and for Paper &Ca. on Account of Public Service.

1. The Diary of this date was kept by Gouverneur Morris. See Diary, August 7 and 21.
2. Secretary of Congress.
3. Richard Phillips, otherwise unidentified, left Hartford, Connecticut, to become

steward to the president of Congress in July 1779 and served until at least 1785. Memorials of Phillips to Congress, February 15, 1780, and February 10, 1785, PCC, no. 42, VI, 236–237, 294; *JCC,* XV, 1225.

4. Late in July RM had ordered the 32-gun frigate *Trumbull,* commanded by James Nicholson, to Havana with dispatches and a cargo of flour and bills of exchange to raise capital for the Bank of North America. As the ship cleared the Delaware Capes on August 8, it was chased by the H.M.S. *Iris* and captured during the night after having been dismasted in a storm. News of its capture first appeared in the *New-York Gazette* extraordinary of August 11 and was republished in the *Pennsylvania Packet* on August 16. The "Letters" to John Jay which Gouverneur Morris drafted in consequence and sent to RM (then at Washington's headquarters in Dobbs Ferry, New York) undoubtedly were various copies of the dispatch of August 15 instructing the American minister to Spain not to honor the bills of exchange, a directive which embarrassed RM when the letter was subsequently intercepted and published by the British. Money for the Bank of North America from France arrived with John Laurens at Boston later in the month. Nevertheless, as RM advised Horatio Gates on September 15, the capture of the *Trumbull* was "a great loss to the Public and a disapointment to a most promising plan I had laid for turning . . . our paper into Silver." Paullin, *Navy of the American Revolution,* 238–239; Clowes, *Royal Navy,* IV, 72–73; see also RM to the Governor of Cuba, and to James Nicholson (two letters), all July 17, to Robert Smith, July 17 and 21, and to John Jay, August 15, and notes, Diary, September 18, and RM to the President of Congress, October 1, 1781; RM's letter to Jay was also registered in the Diary, Minutes of Sundry Transactions for 1781, printed at the end of the year.

5. On this subject, see the Governor of North Carolina to RM, August 4, and Diary, August 22, when the matter was further postponed by RM.

6. Colonel Samuel Miles was deputy quartermaster general for Pennsylvania.

To the Commissary General of Issues (Charles Stewart)

Camp [Dobbs Ferry, New York] 15. Augt 1781[1]

Sir

You will find enclosed herewith Copy of a Letter [2] I have just received from Udney Hay Esqr Agent to the State of New York whereby you may perceive the Assurances he gives me of a Supply of 3000 Barrells of Flour being delivered in Behalf of that State for the Use of the Army by the middle of next Month provided he can be supplied with Casks or the Money to pay for them. It was my Intention to have advanced the Money until you informed me that old Flower Barrells sufficient or nearly sufficient are lying at the different Posts on Hudsons River which with some Expence of Cooperage may be made to answer this Purpose. I am therefore to desire you will deliver to the said Udney Hay Esqr or to his Order 3000 of those Barrells or such Part thereof as can be had without Loss of Time and I will write to his Excellency Govr Clinton to supply Mr Hay with what Money may be necessary to pay Cooperage and purchase the Remainder of the Casks if you do not supply the whole Number; [3] for the Demands since made on me for Money will not admit of any Supply to Mr Hay from the little I have with me. I shall depend on this Flour or the greater Part of it and calculate accordingly, therefore you will remember to urge the Delivery of it at the Time mentioned so that no Want may take Place from Neglect or Inattention. I am Sir your very humble servant

Robt Morris

Charles Stewart Esqr
Comy Genl of Issues

ADDRESSED: On public Service/Charles Stewart Esqr/Commissary General of Issues/Camp/Robt Morris ENDORSED: From the Hon Rob Morris/16 [i.e. 15] Augt. 1781
MSS: LS, Stewart Papers, MH; Ofcl LbC, DLC.
1. The text of this letter is in the writing of Richard Peters of the Board of War, who accompanied RM to Washington's headquarters. For the background of this letter, see Diary, August 21.
2. Dated August 15.
3. See RM to the Governor of New York, August 15, and notes.

From Udny Hay[1]

Camp [Dobbs Ferry, New York] 15 August 1781.

Sir

By an Act of the Legislature of this State passed 27th March last; and altered and amended in the month of June, five thousand Eight hundred Barrells of flour, or a quantity of wheat equivalent thereto, was to be collected on or before the first of September next; [2] from every intelligence yet received I have the greatest reason to believe that about three thousand Barrells thereof might be deposited on the Banks of the Hudson by the middle of next month, had I at present a sufficient sum of hard money to purchase the Casks into which it must be put, and would therefore if consistent with your other plans, request you to favour me with a sum sufficient for that purpose, which I will engage to pay as soon as any hard money the property of the State and not appropriated by Law comes into my hands, and should I not receive any, I shall lay the matter before the Legislature at their next meeting, and have not the least doubt but the State will give you Credit for and repay the same as soon as in their power.[3] You are fully sensible, Sir, of the many disapointments that generaly Occurr in collecting Specific supplies by coercive Laws, and will therefore I doubt not make the proper allowance for any failure that may arise for though I think the opinion above given respecting the quantity that may be collected is well founded, and though I know my own determination to use the most vigorous methods in my power to prevent any disappointment, yet so many untoward circumstances may turn up in the present situation of this State, that I must request You to esteem the collection of the three thousand Barrells only as probable, not absolutely certain.[4] I have the honor to be with every sentiment of respect Sir Your most obedient humble servant

Udney Hay

The Honorable Robert Morris Esq.
(Copy)

ENDORSED: Copy/Udney Hay/To Robt. Morris Esqr. 15 Augt. 1781
MSS: Copy, Charles Stewart Papers, MH; copy, George Clinton Papers, N.
1. This letter was in reply to RM's application to Hay "for Supplies on behalf of the State of New York to which he is Agent" (see Diary, August 21). RM enclosed copies of it to Commissary General of Issues Charles Stewart and Governor George Clinton of New York in letters dated August 15.
2. See Laws of the State of New York (Albany, 1886–1887), I, 363–366, 384–385, for the act of March 27, 1781, and the amending legislation of June 29, which is incorrectly dated there. On the amending act, see Votes and Proceedings of the [New York] Assembly [September 7, 1780–June 30, 1781] [Poughkeepsie, 1780–1783?] for June 18 through 29.
3. Of this request RM wrote the following comment in his Diary, August 21: "I intended at first to furnish the Money to pay for Casks, but some observations I made on this Gentlemans Solicitude to get the Money with an apprehension of bad Consequences following such an Advance to a State Agent determined me not to do it." Instead, RM asked Commissary General of Issues Charles Stewart to furnish Hay with the necessary casks. See RM to Stewart, and to Hay, both August 15.
4. This statement was a modification of the more positive assurances which Hay had given to RM earlier in conversation. See RM to Hay, August 15.

To Udny Hay

Head Quarters [Dobbs Ferry, New York] Augt. 15. 1781.

Sir
   I have received your Letter of this Date and am sorry to observe that your Assurances of supplying three thousands Barrels of Flour by the middle of next Month provided you are furnished with Money to pay for the Casks are not so strong and positive in the Letter as they were in Conversation; [1] however the great and increasing Consumption of this Army renders the specific Supplies from your State indispensably necessary and I am compelled to form dependance on these three thousand Barrels being delivered about the Time you mention. The Demands for Money are so numerous and pressing that I do not find it in my Power to supply you with any from the small Sum I have here as was my first intention; but in Order to facilitate your Delivery's I have desired Charles Stewart Esqr. Commy. Genl. of Issues to deliver to you or to your

Order three thousand empty flour Barrels or so many thereof as he may find at the different Posts on the Hudsons River and I have written to his Excellency Governor Clinton requesting that he will cause you to be furnished immediately with so much Money as may be necessary to pay for Cooperage and for so many Casks as Mr. Stewart may fall short, which I have no doubt he will readily comply with, [2] therefore I have referred his Excellency the Commander in Chief and the said Commissary to a full dependance on this flour and if any Disappointment ensues the Army will suffer. I am Sir your most obedient and humble Servant

RM

MS: Ofcl LbC, DLC.
1. See Diary, August 21.
2. RM's letters to both Stewart and Governor George Clinton of New York are dated August 15.

To John Jay[1]

Office of Finance 15th. Augt. 1781.

Sir

Inclosed you have a list of sundry Bills of Exchange drawn on you.[2] I wrote you relatively to these Bills on the twenty ninth day of July last with sundry Enclosures explanatory of my Letter. I am now to inform you that the Advices contained in that Letter must from particular Circumstances be totally disregarded. Should any of the Bills mentioned in the enclosed List come to your Hands you will be pleased to protest them, and assign if you please as a Reason therefor that you have express Instructions to that Purport. The Uncertainty whether you have received my Cypher [3] prevents my using it on this Occasion. The Importance of the Subject obliges me to write and as I send many Copies the Risque of Capture and Inspection is too great to be more particular.

The Gazettes will furnish you with our latest Intelligence. That of New York announces the arrival of near three thousand Hessian Troops and the Capture of the Trumbull Frigate.[4] Neither of these are very agreable Circumstances. However we must wait the Course of Events and struggle as well as we can against adverse Fortune. Our Affairs to the Southern wear no unpleasing Aspect. And altho it is impossible at this Distance to determine what Effect European Movements may have on American Politicks, Our Government acquires daily a Firmness and Stability which will not easily be shaken. I have the Honor to be with great Respect your most obedient and humble Servant.

RM

MSS: Ofcl LbC, DLC; Spanish translation, Papeles procedentes de Cuba, AGI; Sparks transcript of Spanish translation, MH.

1. On August 15, after receiving news of the capture of the frigate *Trumbull*, bound for Havana under the command of Captain James Nicholson with a cargo of dispatches, flour, and bills of exchange, Gouverneur Morris drafted and forwarded this letter to RM, who was then at Washington's headquarters in Dobbs Ferry, New York. The letter was intercepted by the British, probably after receiving the Financier's signature, and published with the accompanying list of bills of exchange in the New York *Royal Gazette* on September 12. To it, printer James Rivington prefaced "The Mystery of Iniquity, or a Warning to all Dealers in Bills with Congress," and in mock praise of American finances exclaimed: "Admirable Financing this, truly Mr. Morris! But what else can be done by the Financier of a Bankrupt Commonwealth." Milking the letter of its propaganda value, Rivington republished it in the *Royal Gazette* on September 15 and again on October 6 after the *Pennsylvania Packet* reproduced it on September 20 with Rivington's comments and a defense of RM's actions. The incident brought members of Congress to the Office of Finance on September 18 for an explanation of the letter. RM replied that he had stopped payment on the bills lest the British attempt to present them for payment. By this time, however, RM had concluded that Captain Nicholson had sunk the bills prior to capture. Jay's acknowledgment of the letter, which was also registered in the Diary, Minutes of Sundry Transactions for 1781, printed at the end of the year, has not been found. See Diary, August 15, and notes, and September 18, and RM to the President of Congress, October 1, 1781.

2. MSS: Ofcl LbC, DLC (two texts); copy, PCC, DNA; Spanish translation, Papeles procedentes de Cuba, AGI; Sparks transcript of Spanish translation, MH. The list, which is omitted here, was also enclosed in RM to Robert Smith, July 21, 1781, and was printed in the New York *Royal Gazette* on September 12.

3. Enclosed in RM to Jay, July 7, 1781.

4. A report of August 11 from the *New-York Gazette* extraordinary announcing the arrival of 3,000 Hessian soldiers and the capture of the *Trumbull* was republished in the *Pennsylvania Packet* on August 16. Similar reports appeared in the *New-York Gazette, and Weekly Mercury* of August 13, in the New York *Royal American Gazette* of August 14, and in the New York *Royal Gazette* of August 15.

To Gouverneur Morris

[*Dobbs Ferry, New York, ca. August 15, 1781.* On this letter, see RM to Gouverneur Morris, ca. August 12, which it countermanded. *Letter not found.*]

To the Governor of New York (George Clinton)

Head Quarters near Dobbs Ferry [New York]
August 15th. 1781

Sir

I have received a letter of this date from Udny Hay Esqr. agent for your State, wherein he assures me that he will deliver on Hudsons River about 3000 barrells of Flour on behalf of the State in part of the Specific Supplies,[1] provided I can advance him Money to pay for the Casks, which I intended to do, untill informed by Charles Stewart Esqr. Commissary Genl. of Issues that there are empty barrells sufficient or nearly sufficient at the different Posts on that River to answer the purpose; as with the expence of a little Cooperage they can be made fit to hold the flour. I have therefore directed the same to be delivered to Mr Hay or to his order and as I find this supply of Flour indispensably necessary to our Army, I am to request the favour of your Excellency to give immediate orders that Mr. Hay may be furnished with Money sufficient to pay the Cooperage and for so many Casks (if any) as may still be wanting. I would not have troubled you with this application but I meet with such pressing demands for Money as will consume the small Sum I have with me, and as I must form a dependance on the Specific Supplies due from this State, I trust that your Excellencys exertions will remove Mr. Hays obstacles, otherwise the army will again suffer.[2] I have the honor to be Your Excellencys Most Obedient and humble Servant

Robt Morris

His Excelly The Governor and Commr in Chief
of the State of New York

P. S. On looking into Mr Hays letter again, I find he has been more cautious in the assurances in his letter than he was in Conversation, therefore I beg leave to enclose a Copy of it.

ADDRESSED: His Excelly/The Governor and Commander in Chief/of the State of/ New York/Robt Morris ENDORSED: Augt 15th. 1781/Mr. Morris (Supt. of Finance)/Letter on the Subject of Flour/&c &c &c
MSS: ALS, Clinton Papers, N; Ofcl LbC, DLC.
1. On specific supplies, see notes to John Morin Scott to RM, May 30, 1781.
2. Finding that the number of empty flour casks that Commissary General of Issues Charles Stewart could supply would not exceed 200, Hay appealed to Governor Clinton on August 21 for hard money to purchase the remainder. There is no record of Clinton's reply, but in the absence of congressional authorization, RM on September 7 refused another request by Hay for money to buy the casks. On October 12 Clinton was informed that as of September 30 Hay had delivered less than 300 barrels of flour and that a large supply was not to be expected from him. Udny Hay to Clinton, August 21, and William Heath to Clinton, October 12, 1781, Hastings and Holden, eds., *Clinton Papers*, VII, 238–239, 395; see also RM to the Commissary General of Issues, and to Udny Hay, both August 15, and Diary, August 21 and September 7.

Diary: August 16, 1781[1]

Received Letter from Superintendant.[2] Decyphered it; sent for Mr Hazlewood;[3] engaged him to procure 1000 barrells of Flour and send it to Trenton &ca; gave him a Note on that Subject. Wrote to Superintendant.[4] Applications from Mr Hillegas[5] Clerks &Ca. for Money; declined. Mr. Milligan[6] on the same Errand.

1. The Diary of this date was kept by Gouverneur Morris. See Diary, August 7 and 21.

2. This letter, dated ca. August 12, has not been found. See Diary, August 21.

3. John Hazelwood, Pennsylvania's commissioner of purchases for the Continental army in Philadelphia.

4. Letter not found.

5. Michael Hillegas, Treasurer of the United States. See Diary, August 11.

6. James Milligan, Auditor General of the United States.

Gouverneur Morris to John Hazelwood

Philada. 16. Augt. 1781.

Mr. Hazlewood will purchase on the best Terms he can and for as long Credit as he can one thousand Barrels of Flour condemn'd for being coarse or specky but of good Quality, sound and sweet.[1] He will have the Hoops driven tight and a lining Hoop put on the heads of each Cask; he will mark the Casks IH [2] and send them with proper Invoices &ca. Numbered to   [3] Neilson Esqr. deputy Quarter Master General at Trenton on the cheapest Terms of Freight &ca. which he can agree for. He will accomplish this Business as soon as possible. And will settle with the Superintendant on his Return the Compensation he is to receive for his Trouble. The Weight of Flour in each Cask will be also marked on it.

MS: Ofcl LbC, DLC.

1. This note to Hazelwood, Pennsylvania's commissioner of purchases for the Continental army in Philadelphia, was sent in response to RM's letter to Gouverneur Morris, ca. August 12, which has not been found and which was subsequently countermanded. See RM to Thomas Lowrey, August 14, and Diary, August 21.

2. Thus in manuscript. See RM to Matthew Ridley, August 21, and notes.

3. Space left blank in manuscript. John Neilson was deputy quartermaster general for New Jersey.

From Gouverneur Morris

[*Philadelphia, August 16, 1781*. On this date Gouverneur Morris made the following memorandum in the Office of Finance Diary: "Wrote to Superintendant." *Letter not found.*]

Diary: August 17, 1781[1]

Applications for Money, and Refusals. Enquired if any State Paper could be borrow'd; advised some Persons to hoard it and to outrun the Appreciation by Sales at a lower rate.[2]

1. The Diary of this date was kept by Gouverneur Morris. See Diary, August 7 and 21.

2. For RM's intention to appreciate Pennsylvania currency, see Diary, July 19, and notes, and RM to Benjamin Franklin, July 21, 1781, and notes.

From William Scott

[*York, Pennsylvania, August 17, 1781.* On August 25 RM wrote to Scott, Pennsylvania's commissioner of purchases for York County: "I have received your Letter of the seventeenth Instant." *Letter not found.*]

From George Washington

Head Quarters Dobbs's Ferry [New York] 17th. Augt. 1781.[1]

Dear Sir

I have in confidence imparted to you the alteration of our late plan and made you acquainted with our intended operations.[2] Besides the provision necessary at the Head of Elk to carry the troops down the Bay a very considerable Quantity will be wanted in Virginia. I should suppose three hundred Barrels of Flour, as many of salt Meat and eight or ten Hhds of Rum would be sufficient at Elk.[3] For what will be consumed in Virginia, I imagine the order must be general, as we can neither ascertain the number of Men which will be drawn together or the time they will be employed.[4]

I have written to the Count de Grasse [5] and have requested him to send up his light Vessels of every kind to Elk, but I would nevertheless wish to have all that may be at Baltimore and the upper parts of the Bay secured. I shall therefore be obliged to you to take measures at a proper time for that purpose. When that time will be and when you shall give orders for the deposit at Elk, I will hereafter inform you.[6]

I shall direct the Quarter Master [7] in due season to take up all the small Craft in Delaware for the purpose of transporting the Troops from Trenton to Christeen.[8] Should he have occasion for advice or assistance from you upon this occasion I must request you to give him both.

I am confident it will be necessary to give the American Troops destined for southern service one Months pay in specie. This will amount to   [9] dollars. If it will be possible for you to procure this sum you will infinitely oblige me and will much benefit the service. I shall also stand in need of a sum of Specie for secret services. I suppose about 500 Guineas.[10] I have the honor to be with sincere Esteem Dear Sir your most obedient servant

Honbl. Robt Morris Esqr.

ENDORSED: Dobbs Ferry Augt 17th 1781/to the honble./Robt. Morris Esqr.
MSS: Dft in the writing of Tench Tilghman, Washington Papers, DLC; Varick transcript, Washington Papers, DLC.

1. RM no doubt received this letter while at headquarters, which he left on August 18. See Diary, August 21.

2. Washington refers to his decision to set aside the projected allied assault on New York City in favor of operations in Virginia. This decision followed the arrival at headquarters on August 14 of intelligence that de Grasse's fleet would be available for operations in the Chesapeake region until mid-October. See headnote and notes to Diary, August 21, and for previous uncertainty, Washington to RM, August 2 (second letter).

3. For RM's arrangements to deposit these supplies, see Diary, August 23 and 24, RM to the Commissary General of Purchases, August 24, and to the President of Delaware, and to the Governor of Maryland, both August 26; for RM's parallel arrangements to transfer provisions southward for the French forces, see RM to John Holker, August 7, and notes, and Diary, August 21, and notes.

4. See RM to the Governor of Virginia, August 23.

5. Washington to de Grasse, August 17, 1781, Fitzpatrick, ed., *Writings of Washington*, XXIII, 7–11.

6. See Washington to RM, August 27.

7. Colonel Samuel Miles, deputy quartermaster general for Pennsylvania.

8. Christiana, Delaware.

9. Space left blank in manuscript. See notes to Diary, September 1–5.

10. On these requests for money, see RM to Washington, August 22, Washington to RM, August 27 (where the request is again repeated), and RM to Washington, August 28 and September 6 (first, second, fourth, and fifth letters).

Diary: August 18, 1781[1]

Applications and refusals as usual for Money. Wrote Superintendant in Cypher.[2]

1. The Diary of this date was kept by Gouverneur Morris. See Diary, August 7 and 21.
2. Letter not found.

From Nathanael Greene

Head quarters High Hills
Santee [South Carolina] August 18th 1781[1]

Dear Sir

I was favord with your letter of the 12th of June by the hand of Governor Rutledge and I am sorry to inform you that the Governor met with none who were willing to interest themselves in the bank.[2] His route was through a tract of Country where the Inhabitants are little acquainted with commerce and therefore not likely to become adventurers in a measure of that sort. But whether it was owing to an objection to this particular scheme or to all projects of this kind that the people manifested no inclination to become interested in the bank I cannot pretend to determine. But certain it is, not a single subscriber could be found, nor a shilling of money raised.

To conduct a war which is carried on so much at arms end as the operations here are, so remote from supplies of every kind, and where the enemy can be reinforced with such facility, and we with such difficulty, and the whole service attended with so many contingencies, and all this to be done without money, and with a force little more than one third equal to the enemies is an unenviable task; and requires more experience and greater abilities than I possess. I find myself frequently ready to sink under the load of difficulties that oppress me, where all our resources depend upon expedients. Hitherto we have combated them with some degree of success; but this cannot be expected to continue without more effectual support. I know that Government is exceedingly embarassed, I feel for them. But it is nothing more than might have been expected from that unhappy policy to say nothing worse of it, I mean sporting with public credit.

No Nation ever had greater resources in the confidence of the people, than Congress had at the beginning of the war, nor would it have diminished to this day had they maintained their own dignity and a due subordination of the States. But the desire of indulging those and easing the people of heavy taxes led to measures that were no less dishonorable than they have been destructive to our true interest. The tender laws and the plan of redeeming the Continental Money forty for one,[3] have been replete with every kind of mischeif. Credit and reputation are much alike either in public or private life. Once lost they are very difficult to be regained; and no advantage obtained at the expence of our credit or reputation can compensate for the loss of them. It was ever my opinion that we ought to have supported the [4] Continental Money; and I am perswaded it would have afforded us the best medium of any plan we had it in our power to adopt. The hopes of benefiting by its appreciation would have supported its credit. If the States could have been prohibited from making Money [5] and the taxes kept in motion the Contin[en]tal money would have afforded a tolerable medium for business of all kinds. The regulating laws [6] were another source of mischief, indeed these and the tender laws were sufficient to stop all intercourse among men, where they could have no election in either price or pay especially where the Legislators of many States discoverd such dishonest intentions. Trade, commerce, and paper Money of all kinds, like religion [7] depend upon the opinion of the people, and where ever compulsion is made use [8] of they soon languish and dye.

I lament exceedingly that Congress have given up so much of their just and necessary prerogative into the hands of the different States; [9] and I am very apprehensive we shall want that force and vigour in our National character which is necessary to our security; and I am not less apprehensive that intestine broils and feuds will frequently convulse the empire for want of a sufficient respect and dependence of the States upon Congress. Politicks is a knotty subject and all general principles liable to many exceptions. Measures which were promising in prospect often terminate in opposite consequences. Perhaps what I conceive now unfavorable may produce National advantages. Time will bring all things to light; at present there rests too heavy a cloud upon the subject for me to penetrate it and therefore I will drop the matter.

When I tell you I am in distress dont imagine I mean little difficulties but suppose my situation to be like a Ships crew in a storm where the vessel is ready to sink and the water gains ground in the hold with every exertion to prevent it. It is a maxim in republican government never to despair of the common wealth nor do I; but I foresee more difficulties than I can readily see how to conquer. I hope to discharge my duty; but events will depend upon the means and upon the hand of providence. If I have any opportunity of obtaining Money and drawing bills on you I shall embrace it. But it is a very uncertain source and therefore I leave you to judge of the prudence of exposing an army to such contingencies.

The Enemy have lately burnt George Town and Dorchester.[10] A great part of their force is in the fork between the Congaree and Santee.

With the warmest wishes for your health, happiness, and success in your public, and private employments I am Dear Sir Your Most Obedient humble Servant

N Greene

Robert Morris Esqr

ENDORSED: [*Probably at a later date*] To Ro. Morris/August 18th. 1781/used/Hints respecting Restraints/on the States &ca
MSS: ADftS, Greene Papers, MiU-C; George Washington Greene transcript, CSmH.
1. Greene, commanding the Southern army, had failed, in a month-long siege during May and June, to dislodge the British from Ninety-Six, a fortified village in backcountry South Carolina. In mid-July he encamped his weary army in the High Hills of Santee, near the confluence of the Wateree and Congaree Rivers, where it remained for rest and rehabilitation during the next six weeks. Ward, *War of the Revolution*, II, 825.
2. In his letter of June 12 RM had explained to Greene that he had given a subscription list for the Bank of North America to Governor John Rutledge of South Carolina, who was to obtain as many subscriptions as possible and to turn over to Greene such proceeds as he should receive. RM was then to pay the amount of the subscriptions into the bank.
3. An allusion to the act of Congress of March 18, 1780, under which Continental currency was revalued at 40 to 1 of specie. See notes to John Morin Scott to RM, May 30, and the Secretary of Congress to RM, June 29, 1781.
4. Transcript: the word "old" restored here. It was excised from the ADftS.
5. That is, issuing paper money.

6. Greene refers to state legislation to control prices, establish and maintain embargoes, and suppress profiteering. Congress itself in 1777 passed several resolutions encouraging the states to take action against hoarders, to fix the value of goods and services, to enact confiscation laws, and to regulate retail trade. Ferguson, *Power of the Purse*, 33; Richard B. Morris, "Labor and Mercantilism in the Revolutionary Era," in Richard B. Morris, ed., *The Era of the American Revolution* (New York, 1939), 94–139.

7. MS: "regilion." Transcript: blank space left for this word.

8. Transcript: this word given incorrectly as "case."

9. Nationalists in this period frequently observed that out of "diffidence" as to its own authority Congress had surrendered powers to the states which it rightly possessed as a central government. See, for example, Alexander Hamilton to James Duane, September 3, 1780, Syrett and Cooke, eds., *Hamilton Papers*, II, 401–402; on the assertion of the implied powers of Congress under the Articles of Confederation, see Merrill Jensen, *The New Nation: A History of the United States During the Confederation, 1781–1789* (New York, 1950), 59.

10. After two encounters with American forces on July 25 and August 2, 1781, the British virtually destroyed Georgetown, South Carolina, in retaliation for the plundering of loyalists by irregulars under Thomas Sumter. Dorchester, about 15 miles northwest of Charleston, was occupied as a British post, but fell to Greene's forces in December 1781. Boatner, *Encyclopedia of the American Revolution*, 335, 420.

From Gouverneur Morris

[*Philadelphia, August 18, 1781*. On this date Gouverneur Morris wrote the following memorandum in the Office of Finance Diary: "Wrote Superintendant in Cypher." For the cipher in which this letter probably was written, see notes to RM to John Jay, July 7, 1781. *Letter not found.*]

Matthew Ridley to Gouverneur Morris

[*Baltimore, August 18, 1781*. On August 21 RM wrote to Ridley: "I returned from Camp last Evening and have now before me your Letter of the eighteenth in answer to Mr. Morris's of the eighth which latter I hereby confirm." *Letter not found.*]

From Benjamin Dudley

[*Boston, August 20, 1781*. On September 5 RM wrote to Dudley: "I am favored with your Letter of the twentieth of August last." Dudley's communication was enclosed in William Gordon to RM, August 23. *Letter not found.*]

From Nicholas Van Dyke

[*Philadelphia, August 20, 1781*. On August 21 RM wrote to Van Dyke: "I am this Instant favored with your Letter of the twentieth requesting me to appoint some Person to purchase Supplies for the Recruits at Christiana Bridge." *Letter not found.*]

Diary: August 21, 1781

With the entry that follows, Morris resumed the Diary in the Office of Finance which Gouverneur Morris had kept in his absence. Consisting principally of the Financier's record of his visit to Washington's headquarters at Dobbs Ferry, New York, including minutes of conferences and transactions in which he participated there between August 11 and 18, the Diary of this date, with its oblique references to the beginning of the Yorktown campaign, represents a turning point in the early history of the Office of Finance.

To achieve his objective of placing Continental affairs on a sound fiscal basis, Morris early had in view a streamlining of army expenditures. He had declared in his letter of May 14, 1781, to the President of Congress, accepting the office of Superintendent of Finance, that "it will be necessary that I should confer with the Commander in Chief on the various Expenditures of the War and the means of retrenching such as are Unnecessary." Shortly thereafter he advised Washington of his intention.[1] Washington, who had welcomed Morris's appointment as Congress's Financier, was impatient for the visit, telling Chevalier de La Luzerne, the French minister at Philadelphia, that "many very essential Matters in the Operations of the Campaign will [depend] upon the Assistance which he will be able to afford us." [2]

Circumstances beyond Morris's control delayed the desired consultation. The Financier did not take the oaths of office until June 27; the task of organizing the Office of Finance, the pressing demands for money from every department of the government, the current needs of the army itself, and the increasing scope of the duties assigned to him by Congress consumed all of his energies.[3] On July 16 Morris recorded in his Diary that La Luzerne, just returned to Philadelphia from Washington's headquarters, "pressed me to go there Assigning many reasons Why my Presence would be usefull." [4] Morris agreed to go to camp, business permitting, and by the last week in July was evidently set to make the journey. Accordingly, Congress on July 26 appointed a committee to confer with him, Washington, and the Board of War on the army establishment for 1782.[5] Following a conference attended by the committee, the board, and Morris, Congress on July 31 directed a member of the board to accompany the Financier to camp. Although Morris was prepared to leave for headquarters the following day, the Board of War did not appoint its emissary, Richard Peters, until August 3.[6] More importantly, demands for money to support current military operations were so urgent that Morris felt compelled to postpone his departure again.[7]

The possibility of transferring military operations from New York to Virginia complicated Morris's departure still further.[8] On August 6 he received a letter from Washington requesting information on the availability of transport vessels and provisions in the Chesapeake region.[9] A round of conferences ensued, and it was not until the following day that the Financier, leaving the management of the Office of Finance to his official assistant, Gouverneur Morris, set out with Richard Peters for Dobbs Ferry, New York.

The initial purpose of the conference was to make plans for the next year's campaign, a subject which Congress had always heretofore postponed until much later in the season.[10] However, the Financier's visit coincided with the final decision to attack the enemy in Virginia, a decision reached following Washington's receipt on August 14 of intelligence that de Grasse's fleet would shortly arrive off Chesapeake Bay and be available for operations there until mid-October.[11] The preparations thus set in motion commanded Washington's time, and it was not until August 21 that he replied to the letter which Morris and Peters had addressed to him on August 13 following their consultations.

Meanwhile, until his departure from headquarters on August 18, Morris conferred with Rochambeau and his staff on the problem of selling bills of exchange and provisioning the French forces, and arranged for additional supplies of flour for Washington's army, all the time rejecting constant applications for money. Returning to the Office of Finance on August 21 as the allied armies crossed the Hudson River at Kings Ferry on their march south, he took immediate steps to forward provisions and hire transports in readiness for their arrival at the Head of Elk.[12] The work of assisting the allied operations with money and matériel, a task which would occupy the next two months, was Morris's contribution to the victory at Yorktown.[13] That victory made it possible for him to develop and present to Congress his long-range financial programs for infusing the American Union with "a proper Political Form and Consistency." [14]

Minutes of Conferences &Ca taken at Camp by the Superintdt.[15]

The Superintendant returned from Camp last Evening, having left this City on Tuesday the 7th. at 11 OClock and Arrived at Dobbs Ferry on Friday Night [16] after a tedious Journey by the way of Trenton, Princetown, Greigs Town, Somerset Court House, Steels Tavern, Pluckemin, Veal Town, Morris Town, Boon Town, Totaway Bridge &Ca being oblig'd to take that rout for safety from the Enemy.[17] Mr. Peters from the Board of War and Mr James Wilson being in Company, Colo. Blaine Commissy Genl.[18] joined us at Prince Town on the road. We crossed Dobbs Ferry on Saturday Morning and arrived at Head Quarters about 10 OClock.[19] His Excelly. The General being out we did not see him untill about One when he returned and gave us a Chearfull and hearty Welcome. We had then an Oppertunity of seeing at his Levee which is held every Day at Head Quarters from Half after One OClock for an hour or an hour and a half, All The General Officers of the American and French Armies, The Commanders of Regiments, Heads of Departments and such Strangers As Visit Camp &Ca. We dined with His Excelly. and the next day [20] Mr Peters and myself had a long Conference with the General relative to the Numbers of which the Army should Consist for the next Campaign and the means of reducing

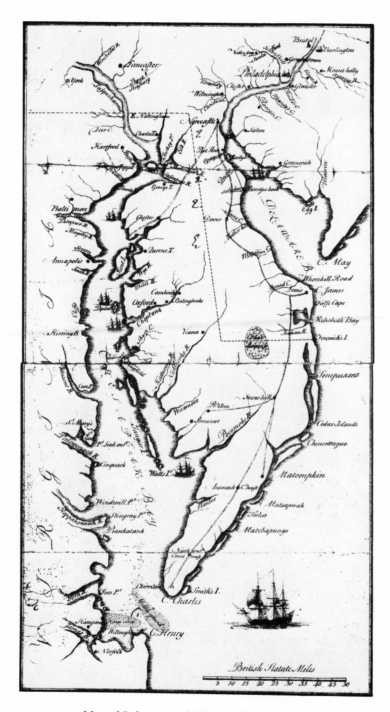

Map of Delaware and Chesapeake Bays, 1781.

the Number of Officers and Augmenting those of the Privates. This Conference branched out into various other Articles respecting departments, Expenditures, Oeconomy &Ca &Ca and therefore was considered by Mr Peters and myself as a general Conversation, but in order to bring the substance of it to the Point on which it Originated we Wrote his Excellency an Official Letter on the Subject [21] the Copy of which is with Mr Peters to be communicated to the Board of War and the Committee of Congress. His Excellency promised an Answer but his whole Attention and time being engrossed by a Variety of Objects whilst we staid at Camp, he could not do it then but has promised to send it after us.[22] On Monday, Tuesday and Wednesday [23] I had several conferences with his Excellency Gen: Washington on the different heads contained in a Memorandum made out here and Which I took with me.[24] They are as follows:

1st. To confer with Genl. Washington on the best means of ascertaining numbers with exactness as on this depend the distribution of Rations, Cloathing, Pay &Ca &Ca.

2d. How to check the Expenditures of Stores and Provisions, Forage &Ca.

3d. The manner of making up Pay rolls, and, Querie, whether Deaths, Desertions and Casualities could not be Converted into a recruiting Fund.

4th. Checks on the Expenditure of Cloathing and how to make the Officers of that Department Accountable.

5th. Oeconomy of Hospitals.[25]

6th. Retrenching the Pay of the Army.

7th. Reducing the Number of Regiments and encreasing the number of Privates in each Regiment.

8th. Officers to keep Rag Rolls. Clothing to be supplied in Lieu of what is lost or sold &c but Stopped from Pay.

9th. To break up all Posts, suffer no Rations or Forage to be drawn but at the Army. Mileage to be allowed Officers or Expresses travelling on Continental Service.

10th. Where Magazines of Provisions shall be established; quantities necessary to be always on hand.

11th. Respecting Contracts whether to be made for Rations or for the several Articles separately.[26]

12th. Respecting Forage and the Quarter Masters Department.

13th. Respecting Sutlers to be Licensed and pay the hard Money into the Military Chest &Ca.[27]

14th. Fixing the Number of the [28] Army for next Campaign.

15th. Steward to the Generals Familey and Estimates for his Table.

16th. To get rid of the Convention Troops by exchange or other-wise.[29]

17th. Exchange and treatment of Prisoners generally.

19th. Transportation of Military and Ordnance Stores to be by Water &Ca.

20th. Letters from the General to the Chevr. pressing him to ex-tend my Credit on France so as to enable me to Compleat my Arrangements.[30]

21st. To hear proposals from the Commanders of the French if they have any to offer in consequence of my Letters to the Chevalier Luzerne,[31] to explain respecting Exchange &Ca.

22d. Post Office. To abolish Franking, Officers letters to be charged and returns of their Accounts to be made Monthly to the Pay Master.[32]

Our Conversations on these Subjects were lengthy and frequently branched out so as generally to Comprehend the present State of our Affairs, the abuses, Mismanagements, Neglects, as also the remedies necessary to be applied, the means of accomplishing them &Ca. Colo. Tilghman took notes of such Conclusions as were agreed to a Copy whereof he gave me and is as follows:

Answers [33]

1st. By regular and accurate Musters, and as it appears that this branch of business has not been as well performed since the annexation of the Mustering and inspectors departments it is proposed again to reestablish the Office of Commissary General of Musters.[34]

2d. By comparing the return upon which the Issues are made with the general returns of the Army and Muster Rolls.

3d. The present Mode of making up payrolls seems as well cal-culated as possible to prevent Frauds and abuses. The Ap-plication of the Money arising from Casualities to a recruiting Fund appears a Plan from which good consequences will result.

4th The only checks must be the Musters. I would observe that Waggoners and all persons not of the line of the Army had better be allowed pay to enable them to find themselves than be supplied by the Public.

5th. Hospitals.

6th. It is thought inexpedient to attempt to decrease the Pay.

7th. Reducing number of Regiments and encreasing number of Men.

8 Provided for by the Inspectorate.

9 This proposal highly Approved as soon as Money can be furnished to defray the Expenses of the Persons mentioned.

10 Places of Deposit to be pointed out hereafter.

11 Contracts for Rations deemed preferable to those for the Articles composing Rations.

12 Quarter Master.

13 Sutlers Unnecessary.

14 Army.

15 The Steward being appointed, the necessary estimates will be made and proper Modes fixed upon for checking and setling his Accounts.

16 Exchange of Convention Troops deemed inexpedient at Present.

22d Post Office.

Several Articles The General required time to think of and finally I gave him a Copy of all my said Notes which he has promised to Answer in writing therefore I postpone all proceedings on these Points untill I shall receive His Excellency's said responses.[35]

On Thursday the 16th instant

I met His Excellency Count De Rochambeau by request at His Quarters, and made a Minute at Camp of what passed at that Meeting of which the following is a Copy.

This day met his Excellency Count De Rochambeau agreable to his request and found at his Quarters himself, Genl. Chattellaux,[36] The Intendant,[37] Treasurer,[38] Colo Menouville [39] and I believe Genl. Viominel [40] but not being well acquainted with these Gentlemen I am not certain of their names. Count Rochambeau told me he had received from the Chevr de La Luzerne Copies of the two Letters I had written to him respecting the Sales of their Bills and of furnishing the Army and Navy with supplies &C.[41] They told me the propositions I had made were perfectly agreable and they conceived were well calculated to promote His Most Christain Majestys Interest as well as the service of the common cause. They Complained of Mr Holker's [42] Conduct towards them, and as I was well acquainted with Mr Holkers transactions I took occasion to explain the same and to assure them Over and Over of what I do most sincerely believe, vizt That Mr Holker is as Honest a Man and as Zealous for the Kings Service as any that ever came from France, however I told them this Subject was Foreign to my present Business in which Mr Holker would have no concern unless they chose to commit anything to him. I observed that being a Minister of the United States, they must be pleased to consider every thing that came from me as flowing from a pure desire to serve the general cause, that I sought no Commission, profit or advantage, that no personal considerations had any influence over me, being only desirous so to unite the Measures for supplying their Army and ours

as that both might benefit thereby. They observed that Messrs.
Wadsworth and Carter [43] had given them much satisfaction and
were very usefull to them. I replyed that I had heard so and hoped
these Gentlemen might continue to supply them as I proposed to
obtain the Supplies for both Armies by Contract [44] and no persons
[were] more suitable to enter into such Contracts than [45] Messrs.
Wadsworth and Carter. I told them I would not undertake this
Business unless the Affairs of the Navy as well as the Army were put
under my direction otherwise I should assume much trouble and
Fatigue for the service of one part of their Force without Effect as
the Affairs of the other would operate to overset my plans. They
replied they could not Answer possitively but they had no doubt
but this Stipulation would be complied with. I desired to be furnished with a list of every Article they wanted and that the Quantities of each daily, Weekly or Monthly required might be Specified,
also the Sum of Money they would require to be furnished Monthly
from the Sale of Bills of Exchange. I told them that it was only a
certain Sum that could be commanded by bills of Exchange, that
the Amount of that Sum depended on uncertain events but a Superior Naval Force on our Coast and a sucessfull Commerce with
the abolishing of Paper Money must inevitably encrease the Demand for Bills and the means of paying for them, that I had to raise
Money for our own Service by Bills and whilst that continued I
would give to each service a proportion of what I raised, that the
Supplies of Money must be paid them at the Current course of
Exchange of which the bills were sold to raise it, but as to the other
Articles, I offered either to Contract for them on their behalf with
Persons whose Characters and Fortunes would secure the performance of their Engagements or if they preferred I would engage
on behalf of the United States to supply those Articles at rates to
be fixed in Livrs of France so that they might deliver me Monthly
the bills for the Amount which should discharge them and the sale
of the Bills would be for the Account of the Continent. This last
Proposal seemed most Acceptable, and they promised to send me
a state of their Drafts that I might carry the same to Phila. for
Consideration in order that final Conclusions might be had when
they came there. I promised them a sight of the Original Contract
made by me for the Supplies at the Post of Philaa: [46] and have since
sent it with permission for them to take a Copy of it. They enquired
relative to the abuses in the management of their Supplies &Ca.
hinted at in my letters to the Chevr. Luzerne to which I replyed that
my Information on that head was general, such as their employing
a number of persons to sell bills, buy supplies &Ca so that they

occasioned a competition in the Agents that tended to lower bills and raise the Prices of the Articles wanted, but they knew best whether it was true or not. I told General Chattelaux that I would give them the same quantity of flour in Maryland as they deliver to the Order of Gen Washington on the North River and have since informed his Excellency thereof.[47]

During my stay at Camp, I had constant applications for Money from almost every body as all had Claims on the Public. I took with me only 150 Guineas and finding so many demands I thought it best to satisfy none, therefore brought the Money back. I had Conferences with the Quarter Master Genl.,[48] Pay Master Genl.,[49] Cloathier Genl.,[50] Commissy. Genl. of Issues,[51] Director Genl. of the Hospitals [52] and with many other Persons but as these chiefly run on the Wants of themselves and others employed in their departments, I could only recommend the Strictest frugality and Oeconomy in their expenditures, that I might thereby be the better Warranted in making reasonable requisitions from the several States, always promising what I Mean most punctually to perform that is, to use my utmost endeavours to establish such revenues as will enable the regular payment of their Salaries and other just demands, but always concluded with Assuring them that this Ultimately depended on the several Legislatures, which could only be induced to grant such revenues from a Conviction that their Grants would be faithfully and frugally used. I made the same Observations to the General Officers and others who spoke to me on Money Matters.

Mr. Thos. Lowrey having come to Camp and finding that the Supplies of Flour already provided were not sufficient, I authorized him to purchase about 700 barrells more than formerly Ordered, so as to make his Supplies Amount on the whole to 4,000 Barrels, all of which is to be charged to the State of Pensylvania on Account of her Specific Supplies. I wrote also to Gouverr. Morris Esqr. to give Orders for the purchase of 1000 barrells of flour at this City and have the same forwarded to Trenton and thence by land Carriage to the Army, but some intended movements of the Army and the other Measures I took at Camp rendering this unnecessary I wrote to countermand it.[53] I applied to Udney Hay Esqr. for Supplies on behalf of the State of New York to which he is Agent. He informed me there was Wheat and flour in Mills and Magazines to the extent of 3000 barrells but that he could not deliver it for want of Casks. I intended at first to furnish the Money to pay for Casks, but some observations I made on this Gentlemans Solicitude to get the Money with an apprehension of bad Consequences following such an Advance to a State Agent determined me not to do it, but in order to facilitate the delivery of the flour I wrote the Commissary Genl. of Issues to deliver him 3000 Old flour Barrells or so many thereof as remained at the several Posts on the North River and Wrote also to His Exy. Govr. Clinton and to Mr Hay himself on the subject, so that I expect this Flour will be in use of the Army in the Months of Septr. and Octobr.[54] And as I understood the French Army were about Moving from their present encampment I proposed to Genl. Chattellaux and desired him to mention it to Count De Rochambeau, that they might deliver any flour they had on hand to the order of His Excellency Genl. Washington and I would deliver them an equal quantity at the place they might want it afterwards; of this I also informed his Ex: G Washington leaving them to finish the Contract when they should find it convenient.[55] The day before I left Camp His Ex: Govr. Clinton came there. I mentioned Mr Hays Affair of the flour; he promised his assistance. We had a good deal of Conversation about Revenue &Ca. This Gentleman appeared to me a true Friend to his Country and Zealous in the general Cause.

On 18th of August

Saturday Morning we took leave of his Excellency Genl Washington and set out for this place escorted by an Officer and twenty light Dragoons for the first Day, after which thinking ourselves out of danger we discharged them and Arrived here on Monday the 20th instant. (Minutes at Camp Concluded)

Waited on His Excelly. The President of Congress to give him information &Ca.[56]

Employed in examining the State of the Money, Sale of Bills and other transactions done in the Office during my absence. Had various fruitless applications made me for Money. Wrote the Honorable Mr Vandyke in Congress.

Wrote Letters to the Govr of Maryland and Mr Ridley respecting Flour &Ca wanted.

Wrote The Board of Treasury on the 4th instant. Omitted inserting in Diary on that Day.

1. See RM to Washington, May 29, 1781 (second letter), also Gouverneur Morris, Tench Tilghman, and Washington to RM, all dated June 4, 1781.
2. Washington to La Luzerne, June 8, 1781, Fitzpatrick, ed., *Writings of Washington*, XXII, 181; see also Washington to RM, July 13, 1781.
3. See, for example, RM to Washington, June 15 and July 23, 1781.
4. See also Diary, July 28, 1781.
5. On this committee and the conference, see Diary, July 31, 1781, and notes.
6. Burnett, ed., *Letters*, VI, 165n. Congressman James Mitchell Varnum of Rhode Island informed Washington that "the detaching Mr. Peters to Camp was a political Manoeuvre of your Friends." Varnum to Washington, August 20, 1781, *ibid.*, 191.

7. "If in my absence, and from that cause, there be any stoppage or considerable delay," RM explained to La Luzerne in a letter of August 2, "the Consequences will be equally injurious to my reputation and to the Public Service."

8. For the background of this strategy, see notes to Tench Tilghman to RM, May 17, and Washington to RM, July 13, 1781; also Washington to RM, August 2 (second letter), and notes.

9. See Diary, August 6.

10. See the President of Congress to Washington, August 3, 1781, Burnett, ed., *Letters*, VI, 164–165.

11. Fitzpatrick, ed., *Washington Diaries*, II, 253–254. "Matters having now come to a crisis and a decisive plan to be determined on," Washington wrote in his diary on August 14, "I was obliged, from the shortness of Count de Grasses promised stay on this Coast, the apparent disinclination in their Naval Officers to force the harbour of New York and the feeble compliance of the States to my requisitions for Men, hitherto, and little prospect of greater exertion in the future, to give up all idea of attacking New York; and instead thereof to remove the French Troops and a detachment from the American Army to the Head of Elk to be Transported to Virginia for the purpose of co-operating with the force from the West Indies against the Troops in that State." *Ibid.*, 254; see also Freeman, *Washington*, V, 309.

12. Now Elkton, Maryland, situated at the junction of the two branches of the Elk River northeast of Baltimore at the head of tidewater on upper Chesapeake Bay. Benson J. Lossing, *The Pictorial Field-Book of the Revolution* (New York, 1851–1852), II, 387.

13. Richard Peters, reminiscing 37 years later about his journey to headquarters with RM, recalled Washington's urgent appeals to them there for provisions, military stores, and money for the Yorktown operations. "Not a single gun was mounted on my arrival at Philadelphia [from headquarters]," Peters wrote, "nor a rammer, nor a sponge, or other article, nor any considerable quantity of fixed ammunition provided. We had chiefly the materials, but no money to enable us to put them together. . . . Mr. Morris supplied the money or the credit; and without derogation from the merit of the assistance rendered by the State authorities, it may truly be said that the financial means furnished by him were the main-springs of transportation and supplies for the glorious achievements which effectually secured our independence, and furnished the foundation of the present prosperous and happy condition of our nation." Richard Peters to W. H. Harrison, January 12, 1818, quoted by William Brotherhead, "Robert Morris," in Henry Simpson, *The Lives of Eminent Philadelphians, Now Deceased* (Philadelphia, 1859), 705–708; a condensed version of Peters' account had been published earlier in John Sanderson, Robert Waln, Jr., and Henry D. Gilpin, eds., *Biography of the Signers to the Declaration of Independence* (Philadelphia, 1823–1827), V, 294.

14. RM's Circular to the Governors of Massachusetts, Rhode Island, New York, Delaware, Maryland, and North Carolina, July 27, 1781.

15. This heading, placed here by the editors, appears as a running head on the second manuscript page of the Diary of this date and is repeated with variations on several succeeding manuscript pages.

16. August 10.

17. This route was similar to the one which Gouverneur Morris had taken and described for RM in a letter of June 4, 1781.

18. Ephraim Blaine, commissary general of purchases.

19. This was on August 11. Washington recorded the arrival of RM and Peters in his diary for that date, but made no further reference to their visit. Fitzpatrick, ed., *Washington Diaries*, II, 253.

20. August 12.

21. Dated August 13.

22. Washington's reply is dated August 21.

23. August 13, 14, and 15.

24. This memorandum, although undated, was almost certainly one of those which RM prepared on August 4 (see Diary of that date). An undated copy in the

writing of Tench Tilghman, Washington's aide, in the Washington Papers, DLC, is entitled "Mr. Morris's Questions," but lacks heads 15–21. All other major discrepancies between it and the text printed in the Diary are noted below.

25. On RM's efforts to achieve economies in the Continental hospital department, see his letter to Doctors Gerardus Clarkson, James Hutchinson, and John Jones, July 17, 1781, and notes.

26. Washington Papers copy: this word given as "severally."

27. Washington Papers copy: this head given as "Sutlers."

28. Washington Papers copy: preceding five words omitted.

29. The convention troops were those British soldiers captured when Major General John Burgoyne surrendered his army to Horatio Gates on October 17, 1777, under the terms of the Convention of Saratoga. By it, the captives were to be marched to Boston, shipped to England, and were enjoined never again to serve in the American war. However, believing that the agreement was far too liberal and that the British did not intend to abide by it, Congress suspended their embarkation, thereby dissolving the convention. Although Burgoyne and some of his officers were permitted to return to England, the prisoners were marched to cantonments in Virginia in 1778 and remained there until recalled to Pennsylvania by a congressional resolution of March 3, 1781. Ward, *War of the Revolution*, II, 537, 540–542.

30. RM's intention to have Washington write such letters was never realized.

31. RM no doubt refers to his letters of August 2 and 4 to La Luzerne. On the matters concerned, see note 44 below.

32. In the Washington Papers copy this article is unnumbered.

33. An undated Dft of this document in Tench Tilghman's writing, entitled "Genl Washington's Answers," is among the Washington Papers, DLC, and is identical to the text printed in the Diary.

34. In June 1779 the officers of the Mustering Department complained bitterly to Congress of their low pay and rations. A committee appointed the following day inquired of Washington whether the department ought not to be abolished. Washington put the question to a meeting of the officers' council at camp, and its decision was that the duties of the department could be handled easily by the inspectors of the army. Accordingly, Congress abolished the Mustering Department on January 12, 1780, and assigned its duties to the inspectors of the army, a decision which Washington came to believe had been a mistake. Memorial of the Deputy Commissary General of Musters Azariah Horton to Congress, June 14, 1779, PCC, no. 41, IV, 67–71; *JCC*, XV, 1274; Washington to Henry Laurens, Joseph Spencer, and Nathaniel Scudder, August 20, 1779, to the Secretary at War, December 28, 1781, and to Baron Steuben, February 4, 1782, Fitzpatrick, ed., *Writings of Washington*, XVI, 134–136, XXIII, 411–412, 483.

35. For Washington's answers to questions 7 and 14, see his letter to RM and Richard Peters, August 21; no further response has been found.

36. François Jean de Beauvoir, Chevalier de Chastellux (1734–1788), joined the French army at an early age and served in the Seven Years War. As major general of the French army in America, he participated in the siege of Yorktown. Returning to France in 1783, Chastellux completed a widely read account of his travels in the United States. Chastellux, *Travels in North America in the Years 1780, 1781 and 1782*, trans. and ed. Howard C. Rice, Jr. (Chapel Hill, N. C., 1963), I, 2–41.

37. Benoît Joseph de Tarlé (1735–1797) entered the French army in 1759, advanced to lieutenant colonel in March 1780, and later that year became adjutant major general and intendant of the French army in America. Balch, *French in America*, II, 235; Contenson, *Société des Cincinnati*, 269.

38. Chevalier César Louis de Baulny had been treasurer or chief paymaster of Corsica before being assigned the same function in the French expeditionary force sent to America under Rochambeau, in which he held the rank of major. After the war Baulny returned to Corsica before becoming treasurer general for the department of war in Paris. Contenson, *Société des Cincinnati*, 136; Gardiner, *Order of the Cincinnati*, 212.

39. François Louis Arthur Thibaut, Comte de Menonville, Rochambeau's aide,

was lieutenant colonel and first deputy adjutant general of the French army in America.

40. Major General Antoine Charles du Houx, Baron de Vioménil (1728–1792) was second in command of the French army in America. On December 1, 1782, he succeeded Rochambeau as commander and in 1783 was promoted to lieutenant general. He died of wounds received while defending the royal family in the Tuilleries *le dix août.* Contenson, *Société des Cincinnati,* 279–280.

41. See note 31 above and note 44 below.

42. John Holker, French consul general, supply agent for the French navy in America, and business partner of RM.

43. Jeremiah Wadsworth and John Carter, contractors for the French army.

44. RM initiated this proposal in a letter of August 2 to La Luzerne, who replied the following day saying he would take up the matter with Rochambeau (see also RM to La Luzerne, August 4, Diary, August 29 and September 1-5, and RM to Matthew Ridley, September 15). Recalling the fate of his proposal, RM wrote to Benjamin Franklin on May 27, 1783, that "Obstacles were raised and objections were made by such as I was induced to suppose were interested in opposing oeconomical Arrangements and therefore I desisted."

45. MS: "then."

46. RM's contract with John Hazelwood and Isaac Serrell of July 19, 1781, has not been found.

47. See note 55 below.

48. Timothy Pickering.

49. John Pierce (d. 1788) of Litchfield, Connecticut, who had been assistant paymaster general of the army since February 10, 1776, was elected deputy paymaster general on June 7, 1779, and paymaster general on January 17, 1781. In a letter of March 15, 1783, RM entrusted him with the task of settling army accounts, which became Pierce's main function after disbandment of the army. By the end of 1785 the office of paymaster general had been subsumed under that of commissioner of army accounts, and on March 23, 1787, Congress joined both duties in a single office, which Pierce held until his death. After the war he joined Daniel Parker and Andrew Craigie in a venture to finance European speculation in American public securities. *JCC,* XXVI, 236, XXX, 417, XXXIV, 150, 392; Heitman, *Register;* East, *Business Enterprise,* 122–123; *Record of Service of Connecticut Men in the . . . War of the Revolution . . .* (Hartford, 1889), I, 98, 143, 313.

50. John Moylan, an Irishman whose family was associated with the firm of Barclay, Moylan and Company in Philadelphia and Lorient, France, had been a merchant at Cadiz before coming to America. On April 17, 1781, Congress elected him clothier general, an office he held until 1783. He was the brother of Stephen Moylan. Thomas Robson Hay, "Letters of Mrs. Ann Biddle Wilkinson from Kentucky, 1788–1789," *PMHB,* LVI (1932), 53n., which is incorrect on the date of Moylan's election.

51. Charles Stewart.

52. John Cochran.

53. RM's first letter to Gouverneur Morris, ca. August 12, reached Philadelphia on August 16 (see Diary, and Gouverneur Morris to John Hazelwood, both August 16). The letter of countermand was probably dated August 15.

54. For correspondence on this subject, see Udny Hay to RM, and RM to Hay, to the Commissary General of Issues, and to the Governor of New York, all August 15.

55. Washington communicated RM's proposal to Rochambeau on August 18, observing that upon the delivery to the Continental army of the two or three thousand barrels of flour which the Financier understood the French to have stored on the upper Hudson, RM would supply the French army with the same quantity "to the southward." The French ultimately furnished over 1,900 barrels of flour. Washington to Rochambeau, August 18, and to Benoît Joseph de Tarlé, August 22, 1781, Fitzpatrick, ed., *Writings of Washington,* XXIII, 16, 37; see also Washington to RM, August 24, Hector Daure to RM, September 16, RM to Daure, September 19, to William Heath, September 17 and 24, and to Matthew Ridley and the Commissary

General of Purchases, both September 20, Heath to RM, September 20 and October 4, and RM to the Commissary General of Purchases, November 13, 1781.

56. At this time RM no doubt delivered Washington's letter of August 17 to President Thomas McKean. See Fitzpatrick, ed., *Writings of Washington*, XXIII, 13–14.

To the Governor of Maryland
(Thomas Sim Lee)

Office of Finance 21. Augt. 1781

Sir

Mr. Morris [1] wrote to you on the eighth a Letter relating to a certain quantity of Flour wanted in your State. In Addition to that Letter I am now to observe that much if not all the flour required of your State will probably be wanted very speedily for the Service of the present Campaign and indeed a considerable quantity of it immediately. Nor is this all. Your Excellency will be pleased to observe that Maryland is to furnish fifty two thousand hundred weight of fresh Beef, four thousand eight hundred Barrels of salted Beef, and five thousand five hundred Barrels of salted Pork.[2] These also will be very speedily wanted and much of the salted Provisions immediately. I must intreat to know what Part of these Supplies can be depended on for the service of the present Campaign and how much thereof is now ready.

If Sir any additional Stimulus were necessary to the Exertions which your Zeal for the general Interests of America will naturally excite I should with the greatest Truth add that the immediate Interest, Ease and safety of the State you preside over are most particularly concerned in the Event of my present Requisitions.[3] I must therefore in the most earnest Manner intreat that you will do every Thing which is possible and I trust you will soon see abundant Cause to justify my present Solicitude.[4]

With all possible Respect I have the honor to be Sir your Excellency's most obedient and humble Servant

RM

ms: Ofcl LbC, DLC.

1. Gouverneur Morris.

2. As required by congressional requisitions of February 25 and November 4, 1780.

3. An allusion to Washington's decision to undertake operations against Cornwallis in Virginia. See headnote and notes to Diary, August 21.

4. See also RM to the Commissary General of Purchases, August 24, and to the Governor of Maryland, August 26 and 28. Governor Lee replied on August 31.

To Matthew Ridley

Office of Finance 21. Augt. 1781.

Dear Sir,

I returned from Camp last Evening and have now before me your Letter of the eighteenth [1] in answer to Mr. Morris's [2] of the eighth which latter I hereby confirm. I am further to request that you will enter into Contracts immediately for three thousand Barrels of Flour. As to the Quality let it be good sound sweet Flour such as no Troops could with any Degree of Propriety refuse. Let it be delivered to you or ready to deliver to your order as soon as possible. Make the Payments as distant as you can in Order that I may have the more Time for the Operations necessary to raise Money. Get the Barrels secured by a lining Hoop on each Head and let them be marked MR [3] and let the Weight and Tare be marked on each. It may be necessary to transport this Flour to the Head of Elk as also salted Provisions and even the Troops which are to the Southward. I am therefore to request that you would immediately engage as many Bay Craft as you can upon the following Terms viz. To be employed at a certain Price per Day payable in hard Money. The Hire to begin whenever they shall receive your Orders and to End when you or any one properly authorized by you shall dismiss them. [4]

I have no Doubt you will exert yourself on this Occasion and Act with all possible Oeconomy and Circumspection both of which I must recommend to you. It may be proper to mention that good Flour such as I have described can be now bought here at fifteen shillings the highest.

I have the honor to be Sir your most obedient and humble Servant

RM

ms: Ofcl LbC, DLC.

1. Letter not found.
2. Gouverneur Morris.
3. The clerk originally wrote "IR," but subsequently expanded the first letter to "M." See Gouverneur Morris to John Hazelwood, August 16.
4. These instructions were in consequence of Washington's letter to RM of August 17.

To Nicholas Van Dyke[1]

Office of Finance 21. Augt. 1781.

Sir

I am this Instant favored with your Letter of the twentieth requesting me to appoint some Person to purchase Supplies for the
Recruits at Christiana Bridge.[2] The State of Delaware is indebted
to the Continent for a considerable Balance of specific Supplies. I
am well content that if the State will furnish Provisions to those
Recruits the Articles so applied shall be deducted from that Balance.
This appears to be the most natural and simple Mode of feeding
them and as such is practiced by other States. I submit it to your
Consideration. With great Respect I have the honor to be Sir Your
most obedient and humble Servant

RM

MS: Ofcl LbC, DLC.
   1. Nicholas Van Dyke (1738–1789) of Delaware, lawyer, judge of admiralty, and
member of the state council, was a delegate to the Continental Congress, 1777–1782,
and later president of Delaware, 1783–1786. *Biog. Dir. Cong.*
   2. Letter not found.

George Washington to Robert Morris
and Richard Peters

Head Quarters Kings Ferry [New York], Augst 21 1781

Gentlemen

I have devoted the first moment of my time which I could command (while the Troops are halted for the french Army at this place)
to give my sentiments unreservedly on the several matters contained in your favor of the 13th Instant.[1] This I will attempt to do,
with all that frankness, and sincerity, which from your own candor
in your communications, you have a right to expect, and for doing
which with the greater freedom, the importance of the Subject will
be my apology. Persuaded that we are influenced by the same motives, and anxious in the pursuit of the same object; I am only
unhappy, that I should be forced to dissent in a single instance, from
the opinion of those, for whose judgment and ability I have the
highest defference, respecting the surest and best mode for attaining that object.

But being at the same time, fully sensible of the necessity of
prosecuting the War with as much vigor as our circumstances will
admit, and of using the strictest œconomy in the prosecution of it;

Upon these very principles, I beg leave to give it as my opinion, that a reduction of the number of Officers and Men as fixed by the last arrangement, or any material alteration of the establishment of the Army for the next Campaign, would not in the present situation of affairs be expedient for the following reasons.

In the first place, because, the Enemy must resolve to prosecute the War, or be disposed to make a Peace, in either of which cases, a respectable Army in the field on our part, will, I conceive, more than compensate the expences of it; and will eventually be the best and most œconomical system of policy we can possibly act upon. For should the Enemy still be determined to carry on the War with obstinacy, not only policy, but even necessity would urge us to keep up a superior Army as the surest and only means of forcing them to a Peace and freeing us from the calamities and expences of the War, as it is evident from many circumstances that they have relied more for success, on our want of exertions, than upon their own Military prowess or resources, and that this has been one principal inducement of their persevering hitherto. But on the other hand, should they be inclined to a Pacification, a powerfull and well appointed Army would both enable us to dictate our own terms at the Negociation and hasten the completion of it.

In addition to this, whoever considers how much more expensive and less serviceable, Militia are than Continental Troops, how heavy and repeated a burden on the public their Bounties are, when they are hired; when Drafted, how disagreeable and frequently distressing for them to be torn from their families to a life with which they are totally unacquainted, how precarious and uncertain the aid is, which may be expected from them in such cases; What glorious opportunities have been lost by us, and what almost ruinous advantages have been taken by the Enemy, in the times of our weakness, for want of a permanent force in the field; will I am persuaded, be convinced, that we ought to have constantly such an army as is sufficient to operate against the Enemy, and supersede the necessity of calling forth the Militia except on the most extraordinary occasions.

I will also beg leave to remind you Gentlemen, of the great reduction of the number of Regiments on the Continental Establishment, viz from 116 to 50 since the year 1777,[2] and to observe, in consequence that, in my opinion, we do not find the Enemy so much exhausted, or their strength so debilitated as to warrant any farther diminution of our established force; by one of the late intercepted Letters from Ld. George Germain, it appears the Enemy considered the number of Men in their Provincial Corps only, greater than the whole number of Men in the service of the Continent,[3] since which time, the reinforcements that have arrived from Europe, amount, by the best accounts I have been able to obtain, to at least 4000 Men.

That the States are able, by proper exertions, to furnish the number of Men required by the last Arrangement of the Army, may I think, rationally be supposed; as the population in many of them have rather encreased than diminished since the commencement of the War; and as the greater part of them do actually, when called upon in an immergency, give a sufficient number of Men for services of short duration, to compleat their Continental Regiments. That the Country abounds with supplies of all kinds is acknowledged from all quarters. Whether the men can be obtained, or the Resources drawn forth is more than I will presume with certainty to determine; but one thing is certain, that it is idle to contend against great odds, when we have it in our power, to do it upon equal, or even advantageous terms.

There are also several Arguments, which I omit to enforce, that might be adduced particularly to prove the impropriety of reducing the Number of Officers, or making any considerable alteration in the system; such as our having found by experience, that the proportion of Officers is not too great for the number of Men; that the same or a greater proportion has been esteemed necessary in other more antient services; and that the full complement is more indispensably requisite in ours, because there are a larger number of Levies and Recruits to train and discipline annually than are to be found in the Regiments of other Nations; and because a greater number of Officers are taken from the Line to perform the duties of the Staff than in most other Services. It is likewise an established fact, that every alteration in the Military System or change in the Arrangement, unless founded in the most obvious principles of utility is attended with uneasiness among the Officers, confusion with regard to the disposition of the Men, and frequently with irregularities and disagreeable consequences before it can be carried compleatly into execution. Perfect Order throughout the whole Army, has but just been restored since the last Arrangement took place. Another innovation, in the present situation might be more Mischeivous in its effect.

Thus I have, Gentlemen, from a desire of faithfully performing my duty, from the experience (of whatever degree it is) which I have acquired in the service of my Country, and from the knowledge I have of the present state of the Army, given my sentiments on the first of your queries, which likewise involves the Answer to the second. With regard to the third, I am of opinion, that the Recruits ought if possible to be engaged for the War or three years; but if this cannot be done that the Community, district, or Class, furnishing a man for a shorter term of service, ought to be compellable to have him replaced by the period, when his time of service expires, [*remainder of sentence in the margin*] and that funds ought to be established (if practicable) for recruiting the Men engaged for short services while they continue with the Army, as it is found by experience, they may be inlisted with more facility and less expence than under any other circumstances. With respect to the 4th, 5th and 6th queries, I am in doubt, whether any alteration can be made on those subjects which shall tend essentially (all things considered) to the public Good. I have the honor to be &c

MSS: Dft in the writing of David Humphreys, Washington Papers, DLC; Varick transcript, Washington Papers, DLC.

1. This reply, received by RM on August 27, was to six queries made by RM and Peters in their letter of August 13, and embraced as well Washington's response to heads 7 and 14 of a memorandum which RM had presented to him at headquarters. See Diary, August 21 and 27, and RM to Peters, August 27.

2. An allusion to the arrangement of 1780, which reduced the number of infantry regiments to 50. See notes to RM and Peters to Washington, August 13.

3. Lord George Germain (1716–1785), British Secretary of State for the Colonies, writing to Sir Henry Clinton on March 7, 1781, about the returns of the provincial forces which Clinton had transmitted, expressed pleasure that "the American Levies in the King's Service are more in number than the whole of the Enlisted Troops in the Service of the Congress." This was an exaggeration. British figures on the enlistment of provincial rank and file in America are: 3,738 in December 1777; 4,628 in June 1778; 6,326 in December 1778; 6,504 in June 1779; 6,757 in December 1779; 8,201 in December 1780; and 8,151 in May 1781. Mackesy, *War for America*, 526; for enlistments in the Continental army, see notes to RM and Richard Peters to Washington, August 13. Germain's dispatch is in Saunders and Clark, eds., *State Records of North Carolina*, XVII, 990–991; on its interception, see Burnett, ed., *Letters*, VI, 147n.

Diary: August 22, 1781

Wrote to His Excellency Genl. Washington stating to him our Want of Money and the disapointments to be expected in consequence thereof.

Addressd Letters (respectively) to the Governrs: of New Jersey and Delaware requesting Specific Supplies.

Waited on His Excellency the President of Congress with Mr Goveurr. Morris on business of a Secret nature.

Had a Conference with The Honorable Mr Sharpe respecting the Transportation of Arms to No. Carolina and perswaded him to wait a While, Money being very scarce.[1]

The Honorable Mr Varnum Communicated his Letters of the 20th and 21st instant to the Commander in Chief.[2] I requested to take Copies thereof which he consented to.

Issued Warrant on Swanwick for £97.16.6 [in] favour of R Humphreys [3] for Plate, Use of Comr: in Chf.

Issued Warrant in favour of Edwd. Moyston [4] for £30.3.3, being Amount of Expences defray'd to and from Camp.

Arranged all the papers, Letters &Ca. that respected my Journey to and business at Camp.[5] Sundry Applications for Money, which I am Obliged to decline granting untill better provided with Funds.

1. On previous arrangements for the shipment of arms to North Carolina, see notes to Diary, July 30, and the Governor of North Carolina to RM, August 4; and Diary, August 15, 1781. See also RM to the Governor of North Carolina, August 29.

2. The letters of James Mitchell Varnum, member of Congress from Rhode Island, to Washington discussing in detail the problems of and proposed changes in the current army establishment are in the Washington Papers, DLC. Brief extracts from the August 20 letter are printed in Burnett, ed., *Letters,* VI, 190–191. Varnum had been a member of the committee Congress had appointed on July 26 to confer with RM, Washington, and the Board of War on army arrangements for 1782. See notes to Diary, July 31, 1781.

3. Richard Humphreys, a Philadelphia goldsmith and silversmith. Alfred C. Prime, *The Arts & Crafts in Philadelphia, Maryland and South Carolina, 1721–1800: Gleanings from Newspapers* (Topsfield, Mass., 1929–1932), I, 72–74.

4. Edward Moyston, RM's steward in the Office of Finance, and possibly the same man who kept the New Tavern, also called the City Tavern or Smith's Tavern, on Second Street in Philadelphia from 1779 to 1787. W. A. Newman Dorland, "The Second Troop Philadelphia City Cavalry," *PMHB,* XLVI (1922), 75n.; see Diary, August 23.

5. See Diary, August 21, for RM's account of his visit to Washington's headquarters.

Circular to the Governors of New Jersey and Delaware

Office of Finance 22nd. August 1781.

Sir

I have already in a former Letter forwarded to your Excellency an account of the Specific Supplies which Congress had demanded from your State.[1] It now becomes my duty again to press for a Compliance with those demands. The Exigencies of the Service require immediate attention. We are on the Eve of the most active Operations, and should they be in any wise retarded by the want of necessary Supplies, the most unhappy Consequences may follow. Those who may be justly chargeable with neglect will have to answer for it to their Country, to their Allies, to the present Generation, and to all posterity. I hope, intreat, expect the utmost possible Efforts on the part of your State, and I confide in your Excellency's prudence and Vigour to render those Efforts effectual. I beg to know most speedily Sir, what Supplies are collected, and at what places, as also the times and places at which the remainder are to be expected. I cannot express to you my Solicitude on this Occasion.

My declaration to Congress when I entered upon Administration will prevent the blame of ill Accidents from lighting upon me, even if I were less attentive than I am; [2] but it is impossible not to feel most deeply on Occasions, where the greatest Objects may be impaired or destroyed by Indolence or Neglect. I must therefore again reiterate my requests; and while I assure you that nothing but the urgency of our Affairs would render me thus Importunate, I must also assure you that while those Affairs continue so Urgent I must continue to importune.[3] With all possible Respect I have the honour to be, Your Excellency's Most Obedient and humble Servant

Robt Morris

His Excellency The Governor of Delaware [4]

MSS: LS, to the Governor of Delaware, Executive Papers, De–Ar; Ofcl LbC, DLC; signed copy with an autograph note by RM, George Washington Papers, DLC.

1. RM refers to his Circular to the Governors of the States, July 25, 1781.

2. A reference to RM's disclaimers of responsibility for financing the current campaign contained in his letters of May 14 and June 30, 1781, to the President of Congress.

3. As noted above, RM sent Washington a signed copy of this letter with the following autograph note subjoined: "This is the Copy of a letter I have written to the Governors of New Jersey, Delaware &ca and I send it to your Excelly that you may enforce the Contents shou'd you have an opportunity." While the American and French armies were en route to Virginia, Washington on September 3 addressed a circular to the governors of New Jersey, Delaware, and Maryland in which he wrote in part: "It is needless for me to trouble your Excellency any further than to enforce in the warmest Terms, the Application of Mr. Morris, which I now take the Liberty to do, and to entreat your Excellency, that it may meet with all that effectual Attention, which the Importance of the Matter requires, and the urgent Importunity of Mr. Morris can expect or wish" (Fitzpatrick, ed., *Writings of Washington,* XXIII, 81). RM's August 21 letter to the Governor of Maryland made an Office of Finance circular to that state unnecessary; replies from New Jersey and Delaware have not been found.

4. The preceding six words are in the writing of Gouverneur Morris. Caesar Rodney (1728–1784), the president of Delaware, was a signer of the Declaration of Independence and member of the Continental Congress, 1774–1776. Thereafter he frequently was elected to Congress, but did not attend. He was president of Delaware, April 1778–November 1781. *Biog. Dir. Cong.;* Burnett, ed., *Letters,* I, xliii, II, xlii, III, lii, VII, lxv.

To George Washington[1]

Office of Finance 22 Augt. 1781

Dear Sir

I arrived in Town the Day before Yesterday. Having taken the earliest Opportunities to acquire Information, I am sorry to inform you, that I find money matters in as bad a situation as possible. The exchange, by the concourse of venders, has run down to five shillings, and bills are offered, at that rate, in such great numbers as to command all the money which is to be disposed of; so that reducing the price of bills still lower would not command money, or answer any other good purpose. The paper of this state is indeed appreciating, but to issue it, in the present moment, would destroy in embryo [2] all my hopes from that quarter, cut off the only resource which I have the chance of commanding, and shake a confidence which has been reposed in me, and which the public interest calls upon me to cherish.[3]

I [am] sorry to observe, in consequence, that you must expect to meet with disappointments: but I assure you, that I will make every possible exertion to place you in the [most] [4] eligible situation which my means will admit of.

I am Your Excellency's Most Obedient and humble Servant

Robt Morris

His Excellency General Washington

ENDORSED: Office of Finance 22 Augt 1781/from/Robert Morris Esqr
MSS: LS, part in cipher, Washington Papers, DLC; Ofcl LbC, DLC; deciphered copy in the writing of Jonathan Trumbull, Jr., Washington Papers, DLC.
1. Except for the dateline, salutation, and the first eighteen words in the writing of Gouverneur Morris and the complimentary close, signature, and addressee's name in the writing of RM, the text of the LS presented here is encoded in Gouverneur Morris's writing. The editors have deciphered it with the code prepared by, and in the writing of, Gouverneur Morris in the Washington Papers, DLC. The cipher is of the same type enclosed in RM to John Jay, July 7, and to Benjamin Franklin, July 13 and 14, 1781. A copy of the Washington cipher that was sent to Nathanael Greene has not been found; see RM to Greene, September 10, and Gouverneur Morris to Greene, September 10 and 11.
2. Deciphered copy: preceding two words omitted.
3. For RM's direction of Pennsylvania finances and his manipulation of the state currency, see the headnote to RM to the Speaker of the Pennsylvania Assembly, June 26; RM to Benjamin Franklin, July 21; and RM's correspondence with the president of Pennsylvania throughout July 1781.
4. This word, supplied from the Ofcl LbC, was omitted from the LS and the deciphered copy.

Lists of Bills of Exchange Delivered to Haym Salomon

Philadelphia, August 22, 1781. Beneath a list of "Bills drawn by Holker fils at sixty Days on Monsr. Boutin Tresorier de la Marine a[t] Paris," is the declaration of Haym Salomon: "Received of the Honble. Superintendant of Finance Bills in my favor to the Amount of fifty two thousand eight Hundred Livres Tournois according to the above List which Sum I promise to Account for to him." Following a second list of "Bills drawn by Holker fils at 60 Days on Monsr Boutin Paris," is the declaration of Haym Salomon: "Received of the Hon. Superintendant of Finance Bills in my Favor to the Amount of twenty one thousand eight hundred Livres Tournois which I promise to Account for to him." [1]

MS: Ofcl LbC, DLC.
1. On these and other bills, see Diary, August 11, Gouverneur Morris to John Holker, August 12, and RM to Le Couteulx and Company, August 26.

From Mathias Slough

[*Lancaster, Pennsylvania, August 22, 1781*. On August 30 RM wrote to Slough: "Your Letter of the twenty second was delivered me some Days since." *Letter not found.*]

Diary: August 23, 1781

Settled the Account of Expences to and from Camp with Edwd. Moyston my Steward who paid the bills and find it right.

Had Applications made me from a Mr Tobine [1] to be employed in this Office, refused; and from a Mr White [2] usually Employed by the Board of War to carry Money to the Army &Ca. Requested employment which I promised when occasion shoud offer.

Colo. Miles applied for Money to pay for 140 Horses wanted by the Quarter Ms. General for the immediate Operations of the present Campaign.[3] I desired him to buy them at 2, 3 and 4 Months Credit but not to give higher Prices for that Credit, and I engage to supply the Money at those periods.

Wrote His Excellency The Governour of Virginia respecting Specific Supplies &Ca.

Wrote The President of the Supreme E[xecutive] Council.

Made application to several persons to borrow State Money and find they have very little of it. My intention in borrowing was to pay the $4/_{10}$ths. without touching the Treasury but as it is Appreciating fast this will be difficult.[4]

Issued a Warrant on Mr Swanwick for £300 in favor [of] S Hodgdon Esqr.[5] (Use of the Army).

Thoms. Smith Esqr. Loan Officer of Pensylvania applied to me for Money on Account of the $4/_{10}$ due from the State of Pensylvania and on settlement it appears that I have paid him 154074 and $^{76}/_{90}$ths on that Account without taking One Dollar from the State Treasury.[6] This being a larger Sum than Mr Rittenhouse could have Issued within the same time from Taxation of Old Continental Money, the Creditors on that Fund have no cause of Complaint and by keeping their respective Warrants they will benefit of the Appreciation; therefore I put him off.

The Honorable Mr. Lovell on behalf of a Committee of Congress applied to me respecting a poor Canadian and a Woman from New York both of whom had equitable Claims on the Humanity and Generosity of Congress who were enclined to grant them Annuities but for want of Funds. I agreed they might draw rations on Account of such Annuities if they should be granted.[7]

Honorable Colo. Bland on behalf of a Committee of Congress applied for payment of an Old Debt assigned by the Original Proprietors to Colo. Spotswood of Virgina. who wants the Money to pay for Accoutrements for two Troops of Horse now raising under his Command by the State of Virginia. I Objected to this payment as being contrary to my Stipulations with Congress, as having no Funds, that can be with propriety applied to payment of such debts and because partial payments of Old Debts would create a Clamour with other Public Creditors and as I wish that Virginia and all the other States would fill up their Quotas of the present Army rather than raise New Corps, I judge the measure impolitic, improper and extravagant, and lastly I cannot Apply any Monies under my Command to this use without doing essential injury to the general Service, or perhaps impedeing entirely the movements intended by his Excelly. the Commdr. in Chief therefore declined this Payment.[8]

Agreed with Mr. Levy Hollingsworth [9] that he should place 300 barrells good flour at the Head of Elk to be held to my Order for which I am to pay the Philadelphia Markett Price discounting Only the Cost of Transportation from thence to this City.

1. Not further identified.

2. Probably John White, an escort employed by the Board of War who delivered $300,000 sent to Georgia by Congress in 1780. *JCC,* XVIII, 966–967.

3. While at Washington's headquarters, RM had agreed to Quartermaster General Timothy Pickering's request that Colonel Samuel Miles, deputy quartermaster general for Pennsylvania, be authorized to purchase between 140 and 150 horses for the Continental artillery. Miles was instructed to complete his purchase in fifteen days and to have the horses ready by September 3. Pickering to Miles, August 17, 1781, WDC, no. 127, p. 213.

4. For RM's direction of Pennsylvania finances, see the headnote to RM to the Speaker of the Pennsylvania Assembly, June 26; Diary, July 19, RM to Benjamin Franklin, July 21, and RM's correspondence with the President of Pennsylvania throughout July 1781.

5. Samuel Hodgdon was commissary general of military stores.

6. See RM to the Treasurer of Pennsylvania, July 16, and to the President of Pennsylvania, August 23, 1781, and the documents cited in note 4 above.

7. The "poor Canadian" was Andrew Pepin, who had joined the American invasion forces and was appointed lieutenant in the 1st Canadian regiment on November 20, 1775. He became a supernumerary on June 23, 1779, his regiment was disbanded at Albany the following year, and he and his large family were directed to Philadelphia where they drew rations from the Continental government. The "Woman from New York" was Mrs. Elizabeth Bergen, who had assisted American officers held prisoner there by the British. Pepin and Mrs. Bergen had petitioned Congress and the Board of War, respectively, for rations for their families. However, the contract for supplying the Continental garrison at Philadelphia which RM signed on July 19 did not provide rations for persons unconnected with the army, and the Board of War recommended instead that Congress grant Pepin "a sum of money" and Mrs. Bergen an annuity of £20 hard money. Congress referred the board's reports to a committee which included James Lovell, whose call at the Office of Finance is recorded in the Diary printed here. Adopting the committee's report, Congress on August 24 awarded Pepin a Treasury warrant for $80 on account and Mrs. Bergen an annuity of $53. Afterwards, Pepin petitioned Congress to settle his accounts, which were referred on October 16 to the Comptroller of the Treasury for settlement in accordance with the terms used in settling the accounts of officers in Hazen's Canadian regiment. Heitman, *Register;* Pepin's memorial to Congress, July 19, 1781, PCC, no. 41, VIII, 148–149; *JCC,* XXI, 784, 816–817, 850–851, 874–875, XXII, 288 and n., XXV, 809n., XXX, 149n., 154n., 209n., 212n., XXXIII, 747, XXXIV, 623; for RM's payments to Pepin, see Diary, September 11 and 14, November 8, and December 21, 1781.

8. On August 21 the Virginia delegates presented to Congress a letter of August 19 from Alexander Spotswood (1751–1818), who had come to Philadelphia seeking funds to equip two legions which Virginia on March 21, 1781, had authorized him to raise for its defense and of which he had been given command. Spotswood's intention was to collect a debt of the United States to a Virginia creditor for £1003.9.6 specie which had been assigned to him. His letter was referred to a committee which included the Virginia delegate Theodorick Bland, whose interview with RM elicited the objections recorded in the Diary printed here. Congress on August 27 rejected Spotswood's request, and explaining this decision to Governor Thomas Nelson, the Virginia delegates cited RM's objections: "The danger of increasing the importunities and discontent of the public Creditors by such a precedent, and the appropriation of every fund to the essential purposes of the Campaign from which it is surmized relief must eventually accrue to Virginia, prevailed over every consideration drawn from the justice of the demand & the use to which it was destined." Spotswood to the Virginia Delegates in Congress, August 19, and the Virginia Delegates to Governor Thomas Nelson, August 28, 1781, Hutchinson and Rutland, eds., *Madison Papers,* III, 229–230, 243. On Spotswood, who had resigned from the Continental army on October 9, 1777, after attaining the rank of colonel, see *ibid.,* I, 226n., III, 37n.; and Heitman, *Register.* For RM's stipulation that he would not be responsible for debts contracted before his administration, see his letter to the President of Congress, May 14, 1781.

9. Levi Hollingsworth (1739–1824), a member of a prominent mercantile family of Philadelphia who came to the city in 1760, was a flour factor with whom RM did a large amount of public and private business. RM placed official government flour exports from Philadelphia in his hands in 1782 and also employed him in subcontracting beef. Hollingsworth was aligned with RM in Pennsylvania politics as an anticonstitutionalist and later became a leader of the Federalist party. East, *Business Enterprise,* 154; Simpson, *Lives of Eminent Philadelphians,* 540; Brunhouse, *Counter-Revolution in Pennsylvania,* 24, 68, 69, 113; RM to Hollingsworth, April 22 and June 1, 1782. On the engagement with Hollingsworth, recorded in the Diary printed here, see Washington to RM, August 17, and notes.

To the President of Pennsylvania (Joseph Reed)

Philada. 23 August 1781

Sir

I have this Day settled an Account with Thomas Smith Esqr. the Loan Officer and have his Receipt for one hundred and fifty four thousand and seventy four Dollars and seventy six ninetieths on Account of the four tenths of the new Emissions due by this State to Congress. As yet, I have not drawn one Shilling from the Treasury of Pennsylvania and am of Consequence so much in advance. There still remains due to Mr Smith on the four tenths a Balance of two hundred and thirty five thousand nine hundred and twenty five Dollars and fourteen ninetieth. Those who have the Warrants on him for this Money are clamorous to obtain Payment.[1]

I had procured on Account of Pennsylvania a considerable Quantity of Flour. In the State of New York one thousand Barrels. In the State of New Jersey four thousand Barrels; and in this City four thousand Barrels.[2] For all these I obtained Credit; and with Respect to the last not finding Consumption for it here I have lately made Payment of Part by the Redelivery of three thousand three hundred and ninety Barrels,[3] which was a desireable Circumstance, first because the Consumption of that Article was and probably would be in Places where it could be so purchased as to save on the Transportation; secondly because the risque of spoiling, or other loss which I began to apprehend was not incurred; and thirdly because, as this Article would probably fall in Price, it might be procured hereafter on easy Terms. My Reasons for purchasing in New York and New Jersey were, that there would be a saving in the Carriage which is a Benefit to the United States and that there would be also a Saving in the Price which is a Benefit to this State. From what has been said, then, your Excellency will perceive that my Credit stands pledged for five thousand six hundred and ten Barrels of Flour. Some of the Payments have already become due and I have found Means to satisfy them. The Rest will shortly be so which will create new Difficulties. Had I drawn Money from the State Treasury at the Time when the Purchases were made, I must have exchanged it for Specie. The rate at those Times was from five to six, and even seven for one; but whenever it shou'd have been known that it was drawn from the Treasury and sold on public Account in all human Probability it would have depreciated still more. The Credit therefore which I have obtained has been beneficial, by giving time for that Change of Opinion which could alone operate an Appreciation.

Had the collection of Taxes taken Place as early as I was induced to beleive it would the Paper would now be nearly if not entirely, equal to Specie. But at the present Rate of Exchange, it will require from eighty to an hundred thousand Dollars to fulfill my Engagements for this flour.

The Payments on my Contracts for Rations [4] will shortly commence and your Excellency, from the former Expenditures at the several Posts will be able to form a more adequate Idea than I can, what those Payments will Amount to. To all this I must add, that I have every Reason to beleive that other considerable Supplies from this State will soon become indispensible and of Consequence the most urgent Demand for Money be immediately created. I have also engaged, if his Excellency Genl. Washington should obtain a Quantity of Flour to be delivered on the North River to the Use of the Army as part of this States Quota of Supplies, to repay the same Quantity of flour to His Order here or on the Chesapeak as he may direct.[5]

I have thought it proper to make this full Communication that the supreme Executive of the State may be informed of what is passing in their Affairs. You will clearly perceive that my Situation is far from agreeable; yet such as it is, I will struggle under it and adopt every Expedient which may probably afford Releif, being determined not to draw Money from the Treasury until the Interest of the State shall Invite or invincible Necessity compel me to it.[6]

I have the Honor to be with all possible Respect your Excellency's most obedient and humble Servant

RM

MS: Ofcl LbC, DLC.
1. See Diary, August 23, and notes.
2. RM refers to the flour he had procured from Philip Schuyler in New York, Thomas Lowrey in New Jersey, and John Holker in Philadelphia.
3. On this transaction, see RM to John Holker, August 7, and notes.
4. RM refers to his contracts for supplying several Continental posts in Pennsylvania.
5. See Diary, August 21, and notes.
6. RM reported more fully on Pennsylvania's accounts with the United States in his letter to the Speaker of the Pennsylvania Assembly, September 28.

To the Governor of Virginia (Thomas Nelson)[1]

Office of Finance 23rd. August 1781.

Sir

I am but just returned from the Head Quarters of the Commander in Chief, where I have been, for some days, in order to confer with him on the various military Operations and Arrangements, as far as they are connected with the duties of my department. Of Consequence, the defence of that valuable Part of Virginia now invaded, became much a Subject of Consideration; and I am happy to inform you, that every Measure will be pursued for its Safety, which is consistent with the general Objects of the War.[2]

The Force in Virginia ought to be very considerable, for Reasons which it is unnecessary to mention to you who are so well acquainted with the Country: But it is necessary to observe that the Supplies to this Force must be proportionably great. I have already done myself the Honour to transmit to your Excellency, an account of the Specific Supplies which have been required by Congress.[3] Virginia stands debited for the whole, and it is not in my power, perhaps not in yours, to State the Credit Side of that Account. Let, however, the Amount of the Articles furnished be what it may, this at least is certain, that I have the Command of no Money from the several States which will serve to maintain a Force in Virginia. Much therefore must depend, on the Provisions and Forage which that State can call forth. It is necessary for me to inform the General, what Reliance can be made on your Resources; and it is also necessary that this information should be just. Your Excellency must perceive that his Arrangements will greatly depend upon my Communications, and therefore you will need no Incitement, to transmit as soon as possible the Answers to my Enquiries. Let me then intreat Sir, to know what quantity of Flour, Beef and Pork both fresh and salted, and what quantity of Hay and Indian Corn, or other Forage, can be delivered by the State of Virginia, at what places, and by what Times. I shall also be happy to be inform'd, where the Tobacco required of your State is deposited, that I may take the proper measures for the Disposal of it.[4]

With all possible Respect I have the Honor to be Your Excellency's Most Obedient and humble Servant

Robt Morris

His Excelly The Governor and
Commander in Chief of the State of Virginia

ADDRESSED: His Excellency/The Governor of the State of/Virginia/Robt Morris ENDORSED: R Morris Esq/dated Aug 23. 1781/On the Matter of Supplies due/from Virginia
MSS: LS, Continental Congress Papers, Vi; Ofcl LbC, DLC.
1. Thomas Nelson (1738–1789), a Virginia merchant, soldier, and signer of the Declaration of Independence, had served as delegate to Congress at intervals from 1775 to 1777 and in 1779. In June 1781 he succeeded Thomas Jefferson as governor

of Virginia, but resigned in November on account of poor health. *DAB;* Burnett, ed., *Letters,* I, lxv, II, lxxii, IV, lxvi.

2. On the transfer of military operations to Virginia, see Washington to RM, August 17, and headnote and notes to Diary, August 21.

3. See RM's Circular to the Governors of the States, July 25, 1781.

4. Governor Nelson replied inconclusively on September 5.

From William Gordon

[*Boston, August 23, 1781.* On September 5 RM wrote to Gordon: "I have received your Favor of the twenty third of August enclosing a Letter from Mr Dudley." Benjamin Dudley's letter to RM was dated August 20. *Letter not found.*]

From the Governor of Massachusetts (John Hancock)

[*Boston, August 23, 1781.* On September 15 RM wrote to Governor Hancock: "I was honored with your Excellency's Favour of the 23rd. August, by the last Post." *Letter not found.*]

Diary: August 24, 1781

Upon Application from the Honorable Mr. Holker by his Agent Mr Turnbull I wrote The Honorable Admiralty Board to return the Bread he had lent for the Use of Frigate Trumbull.[1]

Wrote The President of Nw. Hampshire respecting Salted Provisions.

Wrote Messrs. Langdon and Paul Jones.

Wrote President of Congress for a Salary to be fixed for a Secretary.

Wrote Commissary General of Purchases.

Wrote Board of Admiralty.[2]

The Honorable Mr Matthews called on behalf of a Committee of Congress to know if any Funds under my direction could be applied to discharge two months pay to certain Officers of the Army lately from the Southward who have long been without any pay. I Answered that no Funds for that purpose has yet come into my hands nor do I know where they can be had untill the States will Yield Compliance with the requisitions of Congress.[3] Mr Matthews recommended Mr. Geo: A Hall [4] to be employed by me in this Office &Ca. He also told me the bill I received from the Delegates of So. Carolina on Richards & Co. in New London could only be paid in part.[5]

Colol. E. Blaine returned from Camp and called on me. I informed him of the necessity I shoud be under to sue his Brother Alexr. B[laine], and himself for Damages on Account of their none Compliance with their engagements to Supply the Posts of York Town and Carlisle,[6] but he Answered that his Brother came to this City last Night on purpose to enter into the Contracts and with a View to fulfill his engagements which I am glad of as it relieves me from the disagreable necessity of bringing suits against him.

In Compliance with a request of his Excellency General Washington [7] I desired Colonel Ephraime Blaine as Commissary General to provide Three hundred Barrells of flour, Three hundred barrells of Salt Provisions and Twelve Hogshead[s of] Rum at a Magazine at the Head of Elk and Wrote him a Letter on that subject (as mentioned above). I informed Colonel Blaine of my Agreement with Mr L. Hollingsworth [8] and desired if he could obtain the flour from Delaware or Maryland States, not to suffer the Purchase.

Had a Conference with John Gibson Esqr.[9] respecting the Mode and intention of granting specie Warrants on the Loan Officer in this State [10] and as the matter now appears to me I think it best not to pay more paper Money to said Loan Officer but this requires further Consideration.

Received a Letter from Genl. Thompson [11] respecting Supplies to the Western Department; this was brought by Major Hofnogle [12] and by whome sent it to the Board of War for their Consideration.

1. See Diary, June 23, 1781.

2. Doubtless the same letter mentioned in the first paragraph of the Diary.

3. On August 13 Congress directed the Board of War to draw warrants in new emission money on the paymaster general for six months' pay due to officers of the South Carolina and Georgia lines recently released from British captivity and now in Philadelphia. In apparent ignorance of this action, the officers the same day addressed a memorial to Congress detailing their hardships and requesting rations and arrears of pay. Brigadier General William Moultrie of South Carolina, himself recently paroled, endorsed and enclosed the memorial in a letter of August 16 to the president of Congress, explaining that the depreciated new emission money granted to the officers was inadequate. On August 17 Congress referred his letter and the officers' memorial to a committee which included John Mathews, and on August 20 ordered the Board of War to supply the officers with wood. Despite RM's explanation to Mathews and his policy of not discharging past debts, including army pay, the committee recommended on September 29 that three months' pay be given to these officers, and Congress ordered RM to cash warrants to this amount. Moultrie's letter and the officers' memorial are in PCC, no. 158, fols. 521–526; see also Diary, October 2, 5, and November 2, and RM to the South Carolina Delegates in Congress, November 8, 1781.

4. George Abbott Hall (d. 1791), a merchant of Charleston, South Carolina, and formerly son-in-law of Congressman John Mathews, had been a member of the state Provincial Congress in 1775 and 1776, a commissioner of the South Carolina navy, 1776–1780, and an agent appointed by a committee of Congress ca. 1779 to pur-

chase rice in South Carolina for the Continental army and the French fleet commanded by Comte d'Estaing. Imprisoned at St. Augustine following the fall of Charleston in May 1780, Hall was permitted to return on account of his wife's death. RM appointed him receiver of Continental taxes for South Carolina in January 1782. Hall was collector of customs at Charleston as early as December 1784, was reappointed by President Washington, and served until his death. "Historical Notes," *S. C. Hist. and Gen. Mag.,* VII (1906), 103; Mabel L. Webber, ed., "Josiah Smith's Diary, 1780–1781," *ibid.,* XXXIII (1932), 198n.; A. S. Salley, Jr., ed., *Journal of the Commissioners of the Navy of South Carolina, October 9, 1776 . . . [to] March 23, 1780* (Columbia, 1912–1913), I, 3, 16, 65, 76–77, 146, II, 79; *JCC,* XVI, 314; Ralph Izard to Thomas Jefferson, June 10, 1785, and enclosure II, Boyd, ed., *Jefferson Papers,* VIII, 195, 199–201; Syrett and Cooke, eds., *Hamilton Papers,* X, 430n.; Diary, September 21, 1781, and January 14, 1782, and RM to the Governor of South Carolina, January 14, 1782. RM's first letters to Hall are dated January 18, 1782.

5. On this subject, see Diary, July 20 and 23, RM to Washington, July 23, and Washington to RM, August 2, 1781 (first letter).

6. See Diary, July 30 and August 1, and RM to William Scott, August 25, 1781.

7. See Washington to RM, August 17.

8. See Diary, August 23.

9. Gibson was a member of the Board of Treasury.

10. Thomas Smith was Continental loan officer of Pennsylvania.

11. Letter not found. William Thompson (1736–1781), an Irishman who emigrated to Carlisle, Pennsylvania, commanded the Pennsylvania rifle regiment (later known as the 1st Continental infantry) at the siege of Boston in 1775 and was promoted to brigadier general in March 1776. Captured during the Canadian expedition in June, he was paroled but not exchanged until October 1780. He died, apparently at Carlisle, on September 3, 1781. *DAB.*

12. Michael Huffnagle (d. 1819) of Pennsylvania, adjutant of the 1st Continental infantry in 1776 and captain of the 8th Pennsylvania in 1777, is said to have retired from Continental service in July 1778, although he is later recorded as a frontier ranger with the rank of major. On September 12, 1781, Huffnagle and Ephraim Blaine entered into contract with RM to provision Fort Pitt. Later, the same Huffnagle, apparently, held several judicial offices in Westmoreland County and in 1788 was admitted to the bar in Allegheny County. Heitman, *Register; Colonial Records of Pennsylvania,* XIII, 157–158, 700; *Pennsylvania Archives,* 2d ser., III, 773, 774, 778, 5th ser., IV, 760; J. W. F. White, "The Judiciary of Allegheny County," *PMHB,* VII (1883), 154.

To the Board of Admiralty

Office of Finance Augt. 24. 1781.

Gentlemen

The Honble. Mr Holker has applied to have the Ship bread he lent for the Use of the Trumbull Frigate replaced [1] and as this ought to be done, I request you will cause that Quantity of fresh bread equal in Quality to be delivered him and if needful I will supply you with the Money to pay for it. I am Gentlemen Your most obedient and humble Servant

R.M

MS: Ofcl LbC, DLC.

1. See Diary, June 23 and August 24, 1781.

To the Commissary General of Purchases
(Ephraim Blaine)

Office of Finance 24. Aug. 1781.

Sir

In a Conference with his Excellency the Commander in Chief he suggested the Propriety of depositing a small Magazine of Provisions at the Head of Elk to Answer the Contingent Demands which might arise during the Course of the Campaign.[1] The Quantity he mentions is three hundred Barrells of Flour and as many of salted Provisions with twelve Hogs heads of Rum. I am to request that you will Cause the Flour and salted Provisions to be procured and placed in proper Stores at the Head of Elk from the Specifick Supplies due by the States of Delaware and Maryland on the Requisitions of Congress of the twenty fifth of February and fourth of November 1780.[2] The Rum I will Cause to be delivered to you in this City on Account of the Supplies due from this State and you will take Care to have it transported thither. I am Sir your most obedient and humble Servant

RM.

MSS: Ofcl LbC, DLC; copy, Executive Papers, MdAA.

1. See Washington to RM, August 17, and notes; also RM to Washington, August 28.

2. Enclosing a copy of RM's letter, Blaine on August 25 informed Governor Thomas Sim Lee of Maryland that he had requested the flour and salted beef from state agents Henry Hollingsworth and James Calhoun and asked for further directions for the purchase of specific supplies. Blaine to Lee, August 25, 1781, *Maryland Archives*, XLVII, 446; see also RM to the Governor of Maryland, August 21, 26, and 28, and for Maryland's response, the Governor of Maryland to RM, August 31, and notes.

Delaware's considerably slower response led Blaine as late as October to press President Caesar Rodney for the supplies due from that state. Blaine to Rodney, October 4, 1781, George H. Ryden, ed., *Letters to and from Caesar Rodney, 1756–1784* (Philadelphia, 1933), 427–428; see also RM to the President of Delaware, August 26 and September 1.

To the President of Congress
(Thomas McKean)

Office of Finance 24th. Augt. 1781.

Sir

The Variety of Business I am obliged to do in Detail, so engrosses my Time, that I cannot pay Attention to those general Arrangements which are the proper Objects of my Appointment. I want now some Gentleman of Character, well acquainted with Accounts and Calculations, in whom I can repose Confidence and who may be trusted by the Public. It is difficult, among the many Things he will have to do, precisely to describe his Duties; but his Education, Abilities and Station in Life must be very superior to those of a common Clerk, of Consequence he must have a superior Compensation for his Labor. I must therefore intreat Congress to fix a Salary for such Person as I have described. He will have the Superintendence of the several Clerks and may therefore be properly stiled a Secretary. I shall also stand in Need of more Clerks; but, as their Salaries are fixed, I shall employ such as I may from Time to Time find necessary, without troubling Congress farther upon that Subject.[1]

With all possible Respect I have the Honor to be Sir your Excellency's most obedient and humble Servant

Robt Morris

His Excy The President of Congress

ENDORSED: Letter of 24 Augt. 1781/Superintendant of Finance/Read 24/Mr Bee/Mr Osgood/Mr Sherman/To be allowed a Secretary/to have his salary fixed
MSS: LS, PCC, DNA; Ofcl LbC, DLC.
1. This letter, the text of which is in the writing of Gouverneur Morris, was read in Congress on August 24 and referred to a committee which consulted RM on August 27 but failed to persuade him to suggest a sum for the secretary's salary. On the same day the committee delivered its recommendation that RM be authorized to appoint a secretary, although it appears from the manuscript report that the salary of $1,000 it authorized was filled in at a later date, probably on September 11 when the report was approved by Congress. RM's appointee was James McCall. Diary, August 27, 1781, and February 21, 1782; the committee's report is in PCC, no. 19, IV, 325.

To John Langdon and John Paul Jones

Office of Finance 24. August 1781.

Gentlemen

Having perused the enclosed [1] you will please to Seal and deliver it. When you shall have got the Beef into your hands if you are to feed the Workmen employed on Board of the America it may be applied for that Purpose otherwise it must be sold and the Produce of the Sales applied to the Completion of that Ship.[2] I have the Honor to be Gentlemen, &ca. &ca. &ca.

R.M

MS: Ofcl LbC, DLC.
1. RM to the President of New Hampshire, August 24.
2. On the *America*, see notes to John Langdon to RM, April 20, 1781.

To the President of New Hampshire
(Meshech Weare)

Office of Finance 24. August 1781.

Sir

I do myself the Honor to enclose to your Excellency the Copy of a Letter from the Commander in Chief.[1] I have the request in Consequence of it that you will cause the Beef mentioned in it to be delivered to John Langdon Esqr. and a Duplicate of his Receipt therefor to be transmitted to me.[2]

I have the Honor to be your Excellency's most obedient Servant

R.M

MS: Ofcl LbC, DLC.

1. Washington to RM, August 5.
2. See RM to John Langdon and John Paul Jones, August 24, in which RM enclosed this letter.

From George Washington

Head Quarters Kings Ferry [New York] 24th. Augt. 1781.

Dear Sir

Immediately after you left Camp I applied to Mr. Tarlé the French Intendant and requested to know the quantity of Flour which he could spare us and where he would wish to have it replaced.[1] I have not been able to ascertain either of these points, but from a conversation which passed yesterday between Mr. Tarle and Colo. Stewart [2] on the subject, I do not imagine we shall obtain more than 1000 or 1200 Barrels in this quarter; and as the whole or the greater part which is to be given in return will be wanted ⟨upon the Delaware, the Head of Elk or in Virginia⟩ to the southward, I think you may with safety prepare a few hundred Barrels in Philada, at which place the French will have a quantity of Bread Baked and the remainder at the Head of Elk and upon Chesapeak. The Moment I know with more certainty, I will inform you.

We have been delayed here longer than I expected by the difficulty of crossing the North River. The American Troops march tomorrow Morning and I hope by the time we reach Springfield [3] we shall hear of the arrival of the fleet in Chesapeak. After that, our design may be unmasked. It will take a very considerable number of Craft to carry us down the Delaware and I shall be obliged to you for keeping in mind my request that you would assist the Qr.

Mr. [Quartermaster] in procuring them and the Vessels in Chesapeak should he call upon you for that purpose.[4] I am &c

Robt. Morris Esq.

ENDORSED: Kings Ferry 24th. Augt. 1781/to/Robt. Morris Esqr.
MSS: Dft in the writing of Tench Tilghman, Washington Papers, DLC; Varick transcript, Washington Papers, DLC.
    1. While at Washington's headquarters, RM suggested to Major General Chastel-
lux that since the French forces were moving south, the flour they had on hand be
turned over to the American army remaining in New York and replaced by RM's
delivery of flour elsewhere. See Diary, August 21, and notes; Washington's letter
to Benoît Joseph de Tarlé, intendant of the French army in America, dated August
22, 1781, is in Fitzpatrick, ed., *Writings of Washington*, XXIII, 37.
    2. Charles Stewart, commissary general of issues.
    3. In Essex County, New Jersey.
    4. The request is in Washington to RM, August 17; see also Washington to RM,
August 27.

Diary: August 25, 1781

    Issued a Warrant on Mr Swanwick for £150 in favour of Mr Scott
of York Town having received a Letter respecting Supplies for that
Post,[1] and sent the Money With my Answer of this Date per Michael
Hohn Esqr.[2]

    In Consequence of a Report of the Treasury Board refered by
Congress to me to take Order,[3] Issued a warrant on Mr Swanwick
for £75 Specie in favour of Richard Philips, Stewd. of the Presidents
Household, he to be accountable, and required an Estimate of One
Months Expence thereof.

    This Day Waited on his Excellency The Minister Plenipotentiary
of France [4] to Congratulate him on its being the Anniversary of St
Louis the Saints day of His Illustrious Monarch and partook of an
Elegant Entertainment provided by his Excellency on the Occasion.

    1. The letter of August 17 from William Scott, Pennsylvania commissioner of
purchases for York County, has not been found.
    2. Michael Hahn, a merchant and store owner of York, Pennsylvania, was a captain
in the York County militia. Previously he had been elected to the assembly in 1777;
later he was a judge of the county court of common pleas. George R. Prowell, *History
of York County, Pennsylvania* (Chicago, 1907), I, 654–655; *Journals of the House of Representatives of Pennsylvania, 1776–1781*, 108; *Pennsylvania Archives*, 2d ser., III, 744, 3d
ser., VII, 65, XXI, 6, 330, 6th ser., II, 427, 431, 478.
    3. Congress on August 21 referred to RM for execution part of the Board of
Treasury's report of August 20, not found, recommending that money be furnished
to the steward of the president of Congress.
    4. Chevalier de La Luzerne.

To William Scott[1]

Office of Finance Augt. 25. 1781.

Sir

I have received your Letter of the seventeenth Instant [2] by Mr Hahn and am much obliged by your having complied with my Request and supplied the Post at York Town.[3] My Absence from this Place for upwards of two Weeks past [4] prevented me from calling on Mr Alexr. Blaine to fulfil his Engagement but on the Receipt of your Letter I had determined to take the necessary Steps for that Purpose.[5] But Yesterday his Brother the Commissary General [6] called and told me he was come to this City on purpose to finish the Contract and that he had been purchasing Cattle and otherwise preparing the necessary Supplies. So that I expect he will speedily releive you from this Business and on this Account I suppose a smaller Sum of Money than you mention may do for the present; had not this been the Case I should have sent you three hundred pounds. As it is I will send you one hundred and fifty by Mr Hahn and as soon as Mr Blaine begins the Supplies you will be pleased to send down the Accounts and Vouchers for what you have supplied since the Time mentioned in my former Letter. I will have them directly Examined, settled and the Balance shall be paid to you or your Order without delay [7] therefore I pray you to Continue the Supplies until Mr. Blaine begins and you will further serve your Country and oblige Sir your most obedient and humble Servant

R.M

MS: Ofcl LbC, DLC.

1. Scott was Pennsylvania commissioner of purchases for York County.
2. Letter not found.
3. See Diary, July 10, 1781.
4. RM had been at Washington's headquarters in Dobbs Ferry, New York. See Diary, August 21.
5. On Alexander Blaine and the contract to supply the Continental post at York, see Diary, July 30, and August 1 and 24, 1781.
6. Ephraim Blaine, commissary general of purchases.
7. See Diary, September 15.

From Matthew Ridley

[*Baltimore, August 25, 1781.* On August 27 RM replied to Ridley's "Letter of the twenty fifth Instant." *Letter not found.*]

Diary: August 26, 1781

Wrote His Excellency The Governour of Maryland respecting Specific Supplies.

Wrote His Excellency the Governour of Delaware respecting Specific Supplies.

Wrote Messrs. Le Couteulx & Co. Bankers, Paris, advising of Bills drawn.

To the President of Delaware (Caesar Rodney)

Office of Finance 26. Augt. 1781.

Sir

By the Resolutions of Congress of the fourth of November last the State of Delaware is required to furnish eight hundred Barrels of Pork,[1] none of which as I am informed has yet been delivered. I am therefore now to request that it may be delivered to the Order of Colo Blaine Commissary General of Purchases.[2] If the whole Quantity cannot be immediately supplied I must then desire that the Commissary may have as much as possible. The Necessities of the Service render a compliance with this Request so essential that I perswade myself of your Excellency's Exertions to prevent a Disappointment.[3]

With all possible Respect I have the honor to be Sir your Excellency's most obedient humble Servant

RM.

MS: Ofcl LbC, DLC.
1. See *JCC*, XVIII, 1013.
2. See Washington to RM, August 17, and notes, RM's Circular to the Governors of New Jersey and Delaware, August 22, and RM to the Commissary General of Purchases, August 24, and notes.
3. RM addressed President Rodney again on September 1.

To Le Couteulx and Company

Office of Finance, Philadelphia, August 26, 1781. Encloses a copy of a list of bills of exchange totalling 521,634 livres, 16 sous, and 8 denier tournois, drawn on them to August 2.[1] Also encloses and asks them to honor a list of bills of exchange totalling 201,323 livres, 8 sous tournois, drawn on August 10 at sixty days' sight in Haym Salomon's favor and sold after RM's departure for Washington's headquarters. Their punctual payment is made possible by Chevalier de La Luzerne's agreement to deposit 500,000 livres with them. They have already received one million livres subject to RM's drafts,[2] which he will continue to forward as circumstances require. Instructs them to refuse "as a fraud" the bill of exchange for 500,-000 livres which he drew on them July 17 in favor of Robert Smith because it "is either sunk or has fallen into the Enemies hands." [3]

MS: Ofcl LbC, DLC.
1. This enclosure and the one mentioned in the next sentence have not been found.
2. See RM to La Luzerne, June 8, La Luzerne to RM, June 9, RM to La Luzerne, July 2, and Barbé-Marbois to RM, July 3, 1781.
3. On this bill of exchange, which RM sent to Havana on the frigate *Trumbull,* see RM to Smith, July 17, 1781. On the capture of the *Trumbull* and its consequences, see Diary, August 15, and notes, and RM to John Jay, August 15, and notes. RM sent Le Couteulx and Company an additional list of drafts drawn on them in his letter of September 5.

To the Governor of Maryland
(Thomas Sim Lee)

Office of Finance 26. August 1781

Sir,

I wrote you on the twenty first Instant and informed you that the Flesh due by your State would be speedily wanted and much of the salted Provisions immediately. I am now to request that the whole may be delivered to the Order of Colo. Blaine the Commissary General as fast as it can be collected.[1] I am your Excellency's most obedient Servant.

RM.

MS: Ofcl LbC, DLC.
1. See Washington to RM, August 17, and notes, and RM to the Commissary General of Purchases, August 24, and notes, and to the Governor of Maryland, August 28. Governor Lee replied on August 31.

Diary: August 27, 1781

Prepared Plan for arangeing the Treasury Department. Met Messrs. Sherman, Bee and Osgood [1] on that Subject and on my Letter to Congress of the 24th; [2] confered with them on the Modes of adjusting the several public Accounts. They pressed me to mention a Sum as the Salary for my Secretary which I declined. Explain my Ideas on the Arrangement of the Treasury which they appeared to Approve; transmitted them the Plan.[3]

Sent for Mr Haym Solomon the Jew Broker, who informed me

that he had sold small sums of the Pensylvania State paper at two Dollars for 1 of silver and that he Offered to purchase said paper at $2^1/_2$ for One agreable to Orders I had before given him, and I think it best to continue my Orders on this footing untill the Collection of Taxes Commences. He informed me that bills of Exchange continued to pour in our Market from the Eastern States and other places where the French Bills had been sold or paid and that the best bills of 30 days Sight on France are now selling at 4/6 to 4/9 per five Livres.[4] Mr Josephson [5] says the same and Mr Isaac Moses [6] who offers to purchase bills from me says he can purchase with Cash in hand for 4/6. Mr Moses having an Order on me by Colo. Miles [7] for Amount of Oznaburgs [8] bought sometime, to make sand bags for the intended siege of N York,[9] he requires payment or Offers to take bills for Lrs. 30,000 to Discount this balance and pay the remainder in six Weeks; [10] after much altercation agreed with him at 5/6 to stay Six Week. Sold bills for Lrs. 5,400 at 5/ to pay Mr Ridley for flour purchased at Baltimore and received advice from him [11] that he could not get flour fit for Mr Holkers use from the Goverment of Maryland, therefore he had bought about 1000 barrels at 12 per Ct [12] and Casks 2/9d.[13]

Messrs. Hazlewood and Blackstone presented their Accounts as Contractors for five Weeks Rations and granted them a Warrant on Mr Swanwick.[14]

Issued my Warrant on Swanwick for £250 Specie in favour of Messrs. Hazlewood and Blackston.

Received a Letter from His Excellency Gen: Washington to Mr Peters and myself in Answer to one we Wrote him at Camp.[15] I sent the Generals Letter enclosed in a few lines of this date to Mr Peters requesting him to furnish me with Copies of both these letters.

Wrote Matthew Ridley Esquire respecting Flour, Vessels &Ca.

1. Roger Sherman (1721–1793), Connecticut merchant, lawyer, legislator, and jurist, signed the Declaration of Independence and served in Congress, 1774–1781 and 1783–1784. *DAB.*

Thomas Bee (1725–1812) of South Carolina, Oxford–educated lawyer and planter, was a state legislative councillor, 1776–1778, lieutenant governor, 1779–1780, and a delegate to Congress, 1780–1782. *Biog. Dir. Cong.*

Samuel Osgood, previously identified, was a Massachusetts congressman.

2. The committee's report on RM's letter is discussed in notes to RM to the President of Congress, August 24.

3. See notes to the Plan for Arranging the Treasury Department, August 27, for a discussion of congressional action.

4. On the rates at which bills of exchange on France sold for Pennsylvania currency, see notes to Gouverneur Morris to RM, August 8. For Salomon's previous dealings with the Office of Finance, see Diary, August 8, 9, and 10, and Gouverneur Morris to RM, August 8, and to Salomon, August 10.

5. Manuel Josephson (ca. 1729–1796), a German-born sutler at Fort Edward during the French and Indian War, was a merchant and leader of the Jewish community in New York City on the eve of the Revolution. In 1776, prior to the city's evacuation by the Continental army, he moved to Philadelphia. Although suspected of being a loyalist, for which he was imprisoned on one occasion, Josephson, who was noted for his Hebraic learning, subsequently became an important figure in the Philadelphia Jewish congregation and in 1790 sent congratulations to President Washington on behalf of the Jews of New York, Philadelphia, Richmond, and Charleston. Joseph R. Rosenbloom, *A Biographical Dictionary of Early American Jews: Colonial Times Through 1800* (Lexington, Ky., 1960), 77; Jacob R. Marcus, *The Colonial American Jew, 1492–1776* (Detroit, 1970), II, 710, 1010, 1076, 1084, III, 1294; Erastus Knight, comp., *New York in the Revolution as Colony and State: Supplement* (Albany, 1901), 144, 240.

6. Isaac Moses (1742–1818), a prominent member of New York City's Jewish community, was an auctioneer and merchant heavily involved in international trade as a partner of Samuel and Moses Myers of Amsterdam. He went bankrupt in 1786. Syrett and Cooke, eds., *Hamilton Papers*, III, 26n., 600n.; Alexander Hamilton to Jeremiah Wadsworth, April 7, 1785, *ibid.*, 601–603; Rosenbloom, *Biographical Dictionary of Early American Jews*, 120.

7. Colonel Samuel Miles, deputy quartermaster general for Pennsylvania.

8. A variant of osnaburg, a coarse linen cloth whose name is derived from Osnabrück, a town in northern Germany where it was manufactured. *OED*.

9. A reference to the allied plan which was scrapped in favor of operations in the Chesapeake region. See the headnote and notes to Diary, August 21.

10. See Diary, August 31.

11. Matthew Ridley to RM, August 25, not found.

12. Shillings per hundredweight.

13. On Ridley's flour purchases for John Holker, see RM to Holker, August 7, and notes.

14. John Hazelwood and Isaac Serrell signed a contract with RM on July 19, 1781, to supply rations to the Continental post at Philadelphia, but it is apparent from this Diary entry that Presley Blackistone of Philadelphia, a cordwainer by trade who had been assessor and commissioner for Philadelphia county in 1779, subsequently assumed Serrell's obligations. On Blackistone, see *Pennsylvania Archives*, 3d ser., XIV, 169, 234, 470, 474, 746, XV, 185, XVI, 323, 740.

15. See RM and Richard Peters to Washington, August 13, and Washington's reply of August 21.

To John Davidson

[*Philadelphia, August 27, 1781.* This letter, addressed to Davidson at Annapolis, Maryland, requested him to pay money to Matthew Ridley for the purchase of flour. See RM to Ridley, August 27, and notes. *Letter not found.*]

SOURCE: ALS, sold by Anderson Auction Company, November 25, 1907, lot 168.

To Richard Peters

Office of Finance August 27. 1781.

Dear Sir,

You will find herein the General's Letter in Answer to that which we wrote at Camp [1] and as I have no Copies I shall be obliged if you will Order Copies of both to be made out and sent to me as speedily as possible. I think also it may be well to communicate these Letters to the Committee of Congress [2] that we may have a further Conference if thought necessary. I am Sir your most obedient and humble Servant

RM

MS: Ofcl LbC, DLC.
    1. See RM and Peters to Washington, August 13, and Washington's reply of August 21.
    2. On this committee, see Diary, July 31, 1781, and notes.

Plan for Arranging the Treasury Department[1]

[Philadelphia, August 27, 1781]

In Arranging the Treasury, it is proper to consult Oeconomy, as far is consistent with the Principles of Justice, and the dispatch of Business.

To employ a number of Persons, for performing the same service, is equally dilatory and expensive. Neither will Experience warrant the Idea, that Justice will be more impartially administered by many, than it is by a few, or even by a single Person. On the Contrary, it too frequently happens, that Partiality as well as Neglect are the Attendants of large Boards. If this has not happened in America, it must be Attributed to a Peculiarity of Circumstances, which, as it can seldom happen, ought never to be depended upon. Simplifying public Offices, and the Modes of transacting public Business, seems also to be peculiarly necessary to the United States; because the accumulated Mass of Things which now call for an Adjustment, will no longer admit of Delay; because, it will be difficult, if not impracticable, to find a great number of Men properly qualified; and because, Complexity which is the Parent of Mistery and Concealment, is ill suited to a Goverment like ours. Congress ought to know their own Affairs generally, if not particularly, and therefore, as the Members of that honorable Body are frequently changed, that general knowledge ought to be easily acquired. The People ought to know how Money Matters are transacted, and the Public Debtors and Creditors ought to be disincumbered from useless Ceremonies, while at the same time they are obliged to adhere to necessary Forms.

The Treasury Office divides itself into three Branches, 1st the Liquidation of Accounts, 2dly. Keeping the public Books, and 3ly. the Custody of public Money. These Branches, altho distinct, ought however to be so connected as that the different Parts may form one whole. It may be supposed that the Superintendant of the Finances ought to be the Link of this Connection, but a little Consideration will shew that to be impossible. Attention to the Revenues and Expenditures of a large Country, and what is more, of a new Country, Devising ways and Means to check the one, and to extend the other; the Cherishing and Support of public Credit, Or rather the Restoration of Credit in the midst of new Expences and old Debts, the Ravages of War and the Waste of Invasion: these alone are Objects large enough to fill the most capacious Mind, Minute enough to occupy the most unwearied Attention. And yet these form but a part of the Duties of a Superintendant. He ought not, therefore, to be called on for any Thing more, as to the Treasury department, than to institute such Orders and Regulations for the conduct and dispatch of Business, as Time and Circumstances may require. For the other Purposes above Stated, a Gentleman of Character, Sense, Knowledge, and unblemished Reputation, A Gentleman well acquainted with Business and particularly with Accounts, industrious himself and firm in exacting a Performance of their Duty from others, such a Gentleman should be chosen as a Comptroller.

The Comptroller should have a general Authority to inspect and superintend the whole Department, to see that the public Accounts are expeditiously and properly settled, accurately and safely kept, and the Balance of the public Monies always in the Hands of the Treasurer.

To the Comptroller every Account ought to be delivered, in the first Instance, and he should hand it to such Clerk for examination, as he should think most proper for that purpose; naming also the Auditor to whom the Clerk shall transmit it. As there can be no doubt, that the Party will take care of his own private Interest, so it should be the Duty of the Clerk, to guard the Interests of the Community. Every Account ought to be first stated in one certain form, so that a Person once acquainted with that Form, could go through all the public Accounts with equal Facility. This Form ought also to be easy, simple, and clear. After the Account is stated, the next Object is to examine it numerically, and correct the Arithmetical Errors, if there be any. It ought then to be considered in two principle Points of View; first as to the Validity of the Vouchers, and secondly as to the Propriety of the Charges which they are adduced to support. Throughout the whole of this Examination, the Clerk ought to make and note every objection, and then send the Account with his Remarks to the Auditor, who should hear the Party, and the Clerk, and determine upon the Objections made, after which the Account ought to be transmitted to the Comptroller, and a reasonable Time given to the Party to appeal from the Auditors Judgment. If such appeal be made, the Comptroller ought,

Openly and Publickly, to hear the Party and the Clerk, and finally to decide. From what has been said it will appear, that the Number of Auditors and Clerks must be indefinite, but that of the Clerks will necessarily exceed that of the Auditors. These Clerks ought, for very evident Reasons, to be appointed by the Comptroller; but the Number of them ought to be regulated by the Superintendant. It would not be proper that the Appointment of Auditors should also be in the Comptroller, as that Officer would then be uncheckd, but it might properly be entrusted to the Superintendant.

After an Account has been finally adjusted on Appeal, or remained the Stipulated Time before the Comptroller, it should be, by him, transmitted to the Register or keeper of the Treasury Books to be entered of Record, and a Note of the Balance should be, by the Comptroller, transmitted to the Superintendant to make out the proper Warrants.

The Register, or Book Keeper, who ought to be a very good Accomptant, faithful, Just, accurate, attentive and industrious; should be appointed by Congress, and have the appointment of the Clerks necessary in his Office. He should keep all the public Accounts, both of Receipts and Expenditures, and every Warrant drawn on the Treasurer, or others by the Superintendant, should be entred and countersigned by the Register. The Treasurer should receive and keep the public Monies, and pay them out on the Warrants of the Superintendant, countersigned by the Register, he should appoint his own Clerks, in like Manner with the Register, his Books and Accounts ought always to be Subject to the Inspection of the Comptroller, and he should be at all times Obliged to shew the Comptroller that he is in Possession of the Cash which appears on the Balance of his Accounts. It is needless to add, that this very important Officer ought to be appointed by Congress.

These are the out Lines of a Plan which, if it has nothing else to recommend it, is at least simple and easily comprehensible. Time will discover its Deficiencies, and they may then be remedied. To go deeply into the Detail of a System, is dangerous; because it may on Experiment be found inconvenient, and it is always easier to add, than to alter. The Merit of this plan, if it has any, can only be determined by Experience, and Experience alone can fully unfold its Faults. It will not be very expensive, and gives fair Oppertunities for obtaining Speedy Justice, both to Individuals and to the United States.

ENDORSED: A plan for regulating/the business of the treasury/Office/Aug 27. 1781/Referred to Mr Duane/Mr Clymer/Mr Bee
MS: D, PCC, DNA.

1. The creation of the Office of Finance and the election of RM as Superintendent of Finance by Congress in February 1781 foreshadowed the dissolution of the Board of Treasury and the reorganization of the department over which the board presided (see notes to RM to the Board of Treasury, June 8, 1781, for a discussion of the evolution of Continental treasury administration). At RM's request, however, Congress on July 24 continued the board in the discharge of its duties until he could make new arrangements. These the Financier contemplated for at least six weeks (see Diary, July 11 and 23, 1781) before they materialized in the proposals presented here. The plan for reorganizing the Treasury Department, drafted by RM on August 27 (see Diary of that date), was an effort to inject the dominant goals of his administration—economy, efficiency, and fiscal reform—into the day-to-day management of the financial affairs of the Continental government.

The Financier transmitted the plan to a committee of Congress which conferred with him on the subject (see Diary, August 27). After referral to another committee on the same day, the plan was reintroduced on September 10 in the form of an ordinance drafted by James Duane. As adopted by Congress on September 11, it contained only two significant variations from RM's plan. Congress provided that the Treasurer could issue public funds on treasury warrants drawn by its president as well as by RM and reserved to itself the election of auditors, which RM suggested he be allowed to appoint. Apart from these changes, the ordinance remained, in the Financier's words, "nearly Conformable" in style and substance to his plan (see RM to the Governor of Massachusetts, September 15).

The reorganization of the Treasury Department spanned several months. After assigning salaries to the various offices on September 11 and electing Joseph Nourse Register and reelecting Michael Hillegas Treasurer on September 19, Congress on October 8 appointed a committee to take charge of treasury papers until the newly elected officials assumed their duties. On October 13, after William Churchill Houston, member of Congress from New Jersey, declined the office of Comptroller, Congress chose former Auditor General James Milligan; for auditors it selected William Govett on October 23 and William Geddes and John Dyer Mercier on January 28, 1782. This arrangement of the department stood until RM's resignation on November 1, 1784, when a revived Board of Treasury, established by a congressional resolution of the preceding May 28, assumed his duties and powers. *JCC,* XXI, 1006; see also Diary, August 28, October 12, 22, 27, 29, and November 14, 1781.

To Matthew Ridley

Office of Finance August 27th. 1781.

Sir,

Your Letter of the twenty fifth Instant [1] shews me clearly that I must not depend on the Supplies of your State for any Part of the three thousand Barrels of Flour which I am to deliver to Mr Holker.[2] Wherefore I not only approve of the Engagements you have made for one thousand Barrels at twelve Shillings per hundred weight but request you will without loss of time procure the remaining Quantity so as to have ready for Mr Holker's Order in the whole three thousand Barrels of Flour such as you mention; altho I do not remember that those lining hoops on each Head was any Part of our Agreement, nevertheless you may compleat the whole in that Way, telling me what part of the two Shillings and nine pence Cost of Casks is occasioned by the extra Cooperage. By your Letter to

Mr Holker [3] it seems you did not understand whether my Order was intended for three thousand Barrels in Addition to the first two thousand or not; But you will now clearly understand that three thousand Barrels is the Amount of my Engagement to him and the whole of what you are to purchase.[4] This Flour ought to be ready by the first of September; however if it is ready to deliver when he calls for it that may do, but there is no knowing how soon that call may be made consequently not a Moments Time to be lost. I observe you write to Mr Holker for Money on this Occasion which was very unnecessary as I shall always be ready to fulfill my own Engagements and at the same time I am rather disappointed having been told repeatedly that flour might be obtained for a Month, six Weeks and two Months Credit in your Country and in this and other Places I have met with no Difficulty in obtaining such Credits which facilitate Business whilst Money is so extremely scarce. It happens that I can send you the Sum required instantly if Conveyance can be found which shall be immediately sought after, and I shall continue sending until you are fully reimbursed therefore do not hesitate to purchase the rest of the Flour on the best Terms instantly.[5]

What can put it into the Heads of either Farmers or Millers that prices are to rise? when every Part of the Country from one End of the Continent to the other is so full of Wheat that an Army of ten times the Number of ours could not possibly consume a tenth of the Surplus and when even if your Ports [6] were open, all the Shipping that belongs or Resorts to America could not carry it off, if employed solely in that Business; besides if there were no other Obstacle Money cannot be found fast enough to raise prices even if the Plenty was less visible than it is and I shall not be surprized to see flour at ten shillings per Cwt. altho I do not wish it. Nor will I attempt to lower it, being desirous the Country should obtain Prices to sweeten Labor and enable them to pay Taxes freely. I have desired Mr Stephen Steward junr.[7] and Mr John Davidson [8] of Annapolis to pay you some Money and if they do you will grant them receipts or Drafts as they choose. Furnish me an Invoice of this Flour soon as you can, and oblige Sir your obedient humble Servant.

RM

MS: Ofcl LbC, DLC.

1. Letter not found.
2. See RM to John Holker, August 7, and notes, and to James Calhoun, August 28.
3. This letter has not been found.
4. This point was unclear in Gouverneur Morris to Ridley, August 8, and RM to Ridley, August 21.

5. See RM to John Holker, August 29.

6. MS: "Posts."

7. RM's letter to Stephen Steward, Jr. (d. 1797), has not been found. His father Stephen (d. 1791) was a leading Baltimore merchant frequently associated with RM in privateering ventures. On August 28 RM requested the Stewards to assist in the collection of transport vessels at the Head of Elk for Washington's troops. *Maryland Archives*, XXI, 432, XLV, 246, 432; East, *Business Enterprise*, 160, 171; Ver Steeg, *Morris*, 14, 15; RM's Circular to Stephen Steward and Son, Jonathan Hudson, David Stewart, and Samuel Smith, August 28; see also the following note.

8. RM's letter to John Davidson (d. 1794), a Scots-born merchant of Annapolis, Maryland, has not been found. In 1772 Davidson formed a business partnership with Charles Wallace and Joshua Johnson which lasted until 1777, but he continued to operate the firm's store at Annapolis with his brother Samuel until 1784. With a group which included RM and Stephen Steward, probably the elder, Davidson owned the sloop *Porpoise*, which received a privateer commission from Maryland on January 1, 1781. Before his death, Davidson invested heavily in Washington City, Maryland, real estate. *Maryland Archives*, XLV, 258–259. For information on Davidson, as well as on Stephen Steward, Jr., in the preceding note, the editors are indebted to Mrs. Bryce Jacobsen of the Maryland Hall of Records and Edward C. Papenfuse, Jr., of the *American Historical Review*.

To Stephen Steward, Jr.

[*Philadelphia, ca. August 27, 1781.* This letter undoubtedly was similar to the one RM addressed on this date to John Davidson. See RM to Matthew Ridley, August 27. *Letter not found.*]

From the Board of War

[*Philadelphia, August 27, 1781.* On August 28 RM wrote to the Board of War: "I am favored with your Letter of the twenty seventh." *Letter not found.*]

From George Washington

Chatham [New Jersey] 27th. August 1781.

Dear Sir

Accounts brought by several Vessels to Philada. and to the Eastward leave little doubt but that the Count de Grasse must have already arrived in the Chesapeak, or that he must be very soon there.[1] The Count de Rochambeau and myself have therefore determined that no time ought to be lost in making preparations for our transportation from Trenton to Christiana and from the Head of Elk down the Chesapeak. I have written by this opportunity to Colo. Miles and have directed him immediately to engage all the proper kind of Craft for the navigation of the Delaware which can be found in Philada. or in the Creeks above and below it, and as your advice may be useful to him, more especially so far as respects procuring the Vessels at a distance from Philada., I have desired him to wait upon you for that purpose.[2]

I shall also be obliged to you for using your influence with the Gentlemen of Baltimore to permit any Vessels which may be in that port to come up to Elk to assist us in transportation.[3] I have little doubt, from the chearfulness with which they furnished the Marquis last Winter,[4] but they will comply with your requisition on the present occasion. But lest there should be a necessity for the interference of the Executive of the State, I have written to Governor Lee upon that and other matters.[5] I inclose the letter under flying seal for your information, and you will be good enough to forward it by a Chain of Expresses which is established. Any Vessels which may be procured in Chesapeak should rendezvous as soon as possible in Elk River.

You will be pleased to make the deposit of Flour, Rum and Salt Meat at the Head of Elk which I requested in a former letter.[6]

I am very fearful that about 1500 Bbls of salt provisions and 30 Hhds of Rum which I directed to be sent from Connecticut and Rhode Island under Convoy of the Count de Barras would not have been ready when the Fleet sailed from Newport.[7] Should that have been the case, the disappointment will be great. I would wish you to see whether a like quantity of those Articles can be procured in Philada. or in Maryland, if we should find that they have not gone round from the Eastward.

I must entreat you if possible to procure one months pay in specie for the detachment which I have under my command; [8] part of those troops have not been paid any thing for a long time past, and have upon several occasions shewn marks of great discontent. The service they are going upon is disagreeable to the Northern Regiments, but I make no doubt that a douceur of a little hard money would put them in proper temper. If the whole sum cannot be obtained, a part of it will be better than none, as it may be distributed in proportion to the respective wants and claims of the Men.

The American detachment will assemble in this neighbourhood to day. The French Army tomorrow.[9] I have the honor to be &c

Robt. Morris Esq:

ENDORSED: Chatham 27th. Augt. 1781/to/Robt. Morris Esq./to procure transports/provision &c
MSS: Dft in the writing of Tench Tilghman, Washington Papers, DLC; Varick transcript, Washington Papers, DLC.
    1. De Grasse's fleet arrived off the Virginia Capes on August 26 and at the en-

trance to Chesapeake Bay on August 30. Washington received confirmed intelligence of de Grasse's arrival on September 5 at Chester, Pennsylvania, while on his way to the Head of Elk. Freeman, *Washington*, V, 320–321 and n.; Ward, *War of the Revolution*, II, 884–885; Fitzpatrick, ed., *Washington Diaries*, II, 258; see also the September 7 postscript to RM to Benjamin Franklin, August 28.

2. On August 27 Washington directed Colonel Samuel Miles, deputy quartermaster general for Pennsylvania, to collect vessels at Trenton for the transportation of the army to Christiana, Delaware. Miles conferred with RM the following day and by August 30 had engaged at Philadelphia a total of 31 assorted craft with an estimated capacity of 4,150 men. Fitzpatrick, ed., *Writings of Washington*, XXIII, 54–55, 71n.; Diary, August 28.

3. See RM's Circular to Stephen Steward and Son, Jonathan Hudson, David Stewart, and Samuel Smith, and RM to Matthew Ridley, to Washington, and to Donaldson Yeates, all August 28, and Diary, August 31, and notes.

4. Major General Marie Joseph Paul Yves Roch Gilbert du Motier, Marquis de Lafayette (1757–1834), of the Continental army went back to France in 1779, where he was consulted about arrangements for the expeditionary force about to be sent to America under Rochambeau. He returned to America in April 1780 to prepare for its arrival and subsequently served as liason between Washington and the French command. On February 20, 1781, Washington ordered him to Virginia in an effort to capture Benedict Arnold. Marching his detachment from Peekskill, New York, Lafayette arrived on March 3 at the Head of Elk, whence his men were conveyed to Annapolis in boats. In response to the appeal of Dr. James McHenry, Lafayette's aide, and Lafayette's pledge to ensure repayment of $10,000 out of his personal fortune if necessary, the merchants of Baltimore advanced funds to provide supplies for the expedition. On May 24 Congress registered on the *Journals* its "just sense of the patriotic and timely exertions of the Merchants of Baltimore." After Cornwallis's army retired to Yorktown early in August, Lafayette's force checked his movements until the arrival of the allied forces under Washington, Rochambeau, de Grasse, and de Barras. *DAB;* Washington to Lafayette, with Instructions, both dated February 20, 1781, Fitzpatrick, ed., *Writings of Washington*, XXIII, 253–256; Ward, *War of the Revolution*, II, 870; Louis Gottschalk, *Lafayette and the Close of the American Revolution*, corrected ed. (Chicago, 1965), 197–198; J. Thomas Scharf, *History of Maryland from the Earliest Period to the Present Day* (Baltimore, 1879), II, 445–446.

5. Washington to Governor Thomas Sim Lee of Maryland, August 27, 1781, Fitzpatrick, ed., *Writings of Washington*, XXIII, 57–58.

6. See Washington to RM, August 17, Diary, August 24, and RM to the Commissary General of Purchases, August 24, and to James Calhoun, August 28.

7. Jacques Melchior, Comte de Barras Saint-Laurent, commander of the French squadron at Newport, sailed from Rhode Island on August 24 with fourteen warships carrying the provisions to which Washington refers, siege artillery, and some 600 troops, and arrived safely in the Chesapeake on September 10. Hutchinson and Rutland, eds., *Madison Papers*, III, 248n.; Washington to Nathanael Greene, September 4, 1781, Fitzpatrick, ed., *Writings of Washington*, XXIII, 85; Freeman, *Washington*, V, 333, 512; see also the September 7 postscript to RM to Benjamin Franklin, August 28. For sketches of Barras, see Balch, *French in America*, II, 45–46; Contenson, *Société des Cincinnati*, 136; and Gardiner, *Order of the Cincinnati*, 115.

8. Washington first made this request in a letter to RM of August 17. See also RM to Washington, August 22 and 28, and Diary, September 1–5, and notes.

9. RM received Washington's letter from Colonel Samuel Miles on August 28 and replied the same day. See Diary, August 28.

Diary: August 28, 1781

Had a Conference with Mr Duane and Mr Clymer respecting Money to pay Genl St. Clairs new Levies,[1] and told them I had none that could be so applied and respecting the Duties of Auditor of Accounts Agreable to the plan Offered for Establishment of the Treasury Office &Ca &Ca.[2]

Held Conference with the Board of War respecting Cloathing, and advised to Wait untill we hear what is on board the Ship at Boston.[3]

Mr. Moylan Cloathier General very pressing to have the Salarys fixed for Officers in his Department.[4]

Mr. Danl. Broadhead entred in this Office as one of my Clerks.[5]

Ordered that Mr. Swanwick make up £1500 Specie for Mr Ridley on Account of his Flour Purchases,[6] and sent it by Mr Benjamin May of Baltimore.[7]

Received a Letter from His Excelly. G: Washington dated at Chatham N. Jersey the 27th.

In Consequence of a Letter this day received from the Commdr in Chief, Wrote Letters, To

The Governour of Maryland respecting Supplies, Troops &Ca.

Mr Calhoun Agent of that State, on the Subject of Flour &Ca.

Mr Ridley respecting Vessells to Convey Troops &Ca.

Mr Stephen Stuart and Son, Jonthn. Hudson, D Stewart and Colo Smith (Circular).

Mr William Smith [8] (all these Gentlemen addressed on the subject of procuring immediatly Vessells to Transport Troops &Ca. strongly requesting their Exertions).[9]

Mr Donaldson Yates Q[uarter] Master for Maryland and Delaware on same subject.

His Excellency Genl. Washington in Answer to his favour of the 27th instant.

The Board of War, respecting Money &Ca.

Colo. Miles called to Consult on the General's orders to him.[10] I advised him to apply to the honble Council for their assistance,[11] desired him to fit the continental Schooners and to promise payment to all Craft he should hire in a Month or 6 Weeks. Offered to Join in such promise and engaged to Supply the Money; advised him to procure long and short Forage &Ca. and that he should take up Brigs and Schooners not exceeding 100 Tons, to go to Bordentown and thence to Wilmington &Ca.

Mr. Philips, Steward of the Presidents Household deliverd me on a bit of Paper as an Estimate of the Monthly expences amounting to 620 hard Dollars [12] which I think extravagent and will apply to the President about that Matter.

A thousand Applications, and my Refusals, for Money which become very troublesome and disagreable to me; the Parties ought to have their just Right but it is not in my power to give them any relief.

Mr. Dering, Contractor for Lancaster, brought in his Account for last Months Rations. I agreed to advance £250 Specie on this Account and will Issue my Warrant on Mr Swanwick for this Sum on a New Impression of Copper plate taken and on Occasions will Issue them payable to the Bearer at Sight. I have had this Plate Cut and shall Issue these Warrants merely as preparatory to the introduction of Bank Notes which I hope soon to see Established as part of the Circulating Medium of America. [13]

Issued my first Warrant from impression of Copper Plate, on Mr Swanwick in favour of Henry Dering for £250 payable at Sight.

Wrote Mr Rawleigh Colston of Cape Francois, respecting Public Cloathing. [14]

1. Arthur St. Clair (1736–1818), a Scots-born officer in the British army during the French and Indian War, resigned his commission in 1762 and bought an estate in western Pennsylvania, where he became an important political figure. Serving in the Continental army from 1775 until the close of the war, St. Clair attained the rank of major general in 1777, but his military career was set back when he was compelled to surrender Fort Ticonderoga to the British. Although exempted from charges of misconduct by a court-martial in September 1778, he was thereafter assigned minor functions. In February 1781, Washington put St. Clair in charge of recruiting Pennsylvania troops for the Continental line, and on August 22 directed him to assemble the recruits raised under an act of Pennsylvania of June 25, 1781, and to march them southward to participate in the Virginia campaign. In view of the mutiny of the Pennsylvania line on January 1, 1781, St. Clair was sensitive to the pressing need to pay the recruits, and on August 28 he applied to Congress for assistance. Congress referred his application to a committee which included James Duane and directed it to confer with RM. As this Diary entry indicates, the Financier told the committee he had no money for the purpose, whereupon Congress the next day besought the Supreme Executive Council of Pennsylvania to supply the funds. No response by the council is on record, but on September 8, apparently, RM decided to make the money available. St. Clair still had to make repeated visits to the Office of Finance and pare his request to exclude new recruits who had not yet spent their bounty, but finally, on October 3, RM gave him a warrant for a month's pay to the troops. *DAB;* William Henry Smith, ed., *The St. Clair Papers: The Life and Public Services of Arthur St. Clair, . . . with his Correspondence and Other Papers* (Cincinnati, 1882), I, 109–112, 559–560; Mitchell and Flanders, eds., *Statutes of Pennsylvania,* X, 344–349; Washington to St. Clair, February 3 and August 22, 1781, Fitzpatrick, ed., *Writings of Washington,* XXI, 175–176, XXIII, 38–39; President Thomas McKean of Congress to President Joseph Reed of Pennsylvania, August 30, 1781, Burnett, ed., *Letters,* VI, 204; Diary, September 8, 9, 11, and 21, and October 2 and 3, 1781.

2. See RM's Plan for Arranging the Treasury Department, August 27, and notes. George Clymer was a member of the committee to which Congress referred the plan.

3. Probably a reference to the store ship which accompanied the *Magicienne*. See RM to Benjamin Franklin, August 28.

4. Congress reorganized the Continental Clothing Department on June 18, 1781, but had not yet assigned salaries to its personnel. See Diary, August 31, and on the departmental reorganization, notes to Diary, July 21, 1781.

5. Very likely Daniel Brodhead, Jr., first lieutenant in the 3d Pennsylvania regiment, who was captured at the surrender of Fort Washington on November 16, 1776, and exchanged on August 26, 1778, but who apparently did not die "shortly afterwards" as indicated by Heitman. Although he became a supernumerary officer in 1778, Brodhead claimed the rank of captain and sought the assistance of his father (see notes to Diary, July 6, 1781) in unsuccessfully seeking a military post from Washington. Brodhead took the oath of allegiance and office as an Office of Finance clerk on March 18, 1782. Brodhead's memorial to Congress, [ca. July 29, 1780], PCC, no. 41, I, 305–308; Heitman, *Register;* Daniel Brodhead (Sr.) to Washington, April 3, 1779, Washington Papers, DLC; Washington to Daniel Brodhead (Sr.), May 3, and to the Board of War, May 5, 1779, and to Samuel John Atlee *et al.,* February 28, 1781, Fitzpatrick, ed., *Writings of Washington,* XIV, 480, 502, XXI, 317; *JCC,* XVII, 679, 710, XVIII, 902; Brodhead's oath is in PCC, no. 195.

6. See RM to Matthew Ridley, August 27.

7. Benjamin May, who settled in Baltimore in 1775, has not been further identified. J. Thomas Scharf, *The Chronicles of Baltimore* (Baltimore, 1874), 64, 139.

8. Letter not found.

9. Closing parenthesis supplied.

10. See notes to Washington to RM, August 27, for Washington's orders to Colonel Samuel Miles, deputy quartermaster general for Pennsylvania.

11. For months Miles had been acting in close concert with the Supreme Executive Council of Pennsylvania in purchasing or impressing transports of all kinds, including water craft. See President Joseph Reed of Pennsylvania to Miles, April 21, 1781, *Pennsylvania Archives,* 1st ser., IX, 95.

12. RM had requested this estimate on August 25. See Diary of that date.

13. On "Morris's notes," see notes to Diary, July 27, 1781.

14. This letter is dated August 29.

To James Calhoun[1]

Office of Finance August 28th. 1781.

Sir

By your Answer to Mathew Ridley Esqr respecting the Flour I requested might [be] delivered to him by the Government of Maryland, I observe that the Quality of the public flour is not such as will Answer the Purpose intended, therefore I have taken other Measures for procuring that supply.[2]

This Circumstance however will not lessen my Demands on your State to which I understand you are the Agent. I have lately written several Letters to his Excellency the Governor [3] informing him that the balance due to the United States upon the Requisitions for Specific Supplies by Congress from Maryland will now be wanted for the Public Service. I am authorized and directed to Collect the Balances due from every State. With some I have already succeeded to very considerable Amounts and the main Army is entirely fed thereby. The State of Maryland is so immediately connected with those Operations that will now demand her Supplies and the Security of her Citizens so immediately dependent on them, that I expect the most chearful acquiescence both on the Part of the Government and People.

Colo. Blaine will have applied to you by my Orders for salted Provisions &Ca.[4] But that I may be fully and well informed what dependance to place on your Delivery's I must State to you, that by the Act of Congress of the 25th. February 1780 Maryland was called upon to deliver to the Use of the United States one Thousand hhds: Tobacco, forty thousand Cwt. of Beef, two hundred Tons of Hay, Twenty thousand Barrels of Flour, fifty six thousand one hundred and sixty two Bushels of Corn. And by the Act of the fourth November 1780 Maryland is further called upon to deliver to the Use of the United [States] four thousand eight hundred Barrells of Beef, five thousand five hundred Barrels [of] Pork, twelve thousand Cwt. of Beef, four thousand Bushels of Salt, seventeen thousand and seven Gallons of Rum, [and] twenty thousand Barrels of Flour.[5] What Part of these Delivery's have been complied with I do not yet know, His Excellency the Governor not having yet replied to my Letter [6] on that Subject,[7] but being certain there must remain heavy Balances due in every Article to the United States, I request your immediate Information of the Quantities you are prepared to deliver to each, and the Prospects you have of collecting the Remainder. The Calls for Flour and fresh Beef will be immediate and Constant; the other Articles will also be necessary very soon and I hope you will be every Way prepared to Answer the pressing Demands which will speedily be made upon you.[8]

I am Sir your most obedient and humble Servant.

RM

MSS: Ofcl LbC, DLC; copy, Executive Papers, MdAA.

1. James Calhoun (d. 1816), a prominent Baltimore merchant, was a member, later chairman, of the Baltimore County Committee of Observation in 1776–1777. The Maryland Council appointed him Baltimore county collector of clothing for the Continental army in November 1777, deputy quartermaster general for the Western Shore ca. 1778 (he received a Continental commission from Quartermaster General Nathanael Greene in September 1779), and quartermaster general of the state militia in May 1779. For a time in 1780 Calhoun was also commissary of purchases for Baltimore County. Together with a number of Baltimore merchants, Calhoun loaned money to Lafayette in April 1781 for the purchase of provisions for his army (see notes to Washington to RM, August 27) and was one of a citizens' committee which presented Washington with an address on his arrival in Baltimore on September 8. RM addressed Calhoun in his capacity as state agent. Calhoun held a variety of municipal offices before being elected Baltimore's first mayor in 1797. *Maryland Archives*, XII, 524, 532, XVI, 46, 47, 48, 98, 106, 426, XXI, 167–168, 431, 530; *Calendar of Maryland State Papers* (Annapolis, 1943–1958), no. 4, pt. 3, The Red Books, 113; Scharf, *Chronicles of Baltimore*, 71, 169, 178, 262, 282, 382; Scharf, *History of Maryland*, II, 207, 379n., 445, 457–458.

2. See RM to Matthew Ridley, August 27, and to John Holker, August 7, and notes.
3. See RM to the Governor of Maryland, August 21, 26, and 28.
4. See RM to the Commissary General of Purchases, August 24, and notes.
5. See *JCC,* XVI, 197, XVIII, 1013.
6. MdAA copy: "Letters." See note 3 above.
7. Governor Thomas Sim Lee replied on August 31.
8. For the Maryland Council's orders to Calhoun, see the Governor of Maryland to RM, August 31, and notes.

Circular to Stephen Steward and Son, Jonathan Hudson, David Stewart, and Samuel Smith[1]

(Circular) Office of Finance 28th. Augt. 1781.

Sir,

The Commander in Chief of the American Armies having determined to give every Aid in his Power to the States of Maryland and Virginia has in Consequence detached a considerable Body of Men which will be at the Head of Elk by the fifth of next Month. Mr. Donaldson Yeates the Quarter Master of Maryland and Delaware is employed to procure Vessels for the Transportation of these Troops.[2] Many will be required as the Detachment will be from six to seven thousand strong. When I consider how deeply the Inhabitants of your Town are interested in the Success of these Operations,[3] when I reflect on their Disposition to serve the Cause manifested on former Occasions and when I add that Expedition is of the last Importance on the present Occasion I cannot doubt that they will exert themselves to the utmost. I promise myself your Assistance in the fullest Degree and I have every Hope that you will both publickly and Privately have reason to be convinced that your Efforts could never be better applied. I am very respectfully &c &ca.

RM

MS: Ofcl LbC, DLC.
1. Of these Baltimore merchants, Stephen Steward and Son and Jonathan Hudson have been previously identified. David Stewart, a Scottish emigrant, was a prominent merchant and privateer-owner who had been Baltimore agent for RM and William Bingham. The identity of the last addressee, referred to in the Diary of August 28 as "Colo Smith" and in the manuscript heading of this letter as "Mr Smith," is very likely Samuel Smith (1752–1839), a merchant in the family firm of John Smith and Sons. After distinguished service in the Continental army, Smith resigned his commission in 1779 to resume his business activities. He engaged in privateering ventures and became state supply and ship repair agent and, in the summer of 1781, Maryland's agent for the procurement of military supplies for the troops of the state line, in which capacity he supplied matériel for the Yorktown campaign. Smith began a long and notable career in the United States Congress in 1793. On Stewart, see RM to [John Hancock?], January 7, 1777, Hubertis Cummings, ed., "Items from the Morris Family Collection of Robert Morris Papers," *PMHB,* LXX (1946), 188, 192; "Two Jacobite Convicts," *Maryland Historical Magazine,* I (1906), 351; and *Maryland*

Archives, XXI, 181, 189, 298, 369, 508. On Smith, see *DAB;* for his business activities during the Revolution, see Frank A. Cassell, *Merchant Congressman in the Young Republic: Samuel Smith of Maryland, 1752–1839* (Madison, Wis., 1971), 38–39, and John S. Pancake, *Samuel Smith and the Politics of Business, 1752–1839* (University, Ala., 1972), 27–30.

2. See RM to Donaldson Yeates, August 28. For the background of RM's request, see Washington to RM, August 27.

3. RM elaborated on this point in his letter to Matthew Ridley, August 28.

To the President of Congress (Thomas McKean)

In this letter concerning the settlement of state accounts with the United States, Morris unveiled another segment of his plan for reconstructing the Union.[1] Uncertainty as to each state's contribution to the war effort and what its share of the common expenses should be had allowed every state government to take the position that it had made greater sacrifices than others, that accounts might never be settled, and that it was therefore justified in withholding full payment of Continental requisitions. Boldly pressing for an immediate and final solution of the vexing problems that had hitherto kept everything relative to the settlement of state accounts with the Union in suspension, Morris tried in this letter to override conflicts of state interest and to forestall a long negotiation. Admitting that any rules which could be adopted would in some degree be inequitable, he demanded an immediate and conclusive settlement on the grounds that the longer a decision were delayed the more inequitable it would be. Although Congress, under prodding from Morris, passed an ordinance early in 1782 for settling state accounts, it carefully avoided any determination of the issues he discussed in this letter, and a final settlement was not concluded until 1793.

Of ultimately greater significance was Morris's insistence that the so-called "public" domestic debt, consisting at this time only of loan office certificates but which was to grow hugely by accretion as Continental commissioners settled civilian and military claims after the war, be exempted from the apportionment of war expenses and reserved for payment solely by Congress. His purpose was to vest in Congress, rather than in the states, that federal debt which was the cornerstone of the Nationalists' demand for federal taxes to strengthen the central government. That the proposed federal tax, the impost amendment now before the states for ratification, was intended to be only the first of such taxes was here revealed by Morris in his proposal for land, poll, and excise taxes to be granted to Congress.

Office of Finance 28th. August 1781.

Sir

My circular Letter to the Governors of the several States, of the 25th. of July, a Copy whereof was sent to Congress on the 6th. of August,[2] contains a solemn assurance that all the Accounts of the several States, with the United States, should be speedily liquidated, if I could possibly effect it; and that my Efforts for that Purpose should be unceasing. If after this Declaration, I could possibly have forgotten it, the Reference made to me, on the twenty third Instant, of two Letters from the State of Massachusetts and of a Report on them of the 14th. Instant, would have called for an immediate Attention.[3]

I have thought much on this Subject, and feel very anxious about it. The Settlement of those Accounts is of the utmost Importance; for untill it be completed the States will perswade themselves into an Opinion that their Exertions are unequal. Each will beleive in the Superiority of its own Efforts, Each claim the Merit of having done more than others, and each continue desirous of relaxing to an Equality with the supposed Deficiencies of its Neighbours.[4] Hence it follows that every Day they become more and more negligent, a dangerous Supineness pervades the Continent, and Recommendations of Congress, capable in the Year 1775, of rousing all America to Action, now lie neglected. This is the inevitable Consequence of such Opinions. The Settlement of former Accounts being considered as a Thing forgotten, Men naturally reason from them to those which are now present, conclude that they also will drop into Forgetfulness, and consider every Thing not furnished as so much saved. The Legislatures will not call forth the Resources of their respective Constituents. The public Operations languish. The Necessity of Purchasing on Credit enhances the Expence. The Want of that Credit compels to the Use of Force.[5] That Force offends. The Country is daily more plunged in Debt, and its Revenues more deeply anticipated. A Situation so dangerous calls for more accurate Principles of Administration, and these cannot too Speedily be adopted.

The Settlement of Accounts is the first Step; but it is necessary not only that this Settlement be speedy, but also that it be final. For if it be not Final, disputes on that Subject will have the same baleful Influence with those now subsisting. Disunion among the States must follow in the Event. Disgust must take Place in the Moment. The same opprobrious Indolence will continue. And in the mean time, it is to little Purpose that our Country abounds with Men and Subsistence, if they cannot be called forth for her Defence.

All the Requisitions made by Congress upon the several States contain a Provision for a future Liquidation, when the quotas shall have been ascertained according to the Articles of Confederation.[6] The evil Consequences which have followed from this, are very evident, and the great Advantages which would have resulted from rendering every Apportionment final and conclusive, are equally evident. But those who on such Ground build a Censure against

Congress, ought to consider that they could not act otherwise before the Confederation was compleated.[7]

The Changes which have already happened in the affairs of the several States, at the different Periods of the War, are so great that any apportionment formerly made, however equitable then, would be inequitable now. To determine the quota therefore from the present Situation, or from any particular Moment of the past, must be equally improper. But the quotas must be determined at some Period or other. If we suppose it already done, we shall clearly see how many Inconveniences would have been avoided, and how many advantages gained. True it is, that let this final adjustment of the quota take Place when it will, Difficulties will arise, by reason of those Changes in the Circumstances of the several States which [have] been already mentioned. But those Difficulties will be daily increased, and become at length insurmountable. If a final Determination of past quotas were made now, it must be arbitrary in some Degree; but if we carry our Ideas forward to the end of several years, it must be still more arbitrary. To attempt a Settlement of Accounts subject to after Revision, and after Determination is still worse; for it is liable to every Objection which lies against leaving them unsettled, to every Difficulty which could attend the final Settlement, and has the additional Evil, that by placing the several precise Ballances immediately before the Eyes of Congress, they could take no Step which would not be charged with Partiality.

I will dwell no longer upon this Subject, for I trust the United States in Congress will agree with me in one leading Position. That, after taking a general View of the past from the Commencement of the War to the present Moment, a certain Rate or quota should be established, for each State, of the whole Expence now incurred, excepting thereout the public funded [8] Debt of the United States.[9] I will presently assign the Reasons for this Exception, but that general Position which I have advanced, is the Corner Stone of the whole Fabrick.[10] Without it Nothing can be done, which had not better be left [11] undone. At least such is my Conviction. For these Things appear [12] with the Force of irresistable Conclusion. 1st. That while a Demand of Congress is the meer Request of a Loan, instead of a compleat apportionment of Expence,[13] it will not be attended to. 2ly. That while from the unsettled State of Public accounts, the Individual States are led to suppose that there is a Ballance in their Favor, by superior Exertions for which they neither have nor are like to have any Credit, they will relax their Efforts. 3ly. That the final Settlement of these accounts cannot take Place, untill the quotas be finally adjusted. 4ly. That a Settlement of Accounts which is not final, will [14] be so much Labor, Time, and Expence not meerly thrown away, but employed to pernicious Effect. 5ly. That Congress are less capable to determine on the exact Proportions of past Expences now, than at any former Period. And 6ly. That every Days delay will increase their Incapacity. I feel therefore a Demonstration that the past Circumstances and Situations of the several States should be candidly reviewed: That the Apportionment of all the past Expences should be made now: And that it should be final. Thus, if the whole Expence be stated at 100, each State shou'd be declared chargeable with a certain Number of Parts of that hundred; and thus a Standard will be established by which to determine the Proportions, let the amount be what it may. I know it is not possible to do strict Justice, but it is certain that less Injustice will be done in this Mode, than any other; and that without adopting it nothing effectual can be done.

After the Proportion is fixed, the Principles on which to admit the various Charges will next come into Consideration.[15] I know it will be difficult to draw such a Line as will apply to all Cases, or which will be absolutely just, even in those to which it does apply. Yet neither of these Objections ought to prevent Congress from laying down the general Rules which shall on the whole appear to be most equitable.

The various Requisitions have been made payable at certain Days. The value therefore of the Demand ought to be estimated at the Day of Payment fixed for each, and the proper Mode of doing this, would be by the Table of [Depreciation] [16] formed the 29th July 1780, in Pursuance of the Act of Congress of the 28th of June preceeding.[17] It is possible that this Table is not perfect, but we must remember that it has been fixed by Authority of the United States, and acted upon. It ought therefore to be adhered to; for there is always less both of Inconvenience and Danger in pursuing an established Rule, than in the frequent Change of Rules; because the former is at the worst only a partial, but the latter is a general Evil. Assuming then this Table as a standard, the Account of the Requisitions previous to the 18th. March 1780, will stand thus.

By the Resolutions of the 22nd. November 1777 there is payable as follows:

			Dollars.Ninetieths
1 January	1778.	1.250.000 Dollars equal to.....	857.222.20.
1 April	1778.	1.250.000 Dollars equal to.....	621.423.55.
1 July	1778.	1.250.000	412.864.52.4
1 October	1778.	1.250.000	268.472. 2.

By the Resolutiòns of 2nd. Jany. 1779 and 21st May 1779 there is payable by

1 January　　1780. 60.000.000[18] Dollars equal to . . . . 2.042.500.

By the Resolution of the 6th. October 1779 payable by

1 February 1780. 15.000.000　Dollars equal to . . .　451.041.60
1 March　　1780. 15.000.000. . . . .　equal to . . .　401.458.30[19]
　　　　　　　　　　　　　　　　　　　　Dollars　5.054.982.39.4

Thus the whole Demand made on the States, from the Beginning of the War to the 1st March 1780, is but little more than five Million of Dollars. And yet this Demand, moderate as it is, has not been complied with.

By the Resolutions of Congress on the Subject of Requisitions it is provided, that Interest at six per Cent shall be charged on the Sums due, and allowed on the Sums paid.[20] The Sums paid do in no Instance amount to the Value of the Demand, but each State has an Account against the Union for Advances, by Supplies furnished of various kinds, and by payments made to Militia. As no Taxes were laid by the States, the Sums they expended were procured, partly from the Continental Treasury and partly by the Emission of State Currency, which tended to depreciate the Continental Paper and impede its Circulation. A Consideration of the Mischiefs arising from this Circumstance, will much diminish the Merit which is assumed from those Advances. If the State Paper had not been issued, the same Services might have been performed by an equal Sum of Continental Money, and the general torrent of Depreciation would have then swept away those Expenditures which now exist as State Charges. From hence it might, in Strictness, be inferred that the Continent should [21] be charged for the Amount of [22] Paper advanced, and that amount be estimated at its Value when redeemed by the State, especially as Congress have not only urged the States not to emit Money, but even to call in what they had already emitted. But this Inferrence would perhaps be rather too Strong. No such Idea has been formerly advanced by Congress, and therefore the States, not having had due Notice, might conceive the Determination, at this Period, to be inequitable.

On the whole therefore it may be proper to Estimate the Sums paid by them according to the Rule already noticed,[23] especially as the Method of redeeming the old Continental formerly adopted [24] will, if pursued, work some Degree of Equality. For it will create a

Demand for the old Money in those States which, by the amount
of their own Emissions, have expelled it from themselves, and
forced it upon their Neighbours. There must however be a Distinction made in the Advances of the several States. Much of them has
been for the Support and pay of the Militia, and much of that for
the private Defence of particular States, and of that again a Part has
frequently been unnecessary.[25] To go at this late Period into a close
Investigation of the Subject is impracticable, and perhaps dangerous. Neither would it a[nswer] any valuable Purpose. Some general
Rule therefore must be adopted, and Propriety seems to require
that Credit should be given only for those Expenditures on Militia
which were previously authorized and required by express Resolutions of Congress. With Respect to all other Articles, there is also
to be noted a Distinction between those which were furnished by
the several States previously to the twenty second of November
1777, when the first demand of Money was made, and those made
subsequently to that Period. I would propose that the former, as
also the Militia Expences not expressly authorized as above mentioned, should be taken together into one Account, and the Specie
Value of the whole estimated. That the amount of both, throughout
America, should be apportioned by the same Standard with the
other Expences; and that the several [26] Expenditures of each State
should be settled, and liquidated with it's proportional Part of the
whole, and the several Ballances carried to their respective Debits
and Credits in the general Accounts. These Ballances should bear
Interest at 6 per Cent to the 18th. of March 1780. Thus, suppose
the whole of those Expences should amount to one Million Dollars,
and that the State A be held to pay nine, and the State B ten, parts
out of every hundred. The State A would be accountable for ninety
thousand Dollars, and the State B for one hundred thousand Dollars. And if it should appear that the former had paid one hundred
thousand, and the latter only ninety thousand, the former would be
credited, and the latter debited, ten thousand Dollars, with 6 per
Cent Interest.

I would propose that the Advances made by the several States,
subsequent to the twenty second of November, and prior to the
18th. March 1780, excepting those to Militia not authorized, should
be estimated as aforesaid, and carried to account regularly upon the
advances of Money made to each from the Continental Treasury,
and the apportionment of the several Demands made by Congress,
in like Manner with the Monies paid to their Order. And that Interest, at six per Cent, should be charged or credited upon the several
Ballances, untill the Eighteenth of March 1780.

I would further propose, that on that Day these Ballances and those before mentioned should be liquidated together, and the final Capitals be considered as principal Sums, bearing Interest at six per Cent. Thus supposing the State A in one account to be credited ten thousand Dollars, amounting with Interest to eleven thousand, and debited in the other account five thousand, amounting with Interest to Six; in that Case, the final Ballance on the 18th. March 1780 would be a credit of five thousand Dollars.

On the eighteenth of March, we come to a new and more enlightened Era of Public Accounts.[27] The Apportionment formerly mentioned, as preliminary to a Settlement, will determine the quota due by each State for the 200.000.000 of old Continental, which was then [28] valued at forty for one. These Resolutions of the 18th. of March 1780, not having been fully complied with,[29] there appears to be a Propriety in the following Plan. 1st. To charge the several States with their Proportions of it at that Rate. 2ly. To fix some future day for the full Compliance with the Resolution. 3ly. To receive old Paper, at the rate of forty for one, in discharge of those Proportions, untill that Day. And 4ly. To charge the Ballances then unpaid in Specie, with a Debit and Credit of Interest, at six per Cent, in the manner before mentioned.

I am sensible that many Persons now condemn the Resolutions of the 18th. of March, and among these are found some of those who warmly advocated it previously to that Period. It is not my Business to enter into Arguments on that Subject. Be those Resolutions wise or unwise, they are Acts of the Sovereign Authority, which have been obeyed by some, if not by all; and therefore those who have obeyed, ought not to suffer for their Obedience. They are Acts for the Redemption of Bills issued by that Sovereign, and they have formed the Standard of public Opinion with Respect to those Bills. If therefore, for arguments sake it were admitted that, the Measure was impolitic and unjust; yet now that it has taken Place, there would certainly be both Injustice and bad Policy in altering it. The respective States have either obeyed it in the whole, or in Part, or have totally neglected it. The first have a Right to insist on a Compliance with it. The second must have so far accommodated themselves to it, as that interior Mischiefs would arise from changing the System. And the last, whatever may be their Claim to superior Wisdom, will at least acknowlege that the Precedent of Disobedience once established, our Union must soon be at an End, and the Authority of Congress reduced to a metaphisical Idea. Besides, the Claim of such States must ultimately rest on the Foundation of their own Neglect; and as this will allways be in their own Power, it will be sufficient to rear any Argument, for any Purpose.

By the Resolutions of the 18th. March 1780, 10.000.000 Dollars of new Paper were to have been issued, whereof 4.000.000 were to be at the order of Congress.[30] By the Resolution of the 26th. of August 1780, 3.000.000 more were demanded. By the Resolutions of the 4th. of November 1780, besides the Specific Supplies, an additional Demand was made of 1.642.987$^2/_3$ Dollars in Money, and by the Resolutions of the 16th March 1781, 6.000.000 more are required. These Sums amount in the whole to fourteen Million six hundred and forty two thousand nine hundred and eighty seven Dollars and two thirds. A very small Part of this Sum has yet been paid, but admitting that there may have been circulated, by the United States, two million six hundred and forty two thousand nine hundred and eighty seven Dollars and two thirds; twelve Millions would still remain due. If from this we deduct the whole of the New Emissions, it would leave a Ballance of two Millions. I propose therefore the following Plan. 1st. That no more of these New Emissions be used, on any Pretence. 2ly. That as fast as the old Continental Money is brought in, the several States be credited for the New Emissions to have been Issued, as Specie, agreeably to the several Resolutions of Congress upon that Subject. And 3ly. that on all those Requisitions last mentioned, the Money of the new Emissions of any particular State be received as Specie. It is true that these Propositions are liable to exception but they have the great Advantage of being consistent with former Resolutions of Congress, which should always be attended to as much as possible. I am sure that Congress must be convinced of this, for they are not to learn, that Authority is weakened by the frequent Change of Measures and Pursuits; That such Changes injure the Reputation of the Supreme Power, in the Public Opinion; and that Opinion is the Source and Support of the Sovereign's Authority. It is further to be observed, that the Motives for complying with the Resolutions of the 18th. of March will, if the above Plan is adopted, become very strong; for, in that Case, every forty Dollars of old Continental paid by a State, will produce to the Credit Side of its account three Dollars in Specie. Because, in the first place, the whole proportion of old Continental being charged at forty for one, and receivable, untill a certain Day, at the same Rate, that payment will so far operate a Discharge of one Dollar; and, in the second Place, it will entitle the States to two Dollars of the new Emission, which, not being issued, will also be carried to its Credit upon the several Requisitions. It will be in the Wisdom of the United States in Congress assembled to determine whether after the Expiration of the Day to be fixed for the above Purpose, they will permit the Possessors of old Continental Money to bring it in on Loan, at the Rate of forty for one.[31] It is true that this might operate against those States who have not complied with the Resolutions of the 18th. of March 1780, and who have not now the old Continental to comply with it; but it is entirely consistent with the former Resolutions of Congress, and the States are themselves blameable for the Neglect. Besides, those who now hold the Continental Money, do it either from Choice, because of their Confidence in Congress, or from Necessity, because it has been poured in upon them from those Places where it was of inferior Value; and this Inferiority was owing to the neglect of those States, in not passing the Laws which Congress had recommended. There is therefore a Degree of Justice and Firmness in that Measure, which will create Confidence in the future Acts of the United States.

Whatever Principles may be established for settling these accounts, and however just they may be, many Doubts will arise in the application of them. It must always be remembered that the States are Independent; and that while they are pressed to a Compliance with their Duty, they must have full Evidence that Congress act fairly. It might therefore be proper that for the Settlement of their Accounts Commissioners should be chosen as follows, one by the State, one by the United States, and one by the other two, and the Decission of the Majority to be final.

Hitherto I have taken no Notice of the Specific Supplies called for from the several States.[32] Many of these have been furnished, and many remain to be provided. I would exclude them entirely from the other Public accounts. But as the apportionment, so often mentioned, will give a Rule to go by; I shall continue to press for the Supplies, or where they are not wanted, make such Composition with the States, in Lieu of those which remain to be furnished, as the Public Service shall render most eligible.

I have observed that the Public Debts ought to be excepted from the apportionment of past Expences.[33] The Reason is clear. Those Debts, or at least a great part of them, may subsist untill the relative Wealth of the States has entirely changed. Those who are now most rich, may then be poor, and those who are poor, become rich. This is not all. These Debts are hitherto unfunded. The Creditors have indeed the general Promise of Government, and some of them have Certificates, as the Evidences of that Promise, but untill Measures are taken to provide Solid Funds,[34] for the final Payment, the public Credit must languish. To an enlightened Mind it is needless to dilate the advantages resulting from national Credit. Congress will doubtless pursue the Steps necessary for it's perfect Establishment. And this cannot be otherwise accomplished than by raising Taxes, in hard Money, from Sources which must be productive and increasing. Those Taxes must be so bound to the Public Creditors for the Debts due to them, that the Produce cannot be diverted. These Taxes ought to be raised from the same Articles, at the same Rates, and in the same Manner, throughout the whole Confederation, and consequently a present apportionment of the Public Debts, will be as unnecessary, as it would be unjust.

I think it my Duty while I am upon this Subject, to mention my Opinion that, in addition to the five per Cent called for on articles Imported, and on Prizes and Prize Goods, it would be proper to appropriate to the payment of the Public Debts a Land Tax, a Poll Tax, and Excise on Spirituous Liquors.[35] I readily grant that neither of these Taxes would be strictly equal between the States, nor indeed can any other Tax be so, but I am convinced that all of them taken together would be as nearly equal, as the fluctuating nature of human Affairs will permit. I am however to observe, in addition, that the Land Tax should be laid at a certain Rate by the acre, because the superior Certainty of such a Tax would give it the preference of others, altho it cannot perhaps be so great as might have been expected.[36] Whatever Inequalities may remain, must be adjusted among Individuals by the several States in raising their quotas, and altho those quotas will be most considerable during the War, yet it must be remembered that, after the Conclusion of it, such Sums will be necessary for the establishing a Marine, and other national Purposes, as will still enable the States to continue their Interior Regulations for equalizing the general Taxes.

Among the Public Debts there are a considerable Number of Certificates, given by Public Officers to the Citizens of the several States, for Articles occasionally taken to the public use.[37] With Respect to these Certificates, it is unnecessary to mention that they have anticipated the Revenue, and brought us to the Brink of Destruction. But it is time to pay a particular Attention to them. Many ways may be fallen upon for their Liquidation, all of which perhaps are justly exceptionable. 1st. They may be consolidated with the rest of the Public Debt, and be made payable at a future Period, but this could only be by forcing a Loan from the People, many of whom are unable to make it, and of Consequence it would be a hard Measure, if not an unjust one. Perhaps it could not be executed, for Laws repugnant to the general Feelings of Mankind are a dead Letter.[38] 2ly. Another Mode is by receiving them in Taxes; but this is very dangerous for several Reasons, among which the following are cogent. The public Revenue will not bear such a heavy Deduction as those Certificates would create, and the Collectors of Taxes would be liable to be defrauded themselves, or the Remedy for that would give them Opportunities of defrauding the Public, which, considering the natural Bent and Disposition of many men, ought to be carefully provided against. A third Mode would be turning over the Holders of these Certificates to their respective States, and giving Credit for them on account of the specific Supplies.[39] This may in some Degree become necessary in Cases, where the Negligence of the States on the one Hand, and the Necessities of the Army on the other, have compelled to seize by Force, what ought to have been collected by Law. But in many Cases it cannot be done, and it would be improper in many others where it is practicable. Among the bad Consequences which attend the present Mode of supplying our Armies or rather leaving them to supply themselves, one, of no small Magnitude, is that the Officers who are compelled to the melancholy duty of plundering their fellow Citizens, endeavour by the Sum of their Certificates to compensate for the Manner of taking, as well as for the Value of the Thing taken.[40] Nor is that all. Where there is a Disposition for Fraud, an ample Opportunity is afforded to commit it. Whatever may be the Cause, I am informed that these Certificates are for Sums vastly beyond the Value of the Services and Articles obtained for them. The respective States would naturally be led to give to these Certificates their specified Value, and it cannot be expected that they will scrutinize them so rigidly as they ought, if they are to be accepted in discharge of Demands existing against the particular State.

To all these Modes there are also some farther Objections, among which It is my Duty to state the following. The accounts of the several Staff Officers still remain unsettled.[41] The Certificates given by them, if they are to be paid by the Public, ought to be carried both to the Debit and Credit of their Cash accounts, and the articles obtained carried to their Debit in the account of Expenditures. Of Consequence, the amount of these last Debits must depend much upon the amount of the Certificates, and therefore, either the Certificates given should be known and the account settled with those Charges, or the account should be settled, and no other Certificates allowed but such as are charged in it.

A further Mode of liquidating these Certificates would be by purchasing them from the Holders, but it is needless to state any other Objections to it, than the Want of Money which is felt thro all our Operations. There still remains this Method. 1st. That at present those Certificates should neither be receivable in Taxes nor transferable. 2ly. That they should be taken up and examined, in the Course of settling the Public Accounts. 3ly. That they should be brought to the Amount in Specie, which if the Article procured or Service performed, was reasonably worth. 4ly. That where the Sum due to any Person, on Certificates, is small, a Bill for the Amount should be given, payable at the Distance of a year. 5ly. That where the Sum is large, it should be divided into five different Parts, and Bills given payable in one, two, three, four and five Years, calculating on each Part an Interest of six per Cent, and adding it to the amount. As if for Instance the Sum were £100, then the Bills would be for twenty one Pounds four Shillings, twenty two pounds eight Shillings, twenty three pounds twelve Shillings, twenty four Pounds sixteen Shillings, and twenty five Pounds. 6ly. That these Bills should be drawn payable to the Bearer, and in such Form as not to be counterfeited, without great Difficulty. 7ly. That they should be receivable in Continental Taxes, within any of the States, as Cash, at the Times when they are respectively due; or if not so received, be payable by the continental Treasurer, or any receiver of the Continental Taxes, on Demand; after collecting the Taxes in which they were respectively receivable. In this Way a Credit would be obtained, not only without Injury, but probably with advantage to the Individual. The anticipation of the Public Revenue would not be very great, and as a List of these Notes would be kept, the amount of every years anticipation would be accurately known. Exceptions may probably be found even to this Mode, but unfortunately for us we have only an Alternative of Difficulties. All which human Prudence can do in such Cases, is to chuse the least.

With perfect Esteem and Respect I have the Honor to be Sir Your Excellency's most obedient and humble Servant

Robt Morris

His Excellency The President of Congress

ENDORSED: Letter from the Superintent./of Finance August 28th. 1781/Stating necessity of liquidating/the accounts of States to US,/suggesting principles on which they should/be settled and proposing new funds/for discharging public debt
MSS: LS, PCC, DNA; Ofcl LbC, DLC; copy, Bache Collection, PPAmP; copy, Records of the Supreme Executive Council, RG 27, PHarH.
1. For a general discussion of the settlement of state accounts and the Nationalists' reservation of the public debt to be paid exclusively by Congress, see volume I of this series, xx-xxi, xxii-xxiii, notes to RM's Circular to the Governors of the States, July 25, 1781, and Ferguson, *Power of the Purse,* 143–145, 203–219, 306–325, 332–333.
2. See RM to the President of Congress, August 6.
3. The first of these letters, from a committee of the Massachusetts legislature to the state's delegates in Congress, dated May 24, 1781 (see RM to the Governor of Massachusetts, September 15, and notes), was laid before Congress on June 27 and referred to a committee of five; the second, from Governor John Hancock to the President of Congress, dated June 18, 1781, was read in Congress on July 16 and referred to the same committee. Neither of these letters has been found, but the second may have accompanied a letter from another committee of the Massachusetts

General Court to its delegates in Congress whose date, although ambiguous, probably was June 18. It is doubtful that RM read this letter, but its contents, which
concerned the exchange of old Continental for new emission money as provided by
the act of Congress of March 18, 1780, undoubtedly was the subject of the two
above-mentioned communications.

Under the act of March 18, 1780, old Continental currency was valued at 40 to
1 of the new emission, but its worth soon plummeted to as low as 150 to 1. Since
Massachusetts had pledged to redeem the old money at 40 to 1, large amounts of
it entered the state, particularly from Connecticut and Pennsylvania. "It is the opinion of our best judges," the General Court complained, "that the whole personal
property of this State has lessened one fourth Part within six weeks and what we have
lost has been added to the property of the Inhabitants of these delinquent States."
Not only was property acquired by purchases in this cheap money, but the influx
depreciated the value of Massachusetts' new emission. In consequence, state taxes
drew into the Massachusetts treasury a surplus of old Continental money far in excess
of its quota. To reduce the flow, the General Court on July 6, 1781, revalued its new
emission at $1^3/_4$ to 1 of specie, effectively setting the value of old Continental money
at 75 to 1, and removed all tender laws that had sustained the new emission. Prior
to this action, however, Massachusetts had delivered $12,984,000 in old Continental
money under the act of March 18, 1780, and before the end of 1781 was credited
with nearly its entire quota of $29,861,000. If Congress could be persuaded to
adhere to the 40 to 1 ratio it had originally assigned to old Continental money, or
to any approximation of this figure, Massachusetts stood to gain a large credit in the
settlement of state accounts or would be able to compel other states to purchase
currency from her at that ratio to fulfill their quotas.

Following the committal of the General Court's May 24 letter, Samuel Osgood,
a Massachusetts congressman and a member of the committee to which the letter
had been referred, took up the subject with John Lowell, a member of the committee
of the Massachusetts legislature. "As the Report now stands," Osgood wrote on July
10, "every state is to be credited for all the old they can procure, previous to the
first of November next, at 75 for 1. This will afford our State Relief with Respect
to the Sum it may have, over and above the Requisition of Congress." Nevertheless,
Osgood was uncertain whether the report would pass as it stood. The final version,
which has not been found, was presented on August 7 (not August 14 as mistakenly
given in the text of RM's letter), debated on August 23, and referred to RM.

On the same day that RM completed his report in the form of the letter to the
president of Congress printed here, Osgood succinctly summarized RM's views for
Lowell. From a conversation with the Financier, Osgood found it "to be his prevailing opinion, that the resolve of the 18th of March must be adhered to; so far as it
respects calling in the old money at least: and that a farther day should be given,
after which the delinquent States shall be held to pay to the United States specie
in lieu of the old money, making twenty old continental dollars equal to one dollar
in specie, agreeable to the principles of said resolve." (The act of March 18, 1780,
had authorized the states to issue new emission currency equal in value to specie
in place of $200 million in old Continental money to be withdrawn by state taxes,
a ratio of 20 to 1.) "Whether, if the Financier proposes a rigid adherence to said
resolve, it will meet with the approbation of Congress," Osgood continued, "time
only will determine. I flatter myself the Financier is not unacquainted with our
exertions, and that he is heartily disposed to adjust matters equitably between the
States; it lays with him, and I believe he is fully impressed with the necessity of a
speedy settlement of the accounts of the States; more especially since the resolves
of the 25th of February (respecting specified requisitions) and of the 18th of March,
1780; until he has made his arrangements no step can be taken by Congress. . . .
I have no doubt but Mr. Morris will render us great service, and I hope we shall use
our utmost endeavours to support him."

RM continued to receive documents on Massachusetts' case. On September 10

Congress transmitted resolutions of the Massachusetts House of Representatives of June 30, 1781. Precisely which resolutions these were is uncertain. One may have been that giving directions concerning the receipt of old Continental money by committees empowered to sell loyalist estates; another resolution introduced the same day in a committee report called for the appointment of a committee of both houses to write to Congress on the subject of Continental currency, a resolve which the General Court passed on July 6. It is further unclear whether RM had completed the August 28 letter printed here before receiving these resolutions on September 12 or whether he revised the letter to reflect them; his statement to Congress on November 5 that "my Sentiments on the Subject of those resolutions are fully contained in the Letter" is inconclusive on this point.

In any case, RM did not transmit his letter to Congress until November 5, explaining that "Congress were so much engaged that, as well from that as other circumstances, those Matters which it relates to could not properly be brought before them" and because none "of the Subjects it relates to had been in agitation before the United States." The Yorktown campaign also demanded much of RM's time. Reporting to Samuel Adams on the Massachusetts resolutions, Congressman James Lovell wrote on September 15 that "The Financier has been so pressed by the Business of the moving Army that he has had almost no Leisure to plan Systems till within a Day or two, and I now know that he has digested the Business which you wrote about." Another of the "circumstances" that may have led RM to retain the letter was the likelihood of the unsympathetic hearing it would receive in Congress, for, as Lovell pointed out on September 15, only seven states were represented, and these were for the most part "Culprit states" which had not complied with the act of March 18, 1780, and which could not be expected "to vote for Justice to Massachusetts." Ferguson, *Power of the Purse,* 205–206; John Lowell *et al.* to the Massachusetts Delegates in Congress, [June 18, 1781?], and Governor John Hancock to the President of Congress, June 25, 1781, Edwin M. Bacon, ed., *Supplement to the Acts and Resolves of Massachusetts, . . . 1780–1784* (Boston, 1896), 64–67; *Acts and Laws of Massachusetts,* 1780–1781, pp. 488–490, 681–682, 702–703; Walter Lowrie, Matthew St. Clair Clark *et al.,* comps., *American State Papers: Documents, Legislative and Executive, of the Congress of the United States* (Washington, 1832–1861), class 3, Finance, I, 58; Samuel Osgood to John Lowell, July 10 and August 28, 1781, and James Lovell to Samuel Adams, July [September] 15, 1781, Burnett, ed., *Letters,* VI, 141, 149, 219–220; Massachusetts House of Representatives, Journals, June 30, 1781, M–Ar; see also RM to the Governor of Massachusetts, September 15, and notes, and Diary, July 28 and September 28, 1781; for the Financier's further recommendations on the settlement of state accounts with the Union, see RM to the President of Congress, November 5 (enclosing the August 28 letter printed here) and December 10, 1781; on the act of March 18, 1780, see the sources cited in note 27 below. For further discussion of this letter to the president of Congress, a copy of which was enclosed in RM to Benjamin Franklin, November 27, 1781 (first letter), and of Congress's response, see Ver Steeg, *Morris,* 90–96; and Ferguson, *Power of the Purse,* 203–219. The actual process of settling state accounts with the Union was initiated by Congress's ordinance of February 20, 1782.

4. See, for example, the President of Pennsylvania to RM, July 27, 1781.

5. On impressments, see notes to RM to Washington, May 29 (first letter), and the Secretary of Congress to RM, June 29, 1781.

6. As did the requisition of October 30, 1781 (*JCC,* XXI, 1090–1091). The amount for which each state was liable under Continental requisitions was therefore tentative.

7. The Second Continental Congress adopted the Articles of Confederation on November 15, 1777, but they did not receive unanimous state ratification until Maryland signed on February 27, 1781. Congress announced final ratification on March 1 and met the following day as "The United States in Congress Assembled."

8. Ofcl LbC and PPAmP copy: the word "funded" omitted.

9. In referring to "the public funded Debt of the United States," RM engaged in what appears to be calculated exaggeration. The debt which RM exempted from apportionment among the states and claimed as the sole responsibility of Congress, to be paid by means of federal taxes, consisted at this time of loan office certificates, the government bonds of the Revolution, whose specie value was about $11 million. As the impost, the projected federal tax, still awaited unanimous ratification by the states, the public, or Continental, debt was, contrary to RM's allusion, still unfunded. RM's further discussion of the debt appears later in the letter.

10. Ofcl LbC: a blank space left for the preceding five words.

11. Ofcl LbC: a blank space left for the preceding three words.

12. Ofcl LbC: a blank space left for the preceding two words.

13. Ofcl LbC: a blank space left for this word.

14. Ofcl LbC: a blank space left for the passage beginning with the next word ("be") and continuing up to and including the sentence ending with the word "Incapacity."

15. These were charges made by states for expenditures in the general welfare for which they were prepared to claim credit in the settlement of accounts. Under Article VIII of the Articles of Confederation, such claims were limited to expenditures specifically allowed or authorized by Congress. This strict definition could not be maintained; before the final settlement in 1793 it was relaxed to permit the inclusion of unauthorized expenditures. See Ferguson, *Power of the Purse,* 203–219, 322–324.

16. Supplied from the Ofcl LbC; also in PPAmP copy. The DNA and PHarH texts have "Appreciation," undoubtedly a clerk's error.

17. RM was proposing that state payments on old Continental money requisitions be valued according to the table of depreciation which Congress had applied to loan office certificates. On June 28, 1780, Congress adjusted the value of loan office certificates to correspond with the value of the depreciated currency with which they had been purchased. All certificates issued before September 1, 1777, when the currency depreciation was presumed to have begun, were rated at face value in specie; those issued thereafter were rated according to a table of depreciation which registered the declining value of Continental currency up to March 18, 1780, after which all certificates were valued at $40 to $1 of specie. Actually, this table of depreciation greatly underestimated depreciation and overestimated the value of currency received by the government. See Ferguson, *Power of the Purse,* 68–69.

18. PPAmP copy: this figure incorrectly given as "6,000,000."

19. Ofcl LbC: this figure incorrectly given as "401.450.30."

20. See *JCC,* IX, 955. Strictly speaking, the resolutions allowed 6 percent interest on sums which the states paid in but did not mention charging the states interest on unpaid requisitions.

21. Wharton, ed., *Rev. Dipl. Corr.,* IV, 671, silently added the word "not" at this point. The editors believe the unamended text to be the correct version, particularly since the negative does not appear in any of the extant manuscript texts.

22. Ofcl LbC and PPAmP copy: the word "State" inserted here.

23. That is, by the table of depreciation referred to in note 17 above.

24. That is, by the states' payment of requisitions in old Continental money.

25. See note 15 above.

26. Ofcl LbC and PPamP copy: the word "actual" is inserted here.

27. On the act of Congress of March 18, 1780, see notes to John Morin Scott to RM, May 30, and the Secretary of Congress to RM, June 29, 1781.

28. Ofcl LbC: the preceding three words omitted.

29. Congress had contemplated the withdrawal of $200 million in old Continental currency by April 1781 and its replacement by $10 million in new emission money. Up to the end of 1781, when the plan could be presumed to have had any chance of success, state withdrawals of the old currency were not enough to reduce significantly the volume of old currency in circulation nor to support the value of what

new emission money was issued. A Treasury statement of 1790 credits the states with deliveries of only $54,993,000 before the end of 1781. Another $64,466,000 was retired during the Confederation period after the money had become virtually worthless and had passed out of circulation. Lowrie and Clark, comps., *American State Papers,* class 3, Finance, I, 58–59; the failure of the act of March 18, 1780, is analyzed in Ferguson, *Power of the Purse,* 57–66; see also notes to the Secretary of Congress to RM, June 29, 1781.

30. According to the Treasury statement cited in the preceding note, Congress realized $1,592,222, some of it after 1781, from new emission money made available under the act of March 18, 1780.

31. No decision on the rate at which old money in the hands of individuals was to be valued was made during the Confederation. Under the funding act of 1790, individuals were allowed to subscribe old Continental money at the rate of 100 to 1. Although the destruction of early Treasury records made calculations conjectural, it was hypothecated in 1843 that only $6 million in old Continental currency was subscribed under the funding act and that $70 to $80 million was so widely dispersed that it was never presented. A Treasury statement of the same year, which placed the total emissions of old Continental at $242 million, estimated that $73.8 million remained unredeemed. Jonathan Elliot, *The Funding System of the United States and of Great Britain* (Washington, 1845), 11, 12, 13; Ferguson, *Power of the Purse,* 295–297; see *JCC,* XXVII, 936.

32. On specific supply requisitions, see notes to John Morin Scott to RM, May 30, 1781.

33. See notes 1 and 9 above.

34. RM refers to the proposed impost amendment of February 3, 1781, as well as to other federal taxes he recommends in this letter. See the headnote to RM's Circular to the Governors of Massachusetts, Rhode Island, New York, Delaware, Maryland, and North Carolina, July 27, 1781.

35. On the significance of these proposals, see the headnote to this letter.

36. Under the Articles of Confederation the apportionment of the expenses of the Union was to be based on the value of land and its improvements, including buildings—a rule which gave rise to controversy. The New England states, whose land was relatively highly improved, preferred an apportionment based on a uniform rate on acreage, whereas the southern states wanted improvements as well as acreage included. Ferguson, *Power of the Purse,* 165.

37. On the certificate debt arising from impressment and its obstruction of the withdrawal of old Continental currency under the act of March 18, 1780, see notes to the Secretary of Congress to RM, June 29, 1781.

38. It is noteworthy that RM contemplated excluding certificates given for impressments from the public debt, which, according to his plans, was to be funded by Continental taxes. See the following note.

39. Ultimately, the redemption of the certificate debt followed very largely the methods of liquidation that RM reviewed above and found wanting. Certificates were made receivable by Congress in state payment of old Continental money requisitions after the money was worthless and the requisitions no longer functional in raising revenue. They were redeemed by the states, which received them for taxes or converted them into state debts, for which the states received credit in the final settlement of state accounts in 1793. The remainder of the certificate debt, amounting to about $3.7 million specie after their value was determined by Continental commissioners under the ordinance of February 20, 1782, was incorporated into the public, or Continental, debt and funded in 1790. Ferguson, *Power of the Purse,* 63–65, 67–68, 179–186.

40. On this point, see *ibid.,* 63–64.

41. Congress on February 27, 1782, directed RM to appoint commissioners to settle accounts in the Quartermaster, Commissary, Hospital, Clothing, and Marine Departments. See *ibid.,* 188–193.

To Benjamin Franklin

Philada. 28th. August 1781.

Sir

Herewith I send you No. 1 and 2, Triplicates of my Letters of the thirteenth and fourteenth July last, [and] No. 3 and 4, Duplicates of my Letters of the nineteenth and twenty first of July last. I have not yet executed the Plan mentioned in mine of the twenty first of July of drawing Bills on you for Reasons which it is not necessary to enumerate at present.

Since my Letter to you of the eighth of June last I have found it necessary to apply to the Minister of his most Christian Majesty in this Place to direct another of five hundred thousand Livres with Messrs. Le Couteulx & Co.[1] and I am now drawing Bills for that Sum wherefore I must pray your Excellency to take Measures that they be put in Cash to Answer my Drafts. Altho I have no Doubt that this will be done on the Chevalier de la Luzernes Application yet as his Letters may miscarry or other unavoidable Misfortune happen I take this additional Precaution because it is of the utmost Importance to the United States that these Bills be duly honored.

The last Advices from Europe inform us of Mr Neckars Resignation or Removal[2] which Occasions much Speculation as to the Causes which produced this Event. I should be glad to hear from you on that Subject.

We learn from Boston the Arrival of the frigate Magicienne[3] with a large Store Ship laden with Cloathing &ca. for the United States; another Store Ship put back to Corunna as is said having been dismasted in a Gale of Wind.[4] If this be so it is a loss which will be more easily supplied than that of the Fayette which Ship we are now informed was taken and carried into England.[5]

Colo Laurens's Embarkation on Board a frigate for this Place with Money is also announced and I hope she will speedily arrive.[6] The Boston Account of the sixteenth of August mentions the arrival of the Magicienne in fifty Days. If Colo. Laurens had then sailed he must now have been out sixty two Days which is a very long Period for a single Frigate to be engaged in that voyage. If that Frigate arrives safe with five hundred thousand Dollars which is as I am informed on Board of her it will releive me from many very great Difficulties which I have now to struggle with, and give a much better appearance to our Affairs as it will enable us to operate with far more Vigor and Activity.

It is now a very long Time since we have had any Tidings of Mr.

Adams. We have indeed been informed (tho not from himself) that he had opened a Loan for a Million of Florins: but we are much in the Dark as to the Success of it as well as many other Particulars relative to his Situation which would be very interesting.[7]

September 7th. 1781.

Since writing the above Letter Colo Laurens has come to this City from Boston at which Place he arrived in the Resolu with the two Store Ships under her Convoy after a Passage uncommonly tedious.[8] It is certainly unnecessary to mention how great Pleasure we have received from this Occurrence.

Another equally pleasing is the Arrival of the Count de Grasse in Chesapeak Bay on the thirtieth of August with twenty eight Sail of the Line to wit, one of one hundred and ten Guns, three of eighty four Guns, nineteen of Seventy four Guns, four of sixty four Guns and one of fifty. The Count de Barras sailed from Rhode Island on the twenty fourth so that probably he has before this made a Junction with the Count de Grasse altho he had not on the thirty first of August.[9] A Detachment of about seven thousand Men is on the Way to Virginia of which about two thousand five hundred were at the Head of Elk yesterday. As many more must have arrived there by this Evening and the Remainder to Morrow. There are landed from the Fleet three thousand Men and we are told these will receive an addition of one thousand five hundred Marines besides the Army under the Command of the Marquis de la Fayette which was before in Virginia and consists of about five thousand including the Militia. My Lord Cornwallis was entrenched at York in Virginia with five thousand Men. General Washington takes the Command of the Southern Army in Person. The Fleet under the Count de Grasse took on its way a Packet from Charlestown to Great Britain on Board of which was Lord Rawdon.[10] From this Combination of circumstances you will perceive that we have Reason to flatter ourselves with the Expectation of pleasing Occurrences.

With the greatest Respect, I have the Honor to be Sir your Excellency's most obedient and humble Servant [11]

RM

MS: Ofcl LbC, DLC.

1. RM applied to Chevalier de La Luzerne for a second deposit of 500,000 livres with Le Couteulx and Company in a letter of July 2, 1781. An earlier request had been made in a letter of June 8.

2. Jacques Necker, French Director General of Finance, resigned on May 19, 1781.

3. The 32-gun frigate *La Magicienne* was subsequently captured by the *Chatham*, a British ship of 50 guns, on September 2, 1781, while leaving Boston harbor with a convoy of American vessels. The Virginia Delegates in Congress to Governor

Thomas Nelson, September 18, 1781, Hutchinson and Rutland, eds., *Madison Papers*, III, 258, 260n.

4. This vessel has not been further identified.

5. On the capture of the *Lafayette*, see notes to RM to Washington, July 2, 1781.

6. On the European mission of John Laurens, see notes to RM to Franklin, July 19, 1781; RM's September 7 addendum to the letter printed here and note 8 below; and Laurens to the President of Congress, September 2, 1781, Wharton, ed., *Rev. Dipl. Corr.,* IV, 685–692.

7. John Adams, American minister for negotiating a treaty of amity and commerce with the Netherlands, previously had been commissioned by Congress on June 20, 1780, as agent to negotiate a Dutch loan, superseding Henry Laurens. Inaccurate reports that he had succeeded in opening a loan circulated widely early in 1781, but it was not until June 11, 1782, that Adams contracted a loan of 5 million guilders, the first loan secured solely on the credit of the United States. The contract, which Congress ratified on September 14, 1782, is in PCC, no. 135, I, 82–90. Adams to Franklin, April 16, 1781, and to Robert R. Livingston, June 9 and July 5, 1782, Wharton, ed., *Rev. Dipl. Corr.,* IV, 363–364, V, 482–483, 594–595; Ferguson, *Power of the Purse,* 128.

8. Laurens sailed from Brest on June 1 aboard the French frigate *La Résolue,* commanded by Chevalier de Langle, which with the transports *Olimpe* and *Cibelle,* arrived at Boston on August 25. Laurens to the President of Congress, September 2, 1781, Wharton, ed., *Rev. Dipl. Corr.,* IV, 692.

9. The fleet under Comte de Barras joined de Grasse's force in the Chesapeake on September 10. See notes to Washington to RM, August 27.

10. Lord Francis Rawdon–Hastings, British commander in South Carolina, departed for England in the summer of 1781 on account of poor health and was, in fact, captured en route by a French privateer, taken to Brest, and eventually exchanged. *DNB.*

11. RM registered this letter and its September 7 addendum in the Diary, Minutes of Sundry Transactions for 1781.

To the Governor of Maryland
(Thomas Sim Lee)

Office of Finance Philada. Augt. 28th 1781.

Sir

Whilst I was at Head Quarters near Dobbs's Ferry the Determination was taken by His Excellency the Commander in Chief to send a very Considerable Force against the Enemies Troops under Earl Cornwallis in Virginia; [1] and immediately on my return hither I did myself the honor to address your Excellency respecting the Specific Supplies due from the State of Maryland to the United States, upon the Requisitions of Congress of the 25th. February and 4th. November 1780: [2] well knowing the whole Balances due on those calls of Congress would now become absolutely necessary to the intended Operations. I am very Sensible that your Government have upon all Occasions executed Demands of Congress with a decission and Vigor which does them honor, and on that Account I should decline saying any thing, calculated to stimulate their present exertions, did I not know that every thing depends thereon. Virginia, North and

South Carolina have long subsisted large Armies, and that expence of Provisions must come to their Credit. The New England States, New York, New Jersey and Pennsylvania have supported and must continue to Support the Main Army. Pennsylvania will also contribute towards the Support of the Southern Army and her Supplies will be directed both ways as Circumstances may require. Delaware and Maryland must chiefly be depended on. Virginia and No. Carolina will I hope continue to do all they can. But your Excellency must be perfectly Sensible that I have not any Funds wherewith to purchase Supplies, no State in the Union having hitherto supplied me with Money except Pennsylvania. But as the Money of that State is (in Consequence of Plans adopted for that Purpose) very rapidly rising in Value, it would be improper to call it into circulation at present when it is at the Rate of only two for one, tho it has been as low as seven, because the public Interest would thereby be injured and indeed I might be charged with defeating the Measures I myself had taken in the very moment when they bid fairest for Success.

The Security of your State, the safety of Individuals and their Property are so immediately connected with the present Operations that I perswade myself your Excellency will receive every Aid and support in your Exertions that you can wish both from public Bodies and Individuals. My dependance therefore on receiving the Supplies from your State seems well founded.

I have the Honor to transmit your Excellency herewith a Letter from the Commander in Chief on the same Subject which will add weight to my Intreaties.[3] I have written to Donaldson Yeates Esqr. Qr. Master of the States of Maryland and Delaware to procure immediately as many Craft or Vessells suitable for transporting the Troops from the Head of Elk to Virginia as will carry about [7000] [4] Men with the necessary Provisions and Apparatus.[5] I have written to Mr Ridley, William Smith Esqr. and some others in Baltimore to Assist in procuring these Vessels [6] and should any Application to your Excellency be necessary on this Subject I perswade myself that the Authority of the Government or weight of its influence will be brought in Aid of the Quarter Masters Endeavors to procure the Shipping. I have also written to Mr Calhoun to know what Part of the specific Supplies he has Ready and what Prospects for the Remainder.[7] He must bestir himself as indeed must every Person on whom the procuring of those Articles depends.

While the Demands for the Campaign are constantly transmitted to me and so much depends upon the Measures I am continually taking to œconomize the public Funds and facilitate our military

Operations your Excellency will perceive that full, early and accurate Intelligence upon the various Objects of my Department is of the utmost Importance. I must therefore reiterate my Requests for it. To act from Necessity and on the Spur of Occasion is not only the Source of Waste and Extravagance but frequently Defeats Plans otherwise the best concerted, while on the other Hand that timely forecast and early Provision which compleat Knowlege of Circumstances can alone permit of will save much Public Money and go very far to ensure Victory to our Arms.[8] I am with great Respect your Excellency's most obedient and humble Servant

RM

MSS: Ofcl LbC, DLC; copy, Vertical File, MdHi.

1. See Washington to RM, August 17, and headnote to Diary, August 21.
2. This letter is dated August 21. RM addressed another letter to Governor Lee on August 26.
3. Washington to Governor Thomas Sim Lee, August 27, Fitzpatrick, ed., *Writings of Washington*, XXIII, 57–58. See Washington to RM, August 27.
4. Supplied from MdHi copy. Ofcl LbC: "seven hundred."
5. See RM to Donaldson Yeates, August 28.
6. See RM to Matthew Ridley, to William Smith (not found), and Circular to Stephen Steward and Son, Jonathan Hudson, David Stewart, and Samuel Smith, all August 28.
7. See RM to James Calhoun, August 28.
8. Governor Lee replied on August 31.

To Matthew Ridley

Office of Finance 28th. Augt. 1781.

Sir

On the twenty first Instant I wrote you and requested you would immediately engage as many bay Craft as you could upon the following Terms to wit, to be employed at a certain Price per Day payable in hard money. The hire to begin whenever they should receive your Order and to End when you or any one properly Authorized by you should dismiss them.

I now write by Express to Donaldson Yeates Esquire the Quarter Master at the Head of Elk to collect as many Vessels as he can at that Place by the fifth of next Month and to apply to you and to William Smith Esqr. of your Town to whom I have also written upon the Subject for your Advice and Assistance.[1] I am now therefore to request that you will converse with Mr Smith on the Subject and exert yourself to procure as many Vessels as you can to transport Troops from the Head of Elk to Virginia. Let them be at the Head of Elk by the fifth of September and as soon after as possible. The Detachment to operate in Maryland and Virginia will be from six to seven thousand Men. You will therefore be able to judge of the

Number of Vessels necessary for this Transportation. I pray you engage them on as good Terms as you can and obtain Credit if possible which under present Circumstances will be a great Releif to me and cannot be very inconvenient to the Individuals. I expect your greatest Exertions on this Occasion. You may insure all the Vessels against Capture if that will either facilitate the hireing or obtain it on better Terms. I should suppose the patriotic Inhabitants of Baltimore would make every possible Effort to afford Assistance on this Occasion and certainly if they have a due Sense of their own private or public Interest they would even find Vessels for Nothing rather than not seize the present favorable Moment of clearing Virginia from the Enemy, opening the Navigation of the Chesapeak and setting the whole System of your Commerce once more in motion.[2] I am Sir very respectfully your most obedient and humble Servant

RM.

P.S. It is the proper Business of the Quarter Master to procure these Vessels, and Nothing but my Solicitude for the Good of the Service could have induced me to mention it to you. Should you engage any Vessels before he arrives you will turn them over to him.

MS: Ofcl LbC, DLC.
   1. See RM to Yeates, August 28. RM's letter of the same date to William Smith has not been found.
   2. See RM's Circular to Stephen Steward and Son, Jonathan Hudson, David Stewart, and Samuel Smith, August 28.

To William Smith

[*Philadelphia, August 28, 1781.* RM registered this letter in his Diary of this date. See also RM to Matthew Ridley, and to Donaldson Yeates, both August 28. *Letter not found.*]

To the Board of War

Office of Finance 28th. August 1781.
Gentlemen
   I am favored with your Letter of the twenty seventh [1] but I cannot possibly return you a decided Answer. Whether or not either Money or Credit can be obtained to purchase the tents you mention must depend upon the Sum they will Cost. I pray you therefore to let the Estimates be made out and sent to me as soon as you conveniently can, and I shall then be better able to determine what can be done.[2] I am respectfully, &Ca. &Ca.

RM.

MS: Ofcl LbC, DLC.
1. Letter not found.
2. See the President of Pennsylvania to RM, September 4, and notes, Diary, September 8, and RM to the President of Pennsylvania, September 12.

To George Washington

Office of Finance
Philadelphia August 28th. 1781.

Dear Sir

Your favour of the 27th. from Chatham, has just been delivered me by Coll. Miles, and in consequence, I have advised him to secure the assistance of the President and Council of this State, in case it should be necessary; but, as a preferable Mode of procuring the Craft, I advise his engaging to pay them in a short time after the Service is performed and, if needfull, I shall join in this assurance, and finally see it performed.[1] I directed the Commissary General, immediately on my return from Camp, to cause the deposite of three hundred Barrels of Flour, three hundred Barrels [of] Salt Meat, and twelve Hogsheads of Rum to be made at the Head of Elk; and pointed out the Means of obtaining them.[2] For this purpose, he sent down a Deputy [3] some days since; and I expect all will be ready there. I am much more apprehensive on the Score of Craft, both in Delaware and Chesapeak. I have written to the Quarter Master of Maryland and Delaware, Mr. Donaldson Yates, to exert himself in procuring the Craft. I have written to the Governor, and to several of the most eminent Merchants in Baltimore, to extend their assistance and influence in expediting this business.[4] Foreseeing the necessity of Supplies from Maryland and Delaware, I have written, in the most pressing Terms, to the Governors and Agents to have the Specific Supplies required of them by Congress in readiness for Delivery to my order, and now that your Movements must be unfolded to them, I shall still more strongly shew the necessity and stimulate their exertions, by holding forth what is due to their own immediate Interest and Safety.[5] But still I fear you will be disappointed, in some degree, as to the Shipping, and that I shall be compelled to make purchases of provisions, which if it happens must divert the Money from those payments to the Army that I wish to make. I have already advised your Excellency of the unhappy situation of Money matters,[6] and very much doubt if it will be possible to pay the Detachment a Months pay as you wish, therefore it will be best not to raise in them any expectation of that kind. Should it come unexpectedly so much the better. I do not think it practicable to provide the Salt Provisions here, even if a disappointment happens in New England [7] but have particularly recommended attention to this Article in Maryland, which is to furnish 10.500 [8] barrels of Beef and Pork.

No News here yet of the Count De Grasse; [9] but I have had occasion to lament, that too many People have for some days past seemed to know Your Excellency's intended Movements.

This City is filled with Strangers, so that Coll. Miles cannot procure private Lodgings, and my Family being chiefly at Springetsbury, affords me the Opportunity of appropriating my House in Town [10] to your Use. I believe we can accommodate Your Aids &ca with Matrasses, but our Beds are chiefly in the Country, and as what I have cannot possibly be appropriated to a better use, I beg Your Excellency will Consider and use my House, and what it affords as Your own. [11] I have the honour to be Your devoted Servant

Robt Morris

His Excy General Washington

ENDORSED: Office of Finance 28th August 1781/from/Robert Morris Esqr
MSS: LS, Washington Papers, DLC; Ofcl LbC, DLC.
1. For a more detailed summary of RM's advice to Colonel Samuel Miles, see Diary, August 28.
2. See RM to the Commissary General of Purchases, August 24.
3. Not further identified.
4. These letters are RM to Donaldson Yeates, to the Governor of Maryland, to William Smith (not found), to Matthew Ridley, and Circular to Stephen Steward and Son, Jonathan Hudson, David Stewart, and Samuel Smith, all dated August 28.
5. See RM to the Governor of Maryland, August 21, 26, and 28, to the Governor of Delaware, August 26, and to James Calhoun, August 28.
6. See RM to Washington, August 22.
7. In his August 27 letter Washington expressed the fear that a quantity of salt provisions from Connecticut and Rhode Island would not have arrived in Newport before the French fleet there under Comte de Barras sailed for Chesapeake Bay.
8. Ofcl LbC: "ten thousand." In his letter to the Governor of Maryland of August 21, RM requested a total of 10,300 barrels of salted beef and pork.
9. On de Grasse's movements, see notes to Washington to RM, August 27.
10. Until 1785 RM lived in a house on Front Street below Dock Street. Oberholtzer, *Morris*, 291, 294.
11. Washington accepted RM's offer. See Diary, August 30.

To Donaldson Yeates[1]

Office of Finance 28th. Augt. 1781.

Sir

The Express which carries this Letter will bring you one from Colo. Miles on the same Subject. [2] It is necessary that Vessels be procured as speedily as possible to transport a Body of from six to seven thousand Men from the Head of Elk to Virginia with their necessary Apparatus. You will therefore collect them at the Head of Elk on the fifth of September and as soon after as may be engage them by the Day on the cheapest Terms you can to be paid in hard Money. And obtain as long a Credit as possible. There will be little or no Risque of the Vessels and therefore you may insure them to the Owners if that will tend to obtain them either sooner or cheaper. The Express has Letters to William Smith and Mathew Ridley Esqrs. of Baltimore Town on this Subject and they will give you their Advice and Assistance as will some other Gentlemen to whom I have written should either be necessary.[3] He has also Letters to His Excellency the Governor of Maryland [4] who will I am confident give every Aid which the Executive Authority of the State can afford. You will therefore either apply to the Governor or not as Circumstances shall require.[5]

Any Engagements you enter into on this Occasion shall be fulfilled: but I must again Request that you will be as œconomical as the Nature of the Business will permit. I expect and rely on the Exertion of your utmost Industry and Attention and am Sir very respectfully your most obedient and humble Servant.

RM

MSS: Ofcl LbC, DLC; copy, Manuscript File, WDC, DNA.

1. Donaldson Yeates (1729/30–1796) was a Delaware-born saddler who moved to Kent County, Maryland, in 1766, inherited land, and became involved in business enterprises. In August 1780 Quartermaster General Timothy Pickering appointed him deputy quartermaster general for Maryland and Delaware, in which capacity RM addressed him at the Head of Elk. Yeates retained this position until 1783, subsequently was commissioned a colonel in the Maryland militia, and later served as a delegate to the Maryland convention which ratified the Federal Constitution and as a presidential elector in 1792. Gregory B. Keen, "The Descendants of Jöran Kyn, the Founder of Upland," *PMHB*, V (1881), 221–222; Timothy Pickering to Yeates, August 22, 1780, and August 2, 1783, WDC, no. 126, pp. 35–37, and no. 87, p. 83.

2. The letter from Colonel Samuel Miles, deputy quartermaster general for Pennsylvania, to Yeates has not been found. See Diary, and RM to Washington, both August 28.

3. These letters are RM to William Smith (not found), to Matthew Ridley, and Circular to Stephen Steward and Son, Jonathan Hudson, David Stewart, and Samuel Smith, all dated August 28.

4. RM's letter to the Governor of Maryland, August 28, enclosed a letter from Washington to the governor of August 27.

5. See the Governor of Maryland to RM, August 31, and notes.

From William Carmichael

[*San Ildefonso, August 28, 1781*. In this letter Carmichael wrote in part: "The negotiations for a Peace are on foot. It is the opinion of some persons well Informed that Peace will take place before the opening of another Campaign, or that the Greater Part of Europe will be involved in the War. This I do not give as my opinion, for altho' the Northern Powers already look forward with jealousy to the prospect of our Interfering & Depriving them of a market for some of the principle Staples of their Commerce, I cannot think they will join in a war to save from Ruin a Nation which has shown so strong a disposition to arrogate to itself the right of controlling that of others." [1] *Letter not found.*]

SOURCE: ALS, sold by Stan. V. Henkels, January 16, 1917, lot 109.
1. The extract printed here is from Henkels' catalogue.

From the President of Pennsylvania
(Joseph Reed)

[Philadelphia, August 28, 1781]

Sir

We duly received and acknowledge the Communication made to us in your Favour of the 23d. Instant. We have not been without Apprehension that the Nature and Extent of your Engagements would make some speedy Assistance from the State convenient if not indispensably necessary; we have not therefore ceased urging the Commissioners of the Taxes to proceed with all possible Dispatch, expecting from their Exertions not only a Supply for the Treasury but an immediate Effect on the Credit of the Paper. Should our Hopes on the latter Point be realized we trust that with the Powers you possess over the Treasury, and the Advances that may be made you will be enabled to proceed in your proposed Plan. Since we wrote you last we have the Satisfaction to learn that there is great Reason to believe Mr Searle has succeeded in a Part of his Mission, viz, the Procurement of Military Stores and other Articles which will relieve our Treasury from some present heavy Expenditures and of course enable it to give you more ample and solid Support.[1] The Letters having been thrown overboard in Consequence of Capture we have no farther Particulars than from Captain Mason's [2] verbal Account who also adds that Capt. Gillam [Gillon] in a Vessel of respectable Force was taking in the Stores on Account of the State and to sail in such a Time as to give us Reason to expect them daily.[3]

I am Sir, with much Respect Your Obedient Humble Servant

Hon. R. Morris Esqr
Superintend. &c.

ENDORSED: 1781 August 28th. To/Honble Robert Morris/Superintendant &ca.
MS: ADft, Records of the Supreme Executive Council, RG 27, PHarH.

1. On the European mission of James Searle, see notes to the President of Pennsylvania to RM, July 27, 1781, and note 3 below.

2. Probably Captain Thomas Mason, a ship captain and self-proclaimed "man of propperty" who, as a partner of RM and Jacob Winey, had undertaken a successful voyage to Europe in 1775 on behalf of Congress in order to procure arms and ammunition for the Continental army. A dispute over the settlement of Mason's accounts with RM and Winey lingered on until 1784.

Sailing from the Texel in the Netherlands on May 29, 1781, Mason reached the Delaware capes safely, only to be captured there by the British man-of-war *Suffolk* on June 8, just prior to which Mason destroyed "a very large Bag of Letters," some of which probably contained news of Searle. Mason arrived in Philadelphia on August 23 under a flag of truce from Bermuda. The Journal of Captain Thomas Mason, [July 10, 1775–February 2, 1776], Clark and Morgan, eds., *Naval Documents*, I, 1127–1128, II, 730, 789–791, III, 462, 1103; RM to Mason, March 12, 1776, Mason to RM, April 26, 1776, and March 10, 1783, RM to Mason, and to Jacob Winey, both March 10, 1783, RM to Mason, July 11 and December 28, 1784, all in the Henry Pleasants, Jr., Collection, PHi; James Lovell to Elizabeth Dana, August 23, and to Abigail Adams, August 24, 1781, Burnett, ed., *Letters*, VI, 194, 195–196.

3. Captain Alexander Gillon, who had been in Europe to purchase military supplies for South Carolina, sailed from Amsterdam in the frigate *South Carolina* in August 1781 with military stores for his state. On board was James Searle, who was returning to Pennsylvania from his unsuccessful mission, about which President Reed was overly sanguine. Following a six-week cruise in European waters in search of enemy prizes, Gillon put into Corunna, Spain, in September. There Searle disembarked and, after Gillon set sail without him, eventually returned empty-handed to Philadelphia. Gillon meanwhile went on to capture prizes in the Caribbean and lead a Spanish expedition which seized the Bahamas from the British. He finally reached Philadelphia with his cargo in May 1782. See notes to Benjamin Franklin to RM, July 26, 1781 (second letter); and Hutchinson and Rutland, eds., *Madison Papers*, IV, 112n.–113n., where Gillon's adventures are described at length.

Diary: August 29, 1781

Thos. Lowrey Esqr. of New Jersey this day informed me that his purchase of flour in that State was Stopped by the buyers for the French Army giving 21/ per Ct [1] for flour that he was before obtaining readily at fifteen Shillings.

The Honorable Mr Matthews and Mr Sherman called as a Committee to confer relative to the means of Supplying the honorable Chrisr. Gadsden Esqr. Lieut Goverr and 4 Members of the Privy Council of So Carolina with each £100 to carry them home, the State to be chargeable for that Money and to repay the same into the Military Chest &Ca.[2] I informed them I had no Money at present for such purpose but if Congress thought proper to Grant a Warrant on the Contl. Treasurer with Orders to apply to me I would pledge my Credit untill Money could be Obtained &Ca.

Received a Letter from the Purveyor of the Hospital &Ca.[3]

His Excelly. The Minister of France introduced a French Commissary of the Army [4] and requested my Advice and Assistance in his favour.

Colonl. Blaine called at my request and conferred with him respecting Supplies for ours and the French Army &Ca.[5]

The Honorable Mr Lovell called for the Letters from Mr Jay; [6] in consequence I now return him by Mr Broadhead all the Letters from Dr. Franklin, Mr Jay and Mr Adams, which he had sent for my inspection.

Wrote to Genl. Schuyler in reply to his Letter, 6th of August.[7]

Wrote to Mr. Dunning of the State N York in reply to his Letter of 27th. July.[8]

Wrote to Honorable Mr Holker in reply to his Letter of 10th instant.[9]

Wrote to His Excellency Thomas Burke Esqr. Governour of No. Carolina.

Sent twice this Day for the Cloathier General but could not find him.[10]

1. Hundredweight.

2. Following the surrender of Charleston, South Carolina, to the British on May 12, 1780, the state government collapsed and many prominent officials were imprisoned. In violation of the articles of capitulation, a number of the prisoners were sent to St. Augustine, whence by release, exchange, or parole they made their way to Philadelphia. Among these were Lieutenant Governor Christopher Gadsden (1724–1805), prominent South Carolina merchant and leader in the Revolution, and Thomas Ferguson (1725/26–1786), Richard Hutson (1748–1795), Benjamin Cattell (1751–1782), and the historian David Ramsay (1749–1815), all members of the South Carolina Privy Council. On August 25, 1781, they petitioned Congress to assist their return to South Carolina to work for its recovery from the enemy and the restoration of the state government. Their letter was referred on August 27 to a committee of three, including John Mathews of South Carolina and Roger Sherman of Connecticut, which was ordered to confer with RM. Apparently without consulting the Financier, the committee recommended on August 28 that Congress instruct RM to pay each of the petitioners $266 in specie, to be charged to South Carolina, and that the Board of War provide them with a wagon and team. At the committee's request, Congress recommitted the report, and on the following day, as this Diary entry records, Mathews and Sherman conferred with RM. After considering the committee's second report on August 30, Congress approved RM's suggestion that the warrants be drawn on the Treasury, presumably to be discharged by Morris's notes. The South Carolinians, however, were dissatisfied with this arrangement, so RM finally gave them hard money with the suggestion that it be repaid by advances of the state government to Major General Nathanael Greene. Gadsden et al. to the President of Congress, August 25, 1781, PCC, no. 72, pp. 538–541; Diary, September 8, and RM to Nathanael Greene, September 10. On Gadsden, Hutson, and Ramsay, see DAB; on Ferguson, see Reynolds and Faunt, comps., Biog. Dir. S. C. Senate, 216–217; on Cattell, see Mabel L. Webber, ed., "Register of St. Andrew's Parish, Berkeley County, South Carolina, 1719–1774," S. C. Hist. and Gen. Mag., XIV (1913), 95, and "Order Book of John Faucheraud Grimké, August 1778 to May 1780," ibid., XVI (1915), 125n.

3. Thomas Bond, Jr. Letter not found.

4. The French army official introduced by Chevalier de La Luzerne has not been further identified.

5. On RM's proposal to supply the French army, see RM to La Luzerne, August 4, and Diary, September 1–5.
6. See Diary, July 5 and 6, 1781. Congressman James Lovell of Massachusetts was regularly assigned to committees dealing with foreign affairs.
7. Philip Schuyler's letter has not been found.
8. William Denning's letter has not been found.
9. John Holker's letter has not been found.
10. John Moylan.

To Rawleigh Colston

Office of Finance Philada. 29. Augt. 1781.[1]

Sir

I received a few Days since your Letter of the fourteenth of July last.[2] I am much obliged by the Offer you make of the thirty six Bales of coarse Cloth for the Use of the United States. The Contracts made in Europe for Cloathing and other Articles render it unnecessary and indeed improper to make Purchases elsewhere. Should you think proper to send the Cloth to this Port it will probably meet a very good Market and if the public should contrary to my Expectations stand in Need of it, I shall then be well disposed to make the Purchase. I am very respectfully Sir your most obedient and humble Servant

RM.

MS: Ofcl LbC, DLC.
1. RM registered this letter in his Diary, August 28.
2. Letter not found.

To William Denning

Office of Finance 29th. August 1781.

Dear Sir,

Since my return from Camp I have received your Favor of the twenty seventh of July last.[1] I am sorry you are disappointed in your Intention of coming to Philadelphia but hope shortly to see you and converse on the several Matters mentioned in your Letter.

With Respect to what you say concerning the Bank [2] I Answer that if a Quantity of Flour be delivered to the Commissary of Issues [3] and the Account thereof transmitted to me with the proper Vouchers of that Delivery and of the Price being the then Market Price I will readily Pay the Amount to the Bank on any Subscription which may be made by the Proprietor of the Flour.

I am Sir respectfully your most obedient and humble Servant.

R.M

MS: Ofcl LbC, DLC.
    1. Letter not found.
    2. The Bank of North America.
    3. Charles Stewart.

To John Holker

Philada. August. 29th. 1781.

Sir,

Your Letter of the tenth Instant[1] was delivered to me a few Days ago being after my return from Camp on the twenty first Instant, and I hereby recognize the Bargain that was made in my Absence by my official Assistant on behalf of the United States.[2] The Information I had from his Excellency the Commander in Chief whilst at Camp induced me on my Return here to direct Messrs. Ridley and Pringle to purchase the whole of the three thousand Barrels of flour in Maryland as they will there be most convenient to the Use for which they are intended.[3] I communicated this to His Excellency the Minister of France [4] who agreed to the Propriety of the Measure. As the Flour provided by the State of Maryland proves too Coarse to Answer the agreement made with you I send money to effect the whole purchase and I have no doubt but the Flour will be ready for delivery as fast as you will want it. I have the Honor to be Sir your most obedient and humble Servant.

RM.

MS: Ofcl LbC, DLC.
    1. Letter not found.
    2. Gouverneur Morris noted the arrangements in the Diary of August 8; see also his letters to the Governor of Maryland and Matthew Ridley of the same date, and RM to Holker, August 7, and notes.
    3. See RM to Matthew Ridley, August 21 and 27.
    4. Chevalier de La Luzerne.

To the Governor of North Carolina (Thomas Burke)

Office of Finance 29th Augt. 1781.

Dear Sir,

I received your Letter dated at Wake Court House the eleventh of July last.[1] On that Day I left this City to go to Camp. This Circumstance prevented my answering of it immediately and the Business I there became engaged in has prohibited my answering it properly until the present Moment.

The Comparison you draw between our respective Situations is I fear too just and therefore I will not dwell upon it. Whatever may be the Fate of that Business which is committed to my Care I sincerely Wish that your Government may be as quiet as it promised to be tempestuous.[2] You assign the best Reasons for your Acceptance and while such Principles actuate a Man's Conduct he may be unfortunate but he must be respectable.

Your Application on the Subject of Arms has commanded my serious Attention,[3] and I lament that the State of the Public Treasury is so low as to leave me little more than empty Wishes towards the releif of your Wants. I should have made an Exertion in favour of your request, but it gives me infinite Pleasure to inform you that the Measures taken by the Commander in Chief in Conjunction with the Count de Grasse will probably free the State you preside over both from Invasion and Apprehension and give you Leizure and Opportunity to provide against the future Efforts of our Enemy.

With all possible Esteem and Respect I have the Honor to be Sir your most obedient and humble Servant

R.M

MS: Ofcl LbC, DLC.
1. As RM's following sentence indicates, he received Governor Burke's July 11 letter, which has not been found, on August 7.
2. Burke had been elected governor on June 25, 1781.
3. On the pending shipment of arms to North Carolina, see Diary, August 22, and notes.

To Philip Schuyler

Office of Finance 29th. Augt. 1781.

Dear Sir

I was favored with your Letter, dated the sixth Instant at Albany,[1] when I was at Camp. I could not then learn that any Flour had been delivered by your Order tho I made Enquiries on that Subject. You mention that the Payments are to be made in August but as yet I have neither received the Accounts nor any Order either for Bills or Money. When any appear they shall be duly honored. In the Interim I should be glad to be informed whether you expect that I should send you the Money or whether you will yourself send for it, lastly whether you can point out any Mode of Payment for both the Flour and Batteaux in this Place which will be entirely convenient to you.[2]

I am happy to learn that the Prospects from the present Crop are as favorable in your State as they are elsewhere. The late Movements of the General having greatly diminished the Consumption in your State,[3] I expect that the Supplies already provided together with the specifick Supplies due by the State will be more than sufficient for General Heath's Army [4] and the several Posts. If not I shall perhaps be induced to trouble you again; but as that will depend on the Prices, I shall be glad to hear from you upon that Subject.

I lament with you the Ravages of the Enemy. They are to be expected and will doubtless continue until the States by generous Supplies of Revenue shall have enabled the Congress to take effectual Measures for expelling our cruel Invaders. Every good American must ardently wish for that Event and will therefore do every Thing which is proper to effect it. The uniform Tenor of your Conduct demonstrates that on this as on every other Occasion your best Services may be relied on. I am Sir with great Respect Your most obedient and humble Servant

RM.

MS: Ofcl LbC, DLC.
  1. Letter not found.
  2. On the subjects of flour and bateaux, see RM to Schuyler, July 21, 1781.
  3. Having abandoned plans to attack New York, Washington was leading a detachment of 7,000 men to Virginia for joint operations with Rochambeau and de Grasse against Cornwallis.
  4. William Heath (1737–1814), farmer, politician, and soldier of Roxbury, Massachusetts, had received successive state commissions of brigadier and major general of the army before Boston in 1775. When the Continental Congress assumed authority over this army, Heath became brigadier general in June and major general the following year. After he bungled an attack on Fort Independence in January 1777, Heath was found to be unsatisfactory as a field commander and was assigned to staff duties. He commanded the Eastern District, 1777–1779, and the lower Hudson region, 1779–1783. Upon his departure for Virginia, Washington on August 19 left Heath in command of the army remaining in the Middle Department. *DAB;* Washington to Heath, August 19, 1781, Fitzpatrick, ed., *Writings of Washington,* XXIII, 20–23.

From Thomas Bond, Jr.

[*Philadelphia, ca. August 29, 1781.* In his Diary for this date RM wrote: "Received a Letter from the Purveyor of the Hospital &Ca." *Letter not found.*]

From John Skey Eustace[1]

Augusta, Georgia, August 29, 1781. Only the last manuscript page of this letter has been found. On it Eustace wrote in part: "To you, Sir, do I owe the happiness I now enjoy from the society of an only

Parent and fellow-suffering Countrymen; to you therefore are my wishes for every public and private bliss most justly due." [2] On the cover, Eustace inscribed a note to Congressman Edward Telfair [3] of Georgia requesting him "to forward this letter agreable to its address and to accept the Colonel's respectfull compliments to Mr: Telfair and his colleagues." [4]

ADDRESSED: (Private)/Honorable Robert Morris Esqr:/Minister of Finance/Philadelphia/By Express ENDORSED: Georgia August 29th. 1781/J. S. Eustace
MS: ALS, incomplete, Robert Morris Papers, DLC.
1. John Skey Eustace (d. 1805) of Georgia, the adopted son, declared heir, and aide-de-camp to Major General Charles Lee in 1776 and 1777, became aide to Major General John Sullivan and was breveted major in the Continental army by Congress on November 7, 1777. The Eustace-Lee friendship, through which Eustace probably became acquainted with RM, dissolved in 1779, and Eustace became aide to Major General Nathanael Greene. Congress accepted his resignation from the army on January 27, 1780. Heitman, *Register;* John R. Alden, *General Charles Lee: Traitor or Patriot?* (Baton Rouge, La., 1951), 285, 351n.–352n.
2. The following description of the entire manuscript letter appeared in Stan. V. Henkels, *Catalogue No. 1183: The Confidential Correspondence of Robert Morris . . . sold . . . Jan. 16th, 1917* [Philadelphia, 1917], 186–187: "Expressing in beautiful language his heartfelt thanks for pecuniary assistance which Morris extended to him. He mentions the British being forced out of Georgia, has left the citizens, who were loyal to America, with very little specie and the Continental money could not be negotiated, consequently the inhabitants are much distressed; but he says the Legislature has elected a Governor and that order will soon be established, and as soon as they are supplied with requisites for taking the field the men will march against the enemy."
3. Edward Telfair (1735–1807) of Georgia, a Scotsman who emigrated to America in 1758 as a factor for a British firm and eventually established a business in Savannah in 1766, became active in the resistance to Britain and held local offices before serving as a delegate to Congress, 1778–1782, 1784–1785, and 1788–1789. A signer of the Articles of Confederation, Telfair later was a delegate to the state convention called to ratify the United States Constitution and served as governor of Georgia. *Biog. Dir. Cong.*
4. This letter may have been that delivered by Telfair on September 25 (see Diary of that date). Eustace addressed RM again on November 1, 1781, and February 5, 1782.

From William Gordon

[*Boston, August 29, 1781.* On September 11 RM wrote to Gordon: "I have the Pleasure to acknowlege the Receipt of your Favor of the twenty ninth of August last, relating to Mr. Dudley." *Letter not found.*]

From John Hathorn and Isaac Nicoll

[*Orange County, New York, August 29, 1781.* On September 18 RM wrote to Hathorn and Nicoll: "I have received the Letter you was so kind as to write to me on the twenty ninth of August last." *Letter not found.*]

From the Navy Board of the Eastern Department

Navy Board Eastern Department
Honble. Robert Morris Esqr.   Boston 29th. August 1781
Sir

This Evening we are honored with your favors of the 2d. July [1] and 4th. Augst. by Capt John P Jones, the former inclosing a resolve of Congress of the 20th. June authorizing you to take Measures for the Speedy Launching and Equipping the America for which purpose the proceeds of the Alliances Prizes are directed to be appropriated.[2] Previous to this resolve we were under the necessity of calling the greater part of the proceeds of one Small Prize out of the agents hands [3] (being the only one that arrived in port) which the Continent had any Share in with Views of fitting the Alliance and Deane as far as so Small a sum would go.[4]

Agreeable to your last letter we shall in the Morning deliver your Inclosed Letter to his Excellency the Governor and Council of this Common Wealth [5] and make the most pressing Application for money to compleat the Equipment of those Ships; most Sincerely wish may meet with Success and shall take the Earliest oppertunity of informing you and of transmitting an Account of what we receive and the Expenditure thereof in which we shall observe the greatest frugality and all possible dispatch; shall afford Capt. Jones all the Assistance in our power. The Alliance is compleatly Coppered and off in the Stream; none of the Copper Bar was made use of.[6] We have the honor to be with great esteem Sir your most obedient humble Servants.

Wm Vernon
J Warren

MS: LbC, Letterbook of the Navy Board of the Eastern Department, DLC.
   1. Letter not found.
   2. This act was passed on June 23. See notes to RM to the President of Congress, June 22, 1781 (second letter).
   3. John Bradford was Continental prize agent for Massachusetts.
   4. The Navy Board had previously reported to RM in a letter of July 16, 1781, that it had disposed of the *Alliance*'s prize money.
   5. See RM to the Governor of Massachusetts, August 4.
   6. See RM to the Navy Board of the Eastern Department, August 4, and notes.

Diary: August 30, 1781

Wrote Matthias Slough Esquire of Lancaster.

Colonl. Blaine informed me that 500 barrells of flour and some Salt Provisions and Rum are deposited at the Head of Elk agreable to the desire of the Comr. in Chief; [1] had some Conference with the Colo. respecting Salt and Salt provisions.

Conference with the Revd. Mr Witherspoon,[2] of Money, Taxes &Ca &Ca.

Various Applications for Money from Commissary of Military Stores,[3] Officers and others, but was Obliged to resist all; shall be compelled to Force the Sale of Bills to raise Money.

Went out to Meet His Excellency General Washington who arrived in this City about One OClock [4] amidst the universal acclamations of the Citizens who displayed every mark of Approbation and Joy on the Occasion. His Excellency alighted at the City Tavern, received the Compliments of many Gentlemen that went out to escort him and of others who came there to pay their respects, and then adjourned to my House with his Suite, Count De Rochambeau, the Chevr Genel. Chattellaux, Genl Knox,[5] Genl Moultrie [6] and others to Dinner. The Owners of several Ships in the harbour ordered them out in the Stream and fired Salutes Whilst we Drank The United States, His Most Christain Majesty, his Catholic Majesty, the United Provinces, the Allied Armys, Count De Grasse['s] speedy Arrival &Ca.[7]

1. See Washington to RM, August 17 and 27, and RM to the Commissary General of Purchases, August 24.

2. Dr. John Witherspoon (1723–1794), a Scottish Presbyterian clergyman who emigrated to America in 1768, became president of the College of New Jersey, and eventually took up the American cause against England. From June 1776 to November 1782 he served (with some intermissions) as a delegate from New Jersey to the Continental Congress, where he signed the Declaration of Independence and drafted the revised peace instructions of June 1781. *DAB.*

3. Samuel Hodgdon, whose application to RM probably concerned money needed for "garrison Carriages, with their implements," estimates of which had been approved by the Board of War. See Hodgdon to the Board of War, August 28, 1781, WDC, no. 92, p. 114.

4. Washington mistakenly recorded in his diary that he arrived in Philadelphia on August 31 in time for dinner. Fitzpatrick, ed., *Washington Diaries,* II, 258; Freeman, *Washington,* V, 317n.

5. Brigadier General Henry Knox (1750–1806) directed artillery operations in almost every campaign in the northern theater of the war, became friend and adviser to Washington, and was promoted to major general on March 22, 1782, retroactive to November 15, 1781. He served as Congress's Secretary at War from 1785 to 1789 and in the same position under President Washington until 1794. *DAB.*

6. Brigadier General William Moultrie (1730–1805), planter, legislator, and soldier of South Carolina, was captured by the British when Charleston fell in 1780.

Released on parole in a cartel of May 1781, he sailed for Philadelphia in June, was finally exchanged in February 1782, and promoted to major general on March 22, retroactive to November 14, 1781. *DAB;* William Moultrie, *Memoirs of the American Revolution* (New York, 1802), II, 198–200; see also notes to Diary, August 24.

7. De Grasse arrived in Chesapeake Bay on this date (see notes to Washington to RM, August 27). Another participant in the day's festivities, Baron Ludwig von Closen, an aide-de-camp to Rochambeau, described the "excellent repast" served by RM at which "we had all the foreign wines possible with which to drink endless toasts." See Evelyn M. Acomb, trans. and ed., *The Revolutionary Journal of Baron Ludwig von Closen, 1780–1783* (Chapel Hill, N. C., 1958), 116–117.

To Mathias Slough

Office of Finance Aug: 30. 1781.

Dear Sir

Your Letter of the twenty second [1] was delivered me some Days since but the constant hurry I am kept in has prevented me from preparing an Answer until the Moment your Son [2] has called for it. He is waiting and I must be brief.

The Plantation must wait for more Leisure.[3] I thank you for the Recruits [4] and will take Information respecting the excise on Liquors supplied to the Troops and you shall hear from me on that Head.[5] The present Movements of the Army require Money from me so fast that it will be inconvenient to part with it at present. Tell me what Price you can convert State Paper to hard; it is here two for one and will be equal if the Collection of Taxes is pushed with Vigor.

I am Sir your most obedient and humble Servant

RM.

MS: Ofcl LbC, DLC.

1. Letter not found. Slough was contractor for the Continental post at Reading, Pennsylvania.

2. Not further identified.

3. The plantation, very likely that at French Creek in Chester County, Pennsylvania, apparently included a farm in poor condition and a powder mill said to have been destroyed. The powder mill, one of several in the area, probably was built early in the Revolution, perhaps wholly or partially under the auspices of the Pennsylvania Committee (later Council) of Safety. Title to the property, which was vested in a group headed by Owen Biddle, who had been a member of the committee, 1775–1777, was subsequently conveyed "to the Board of War in Trust for the United States." On November 8 RM instructed the board to sell the plantation. Diary, November 2, and RM to the Board of War, November 8, 1781; see also *Colonial Records of Pennsylvania,* X, 550, XI, 49, 58.

4. The allusion is obscure, but possibly refers to a body of 100 recruits at Reading which were thought by the Board of War to be needed at Lancaster, York, and Hanover to guard against a possible attempt by the British to free the Convention prisoners incarcerated there. See J. Moore to William Irvine, and James Wood to Irvine, both dated August 8, 1781, F. D. Stone, ed., "Extracts from the Papers of General William Irvine," *PMHB,* V (1881), 263, 264; and Irvine to President Joseph

Reed of Pennsylvania, August 9, William Atlee to Reed, August 9, Adam Hubley to Reed, August 12, and Reed to Irvine, August 27, 1781, *Pennsylvania Archives,* lst ser., IX, 345–346, 347, 351, 373.

5. On Pennsylvania's excise tax on liquors, see RM to the President of Pennsylvania, August 31, and notes. RM's next letter to Slough, dated September 10, has not been found.

From James Calhoun

[*Baltimore, August 30, 1781.* On September 5 RM wrote to Calhoun: "I am favored with yours of the thirtieth of August last." *Letter not found.*]

From Gerardus Clarkson, James Hutchinson, and John Jones

Philadelphia 30th: August 1781

Sir,

The letter you honored us with on the 17th. of last month,[1] wou'd have met an earlier acknowledgement, had wee concieved it to be of more immediate necessity, but that consideration joined to our own private occupations have defered it until now. Impressed with a high sense of the flattering opinion you are pleased to entertain of our abilities, and the truest zeal for our countrys service, wee shall with great pleasure afford you every information in our power on the subject you request, happy, if our endeavors may in the least degree contribute to lighten that oppressive load, which a country sinking under the weight of its own derangements have intreated you to sustain.

The plan of arrangement proposed by Dr. Tilton is so conformable to our own Ideas of health and oeconomy, that wee think it requires no essential alteration, except in the number of Hospital Surgeons, which wee think may be reduced to ten, including the Senior Physician and Surgeon. The reason of this reduction, is founded on the soundest principles of health and oeconomy. All the art of Physic never has, and probably never will, be able, to counteract the fatal effects of foul air, arising from great numbers of sick persons crowded together in large Hospitals; where indeed, they are attended with much greater ease by the Physicians and Surgeons, but surely convenience is to be sacrificed to health, the grand object of all medical enquiries.

To prevent therefore, the necessity of large Hospitals, distinct and distant from the Army, wee propose that all acute diseases, as well as wounds which are likely to terminate in a short time, shou'd be treated by the regimental Surgeons in the vicinity of the camp, where besides the Hospital tents, Churches, barns, and other large buildings may be appropriated for the purpose, and in cases of exigincy, detachments may be made from the General Hospital, to assist the regimental Surgeons, who, will not commonly want such assistance, as the thinness of the American regiments in general,[2] makes the proportion of Surgeons in them, much greater than in the Brittish Army.

Respecting the quantities of Medicine necessary for the army, it must be observed that no accurate calculation of its expence can be made, until a Hospital dispensatory composed on the principles of health and simplicity is adopted by the medical board, and the Surgeons of the Hospital as well as regiments, obliged to conform to it in their prescriptions, and this wee think a most essential article in the new plan of arrangement. Wee imagine however that £1000 Sterg. properly laid out will furnish the Army with all necessary medicines for one year.

The wine, spirits, sugar and other articles allowed in diet to the sick, from a calculation of the daily consumption may amount to £1000 Sterl.; as to tea, coffee and chocolate, though long habit has rendered them in a certain degree articles of necessity, and of course some indulgence must be allowed to individuals, yet wee are clearly of opinion that a gruel or caudle made of fine indian meal, is a much more proper diet for a sick soldier than tea or coffee, which are never used in any European Hospital that wee are acquainted with, excepting to the Matron, nurses or necessary officers of the Hospital.

Should any objections be made to this plan of arrangement, as it is very probable there will,[3] wee shall at all times be ready to answer them, and upon every occasion be proud to afford you every information and assistance in our power.[4]

With every sentiment of respect and esteem wee have the honor to be Sir Your Most Obedient Humble Servant

John Jones
Gerards. Clarkson
James Hutchinson

[ENCLOSURE]

Remarks of Gerardus Clarkson, James Hutchinson, and John Jones on James Tilton's Observations on Military Hospitals and Plan of Arrangement[5]

[Philadelphia, ca. August 30, 1781]

Remarks on Dr. J. Tilton's Observations on Military Hospitals, and on his Plan of Arrangement.

Observations page 1, 2, 3, 4, and 5.[6]

Dr. Tilton has made several Judicious observations to shew the propriety of keeping the Direction of the practice and the purveyorship of the Hospital in different hands. We need add nothing on this subject. These branches are at present seperated, and we flatter ourselves they will continue so; Congress were convinced by fatal experience, that they ought not to be united, and seperated them in February 1778.

Observations page 5, 6, 7, and 8.

The Arguments offered in favour of increasing the Regimental practice; and against accumulating the sick in General Hospitals are convincing; and apply particularly to the American Army, where we have less conveniences for a General Hospital, and a greater number of Regimental Surgeons in proportion to the number of men, than any other Army in the world, and of course they ought to be better able to take care of the sick in Camp (in Hospital Tents provided for that purpose) in which they will be less liable to infection, from the smallness of the number under each Surgeon, and it will be the duty of the Officers as well as the Surgeon to see the men properly attended. In those fatal years 1777 and 1778 when most of the sick were sent to General Hospitals, the Regimental Surgeons had no duty, and held perfect sinecures. We are clearly of Opinion that all acute Diseases, and all Diseases which from their nature are likely to terminate in a short time, should be taken care of in Camp, and that none should be sent to the General Hospital but Chronic complaints, wounded men who were not in a situation to recover speedily, and those persons whose complaints will continue a considerable length of time, unless a General Action or long march should make it necessary to disencumber the Army of its sick, of which the Commander in Cheif will be a Judge. We cannot dismiss the subject without forcibly inculcating this principle; that as few as possible be sent to the General Hospitals, and as many as possible taken care of in Camp, for in large and crouded Hospitals it is impossible to prevent infection, and soldiers who are afflicted

Dr. Craik [7] has pursued this plan during the early part of this Campaign and found the greatest advantages result from it;

with diseases not in themselves dangerous, on coming into the he did not send ten men to the General Hospital for several weeks previous to the movement of the Army. Hospital take the infection, and are lost to the United States; America has already lost more men from this cause than from the sword of her Enemies, and Humanity, Oeconomy, and sound Policy, make it necessary, that we should lessen the Hospital practice and encrease that of the Regimental Surgeons.

It is absolutely necessary that all districts should be abolished. We Observations part of page 8, and 9. cannot conceive what could ever give rise to this division, which encreases the expence, Multiplys the Officers, and prevents any system or regularity taking place in the Medical department; before September 1780 the United States were divided into four districts or departments. Congress have lessened the Absurdity by lessening the number but have not yet removed it. For should it so happen that the Army of the United States should remove to the Southward of Virginia, all the Gentlemen belonging to the Hospital Department in the Northern district would be Idle, and the sick of the Army would be attended by the Physicians and Surgeons of the Southern Observations part of page 8, and 9. district; the same with the Southern department should the whole Army be to the Northward of North Carolina as the Medical Gentlemen are not obliged to do duty, nor can they be ordered by any person not belonging to their respective department; hence it follows, that double the number necessary must be constantly employed; The purveyors will provide stores in each district, the Apothecary Medicine and Instruments, and the same with the whole Hospital Apparatus; add to this when the whole Army removes from one district to another, as the Physician[s] and Surgeons of the Hospital cannot move with it, they will be deprived of the Assistance of those who have been long acquainted with them and their diseases, and fall into the Hands of Strangers. We are therefore of Opinion that all districts or division of departments should be abolished, and that the Officers of the Hospital should form one department, connected with the Army, divisible with the Army, to move with it, be detached with a detachment, be confined to no place or district, but sent wherever the Army is sent, subject to the same orders from the Commander in Cheif, and liable to go to any post or part of the United States which the service may require, under one head who is to be accountable; by which complexity, profusion and extravagance will be avoided, simplicity, Oeconomy and regularity may be introduced, and we believe the good of the service will be promoted.

We agree with Dr. Tilton that the flying Hospital should not form Observations page 9th. a seperate department from the General Hospital under a distinct head; but we are of opinion great advantages may result from an institution of this sort during a Campaign and therefore would recommend, that a number of Hospital Tents or Marques be procured, which together with Medicines, Instruments and Stores be always an appendage to the Army; to take the sick from Regimental Surgeons on a march, or whenever it is necessary to disencumber the Army, and to form a Temporary, convenient, and immediate receptacle for wounded, in case of an Action where every necessary aid can be afforded. One Hospital Surgeon with his mates should be always with the Army, to attend to the Regimental Surgeons, and to prevent improper objects being sent to the General Hospital; and all Surgeons having no Hospital under their charge should attend the Army, and never be absent, without leave from the Director or in his Absence superior Surgeon and Commander in Cheif.

Observations page 9, 10, 11, and 12.   We are convinced there would be a propriety in establishing a Medical board in the manner proposed by Dr. Tilton, and as we have pointed out the necessity of encreasing the duty of Regimental Surgeons by taking care of as many sick as possible in Camp, and sending as few as possible to the General Hospital, it will be proper to observe, that great care should be taken to procure men of Abilities for Regimental Surgeons. We apprehend that this has not been heretofore sufficiently attended to, and that the Hospital swallowed up such a large number, under such a variety of pompous Titles, that few were left for the Regimental Duty, who were qualified; we would therefore recommend that the Station of Regimental Surgeon be made as respectable as may be done with convenience, that he should be considered as next in rank to the Surgeons of the General Hospital, and superior to any Hospital mate. That he should be examined and appointed in the manner directed by Dr. Tilton, that his sick should be under his own care, that he shall be accountable to the Director, or in his absence to the Superior Surgeon in Camp and Commander in Cheif, and that he never be dismissed the service without a regular Trial by a Court Martial.

Observations page 12, 13, 14, and 15.   Tho' the number of thirteen Surgeons proposed by Dr. Tilton, is less than any number employed since April 1777 yet we apprehend this number more than is necessary, and that ten Hospital Surgeons with twenty mates will be fully sufficient provided the proposed plan be adopted. If the Army of the United States consists

Observations of 20,000 men, we cannot suppose more than 5,000 to be sick or wounded during a Campaign. (This is a large Allowance.) We have advised that the Hospital Duty should be lessened and the Regimental practice increased, by which means two thirds or three fourths of the sick will be provided for in Camp. Should the number be 5,000 and the Regimental Surgeons take care of 3,000 or 3,500 there will remain but 1,500 or 2,000 for the General Hospital, which will be about 150 or 200 for a Hospital Surgeon and two mates; a number they are (or ought to be) fully capable of attending. It may be expected that on a sudden movement, when the Army is disencumbered of its sick, or after a severe action the number in the Hospitals may be greatly encreased, to which we answer, that in such case, as there will be few or no sick in Camp, a part of the Regimental Surgeons and Mates must by order of the Director, or in his Absence superior Surgeon and Commander in Cheif, be sent to the Assistance of the Hospital Surgeons, which will enable them to take care of all the sick.

We agree with Dr. Tilton in his plan of Arrangement, except with respect to the number of Surgeons, and think there ought to be one Physician in Cheif to the Army and Director of the Military Hospitals, ten Surgeons and twenty Mates for the General Hospital; a Surgeon and one mate to every Regiment; a Purveyor and assistant, and an Apothecary and two Assistants; should any extraordinary occasion occur, the Medical Board may encrease the number of Hospital mates pro Tempore, and give additional Assistants to the purveyor or Apothecary. The Purveyor shall provide all necessaries, Stores &c., and the Apothecary All medicines, Instruments and Dressings &c. but should be supplied with money by the purveyor, with whom he is to be accountable. The Director Should reside in or near Camp, the Purveyor and Apothecary in the place most convenient to provide the Articles belonging to their respective departments (Philadelphia); and an Assistant from each should reside with the Army. *(Plan of Arrangement page 15, 16, 17, 18, 19, and 20.)*

We agree with Dr. Tilton that when a seperate Army is formed and is sent to any distant part of the United States, and is to exist a considerable time, that the Medical Board shall nominate the Hospital Staff &c &c. in the manner proposed in his plan of arrangement; but when a detachment is sent off, we think this would be attended with great inconvenience, and that it would be unnecessary; and that the Director, or in his Absence the Senior Surgeon and commander in cheif, may order without calling a Medical board, such a part of the Medical Staff as they may think necessary for the Occasion. *(Plan of Arrangement page 20.)*

MS: LS, probably in the writing of John Jones, PCC, DNA.

1. In his letter to Clarkson, Hutchinson, and Jones of July 17, RM enclosed James Tilton's Observations on Military Hospitals and Plan of Arrangement and requested their evaluation of it. Following a conference with these three physicians, Tilton addressed RM on August 9, arguing against the relatively minor alterations they proposed. On July 30 RM furnished Clarkson, Hutchinson, and Jones with a letter

of July 26 from Director General of Military Hospitals John Cochran, enclosing departmental returns.

2. On this point, see notes to RM and Richard Peters to Washington, August 13.

3. Implicit criticism is contained in the Director General of Military Hospitals to RM, July 26, 1781.

4. RM received this letter and its enclosure on September 15 (see RM to the President of Congress, September 21). For congressional action on these papers, see notes to RM to Clarkson, Hutchinson, and Jones, July 17, and to RM to the President of Congress, September 21, 1781.

5. MS: D, probably in the writing of James Hutchinson, PCC, DNA. ENDORSED: "Remarks on Dr. Tiltons Observations relative to Military Hospitals."

6. When printing Tilton's Observations on Military Hospitals and Plan of Arrangement as the enclosure to RM's July 17, 1781, letter to Clarkson, Hutchinson, and Jones, for purposes of comparison the editors inserted in square brackets the manuscript page numbers to which Clarkson, Hutchinson, and Jones refer here and below.

7. Dr. James Craik, chief physician and surgeon of the Continental army.

Diary: August 31, 1781

The Cloathier General called for a conference respecting the appointment of Officers in his Department.[1] I desired him to Apply to Congress to fix the Salarys for his Assistant, Deputies and Clerks, and then to inform me by Letter the number he wanted and where they are to Act that I may consider the propriety or impropriety of the appointments he makes.

Went along the Wharves to take a View of the number of Vessells and to Obtain information as to the hire per Ton in case any should be wanting for Transports.

A conference by His Excelly. The Commander in Chief, Count de Rochambeau, Genl. Chattellaux, His Excelly the Minister of France,[2] Govr. Morris Esqr. and myself; respecting the expediency of hiring Transports in Delaware and sending them round to Chesipeak, there to be employed in facilitating the Various Operations of the Army. I was of Opinion against the Measure and gave my reasons founded on the scarcity of proper Vessells, and of Seamen to fitt and mann them, the length of time it would require to get them round, the risque of Capture in going round, the heavy expence &Ca. &Ca. but concluded with an Assurance of my giving every facility should the Measure be Adopted. After much and Various Conversation it was concluded to wait for information from Chesapeak as to the Number or quantity of Tonage that can be procured there, and if any shall be found necessary from Delaware to send such of the River Craft already in the Service as shall be found most suitable.[3]

Generl. Hazen applyed for Money, Goods or Credit on the strength of Certain Specie Certificates bearing Interest granted to his Regiment by Order of Congress.[4] After being earnestly pressd, I refused to come under any other engagement than a promise that my best endeavours shall be used to Obtain the means of paying regularly the interest of these Certificates as they fall due, Which I certainly shall strive very hard to Accomplish.

Issued a Warrant on Mr Swanwick in favour of Isaac Moses for £704 for Oznabrigs delivered to Colo S. Miles Qur. [Quarter] Master [for] Use of Public.[5]

Wrote His Excellency The President of the Supreme Executive Council.

1. On the reorganization of the Clothing Department, see notes to Diary, July 21, 1781. For Clothier General John Moylan's previous interview with RM on this subject, see Diary, August 28.

2. Chevalier de La Luzerne.

3. In view of the shortage of vessels, Rochambeau marched his troops overland to the Head of Elk, while most of the American forces were conveyed by water as far as Christiana, Delaware. Fitzpatrick, ed., *Washington Diaries,* II, 258; Washington to Benjamin Lincoln, August 31, 1781 (two letters), Fitzpatrick, ed., *Writings of Washington,* XXIII, 69–72.

4. On the certificates granted to the regiment commanded by brevet Brigadier General Moses Hazen, see notes to RM to Francis Hopkinson, July 20, 1781.

5. See Diary, August 27, and notes.

To the President of Pennsylvania (Joseph Reed)

Office of Finance 31. Augt. 1781.

Sir,

The Contractor for supplying Rations at the Post of Reading informs me [1] that the Excise Officer at that Place [2] has demanded of him the Excise on the Spirits he is issuing to the Soldiers and as this charge was never in Contemplation of either him or me when the Contract was made he desires my Instructions on that Point because if he pays it must be at charge of the United States and if one State exacts such an Excise every State will do it, and by this Means the State which contains most Troops will raise Revenue on the rest. I beleive this is the first Attempt of the Kind. How far it is warranted by the Law I do not know but I presume the interference of your Excellency and the Hon: Council may be proper and necessary until the Case if required can be considered by the Legislature.[3]

I have the honor to be your Excellency's most obedient and humble Servant

                                                            RM.

ms: Ofcl LbC, DLC.
   1. The letter of Mathias Slough to RM, dated August 22, has not been found. See RM to Slough, August 30.
   2. Not further identified.
   3. The excise on liquors to which RM refers was passed by the Pennsylvania Assembly on April 6, 1781, and extended for ten years the excise which had been passed on March 21, 1772, and was due to expire on April 10, 1782. President Reed informed RM on September 1 that he should seek redress from the assembly. It was not until March 19, 1783, however, that the assembly passed an act providing that contractors employed by RM to furnish rations to the Continental army within the state, upon the settlement of their accounts with the county collectors, were to receive credit for the excise paid on liquors they issued. Mitchell and Flanders, eds., *Statutes of Pennsylvania,* VIII, 204–220, X, 298–301, XI, 53–54.

From the Governor of Maryland (Thomas Sim Lee)

[Annapolis] In Council, 31st Augt. 1781.

Sir,

We have been lately honored with several Letters from you on very important Subjects,[1] but as it was necessary for us to make many Arrangements and Enquiries before we could give you such explicit Answers as we thought necessary or the Subjects deserved, we contented ourselves with adopting the best Measures in our power to perfect the Business without troubling you with unsatisfactory replies, however your favour of the 28th. demands a more immediate Answer. Every Thing that is within our power, and within the exhausted Abilities of this State shall be done chearfully and immediately to promote and render effectual the Expedition which his Excellency Genl. Washington formed against the British in Virginia; in which we are fully sensible the Ease and Safety of this State in particular is deeply interested. The most precise Orders are issued to impress every Vessel within this State and forward them to the Head of Elk without a Moment's Delay;[2] to purchase and seize all the salt Provisions, upwards of five thousand Head of Cattle, and to procure a large quantity of Flour and Forage; Part of these Supplies will be at Elk, Baltimore and George Town, the rest in places convenient to be removed either by Land or Water, as may be found most proper for the Service.[3]

Robert Morris Esq.

MS: LbC, Council Letterbook, MdAA.

1. Presumably the dates of the letters referred to are August 8 (from Gouverneur Morris), 21, 26, and 28.

2. On August 30 the Maryland Council issued warrants to Donaldson Yeates, deputy quartermaster general for Maryland and Delaware, David Poe, assistant deputy quartermaster general for Maryland, and others, requesting and authorizing them to impress transport vessels and send them to the Head of Elk to await Yeates's orders. The following day, however, the Council informed Yeates that it feared the necessary quantity would not be procured. *Maryland Archives,* XLV, 588, 593; see also RM to Yeates, August 28.

3. On August 30 the Maryland Council sent to state agent James Calhoun £250 in new emission money and ordered him to deposit at Baltimore, Georgetown, and Head of Elk all the state-owned flour and meat provisions (including 2,000 head of beef cattle) collected from the county commissioners in his district. *Ibid.,* 589–590; for the Council's orders of the same date to state agent Henry Hollingsworth and the county commissioners, see *ibid.,* 589, 590–591; see also RM to the Commissary General of Purchases, August 24, and to James Calhoun, August 28. RM received Governor Lee's letter on September 2 and replied on September 5.

From Philip Schuyler

Albany [New York] August: 31st. 1781

Dear Sir

On the 18th Instant I was advised that you was at head quarters, and hastened down but when I reached Kings Ferry you had already left It.[1] Not being able to procure a person there whom I could venture to recommend to you as proper to send the money by for the payment of the flour purchased by Mr Cuyler on my account,[2] I brought the account and Certificates back with me to this place, and now inclose the former and Copys of the latter by Mr John Van Woort,[3] a careful and sober person and for whose honesty I will be responsible. I have agreed to allow him at the rate of 20/ currency per day Including all expences.

I have not yet seen any advertisement of yours offering a Contract for the supply of the Army, but have understood that you proposed the contractors should both furnish and Issue the provisions to the Army. This certainly will Induce most to a public saving, If It is practicable, but I believe it will be exceedingly difficult to Estimate the value of a ration, as that value will vary not only in proportion to the distance, or vicinity where the principal part of the Issues may be made, from Navigable waters, from the near or more [remote?] operations of the Army to States which can furnish the most capital necessarys, but also from the more or less frequent Movements of the Army which will ever create a very extra expence. These difficulties might however I conceive be avoided and the Contractors still Issue the provision, If certain prices were allowed at one or more fixed places in each state, and the expence of transportation thence to the Army charged by the Contractors, but I am on a subject to which you have doubtless already turned your closest attention and consequently seen every side of it.

The Oneida and Tuscarrora Indians who have so firmly adhered to our cause as to be driven from their country are now resident at Schenectady.[4] Congress has long since ordered them provisions out of the public Stores,[5] but as there has seldom been a sufficiency for the troops, those distressed unhappy people have frequently nay I may with great truth say almost continu[a]lly experienced a famine, in a greater or lesser degree. They complain grieviously And Justly that having made every sacrifice for us they are now neglected. Honor, Justice, and Gratitude all combine in calling on us to afford them a comfortable subsistance and as It may be some time before you can arrange matters so as that they will be properley furnished under a contract, In the mean time If you approve, I will agree with some one to furnish them on the same Conditions per day that you may give others in this Quarter, or If you think it more Eligible to determine a price per day I will attempt to make the Agreement.

You will [perceive?] that Mr Cuyler charges five per Cent Commissions which he assured me the french agents who purchased flour here were allowed.

I have not been able fully to collect the Accounts of the workmen employed in constructing the 107 batteaus at this place, but believe 3500 Dollars will discharge the whole Including the nailers, nails, and [illegible] purchased by me. Altho the payments will not become due until after the 15th of October yet, If it is not Inconvenient to you and as this will be a good conveyance I could wish to have It sent.[6] Would It not be proper to order a small Escort to attend Mr Van Woort at least from Morris Town to Hudsons River as since the removal of the Army that road may be infested with Robbers.

I have taken the liberty to draw on you at thirty days sight in favor of Mr Binden [7] for two hundred and twenty Dollars in Specie which I Intreat you to honor.[8]

I am Dear Sir with Sentiments of Great Esteem Your Obedient Servant

Ph: Schuyler

Hon Robert Morris Esqr

ENDORSED: To/Robert Morris Esqr/Aug: 31st 1781
MS: ADftS, Schuyler Papers, N.

1. RM was at Washington's headquarters at Dobbs Ferry, New York, from August 11 to 18. See Diary, August 21.

2. See RM to Schuyler, June 25.

3. The Account of Philip Schuyler, dated August 31, shows $60 specie paid to Jacob Van Woort (also listed in the same account as John Van Woort) for delivering $5,201 specie from Philadelphia to Albany. See also Diary, September 12.

4. In August 1775 a congressional delegation of which Schuyler was a member had won a pledge of neutrality from the Iroquois. Although this understanding remained in force for nearly two years, most of the Iroquois were persuaded by British Indian agents that the westward-moving Americans were their natural enemies, and by 1778 they were actively assisting in British military operations on the frontier. Of the Six Nations, only the Oneidas and Tuscaroras remained friendly to the American side, the Oneidas serving with Continental troops in several engagements of the war, but they were few in number and impoverished. In retaliation against them, Sir Frederick Haldimand, British governor of Canada, in 1780 dispatched an expedition which destroyed Oneida villages and forced them to seek refuge on the outskirts of Schenectady, New York, where they lived in squalor and neglect (see note 5 below). Barbara Graymont, *The Iroquois in the American Revolution* (Syracuse, N. Y., 1972), 60–61, 69, 71–74, 100, 111, 112, 149, 233–236, 242–244; Ward, *War of the Revolution*, I, 143–144, II, 480, 547, 564, 566–567, 650.

5. Congress on March 24, 1779, empowered its commissioners for Indian affairs in the Northern Department, of whom Schuyler was the leading member, to furnish supplies and provisions to "our faithful friends the Oneidas and other friendly Indians." However, by the date of Schuyler's letter printed here, Congress still had not appropriated funds nor acted on a committee report of April 30, 1781, recommending that it approve measures for relieving the Oneidas and Tuscaroras taken by Schuyler with the concurrence of the New York State Legislature, that the expenses incurred be considered as a charge against the United States, and that Schuyler be furnished with $1,000 in bills of exchange on France for money he had advanced for the purchase of blankets. *JCC,* XX, 465n., XXI, 901; see also RM to Schuyler, November 16, and Schuyler to RM, December 1, 1781.

6. See RM to Schuyler, July 21, 1781.

7. Joseph Bindon, a Quebec merchant who took up the American cause, assisted the Continental forces which besieged that city in 1775–1776, and removed thereafter to the United States. In October 1782 RM appointed him commissioner for settling the accounts of the Clothing Department, an office he held until 1786, when Congress consolidated the number of commissioners for settling the accounts of the staff departments. Memorial of Bindon *et al.* to Congress, April 18, 1783, PCC, no. 41, II, 134–135; RM to the President of Congress, October 11, 1782; *JCC,* XXX, 130–131, 135n., 158–159, 202–203, 239–240.

8. RM received this letter on September 8 and replied on September 14. See also Diary, September 12 and 14.

Account of Philip Schuyler

[*August 31, 1781*]. The first entry in this account with RM for flour purchases is for August 31, the last for September 24, 1781.[1]

MS: DS, Schuyler Papers, NN.

1. See Schuyler to RM, August 31.

From William Thompson

[*Carlisle, Pennsylvania? August 1781.* In his Diary for August 24 RM wrote: "Received a Letter from Genl. Thompson respecting Supplies to the Western Department." *Letter not found.*]

Diary: September 1–5, 1781

During these Five days my time and Attention has been so entirely engrossed in Assisting the intentions and Movements of the Commander in Chief, in hearing the Applications of every Department and of almost every Officer for Money, and in giving those Answers which Necessity and inability to Comply with most of their requests dictated, that it was not practicable to keep any regular Minutes of the several Transactions that have taken place during that time, wherefore I must upon recollection insert the best Account of them that my Memory will enable.

His Excelly. The Commander in Chief, having repeatedly urged both by Letter and in Conversation the necessity of paying a Months pay to the Detachment of Troops Marching to the Southward under Command of Major Genl. Lincoln,[1] and my Funds and resources being at this time totally inadequate to make that advance, and at the same time Answer the Various Calls and demands that are indispensible, I made Application to His Excelly. Count Rochambeau for a Loan of 20.000 hard Dollars for such time as His Military Chest could without inconvenience spare that Sum, promising repayment at the time they should fix. I was desired to meet the Count at His Excellencys the Chevr. De la Luzerne's House which I did on Wednesday the 5th instant. When I met the said Minister, Count De Rochambeau and Genl. Chastellux, they informed me of their strong desire to comply with my request, but that their Treasury was at present not well filled considering the daily drains from it and that altho they had Money arrived at Boston it would require Six or Eight Weeks to get it from thence; that altho they expected Money by the Fleet of Compte De Grasse yet it was not then Arrived and of course that supply less certain than the other;[2] That the Intendant Monsr   [3] and the Treasurer[4] were set out for the Head of Elk and their Consent was necessary, however they concluded this subject with requesting that I would ride down to Chester where we should Overtake those Gentlemen and if it were possible on consideration of all circumstances they would supply the Money I required, His Excellency Genl. Washington being extremely desirous that the Troops should receive their Months Pay as great S[y]mptoms of discontent had Appeared on their passing through this City without it. This affair being considered of great importance I desired Mr Governeur Morris my Assistant to accompany me on account of his speaking fluently the French Language. We set out at 3 OClock for Chester and on the Road met an express from His Excellency Genl. Washington (who had left us in the Morning to join his Troops at the Head of Elk) with the agreable News of the safe arrival of Count De Grasse and his Fleet in Chesapk. This News I received with infinite Satisfaction on every account, and amongst the rest, one reason, was the facility it would give the French Treasury in Complying With My Views and this I found was actually the case as His Excelly. Count De Rochambeau very readily agreed at Chester to supply at the Head of Elk 20.000 hard Dollars [5] to such Person as I should appoint to receive the same, I engaging to replace the same sum in their Treasury by the 1st. day of October next which I agreed to and after dispatching some advices to the Commander in Chief and to Mr Ridley of Baltimore [6] on Thursday forenoon I returned to this City about 12 OClock having been impeded in my Journey by meeting the last Division of the French Army, their Artillery and Baggage on the Road. On my return I immediately dispatchd Mr Philip Audibert Depty. Paymaster General to the Head of Elk with Orders to receive the Money, pay the Troops &Ca. agreable to instructions given him in Writing.[7] In the Conferences with his Excellency Count De Rochambeau and Genl Chastellux they asked whether if upon any Occasion their Treasury should stand in need of temporary Aids, I thought they could procure such Loans in this City. I answered that Money is very scarce, that the People who have property generally keep it employed and that no certain dependance can be placed on any given Sums but that I knew the People to be very generally disposed to Assist Our generous Allies and should such Occasions Offer I was certain they would exert themselves, and as to my own Part they Might on every Occasion Command my utmost Services, assistance and Exertions both as a Public Officer and as an Individual. I mentioned to them again the Affair of Exchange [8] shewing that they had reduced the price of Bills from 6/ which it had been raised to by my Measures, to 4/7d. and requested that in future when they expected to raise Money by Bills they should in good time previously lodge them with the Minister [9] and that on his giving me timely Notice I would cause the most advantageous Sale to be made of them and deliver him the Money without any other charge or deduction than the Expence of Brokerage. I Observed that this Mode of proceeding was now become essentially necessary as there is no general Markett for Bills of Exchange to the Southward, but that Philadelphia in that respect is as Boston is to the Eastern States. They answered that they expected to procure their Supplies with Money without occasion to draw Bills, but if it happened otherwise they would pursue my Advice. I told them in regard to the Articles of Provisions, Forage, Wood, Transportation &Ca. &Ca. necessary for their Army and which when at Camp I had proposed to procure for them on the same terms as for the Contl. Army by Contract,[10] I proposed to postpone that matter as it might be best to continue their present method of supplies during the Active Scenes they are like to be engaged in as their present Agents [11] have given satisfaction and are acquainted in the Country where they are going and that I could advertize for Proposals to supply them the ensuing Winter &Ca laying before them such Offers or proposals as I should receive. This Appeared very Satisfactory, and here we rested that subject for the present.

Colol. Pickering and Colo. Miles frequently called for Advice and Assistance in the execution of their duties which I gave them readily and engaged to pay the hire of the Vessells taken as Transports, hire and Cost of Horses and Teams necessary for transportation &Ca &Ca.

Colol. Blaine and Colo. Stewart as Commissaries Genl. of Purchases and Issues frequently calld for advice, Assistance &Ca which I constantly gave them and Authorized Colo Blaine to purchase Rum for the Soldiers &Ca.[12] All these Staff departments press hard for a Months pay to the Sundry Persons employed therein and I think their solicitations ought to be complied with if possible.

Wrote a Letter to the Governour of Delaware dated 1st. Septbr.

Issued a Warrant on Mr Swanwick for £150 in favour of S Hodgdon for Military Stores purchased by him for use of the Army. Sept. 1st.

Issued a Warrant on Mr Swanwick for £150 in favour of Colo Miles being for immediate charges of the Quarter Masters Department at this Post.

Wrote a Letter to Genl Schuyler dated 4th instant.

Issued a Warrant on Mr Swanwick dated 4th instant in favour of Colo Pickering for £187.10.

Issued a Warrant on Mr Swanwick dated 4th instant in favour of Philips, Steward to The Presdt. of Congress, for Household Expences. £75.

Wrote a Letter to Mr. Philip Audibert Depty. P[ay] Master.[13]

Wrote a Letter to Mr Wendall, Portsmouth, N Hampshire.

Wrote a letter to Messrs. Ridley and Pringle, Baltimore.

Issued a Warrant on Mr Swanwick, dated 5th. instant in favour of Jno Hazlewood Contractor for the Post of Philadelphia. £200.

a Warrant on Mr. Swanwick, dated 5th instant in favour of P. Goffigan, Pilot for the French Fleet.[14] £15.

a Warrant on Mr Swanwick, dated 5th instant in favour of E. Blaine Commy. Gl. of Purchase[s]. £375.

Wrote a Letter to Mr. Benjamin Dudley, Boston, dated 5th instant.

Wrote a Letter to Mr. Calhoun, Agent of State [of] Maryland, Baltimore, 5th instant.

Wrote a Letter to Doctor Wm Gordon, Boston, 5th instant.

Wrote a Letter to Messrs. Le Couteulx & Co. Bankers Paris, 5th instant.

Wrote a Letter to Major Genl Heath Commanding the No. Army, 5th instant.

Wrote a Letter to The Chevr. De Chastelleux, Genl of H[is] M[ost] C[hristian] M[ajesty's] Forces at the Head of Elk.[15]

1. See Washington to RM, August 17 and 27.

2. De Grasse, who arrived in Chesapeake Bay on August 30 (see notes to Washington to RM, August 27), brought 1.2 million livres, 800,000 of them in silver, which he had borrowed at Havana. Charles Lee Lewis, *Admiral de Grasse and American Independence* (Annapolis, 1945), 137–138; Hutchinson and Rutland, eds., *Madison Papers,* III, 263n.

3. Space left blank in manuscript. Major General Benoît Joseph de Tarlé was intendant of the French army in America.

4. The treasurer of the French army in America was Chevalier César Louis de Baulny.

5. The sum furnished by Rochambeau actually totalled $26,600, but even this was insufficient. Putting aside other demands on him, RM used all the funds at his command to supply the deficiency, which amounted to $6,200. This payment was the first in specie to any Continental troops. On September 20 La Luzerne permitted RM to delay repayment of the loan until the French specie which John Laurens had brought to Boston should reach Philadelphia. See Diary, September 9, 11, and 20, and December 1, RM to Philip Audibert, September 4 and 6, to Rochambeau, September 6, and to Washington, September 6 (first, second, fourth, and fifth letters), Washington to RM, September 6 (second letter) and 7 (first letter), Benjamin Lincoln to RM, September 8, and RM to Washington, September 10, to Lincoln, September 11, to La Luzerne, September 20, to Baulny, October 1 and 30, and to Rochambeau, October 1 and 18, and November 15, 1781; Freeman, *Washington,* V, 323. For still further requests for a month's pay to men who did not receive payment at the Head of Elk, see Washington to RM, October 1 (first letter), and Diary, December 1 and 14, 1781.

6. These were RM to Washington (first, second, and third letters), and to Matthew Ridley, all September 6.

7. RM to Philip Audibert, September 6. See also RM to Washington (fourth and fifth letters), and to Rochambeau, all September 6.

8. On RM's efforts to arrange for the sale of bills of exchange in concert with the French, see RM to La Luzerne, August 2, and notes.

9. Chevalier de La Luzerne.

10. On RM's plan to supply the French forces by contract, see Diary, August 21, and notes.

11. Jeremiah Wadsworth and John Carter were principal agents for supplying the French armies. See notes to RM to Washington, July 23, 1781, and Diary, August 21.

12. See Diary, September 7 and 11. William Turnbull and Company supplied the rum to Blaine.

13. This letter and those to John Wendell and Ridley and Pringle, also mentioned in Diary, are dated September 4.

14. Peter Goffigan has not been further identified. See John M. Taylor to RM, September 4, and RM to Chevalier de Chastellux, and to Chevalier de La Luzerne, both September 5.

15. This letter is dated September 5.

To the President of Delaware
(Caesar Rodney)

Office of Finance 1 Sepr. 1781.

Sir,

I have frequently written to your Excellency on the Requisitions made by Congress from your State.[1] I have pressed upon you as urgently as I could the Necessity of a Compliance with those Requisitions. The Moment is now arrived when that Compliance must be insisted on. A considerable Detachment of the Army is on its March to the Southward and must be supported. By the Resolutions of the fourth November 1780, Delaware is to furnish eight hundred Barrels of Pork or four hundred Weight of fresh Beef in Lieu of each Barrel of Pork, two thousand Gallons of West India Rum and five hundred Bushels of Salt. These Articles in particular are immediately wanted, and if the Legislature have neglected to pass the proper Laws, or if there has been any Neglect in the Execution of those they have passed the Persons who are in Fault must be responsible for the Consequences to their suffering fellow Citizens. It is needless to say that a Body of Soldiers will not Starve in the midst of a plentiful Country. I hope most ardently that your timely Endeavors will have spared the Necessity of military Collection. If not I still hope that the military Force will be exerted with all possible Mildness. But at any Rate the public Service must not Suffer.[2] With all possible Respect I have the Honor to be Sir your Excellency's Most obedient and humble Servant

RM.

MSS: Ofcl LbC, DLC; Bancroft transcript, NN.

1. See RM's Circulars to the Governors of the States, July 6, 16, and 25, his

Circular to the Governors of New Jersey and Delaware, August 22, and his letter to the President of Delaware, August 26.

2. See RM to the Commissary General of Purchases, August 24, and notes. Delaware passed no emergency legislation in response to this appeal. It was not until November 13 that the legislature voted to raise £23,625 specie in 1782 for congressional requisitions; taxpayers were permitted to pay a portion of their assessment in wheat, flour, pork, or beef. *Laws of the State of Delaware* [October 14, 1700–August 18, 1797] (New Castle, Del., 1797), II, 751–762.

From John Jay[1]

San Ildefonso, September 1, 1781. The arrival of Major David S. Franks with dispatches "last Evening" will result in "long Letters to Congress and your self." [2] Will dispatch Franks as quickly as circumstances will permit. The bills of exchange drawn on Jay "far exceed the Funds for their Payment; and unless other than Funds in the air, are afforded me Protests will probably end this game of Hazard." Franklin cannot continue to make advances to him without Congress's order. From Spain's mismanaged finances and poor credit he has "but little hopes of Loans or Subsidies," but will do everything in his power.[3] He has neither sold nor pledged Congress's "Ships on the Stocks." [4] "This Court," Jay concluded, "seems determined to do nothing untill the Campaign ends." In a postscript of September 8 Jay declared that between $68,000 and $70,000 in bills of exchange "are now utterly unprovided for."

MS: ADft, with interlinear encoding in part, Jay Papers, NNC.

1. This letter is under publication restrictions. Four of its five paragraphs and the postscript are encoded interlineally in Office of Finance Cipher no. 1, which is discussed in notes to RM to Jay, July 7, 1781.

2. The dispatches carried by Franks were RM's letters to Jay, July 4, 7, 9, 13 (two letters), and possibly 15, and to Franklin, July 13 and 14, 1781. No "long Letters" of Jay's in reply to RM have been found; Jay wrote letters to the President of Congress on September 20 and October 3 and 18, 1781, all in Wharton, ed., *Rev. Dipl. Corr.*, IV, 716–718, 738–765, 784. For the date of Franks's arrival, cf. *ibid.*, 716, 784.

3. RM had written at length to Jay on July 4, 1781, about the negotiation of a loan from Spain.

4. In a letter of November 6, 1780, Jay transmitted Spain's offer of a future loan, which Congress might anticipate by drawing bills against it, on condition that the United States build and equip several frigates and a number of smaller vessels to be manned by American seamen and to cruise under Spanish colors against the British East Indies fleet. Jay was decidedly averse to the idea, but Congress on May 16, 1781, authorized him to turn over to Spain, on the best terms he could get, the ship *America*, then under construction at Portsmouth, New Hampshire, along with the materials assembled to complete her. On May 28 Congress postponed action on a proviso that the value of the ship, without rigging or armament, be fixed at 100,000 Spanish milled dollars and a further stipulation that no American seamen could be provided. Not long afterward, however, on June 23, Congress, at RM's request, directed the Financier to launch and equip the *America* for the use of the

Continental navy with money derived from prizes captured by the *Alliance*. The only other ship on the stocks at the time of RM's election as Agent of Marine on September 7 was the frigate *Bourbon*, which was under construction at Chatham, Connecticut. Jay to the President of Congress, November 6, 1780, Wharton, ed., *Rev. Dipl. Corr.*, IV, 115, 117–118; *JCC*, XX, 497; Paullin, *Navy of the American Revolution*, 235; *Dict. Amer. Naval Ships*, I, 146.

From John Jay[1]

San Ildefonso, September 1, 1781. Will request Richard Harrison at Cadiz to send three dozen blankets and Joshua Johnson [2] at Nantes to send the same with 150 yards of coarse linen for his father's family. Asks RM to inform his brother Frederick when the goods arrive.[3] Major Franks has received the £20 sterling, and RM is asked to pay Kitty Livingston an equal sum "for the same use as before." RM will "soon hear more particularly."

MS: ADft, Jay Papers, NNC.
    1. This letter is subject to publication restrictions.
    2. Joshua Johnson (1742–1802) of Maryland, who was the younger brother of Governor Thomas Johnson and whose daughter, Louisa Catherine, later became the wife of John Quincy Adams, was a member of the Annapolis commercial firm of Wallace, Davidson, and Johnson before the Revolution. In 1770 he went to London where he engaged in business, remaining there until the outbreak of war, when he moved with his family to Nantes. From 1778 he acted as an agent to procure money and military supplies for the state of Maryland. On September 29, 1779, Congress gave him the task of examining accounts of American commissioners and commercial agents in Europe before they were transmitted to the Board of Treasury for settlement. Johnson accepted the appointment, but when Silas Deane returned to France, Johnson refused to review his accounts, and it appears that he made no progress with other foreign accounts because his duties entailed removal from Nantes to Paris, which he refused. Although Congress on August 24, 1781, authorized him to audit the accounts of Jean Daniel Schweighauser against the frigate *Alliance*, Johnson's appointment was superseded the next year by the election on November 18, 1782, of Thomas Barclay as general commissioner to settle accounts in Europe. After the war, Johnson returned to London, where he served as American consul, 1790–1797. Butterfield, ed., *Adams Diary and Autobiography*, II, 300n.; Sullivan, *Maryland and France*, 53; Rhoda M. Dorsey, "The Pattern of Baltimore Commerce During the Confederation Period," *Maryland Historical Magazine*, LXII (1967), 127; Johnson to the President of Congress, April 12, 1780, PCC, no. 78, XIII, 139–142; Johnson to Benjamin Franklin, February 29 and July 1, 1780, I. Minis Hays, comp., *Calendar of the Papers of Benjamin Franklin in the Library of the American Philosophical Society* (Philadelphia, 1908), II, 220, 267; Silas Deane to RM, September 10.
    3. Two invoices of goods shipped by Wallace, Johnson, and Muir by Jay's order and consigned to RM, both dated September 15, 1781, are among the Jay Papers, NNC.

From the President of Pennsylvania (Joseph Reed)

[Philadelphia, September 1, 1781]

Sir

We duly received your Favour of this Morning [1] and should be glad to facilitate the Business of the Contractor [2] if it is in our Power: But upon considering the Act of Assembly creating the Excise [3] we apprehend it would be an Extension of Authority in which we are not warranted. How far it may be a general Inconvenience or produce Difficulties between the States we cannot pretend to say, but we think the Indulgence very capable of Abuse and therefore more proper for the Consideration of the Legislature who if they deem a Relaxation expedient will at the same Time guard against any [Perversion?] to undue Purposes.

I am Sir &c

The Hon. R. Morris

ENDORSED: 1781/September 1st. To/Honble Robert/Morris Esqr./Superintendant of finance
MS: ADft, Records of the Supreme Executive Council, RG 27, PHarH.
1. RM's letter is dated August 31. This answer was probably drafted the same day and the recipient's copy dated and sent on September 1.
2. See RM to Mathias Slough, August 30.
3. See notes to RM to the President of Pennsylvania, August 31, for a discussion of the excise law.

From Ridley and Pringle

[*Baltimore, September 1, 1781.* On September 4 RM wrote to Ridley and Pringle: "Your several Letters to the first Instant have been received." Aside from the communication of this date, the last recorded letter of Ridley to RM, dated August 25, was acknowledged in RM's reply of August 27. *Letter not found.*]

From Oliver Ellsworth[1]

[*September 3, 1781.* On September 18 RM wrote to John Lloyd, Jr.: "I have been favored with your Letter of the fifth Instant, enclosing one from the honorable Mr. Elsworth of the third." RM requested Lloyd to assure Ellsworth "that it will always give me a very particular Pleasure to attend to his Recommendations and forward his Views, as far as may lay in my Power," an indication that Ellsworth's letter probably was addressed to the Financier. *Letter not found.*]

1. Oliver Ellsworth (1745–1807), lawyer, legislator, jurist of Connecticut, and member of Congress, 1777–1784, had left Philadelphia prior to August 28. His later career included service as a delegate to the Federal Convention of 1787, as United States senator, and as chief justice of the United States Supreme Court. *Biog. Dir. Cong.;* Burnett, ed., *Letters,* VI, xliii.

To Philip Audibert

Office of Finance September 4. 1781.

Sir

I want an Estimate of one Months pay for the Officers and Men of the Detachment now marching to the Southward under Major General Lincoln, and suppose you can furnish an accurate one this day,[1] but as it is uncertain whether the Money can be obtain'd speedily to make the payment, You will be silent on the Subject. I am Sir Your Obedient Servant

Robt Morris

Mr. Philip Audibert
Depy. Pay Master General

ENDORSED: Phila. Sept. 4 1781/from Mr Morris/Copied
MSS: LS, Manuscript File, WDC, DNA; Ofcl LbC, DLC.
1. See Diary, September 1–5, for the background of this request, and RM to Audibert, September 6, for his failure to comply.

Circular to the Governors of the States

(Circular)   Office of Finance 4th. Sepr. 1781.
Sir

I do myself the Honor to enclose the Plan of a National Bank which I laid before the United States in Congress Assembled on the seventeenth Day of May last, and which was adopted by them on the twenty sixth.[1] I have now the Pleasure to inform your Excellency that an Election for Directors will be held in this City on the first Day of November next.[2]

It is of Importance that the Execution of this Plan be facilitated as much as possible and particularly that Part of it which relates to the Currency of the Bank Notes.[3] The Inhabitants of the United States already suffer from the want of a circulating Medium. Of

Consequence the Taxes must soon press heavily upon the People. My feelings conspire with my Duty in prompting [me] to alleviate those Burthens, therefore I pray the speedy Attention of your Legislature to that Resolution by which the Notes are to be receivable in Payment of all Taxes, Duties and Debts due or that may become due or payable to the United States.[4]

I do not Doubt either the Credit or currency of Bank Notes; but I wish to render them equally useful to America in the Individual as well as collective Capacity and to supply the Necessities of the Husbandman as well as the Merchant. I shall not at present mention the other Articles to be attended to.[5] Nor will I adduce any Arguments in Favor of my present Proposition as it is evidently calculated for the Ease and Benefit of the People you preside over. I hope however that your Legislature will not only pass the proper Laws to make bank Notes receivable in the Manner mentioned in the Resolution but that it will be done soon.[6] With all possible Respect I have the Honor to be your Excellency &ca. &ca.

RM

MS: Ofcl LbC, DLC.

1. The allusions are to RM to the President of Congress and the Plan for Establishing a National Bank, with Observations, both May 17, and to the Report of a Committee of Congress on the Plan for Establishing a National Bank, May 26, 1781. Other important documents on the bank are RM's address, To The Public, May 28, his Circular on the National Bank, June 11, and RM to Marquis de Barbé-Marbois, and Queries and Answers on the National Bank, both July 21, 1781.

2. The results of this election are recorded in the Diary, November 1, 1781.

3. Article 11 in the Plan of the Bank, May 17, 1781 (article 12 in the published plan), provided "That the Bank Notes payable on demand shall by Law be made receivable in the Duties and Taxes of every State in the Union and from the respective States by the Treasury of the United States as Specie."

4. See the Report of a Committee of Congress on the Plan for Establishing a National Bank, May 26, 1781.

5. After the bank's formal incorporation on December 31, 1781, RM requested a full compliance with the congressional resolutions of May 26. See his Circular to the Governors of the States, January 8, 1782.

6. Article 11 of RM's Plan of the Bank, quoted in note 3 above, implied acceptance of the bank's notes for all state taxes; however, the congressional endorsement of the bank plan adopted on May 26 recommended only that the notes be received in payment of taxes or duties collected by states for the use of Congress or in payment of debts due the federal government. In terms of Congress's stipulation, the response of the states to RM's request was fairly positive. The first to act was Connecticut, which on January 10, 1782, levied a tax for the state's quota of congressional supplies in 1782, for which notes of the Bank of North America were acceptable. Both Massachusetts and New York granted the bank charters of incorporation and prohibited other banks during the war. Although Massachusetts made bank notes receivable in payment of two current tax levies, its act of incorporation, passed on March 8, 1782, restricted their acceptance to "the Payment of all Taxes, Debts and Duties, due, or that may become due, or pay[a]ble to or for Account of the . . . United States." New York's act of incorporation, adopted on April 11, 1782, con-

tained a similar provision. The New Hampshire General Assembly resolved on June 25, 1782, that the bank's bills were to be received at the state treasury in lieu of specie for all taxes. Pennsylvania, which chartered the bank on April 1, 1782, made no special provision for the acceptance of bank notes in payment of duties or taxes; however, RM's management of the state's finances probably made such a statement supererogatory. New Jersey complied with RM's request on May 30, 1782, incorporating the bank and authorizing acceptance of its notes for all state taxes and debts owed to the state. North Carolina, although it declared in April 1782 that the congressional act of incorporation was operative as though by state law, neglected to specify receipt of the bank's notes for taxes. The other states took no action on RM's request in 1782. C. J. Hoadly and Leonard W. Labaree, eds., *The Public Records of the State of Connecticut* (Hartford, 1894–1951), IV, 8; *Acts and Laws of Massachusetts, 1780–1781*, pp. 579–581, 935–936; *Laws of New York*, I, 462–465; Nathaniel Bouton *et al.*, eds., *New Hampshire State Papers* (Concord, etc., 1867–1943), VIII, 945; Mitchell and Flanders, eds., *Statutes of Pennsylvania*, X, 406–408; Peter Wilson, comp., *Acts of the Council and General Assembly of the State of New Jersey from the Establishment of the present Government . . . to . . . the 14th Day of December, 1783* (Trenton, 1784), 262–263; Saunders and Clark, eds., *State Records of North Carolina*, XXIV, 446.

To Ridley and Pringle

Office of Finance Philada. 4. Sepr 1781.

Gentlemen

Your several Letters to the first Instant [1] have been received and your Drafts accepted except the one of fifty Pounds which you mention to have taken up again; this was unnecessary as it should also have been paid, altho I shall readily acknowlege to you that the Demands for Money in consequence of the present Movements of the Army come faster than I could Wish and therefore Accomodation in Time of Payment is very agreeable. I must request you will continue your Purchase and Collection of Flour until you shall have the three thousand Barrels ready for Mr Holker's call,[2] As I have assured him and the Minister,[3] that the whole quantity would be ready on Demand.

I am Sorry the Prospect of Craft to Transport the Troops did not extend beyond a sufficient quantity for two thousand Men; [4] however if Baltimore supplies so many I expect the other Parts of your State will furnish the remainder as they will doubtless be turning out of all your Rivers the Moment it shall be certain that we are Masters of the Navigation. You will certainly continue your Exertions to effect this Business compleatly. I am Gentlemen your obedient Servant

RM.

MS: Ofcl LbC, DLC.
1. Letters not found.
2. On this transaction, see the letters cited in notes to RM to John Holker, August 7.

3. Chevalier de La Luzerne, French minister to the United States.

4. In letters of August 21 and 28, RM had requested Ridley to assemble transport vessels at the Head of Elk by September 5 for a force of 6,000 to 7,000 men.

To Philip Schuyler

Office of Finance
Philadelphia September 4th. 1781.

Sir

I had the honor to write you a few days since,[1] and shall now employ very little of your time. Enclosed you will find a draft of Coll. W. S. Smith[2] this date at Sight on Morgan Lewis Esqr.[3] of Albany in my favour for Fifty Pounds Pennsylvania Currency in hard Money, Dollars at 7/6 each.[4] I have endorsed the same payable to your order and Charged you for the amount not doubting but it will be duly acquitted.[5] I am Dear Sir Your Obedient Servant

Robt Morris

The Honble. General Schuyler

ENDORSED: From Robert Morris Esq/Sept. 4th 1781
MSS: LS, Schuyler Papers, NN; Ofcl LbC, DLC.

1. See RM to Schuyler, August 29.

2. Lieutenant Colonel William Stephens Smith (1755–1816) of New York fought in many engagements of the Revolutionary War and served on the staffs of Generals John Sullivan and Lafayette before becoming an aide to Washington in July 1781. Washington appointed him commissary of prisoners in September 1782, in which capacity RM corresponded with him, and in 1783 entrusted him with the supervision of the British evacuation from New York City. Smith married Abigail, the daughter of John Adams, in 1786, held a number of federal offices under the Constitution, and was a Federalist congressman, 1813–1816. *DAB;* Washington to Smith, September 7, to Abraham Skinner, September 22, and General Orders, September 22, 1782, Fitzpatrick, ed., *Writings of Washington,* XXV, 133–134, 185–186, 188–189.

3. Morgan Lewis (1754–1844) of New York, son of Francis Lewis, attained the rank of colonel in the Continental army and was deputy quartermaster general in the Northern Department, a post to which he was appointed on September 12, 1776. Following the war he became an important figure in New York politics. *DAB.*

4. This draft, in the writing of John Swanwick, signed by William Stephens Smith, endorsed by RM, and dated at Philadelphia, September 4, 1781, is in the Lafayette Papers, InU.

5. See RM to Schuyler, September 14.

To John Wendell

Office of Finance 4 Sepr. 1781.

Sir,

I had the Pleasure of receiving your Letter of the thirtieth day of July last[1] upon my Return from Camp to this Place. I should sooner have acknowleged the Receipt but a variety of Business has engrossed my Attention to such a Degree that I have been obliged to neglect it until the present Moment.

I have little Doubt with you but that the Enemy have taken every Measure in their Power to ruin the Credit of our Money. But I hope and trust our future Measures will be so supported by plain and evident Reason that their Arts will be unavailing and indeed produce the contrary Effect. In the Interim the Efforts of yourself and other friends of the Public will combat effectually against their Insidiousness. I have the Honor to be very respectfully Sir your most obedient and humble Servant

RM

MS: Ofcl LbC, DLC.
   1. Letter not found.

From Horatio Gates

[Berkeley County, Virginia] 4th. Sept. 81 [1]

Dear Sir,

This Letter will I hope find you Happily returned to Mrs Morris, & that very [2] Beneficial Effect has resulted from your Eastern Tour.[3] —Paper Money has no Circulation here, or next to none. The Continental Currency being at 600 for One, & will only pass at that Rate for a few Home made Articles; for Foreign Manufactures, at The Taverns or for Labour, it will not pass at all; have you read the protest of Certain of the Members of the Legislature of Virginia against the Late Tender Law; [4] If you have, you will think, after all allowance is made for Party Spirit, that Avarice and Fraud have got a Severe Rap upon the Knuckles:—Your Obliging Letter of the 14th June [5] was Six Weeks finding its way to me, & I even then recovered it by mere chance—Neither Congress, nor General Washington, have condescended to Answer the Letters I wrote them upon My leaving Philadelphia; [6] is a sword to be kept continually hanging over my head, and the Hand that holds it to remain forever unseen; Conscious that I deserve to be Generously dealt with by Our Rulers, why am I so Barbarously Used—can you answer me these Questions —In regard to General Lee [7] I must refer you to the Bearer [8] who knows full as much of Him as I do.—Ever since I read of the Capture of the Trumbull, I have been in pain for your sons; as I think you told me they were to go with Mr. Ridgely to France in that Frigate: [9] Mrs. Gates requests you will make our Compliments Acceptable to Mrs. Morris;—My letter to Mr. Peters [10] which I desire him to shew

to you only; furnishes good Reasons for my saying, I know not when
I shall be out of your Debt,[11] but of this be assured, I will pay you
the moment I am Able. I am Dear Sir Your much obliged Humble
Servant

Horatio Gates.

Honble: R. Morris Esq.

PRINTED: "Notes and Queries," *PMHB*, XXXVII (1913), 123–124. MSS: ADft dated
"4th: Sepr: 81," incomplete, Gates Papers, NHi; ADft dated "Septr. 1781," incomplete, Gates Papers, NHi.

1. Internal evidence suggests that the text reprinted here, which is fuller than the
two incomplete autograph drafts noted above, probably was based on a more advanced draft of the letter or on the copy RM received and to which he replied on
September 15.

2. Both autograph drafts: "every."

3. An allusion to RM's visit to Washington at his headquarters in Dobbs Ferry,
New York. See Diary, August 21.

4. The "protest" to which Gates refers may have been the message sent by the
Senate of Virginia to the House of Delegates on March 13, 1781, rejecting clauses
in a supply bill passed by the house on March 10 punishing counterfeiters of Continental and state currency as felons and making such paper money legal tender in
the payment of debts. See *Journal of the House of Delegates of Virginia, March 1781 Session*,
in *Bulletin of the Virginia State Library*, XVII, no. 1 (January 1928), 20, 23–24, 27, 50;
William Waller Hening, ed., *The Statutes at Large; Being a Collection of All the Laws of
Virginia, from the First Session of the Legislature, in the Year 1619* (Richmond, etc., 1810–
1823), X, 397–400.

5. Gates probably refers to RM's letter of June 12, which he otherwise failed to
acknowledge.

6. These letters, dated May 22, concerned Gates's demand for a court of inquiry
into his conduct at the battle of Camden as provided by a congressional resolution
of October 5, 1780. Washington had already informed Gates on May 12 that no
formal inquiry could take place until charges were preferred against him, that none
had been, and that he would not bring any; and Congress, in response to an earlier
letter from Gates, had declared on May 21 that its resolution for inquiry did not
suspend Gates from his command as major general in the line, and that he was free
to go to headquarters to assume whatever command Washington might assign to
him. Gates nevertheless informed Congress on May 22 that he could not accept its
"Indulgence" until an inquiry had cleared his reputation and restored him to the
army's confidence. "I see a Sword Hanging over my Head," he wrote. "The Hand
that holds it is invisible." To Washington, Gates objected that the May 21 resolution
"dooms me to Temporary Disesteem, and Loss of Confidence. . . . Convinced that
you have done every thing which propriety could admit, to protect Slandered Officers
against Anonymous Accusations, I will set out tomorrow morning for Virginia, where
I shall wait for your Excellencys Orders." Gates's letter to Congress evoked a motion
submitted on May 24 by James Mitchell Varnum of Rhode Island providing for the
repeal of so much of the resolutions of October 5, 1780, relating to the inquiry into
Gates's conduct, but it was not approved. Gates to the President of Congress, May
18 and 22, 1781, PCC, no. 154, II, 355, 357–358; the President of Congress to Gates,
May 22, 1781, Burnett, ed., *Letters*, VI, 94–95; *JCC*, XX, 533n.; Washington to the
President of Congress, May 8, and to Gates, May 12, 1781, Fitzpatrick, ed., *Writings
of Washington*, XXII, 59, 76–78; Gates to Washington, May 22, 1781, Washington
Papers, DLC; Gates to RM, June 3, 1781, and notes.

7. In his June 12, 1781, letter to Gates, RM had expressed the desire to hear "some
more pleasing accounts of our Friend [Charles] Lee" than Gates had supplied in his

June 3 letter. In the incomplete ADft dated "Septr. 1781," Gates wrote and then excised the following passage: "You ask me after General Lee; he was a few days ago at Home but with Him I neither have, nor desire to have any sort of Communication; but I am told he is writing a Treatise for the Press, in which I conclude, all Those he does not like, will be treated with all the Acrimony of his Dislike."

8. In the incomplete ADft dated "Septr. 1781," Gates refers to the bearer as "⟨James⟩ Mr: Nourse," no doubt James Nourse, on whom see notes to Charles Lee to RM, June 16, 1781.

9. On the capture of the frigate *Trumbull*, which was bound for Havana, see notes to Diary, August 15. RM sent his two sons to Europe later in the year under the care of Matthew Ridley. See RM to Ridley, and to Benjamin Franklin, both October 14, 1781.

10. Gates's letter to Richard Peters, a member of the Board of War, is dated September 4, 1781, and is in the Peters Papers, PHi.

11. About May 1781, Gates incurred a personal debt to RM for an undisclosed sum said to have been spent for public purposes. Writing to the Financier a year later, he apologized for not repaying it. He proposed that his accounts with the government for military services be laid before Congress along with a request that Congress authorize payment of a sufficient portion of the balance due him to cover his debt to RM, which he could then turn over to the Financier. RM subsequently informed Gates that even after his accounts were settled, he could receive no payment for any balance due up to the end of 1781; however, the balance would be set at interest, and he was entitled to receive current pay for the first two months of 1782. Gates to RM, [May 12, 1782?], Gates Papers, NHi; RM to Gates, May 31, and Gates to RM, June 14, 1782.

From the President of Pennsylvania
(Joseph Reed)

[Philadelphia, September 4, 1781]

Sir

Genl. St. Clair has been very pressing to give up a Number of Tents the Property of the State for the Service of the United States.[1] The great Difficulty we have had to equip the Militia, the low State of our Treasury which forbids a Hope of soon replacing them, and the Impracticability of taking the Militia into the Field in Case of Necessity without Covering would have made our Compliance very reluctant if he had not accompanied his Request with an Assurance that you would in a short Time replace them. Our Anxiety to forward the Troops in a proper Manner and the present Emergency have induced us to give them up. At the same Time we must express our earnest Desires that you would as soon as possible relieve us from our Apprehensions of the Difficulty which will ensue if the Militia should be called out in an unprovided State.[2] I am Sir Your Humble Servant

JR.

ENDORSED: 1781 September 4th To/Honble Robert Morris/Superintendant of finance
MS: ADftS, Records of the Supreme Executive Council, RG 27, PHarH.
   1. On September 4 Major General Arthur St. Clair inquired of President Reed whether the Supreme Executive Council had agreed to "Mr. Morris's proposal about the Tents" needed for the Pennsylvania troops under his command which were ordered to Yorktown and, if so, requested their delivery to him. RM's proposal is not recorded in his correspondence or Diary, but he apparently promised to replace tents furnished to St. Clair by the state. As Reed notes in this letter to RM, the Council on the same day provided St. Clair with 86 tents that were to be replaced by RM. On September 8, having decided that the Council should retain its tents for the militia's use, RM ordered Colonel Samuel Miles, deputy quartermaster general for Pennsylvania, to furnish St. Clair with 100 tents. St. Clair to Reed, September 4, 1781, *Pennsylvania Archives*, 1st ser., IX, 386–387; *Colonial Records of Pennsylvania*, XIII, 47; Diary, September 8, and RM to the Board of War, August 28, and to the President of Pennsylvania, September 12.
   2. RM replied on September 12.

From Matthew Ridley

[*Baltimore, September 4, 1781.* From Chester, Pennsylvania, on September 6 RM wrote to Ridley: "I received yours of the fourth last Evening at this Place and sincerely rejoice with you in the agreable Inteligence it contains." *Letter not found.*]

From John M. Taylor[1]

Philadelphia, Tuesday Morning, [*September 4, 1781*]. "The Bearer Peter Goffigan who I informed you of two days ago will hand you this; he wishes to be employed as a Pilot for the French. I beleive him to be one of the best Pilots (particularly for Chesapeak Bay) of any now to be found." [2]

MS: Ofcl LbC, DLC.
   1. Possibly John Man Taylor, a Philadelphia merchant and broker who later acquired holdings of $50,000 in the public debt. Syrett and Cooke, eds., *Hamilton Papers*, XI, 336n.; Ferguson, *Power of the Purse*, 280; Campbell, *Sons of St. Patrick*, 534.
   2. See Diary, September 1–5, and RM to Chevalier de Chastellux, in which the letter probably was enclosed, and to Chevalier de La Luzerne, both September 5.

To James Calhoun

Office of Finance 5th. Sepr. 1781.

Sir,

I am favored with yours of the thirtieth of August last [1] and am much obliged by the early Attention you have paid to mine of the twenty eighth. I hope you will continue to exert yourself in the

Service of your Country and to merit the Acknowlegements of her Servants.

By a Letter from Governor Lee of the thirty first of August I find that the Council have directed the Impressing of Salted Provisions. Some of it will be necessary to make up the Quantity required at the Head of Elk of which you will receive Notice from the Commissary General.[2]

I am Sir your most obedient and humble Servant

RM

ms: Ofcl LbC, DLC.
    1. Letter not found.
    2. In addition to the correspondence mentioned in this letter, see RM to the Commissary General of Purchases, August 24, and to the Governor of Maryland, August 21, 26, and 28.

To Chevalier de Chastellux

Office of Finance
Philadelphia 5th. Sepr. 1781.

Sir

By the enclosed Papers [1] you will perceive that the Bearer hereof Mr Peter Goffigan is one of the best Pilots for Chesapeak Bay and he tells me he is equally well acquainted with the Coast of Virginia, Carolinas and Georgia wherefore I sent him to the Chevr. Luzerne supposing he might be usefully employed for the service of your Fleet. His Excellency in his Note of this Morning [2] replys that he is not a Judge of the Services he may be of but desires I should furnish a Horse and some Money to Mr Goffigan and send him to you at the Head of Elk. The Horse I think unnecessary as he can go by the Stages but he could not depart with a smaller Sum than forty hard Dollars which I have given to him in part Payment of such Service as you may employ him in. This Sum can be deducted from his future Pay, and the Chevr. refers me to you for Reimbursement. You will fix the Terms of his Service with himself.

I have the Honor to be with great Attachment Dear Sir your obedient humble Servant

RM.

PS. I pray you to shew these Letters to His Excellency Genl Washington in Order that he may employ this Person if he should find it necessary in the first Instance for piloting down the Craft with the Troops &Ca. which may be very useful altho I do not suppose he will become most so on board the Fleet.

MS: Ofcl LbC, DLC.
1. Probably John M. Taylor to RM, September 4, and RM to Chevalier de La Luzerne, September 5. See also Diary, September 1–5.
2. Letter not found.

To Benjamin Dudley

Office of Finance 5. Sepr. 1781.

Sir,

I am favored with your Letter of the twentieth of August last.[1] There are many Reasons why I wish rather to see you as soon as you can conveniently come forward than at a later Period. I am therefore to request that you may not delay your Journey longer than may be absolutely necessary.[2] I am most respectfully Sir your most obedient and humble Servant

RM

MS: Ofcl LbC, DLC.
1. Letter not found.
2. See notes to Diary, July 16; and RM to William Gordon, September 5, 1781.

To William Gordon

Office of Finance 5th. Sepr. 1781.

Sir

I have received your Favor of the twenty third of August enclosing a Letter from Mr Dudley.[1] I am much obliged, by your kind and polite Attention for which I pray leave to return you my Thanks. The sooner Mr. Dudley comes forward the sooner [he] will have an Opportunity of [2] remedying the State of his Finances which now calls for that Interposition of Mr Bradford [3] and yourself which you have been so kind as to Promise.[4]

Should you come to this City as you seem to have determined It will give me a very particular Pleasure to see you and Personally to make my Acknowlegements for your Favors. I am respectfully Sir your most obedient and humble Servant

RM

MS: Ofcl LbC, DLC.
1. Both Gordon's letter and Benjamin Dudley's August 20 letter to RM have not been found.
2. MS: "or."
3. John Bradford was Continental prize agent for Massachusetts.
4. See notes to Diary, July 16; and RM to Benjamin Dudley, September 5, 1781.

To William Heath

Office of Finance
Philadelphia Sept 5th. 1781

Sir

His Excellency The Commander in Chief departed hence this Morning for the Southward and I believe he wrote to you respecting the Supplies of Cattle which it will be necessary to forward from your's to the Use of the Southern Army.[1] I know it was his intention to Write on this Subject but as his Attention was called by a multitude of Objects, I beg leave to observe that such Supplies will be absolutely necessary as Meat is the only Article which we cannot depend on the Southern States to Supply. The Commissary General[2] thinks One hundred head of Cattle per Week will be necessary and that you will be able to spare that quantity from the number that will be furnished by the Eastern States. I do not pretend to decide on this point but I am Confident you will be entirely disposed to relieve the Wants of the Commander in Chief as far as in your power,[3] and you may also assure yourself that I am entirely disposed to Assist your Command in all things wherein I can be usefull.[4] And that I am with much Esteem Sir your Obedient humble servant

Robt Morris

The Honorable
Major Genl. Heath
Commanding the Northern Army

ENDORSED: From Mr. Morris/respecting Cattle for the/Southern Army/Sept: 5th. 1781
MSS: LS, Heath Papers, MHi; Ofcl LbC, DLC.
1. Washington ordered Heath on September 4, 1781, to forward cattle supplied by the New England states at the rate of 100 a week. Fitzpatrick, ed., *Writings of Washington*, XXIII, 86–87.
2. Ephraim Blaine, commissary general of purchases.
3. Difficulties in driving cattle southward are apparent in RM to the Governor of New Jersey, and to the Governor of New York, both September 6, and Heath to RM, October 4 and 17, 1781.
4. Heath replied on September 12.

To Chevalier de La Luzerne

[*Philadelphia*], *Wednesday Morning*, [*September 5, 1781*]. "Mr. Morris presents his Compliments to His Excelly. the Minister of France and sends the Pilot abovementioned [1] because he beleives the Character given of him by Mr Taylor to be just. The Minister can best determine if his Services may be wanted." [2]

MS: Ofcl LbC, DLC.
1. Peter Goffigan. See John M. Taylor to RM, September 4.
2. This letter probably was enclosed in RM to Chevalier de Chastellux, September 5. La Luzerne's reply of the same date has not been found.

To Le Couteulx and Company

Philada. 5th. September 1781.

Gentlemen

I have already written you by this Conveyance [1] and now add these Lines to enclose you a further List of Bills from No. 159 to 173 inclusive amounting to seventy seven thousand seven hundred Livres Tournois.[2]

The great Delay the Franklin has met with [3] gave Occasion to this further Draft on you and I depend these Bills will meet due honor on their being presented for Acceptance. I am Gentlemen your obedient humble Servant

RM.

MS: Ofcl LbC, DLC.
1. RM probably refers to his letter of August 26.
2. Enclosure not found.
3. The *Franklin* arrived at Philadelphia on June 21 after a protracted voyage from France. RM, however, might have had in mind the delay arising from a suit brought in a Philadelphia court attaching part of its cargo, consisting of clothing owned by the state of Virginia, which had been consigned to him. For details on this matter, see the Virginia Delegates in Congress to the Supreme Executive Council of Pennsylvania, [ca. July 9, 1781], and to Thomas Nelson, August 20, 1781, Hutchinson and Rutland, eds., *Madison Papers,* III, 184–185, 231.

To the Governor of Maryland
(Thomas Sim Lee)

Office of Finance 5. Sepr. 1781.

Sir

I was honored with your Letter in Council of the thirty first of August last by Express on Sunday Evening. I pray leave to return you my sincere Acknowlegements for it and to assure you that I derive the most Sensible Pleasure from those Promises of Vigor and Exertion which it contains. I shall rely entirely on those Promises and hope that the punctual Performance will spread Ease and Plenty thro our Camp.

The Situation of Maryland is so different at present from what it was that I cannot ask for the supply of Rum required by Congress; but as a great Quantity of Wiskey is made in your State I wish that agreably to these Resolutions of twenty fifth February and fifth November 1780 Whiskey may be supplied in Lieu of Rum. This will answer the Purposes of the Soldiery as well as the other and I will provide Rum for the Officers in this City. I have communicated your Letter to the Commander in Chief and he either has already written or will write by this Post upon the Subject [1] wherefore it is unnecessary for me to mention the Pleasure he has received from the Contents.

I am very respectfully your Excellency's Most obedient and humble Servant.

RM

MS: Ofcl LbC, DLC.
1. While writing to Governor Lee from Mount Vernon on September 11 in praise of the "Spirit of Exertion" prevailing in Maryland and "the happy Prospect of receiving very effectual Supports from you," Washington begged for "the most expeditious Relief" in the form of provisions for the army, particularly flour. Four days later, Washington wrote from his headquarters at Williamsburg that supplies expected in Virginia had failed, and urged Lee to forward all the provisions he could. Washington to Governor Thomas Sim Lee, September 11 and 15, 1781, Fitzpatrick, ed., *Writings of Washington*, XXIII, 112, 115–116.

From Chevalier de La Luzerne

[*Philadelphia, September 5, 1781.* In a letter of this date to Chevalier de Chastellux, RM acknowledged the receipt of a "Note of this Morning" from La Luzerne concerning Peter Goffigan, a pilot recommended to RM by John M. Taylor in a letter of September 4. *Letter not found.*]

From John Lloyd, Jr.

[*Danbury, Connecticut? September 5, 1781.* On September 18 RM wrote to Lloyd: "I have been favored with your Letter of the fifth Instant, enclosing one from the honorable Mr. Elsworth of the third." *Letter not found.*]

From the Navy Board of the Eastern Department

Navy Board Eastern Department
Honble. Robert Morris Esqr.   Boston Septemr. 5. 1781
Sir

Since our last of the 29th. Ultimo we have delivered your Letter to the Governor; [1] this we did the next morning after we received it but not having any Answer have made our Application to him this day desiring he would inform us what dependence we might make on receiving from the Treasury of this Common Wealth a Supply of money for fitting out the two Frigates in this harbour; if we should receive an Answer before the post goes we shall Inclose you a Copy; [2] whether we do or not our knowledge of the State of the Treasury is such as makes it our duty to tell you that very little Confidence can be placed in being Supplyed from that quarter unless some extraordinary Change takes place in the paper money and as delays contract in their operation those Advantages you mention as the Consequences of dispatch we wish to avoid them and flatter our selves some other resource will be devised; to be sure this will be Slow if ever Sufficient. The Alliance is in the Road and if we had money might be soon Equipped and Manned; the last is the principal business and requires more time than all the rest and yet it cannot be begun with any success untill we are able to pay the Bounties. One Side of the Deane is cleaned and she will soon be in a Condition to enter men. Inclosed you will please to find a recommendation of the Governor and Council for the Exchange of Capt. Edwards who was taken by the Alliance; great numbers of merchants &c have Joined in an Application for that purpose and so universal is the desire that he may be permitted to go in the Cartel bound to Nfoundland that there is no resisting it. [3] We have therefore Complyed and at present propose to take his parole to be Exchanged for Capt. Nicholson [4] or Harding [5] as Congress shall choose; you will therefore please to give the necessary directions. We are Sir with respect Your most humble Servants

Wm Vernon
J Warren

MS: LbC, Letterbook of the Navy Board of the Eastern Department, DLC.

1. Writing to the Navy Board on August 4, RM enclosed a letter of the same date to Governor John Hancock of Massachusetts requesting the state to furnish the board with funds to equip the frigates *Alliance* and *Deane* for sea.

2. The governor's answer was a promise to lay the matter before the next session of the legislature. See the Navy Board of the Eastern Department to RM, September 12.

3. Captain Sampson Edwards (1745–1840) commanded the British man-of-war *Atalanta*, which, with the *Trespassy*, was captured on May 28, 1781, by Captain John Barry of the *Alliance*. While the British prisoners taken in this engagement were placed on board the *Trespassy* and dispatched for Saint John, Newfoundland, on May 30 in conjunction with a cartel for the exchange of American prisoners there, Captain Edwards was taken to Boston on the *Alliance*. When it became known that Rear Admiral Richard Edwards (d. 1794), commanding officer at Saint John, desired the exchange of his nephew, the merchants of Boston and Salem petitioned Governor John Hancock and the Massachusetts Council to expedite the exchange of Captain Edwards in consideration for the admiral's "Humanity and Kindness" to, and his efforts "to alleviate the Horrors of War" for, American prisoners held there. This "Friend to the Rights of Humanity," declared the petitioners, "has for two years past immediately released the Prisoners taken by those under his Command and sent them home in Cartel Ships without waiting for any to return in Exchange." On August 27 the Council ordered copies of the petitions sent to the Navy Board with the recommendation that it exchange Captain Edwards "for an Officer of equal Rank and permit him to return to Newfound Land by the Cartel destined for that Place." William Bell Clark, *Gallant John Barry, 1745–1803: The Story of a Naval Hero of Two Wars* (New York, 1938), 221–226; Clowes, *Royal Navy*, III, 415, 567, IV, 195; the undated petitions of the merchants of Salem and Boston and the action of the Massachusetts Council are in Massachusetts Archives, CLXXI, 474–478a, M-Ar; see also notes to RM to the President of Congress, June 22, 1781 (first and second letters).

4. Captain James Nicholson, commanding the frigate *Trumbull*, was captured by the British en route to Havana early in August (see notes to Diary, August 15). Evidently soon paroled or exchanged, he was in Philadelphia in November (see Diary, November 17, 1781). For RM's efforts to secure his release, see RM to the President of Congress, September 24, to the Navy Board of the Eastern Department, September 25, and to the Board of War, September 25 and 29.

5. Captain Seth Harding (1734–1814) of Connecticut, a successful captain in the state navy during the early years of the Revolution, was selected by Congress on September 25, 1778, to command the Continental frigate *Confederacy*. He raided merchant vessels and did convoy service until his vessel was captured on April 14, 1781. Taken to New York, Harding was immediately released on parole and went to New London, Connecticut, where he remained until his exchange, which was delayed until May 1782 because the Americans had not captured a British naval prisoner of comparable rank. *DAB;* James L. Howard, *Seth Harding, Mariner: A Naval Picture of the Revolution* (New Haven, 1930), 144–153.

From the Quartermaster General
(Timothy Pickering)

Philadelphia Septr. 5. 1781

Sir

Two deputy waggon masters and one deputy commissary of Forage for themselves and seven conductors and forage masters, one clerk to the Waggon master General and four expresses, took up cloathing yesterday to the amount of the inclosed orders.[1] The Deputy Waggon Masters and Deputy Commissary of Forage have exceeded in value what I expected they would purchase for themselves and their conductors and forage masters: but this it seems they thought was the only opportunity they should meet with of getting cloathing; and as the same is furnished as so much pay it would be immaterial, were it not for the present scarcity of Money. I directed my pay Master [2] to get the time of payment postponed as long as possible: but he could obtain credit only to the days mentioned in the orders. I have the honour to be very respectfully Sir your most obedient Servant

TP. QMG

MS: LbC, WDC, DNA.

1. The order, which has not been found, was probably that for £37.10 referred to by RM in his Diary, September 8.

2. Peter Anspach of New York, probably a descendant of early eighteenth-century Palatine emigrants, was paymaster of the Quartermaster Department, a position he apparently held as early as April 1778 and retained until 1783 or early 1784. In May 1784 he is referred to as assistant quartermaster. He also held a lieutenant's commission in a New York artillery regiment in 1782 and 1783. Walter A. Knittle, *The Early Eighteenth Century Palatine Emigration: A British Government Redemptioner Project to Manufacture Naval Stores* (Philadelphia, 1937), 283, 293; Heitman, *Register;* Anspach to John Marston, April 24, 1778, "Notes and Queries," *PMHB,* XXXVI (1912), 502; Anspach *et al.* to Thomas Mifflin, March 8, 1780, PCC, no. 78, XVI, 13–16; John Lamb to George Clinton, August 10, 1781, Hastings and Holden, eds., *Clinton Papers,* VII, 188; Pickering to Anspach *et al.,* June 17, 1782, to Anspach, July 3 and December 13, 1782, and May 4, 1784, WDC, no. 85, pp. 42, 72–73, no. 90, p. 57, and no. 88, p. 24.

From the Governor of Virginia (Thomas Nelson)

Richmond, Septr. 5. 1781

Sir

Your Letters of July 16th. and Augt. 23d. with a Copy of July 25, the original of which has not been received,[1] are all come to hand. At present I can do little more than acknowledge the Receipt of them, but shall lose no Time in paying that Attention to their Contents, which their Importance requires. A Person has been for some Time employed in liquidating the Accounts between the United States and this State.[2] Another is engaged in settling the Accounts of the Specific Supplies furnished by this State.[3] Both these, as soon as they are finished, shall be transmitted to you. In general I may observe that this Country has far exceeded the Requisitions of Congress in its Advance of most of the Specific Supplies.[4]

The Assembly of this State meets on the first Day of October. If you can be enabled to execute the Duties of your Office agreeably to your Wishes, I am persuaded America will feel the good Effects of it; and I hope you will believe that private Friendship as well as Regard for the public Welfare will prompt me to lend you every Assistance which my Situation and Abilities give me the Power of furnishing.[5] I am &c.

Robert Morris

ENDORSED: To Honble. Robert Morris Esqr./Superintendant of Finance/Septr. 5. 1781
MS: ADft, Vi.
1. RM's letters of July 16 and 25, 1781, were circulars to the governors of the states. Gouverneur Morris sent a copy of the July 25 circular to Governor Nelson on August 11. RM's letter of August 23 requested the delivery of specific supplies for the operations against Cornwallis in Virginia.
2. On the settlement of state accounts with the Union, see notes to RM's Circular to the Governors of the States, July 25, and RM to the President of Congress, August 28, 1781.
3. On specific supply requisitions, see notes to John Morin Scott to RM, May 30.
4. Here the following words were excised: "except in Salt, and in that Article there is just a small Deficiency." In their place were substituted the words "when we have fallen short in one we exceeded in others," also struck out.
5. RM replied on September 18.

Diary: September 6, 1781

Wrote 4 Letters to His Excellency The Commdr. in Chief of this date.[1]
Wrote a Letter to the Governour of the State of N York.
Wrote a Letter to Matthew Ridley Esqr. Baltimore.
Wrote a Letter to Mr P. Audibert, Depty. P[ay] Master.
Wrote a Letter to His Excellency, Count De Rochambeau.
Wrote a Letter to The Governour of New Jersey.

1. The first two of these four letters to Washington were written at Chester, Pennsylvania, the last two at the Office of Finance. Except for a fifth letter concerning a deserter, designated by the editors as the last Chester letter, the correspondence is arranged according to the Official Letterbook sequence.

To Philip Audibert

Office of Finance 6. Sepr 1781.

Sir,

With this Letter I deliver you a Letter to His Excellency the Count de Rochambeau.[1] In Consequence of which he will give you the Sum of twenty thousand Dollars for the Purpose of paying one Month's Pay to the Officers and Soldiers of the Line under the Command of Major Genl Lincoln, for which Sum you will give duplicate Receipts.[2]

I did expect that in Consequence of my Instructions to you [3] I should have received a Return of the precise Sum Necessary for the above Purpose, and I am much disappointed to learn that no such Return is made out.

I deliver you a Letter to the Commander in Chief which you will take Care of.[4] When you have received the Money from the Count you will take Genl Washington's Orders for the Disposition of it and having paid the military Officers and the Soldiers their Month's Pay bring with you your Accounts and Vouchers with whatever Balance may be remaining. Return as speedily as you can and upon your Return I will give such further Directions as may be necessary.

I am Sir your most obedient and humble Servant

RM.

MSS: Ofcl LbC, DLC; copy, Manuscript File, WDC, DNA; copy, Washington Papers, DLC.

1. RM to Comte de Rochambeau, September 6. Audibert was deputy paymaster general.
2. See Diary, September 1–5, for the background of this transaction.
3. See RM to Audibert, September 4.
4. RM to Washington, September 6 (fourth letter), in which a copy of this letter to Audibert was enclosed. Audibert also delivered RM's fifth letter of that date to Washington.

To the Governor of New Jersey (William Livingston)

Office of Finance 6th. September 1781.

Sir

The Commissary General has just now, by Letter,[1] given me the disagreeable Information, that from the Want of Money to Pay the Pasturage of Cattle thro your State, the Droves intended for the Support of the Army now acting to the Southward cannot be brought on; to the very great Detriment of the Service.[2] Under such Circumstances, it becomes my Duty to pray your Assistance, and I know but two Modes in which the Object can be accomplished. The one is by the Payment of the Money to the Commissary for the Purpose. But this I fear will not be in your Power, I therefore only mention it as preferable to all others if practicable. The other Mode is by granting Warrants to impress Pasturage. I presume the State have undoubtedly vested your Excellency with sufficient Powers for the Purpose, and therefore I must pray that you will exercise them.[3]

This Letter will be delivered you by Mr. Morton,[4] one of the Commissary's Deputies who will wait your Excellency's Orders. With all possible Respect I have the Honor to be Sir Your Excellency's Most Obedient and humble Servant

Robt Morris

His Excellency
The Govr. of New Jersey

ENDORSED: Letter from Mr Robert/Morris 6 Sepr 1781
MSS: LS, William Livingston Papers, NN; Ofcl LbC, DLC.

1. Letter from Commissary General of Purchases Ephraim Blaine not found.

2. On the supply of cattle for Washington's Virginia operations, see RM to William Heath, September 5, and Heath to RM, September 12.

3. New Jersey had instituted a coercive procurement system, but the impressment powers associated with it were not lodged in the governor, but rather in a state superintendent of purchases and county contractors created by an act of December 25, 1779. The contractors were at first empowered to buy supplies with paper money or certificates, the inhabitants being subject to fine if they refused to sell, and to impress wagons, teams, and boats to transport the supplies. In subsequent acts the legislature enlarged the impressment powers of the contractors, who were the agents entrusted with the state's compliance with congressional specific supply requisitions, by authorizing them to impress any kind of supplies and transport, as well as pasturage for horses and cattle, and to make payment in certificates at adjudicated prices. At the time RM wrote this letter, however, the legislature was backing away from this arbitrary procedure. By an act of June 8, 1781, the legislature curtailed the powers of the contractors, discontinuing impressments, and on December 29, 1781, abolished the offices of superintendent of purchases and county contractors. *Acts of the General Assembly of the State of New-Jersey, At a Session begun at Trenton on the 26th Day of October, 1779* . . . (Trenton, 1780), 41–47, 69–72, 116–120; *Acts of the Fifth General Assembly of the State of New-Jersey, At a Session begun at Trenton on the 24th Day of October, 1780* . . . (Trenton, 1781), 6–10, 80–81; *Acts of the Sixth General Assembly of the State of New-Jersey, At a Session begun at Trenton on the 23d Day of October, 1781* . . . (Trenton, 1782), 47.

4. George Morton, cashier and bookkeeper in the office of the commissary general of purchases at Philadelphia. See the Roster of the Commissariat of Purchases, July 1, 1781, enclosed in the Commissary General of Purchases to RM, July 2, 1781.

To the Governor of New York
(George Clinton)

Office of Finance 6. Sepr. 1781.

Sir,

The Commissary Genl.[1] will have Occasion to employ some Persons to drive Cattle from the Eastward to the Head of Elk for the Supply of the Southern Army.[2] As he has no Money they will necessarily Want it. I hope the Treasury of New York will be in such Situation as will enable you to make the necessary Advances which cannot be considerable. This I must entreat you to do as it will be of very great Benefit to the Public Service. Any Monies paid to this

Use shall be carried to the Credit of the State upon the Requisitions of Congress. With very great Respect I have the Honor to be your Excelly's most obedient and humble Servant

RM

MS: Ofcl LbC, DLC.
1. Commissary General of Purchases Ephraim Blaine.
2. See RM to William Heath, September 5, and Heath to RM, September 12.

To Matthew Ridley

Chester [Pennsylvania] 6. Septemr. 1781.

Dear Sir,

I received yours of the fourth last Evening at this Place [1] and sincerely rejoice with you in the agreable Inteligence it contains.

I beg you will exert yourself to compleat the three thousand Barrels of Flour mentioned in former Letters as soon as possible they being intended for the Use of the Fleet.[2] After it is done let me know whether more can be had for the same Price because I may perhaps have Occasion to Order more in which Case I shall probably apply to you. I am very respectfully Sir your most obedient and humble Servant

RM.

MS: Ofcl LbC, DLC.
1. Letter not found. See Diary, September 1–5, for RM's journey to Chester.
2. On this transaction, see the documents cited in the notes to RM to John Holker, August 7.

To Comte de Rochambeau

Office of Finance 6 Sepr. 1781.

Sir,

In Consequence of the Conversation I had the Honor to hold with your Excellency Yesterday and of your Promise to Supply to the United States the Sum of twenty thousand Dollars for an immediate Purpose to be replaced on the first Day of October next,[1] I have directed Mr Philip Audibert the Bearer of this Letter to wait upon you.[2] I shall be much obliged to your Excellency if you will be pleased to direct that the above Sum be paid to Mr. Audibert and that duplicate Receipts be taken of him one of which I pray may be transmitted to me. I will take Care that the Money be replaced, at the Time agreed upon.[3] With every Wish for the most brilliant Success to the allied Arms and for your own personal Glory I am very respectfully Your Excellency's Most obedient and humble Servant

RM.

MSS: Ofcl LbC, DLC; copy, George Washington Papers, DLC.

1. For details of this conversation and agreement, see Diary, September 1–5.

2. See RM to Philip Audibert, September 6.

3. A copy of this letter was enclosed in RM to Washington, September 6 (fourth letter).

To George Washington

[Chester, Pennsylvania, September 6, 1781]

Dear General [1]

Permit me most sincerely to congratulate you on the Arrival of the french Fleet and to express my warmest Wishes for the Success of your future operations.[2]

As soon as I arrive at Philadelphia I shall give Directions for the Deputy Paymaster to repair to the Head of Elk and make Payment of a Month's Pay in Specie to the Detachment under the Command of Genl. Lincoln.[3] I wish the States had enabled me to do more, but it is to be lamented that the Supineness of the several Legislatures still leaves the Servants of the Public to struggle with unmerited Distresses. It shall however be a Part of my Business to rouse them into Exertion and I hope soon to see the Army better paid than heretofore, and I confide that your Excellency will with every other Public Officer exert your Influence to aid me in this necessary Task.

With the greatest Respect I have the Honor to be your Excellency's most obedient and humble Servant

Robt Morris

His Excellency Genl. Washington

PS. I shall send the 500 Guineas by the Pay Master, as they were left behind by your Excy.[4]

ENDORSED: Chester 6th. Septemr 1781/from/Hono Robt Morris Esqr/answered previous to [Receipt?]

MSS: LS, Washington Papers, DLC; Ofcl LbC, DLC.

1. Except for the postscript (see note 4 below), the text of this letter is in the writing of Gouverneur Morris, who accompanied RM to Chester. See Diary, September 1–5.

2. It was while riding three miles south of Chester on September 5 that Washington received dispatches from an express announcing the arrival of de Grasse's fleet in Chesapeake Bay. On the day this letter was written, Washington travelled via Christiana, Delaware, to the Head of Elk on the Chesapeake, in Maryland, where he replied to RM on September 7. Freeman, *Washington*, V, 321, 323.

Jean Baptiste Donatien de Vimeur, Comte de Rochambeau. Drawing by Gabriel Jacques de Saint-Aubin.

3. See RM to Philip Audibert, September 6. For RM's conference with Rochambeau at Chester on September 5, during which he secured a loan of $20,000 for payment to American troops detached to Virginia, see Diary, September 1–5.

4. This postscript, in RM's writing, was omitted from the Ofcl LbC. In his letter of August 17, Washington had requested 500 guineas in specie for secret services.

To George Washington

Chester [Pennsylvania] 6 Sepr. 1781.[1]

Dear General

Since writing my Letter of this Morning [2] I reflect that as it is now late and it may be long before Mr. Audibert the Paymaster can get down, I wish therefore that if in the intermediate Time you should find it necessary you would direct the Receipt of the Money by some trusty Person and the Payment of the Month's Pay. Audibert will bring the Order for receiving it &ca. and the Accounts can be then adjusted. I am respectfully your most obedient and humble Servant

Robt Morris

MSS: LS, Vail Collection, NHi; Ofcl LbC, DLC.
    1. The text of this letter is in the writing of Gouverneur Morris.
    2. See the preceding letter.

To George Washington

Chester [Pennsylvania] 6 Septr. 1781.

Several Worthy People and particularly the Romish Priest [1] and Mrs. Fitzsimmons [2] have interested themselves in favour of a Criminal under Sentence of Death for Desertion. I dont know his Name but he is in Philada Goal.[3] Your Excy is the best judge of propriety in such cases and I am sensible of the impropriety of such applications but as I promised to speak to your Excy and lost the Opportunity I desired Colo. Smith [4] to mention it and now repeat the matter that I may not have to accuse myself of Neglect. This is a Young Man and may become a good Soldier hereafter. Tomorrow is fixed for his Execution, therefore if Mercy is extended the order shou'd be instantly sent.[5] I ever am Your Excys Sincere and devoted Servant

R Morris

His Excy Genl. Washington

MS: ALS, Washington Papers, DLC.
    1. Probably either the Reverend Ferdinand Farmer (1720–1786) or the Reverend Robert Molyneux, the two Roman Catholic priests in Philadelphia during the Revolu-

tion. J. Thomas Scharf and Thompson Westcott, *History of Philadelphia, 1609–1884* (Philadelphia, 1884), II, 1372; John F. Quirk, "Father Ferdinand Farmer, S.J.: An Apostolic Missionary in Three States," United States Catholic Historical Society, *Historical Records and Studies,* VI, pt. 2 (1912), 235–248.

2. Mrs. Catherine Meade Fitzsimons was the wife of Thomas Fitzsimons (1741–1811), an Irish Catholic who emigrated to Philadelphia in his youth, became a successful merchant, soldier, and politician, represented Pennsylvania in the Continental Congress, 1782–1783, and in the United States Congress, 1789–1795, was a director of the Bank of North America from its inception until 1803, and went bankrupt in 1805 as as result of his involvement in RM's land speculations. *Biog. Dir. Cong.; DAB;* Lewis, *Bank of North America,* 120; William Graham Sumner, *The Financier and the Finances of the American Revolution* (New York, 1891), II, 292, 293, 294.

3. Obsolete form of "gaol." *OED.*

4. Lieutenant Colonel William Stephens Smith, an aide to Washington.

5. Washington's reply of September 7 (second letter), enclosing a pardon, has not been found. It reached the Office of Finance on September 8, the day after the nameless deserter had been executed. See Diary, and RM to Washington, both September 10.

To George Washington

Office of Finance
Sept 6th. 1781

Dear General

I had the Honor to send you two Letters [1] this Morning by Major Clarkson.[2] This will be delivered you by Mr Audibert the Paymaster and encloses No 1 a Copy of my Letter to him and No 2 a Copy of my Letter to the Count de Rochambeau.[3]

As it was not in Contemplation to make any Payments to the Civil Staff of the Detachment so the Heads of the Departments have made their seperate Applications to me for Money and I shall let them have what may prudently be spared.[4]

It is possible that the Sum of twenty thousand Dollars may be insufficient in which Case I am to request of your Excellency that you would make Application to the Count for the Deficiency and I will readily replace the Whole on the first of October.[5] I am with the greatest Respect and sincerest Attachment your Excellency's most Obedient

Robt Morris

His Excellency George Washington Esqr.
General and Commandr. in Chief &Ca &Ca.

ENDORSED: Office of Finance 6th Sepr 1781/from/Hono. Robt Morris Esqr/answered
MSS: LS, Washington Papers, DLC; Ofcl LbC, DLC.

1. See RM to Washington, September 6 (first and second letters).

2. Major Matthew Clarkson (1758–1825) of New York, who fought at the battles of Long Island and Saratoga, had been aide-de-camp to Benedict Arnold. Reproved

by Congress in 1779 for showing disrespect to the civilian authorities of Pennsylvania, Clarkson was summoned before Congress and reprimanded from the chair. At his request, Congress approved his transfer to the southern army where he served until the end of the war on the staff of Major General Benjamin Lincoln, in which capacity he was the bearer of the letter printed here. Following Lincoln's election as Secretary at War, Clarkson became assistant secretary late in 1781 or early 1782. On July 2, 1782, Congress granted his request for a leave of absence from the army to serve as a volunteer in the combined French and Spanish forces in the West Indies. *DAB; JCC,* XIII, 247–250, 360–362.

3. See RM to Philip Audibert, and to Comte de Rochambeau, both September 6.

4. See, for example, the applications of Commissary General of Purchases Ephraim Blaine and Commissary General of Issues Charles Stewart in the Diary, September 1–5, 7, and 9, and that of Quartermaster General Timothy Pickering in his letter to RM, September 6.

5. For the background of RM's loan from Rochambeau for one month's pay for the troops marching south for operations against Cornwallis in Virginia, see Diary, September 1–5, and notes.

To George Washington

Office of Finance 6th. September 1781.

Dear General

The bearer Mr. Audibert will deliver you five hundred Guineas as for secret Service Money according to the request made in your Letter of the 17th. of August last from Dobbs's Ferry.[1] I had directed Mr. Audibert to bring with him the ballance which might remain of the 20,000 Dollars after paying the Troops, but upon Consideration I think it will be best if there be any Ballance that it should be paid to the Use of your Excellency's Table.

You will perceive by my Letter to Mr. Audibert[2] that he is directed to take your Order wherefore I am now to request that your Excellency will be pleased to order the Payment of this Ballance for the Purpose above mentioned and direct a proper Receipt to be given to the Paymaster.[3] I am respectfully Your Excellency's Most Obedient and humble Servant

Robt Morris

His Excellency General Washington

ENDORSED: Office of Finance 6th Sepr 1781/from Hono Robert Morris Esqr/answered
MSS: LS, Washington Papers, DLC; Ofcl LbC, DLC.

1. See RM to Washington, September 6 (first letter), and Washington to RM, September 7.

2. RM to Philip Audibert, September 6.

3. Because the sum ultimately required for one month's pay exceeded the amount furnished by Rochambeau, no balance remained. See notes to Diary, September 1–5.

From the Commissary General of Purchases
(Ephraim Blaine)

[*Philadelphia, September 6, 1781*. See RM to the Governor of New Jersey, September 6, for the receipt and purport of this letter. *Letter not found.*]

From the Quartermaster General
(Timothy Pickering)

Philada. Septr. 6. 1781

Sir

Since the Estimate of pay necessary for my department was laid before you,[1] I have received some fresh applications from persons for whom I at first thought it was not so necessary to provide, particularly the conductors of ox teams: but as the object of their march could not be announced, they came on not so well provided as they ought to have been. However, if they can receive each one months pay they will make that suffice for themselves and their teamsters to whom they are answerable for their pay.

The director of my artificers with sixteen men has joined since the former estimate was made. The superintendant of the horse yard and his people had not come up, and I forgot them.

As you proposed making up a months pay for the detachment, I have added my deputy and Assistant to the present list; and if a months pay could be allowed to me it would greatly oblige me.

I do not know whether other staff officers have received more or less pay than those in my department: but excepting about half a months pay which I long ago gave the latter in paper money, I believe they have received nothing these eighteen months. The situation of officers of the line is much more eligible, for they have received several months pay within that time from their respective states, besides cloathing.[2] I have the honour to be very respectfully Sir your most obedient servant [3]

Tim: Pickering
QMG

MS: LbC, WDC, DNA.
   1. This estimate has not been found.
   2. Congress on April 10, 1780, authorized the states to pay current salaries due to their troops in Continental service who were enlisted for three years or for the duration of the war. State contributions, however, did not go to regiments not attached to state lines, nor to military personnel drawn from the lines to serve in

the Quartermaster or other departments connected with the army, a policy which Washington deplored as destructive of morale. The general army reorganization of October 3, 1780, consolidated all Continental troops except Hazen's regiment into state lines but still left staff officers unattached. In 1782 Congress, at RM's recommendation, insisted upon centralized Continental disbursements and withdrew its authorization of direct state payments to the troops. See Ferguson, *Power of the Purse*, 50, 141–142; Washington to the President of Congress, April 3 and August 20, and to John Sullivan, December 17, 1780, Fitzpatrick, ed., *Writings of Washington*, XVIII, 207–211, XIX, 402–413, XX, 488–491; *JCC*, XXIII, 631.

3. No reply to this letter has been found, but see Diary, September 11.

From George Washington

Christiana [Delaware] 6th. Septr. 1781

Dear Sir

Capt. Machin [1] of the Artillery is detached to pursue some deserters from that Corps; he will have occasion for some Money for expences. If you can advance him about £10. it will be sufficient,[2] and will oblige the public as well as Dear Sir Yours

G. W

Honble. Robert Morris

ENDORSED: Christina 6th Sep 1781/to/Hono Robt Morris Esqr.
MSS: Dft in the writing of David Cobb, Washington Papers, DLC; Varick transcript, Washington Papers, DLC.

1. Thomas Machin (d. 1816) of Massachusetts, a second lieutenant in a Massachusetts artillery regiment at the battle of Bunker Hill, became a lieutenant in Henry Knox's regiment of Continental artillery in December 1775, attained the rank of captain on August 21, 1780, and served until June 1783. Heitman, *Register*.

2. RM received this letter and complied with Washington's request on September 7. See Diary of that date.

From George Washington

Head of Elk [Maryland] 6th Septemr 1781.

Dear Sir

Every Day discovers to me the increasing Necessity of some Money for the Troops. I hope by this Time you are provided to give a Month's Pay. I find it of the last Importance to hasten forward myself to join the Marquis [1] as soon as possible. I may leave this in a few Hours. I cannot do It however, without intreating you in the warmest Terms to send on a Months Pay at least, with all the Expedition possible.[2] I wish it to come on the Wings of Speed. I am Dear Sir &c

GW

Hono Robt Morris

ENDORSED: Head of Elk/6th Sepr 1781/to/Hono Robt Morris
MSS: Dft in the writing of Jonathan Trumbull, Jr., Washington Papers, DLC; Varick transcript, Washington Papers, DLC.
1. Marquis de Lafayette.
2. See Diary, September 1–5, and notes, and RM to Washington, September 6 (first, second, fourth, and fifth letters).

Diary: September 7, 1781

Wrote a Letter to The honorable James Lovell Esqr. respecting Mr Bingham &Ca.

Issued on Mr Swanwick per Genl. Washingtons Order in favor of Capt Mackin of Artillery £10.[1]

Issued a warrant on Mr Swanwick in favour of Colo Pickering Q[uarter] M[aster] Genl. £18.15.

Issued a Warrant on Mr Swanwick for my Expences and Assistants to Chester, on Public Business. £27.1.[2]

Had received early this Morning a Letter from the Commander in Chief,[3] requesting that the above ten pounds to be paid to Capt Mackin who is detach'd in search of Deserters from his Corps.

Wrote a Letter to Wm. Turnbull and Co.

Charls. Stewart Esqr., Commissary Genl. of Issues, applied for Money for his department; postponed untill tomorrow.[4]

Received a Letter from His Excellency The Commander in Chief, urging me to send forward a Months pay for the Troops under Genl. Lincoln.[5] This being done already and Mr Pierce the Paymaster Genl. calling at the same time I desired him to proceed immediately to the Head of Elk to compleat the payment of the Troops agreable to the instructions given his Deputy Mr Audibert.[6] Mr Pierce tells me that he has Money with him to pay the Troops of the Connecticut line a Months pay having received the same from that State. Wherefore I desire him to pay them only One Months pay that they may be on a footing with the rest and the State shall have Credit with the United States for the Money he will retain on that Account.[7]

The honble. Mr. Jenifer made application to have Mr Stone [8] of Maryland his relation employed as a Clerk in this Office and if his Abilities equal the Duties he has to perform I shall be glad of a Person of his Character; he is to come on Tryal.

Colol Blaine Commissary Genl. applied respecting Rum. I agreed to pay his engagements for that Article.[9]

Several Applications respecting the Bills drawn at Charles Town by Genl. Lincoln and accepted by the Treasury Board but not being prepared to Complete that Business, Obliged to put them off with a Promise to do it soon as in my power.[10]

Received a Letter from Colo. Pickering the Q[uarter] Ms. [Master] Genel. to Supply Fifty Dollars for the use of Mr Dewit [11] The Military Surveyor which I complied with.

Mr. Scott of York Town calld about his Account of Supplies at that place from July 20th untill the Contract took effect.[12] Referred the Settlement to Colo Morgan [13] on behalf of the State and promised on receipt of his Certificate to pay the Balance.

Mr. Blaine calld about completeing the Contract for Fort Pitt. Proposed some Amendants to the additional Articles sent from the Board of War and transmitted them to the Board.[14]

Colol. Hay applies for Money to buy Flour Casks to contain the flour called for by Congress from the State of New York.[15] I decline it because no Provision is made by Congress for the purpose and every State may make a like Application. He then requested a Sum sufficient for that Purpose to be advanced for the purchase of Forage which he can Obtain on State Certificates and would apply the Money in purchasing Casks. I decline it, declaring I will never grant Money ostensibly for one purpose and really for another. He then mentions that the State has furnished beyond its Proportion of Forage and may by the public Wants be called on to do it again. I agree to receive one Article in Lieu of another according to the Proportion fixed by the Prices of the several Articles of specific Supplies in the Resolutions of Congress.[16]

Conferred with Mr Brown [17] on the means of adjusting the Affairs of the Marine. With Genl. Varnum and Mr Cornell [18] on the Ways and Means of bringing forward the Money from Boston.[19] With the latter about liquidating his Warrant.[20] With Mr Duane respecting an Advance of Money to Colo Laurens.[21] Received a Note from the Chevr. Dubuisson requesting Bills at a long Sight in discharge of his Pay due [22] which I declined and referred him to the Treasury for a Certificate in the usual Form. Examined the House where the Board of Admiralty sat; determined to give it up and save the Rent to the public.[23]

1. See the fifth paragraph of this Diary entry.
2. For RM's journey to Chester, Pennsylvania, see Diary, September 1–5.
3. Washington to RM, September 6 (first letter).
4. See Diary, September 9.
5. See Washington to RM, September 6 (second letter).
6. See RM to Philip Audibert, September 6.
7. On state payments to troops in the Continental line, see notes to the Quartermaster General to RM, September 6.

8. Walter Stone (d. 1791), a member of a prominent Maryland family and the nephew of Daniel of St. Thomas Jenifer, a member of Congress from Maryland, was hired as a clerk in the Office of Finance on September 18. Although Jenifer believed RM would be "the means of making [Stone's] fortune," such was not the case, and he continued as clerk until June 1782 when he left to join his brothers in an abortive venture in Maryland tobacco. In March 1783 Stone became a clerk in the office of the Secretary for Foreign Affairs, but later that year returned to Maryland where he worked as a clerk in the state government, a position he held until May 1784. Thereafter he established himself in business and maintained an occasional correspondence with RM. Butterfield, ed., *Rush Letters*, I, 575n.; Sanders, *Executive Departments*, 111n.–112n.; Daniel of St. Thomas Jenifer to Thomas Stone, July 23, 1781, Sir Henry Clinton Papers, MiU-C; Walter to Thomas Stone, June 27, 1782, Stone Family Papers, MdHi; Thomas to Walter Stone, March 30, 1783, MdBJ-G; RM to Walter Stone, December 5, 1790, Gratz Collection, PHi; Diary, September 17 and 18, 1781, and March 26, 1782. The editors are indebted to Mrs. Jean H. Vivian of Plateville, Wisconsin, for the research on which this note is based.

9. See Diary, September 1–5 and 11.

10. For the background of this subject, see Diary, July 25 and 28, and RM to the President of Congress, July 25, 1781, and notes. Later references to these bills may be traced in RM to the President of Congress, September 28, and Report of a Committee of Congress, October 8, 1781.

11. Letter not found. Simeon DeWitt (1756–1834), a New York surveyor and mapmaker, had been appointed assistant to Robert Erskine, geographer of the Continental army, in 1778, and on Washington's recommendation was elected by Congress on December 4, 1780, to succeed the deceased Erskine. Accompanying the detachment of the Continental army marching from New York to Virginia for operations against Cornwallis, DeWitt and his assistants were ordered to survey the surrounding country, for which purpose he wrote from Trenton requesting money from Quartermaster General Timothy Pickering, who applied to RM. In May 1784 DeWitt became surveyor general of New York, an office he held for fifty years. *DAB;* Washington to the President of Congress, November 26, 1780, Fitzpatrick, ed., *Writings of Washington*, XX, 400; DeWitt to Pickering, August 31, 1781, Manuscript File, no. 23980, WDC.

12. See RM to William Scott, August 25.

13. Colonel Jacob Morgan, Jr., superintendent of the Pennsylvania county commissioners of purchases.

14. These contract amendments have not been found. RM advertised for the Fort Pitt contract on July 14 and completed it with Commissary General of Purchases Ephraim Blaine and Michael Huffnagle on September 12. See Diary of that date.

15. For the exchanges between RM and Udny Hay, New York State supply agent, at Washington's headquarters in Dobbs Ferry, New York, see Hay to RM, RM to Hay, to the Governor of New York, and to the Commissary General of Issues, all August 15, and Diary, August 21.

16 The specific supply requisitions of February 25 and November 4, 1780, evaluated in specie the articles requested of the states.

17. John Brown (1748–1833) of Pennsylvania was born in Ireland and emigrated at an early age to Philadelphia where he was employed by Willing, Morris and Company. No doubt because of RM, who later acknowledged that he "knew him well and reposed perfect confidence in him," Brown became secretary of the Marine Committee of Congress not long after its establishment in December 1775 and for a time was clerk to the Secret Committee of Trade and its successor, the Committee of Commerce. Brown was appointed secretary of the Pennsylvania Board of War in 1777 and, like RM, was an anticonstitutionalist in state politics. Upon the reorganization of the Marine Department, Congress, on December 3, 1779, elected him secretary of the Board of Admiralty, a position he held until RM's appointment as Agent of Marine on September 7. Thoroughly conversant with Continental naval matters,

Brown was sent to Boston later in the month by RM to report on conditions in the department and to speed its consolidation under his authority. Emelin Knox Parker, "A Biographical Sketch of John Brown," revised (typescript, Carlisle, Pa., 1935), in PHi; Campbell, *Sons of St. Patrick,* 100; *JCC,* XI, 658, XIII, 81, 165, 166, 169; Paullin, ed., *Out-Letters,* II, *passim;* see also notes to John Langdon to RM, April 20, 1781; headnote to RM to the President of Congress, September 8; Diary, September 17 and 19; and RM to Brown, September 19.

18. James Mitchell Varnum of Rhode Island was major general of the state militia and a member of Congress. Ezekiel Cornell (1733–1800) of Rhode Island was brigadier general of the state's forces from 1776 until 1780, when he was elected to Congress. On November 21 Congress named him one of its members of the Board of War and on December 29 a noncongressional commissioner of the board, an appointment which vacated his seat in Congress. He remained on the board until November 19, 1781, when he resumed his seat in Congress. RM appointed Cornell inspector for the main army on September 19, 1782. *Biog. Dir. Cong.;* Burnett, ed., *Letters,* V, 506n., VI, li; RM's Commission to Cornell, September 19, 1782.

19. An allusion to the specie from France which arrived at Boston with John Laurens on August 25. For its transportation to Philadelphia, see Diary, September 10.

20. On the motion of James Mitchell Varnum, Congress on September 10 recommended to Rhode Island that it pay a warrant for $557 specie, originally drawn in Cornell's favor on the Pennsylvania loan office, and charge this sum against the United States.

21. James Duane, a member of Congress from New York, headed a committee appointed on September 3 to consider Colonel John Laurens's report on his European mission. The subject of the conversation was no doubt Laurens's expense account, which, according to Duane, amounted to less than 300 guineas and the balance of his salary during his absence. On September 8 RM authorized an advance of $720 in hard money against the salary due him. See Diary, September 8; and James Duane to Robert R. Livingston, September 11, 1781, Burnett, ed., *Letters,* VI, 216.

22. Letter not found. Following his exchange (see notes to Diary, August 9), Chevalier Charles François Dubuysson des Hays asked Congress on August 31 for permission to return to France with Congress's testimonial of his services and to discharge his back pay in bills of exchange. Congress on September 4 and 5 responded with a handsome tribute and authorized the Board of War to place him on an equal footing with other army officers with respect to his back pay, to liquidate his pay in specie up to that date, and to award him a certificate for the balance, but did not give him bills of exchange. Nor, as this Diary entry shows, would RM advance any bills of exchange against his back pay. Dubuysson to the President of Congress, August 31, 1781, PCC, no. 78, VII, 403–404.

23. See Diary, September 22 and 24.

To James Lovell

Philadelphia September 7th. 1781.

Sir

Agreeable to your desire I have had a Conference with Mr Bingham relative to his demands on the Public in Compensation of his Services as Political Agent in Martinique to the Committee of Secret Correspondence.[1] I have also seen a Copy of the Instructions given him at his departure for that Island.[2] And I recollect perfectly well

that it was then the intention that the Committee of Secret Correspondence should pay his expences, and the Secret Committee by
employing him for Commercial purposes and allowing the usual
Commissions on their business would afford a sufficient Compensation for his time &c. The Expences he has Charged being already
allowed I need only observe that Mr. Bingham alledges he has not
made a Charge of more than one third of what he actually expended
during his residence in Martinique,[3] altho' the amount of that
Charge is I am perswaded as much or more than either the Committee or himself expected it to be, but it seems living is much dearer
there then he or they Supposed.

The Committee of Secret Correspondence did not contract to pay
Mr. Bingham any Salary nor had they Authority to do it therefore
it must have been their intention and his expectation that he should
receive a farther Compensation from Congress if their allowances
in the way I have mentioned proved insufficient. It is very certain
that the emoluments arising to Mr. Bingham from the Commercial
business of Congress fell short of what was expected, and it is
equally Certain that the inconvenience arising from his constant
Advances and Consequent distresses must far outballance the Commissions he drew. At the same time I must confess that the aggre-
gate Sum of Mr. Bingham's Charges for Expenses, Commissions
and Salary Amounts to more Money than at the time of his Appointment I had any Idea of; to this he Answers that his living Cost much
higher than we could then Suppose, that his Commission was ab-
sorped in losses and disappointments Consequent to his advances,
and the Salary he charges far short of what has been allow'd other
Gentlemen who had much less trouble and were not more usefull.
I am Sir Your very Obedient Servant

Robt Morris

The Honorable
James Lovell Esqr.

endorsed: Sept. 7. 1781/Hon: R Morris/respecting Mr. Bingham's/Salary and Expences.
mss: LS, PCC, DNA; Ofcl LbC, DLC.
    1. See Lovell to RM, July 5, 1781, and notes, for a discussion of William Bingham's
claims, and Bingham to RM, August 7.
    2. RM probably refers to the Committee of Secret Correspondence (Benjamin
Franklin, Benjamin Harrison, John Dickinson, and RM) to Bingham, June 3, 1776,
Simon Gratz Collection, PHi.
    3. If RM refers to Bingham's claim for living expenses, there is a discrepancy
between his statement and Bingham's declaration, made in his August 7 letter to
RM, that he had charged only £110,000 of a total of £161,000 livres of Martinique,
or a little more than two-thirds of the expenses.

To William Turnbull and Company

Office of Finance 7th. Septemr. 1781 [1]

Gentlemen

Your Letter of the twenty third of August last to the Secretary of the Admiralty was laid before Congress, and by that honble. Body referred to me.[2] I think the shortest way to accomplish the Business is to request you will purchase the same quantity of Bread and Flour of equal Quality with that which Mr Holker kindly lent to that Board [3] and on your rendering the Accounts for the same I will cause the Amount to be immediately paid.

I trust that your Regard to the Public Interest added to the usual considerations of mercantile Oeconomy will induce you to procure these Supplies on the best Terms, And remain Gentlemen your obedient Servant

RM.

MS: Ofcl LbC, DLC.
1. A memorandum of this letter appears in the Diary, September 8.
2. Turnbull's letter to John Brown, which has not been found, was referred to RM by Congress on August 25.
3. On this transaction, see Diary, June 15, 23, and 30, July 14, and August 24, 1781.

From Chevalier Dubuysson

[*Philadelphia, September 7, 1781.* In his Diary of this date RM wrote: "Received a Note from the Chevr. Dubuisson requesting Bills at a long Sight in discharge of his Pay due." For RM's response, see Diary, September 7. *Letter not found.*]

From the Quartermaster General (Timothy Pickering)

[*Philadelphia, September 7, 1781.* RM entered the following memorandum in his Diary on this date: "Received a Letter from Colo. Pickering the Q[uarter] Ms. [Master] Genel. to Supply Fifty Dollars for the use of Mr Dewit The Military Surveyor which I complied with." *Letter not found.*]

From George Washington

Head of Elk [Maryland] 7th Septemr 1781

Dear Sir

I have received your two favors of Yesterday No. 1 and 2.[1]

I find myself so pressed by Circumstances, that It will be impossible for me to stay at this Place 'till the Payment of the Money comitted to Mr Audibert can be effected. I must leave the Head of Elk this Afternoon or early Tomorrow Morning. I shall however leave Instructions with G[eneral] Lincoln to do all that is necessary on the Occasion.[2]

The Sum of 20,000 Dollars will fall much short of the Sum necessary.[3]

The 500 Guineas on my own Account I have received.[4]

I have the Honor to be &c

GW

Hono Robt Morris Esqr

ENDORSED: Head of Elk. 7th Sepr 1781/to/Hono R Morris Esqr
MSS: Dft in the writing of Jonathan Trumbull, Jr., Washington Papers, DLC; Varick transcript, Washington Papers, DLC.
1. A reference to RM to Washington, September 6 (first and second letters).
2. Before leaving Head of Elk on September 8, Washington issued instructions to Paymaster General John Pierce for distributing the month's pay to the troops. See Washington to Pierce, September 8, 1781, Fitzpatrick, ed., *Writings of Washington,* XXIII, 107.
3. A prediction that proved to be correct. See notes to Diary, September 1–5.
4. RM replied on September 10.

From George Washington

[*Head of Elk, Maryland, September 7, 1781.* This letter, which was in reply to RM to Washington, September 6 (third letter), and contained a pardon for a deserter jailed in Philadelphia and sentenced to death, was received by RM on September 8. See Diary, and RM to Washington, both September 10. *Letter not found.*]

Diary: September 8, 1781

Issued a Warrant on Mr Swanwick in favour of Colo J Laurens for £270 on Account of The U. States.[1]

Issued a Warrant on Mr Swanwick in favour of P Anspach, per Colo Pickerings Order £37.10.[2]

Issued a Warrant on Mr Swanwick in favour of Saml. Hodgdon £187.10.[3]

Colol. Jno Laurens applied for Money on account of 9 Months pay due to him. I answerd that I cannot consistently order the pay, therefore offered my private purse, which he declined and I directed the above advance of 720 hard dollars on Account of the U States for which he is to Account.[4]

Mr. Turnbull on behalf of Mr Holker for a return of the Bread and Flour lent by him to the Admiralty Board. Wrote him an Order to purchase the same on the best terms and promised to pay the Amount.[5]

Directed Mr Swanwick to pay in State Money at two for One Sundry Warrants in the hands of Officers of the civil List who are in distress for want of their Money.[6]

The State Agent of Virginia Mr Thomas Pleasant [7] Offered me a Draft on his principal Mr Ross [8] for Amount of my Advances to their Delegates which he assures me will be paid, and therefore I accept it with intention to remit the same for the Use of the Commander in Chiefs Table.[9]

Genl. St Clair called for Money to move his Detachment. I require an estimate of the Sum Wanted; [10] at his request I have given Colo. Miles orders to provide 100 Tents &Ca.[11]

The Honorable Mr Matthews [12] called on me this Evening to offer the Services of a Gentleman for supplying the Southern Army With Provision, &Ca but as I have no Funds provided by Congress for that purpose and as the Southern States have no other way of furnishing their Quota of Specific Supplies than by feeding that Army, I necessarily declined Medling with that Business.[13]

Met with The Honorable C. Gadsden Lieut. Govern. and four of the Council of So Carolina respecting the advance ordered to them by Congress and finding them very Averse to the Measures which had been proposed by the Honble Mr Matthews for procuring that Money upon Acceptances of mine in their favour and having observed at a former interview how much their Feelings were hurt by this proposal I determined to supply the Money and told them so, which seemed very satisfactory. I requested that the Money might be repaid by the State soon as Convenient And if given to Genl. Green his draft on the Treasurer would be satisfactory.[14]

Wrote a Letter to His Excellency The President of Congress.

1. See Diary, September 7, and notes, and the fourth paragraph of this Diary.
2. See the Quartermaster General to RM, September 5.
3. Hodgdon was commissary general of military stores.
4. See note 1 above.

5. Undoubtedly RM to William Turnbull and Company, September 7.

6. Congress on July 10 appointed a committee to confer with RM "on the means for paying the salaries due to the civil officers and clerks of the boards or offices immediately under Congress." Following the committee's report, Congress on July 30 directed RM to discharge the back pay and future salaries of officers on the civil list. Following a report of the Board of Treasury on August 2, however, the board was put in charge of the matter. Its warrants for salaries due were to be drawn on the Continental loan office of Pennsylvania, and the loan officer, if he found it convenient, could discharge the warrant in new emission money, whose value was to be calculated according to a scale of depreciation drawn up monthly by the board. Presumably, this arrangement interfered with the Financier's disposition of the funds which Pennsylvania had placed under his management, for on August 24 Congress rescinded its directive to the board and restored to RM responsibility for supporting the civil list.

7. Thomas Pleasants, Jr. (ca. 1737–1804), a Virginia planter and merchant, was a state commercial agent acting under David Ross (see note 8 below). Hutchinson and Rutland, eds., *Madison Papers*, III, 87n.

8. David Ross (ca. 1736–1817), a merchant of Petersburg, Virginia, who owned ships, plantations, and an iron mine, was the state's commercial agent from December 27, 1780, until May 24, 1782, in which capacity he corresponded with RM. *Ibid.,* 60n.

9. See RM to Washington, September 13.

10. For the background of St. Clair's application, see notes to Diary, August 28.

11. See the President of Pennsylvania to RM, September 4, and notes.

12. John Mathews, a South Carolina delegate to Congress.

13. RM did not extend army supply contracts to the southern states until 1783. Ver Steeg, *Morris,* 161–162.

14. See Diary, August 29, and notes, and RM to Nathanael Greene, September 10.

To the President of Congress
(Thomas McKean)

In this letter Morris accepted the duties of Agent of Marine which Congress assigned to him on September 7. Upon his assumption of the office, the functions of the Board of Admiralty, the regional navy boards, and other civil officers of the Marine Department were to cease and all the papers of these agencies were to be delivered to the Financier.[1]

The creation of a Secretary of Marine and other "great officers of state"[2] had long been contemplated by those who wished to instill energy and vigor into Continental government. While the consolidation of executive departments under single individuals was under discussion in Congress in 1780 and 1781, Gouverneur Morris drew a composite portrait of the man most qualified to manage the Continental naval business. "A Minister of the Marine," he wrote, "should be a man of plain good sense, and a good economist, firm but not harsh; well acquainted with sea affairs, such as the construction, fitting, and victualing of ships, the conduct and manœuvre on a cruise and in action, the nautical face of the earth, and maritime phenomena. He should also know the temper, manners, and disposition of sailors; for all which purposes it is proper, that he should have been bred to that business, and have followed it, in peace and in war, in a military, and commercial capacity. His principles and manners should be absolutely republican, and his circumstances not indigent."[3]

By most of these standards, which were probably not drawn with him in mind, Robert Morris was peculiarly suited to administer the naval affairs of the United States. When, in December 1775, Congress appointed him to the committee which the following year became known as the Marine Committee, Morris already had over fifteen years of experience in the management of merchant ships as a partner in the firm of Willing and Morris. Thenceforth, he played a significant role in the development of the infant American navy, serving for a time as vice-president of the Marine Committee. During the winter of 1776–1777 when Congress withdrew from Philadelphia to Baltimore, he directed the Continental navy virtually unaided.[4] His retirement from Congress in November 1778 left a gap in naval administration which was not easily filled. "Mr. Morris has left the Marien," an acquaintance reported, "and Every thing is Going to the devel as fast [as it] can." [5]

The following autumn, on October 28, 1779, Congress reconstituted the Marine Department by establishing a Board of Admiralty to supersede the Marine Committee, but the dissolution of the board was in turn forecast on February 7, 1781, when Congress, which had embarked upon a general reorganization of its executive departments, provided for a Secretary of Marine, as well as a Superintendent of Finance and a Secretary at War. The resolution creating the office of Secretary of Marine declared "that it shall be the duty of the Secretary of Marine, to examine into and report to Congress the present state of the navy, a register of the officers in and out of command, and the dates of their respective commissions; and an account of all the naval and other stores belonging to that department; to form estimates of all pay, equipments and supplies necessary for the navy; and from time to time to report such estimates to the Superintendant of Finance, that he may take measures for providing for the expences, in such manner as may best suit the condition of the public treasury; to superintend and direct the execution of all resolutions of Congress respecting naval preparations; to make out, seal and countersign all marine commissions, keep registers thereof, and publish annually a list of all appointments; to report to Congress the officers and agents necessary to assist him in the business of his department; and in general to execute all the duties and powers specified in the act of Congress constituting the Board of Admiralty." Despite the last clause, it is significant that Congress did not specifically authorize the Secretary of Marine, as it had the Marine Committee and the Board of Admiralty, to direct the movements of Continental vessels.[6] On February 9 Congress voted an annual salary of $5,000 for the office (reduced to $4,000 specie on October 1) and on February 27 offered the post to Major General Alexander McDougall, who declined it rather than give up his rank in the army. Meanwhile, naval affairs continued under the direction of the Board of Admiralty, the navy boards, and Continental agents.

It was not until June that the movement for reconstituting the Marine Department made further headway in Congress. Most of the proposals introduced exhibited a tendency to put Morris in charge of marine affairs and to enlarge his discretionary authority in handling them. A motion of Meriwether Smith of Pennsylvania criticizing the "inefficient and expensive" management of the Continental navy, considered June 28, provided for the dissolution of all existing boards, entrusted Morris with the settlement of their accounts, and recommended that until the election of a

Secretary of Marine, the Superintendent of Finance be authorized to appoint "some discreet Agent to manage the Navy of these States under his order and Inspection." [7] The committee to which this motion was assigned reported the substance of Smith's original proposals on July 6 with additional recommendations that the election of the Secretary of Marine be postponed until November and that, in the meantime, Morris be specifically empowered to fit out and employ American naval vessels. Postponement of the Secretary's election was apparently favored by those who wanted to place the navy permanently under Morris's direction. However, in a roll call vote in which approval required the assent of a majority of the states, the proposal to entrust naval affairs to Morris was defeated by a sectional vote of five (Pennsylvania, Maryland, Virginia, North Carolina, and Georgia) in favor against four (New Hampshire, Massachusetts, Connecticut, and Delaware) opposed, with South Carolina divided. Rhode Island, with only one delegate in attendance, was unable to vote, and New York and New Jersey were unrepresented.

This vote notwithstanding, a committee report of July 18 showed a steady drift toward Morris. It was proposed that, instead of a Secretary, Congress appoint an "Agent" of Marine and give him unhampered power to "direct, fit out, equip *and employ* the several vessels of war belonging to these States." Although not formally adopted at this time, the idea of an Agent of Marine foreshadowed Morris's appointment, as did Congress's increasing delegation of naval responsibilities to him. At Morris's request, Congress had assigned Continental prize money to him on June 23 for the completion of the frigate *America* under construction at Portsmouth, New Hampshire, and on July 11 had placed the frigate *Trumbull* under his orders.[8] By this time, the Board of Admiralty was virtually defunct. After receiving the board's last official report on July 7, Congress granted one of its members, William Ellery, a leave of absence on July 9, accepted the resignation of another member, Francis Lewis, on July 17, and on the following day transferred the care of marine prisoners to the commissary of prisoners acting under the Board of War. The admiralty seal was ordered to be deposited with the secretary of Congress.

Faced with the difficulty of selecting a competent Secretary of Marine and the high expense of his salary at a time when its pitifully small navy—by this time reduced to two ships [9]—did not require a high-level appointment, Congress was governed by expediency.[10] On August 29 it resolved to appoint an Agent of Marine at an annual salary of $1,500 to "direct, fit out, equip and employ" American naval vessels, to supervise the sale of Continental prizes, and deposit the proceeds with the Superintendent of Finance. The functions of the Board of Admiralty, the navy boards, and all civil officers appointed under them were to cease with the election of the agent, who was to settle their accounts. In one respect the act fell short of previous resolutions; although the Agent of Marine was given general authority over Continental vessels, he was required to exercise it "according to such instructions as he shall, from time to time, receive from Congress."

Morris was elected Agent of Marine on September 7 when Congress, "not being able to agree on the Person at the Day of Election . . . thought proper to devolve the Duties of that Station pro tempore on the Superintendant of Finance." [11] Quickly calling the attention of Congress to the restrictions on his powers, Morris pointed out in a letter of September 10 that while the reorganization of the Marine Department was pending he had outfitted the *Alliance* and the *Deane* for a cruise.[12] He requested Congress's wishes in the matter, or, if it were intended that he have control over these ships, that his authority be explicitly confirmed. Congress's response on September 12 went beyond Morris's letter of request and authorized him to fit out and employ all Continental ships of war "in such manner as shall appear to him best calculated to promote the interest of these United States."

"I accepted the Marine Agency," Morris later recalled, "simply with a View to save the Expence of the Department." [13] Besides saving Congress the expense of his salary as agent, Morris consolidated the finance and marine offices by moving the Office of Finance to the quarters formerly occupied by the Board of Admiralty.[14] On September 19 he began to dispatch orders for the dismissal of the navy boards and Continental marine agents, the settlement of their accounts, and the collection of their books and papers.[15] Internal resistance to the reorganization lingered at the Navy Board of the Eastern Department at Boston, which, by agreement, continued to outfit ships until March 1782.[16] As Agent of Marine, however, Morris remained in control of naval affairs until his resignation as Superintendent of Finance on November 1, 1784.

Office of Finance 8th. Septembr. 1781.

Sir

I received last Evening an Act of the United States in Congress assembled of the 7th. Instant by which it is resolved that untill an Agent of Marine shall be appointed by Congress, all the Duties, Powers and Authority assigned to the said Agent be devolved upon and executed by the Superintendant of Finance.

There are many Reasons why I would have wished that this Burthen had been laid on other Shoulders or that at least I might have been permitted to appoint a temporary Agent untill the further Pleasure of Congress. As it is I shall undertake the Task however contrary to my Inclinations and inconsistent with the many Duties which press heavily upon me, because it will at least save Money to the Public.

But on this Subject I have to observe that true Oeconomy according to my Ideas of it consists in employing a sufficient Number of proper Persons to perform the Public Business. I wish the accounts of the Marine Department may be speedily Settled. I am sure I need not hint to Congress my anxiety to see Measures taken and steadily pursued for adjusting all the Public Accounts. I am sure they must participate in every Sentiment of Concern which I feel on that Occasion. I am sure that it will meet with every expeditious Attention which the Importance of it can demand.[17]

I am Sir with all possible Respect Your Excellency's Most Obedient and humble Servant

Robt Morris

His Excellency The President of Congress

ENDORSED: Letter Sept 8. 1781/Super: finance/Accepting the Office of Agent/of Marine and urging the settle/ment of accounts of Marine department
MSS: LS, PCC, DNA; Ofcl LbC, DLC.

1. For a fuller discussion of some of the agencies and individuals in the Marine Department, see notes to John Langdon to RM, April 20, Diary, June 23 and 29, and RM to John Bradford, June 27, 1781. The evolution of Continental marine administration up to 1781 may be traced in detail in Sanders, *Executive Departments,* ch. ii, and Paullin, *Navy of the American Revolution,* chs. i, iii–vii.

2. A phrase used by Alexander Hamilton in a letter to James Duane, September 3, 1780, Syrett and Cooke, eds., *Hamilton Papers,* II, 408.

3. As quoted from an undated document in Jared Sparks, *The Life of Gouverneur Morris, with Selections from His Correspondence and Miscellaneous Papers* (Boston, 1832), I, 229–230.

4. For RM's work on the Marine Committee, a subject which has never been fully treated, see Oberholtzer, *Morris,* 24–26, and Paullin, *Navy of the American Revolution,* 86, 90, 173–176.

5. Thomas Bell to John Paul Jones, November 1778, quoted in Morison, *John Paul Jones,* 180.

6. See Paullin, *Navy of the American Revolution,* 188, 217.

7. Another motion, by James Madison, probably drafted on June 28 as a substitute for Smith's, proposed that until the election of a Secretary of Marine, "the management and direction of the navy" be committed to the Superintendent of Finance or his agents. It is doubtful whether Madison actually introduced his motion. On June 29, however, a committee appointed to consider a motion of Theodorick Bland of Virginia recommended the active employment of the Continental navy in preparation for joint operations with the French fleet, suggested that the Board of Admiralty deliver to the Financier a review of the vessels of the Continental navy and an estimate of the money needed to equip them for operations, and proposed that RM report to Congress "the ways and means for fitting the said vessels for sea." Congress never acted on the committee's report. On Madison's motion, see *JCC,* XX, 708n.; and Hutchinson and Rutland, eds., *Madison Papers,* III, 167n.–168n.

8. See RM to the President of Congress, June 22, 1781 (first and second letters), and to the Board of Admiralty, July 11, 1781, and notes. For RM's orders regarding the *Trumbull,* see RM to James Nicholson (two letters), and to Robert Smith, all July 17, 1781.

9. The New York Delegates in Congress to the Governor of New York, September 9, 1781, Burnett, ed., *Letters,* VI, 214–215. Besides the 74-gun frigate *America* on the stocks at Portsmouth, New Hampshire, and the frigate *Bourbon* under construction at Chatham, Connecticut, the two ships in active service were the 36-gun frigate *Alliance* and the 32-gun frigate *Deane,* both of which were awaiting orders at Boston. The 28-gun frigate *Trumbull,* dispatched to Havana by RM, had been captured by the British. See Diary, August 15, and notes; notes to John Jay to RM, September 1 (first letter); and Paullin, *Navy of the American Revolution,* 235.

10. "When the number of our ships and the Circumstances of our Treasury Justify it," Congressman James Duane of New York wrote, "the Appointment of the Minister of the Marine will be seasonable." Duane to George Washington, September 9, 1781, Burnett, ed., *Letters,* VI, 215; see also RM to John Bradford, September 22.

11. RM to John Bradford, September 22.

12. See RM to the Navy Board of the Eastern Department, and to the Governor of Massachusetts, both August 4.

13. RM to Alexander Hamilton, April 16, 1783.

14. See Diary, September 7, 22, and 24.

15. For these orders, see RM to John Brown, September 19, 21, and 22 (three letters), to John Bradford, September 21 and 22, and to John Barry, to the Governor of Massachusetts, to the Navy Board of the Eastern Department, and to Samuel Nicholson, all September 21.

16. Paullin, *Navy of the American Revolution,* 227; William Vernon to John Adams,

April 26, 1782, "Papers of William Vernon and the Navy Board, 1776–1794," Rhode Island Historical Society, *Publications,* n.s., VIII (1900), 273–274. See also the Navy Board of the Eastern Department to RM, February 6, and RM to the Navy Board of the Eastern Department, March 25 and 26, and to John Brown, March 25 and 26, 1782.

17. This letter was read in Congress on September 10. See the endorsement to RM to the President of Congress, September 10.

To the Secretary of Congress (Charles Thomson), with Reply

Saturday Morning [*Philadelphia, September 8, 1781*]. "Mr. Morris's Respects wait on Mr: Thomson. Mr. Thomson has forgotten to send the Account of the Money on board the Resolué the Captains Re [ceipt] and Treasurer's Note. These are immediately wanted." Thomson's subjoined reply of the same date is as follows: "Sent the two papers above referred to N[umbers] 6 [and] 7."[1]

ENDORSED: Letter from R Morris/to Chas Thomson 1781
MS: Letter in the writing of Gouverneur Morris, with autograph reply, PCC, DNA.
1. John Laurens, who accompanied the French treasure carried on the *Résolue,* described the two documents sent to RM by Thomson as follows: "No. 6 is the Chevalier de l'Angle's receipt for the specie on board the frigate *Resolue;* No. 7, the copy of the treasurer's note at Brest." Laurens enclosed them in his letter to the president of Congress of September 2 (Wharton, ed., *Rev. Dipl. Corr.,* IV, 691). The presumption from Thomson's reply to RM must be that the two papers he sent constituted "the Account of the Money on board the Resolué." Concerning related documents Bray Hammond wrote in 1957: "The bill of lading for this specie, put on board *La Résolue* at Brest, the receipt given for it by Governor John Hancock of Massachusetts in Boston, and the receipt given for it by Tench Francis in Philadelphia for Robert Morris . . . are displayed in Carpenters' Hall, Philadelphia." A recent search, however, failed to locate them. Bray Hammond, *Banks and Politics in America from the Revolution to the Civil War* (Princeton, 1957), 50n.; see RM to Tench Francis, September 11 (first letter), and notes, and to Chevalier de Langle, and the Governor of Massachusetts, both September 11.

From César Louis de Baulny

[*September 8, 1781.* On October 1 RM wrote to Baulny: "I was honored with your Favor of the eighth of September last." *Letter not found.*]

From the President of Delaware (Caesar Rodney)

[*Dover, September 8, 1781.* In his Diary, September 11, RM wrote: "Received a Letter from His Excellency Caesar Rodney respecting

Supplies; looks well, but does not require an immediate Answer; dated 8th: instant." *Letter not found.*]

From Benjamin Lincoln

Head of Elk [Maryland] 8th: Sept 1781

Sir

His Excellency General Washington left this place at 4 oClock this morning and directed me to give warrants on Mr. Pierce [1] for the payment of the troops one months pay. Several Corps have been paid. I am just now informed by the paymaster that he has received of Count Rochambeau twenty six thousand and six hundred Dollars,[2] that the several pay abstracts amount to about thirty thousand exclusive of the Military staff and the Corps of sappers and miners which will amount [to] two or three thousand more so that the paymast[er] is short about six thousand dollars; this is embarrassing indeed for part of the troops received their pay before Mr Pierce discovered that the ballance would be against him; it will be difficult if not impossible for us to keep the men quiet who do not receive their pay. I therefore must entreat that six thousand dollars may be sent to the paymaster as soon as possible; the good of the service certainly requires it.[3] I have the honor to be Sir with the highest Esteem your most obedient Servant

BL

Robt. Moriss Esqr.

ENDORSED: Copy to Mr. Morris/Septr. 8th. 1781
MS: ADftS, Lincoln Papers, MHi.
    1. John Pierce, paymaster general.
    2. For details of RM's loan from Comte de Rochambeau to supply one month's pay in specie for the Continental troops marching southward to Virginia, see Diary, September 1–5, and notes, and documents cited there.
    3. RM supplied $6,200 to meet the deficiency. See RM to Lincoln, September 11.

From John Neilson

[*Trenton, New Jersey, September 8, 1781.* On September 17 RM wrote to Neilson: "I am to acknowlege the Receipt of your Letter of the eighth Instant." On the contents of Neilson's letter, see RM to the Governor of New Jersey, September 17. *Letter not found.*]

Diary: September 9, 1781

Colonl. Charles Stewart [1] applied for Money for his department alledging his being obliged to follow the Army. I told him to borrow 400 hard Dollars and draw upon me for them; these dollars are to pay his Officers &Ca.

Genel. St Clair called with an Estimate of pay for his Detachment which I am not yet provided for. [2]

Mr. Audibert the Deputy Paymaster Genel. came up from the Head of Elk for more Money. [3] The Sum supplied there by Order of Count de Rochambeau altho exceeding the 20,000 dollars he agreed to lend me, proves insufficient and the Paymaster Genl. Mr Pierce Writes for about 6500 drs. more. [4]

Received a Letter from Colo. Jno Laurens to the Chevr. de L'angle Commandant of the French Frigate Resolue at Boston. [5] Received also an Account from Colo. Laurens for the Expences of an Express at the City Tavern. This Express Travell'd with Colo. Laurens from Boston and brought the dispatches which were Bulky. I shall direct Mr Swanwick to pay this Account, Amounting to £5.11.3.

1. Commissary general of issues, whose application is first mentioned in Diary, September 7.
2. This estimate was requested by RM on September 8 (see Diary of that date). On the subject of pay for Major General Arthur St. Clair's troops, see notes to Diary, August 28.
3. See Benjamin Lincoln to RM, September 8, and Diary, September 1–5, and notes.
4. It is uncertain whether John Pierce addressed his request to RM; in any case, no such letter has been found.
5. The letter from John Laurens to Chevalier Paul Antoine Marie Fleuriot de Langle (1744–1787) has not been found. Langle, who entered the French navy in 1758, had held a number of commands during the war before being assigned the task of shipping 2.5 million livres in specie to the United States aboard the *Résolue* and convoying two ships with stores valued at 2.2 million livres. On the mission of John Laurens, who landed at Boston with Langle, and the specie shipment, see notes to RM to Benjamin Franklin, July 19; Franklin to RM, July 26 (second letter); and notes to RM to Franklin, August 28, 1781. On Langle, see Hoefer, ed., *Nouvelle biographie générale*, XXIX, 414–416; sketches also appear in Contenson, *Société des Cincinnati*, 179, and Gardiner, *Order of the Cincinnati*, 139. For RM's arrangements for transporting the specie from Boston to Philadelphia, see RM to Tench Francis, September 11 (first letter), and notes, and the documents cited there.

From John Paul Jones

[*Portsmouth, New Hampshire, September 9, 1781.* On September 25
RM wrote to Jones: "Your Letter of the ninth Instant came to Hand
by Yesterdays Post." *Letter not found.*]

Diary: September 10, 1781

This Morning had a pretty long Conversation with Jno. Gibson
Esqr. respecting the Mode of settling Public Accounts, &Ca.[1]

Wrote a Letter to His Excellency Genl. Washington in reply to
his two of 7th instant, and here I must observe that one of those
letters respected a Criminal under Sentence of death.[2] The letter
came to hand on Saturday $^3/_4$ after 11:OClock in the forenoon and
as it contained a pardon, I instantly sent it (by Mr John Brown
Secrety. of the Marine Department) for Genl St Clair whom he could
not find but calling at the Goal[3] he was informd the Criminal had
been executed the day before.

Wrote Letters, to His Excellency the President of Congress.

To Matthias Slough Esqr. Lancaster.[4]

To The Honorable The Board of War.

To The honorable Major Genl. Green, at the Southward.

Received a Letter from the Contractor at Lancaster[5] and Ordered Mr. Swanwick to pay him from 1500 to 1600 dollars on
Account.

Chrisr. Lutz[6] who supplied the Post at Reading from the 20th.
July untill the Contractors begun the Business. He called for the
Balance due him as settled by Colo Jacob Morgan[7] on behalf of the
State of Pensylvania and Orderd him payment £80.16.5$^3/_4$.

Capt. James Willing[8] called to inform of his being exchange[d]
and about his Accounts which I desired might be prepared with
proper Vouchers &Ca in Order for settlement.

Mr. Danl. Clark[9] as Attorney to Oliver Pollock Esqr.[10] came to
Solicit payment of the Debt due to the latter who is like to be ruined
for want of it.

John Gibson Esqr. applied for a Sum of Money about 1900 dollars
to be paid a Spaniard that assisted in the defence of Charles Town
and whose demand Amounts to more than double the Sum he now
asks for, but he is willing to relinquish the other part of his Claim
on being paid this, either in Money or a Bill on Hava. [Havana]
Which I agreed to Supply.[11]

Constant applications for Money some of Which I supply and some must Wait untill Money Comes in.

For Three days past I have been anxiously looking out for a proper person to send to Boston to receive and bring forward to this City the Money lately Arrived there in the Frigate Resolue Capt De L'angle,[12] and as I propose to have a part of that Money invested at Boston in bills of Exchange drawn by Authority of His Most Christain Majesty or of the Honorable Congress at such prices as I judge will produce a Profit upon being sold here, it is therefore necessary to have a gentleman of approved honour and Honesty, of Mercantile knowledge and Abilities and of such an Active Indefatigueable disposition as will be able to surmount difficulties and guard against dangers on the Road, in short a person who has resources in himself to surmount all Obstacles so as finally to accomplish this Business to universal satisfaction by delivering the Treasure safely in this City. Many Gentlemen have Occurred but some are unable to perform this Task, others so engaged that they cannot undertake it, and I have been in much anxiety on the Subject. In the midst of this Anxiety seeing Tench Francis Esqr. and knowing that he possesses the Talents, Abilities and resources necessary I thought of him as entirely proper in every respect. I put the question and he readily declared that he was willing to serve His Country in anything within his Power and that he would most readily go upon this Service. I thought the proposal was pleasing to him as it afforded an Opportunity to shew his firm attachment to the cause of America which some few of his Actions early in the Contest, flowing from an uncommon Warmth of Temper, had rendered dubious in the Eyes of many People [13] but for my Own part as I am fully convinced of his Zeal and Attachment to the interest of the United States, I employ him with pleasure having full Confidence in his Fidelity, Integrity and Abilities. For these reasons, I have agreed with him to proceed tomorrow for Boston and for the greater security of the Treasure I shall direct Major Saml. Nichols [14] of the Marines to go with him to Aid and Assist him throughout. I shall apply to the Board of War to Order such an Escort of dragoons from Boston to Philadelphia as they shall deem sufficient, to write to the commanding Officer at Boston to supply an Ample Guard whilst there also to supply Arms and Ammunition to the Teamsters that they may be in Condition to join the Escort in defence of the Treasure should they be attacked on the Road, and to the honorable General Heath to supply such a Guard of infantry whilst this Money is Travelling through the dangerous part of the Road and to take such other measures as he may judge will render it perfectly safe against every attempt of the Enemy and secure it from all Thieves whatever.[15] I propose that as many bills of Exchange drawn as already mentioned shall be Bought as can be obtained at the price of 75 dollars for Lrs. 525 or any price more in favour of the purchase, for these Reasons: the Sum to be risqued in Waggons and the Weight to be drawn will be lessened, a Profit will certainly result on such purchase and resale here,[16] which will apply towards the Cost or Expence of this Transportation, And by taking the bills of Exchange out of the hands that mean to resell them I shall thereafter be able to establish a more favorable rate of Exchange for those Bills which I am to draw on Account of the United States especially as the Count de Rochambeau has assured me that their Service can be carried on for a long time without their drawing bills again.[17] I propose that Mr Francis should purchase in Boston as many Ox Teams as may be necessary to bring forward this Money by Which I think much expence will be saved for the Oxen will be worth more Money here after performing the service than their first Cost. The Teamsters must be hired and they must be sober, honest and industrious Men if possible. The Bodies of the Ox Carts, We propose, should be taken off and in its place have a Chest fixed on the Axle and on the Tongue so made as just to receive the small Boxes in which the Money must be packed, as many of them as will make about a Ton weight, then the lid of the Chest well Nailed on and finally the whole Chest secured by Iron straps fixed round and lengthways and Welded so that it will be impossible to open or take them off the Carriage untill they arrive here at the Journeys end. The rout I shall recommend is pointed out by Ezekl. Cornell Esqr. Member of the Board of War who is well acquainted with the Country &Ca.[18] Genl Heath will doubtless give the Officers of the Escort the proper Orders for mounting Guard at all Stages and taking proper Positions for safety on the March. Therefore with all these precautions and that attention and industry which I expect from the persons employd we shall in due time be able to apply this Treasure to the Service of the United States which now stands much in need of it. I sent for Major Nicholls [Nicholas] who chearfully agrees to the Journey and says he can be ready tommorrow.[19]

His Excellency The Minister of France [20] applied to me for some Money to supply the Hospital of some Sick Troops and other stragglers left by their Army, the Treasurer of Which [21] had neglected to leave Money for this Purpose. I chearfully embrace the Opportunity of doing this little service to which they are so well entitled.

Colol. Grayson [22] called to inform me he could not dispose of the paper Money which I had paid him at two for one but that he could get the Value advanced for a few days. I desired him to do so, to deposit the money with his Friend and if by that time he could not dispose of it at two for One I would repay the Specie.

In the hurry of Constant applications and interruptions I find it impossible to keep Minutes of occurences as they happen and they are too numerous for Memory to retain even for a short time because fresh matter comes forward every moment, therefore I write Letters, Notes and give Orders or Answers some of which may possibly be Omitted but all of which tend to promote the Public Service.

1. RM's interview with John Gibson, a member of the Board of Treasury, may have been occasioned by the impending reorganization of the Treasury Department, accomplished by congressional ordinance on September 11. See notes to RM's Plan for Arranging the Treasury Department, August 27.

2. Washington's letter about the criminal has not been found. See RM to Washington, September 6 (third letter).

3. Obsolete form of "gaol." *OED.*

4. Letter not found.

5. Henry Dering. See notes to Diary, July 16, 1781.

6. That is, Nicholas Lutz. See notes to Diary, July 10, 1781.

7. Colonel Jacob Morgan, Jr., superintendent of the Pennsylvania county commissioners of purchases.

8. Captain James Willing (1751–1801), brother of Thomas Willing of Willing, Morris and Company, had been a trading partner of Oliver Pollock (see note 10 below) in New Orleans in 1772, lived in Natchez for several years, and returned to Philadelphia in 1777. Later that year, Willing was commissioned a captain in the Continental navy by the Commercial Committee of Congress and ordered to equip a small force at Fort Pitt for the reduction of West Florida and the transport of military stores collected at New Orleans for Congress by Bernardo de Gálvez, governor of Louisiana, with the support of Pollock, then American agent at the port. Willing's expedition left Fort Pitt on January 10, 1778, plundered the loyalists of West Florida (but failed to win that colony for Congress), captured several British prizes on the Mississippi, safely reached New Orleans, and induced Spain to violate its neutrality. Blocked by British forces from returning with the supplies up the Mississippi, Willing left New Orleans for Philadelphia on November 15, 1778, but was captured by the British, imprisoned in New York City, and eventually paroled and permitted to go to Philadelphia until his exchange. Willing's October 1781 petition to Congress requesting settlement of his accounts was referred to the Comptroller of the Treasury, but as late as 1785 they were still not settled. His request for a commission in the Continental line and "such other relief. . . as to equity may seem meet" appears not to have been approved. James Alton James, *Oliver Pollock: The Life and Times of an Unknown Patriot* (New York, 1937), 117–125, 147, 156; Reuben Gold Thwaites and Louise Phelps Kellogg, eds., *Frontier Defense on the Upper Ohio, 1777–1778* (Madison, Wis., 1912), 191n.–193n.; John Caughey, "Willing's Expedition Down the Mississippi, 1778," *Louisiana Historical Quarterly,* XV (1932), 5–36; Willing's memorial to Congress, [October 1781], PCC, no. 42, VIII, 237–240; *JCC,* XXI, 1079, XXVIII, 172n., 459n., XXIX, 620n., 663n.

9. Daniel Clark (d.1799), an Irish-born Philadelphia merchant who later resettled in New Orleans, had advanced 40,000 Mexican dollars from his private fortune to the state of Virginia for military operations in Illinois and claimed to have loaned 54,981 milled dollars to Oliver Pollock for outlays on behalf of Virginia (see note 10 below). In 1782 Clark became RM's agent in Virginia for the tobacco contract

concluded with British merchants under the terms of the capitulation at Yorktown. Campbell, *Sons of St. Patrick*, 104; Hutchinson and Rutland, eds., *Madison Papers*, III, 256n.–257n.; RM to Clark, April 10, 1782.

10. Oliver Pollock (ca. 1737–1823), an Irish merchant who emigrated to Philadelphia ca. 1760 and thence to New Orleans in 1768, won the freedom to trade in Louisiana by helping to provision the governor's army in 1769. Following the outbreak of the American Revolution, Pollock's influence with successive governors of Louisiana was responsible for Spanish assistance to American frontier posts, including, by 1778, some $70,000 in supplies advanced on Pollock's credit by Governor Bernardo de Gálvez. As commercial agent of Congress at New Orleans, an appointment he received early in 1778, Pollock advanced some $300,000 for Congress and the state of Virginia (to the latter for the operations of George Rogers Clark), but by 1781, because their promised remittances failed to materialize, his credit had become exhausted, a development that occasioned Daniel Clark's call on RM.

On the recommendation of the Commercial Committee, Congress on February 6, 1781, already had ordered the Board of Treasury to pass to Pollock's credit $37,836 specie against the United States, the sum to bear an interest of 6 percent until paid. Following his interview with RM, Clark petitioned Congress for the payment of Pollock's claims. His memorial was referred to the Commercial Committee, which recommended on October 11 that the Treasury enter on its books a further specie credit for Pollock of $21,419 with 6 percent interest from February 6. Congress approved this on November 7 with instructions enjoining RM from paying any part of this sum until the measures taken by Pollock to reimburse Gálvez for his outlays had been ascertained. Meanwhile, Clark's efforts for Pollock in Virginia won from the state legislature in December a promise to pay $35,000 of what it owed him. While RM continued in office, he supported Pollock's claims both against the United States and Virginia.

Hoping to discharge his debts, Pollock accepted the post of commercial agent at Havana tendered by Congress on June 2, 1783. His financial obligations still outstanding, Pollock was imprisoned there for debt, was released eighteen months later through the influence of Gálvez, and returned to Philadelphia to press his claims. In December 1785 Congress awarded him a credit of $90,000, though the sum was not paid until 1791. Following the cession of Virginia's western lands to the United States, Congress paid $108,609 of his claims against the state, which pledged to pay the remainder. Pollock returned to New Orleans in 1790, prospered there as a trader, met all his financial obligations, and later resettled in the United States. *DAB;* Hutchinson and Rutland, eds., *Madison Papers*, III, 256n.–257n.; *JCC*, XXI, 1016, 1046–1047, 1078, XXIV, 372; see in general James, *Oliver Pollock;* for RM's correspondence regarding Pollock's claims, see RM to the Governor of Virginia, January 15 and October 29, 1782, to James Duane, October 11, 1782, and to the President of Congress, October 10, 1783, and September 30, 1784, Pollock to RM, September 10, 1783, and August 28, 1784, and RM to Pollock, September 30, 1784.

11. Prior to the British siege of Charleston, South Carolina, Captain Miguel Lorenzo Ysnardy had delivered to the commanding officer of the city eight cannon owned by the King of Spain along with naval stores from his own stock, and both he and his crew had defended one of the bastions during the siege, which continued until the city fell on May 12, 1780. In response to Ysnardy's petition for reimbursement, Congress on June 21 allowed him the value of the articles he had furnished and also awarded him and his crew the same pay and subsistence as artillery men on active duty. On September 5 Congress approved a report of the Board of Treasury valuing the cannon and stores at $1967 and determining his crew's pay at $2237. "From a desire of shewing his attachment to the American cause," Ysnardy declined to accept the latter sum provided that the claim for cannon and supplies furnished was fully satisfied, terms which RM agreed to on September 18. *JCC*, XX, 602; Diary, September 17 and 18.

12. For the background of this subject, see notes to RM to Benjamin Franklin, July 19; also Diary, September 9, 1781, and notes.

13. RM may allude to suspicions of loyalism that were directed at Francis because

his family had been land agents of the Penn family. Robert C. Alberts, *The Golden Voyage: The Life and Times of William Bingham, 1752–1804* (Boston, 1969), 112n.; see also notes to Gouverneur Morris to RM, June 4, 1781.

14. Samuel Nicholas (d. 1790) of Philadelphia, commissioned captain of marines by Congress on November 28, 1775, was the first commissioned officer in the United States Marine Corps. After serving with distinction in the capture of Nassau in the Bahamas in March 1776, he was promoted by Congress on June 25 to the rank of major. He received various assignments thereafter but gravitated into noncombatant duties because departmental regulations forbade an officer of his rank from serving on a frigate, and there were no ships of larger size in the navy at the time. In August 1781 Nicholas asked to be placed on active duty, observing that service on the *America,* a ship-of-the-line whose construction was being hastened by RM, would be commensurate with his rank. While Nicholas's request was being considered in Congress, RM selected him because of his "Activity, Spirit and Talents" to accompany Tench Francis on the mission to Boston, a duty which Nicholas "chearfully" accepted. With the Continental navy reduced to two ships, Congress probably saw no reason to continue his service and on November 22 ordered the settlement of his accounts to August 25, 1781, which it fixed as the date of his retirement from service. William Bell Clark, ed., "The Letters of Captain Nicholas Biddle," *PMHB,* LXXIV (1950), 379n.; Nicholas's commission and documents relating to his early service are in Clark and Morgan, eds., *Naval Documents,* II, 1183, IV, 748–752, V, 623; Nicholas to the President of Congress, August 10, 1781, PCC, no. 78, XVII, 301–302; *JCC,* XXI, 851, 884–885, 942–943, 1028–1029; Diary, and RM to Nicholas, both September 11.

15. See RM to the Board of War, September 10, and notes; also RM to William Heath, September 11. For "the commanding Officer at Boston," Colonel Jabez Hatch, see notes to Diary, September 11.

16. At the rate of exchange RM proposed, he would give 7 livres for $1 in hard money, which was more adverse to the United States than the best rate obtained during the war (6$^1/_4$ livres for $1), but better, presumably, than the current exchange in Philadelphia. On rates of exchange, see RM's Circular to the Governors of the States, October 19, 1781.

17. On the adverse effects of competition with French officials in selling bills of exchange, see RM to La Luzerne, August 2, and notes.

18. RM conferred with Cornell about this matter on September 7 (see Diary of that date).

19. For RM's detailed instructions regarding the transportation of the money and the route to be followed as well as an account of the execution of the plan, see RM to Tench Francis, September 11 (first letter), and notes.

20. Chevalier de La Luzerne.

21. César Louis de Baulny.

22. Colonel William Grayson, who on this day resigned from the Board of War (*JCC,* XXI, 945). The subject of his call on RM has not been further identified.

To the President of Congress (Thomas McKean)

[Philadelphia] 10th. September 1781.

Sir

I perceive that by the Act of Congress of the twenty ninth of August last that the intended Agent of the Marine is directed to fit out, equip and employ the Ships and Vessels of War belonging to the United States according to such Instructions as he shall from time to time receive from Congress.[1]

While this Matter was in Suspense I gave Directions for fitting the Alliance and Deane and sending them on a Cruize, not knowing the Determinations which the United States might make, and being convinced that while they lay in Port an useless Expence must necessarily be incurred.[2] Should there be any particular Object in the Contemplation of Congress wherein to employ these Frigates or should they disapprove of the Directions I have given I shall be happy to be favoured with their Orders, and on the other Hand if it is intended that I should employ these Ships from Time to Time as may to me appear most for the public Interest I shall submit whether it might not be proper that such Intention should be explicitly declared.[3]

I have the Honor to be with all possible Respect Sir Your Excellency's Most Obedient and humble Servant.

Robt Morris

His Excellency
The President of Congress.

ENDORSED: 25/Letters Septr. 8. 10. 1781/from Superintendant of Finance/Read 10./Referred to Mr Mathews/Mr Sherman/Mr S. Smith/Sep/10. That he has ordered the/Alliance and Deane to be fitted out/and sent on a cruise and desiring Orders/if Congress have any particular Object/in Contemplation
MSS: LS, PCC, DNA; Ofcl LbC, DLC.

1. For the background of RM's appointment as Agent of Marine, see the headnote to RM to the President of Congress, September 8.

2. See RM to the Navy Board of the Eastern Department, and to the Governor of Massachusetts, both August 4.

3. Congress on September 12 authorized RM to fit out and employ all ships of the Continental navy without its further instructions.

To Nathanael Greene

Office of Finance 10th. September 1781.

Sir

The Departure of your Aid de Camp Coll. Morris [1] gives me an opportunity of mentioning my Letter to you by Governor Rutledge [2] which I am inform'd got safe to hand. While I congratulate you on the many Successes which you have obtain'd under every Disadvantage Let me also congratulate you on the just Sense of your Merit which is now generally diffused. The Superintendant of Finance in particular, Circumstanced as the American Superintendant is, must give the fullest Applause to an Officer who finds in his own Genius an ample Resource for the want of Men, Money, Cloaths, Arms and Supplies.[3] I have made another attempt to place some Money in your hands by requesting the Lieutt Governor and Council of South Carolina to pay you when Convenient £500, this Currency advanced by Order of Congress to them, their State being Accountable; as I presume they will mention the affair you need not.[4] In order that I may maintain a Correspondence with you free from the Danger of Inspection I enclose a Cypher the use of which you will easily perceive.[5] I shall be very glad to hear from Time to Time such things relative to your Situation as it may be useful to the public for me to know. And I am sure your Regard for the Service will readily induce you to take that Trouble.

I hear with much pain that some of the States do not pay that attention to the Mode of Settling public accounts which is necessary to avoid future Litigations with the United States. They must be Sensible that no Vouchers will be admitted for the Specific Supplies other than those Receipts from the Commissaries and Quarter Masters which the Resolutions of Congress have directed.[6] Should you perceive any Negligence of this sort I must intreat you to make Representations on the Subject immediately and at the same time to let me know the Facts that I may myself represent them.

I hope and trust that the arrival of the French Fleet and the ulterior operations which are now commencing in the Chessapeak will greatly relieve you from the Embarrassments you have hitherto laboured under and turn the Scale of Superiority in our Favour thro' the Southern States. I am very respectfully Sir Your most Obedient and humble Servant

Robt Morris

The Honble Major Genl. Greene

ENDORSED: from Mr. R. Morris/Sept. 10th: 1781/[*At a later date:*] Very hansesome Comp/lements from the Superin/tendant of Finance
MSS: LS, Greene Papers, MiU-C; Ofcl LbC, DLC.
1. Lieutenant Colonel Lewis Morris, Jr. (1752–1824), a nephew of Gouverneur Morris, became brigade major of New York militia in June 1776, served as aide to Major General John Sullivan, August 1776–June 1779, and to Greene thereafter until the end of the war, when he settled in Charleston, South Carolina. Heitman, *Register;* Walter W. Spooner, ed., *Historic Families of America* (New York, 1907–1908), III, 219; notes to Diary, September 13.
2. See RM to Greene, June 12, 1781.
3. RM provided Greene with little support, leaving the southern state governments to furnish him with specific supplies. See Diary, September 8.
4. See Diary, August 29, and notes.
5. On this cipher, see Gouverneur Morris to Greene, September 11, in which it was ultimately enclosed.
6. For the Financier's extended observations on the settlement of state accounts with the Union, see RM to the President of Congress, August 28. On later difficulties arising from unauthorized expenditures and the absence of vouchers to support state claims for disbursements, see Ferguson, *Power of the Purse,* 204–205, 207–208, 210–219.

To Mathias Slough

[*Philadelphia, September 10, 1781.* In the Diary of this date RM entered the following memorandum: "Wrote . . . To Matthias Slough Esqr. Lancaster." *Letter not found.*]

To the Board of War

Office of Finance 10th. Septr. 1781.

Gentlemen

I am about to send off for the Money lately arrived from Boston.[1] It will be necessary that while this money is in Boston it should be properly guarded, that the Teamsters should have Muskets, Bayonets, Cartouches and Cartouch Boxes. That there should be a strong Escort of Cavalry to attend it all the Way and that additional Measures should be taken for the Defence of it thro the dangerous Parts of the States of New York and New Jersey. I am therefore to request that you will give the necessary Orders to the Honble. Major Genl Heath and to the commanding Officer in Boston[2] which will be delivered by the Person or Persons I shall employ to go for this Treasure.

I have the Honor to be Gentlemen, very respectfully your most obedient and humble Servant.

RM.

MS: Ofcl LbC, DLC.
1. On this subject and the individuals mentioned below in this letter, see Diary, September 10 and 11, and notes, and RM to Tench Francis, September 11 (first letter), and notes.
2. For the board's orders to William Heath, dated September 11, 1781, see the *Heath Papers*, III, 240–241; and notes to RM to Tench Francis, September 11 (first letter). As noted in the Diary of September 11, the board also addressed a letter to Governor John Hancock of Massachusetts, but neither this letter nor the one to the commanding officer at Boston has been found.

To George Washington

Office of Finance
September 10th. 1781.

Dear Sir

The sole intent of the present is to acknowledge the receipt of your two Letters of the 7th. Instant; that which related to the

Months pay you wou'd see was answer'd by the Steps previously taken,[1] but I am a good deal disappointed and put to inconvenience by the Money at Elk falling short of the Object which obliges me to send Money thither that was absolutely necessary to fulfill my engagements here.[2] I must struggle thro' these difficulties, but the doing so requires that attention and time which ought to be bestowed upon greater objects.

The letter respecting the Criminal was too late,[3] the poor Fellow was gone. I am sorry for it, and remain Your Excellency's Most Obedient humble Servant

Robt Morris

His Excellency General Washington

ENDORSED: Office of Finance 10th Sept 1781/from/Hono Robert Morris Esqr/Answer to mine
MSS: LS, Washington Papers, DLC; Ofcl LbC, DLC.
   1. For RM's efforts to provide one month's pay in specie for the detachment of Continental troops marching south for operations against Cornwallis in Virginia, see Diary, September 1–5, and documents cited there.
   2. See Benjamin Lincoln to RM, September 8, Diary, September 9, and RM to Lincoln, September 11.
   3. Letter not found. See Diary, September 10.

Gouverneur Morris to Nathanael Greene

[Philadelphia, September 10, 1781] [1]

Dear General,

It is a long time since our Correspondence has been broken asunder. I will not now renew it, for your Trouble, but [whenever you shall have] [2] nothing else to do, if such times happen, I will be glad of an Account of your Situation. In explaining my Motive for the Request I shall give you one to comply with it, tho possibly you have a good Disposition for the Purpose without any other Motive than the Request itself. Europe [knows] little of us and Spain knows less of every thing than the Rest of Europe. The extraordinary Success of your Efforts is as striking in the [gross] Amount as it is wonderful in the Detail. A thousand little [Incide]nts must have [fallen within] your Knowlege calculated to shew our national Character and [Circum]stances beyond what can be [conveyed by] any Coloring which general Exploits or Sufferings will a[dmit of. It wi]ll certainly be useful to put these Things in a Train of Communication but that is not all. Even those marked Moments of Action which come singly forward in official Letters must derive much of [their] Beauty and Splendor from the previous Detail of Situation which official [Letters] cannot and indeed ought not to contain. Colo Morris will [carry] with him a Cypher [3] which will put you at your Ease in sending Letters by any and every Conveyance with the only Precaution of Duplicates where the Uncertainty of the Messenger or Importance of the Matter may render it necessary.

There is a Thing in Agitation here which you are concerned in tho probably you do not know of it. I mean the Appointment of a Minister of War. Many Reasons have induced some Persons to think of you for that Office.[4] I know not whether you would chuse to accept of it but I will candidly tell you that I have on every Occasion mentioned you not only as the proper Person but as the only proper Person. I incline to think that it will be disagreable to you to quit [the busy active] Scene of military Exploit and it is therefore probable [that I have] done you an ill office which you know is not an uncommon Circumstance even with the best Intentions.

I will speak [to you with] great Plainness on this Subject. I know I am doing [what is right] and therefore I will make no Apology. On every Occasion of the Sort there are two Classes of Reasons the one private and the other public. I will notice a few of both and place the latter, as of most Weight, in the foremost Place. The Importance of having the Office [of Secretary] of War well filled is too great to need one Moments Question [even with] those who are but slightly informed. But you who in a long Course of Service have seen, heard, felt and tasted the Consequences of an indigested System. You must see that Matter in all its Lights with the Clearness of Intuition. Now I will venture to say that you are the only Man who can fill the office properly. In this I mean no Compliment, and if you suppose me capable of such Prostration you must have a very improper Idea of me or beleive that I have much less Esteem for you than I really have. You have served as a Major General, as a Quarter Master General and as [a Commander in] a seperate Department. You have had an Opportunity of seeing all America, of examining it critically, of knowing its Soil, its Climate, its [Production, its Man]ners, its Roads, its Rivers, its Communications, its [Tillage, its Arts], its Revenues, its Resources of every Kind. I shall not speak of your Qualities because that Subject cannot well be treated without the appearance of some adulation [but] your Opportunities have been such that moderate Talents to say no more of them must have given you the Superiority [over Genius] however splendid and Industry however Persevering. This is not all. You are unexceptionable among the States and will I am well [convinced be attended] to, respected and supported by all. You are a Soldier [beloved by] your fellow Soldiers and your military Character is such that you will be certain of that Deference which is due from subordinate stations to authority immediately delegated by the Sovereign. There is another Matter of very great Consequence. You are [on terms] not of base Intimacy but sincere Friendship with the Commander in Chief. You are capable of and used to Business which is no trifling Consideration. Finally you will I am sure be upon terms of Confidence with the Superintendant of Finance for you are worthy of each other's Confi[dence]. I am sure I need not tell you how important it is for the Ministry of this Country to be upon such [Terms].

As to private Reasons, altho I know they will be of little [Weight yet it is proper] to take Notice of them. I shall say Nothing [on the Subject of Int]erest or Ease. You ought to be above attending to either and [I think] you are. Your domestic [Happiness] will have just as much weight as [it ought] and must [be left to its own Impressions]. Your Reputation [is an Object] which may be [taken either Way. On the one] Hand you will tell yourself that by pursuing Glory in her [favorite Fields] you must inevitably overtake her and snatch a precious [Sprig of Laurel even] from the Grasp of [Misfortune. On the other] Hand I tell you that the World have agreed before we were born never to seperate Events so as to examine how much has been due to Ability and how much to Chance. And this Agreement has been very faithfully adhered to. The greatest Qualities nay more the best Qualities will receive such a jaundiced [Tint] when viewed thro the Medium of Misfortune as frequently to meet unmerited Condemnation. And who is it that can command the Capriciousness of Chance? I know that every Man has a Confidence in his own good Fortune but I am sure that Prudence will, on Reflection, check and repress this instinctive Emotion. It was for Cæsar to cry to the frighted Fisherman, "fear not you are charged with Cæsar and his Fortune." [5] Had the Boat sunk in the Storm it would have happened fortunately for his Fame that nobody could have told the Story. As it was, Success has given to his Confidence the Lineaments of Heroism. Think my [Friend] that a luckless Moment may hand over your good name to the malicious, the envious and the censorious. Think whether it will not be more secured by Retirement. I know there is Something painful, Something which [looks] like a Want of Spirit in that Idea but remember it will be very difficult for you to add to your Military Reputation and of Consequence you play a great Stake against a small one. Besides in accepting the Office, you will have the Road to Reputation Still open and if the Career you can there run is less splendid, that Disadvantage is compensated by the superior Certainty. There Abilities will decide. If Plans are well laid, if they are judiciously combined, if the System be simple,[6] clear, active, methodical, the Head will be entitled to Respect let the Execution of subordinate Parts be whatever it may.

I have said enough, perhaps more than enough, on this Subject. Receive it from your Friend, and dispose of it as you please. Adieu. Yours

Gouv Morris

ENDORSED: From Mr G. Morris/10th Sept. 1781
MSS: ALS, Greene Papers, DLC; George Washington Greene transcript, CSmH.

1. In view of the controversy surrounding appointments to the executive departments created by Congress (see note 4 below), the evident interest of the Office of Finance in those appointments, and the close relationship existing between RM and Gouverneur Morris, his official assistant, the editors present this letter without assuming that it represents in every detail the opinions of the Financier.

2. Many passages of the ALS are difficult to read because of tears, water stains, and faintness of the ink. All such passages, in square brackets, have been supplied from the transcript, which was prepared in the mid-nineteenth century, presumably before the manuscript became worn.

3. On the cipher carried by Lieutenant Colonel Lewis Morris, Jr., Greene's aide, see Gouverneur Morris to Greene, September 11, and notes.

4. Acting to establish single executives to replace standing boards and committees in the administration of its civilian departments, Congress on February 7, 1781, created, in addition to a Superintendent of Finance and a Secretary of Marine (see notes to Diary, February 7, 1781), a Secretary at War and defined his duties and powers. Unable to agree on a candidate, Congress on February 28 postponed the election until October 1 and instructed the Board of War to continue department business. Although Major Generals John Sullivan, Horatio Gates, and William Heath and President Joseph Reed of Pennsylvania were among those mentioned for the office, the principal candidates were Philip Schuyler, Major Generals Greene and Benjamin Lincoln, and Brigadier General Henry Knox. Schuyler was reported to be the choice of RM and his supporters, but he had engaged in bitter disputes with Congress, had been relieved of his command of the Northern Department in 1777, and had resigned his commission as major general in April 1779 following his acquittal by a court-martial. Although Washington urged him to accept the office if chosen, Schuyler was unenthusiastic, having declared previously that he would never again serve under Congress unless his military rank were restored. Although Schuyler apparently continued to be the Financier's personal choice, Gouverneur Morris doubted that he could be nominated, and in March 1781 advised his friend Robert R. Livingston of New York that "Green will be the man." It is apparent from the letter printed here that Gouverneur Morris hoped to draw out Greene on the subject, and although Gouverneur's opinions on this matter cannot be directly equated with those of the Financier, the possibility remains that by this time Greene had become for the Office of Finance a more realistic candidate than Schuyler. Certainly Greene's views on the necessity of strengthening the powers of Congress and his opposition to legal tender paper currency (see Greene to RM, August 18) found favor with RM. Washington refused to recommend anyone even though he was advised that Congress would ratify his choice. Eventually, Greene, Lincoln, and Knox emerged as serious nominees. Since neither Knox nor Greene could be spared from the army, the first because of his proficiency with artillery and the latter because military operations in the south required his presence, Congress on October 30 elected Lincoln, who accepted the office on November 26 and, in accordance with a previous resolution, was permitted to retain his military rank but not his officer's pay. According to Mary-Jo Kline, the election of Lincoln, a New Englander who was

not intimate with the Office of Finance, "may have been a blessing in disguise," for it served to deflect nascent criticism that the executives elected by Congress constituted a junto. In any case, Greene's November 21 reply indicated little enthusiasm for Morris's proposal. Ezekiel Cornell to Governor William Greene of Rhode Island, February 19, John Sullivan to Washington, March 6 and May 17, Schuyler to Washington, April 3, Gouverneur Morris to Robert R. Livingston, March 14, James Mitchell Varnum to Washington, August 20 and October 2, the President of Congress to Benjamin Lincoln, October 31, 1781, and Samuel Osgood to John Adams, December 7, 1783, Burnett, ed., *Letters*, V, 573n., VI, 11–12, 12n., 26n., 90, 191, 231, 254, VII, 379–380; Washington to Schuyler, February 20 and March 23, 1781, Fitzpatrick, ed., *Writings of Washington*, XXI, 261–262, 360; Schuyler to Washington, February 25, 1781, Washington Papers, DLC; Joseph Reed to Nathanael Greene, November 1, 1781, William B. Reed, *Life and Correspondence of Joseph Reed* (Philadelphia, 1847), II, 375–376; Greene to Gouverneur Morris, November 21, and Morris to Greene, December 24, 1781, both in Greene Papers, MiU-C; Mary-Jo Kline, "Gouverneur Morris and the New Nation, 1775–1788" (unpubl. Ph.D. diss., Columbia University, 1970), 216; Sanders, *Executive Departments*, 98–103; Ferguson, *Power of the Purse*, 119–120.

5. This incident is recounted in Plutarch's *Lives,* trans. Bernadotte Perrin (London, 1914–1926), VII, 535, 537.

6. Transcript: this word omitted.

From John Bondfield

Bordeaux 10 September 1781

Sir

The Dutch have given a Sample of what England has to expect by their rupture with that nation.[1] We hope the example will influence on the other branches of Allies. Spain has landed a body of men on Minorca where the force of Great Britain appears too weak to resist and promises to Spain Success.[2] We expect, A[dmiral] Digby is arrived at New York with reinforcements.[3] They are not considerable, but will give Spirits to the Enemy who appear weaker in every quarter than are their adversaries, but meet no decided check from any; from appearances this Campaign must terminate to their loss. Spain lays Siege to Gibraltar and Minorca; carries on both vigorously.[4] Hyder Aly in India has dispossest them of all their possessions on Coromandel Except Madras say [5] Fort St. George.[6] In the West Indies the french fleet is Superior and all their Islands secured from any attack. On the Coast of America the fleets are equal, and if as reported de Grasse passes the Hurrican[e] Months with you, so considerable a force may be expected to act offensively to advantage. Darby is returned to Torbay.[7] The combined fleets of France and Spain have been seen to the westward of Scilly who thereby shut up the English fleet in the Channel, and prevent them from sending any Succours to the besieged places or to their Colonies or Islands, and may possibly intercept some of the homeward bound fleets, particularly that of Jamaica daily expected. Holland works indefatigably to put to sea a force to meet that of Great Britain, to protect her northern Trade and harrass that of the Enemy; notwithstanding all these formidable enemys stocks in England keep up, that of India excepted, which has dropt from 147 to 135. Had M. Necker remained and an able Minister as the head of The finances of Spain, great things might be expected, but unfortunately the officers in place in both Kingdoms give few Striking Marks of their abilities in their respective departments. Spain under pretence of her treasures being in Mexico and would not risk them on the seas, in imitation of America emitted a paper currency which notwithstanding all the assurances of Government is at present 10 Per Cent below par, and promises a further decline.[8] May Success attend your virtuous exertions is the Sincere wish of all your friends, of which class permit me to be enroled, and believe me to be with Sincere attachment Sir Your most obedient Humble Servant

John Bondfield

ADDRESSED: To/The Honble. Robert Morris,/Esq,/Superintendant of the/Finances of the United States/of America,/Philadelphia ENDORSED: Bordx. Augt and Sept. 10/1781/J. Bondfield
MS: LS, Robert Morris Papers, NN.

1. Possibly a reference to the naval engagement off the Dogger Bank in the North Sea, sixty miles east of England, on August 5, 1781, between English and Dutch fleets, in which one Dutch vessel was sunk and heavy casualties were suffered by both sides. Clowes, *Royal Navy*, III, 504–508.

2. On the siege of Minorca, see notes to William Carmichael to RM, August 13.

3. Sent from England to command the North American station, Rear Admiral Robert Digby (1732–1814) arrived in New York harbor on September 24, 1781, with three ships of the line. Hutchinson and Rutland, eds., *Madison Papers*, III, 198n.

4. Following their successful siege of Minorca (see notes to William Carmichael to RM, August 13), in September 1782 Franco-Spanish naval forces resumed operations against Gibraltar, which had been under blockade by the Spanish navy since June 1779. The British successfully resisted a siege which lasted until February 1783 and were confirmed in possession by the peace. James, *British Navy in Adversity*, 188, 302–303, 370–377.

5. Thus in MS.

6. On Haidar Aly, see notes to William Carmichael to RM, August 13. Fort Saint George was an English outpost established in the seventeenth century at Madras, a port on the Coromandel coast in southeast India. *Webster's New Geographical Dictionary* (Springfield, Mass., 1972).

7. After learning of the presence of a Franco-Spanish armada near the Scilly Isles off southwest England, Vice Admiral George Darby (d. 1790) withdrew with the Channel fleet under his command to Torbay on the Devonshire coast on August 24, 1781. Declining to pursue him, on September 5 the Spanish fleet returned to Cadiz, the French to Brest. *DNB;* Clowes, *Royal Navy*, III, 504, 566.

8. On Spain's paper currency, see Silas Deane to RM, February 23, 1781, and notes.

From Silas Deane

Paris Sept. 10th. 1781

Dear Sir

I receiv'd yours of the 7th. of June past, and though I wish'd to hear from you often, yet I never attributed your silence to other than the true Causes, which you have given me in your farewell Letter as you stile it, on Account of your being about to reimbark on the Sea of Politics. It is my Friend a tempestuous Ocean, and I fear not well explored. I am convinced that the motives, which have induced you to engage, are the most honorable, and disinterested, but if you receive the Letter I wrote you the 10th. of June last, you will fully conceive what my apprehensions must be for the issue. My Sentiments unreservedly given in that Letter,[1] anticipate any thing, on the subject in this; but in a word, if the Men who now apply to you in the hour of their discredit, and distress, had in 1778 appointed you to the same important office, which they now force on you, Our National Faith, Credit, and honor would have been preserved, and America would probably have been before this blessed with an honorable and lasting Peace. I sincerely esteem your Abilities, equal to those of Mr. Neckers, but your situation, and undertaking, is widely different. Mr. Necker attempted by lopping off the rotten, and useless branches of an old Tree, in its Nature strong, and vigorous, almost beyond example; to give it fresh force, and consistency. You have to reanimate a young one, which by bad managers, has even before it was well rooted, been lopp'd, peel'd and undermined. The Office you have undertaken is at any Time, and even in old establish'd Nations, accustom'd for Ages, to all the variety of Taxation, and Schemes of Finance, an arduous one, but in the present State of America, it appears to me, a Labor truly herculean. If any Man of my acquaintance is equal to it, You are, and as you are accustom'd to do Business in a clear and regular manner, I presume that one of your first Steps will be to ascertain what the Debt of the public is, at the Time of your entering on their Business, which gives me ground to hope, that my long neglected Account will now be adjusted, and the Ballance paid me.[2] When I returned from America to France,[3] it was on the presumption that such Measures had been taken by Congress, that my Accounts would be audited as soon as ready. You must remember that as Congress insisted on their being transmitted to them, with their Vouchers, before final Settlement,[4] I petitioned to have orders given that the Ballance whatever it undoubtedly appear'd to be, in my favor, should be paid me, on my giving security to be accountable for any Error, that might be made.[5] This was refused me, and on my Arrival in France Mr Johnson would not act as Auditor; [6] he told me he had long before informed Congress of his reasons for declining the Services, and that he doubted not, but that they would either satisfy him, on the subject, or appoint some other immediately. But to my great disappointment and to the almost total ruin of my Affairs, I have been obliged to wait here, it is now Ten Months, with my Accounts ready to be Audited, and settled, without being able to get any thing done, or to touch one Livre of the large Ballances, due to Me.[7] I am informed that the Accounts of Mr. Lee,[8] though neither Audited in Europe, nor offer'd for it by him, have notwithstanding been passed by the Board of Accounts at Phila.[9] This encourages me to send the particulars of mine, and my general Account Current with Congress. As I cannot be present myself, nor send the Vouchers, having no Duplicates of them, it is possible that Congress may object to the ordering Me the whole of the Ballances, without first having the Vouchers examined, and compared with the Charges, but as the smallest examination, will convince them that a large Ballance, is unquestionably due to Me, I trust they will no longer put off, the Appointment of an Auditor, to examine, and close my Accounts, and that in the mean time, they will order Me, an immediate remittance, and impower their Auditor, to pay me with Interest from the Time of the Monies having been due.

I have stated the Commission Account separate. You must remember that the Contracts with me, by the Secret Committee, and the Commissrs. of Commerce,[10] promised me five per Cent on the purchases made by me, in Europe, on Account of Congress, which I have accordingly charg'd. The purchases made after the Arrival of my Colleagues,[11] though I was the acting Person in the greater part of them, and took on me a Business, for which, being entirely independant of my political Commission, I was justly entitled to that Commission, which any other Person would have been allow'd, yet as I did not intend to charge it, at the Time, I have not done it now, though the Expences I have been at in returning, and my Time and Money spent, in attending here for a Settlement, are sufficient to intitle me to such a demand. In my Accounts general of expenditures and disbursements, you will see that all the Money ever paid me, or charg'd me either by Mr. Grand, or Mr Solier [12] the Bankers for Congress amount to £150389.7.11 [13] of which Sum £60932.0.5 is made up of wrong charges, which I have explain'd in the Account, and to the greater part of which, that of Soliers you are knowing. This leaves the Sum of 89457.7.6 for me to Account for; out of this I paid to relief of Prisoners at different Periods £19223.7.10 for the greatest part of which, I have their Vouchers. This sum will not appear extravagant, nor convict me of wasting the public Money, in unnecessary gratuities, when you find that within Two Years after my leaving France, more than twice that Sum was paid for that purpose. I have Mr. Carmichaels [14] Receipts and Accounts for the Money paid him, except for about 1200 Livs. For the Sum of £47899 Livr. 12 Sous 6d paid Officers going out to America, and Americans in Service of Congress, I have their Receipts for the whole; it cannot be expected, that I can have Vouchers for every Article; I have however more than I thought I had, before I examined my Papers. Indeed I do not think that there is Ten Thousand Livres, in the whole for which I have not Vouchers. I have charged my Time up to Jany. last, not doubting but that when Congress see, as they must, from the very first View of the Account, that independant of my Time, and Expences, I have paid out for them near as much Money, as I have ever receiv'd from them, they will think that the Sum charg'd by me for my Time in returning, and settling their Accounts, ought to be allowed. With respect to the Commission Account, You will recollect that on my engaging to come to Europe in Jany. 1776, I receiv'd orders to purchase Goods, to the amount of £40000 Stg. and was promised that the Money should be sent out with me, or remitted so early, that I should not be under the Necessity, of asking any Credit for them, and that at the same time, I was ordered to purchase Brass Cannon, Cloathing, Arms, Tents, &c compleat for an Army of 25,000 Men, and the Commission of 5 per Cent then, and since given to the Agents of Congress, was promised Me. Though pecuniary considerations had very little weight in determining me, to undertake the Voyage, yet my prospects were favorable in that way, as the certainty, as I then supposed of having £40000 Stg. to dispose of in Europe, which must obtain a ready Credit for the other Articles, to a much greater amount, would by the Commission itself, advance my fortune, and by the extent of the Operation, obtain for me no small degree of consideration, in the mercantile World. I need not repeat the History, of what you know perfectly well.[15] In short though disappointed of the Funds promised, and thrown into the most perplex'd, and embarrassing Circumstances, yet I succeeded in obtaining on Credit, more even than I was directed to purchase. Intent solely on fulfilling my Commissions, in the most advantageous manner for my Country, I neglected my private Interest so far, that though it was for a long Time in my power, to have paid myself my just due, out of the public Monies, then in my disposal, yet I never turned a thought that way, but relied entirely on the Justice of Congress, to fulfill their engagements with Me. Some others in public employ, acted a different part, and at all times held Money in advance in their hands; at this Time they find themselves at ease, in their circumstances, and uncensured by Congress or the public Voice. Had I done the same, I might possibly have escaped the obloquy thrown on me, at least I should have escaped the distress in which I have been involved, for two Years past, but I will not add on the subject, least I say something that may tend to irritate others, or myself, and be led to make recriminations, foreign to the affair in hand, which is simply an Account in the settling of which, Facts and Justice, alone are to be attended to.[16] It matters not how obnoxious I have been rendered to many, even of my well meaning Countrymen, nor by what means this has been effected; were I even their Enemy, which it is not possible I can ever be, still honor, as well as Justice would require that what is due to me, should be paid to me. I have for sometime since despair'd of seeing Justice done to my Character, untill the phrenzy and madness of the present Time, is over, and I see by the public Papers, sent over, from Boston, and Phila., that unhappily for our Country as well as well as Individuals, the wish'd for Crisis, is still at a distance; whilst the most respectable Characters in Congress, or in the immediate Service of their Country, are daily traduced, and abused in your Papers, and the Calumnies publish'd with You, transmitted here, to be spread in Europe, and this by Men who from their station, ought to act a very different part; what can I expect? I who have long since been inured to their Calumnies, and have been refused either protection, or Justice, by those from whom I had the greatest right to expect and demand both?

I must patiently wait for better times, with this melancholy consolation that it is hardly possible they can become worse.

I think it is not improper, to make one observation on the subject of my Accounts, before I close. You will see that the whole of my charges for my time including the last Six Months and the Expences of it amount to £51957.13. and that Mr. Izard [17] who receiv'd his Commission at Paris, where he had previously settled himself, and Family, for the sole purpose of educating his Children, and who never took one step, or expended one Livre extra, on Account of his Commission, receiv'd 60000 Livs. of the public Monies, more than two third of the whole Sum which I receiv'd of the Bankers and, for which I am accountable; and further I can but remind you, to look at the Prisoners Accounts, in the Congress Commissioners Books, and you will find very little charged before I left Paris, about two Thousand Livres only, and from my leaving Paris, to the January following more than thirty Thousand Livres are charg'd on that Account only. But I will not add to a Letter, already sufficiently particular, to shew my right to demand a Settlement, and payment of my Accounts and to have that Justice done, which has been so long and so cruelly refused me. I have address'd myself to you, on the supposition that it must lye within your department, to give orders on such subjects. If I am mistaken, You will please to lay this Letter and the Accounts transmitted, before Congress, or that Board which may be charged by them with the management of their concerns of this Nature.[18]

My best Compliments wait on Mrs. Morriss and am with the most Sincere Respect and Esteem Dear Sir Your most Obedient and very humble Servant

Silas Deane

Honble. Robt. Morris Esqr.

P.S. As I stated the General Accounts of Congress many Months since not only up to the Time of my recall, but to the Time of Doctr. Franklins receiving his Commission of sole Minister [19] and delivered him duplicates of the Books, I presume you must have received them before this.

ADDRESSED: To/The Honble Robert Morriss Esqr./Philadelphia
ENDORSED: Paris Septr. 10th. 1781/Silas Deane/respecting his public accounts.
MSS: ALS, Robert Morris Papers, NN; LbC, Deane Papers, CtHi; Force transcript, DLC.

1. Deane's apostasy was disclosed when his June 10, 1781, letter to RM was published in Rivington's New York *Royal Gazette.*

2. On Deane's accounts and their long-delayed settlement, see notes to Deane to RM, February 23, 1781.

3. Deane arrived in France on July 25, 1780.

4. Congress on August 6, 1779, directed "the several commissioners, commercial agents and others in Europe entrusted with public money . . . to transmit, without delay, their accounts and vouchers, and also triplicate copies of the same to the Board of Treasury of these United States in order for settlement," and at the same time excused Deane, then in Philadelphia, from further attendance. Congress also decided to appoint someone to examine such accounts in Europe and "certify his opinion" of them before their transmittal to the United States, and on September 29, 1779, assigned this task to Joshua Johnson.

5. Deane's request to Congress, which apparently failed to act upon it, was made in a memorial of August 16, 1779, in the *Deane Papers,* IV, 68–73; see also *JCC,* XIV, 979, XV, 1041.

6. On Joshua Johnson, see note 4 above and notes to John Jay to RM, September 1 (second letter).

7. On June 26, 1781, Congress elected Thomas Barclay vice-consul in France and on September 12 blandly informed Deane that the appointment took care of his request for a settlement of his accounts. Barclay was promoted to consul on October 5, but not until November 18, 1782, was he formally charged with settling accounts of agents in Europe and then he was empowered to undertake a final settlement of

them prior to transmitting the relevant papers to the Treasury, a procedure that was advised by RM. Ferguson, *Power of the Purse,* 195.

8. Arthur Lee (1740–1792) of Virginia, appointed by Congress on October 22, 1776, to join Benjamin Franklin and Deane as a commissioner to France for obtaining foreign aid, subsequently accused Deane of fraudulently misusing public funds (see notes to Deane to RM, February 23, 1781). After Congress instructed him on June 10, 1779, to return to the United States to support his charges against Deane, Lee was elected to the Virginia House of Delegates, served in the Continental Congress, 1781–1784, and on July 27, 1785, was named a member of the Board of Treasury which managed Continental finances after RM's resignation as Superintendent of Finance. *DAB;* for RM's correspondence with Lee (then chairman of a congressional committee) about Deane's accounts, see RM to Lee, August 29 and October 4 and 11, 1783, and Lee to RM, September 26 and October 9, 1783.

9. On May 29, 1781, Congress accepted Lee's statement of his accounts, requiring only his word of honor in verification of doubtful items, and on August 6 acknowledged a balance of £2,238 sterling due him for his salary and that of his secretary. For the later controversy over payment to Lee, see *JCC,* XXII, 337–338, 404, XXIII, 727–728; and Lee to RM, October 5 and November 2, 1782, and RM to Lee, October 9 and November 18 and 26, 1782, and to the President of Congress, November 14, 1782.

10. Deane refers to his contract of February 19, 1776, with the Secret Committee of Trade and probably with its successor, the Committee of Commerce, which Congress established on July 5, 1777. Deane also went to Europe under contract with the Committee of Secret Correspondence to procure supplies and undertake political activities. See the Secret Committee of Trade to Deane, March 1, 1776, and enclosed agreement, February 19, 1776, and the Committee of Secret Correspondence to Deane, March 2 and 3, 1776, *Deane Papers,* I, 116–118, 119, 123–126; and Ferguson, *Power of the Purse,* 82, 198; on the origin of these committees, see Sanders, *Executive Departments,* 38–45, 78–79.

11. Benjamin Franklin and Arthur Lee.

12. Ferdinand Grand, and possibly Jacques, Jean, or Marc Solier, Protestant merchants of Marseilles. Jacques Solier, with another firm, conducted trading expeditions to the United States during and after the war. Herbert Lüthy, *La banque protestante en France de la révocation de l'Edit de Nantes à la Révolution* (Paris, 1959–1961), II, 91, 111–113, 130–131, 495; Deane to Joseph Reed, 1784, *Deane Papers,* V, 415, 416.

13. Except where Deane states otherwise, the £ sign represents French livres.

14. William Carmichael.

15. See the sources cited in note 10 above.

16. On the Deane-Lee affair, see notes to Silas Deane to RM, February 23, 1781.

17. Ralph Izard (1742–1804) of South Carolina was living in Paris when Congress on May 7, 1777, appointed him commissioner to Tuscany. Tuscany would not receive him, and Izard continued in Paris, attempting to incriminate Franklin and Deane by writing numerous letters to Congress, which led to his recall on June 8, 1779. Prior to his return, however, Congress on August 9, 1780, approved his "faithful endeavours . . . to fulfil the objects of the commission." Izard was elected to the Continental Congress in 1782 and 1783. *DAB.*

18. RM received this letter and the enclosed accounts on January 15, 1782, and immediately forwarded them to Congress with a request for instructions. At his suggestion and apparently without taking any other action, Congress returned the letter to RM. The Financier's prudence regarding communications from Deane arose from the publication of Deane's previous tainted letter to him. See RM to the President of Congress, January 15, 1782 (first letter); *JCC,* XXII, 35n.; notes to Deane to RM, June 10; and Thomas Paine to RM, November 26, 1781; Deane next addressed RM on October 10, 1783.

19. Congress recalled Deane on November 21, 1777, and on December 8 directed the Committee for Foreign Affairs to instruct him to return to America at once, an

order Deane received early in March 1778. Franklin, who was elected sole minister plenipotentiary to France by Congress on September 14, 1778, received his commission in February 1779. James Lovell to Deane, December 8, 1777, and Deane to Conrad A. Gérard, March 9, 1778, *Deane Papers*, II, 267, 389; Carl Van Doren, *Benjamin Franklin* (New York, 1938), 608.

From Henry Dering

[*Lancaster, Pennsylvania, ca. September 10, 1781*. In his Diary of this date RM wrote: "Received a Letter from the Contractor at Lancaster." On Dering, see Diary, July 16, 1781, and notes. *Letter not found.*]

From John Langdon

[*Portsmouth, New Hampshire, September 10, 1781*. On September 28 RM wrote to Langdon: "Your Letter . . . of the tenth September arrived by Yesterdays Post." *Letter not found.*]

From Matthew Ridley

[*Baltimore, September 10, 1781*. On September 15 RM addressed Ridley in reply to his "Letters of the tenth Instant." *Letters not found.*]

Diary: September 11, 1781

Very much employed in preparing the instructions and other letters for Mr Francis and Major Nicholas, who set out on their Journey this day after dinner.[1]

The Board of War having in their Letter[s] to Genl Heath, Govr Hancock and Mr Hutch,[2] inserted the "Bearer" instead of Mr Francis's Name, which they did not know at the time those Letters were Wrote as it was then uncertain whom I shoud get to undertake this Service, I went to the Board of War and informed them that Mr Francis had undertaken it in Company with Major Nicholas and they Wrote Postscripts to their Letters mentioning these Gentlemen properly.

Mr. Nicholson[3] the Gunsmith informed me that there are a Number of Old Gun barrells, Locks &Ca in the Armory not fit to be worked up for Field Service but which might be repaired and sold for the use of Shipping so as to afford the Public much Profit. I will Converse with the Commissary of Military Stores[4] on this Subject.

Capt. Hazlewood applied for money on Account of his Contract and with reluctance I was Obliged to put him off.[5]

Lieutt. Pepin applied for Money, postponed.[6]

It seems as if every Person connected in Public Service entertain an Opinion that I am full of Money for they are constantly applying even down to the common express Riders and give me infinite interruption so that it is hardly possible to attend to Business of more Consequence. I have been Obliged to advance to the Paymaster Genls. department all the Money I had to Complete the payment of a Months pay to the Troops under Genl Lincoln.[7] Mr Anspach Paymaster of Colo Pickerings department applies daily for Money but cannot yet be supplied with the Sums required.[8] Genl St Clair calls again for Money to pay 500 recruits of the Pennsylva. Line to enable them to join the Southern Army, which I hope soon to Accomplish.[9] Received a Letter from His Excellency Caesar Rodney respecting Supplies; looks well, but does not require an immediate Answer; dated 8th: instant.[10]

The Honorable Mr Matthews [11] applied to me last Evening to employ or Contract with a Mr Kercher [12] for supplying the Southern Army &Ca. This rather surprised me because Mr Matthews well knows Congress have not supplied me with Funds sufficiently extensive for such an Undertaking nor can Carolina at present, follow the example of Pensylvania by putting Funds for procuring Supplies into my hands.

This day the Honorable Mr Bee [13] applied to Governeur Morris Esqr. on the same Subject and had a similar reply.

Wrote Tench Francis Esqr. 2 Letters.

Wrote Major Samuel Nicholas.

Wrote Monsr. Chevalier de L'Angle.

Wrote His Excellency The Governour of Massachusetts.

Wrote The Honble General Heath.

Wrote Mr Benjamin Dudley.

Wrote the Reverd. Doctr. Wm Gordon.

Wrote The honble Major General Lincoln.

Issued a Warrant On Swanwick, in favour of Wm. Turnbull & Co for Rum they supplied Colo Blaine £725.11.[14]

Issued warrant On Swanwick, in favour of P Audibert D[eputy] P[ay] M[aster] Genl. for £2325.[15]

1. A reference to the preparations for transporting to Philadelphia the specie at Boston brought from France by John Laurens. See the documents cited in notes to RM to Tench Francis, September 11 (first letter); for the use of this specie in capitalizing the Bank of North America, see the headnote to RM's Plan for Establishing a National Bank, with Observations, May 17, and notes to RM to Benjamin Franklin, July 19, 1781.

2. On these letters, see RM to the Board of War, September 10, and notes. The last addressee no doubt was Colonel Jabez Hatch (ca. 1738–1802) of Boston, lieutenant colonel and colonel of Massachusetts militia, 1776–1780, and deputy quartermaster general for New Hampshire, Massachusetts, and Rhode Island from October 1780 until early 1783. Allen H. Bent, "Col. Jabez Hatch, of Boston, His Ancestry and Descendants," *New-England Historical and Genealogical Register,* LI (1897), 36; Heitman, *Register;* William Heath to the Captain of the Escort, September 1781, Heath Papers, MHi; Timothy Pickering to Hatch, October 2, 1780, and January 26 and June 26, 1783, WDC, no. 126, pp. 115–117, no. 87, pp. 37, 62.

3. John Nicholson, who contracted to supply flintlock muskets to the Pennsylvania militia, was a Philadelphia gunsmith on Front Street from 1774 until 1792. Arthur Merwyn Carey, *American Firearms Makers: When, Where, and What They Made from the Colonial Period to the End of the Nineteenth Century* (New York, 1953), 85.

4. Samuel Hodgdon.

5. John Hazelwood, one of the contractors for the Continental post at Philadelphia. RM made a payment to the contractors on September 20, as recorded in the Diary of that date.

6. See notes to Diary, August 23.

7. See Diary, September 1–5 and 9, Benjamin Lincoln to RM, September 8, and RM to Lincoln, September 11.

8. Probably a reference to the requests contained in the Quartermaster General to RM, September 5 and 6. See also Diary, September 18 and 26.

9. See Diary, August 28, and notes.

10. This letter, from the president of Delaware, has not been found.

11. John Mathews, a member of Congress from South Carolina.

12. Probably Joseph Kershaw (ca. 1728–1791) of Camden, South Carolina, who emigrated from England in the 1750s and became an important merchant and flour miller. During the Revolution he served in a variety of state offices, including the first and second provincial congresses, the legislative council, and assembly. He was a colonel in the state militia from 1776 until his capture at the fall of Charleston in May 1780, and was a frequent supplier of military stores and clothing. Reynolds and Faunt, comps., *Biog. Dir. S. C. Senate,* 251; Heitman, *Register.*

13. Thomas Bee, a member of Congress from South Carolina.

14. See Diary, September 1–5 and 7.

15. This outlay was for completing the payment of one month's pay in specie to the troops marching south to Virginia. See earlier in the Diary of this date and documents cited in note 7 above.

To Benjamin Dudley

Office of Finance 11. Sepr. 1781.

Sir,

If you should not have left Boston before this reaches you I shall be glad that you will come with Tench Francis Esqr. who is the Bearer of it and who is directed to defray your Expences hither.

As the Business on which I want to confer with you is important and will not admit of Delay, I hope to see you speedily.[1] With great respect, I am Sir your most obedient and humble Servant

RM

MS: Ofcl LbC, DLC.
1. This letter was enclosed in RM to Tench Francis, September 11 (second letter);

see also RM to William Gordon, September 11. RM brought Dudley, a metallurgist, to Philadelphia to start a Continental mint. See Diary, July 16, 1781, and notes.

To Tench Francis

Office of Finance 11. Sepr. 1781.

Sir

You will proceed from hence to the Town of Boston in the State of Massachusett's Bay with all possible Expedition and on your Way you will deliver the Letter enclosed to General Heath and concert with him the Measures which may be necessary for the Business entrusted to your Care.[1] Enclosed is an Account of two Million five hundred thousand, two hundred and twenty four Livres eighteen Sous on Board of the french Frigate la Resolûe commanded by Monsr. le Chevalier de Langle together with his Receipt for that Sum also a Letter from Colo. Laurens to him on the Subject and an Order from me in your Favor to receive it, which you will do and give Duplicate Receipts.[2]

By Colo. Lauren's Report to Congress [3] it appears that Notwithstanding this Money was put in double Casks yet the Carriage of it to Brest so injured them that a Part was from Necessity shifted into Boxes previous to the Embarkation as you will see by the Account abovementioned. The Remainder is in a very shattered Condition wherefore great Care and Attention must be paid to the Removal. The Sum is so large that too much Time would be consumed in counting it; I therefore propose that from a thousand to two thousand Crowns be counted and Weighed after which the Remainder may in like Manner be weighed and if the Scales are tolerably good this Mode will determine the Amount with Accuracy.

It is my Intention to have this Money brought from Boston to this Place as soon as the necessary Attention to its Safety will permit. At the same Time I mean to have it transported with the utmost possible Oeconomy. With these Views and with a further View to the public Service in a different Line and on different Principles I desire you to invest as much of it as you can in Good Bills of Exchange drawn by Authority of his most Christian Majesty or of Congress. These you must buy as Cheap as possible, but so as not to exceed the Rate of seventy five spanish Dollars for five hundred and twenty five Livres Tournois.[4]

With Respect to the Remainder I wish it to be brought here in the following Manner. Have small square Boxes made strong of Oak Boards to contain about fifteen hundred to two thousand Crowns each and have large strong Chests made of thick Oak Plank of such

Tench Francis. Miniature by James Peale, 1798.

Shape as may be most proper and of Size to contain about twenty of the lesser Boxes. These larger Chests had best be fixed on the Axell of an Ox Cart from which the Body has been previously removed: they should when closed be strongly strapped about with Iron. Four Oxen led by one horse will then draw it with Ease. The Axle, Wheels and Tongue of the Carts should be very strong and good because the Roads thro which they are to come are very rough. I think it best that the Teams should be purchased and I should prefer Oxen of six Years Old and the Horses from seven to ten years old. Honest Sober Teamsters must be hired on the best Terms in your Power.

Inclosed you have an Order to General Heath for an Escort of Dragoons [5] who will proceed to Boston so as to be ready to set off by the Time you shall have got every Thing in Readiness which I hope and expect will be very speedily. I presume General Heath will give the proper Orders to the Officer commanding the Escort for mounting Guards where you stop and taking proper Positions along the Road but if any Thing of this Sort should be omitted you will yourself apply to the Officer on the Subject and lest he should conceive an Impropriety in the Application shew this Letter to him and request his particular Care and Attention.

From Boston to Philadelphia the following Rout is recommended to me which may nevertheless be altered as Time and Circumstances shall require for greater Safety. From Boston to Worchester [Worcester], to Springfield to Greenwood to Salisbury to Fisk Kill [Fishkill] to New Windsor or Newburgh to Sussex Court House or Newton to Easton to Philadelphia.[6] When you shall have arrived at Salsbury you will send to General Heath and let him know your intended Rout that he may take such Positions from Time to Time as will cover you perfectly and also that he may give you his Directions as to what may be proper for you to do in Order to avoid all Risque, which Directions you will comply with.

I think it would be useful that while you are in the dangerous Parts of the States of New York and New Jersey you should be escorted by an additional Number of Dragoons and also by a Party of Infantry but I shall submit this to Genl Heath who will be the best Judge. At any Rate it will be useful that the Teams Men be armed each with a good Musket and Bayonet because they may then assist the Cavalry in Case of an Attack. The items may be furnished for this Purpose from the Public Magazines and they may be again lodged in the Public Magazines here.

Should you upon Information find that the Weight I propose will be by any Means inconvenient or productive of Delay let the smaller

Boxes contain a lesser quantity so as to accomodate the Matter better and increase the Number of Teams proportionately. On the Road from Boston you will pay the Expences of the Escort &ca. and you will study to render the Expence as light as possible. It may be useful to encourage the Guard with the Hope of Reward; if upon Information you find it proper you may on my Part promise them one Months Pay in Specie on their Arrival at this Place.

Keep all your Motions and Intentions secret and give out that you mean to go from Springfield to Claverack from Claverack to Rhinebeck from Rhinebeck to Esopus from Esopus to Minisink from Minisink to Easton and when you quit this Rout to go to Fiskkill [Fishkill] move with as much Rapidity as your Cattle will permit. Take Care therefore to have good Cattle and spare them in the beginning of the Route.

No Instructions can apply accurately to all Circumstances but what has been said will explain to you my Views. In the various Contingencies which may arise be directed by your own Prudence as shall be best for the Public Interest and Service. You will keep an exact Account of all your Expences which I am convinced will be as moderate as they ought to be and this will accord well with Finances in the State ours are.

I know your Zeal to serve the Public too well to suppose you will look for an extravagant Reward for your Time and Trouble, therefore am Content to leave that Reward to be fixed after your trouble shall be known and your loss of Time ascertained. The Pleasure of serving your Country and the Confidence which is placed in you will be a more agreable Part of your Reward. And I hope the Event will justify that Confidence and give joy to every Friend of the United States. I wish you a Safe, a speedy and a prosperous Journey [7] and I am very respectfully Sir your most obedient and humble Servant

RM.

PS. I have thought proper to join Majr. Saml Nicholas with you in this important Commission; he will go and Return with you; he is instructed to give his Advice and Assistance in everything wherein it may be necessary.[8]

MSS: Ofcl LbC, DLC; extract, William Heath Papers, MHi.

1. For the background of this letter, see Diary, September 10 and 11. RM's letter to William Heath is dated September 11. Francis also carried RM's letters to Chevalier de Langle and to the Governor of Massachusetts, both dated September 11.

2. These enclosures have not been found. See RM to the Secretary of Congress, with Reply, September 8, and notes.

3. John Laurens to the President of Congress, September 2, 1781, Wharton, ed., *Rev. Dipl. Corr.*, IV, 691.

4. RM intended to sell these bills in Philadelphia at a profit. See Diary, September 10, and notes.

5. See RM to the Board of War, September 10, and notes, and note 7 below.

6. Ezekiel Cornell, a member of the Board of War, had suggested this route to RM. See Diary, September 7 and 10, and note 7 below.

7. On their way north Francis and Nicholas delivered the letters of RM and the Board of War to Major General William Heath, whom Washington had left in command in the Middle Department at Continental Village, New York, on the east bank of the Hudson River about three miles north of Peekskill. By September 24 they were in Boston receiving the specie from Governor John Hancock, to whom the French apparently had committed it. Meanwhile, in accordance with instructions of the Board of War, Heath dispatched to Springfield, Massachusetts, ca. September 30 some forty light cavalry under Captain Jeronimus Hoogland of the 2d Continental regiment of light dragoons, and on October 6 100 infantry under Major Amos Morrill of the 2d New Hampshire regiment. There they were to await Francis, who was moving west from Boston via Worcester accompanied by a guard of militia. While retaining the military command of their detachments, Hoogland and Morrill were instructed to follow Francis's directions in all matters concerning the treasure, which they were to defend "at every hazard." Francis informed Heath that he would leave Boston with the treasure on October 4 or 5 and expected to be at Springfield on October 10, but neither the chronology of his movements nor his exact route beyond Springfield are subject to precise verification from available sources.

Conveyed in 14 wagons pulled by 56 oxen and lead horses, the treasure traveled from twelve to fifteen miles a day. Francis was at Washington, Connecticut, about thirty miles from Fishkill, on October 22; at Fishkill, where his guard was to be reinforced by fifty infantrymen, probably by October 24 or 25; on the west side of Hudson River by October 26; and at Chester, in Orange County, New York, about sixteen miles southeast of Newburgh, on October 27, whence he proceeded to Sussex Court House, New Jersey. It is uncertain, however, whether Francis adhered to RM's suggested route through Easton, Pennsylvania, which he wished to avoid because of its "Vile Roads" and "bad Boats." The progress of the convoy through the parts of New York and New Jersey subject to incursion by the British was apparently without incident, and Francis, if he acted on intentions expressed to Heath, probably discharged the dragoons and all but fifty infantrymen upon reaching the Delaware River. The treasure arrived intact in Philadelphia on November 6 and was delivered to Michael Hillegas, Treasurer of the United States, to be subject solely to RM's orders.

On the specie shipment, see Diary, and RM to the Board of War, both September 10, and notes, RM to William Heath, to Chevalier de Langle, to the Governor of Massachusetts, and to Samuel Nicholas, all September 11, to the Governor of Massachusetts, September 18 and October 4, and notes, to Tench Francis, and to the Treasurer of the United States, both November 6, William Heath to RM, September 15 and October 24, and Diary, October 30, and November 6, 7, and 19, 1781; Governor John Hancock of Massachusetts to the President of Congress, September 24, 1781, PCC, no. 65, II, 147; Richard Peters of the Board of War to Heath, September 11, 1781, *Heath Papers*, III, 240–241; Heath to the Captain of the Escort, September 1781, to Hoogland, and to Morrill, both October 6, to the Board of War, October 7 and 24, and to Francis, October 1, 6, 23, and 27, Francis to Heath, September 30, and October 22 and 28, and Hugh Hughes to Heath, October 26, 1781, all in the Heath Papers, MHi; and *Pennsylvania Packet*, November 10, 1781.

8. See Diary, September 10, and notes, and RM to Nicholas, September 11. For additional instructions to Francis on related money matters, see RM to Francis, September 11 (second letter), 15 (two letters), and 22.

To Tench Francis

Office of Finance 11th. Septemr. 1781.

Sir,

Enclosed you have two Letters, the one for Doctr Gordon and the other for Mr Benjamin Dudley.[1] I pray you to enquire at Mr. Bradfords[2] in Boston the Means of conveying these Letters and having read be pleased to seal and send them.

Should Mr Dudley think proper to come on with you you will provide him with a Horse, Saddle &Ca. and defray his Expences on the Road. He will probably be useful to you in putting up the Money as he is an excellent Mechanick and may therefore strike out Hints on the Subject which would escape others. I hope you may find him an useful, agreable and entertaining Companion on the Road.

I am very respectfully Sir your most obedient and humble Servant

RM

MS: Ofcl LbC, DLC.
1. See RM to William Gordon, and to Benjamin Dudley, both September 11.
2. John Bradford, Continental prize agent at Boston, who had brought Dudley to RM's attention. See notes to Diary, July 16, 1781.

To William Gordon

Office of Finance 11th. Septr. 1781.

Sir,

I have the Pleasure to acknowlege the Receipt of your Favor of the twenty ninth of August last, relating to Mr. Dudley.[1] Tench Francis Esqr. the Bearer of this Letter who is charged with the Care of conducting the Money late arrived at Boston to this City will also take Care of Mr Dudley and defray his Expences hither.[2] I shall be glad if Mr Dudley will come with him and afford his Assistance in protecting the Treasure. With very great Respect I have the Honor to be Sir your most obedient and humble Servant.

RM.

MS: Ofcl LbC, DLC.
1. Letter not found.
2. See RM to Tench Francis, September 11 (second letter), in which the letter to Gordon was enclosed, and RM to Benjamin Dudley of the same date.

To William Heath

Office of Finance
Philadelphia Sept. 11th. 1781

Sir

Enclosed is an Order from the Board of War,[1] to send a Party of Dragoons to Boston to escort thence a Considerable Sum of Money belonging to the United States, which I trust you will Comply with in the manner most proper. Mr Francis, the Bearer of this Letter, is charged with the care of the Transportation, and now waits upon you to concert such Measures as may be necessary.

I also enclose an Extract from my Instructions to Mr Francis,[2] which will place you in a Situation to give him the occasional Directions which he may stand in need of, or which the Motions of the Enemy, or other Circumstances may require. I would recommend Secrecy and mention that the Interests of the United States, and of the Army require the greatest Care to be used with Respect to this Money, But your Character Sir renders every such Caution unnecessary, for I am convinced that you will be as forcibly impressed with those Sentiments as I can be.[3] I am very respectfully Sir, your Most Obedient humble Servant.

Robt Morris

Honble. General Heath

ENDORSED: From Mr. Morriss [*remainder cut off*]
MSS: LS, Heath Papers, MHi; Ofcl LbC, DLC.
1. The enclosure, Richard Peters to Heath, September 11, 1781, is in the *Heath Papers*, III, 240–241.
2. The extract from RM to Tench Francis, September 11 (first letter), is printed in *ibid.*, 245–246.
3. Heath replied on September 15.

To Chevalier de Langle

Office of Finance
Philada. Septemr. 11th. 1781.

Sir

The Bearer of this Letter Mr. Tench Francis Has the Honor to deliver to you a Letter from Colo. Laurens relative to the Money laden on Board your Frigate for Account of the United States [1] And he has in Consequence of the enclosed Resolution of Congress [2] my Orders to receive it from you at such Time as shall suit your

Convenience. He will on the Delivery give you the necessary Receipts of which I pray you to take Duplicates and lodge one Copy with his Excellency the Governor of Massachusett's to be forwarded to me.[3]

I am very Sorry that I could not sooner releive you from the Custody of this Money but I do myself the Honor Monsieur le Chevalier to assure you that I have taken my Measures as speedily as I possibly could. Mr. Francis is directed to give to this Business all possible Facility on his Part and I trust you will find him ready to render it as convenient to you as shall be possible.

I cannot omit the present Occasion of testifying my Acknowlegements for your Care and Attention to those Interests of my Country which are committed to you by your Sovereign. Permit me Sir to express my Sincere Wishes for your Prosperity and Glory and to assure you that I am very respectfully your most obedient and humble Servant

RM.

MS: Ofcl LbC, DLC.
1. Letter not found. See RM to Tench Francis, September 11 (first letter), and Diary, September 10.
2. On September 4 Congress ordered the money recently arrived at Boston with John Laurens, aboard the frigate *La Résolue* commanded by Chevalier de Langle, to be delivered to the order of RM, who was "empowered and directed to take charge of the same."
3. See RM to Tench Francis, September 11 (first letter), and to the Governor of Massachusetts of the same date.

To Benjamin Lincoln

Office of Finance
September 11th. 1781.

Sir

Before you can receive this Letter you will have been convinc'd of my attention to yours of the 8th. Instant [1] as I supplied the Pay Master General with Six thousand two hundred Dollars in preference of the many other demands that come on me, and I wish it may always be in my power to answer your desires as expeditiously as in the present Instance for I am very truly Sir Your Obedient humble Servant.

Robt Morris

The Honble. Major General Lincoln

MSS: LS, MB; Ofcl LbC, DLC.

1. In which Lincoln informed RM of the deficiency in specie necessary to complete the distribution of one month's pay to the Continental troops marching south to Virginia for operations against Cornwallis. See also Diary, September 1–5, and notes.

To the Governor of Massachusetts
(John Hancock)

Office of Finance 11th. Sepr. 1781.

Sir,

I do myself the Honor to enclose to your Excellency the Extract of a Letter to the Chevalier de Langle [1] and am to request your Care of the Duplicate Receipts referred to.

I also enclose a Letter from the Board of War requesting a Guard to the Money while it remains in Boston.[2] My intimate Knowlege of your Excellency convinces me that as well in that as in every Thing else where the public Service may be concerned you will exert yourself to the utmost. I therefore make no Apology for recommending Mr Tench Francis the Bearer of this Letter and charged with the Care of the Money to your Excellency's favorable Attention.[3]

I have the Honor to be very respectfully your Excellency's most obedient and humble Servant.

RM

MS: Ofcl LbC, DLC.

1. Dated September 11.

2. The board's letter to Governor Hancock has not been found. See RM to the Board of War, September 10, and notes, and Diary, September 11.

3. On Francis's mission, see RM to Tench Francis, September 11 (first letter), and notes.

To Samuel Nicholas

Office of Finance 11th. Septr. 1781.

Sir,

The United States in Congress assembled having thought proper on the seventh Instant to place the Affairs of the Marine under my Direction [1] I am now to desire that you will repair to Boston in Company with Tench Francis Esqr. who is charged by me with the Execution of an important Business which he will communicate on your Arrival at Boston.[2] From an Opinion of your Activity, Spirit and Talents I have pitched upon you to accompany him and I hope and expect that you will on every Occasion favor him with your best advice and Assistance. He is instructed to defray your Expences from hence until your return to this City. I wish you an agreable Journey and am Sir respectfully your most obedient and humble Servant

RM.

MS: Ofcl LbC, DLC.
  1. See the headnote to RM to the President of Congress, September 8.
  2. For a discussion of Nicholas and this mission, see Diary, September 10, and notes, and RM to Tench Francis, September 11 (first letter), and notes.

Gouverneur Morris to Nathanael Greene

Phila: 11 Sepr: 1781.

Dear General

The enclosed Cypher is that referred to in my Letter [1] as well as in that from the Superintendant of Finance.[2] It is the Cypher also of which the Commander in Chief has one Duplicate and consequently when you shall have received it you will be able to correspond with him for which Purpose you will let him know that you have it.[3]

In order to explain more fully the Use take the following Sentence. *"Sir Henry Clinton threatens an Attack on Philadelphia, by Way of Diversion, in favor of Lord Cornwallis; this has a little intimidated some few Ladies of my Acquaintance."*[4] This being put into Cypher will stand thus. [*Cipher follows.*] I am very truly yours

Gouv Morris

ENDORSED: From/Mr G. Morris/11th Septr. 1781/Cypher
MS: ALS, Greene Papers, MiU-C.
  1. A reference to Gouverneur Morris to Greene, September 10.
  2. See RM to Greene, September 10.
  3. On this cipher, see notes to RM to Washington, August 22.
  4. This sentence alludes to a rumored diversionary movement by the British against Philadelphia, which was discounted by RM and, if this choice of phrase is a clue, by his official assistant as well. See notes to Timothy Matlack to RM, September 11.

From Timothy Matlack[1]

Philadelphia September 11. 1781.

Sir,

By His Excellency the President and Council I am ordered to inform you, that, agreable to the requisition of Congress of the 10th instant, recommending "to the States of New Jersey and Pennsylvania immediately to embody three thousand men each, properly officered and equipped, and to cause them to rendezvous at such place or places as the commanding officer shall direct," [2] they have ordered "three classes of the militia of the city of Philadelphia, four classes of the county of Philadephia, four classes of the county of Chester, four classes of the county of Bucks, three classes of the county of Lancaster, three classes of the county of Berks, two classes of the county of Northampton, the whole of the Light horse of the city and the said counties, the whole of the Light horse of the counties of York and Cumberland and two companies of Artillery. And that the said Militia do rendezvous, as soon as possible, at Newtown in the county of Bucks," which order, it is supposed will produce at least 3000 men.[3] You will perceive, that this communication is now made to afford you the earliest opportunity of making provision for these troops, and should any alteration be made respecting the place of rendezvous you will be immediately informed thereof. I have the honor to be with great respect Your most obedient and very Humble servant

TM Secy.

Hnble R Morris Esqr.

ENDORSED: To Hnble R Morris Esqr/Septr 11. 1781.
MS: ADftS, Records of the Supreme Executive Council, RG 27, PHarH.
1. Matlack was secretary of the Supreme Executive Council of Pennsylvania.
2. This action by Congress was recommended by the Board of War in response to intelligence communicated by Governor William Livingston of New Jersey that Sir Henry Clinton in New York planned to invade New Jersey and attack Philadelphia in an effort to assist Cornwallis by disrupting the flow of American reinforcements to Virginia. Throughout September, in fact, Clinton made preparations to reinforce Cornwallis or launch a diversionary attack on Philadelphia. Congress received advice on September 19 that a British force had already embarked, probably destined for Philadelphia. Its response was to alert the Delaware militia, to request that half of it be brought immediately into the field, and to order the troops of the Pennsylvania line under Major General Arthur St. Clair to rendezvous at Philadelphia instead of proceeding to join Washington's army. RM, who discounted the British threat to Philadelphia, nevertheless cooperated with the alarmed state government in measures for the defense of the city. Clinton's relief force did not actually set sail from New York until October 19, the date Cornwallis surrendered. It arrived at the Chesapeake on October 24, too late to affect the military decision, whereupon it returned to New York. Meanwhile, Congress on September 27 had reassigned St. Clair's troops to Washington's command. Governor William Livingston to President Joseph Reed of Pennsylvania, September 8, 1781, *Pennsylvania Archives*, 1st ser., IX, 393; the Board of War to the President of Congress, September 10, 1781, PCC, no. 148, I, 421; the President of Congress to the Governors of New Jersey and Pennsylvania, September 11, 1781, and to the President of Delaware, September 19, 1781, Burnett, ed., *Letters*, VI, 216, 222; Virginia Delegates to Thomas Nelson, September 11, 1781, Hutchinson and Rutland, eds., *Madison Papers*, III, 253n., 254–255n., 260n., 262n., 288n.; *JCC*, XXI, 974–975. For RM's role in preparations for the defense of

Philadelphia, see the President of Pennsylvania to RM, September 12, 20, 21, and 22, RM to the President of Pennsylvania, September 12, 20, and 23, and October 1, Diary, September 19 and 21, Thomas Paine to RM, September 20, and RM to Paine, September 21, 1781.

3. The Council's order was made on September 11. *Colonial Records of Pennsylvania,* XIII, 52–54.

Diary: September 12, 1781

The Usual Applications for Money this Morning which I shall use my utmost endeavours to procure there being very little on hand this Morning.

Jno. Moylan Esqr. Cloathier General applied respecting the removal of the Cloathing from Boston by Land,[1] but the determination of this Point being with the Board of War I refer him to that Board.

Colol. Miles [2] Applies for Money; Mr Morse, Clerk in the Secretys Office, calls on same subject.[3] Genl Schuylers Express,[4] Mr Lowrey [5] and The Honorable Mr Cattle [6] all of them attending for Money.

Mr. Jno. Brown Secrety. of the Admiralty having supplied Rum and Spirit to the Navy Board at a price in paper Money in   [7] last being then rather cheaper than the Current price and under my promise to see him paid, He now calls for the paper Amounting to £   [8] which I must pay, but as he offers to take Bills of Exchange at 5/6 hard for 5 livres and reduce the paper to hard @ $2^1/_2$ for One I think it for the Benefit of the United States to accept this Offer and will comply therewith Accordingly.[9] And as my want of Money is so pressing I have offered to receive from said Mr Brown about £2000 hard Money which he expects to Collect in a day or two from Persons indebted to him and to deposite Bills of Exchange for that Amount at 5/6 for 5 Livrs. and to give him a draft on Boston for the same Sum he deposites leaveing him at Liberty to use the Money in Boston or the Bills here returning that he does not apply to his Use.[10]

This day executed a Contract with Colol. E. Blaine and Michael Hoofnagle for supplying the Post at Fort Pitt &Ca.[11]

Colol. Blaine shewed me his Account of supplies for the Generals Table &Ca.[12]

Apply'd to by a Powder Maker to Contract for Powder; desired him to go to the Board of War.

Sent Genl. Schuylers Letter to Mr Secrety. Thompson to know what provision is made for the Indians therein mentioned.[13]

Received a Letter from the President of the State of Pennsylvania informing of a Call by Congress for 3000 Militia and a request to provide for them &Ca.[14]

Received a Letter from the Board of War respecting a Contract for Wyoming [15] and Advertized immediately of this date.

Wrote a letter in Answer to that received from the President of Pennsyla.

1. Probably a reference either to the clothing which had arrived at Boston aboard a vessel escorted by the frigate *Magicienne* and/or that which had arrived aboard the *Olimpe* and *Cibelle* with John Laurens on August 25. See RM to Franklin, August 28, and Diary, September 20; John Laurens to the President of Congress, September 2, 1781, Wharton, ed., *Rev. Dipl. Corr.*, IV, 685–692; and invoices of the cargoes of the *Olimpe* and *Cibelle* in PCC, no. 165, pp. 165–176, 223–226. For Moylan's part in arranging for the shipment of this clothing to Philadelphia as well as that arriving in Boston from France and consigned to John Holker, see Diary, September 20, 21, October 29, and November 2, RM to the Clothier General, September 20 and November 2, and RM to Heath, and RM's Agreement with John Holker, both November 2, 1781.

2. Colonel Samuel Miles, deputy quartermaster general for Pennsylvania. See Diary, September 13.

3. On the application of Charles Morse, see notes to Diary, August 8.

4. See Philip Schuyler to RM, August 31, and notes.

5. Thomas Lowrey of New Jersey, a flour purchaser for RM. See Diary, August 21 and 29, and September 13.

6. Benjamin Cattell, a member of the South Carolina Privy Council. See Diary, August 29, and notes.

7. Space left blank in manuscript.

8. Space left blank in manuscript.

9. See Diary, September 13, which records a payment in Pennsylvania currency.

10. See RM to Tench Francis, September 22. The sum received from Brown is there stated as £2,077.18.7 Pennsylvania currency.

11. Contract not found. See Advertisement for Fort Pitt Contract Proposals, July 14, and Diary, July 16, 1781.

12. See Diary, July 6, 1781, and notes.

13. Philip Schuyler's letter to RM is dated August 31. His offer to undertake the distribution of supplies to Indians at Schenectady friendly to the American cause was accepted in RM's reply of September 14. RM's letter to Secretary of Congress Charles Thomson has not been found.

14. This letter is dated September 12.

15. Letter not found.

Advertisement for Wyoming Contract Proposals

Office of Finance, September 12, 1781. This advertisement is identical to that for Reading, Pennsylvania, dated July 14, 1781, with the following exceptions: the proposals for "the post at Wyoming" were to be received at the Office of Finance "until the 1st day of October next"; the rations were to be supplied to "Officers, Soldiers, and others" from "a certain time to be fixed in the contract until the expiration of twelve months thereafter"; the whiskey was to be "good"; and the soap and candles were to be issued "to every seven hundred rations." [1]

PRINTED: *Pennsylvania Packet,* September 15, 1781.

1. This advertisement also appeared in the *Pennsylvania Packet* on September 22 and 27, in the *Freeman's Journal* on September 19 and 26, and in the *Pennsylvania Journal* on September 15, 22, 26, 29, and October 3. It was placed in response to a letter from the Board of War to RM, September 12, which has not been found. See Diary, September 12; negotiations for letting this contract may be traced in RM to Stephen Chambers, October 3 and 8, and Diary, October 8 and November 20, 1781.

To the Secretary of Congress (Charles Thomson)

[*Philadelphia, September 12, 1781.* In his Diary for this date RM wrote: "Sent Genl. Schuylers letter to Mr Secrety. Thompson to know what provision is made for the Indians therein mentioned." Schuyler's letter to RM is dated August 31. See Diary, and RM to Schuyler, both September 14. *Letter not found.*]

Contract with Ephraim Blaine and Michael Huffnagle

[*Philadelphia, September 12, 1781.* In his Diary of this date RM wrote: "This day executed a Contract with Colol. E. Blaine and Michael Hoofnagle for supplying the Post at Fort Pitt &Ca." See Advertisement for Fort Pitt Contract Proposals, July 14, and Diary, July 16, and September 7, 1781. *Contract not found.*]

From the President of Pennsylvania (Joseph Reed)

[Philadelphia, September 12, 1781]

Sir

We yesterday received a Requisition from the Hon. Congress to embody 3000 Men with all Expedition and to cause them to rendezvous at such Place as the commanding Officer shall appoint. We presume this Requisition to be founded on Advices received that Sr. Henry Clinton has in Contemplation some Enterprize as a Diversion in favour of Ld. Cornwallis which if directed against this State will require the utmost Exertions of its Inhabitants.[1] We have in Consequence ordered out so many Classes of the Militia as will make up the Number required or near it and have appointed New-town in Bucks County as the place of Rendezvous. We are very sensible of the Difficulties and Expence that will attend this Measure and therefore shall not direct the actual March untill the Intentions of the Enemy are more clearly ascertained, but as the Arrangement of the Militia for Service is allways attended with some unavoidable Delay we have thought it proper to make every Preparation by which Expence will not be actually incurr'd so that if the Views of the Enemy should point to this State we may not be found wholly unprovided. Under this Consideration we have thought it necessary to communicate to you this Requisition that if there should be a Necessity for this Body of Men to go into actual Service the earliest Opportunity may be afforded of making Provision for them: For which in the present State of our publick Treasury I fear we must very much depend upon your Exertions and Assistance. Should any Alteration of the Rendezvous be made we shall immediately acquaint you therewith.

Inclosed I send you an Extract of a Letter from Gov. Livingston containing the Intelligence received by him from New York [2] and am Sir, Your Most Obedient and very Humble Servant

JR.

ENDORSED: 1781 September 12th. To/Honble Robert Morris/Esqr. Superintendant of Finance.
MS: ADftS, Records of the Supreme Executive Council, RG 27, PHarH.
1. On Clinton's threatened diversionary action and the response of Congress and RM, see notes to Timothy Matlack to RM, September 11, and the documents cited there.
2. The letter of Governor William Livingston of New Jersey to President Reed, September 8, 1781, is in the *Pennsylvania Archives,* 1st ser., IX, 393.

To the President of Pennsylvania
(Joseph Reed)

Office of Finance 12. Sepr. 1781.

Sir,

I am this Moment favored with your Excellency's Letter in Council of this Date enclosing an Extract of the Letter from Govr. Livingston. I thoroughly approve of the Determination of your Excelly. and the honble. Council not to incur any Expence until the Intentions of the Enemy are clearly ascertained. If I were to hazard an Opinion It would be very clear that Sir Harry Clinton has no Views against this State.[1]

Your Excellency must be Sensible that any Expence of Provisions which may be incurred must be defrayed from the Treasury of this State. The Money is already Appreciated to two for one and I am convinced that it will be brought to Par if the Assembly take the further Steps which may be necessary. In this Situation of Affairs you will agree with me that every thing which may retard that desirable Event ought if Possible to be avoided.[2]

As the Place where the Militia will be called to Action will be near the Banks of the Delaware and I can always command as much Flour in this City as will be wanting for an immediate Supply no previous Provision of that Sort is necessary: And as I cannot Doubt that the People will cheerfully bring in their Cattle on the proper Assurances of Payment I conceive it equally unnecessary to take any Steps at present for the procuring of Beef.

I should before this have acknowleged the Receipt of your Excellency's Favor dated in Council the fourth Instant.[3] But I was delayed from the following Cause. On Reflection I thought it possible that the Tents there mentioned might be wanted for the Militia and therefore I directed the Quarter Master to get them made intending if they could be procured in Season not to take the Benefit of your Promise to Genl Sinclair. I am happy now to inform you that they will soon be ready.[4] Permit me Sir at the same time to express my Acknowlegements for the Readiness shewn by the honorable Council to forward the public Service on that Occasion. I have the Honor to be your Excellency's most obedient and humble Servant

RM.

MS: Ofcl LbC, DLC.

1. On Clinton's threatened diversionary movement, see notes to Timothy Matlack to RM, September 11.

2. RM had charge of Pennsylvania's last currency emission. This remark alludes to the prospect that a further emission to support the expense of calling out the militia would tend to decrease the value of the state's currency. On RM's financial arrangements with Pennsylvania, see the headnote to RM to the Speaker of the Pennsylvania Assembly, June 26, and on his plan to appreciate the value of Pennsylvania currency, RM to Benjamin Franklin, July 21, 1781.

3. In this letter President Reed wrote that the Council had made tents available to the troops of the Pennsylvania line commanded by Major General Arthur St. Clair on the assurance that RM would supply others to the militia should it unexpectedly be called out.

4. On these tents, see notes to the President of Pennsylvania to RM, September 4; for RM's orders to Colonel Samuel Miles, deputy quartermaster general for Pennsylvania, see Diary, September 8.

From Benjamin Franklin

Robert Morris Esqr   Passy, Sept. 12. 1781
Sir,

I have received your Letters of July 13, 14, 19 and 21, all at once by Way of L'Orient. The Originals of those you mention to have sent by Major Franks, are not yet come to hand, nor have I heard of his Arrival in Spain.[1]

Your Letters of June 6 and 8 were remarkably lucky in getting to hand. I think I have receiv'd 7 of the Copies you had the Precaution to send of them. I inclose Copies of my Answers.[2]

I have now the Pleasure to acquaint you that I have obtained a Promise of the Sum I wanted to pay the Bills I had accepted for the Purchases made in Holland.[3] So that your supplying me with Remittances for that purpose, which I requested, is now unnecessary, and I shall finish the Year with Honour. But it is as much as I can do, with the Aid of the Sum I[4] Stopt in Holland; the Drafts on Mr. Jay and on Mr Adams, much exceeding what I had been made to expect. I had been inform'd that the Congress had promised to draw no more Bills on Europe after the Month of March last, till they should know they had Funds here: But I learn from Mr Adams that some Bills have been lately presented to him, drawn June 22 on Mr. Laurens who is in the Tower, which make the Proceeding seem extraordinary. Mr Adams cannot pay these Bills, and I cannot engage for them.[5] For I see by the Minutes of Congress you have sent me, that tho' they have stopt issuing Bills drawn on the Ministers at Madrid and the Hague, untill they shall be assured that Funds are provided for paying them, they have left open to be sold those drawn on their Minister at Versailles, Funds or no Funds,[6] which in the Situation you will see I am in by the Letters of M. de Vergennes,[7] terrifys me: For I have promised not to accept any Drafts made on me by Order of Congress if such should be[8] after the Time above mentioned, unless I have Funds in my Hands, or in View to pay them. After its being declar'd to me that such Bills could not be provided for, and my Promise not to engage for them, it will be impossible to ask for the Money, if I should accept them; And I believe those Bills of Mr Ross must go back protested.

The projected Loan in Holland has of late some appearances of Success. I am indeed told, it is agreed to by the States. But I do not yet think it so certain as to venture or advise the Venturing to act in Expectation of it.[9] The Instant it is assured, I will send you Advice of it by every Opportunity; and will from time to time send Parts of it in Cash by such Ships of War as can conveniently take it.

I cannot write to you fully by this Opportunity. I will not however delay acquainting you, that having the fullest Confidence in your Assurances of enabling me to pay them, I shall chearfully accept your Bills for 400,000 livres.[10]

Capt. Gillon has sail'd from Holland without taking under his Convoy the two Vessels that were freighted to carry the Goods purchased by Capt. Jackson in Holland. There has been terrible Management there: And from the Confusions in the Ship, before and when she sail'd, it is a question if she ever arrives in America.[11]

They are hard at Work here in providing the Supplies, to replace those lost in the Marquis de la Fayette.[12]

With best Wishes of Success to you in your new Employment, and Assurances of every Aid I can afford you, I am, Dear Sir,[13]

MSS: ADft, Franklin Papers, DLC; LbC, Franklin Papers, DLC; transcript, incomplete, Levis Collection, PHi.

1. Major David S. Franks had already delivered dispatches to John Jay, American minister to Spain. See Jay to RM, September 1 (first letter).

2. Franklin to RM, July 26, 1781 (two letters).

3. France had stipulated that part of its gift of 6 million livres for the year 1781 was to be applied to the purchase of clothing and munitions needed by the American army and that the remainder was to be subject to Washington's (or Congress's) drafts. John Laurens, during his special mission to obtain French aid, spent 2.2 million livres purchasing army supplies in Holland, and on his return voyage to America carried 2.5 million livres in specie, which was destined to provide most of the initial capital for the Bank of North America. Another 1.5 million livres was deposited at Amsterdam in the care of Laurens's deputy, William Jackson, and also earmarked for shipment to America. These allocations more than used up the French subsidy. However, Jackson laid out an additional £50,000 sterling, most of it for military goods already bought for South Carolina by Captain Alexander Gillon and paid for in bills of exchange on Franklin without the latter's authorization. Franklin was also faced with bills drawn by authority of Congress, not only upon himself for interest due upon loan office certificates, among other things, but upon John Jay, Henry Laurens, and John Adams as well. Before Laurens's departure was known, Franklin applied to Vergennes for permission to hold back 5 of the 6 million livre gift. Vergennes refused to divert the funds from their original purposes and disclaimed any responsibility for drafts in excess of Franklin's current funds. He also took a hard line with respect to the loan pending in Holland under the guarantee of the French government, the proceeds of which France had agreed to advance immediately. Franklin, who had counted on resorting to the loan, was told that it was at the disposal of Congress and that he would have to have specific congressional authority to draw on it.

Franklin took immediate steps to save his credit by arbitrarily stopping the 1.5 million livres at Amsterdam. In response to Franklin's serving notice that he would have to suspend payments after July 10, Vergennes apparently sanctioned the stoppage. On August 23 Vergennes made further concessions, to which Franklin no doubt refers in this letter to RM. He agreed to subsidize Franklin's acceptance of bills drawn by Congress prior to April 1, 1781 (but not beyond that date), to honor bills drawn by order of John Laurens up to 2 million livres, and to replace money expended for the cargo lost aboard the *Lafayette.* John Laurens to the President of Congress, March 20, Vergennes to John Laurens, May 16, Franklin to Vergennes, June 4, Vergennes to Franklin, June 8, Franklin to Vergennes, June 10, to the President of Congress, June 11, to Jackson, June 28 and July 5 (two letters) and 6, to Vergennes, July 6, to Jackson, July 10, and to the President of Congress, July 11, 1781, Wharton, ed., *Rev. Dipl. Corr.,* IV, 317–318, 418–419, 467–468, 484, 485–487, 493, 523, 543–546, 547–548, 557–559; Vergennes to Franklin, June 17 and August 23, 1781, PPAmP; Franklin to RM, July 26, 1781 (second letter); see also note 5 below and, for the later dispute between RM and the French government over the terms of French aid in 1781, including the 6 million livre subsidy, see RM to Franklin, November 27, 1781 (first letter).

4. LbC: this word omitted.

5. In a letter of August 17, 1781, John Adams notified Franklin that bills for 40,958 guilders in favor of John Ross had been drawn on Henry Laurens, then imprisoned in the Tower of London, and asked whether he would pay them. Franklin refused and advised Adams to do the same.

The drafts in question were authorized on November 23, 1779, when Congress voted to draw bills of exchange for £100,000 sterling each on John Jay, minister to Spain, and Henry Laurens, special commissioner to seek loans in Holland, and sell them to raise money. There was no assurance that funds were available to pay the bills; nevertheless, after Laurens's capture, Congress on June 20, 1780, instructed Adams, his replacement, to discharge any drafts on Laurens. On June 4, 1781, RM was given custody of the unsold portion of these bills with instructions to sell the drafts on Jay and Adams only if he had assurance that these ministers had funds to pay them. Although such assurance was lacking, Congress on June 20 empowered RM to give the bills to John Ross in partial payment of his account, on the condition that Ross would not charge the usual damages if they were refused. Adams to Franklin, August 17, 1781, Adams Papers microfilm, reel 104, published (Boston, 1954–1959) by MHi, which owns the originals; Franklin to Adams, August 31, and November 7, 1781, Wharton, ed., *Rev. Dipl. Corr.,* IV, 682, 834–835; notes to the Plan for Establishing a National Bank, with Observations, May 17; and Diary, June 23, and RM to John Jay, June 29, 1781; Ferguson, *Power of the Purse,* 46, 55–56.

6. On April 10, 1781, Congress prohibited the sale of bills of exchange drawn on its ministers in Europe, except for those appropriated to the southern army and those lodged with the Board of War, without its "special direction." The congressional order of April 27, 1781, to which Franklin refers, prohibited the sale of bills of exchange drawn on John Jay or Henry Laurens until further notice, without mentioning drafts on Franklin.

7. Probably an allusion to the letters of June 8 and 17, and August 23, 1781, from Vergennes to Franklin discussed in note 3 above.

8. Here the LbC contains the words "made on me."

9. The loan of 10 million livres was agreed to by the French government and the States General of Holland on November 5, 1781. The sum was to be advanced to the United States by France. Franklin was informed of the success of the loan on November 8. Contract of the United States with France, July 16, 1782, PCC, no. 135, I, 13–14; Franklin to John Laurens, November 8, 1781, Wharton, ed., *Rev. Dipl. Corr.,* IV, 838.

10. As requested by RM in his letter of July 21, 1781, to Franklin.

11. On the activities of William Jackson and Alexander Gillon, see notes to Franklin to RM, July 26, 1781 (second letter), and the President of Pennsylvania to RM, August 28.

12. On the *Lafayette,* see notes to RM to Washington, July 2, 1781, and note 3 above.

13. RM replied on December 3.

From William Heath

Head Quarters Continental Village [New York] Sept. 12th 1781

Sir

I was yesterday honored with yours of the 5th. One Hundred Head of Beef Cattle went from hence this day for the Southern Army. They will be followed by a like number weekly; you may depend upon every attention in my power to insure a punctual Compliance.[1] I thank you for your assurances of affording aid to this Department. We shall need it in the article of Flour.[2] I have the honor to be with much respect and Esteem Sir your most Obedient Servant

W Heath

Honl. Robert Morris Esqr

ENDORSED: To R. Morris Esqr. respecting/the supplies of beef cattle from/the eastern quarter/Sept. 12. 1781.
MS: ADftS, Heath Papers, MHi.
1. On the arrangements for delivery, see RM to Heath, September 5.
2. See RM to Heath, September 17 and 24, and Heath to RM, September 20 and October 4, 1781.

From Isaac Howell and Peter Thomson

[*Philadelphia, September 12, 1781.* On September 20 RM wrote to Howell and Thomson: "I received your Letter of the twelfth to which no reply was made." *Letter not found.*]

From the Navy Board of the Eastern Department

Navy Board Eastern Department
Boston Septemr. 12. 1781

Honble. Robert Morris Esqr.

Sir

Since our last of the 5th Instant The Active Packet Arrived here from France.[1] As we had no directions for sending forward the dispatches by Express and the Post Master here undertook to send them Carefully and with Expedition we delivered them all to him and Inclose to you Copy of a Letter received from Messrs. Sweighauser and Dobree [2] and two original Bills of Loading for the Goods they shipped on board the Active; those designed for the Arsenal we shall deliver to Mr Bradford the Agent; [3] those for the Admiralty we shall retain in our hands and use such as are wanted for the Ships here; there is besides a bill of Loading shewn us by the Captain [4] for ten barrells, fifteen Chests and a bale of Sundry medecines, thirty barrells containing each 450 Sheets of tin, thirty boxes Containing each 225 Sheets of tin, 1 hhd. of wire to be delivered to the Honble. Board of War Philadelphia or the Deputy Quarter Master General of any other department which will be Accordingly delivered to the Deputy Quarter Master here.[5] We have not a Shilling of money for the most pressing Occasion. The Governors Answer to our Application mentioned in our last was that he would lay the Matter before the Assembly at their first meeting (which is on this day) and that he would use his Endeavors to Supply us Agreeable to your Letter [6] but as we wrote you before we see but little reason to make any dependence upon a Supply from that quarter. The post is Arrived and without any of your favors. The Dean has one Side Graved [7] and waits only for Tides to Compleat her which we expect in two or three days. We are with respect Your most obedient humble Servants

J Warren
Wm Vernon

 MS: LbC, Letterbook of the Navy Board of the Eastern Department, DLC.

1. The Continental brigantine *Active* was a packet launched in July 1779 at Marshfield, Massachusetts. Commanded by Captain Corban Barnes (ca. 1733–1807) of Plymouth, formerly a privateer captain, the *Active* sailed to Nantes in 1781. It is very likely that the ship returned from this voyage with the cargo, described in the letter printed here, containing part of the supplies procured by John Laurens. Brought to Philadelphia in accordance with RM's orders, the vessel was subsequently dispatched to Havana and captured en route by the British on March 23, 1782. Available records would seem to indicate that the *Active* and its captains were not considered part of the Continental navy. *Dict. Amer. Naval Ships*, I, 8; Rosa Pendleton Chiles, comp., "Index of Letters of Robert Morris as Agent of Marine, September 8, 1781–October 20, 1784" (typescript, Office of Naval Records and Library, Navy Department, Washington, n.d.), I, 1, in Naval Records Collection, RG 45, DNA, which contains some conflicting and apparently erroneous data on the *Active;* John Laurens to the President of Congress, September 2, 1781, Wharton, ed., *Rev. Dipl. Corr.*, IV, 691. On Barnes, see Clark and Morgan, eds., *Naval Documents*, III, 602–603, IV, 85, 1267, V, 647–648; *Index of Deaths in Massachusetts Centinel and Columbian Centinel, 1784–1840* (Worcester, Mass., 1952), I, s.v. "Barnes, Corban." For subsequent references to the *Active*, see notes to the Navy Board of the Eastern Department to RM, September 29; RM to the Board of War, September 25, to John Brown, September 25 and 26, and November 2, 1781, to John Ross, and to John Hodge, both January 10, 1782, and to George Abbott Hall, January 22, 1782; and Diary, November 7, 1781, and January 10 and 14, 1782.

2. Letter not found. Jean Daniel Schweighauser, a merchant of Basle, Strasbourg, and Nantes who was appointed commercial agent of the United States at Nantes by William Lee in 1778, was remembered by John Adams as "a very solid Merchant

highly esteemed by every body and highly approved by the Court." Schweighauser died prior to 1786, but despite the applications of his descendants, including his son-in-law Dobrée, his accounts for supplying the Continental frigate *Alliance* were not settled until the first decade of the nineteenth century. Lüthy, *La banque protestante en France*, II, 216; Jacob M. Price, *France and the Chesapeake: A History of the French Tobacco Monopoly, 1674–1791, and of Its Relationship to the British and American Tobacco Trades* (Ann Arbor, Mich., 1973), II, 694, 701, 716; William Lee to Richard Henry Lee, March 23, 1778, Ford, ed., *Letters of William Lee*, II, 407–408; James Lovell to James Warren, August 13, 1779, Burnett, ed., *Letters*, IV, 364–365; Butterfield, ed., *Adams Diary and Autobiography*, IV, 52; Schweighauser and Dobrée to Thomas Jefferson, August 5, 1786, Thomas Barclay to Jefferson, February 10, 1787, Burrill Carnes to Jefferson, January 15, 1788, and Jefferson to Schweighauser and Dobrée, March 3, 1788, Boyd, ed., *Jefferson Papers*, X, 192, XI, 134, XII, 515–516, 642–643; *JCC*, XX, 590, XXI, 899, 907, XXX, 400, XXXI, 878–880.

3. John Bradford, Continental prize agent at Boston.

4. See note 1 above.

5. Colonel Jabez Hatch.

6. See RM to the Governor of Massachusetts, and to the Navy Board of the Eastern Department, both August 4.

7. That is, cleaned and waterproofed. *OED*.

From Lewis Nicola

[*September 12, 1781*. On October 12 RM wrote to Nicola: "I had the Honor of yours of the twelfth of September last some time ago." *Letter not found*.]

From the Board of War

[*Philadelphia, September 12, 1781*. On this date RM wrote in his Diary: "Received a Letter from the Board of War respecting a Contract for Wyoming and Advertized immediately of this date." *Letter not found*.]

Diary: September 13, 1781

Issued a Warrant on Mr Swanwick, favour of Jno. Brown, for Rum Supplied, £3083 State Money.[1]

Genl. Varnum delivered me the Report of a Committee respecting Supplies to Genl. Greens Army, and for strengthening the same to be considered.[2]

An Irish Gentleman [3] Offered himself for a Clerk in this Office; am to see him again.

Mr Lowrey applies again for Money.

Colol. Miles applies most pressingly for Money.[4] I consented to his buying Wood for the Barracks and Prisoners.

Doctr. Witherspoon applied to sell me a Bill on Chas. Town as a means of remitting Money to Genl Green, Which I declined as the payment is not certain; he asked me to remit it and if paid there then to pay here; this I agreed to.[5]

Mr. Forman [6] late Commissioner of the Treasury applies for Money due him on Salary and for Supplies &Ca.; gave him expectation of speedy payment of the Salary but told him the other must be Funded.

Colol. Blaine applied for the Balance of a Warrant he has on T Smith Esqr. in State Emission and Ordered him payment.[7] He produced an Order from the Board of War for Money to Buy Articles for Genl. Greens Table but Money being so scarce I promise to have them procured and delivered to Major Burnet, and the Colo. to be charged for the Amount.[8]

Jno. Pierce Esqr.[9] respecting pay of the Army &Ca.

Wrote a Letter to His Excellency General Washington.

1. See Diary, September 12.

2. On September 3 Congress appointed James Mitchell Varnum, a delegate from Rhode Island, one of a committee to confer with Lieutenant Colonel Lewis Morris, Jr., an aide to Major General Nathanael Greene, on matters "relative to the southern department." Because of Lewis Morris's departure from Philadelphia (see RM to Greene, September 10), the committee apparently conferred instead with Major Robert Burnet (d. 1784?), another aide-de-camp sent by Greene to Philadelphia in August to report to Congress on conditions in his army and the Southern Department. The committee's report of September 12 was recommitted and the committee directed to hold further consultations with the Board of War and RM. There is no further mention of the committee's activities, but RM advised Greene in a letter of September 14 that Burnet would return with "some Money and Stores for your Department" (see also note 8 below). On Burnet, who was an aide to Greene from March 23, 1778, until the end of the war, see Heitman, *Register;* William Johnson, *Sketches of the Life and Correspondence of Nathanael Greene* (Charleston, 1822), II, 403–404, 411–412; and Theodore Thayer, *Nathanael Greene: Strategist of the American Revolution* (New York, 1960), 369.

3. Not further identified.

4. See Diary, September 12, 14, and 15, for applications of Thomas Lowrey and Colonel Samuel Miles.

5. See, on this subject, RM to Nathanael Greene, September 14, and Diary, September 14 and 15.

6. Ezekiel Forman (1736–1795) of Maryland had been paymaster of the Eastern Shore militia and a member of the Maryland Council of Safety before Congress elected him a commissioner of the Board of Treasury on November 9, 1779. His activities in the Treasury Department, together with those of fellow commissioner John Gibson, were the subject of an investigation by a congressional committee, which on August 25, 1780, recommended their dismissal. At Forman's request, Congress accepted his resignation on July 24, 1781. Anne S. Dandridge, comp., *The Forman Genealogy* (Cleveland, 1903), 97–98; notes to RM to the Board of Treasury, June 8, and Diary, July 11, 1781.

7. Ephraim Blaine was commissary general of purchases; Thomas Smith was Continental loan officer of Pennsylvania.

8. Acting on a report of the Board of War of September 11, Congress the following day ordered RM to furnish the board with $500 to purchase supplies for Greene's table. See note 2 above, and RM to Greene, September 14.

9. Paymaster general of the Continental army.

To George Washington

Office of Finance
September 13th. 1781.

Dear General

You mention'd to me in Conversation that the Bill I formerly remitted you on Messrs. Richards & Co. of New London had not been paid. I must therefore request that you will give orders for its being returned to me.[1]

Herein you will find the first bill of a Sett drawn by Mr. Thomas Pleasants Junr yesterday at Ten days sight in my favour on David Ross Esqr. Commercial Agent of the State of Virginia [2] for three hundred and twenty Pounds hard Money at the rate of six Shillings per Dollar equal to $1066^2/_3$rds. Spanish Silver Dollars which the Drawer assures me will be punctually paid, and I have charged the same as a Supply for Your Excellency's Table.

Mr. John May [3] of Virginia will pay you thirty Silver Dollars for the same Sum advanced him here for which be pleased to grant him a draft on me and apply it to the same purpose.

I ever am Your Excellency's Most Obedient and humble Servant
Robt Morris

His Excellency General Washington.

ENDORSED: Office of Finance 13th Sepr 1781/from/Hono. Robert Morris Esqr
MSS: LS, Washington Papers, DLC; Ofcl LbC, DLC.

1. See Diary, July 20, and notes, RM to Washington, July 23, and Washington to RM, August 2, 1781 (first letter). Washington returned the bill in his second letter to RM of October 1.

2. On Pleasants and Ross, see notes to Diary, September 8.

3. John May (d. 1790), a Jefferson County, Virginia, surveyor and land speculator who served in the House of Delegates in 1782, later invested heavily in Kentucky lands and was a pioneer settler in the region. Reuben Gold Thwaites and Louise Phelps Kellogg, eds., *Documentary History of Dunmore's War, 1774* (Madison, Wis., 1905), 21n.; Robert A. Rutland, ed., *The Papers of George Mason, 1725–1792* (Chapel Hill, N. C., 1970), I, lxxviii; Earl G. Swem and John W. Williams, *A Register of the General Assembly of Virginia, 1776–1918, and of the Constitutional Conventions* (Richmond, 1918), 15.

Diary: September 14, 1781

Application from Lieutenant Peppin for Money. Ordered him 20 dollars in part of his Warrant.[1]

Mr Peters of the Board of War called respecting the Oneida Indians as they stand in need of Supplies of Cloathing, Paint &Ca.; these I suppose must be supplied. Having sent to Mr Thomson

Secrety. of Congress for the resolutions of the 24th March 1779 I find the Commissioners of Indian Affairs are to order this Tribe Supplies of Provisions from the public Magazines.[2] I answered Genl. Schuyler's Letter on that subject by desiring him to Supply them frugally for the present and to send me an Estimate of a Monthly Supply.

For several days past have been endeavouring to borrow Money but find it very scarce.

Mr. Lowrey applied to me for Money to pay for Flour and Transportation and the Balance being about £8000 to £10,000, I agree to pay him £1,000 tomorrow and give him an Order on Boston for £8,000 being at his own request.[3]

Had Sundry Conferences. Viz. With Solomon the Broker[4] respecting Exchange Money &Ca. With Colo. M Smith[5] an hours Conversation relative to the Revenues of Virginia &Ca. With Doctr. Wetherspoon about some Bills drawn by the Honorable John Matthews Esqr. on Chas. Drayton Esqr. in Chastown So Carolina,[6] Which he requested me to remit to Genl. Greene and pay for here when I should have received advice that they had been paid to him. This I agreed to.[7] Doctrs. Bond and Oliphant[8] calld with an Order of the Board of War of this date and Estimates for Medicine and Stores.[9] I decline paying any Money.[10] Doctr. Jones[11] calls on me; I lay the Estimates before him. He thinks them exorbitant and most of the Medicines mentioned in that Estimate useless.

Dispatch'd Genl Schuylers Express with the Balance due to him for Flour.[12]

Conversed with Mr Peters of the Board of War relative to the Issuing Department; he assures me all Persons that previous to my Contracts had been employed in Issuing Provisions, were now displaced and that the Depty Commissary Genl of Issues and such as are employed under him in this City are those which are necessary to superintend Posts not provided for by Contracts.[13]

Issued a Warrant On Mr Swanwick in favour of Philips, Presidt of Congress, Stewd. for £37.10.

Issued a Warrant On Mr Swanwick in favour of Jno Van Woest, for Genl Schuyler £1950.9.[14]

Issued a Warrant On Mr Swanwick in favour of Colo Miles £30.[15]

Wrote Letters, To Thomas Russell Esqr. Boston, Major Genl. Schuyler and to Major Genl. Green.

1. On Andrew Pepin's application, see notes to Diary, August 23; and Diary, September 11.
2. On this resolution, see notes to Philip Schuyler to RM, August 31; and Diary, September 12.

3. On Thomas Lowrey's application, see Diary, September 12, 13, and 15, and RM to Tench Francis, September 15 (two letters).

4. Haym Salomon, Philadelphia bill broker.

5. Meriwether Smith (1730–1790), a Virginia delegate to the Continental Congress, 1778–1782, and a member of the Virginia House of Delegates, 1776–1778, 1781–1782, 1785 and 1788. *Biog. Dir. Cong.*

6. Charles Drayton (1743–1820), physician, planter, botanist, and artist of Charleston, South Carolina, was a captain of volunteers and supplier of provisions during the Revolutionary War. Later he became lieutenant governor, 1785–1787, a delegate to the state convention to ratify the federal Constitution in 1788, and a state legislator, 1787–1796, 1797–1800. Reynolds and Faunt, comps., *Biog. Dir. S. C. Senate,* 208.

7. See RM to Nathanael Greene, September 14, and Diary, September 13 and 15.

8. Doctors Thomas Bond, Jr., purveyor of the Continental Hospital Department, and David Olyphant (1720–1805) of South Carolina, a Jacobite who emigrated from Scotland shortly after the rebellion of 1745 and established himself as a physician and planter in Charleston. Besides serving in the South Carolina legislature during the Revolution, Olyphant was named director general, physician, and surgeon-in-chief to the Continental hospitals in South Carolina on June 1, 1776. He held this position, in which he claimed autonomy from the director general of the department in Philadelphia, until May 15, 1781, when, following a departmental reorganization, he was named deputy director of the department for the southern army, a post he retained until the end of the war. Reynolds and Faunt, comps., *Biog. Dir. S. C. Senate,* 284; Heitman, *Register;* Olyphant to the South Carolina delegates in Congress, July 16, 1779, his commission of June 1, 1776, and his undated memorial to Congress, [October 1782], are in PCC, no. 72, pp. 515, 518–519, and no. 41, VII, 330.

9. Neither the board's order nor the estimates has been found.

10. See RM to Nathanael Greene, September 14, for a further explanation of this refusal; and Diary, September 21, 24, 26, and 27.

11. Doctor John Jones, whose advice RM had previously sought. See RM to Gerardus Clarkson, James Hutchinson, and John Jones, July 17, 1781, and notes.

12. See below in this Diary, Philip Schuyler to RM, August 31, and RM to Schuyler, and to Thomas Russell, both September 14.

13. Contracts for Continental posts in Pennsylvania. Thomas Jones was deputy commissary general of issues.

14. Schuyler's express was John Van Woort. See above in Diary and notes to Philip Schuyler to RM, August 31.

15. See Diary, September 12 and 13.

To Benjamin Franklin

Office of Finance
Philada. Septbr. 14th. 1781

Sir

I take the Liberty to enclose to you a note of two Books of which I am to request that you will cause three compleat Setts to be purchased on the public account and sent to me by three different Conveyances.[1] I am very respectfully Sir your most Obedient and humble Servant

Robt Morris

His Excy Benjn Franklin Esqr.
Minister Plenipotentiary from the United States
at the Court of Versailles

[ENCLOSURE]

L'histoire des Finances par Monsr. de Forbonnois[2]

Traite des Imposetions dans les differens Etats de l'Europe redigé
par Monsr. Baumont, imprimé a l'Imprimerie royal.[3]

MSS: LS and enclosed D, Franklin Papers, PU; Ofcl LbC, DLC.
    1. Franklin sent, and presumably RM received, the books the following year. See
Franklin to RM, June 25, 1782.
    2. François Véron Duverger de Forbonnais (1722–1800), French treasury official,
advocate of economic reform and state regulation, opponent of free trade, and one
of the chief contemporary adversaries of the physiocrats. The work to which RM
refers is probably his two-volume *Recherches et considerations sur les finances de France,
depuis l'année 1595 jusqu'à l'année 1721* (Basle, 1758), also published the same year
at Liège in six volumes. Henry Higgs, *The Physiocrats: Six Lectures on the French Écono-
mistes of the 18th Century* (London, 1897), 79, 102–104; Bosher, *French Finances*, 100,
126.
    3. Jean Louis Moreau de Beaumont (1715–1785), an official in the French treasury
under Louis XV and XVI and author of *Mémoires concernant les impositions et droits en
Europe* (Paris, 1768–1769) in four volumes. Hoefer, ed., *Nouvelle biographie générale*,
V, 31; Bosher, *French Finances*, 28, 37 and n., 366.

To Nathanael Greene

Office of Finance September 14th. 1781.

Sir

   In my former letters I mention'd that His Excellency Governor
Rutledge would pay you any money he might receive for Subscriptions to the National Bank, also that by order of Congress I had
supplied the Lieutent. Governor and Members of the Council of
South Carolina with five hundred Pounds Currency of Pennsylvania
in Specie which in Convenient Season they will repay to you taking
your draft on the Treasurer of the United States.[1] And herein you
will find a Bill drawn by the Honorable John Matthews Esqr. this
date at ten days Sight on Charles Drayton Esqr. in Charles Town
for one hundred and seventy three Specie Dollars in favour of
Doctor John Witherspoon who has endorsed the same payable to
your Order and is informed that you will be able to obtain payment,
or to Negotiate it so as that the Money will come into your hands.
If this happens be pleased to remit to Doctor Witherspoon your
Draft on the Treasurer of the United States which I have promised
him shall be paid, but if you do not recover the payment be pleased
to return the bill to me with the Reasons for nonpayment.[2] A letter
of advice accompanies the bill and I shall by another Conveyance
send you duplicate of each.[3] Whatever Monies you receive from any
of these Remittances will be charged to you as advances for the
Public Service. Consequently you will cause Accounts of the Expen-

diture to be render'd with the proper Vouchers in due Season. Major Burnett will also receive some Money and Stores for your Department to which I give all the facility in my power,[4] but Doctor Oliphant has sent in Lists of Medicine, Stores and Money as necessary for the Hospital of the Southern Army which I do not so readily acquiesce in, particularly as it is not possible in the present Situation of things to provide such Sums of Money as are called for in many other Departments besides this.[5] But I can with truth assure you I have every disposition to provide for those things that are realy necessary to the use of the Army.[6] I am Dear General, Your Obedient humble Servant

Robt Morris

The Honble. Major General Greene
Commanding the Southern Army.

ADDRESSED: The Honorable/Major General Nathl. Greene/Commanding the Southern/Army/R Morris   ENDORSED: From/Mr. R. Morris/Sept 14th. 1781
MSS: LS, Greene Papers, MiU-C; Ofcl LbC, DLC.
    1. See RM to Greene, June 12, Greene to RM, August 18, and RM to Greene, September 10.
    2. On this transaction, see Diary, September 13, 14, and 15.
    3. Enclosures not found.
    4. On Burnet's mission, see notes to Diary, September 13.
    5. For Olyphant's application to RM, see Diary, September 14, 21, 24, 26, and 27.
    6. This letter undoubtedly was enclosed in RM's communication to Washington, September 18, which has not been found.

To Thomas Russell

Office of Finance
Philada. Septr. 14th. 1781.

Sir,
    Having Occasion to make General Schuyler a remittance on Public Account at a time when the Movements of the Army bear very hard on me, and observing that the Subscriptions to the Bank are going forward in Boston, I have drawn a Bill on you this Date at ten Days sight in favor of Genl Philip Schuyler or Order for three thousand five hundred silver Dollars or other Gold or Silver Specie equivalent which I pray you to honor and redraw on me for the same Sum in favor of Messrs. Clymer and Nixon for the use of the Bank which [will] be punctually paid.[1] I always am Sir your devoted humble Servant.

RM.

MS: Ofcl LbC, DLC.

1. On the remittance to Schuyler, see Philip Schuyler to RM, August 31, and Diary, and RM to Schuyler, both September 14. For a discussion of the Bank of North America and the work of George Clymer, John Nixon, and Thomas Russell connected therewith, see the headnote and notes to RM's Plan for Establishing a National Bank, with Observations, May 17, and notes to John Langdon to RM, July 6, 1781.

To Philip Schuyler

Office of Finance Septembr. 14th. 1781.

Dear Sir

I receiv'd your Letter of the thirty first of August last by Mr. Vanbrunt [1] on the eighth Instant [2] and should have answer'd it immediately had it arrived a little sooner as I kept myself in a State of Preparation for that Purpose. But just before the arrival of Mr. Vanbrunt a very heavy demand was made upon me for the rapid Movement of the Army which has since taken place.[3] This demand was as urgent as it was great and I was unable alike to resist or to answer it. By the greatest Exertions I have at length been able to comply with the General's Views but that Compliance has exposed me almost pennyless to answer Engagements which cannot be violated. That with you is among the Number, and therefore I send you the Ballance due on the account transmitted to me after deducting a Bill remitted you on the fourth Instant drawn by Coll Smith on Mr. Lewis for fifty Pounds of which I now send you the second enclosed.[4]

I wish I could send you also the Money necessary to pay for the Batteux which you estimate at about three thousand five hundred Dollars, but this is impossible. In Order to avoid the sending Expresses for it and the like, I have thought of an Expedient which is this. I enclose you my first and second of Exchange on Thomas Russell Esqr. of Boston.[5] If you find it convenient to receive the Money in that place, You can transmit the Bills for that Purpose, and they will be duly honoured. If not, return it to me and I will pay the Money here as you shall direct. But as there must be constant Demands, for Articles to the Eastward in your State I should suppose it would be even more convenient to have the Money there than here. Your request of a Guard to your Messenger, it is not in my Power to comply with, but I cannot conceive that there is any great Danger, if he Conducts himself with tolerable Prudence, and the Expence of a Guard, even if it could be afforded, would be intolerably great in Proportion to the Sum.

It is my Duty to observe to you, that the Commission of five per

Cent is double the Commission which I have paid in the like Cases, and that I did not when I gave this Order imagine that any Part of the Flour would have been expended at Albany, but hoped that the State of New York would have furnished the necessary Supplies for those Posts most connected with the immediate Protection of her Frontiers, and I expected that the Flour procured by you would have been applied solely to the Support of the Main Army, under the Command of His Excellency General Washington.

With Respect to what you say about the Indians, I have to answer that I have every Inclination to comply with the Promises which may have been made to them, as well from Motives of Gratitude and Justice as of good Policy.[6] On the other Hand, I am sure I need not tell you that strict Oeconomy is necessary in the Conduct of our Affairs. I am therefore to request that you will cause them to be supplied for the present on the most reasonable Terms possible, and that you will be so Kind as to transmit me an Estimate of the Monthly Expence, that I may take the Measures necessary in Consequence of it, either by making Provision for the Service or by laying it before Congress for their Consideration. I have the Pleasure to inform you that Your bill in favour of Mr. Binden has been duly honored. I have the Honor to be with great Respect Sir, Your most Obedient and humble Servant

Robt Morris

ENDORSED: From/Rob Morris Esq/Sept: 14. 1781
MSS: LS, Schuyler Papers, NN; Ofcl LbC, DLC.
    1. Undoubtedly a clerk's error in transcribing the name of John Van Woort. See Schuyler to RM, August 31, and Diary, September 14.
    2. The preceding two words are in the writing of Gouverneur Morris.
    3. The movement of a detachment of Washington's army from New York to Virginia for operations against Cornwallis, some of the financial preparations for which are discussed in Diary, September 1–5, and notes.
    4. On this transaction, see RM to Schuyler, September 4.
    5. See RM to Russell, September 14.
    6. See Diary, September 12 and 14.

From John de Neufville and Company

[*Amsterdam*], *September 14, 1781.* This private business letter discussed the prospects of Dutch cooperation with the United States in prosecuting the war, particularly the exchange of British seamen captured by American privateers for American prisoners in England. Of RM's assumption of duties as Financier the firm writes: "Nothing could give us more real Satisfaction than to be apprised that you had taken upon you the Labourious task of Superintending the finances of the States. Where public Virtue and ability are so Conspicuously blended, one may reasonably hope [for] the happiest effects. We are of Course Sanguine in our Expectations on that event."

MS: LbC, John de Neufville Papers, NHi.

From Anthony Wayne[1]

Wms Burgh [Virginia], 14th Septr, 1781.[2]

Dear Sir,

The arrival of the Count de Grasse with a large fleet of men of war &c must have been announced in Phila long before this period.[3] I wish that the state of our Magazines had been such as to enable us to improve the moment of his arrival, but they were not—and what is *worse* they are *not* even at this moment.

I dont know how it is, but I have not felt so sanguine on the occation as the Naval and land force sent us by our generous and great ally would justify—probably it is occationed by our former disappointments, when matters bore a flattering aspect. The French troops are the finest and best made body of troops I ever beheld. Their officers are gentlemen and I will be answerable for their being soldiers;—we have the highest opinion of their discipline and cannot doubt their prowess. Do you know that notwithstanding all these circumstances I have been extremely uneasy lest the appearance of a British fleet off these Capes should induce the Count to follow them too far and leave an opening for the British to enter to their exclusion. I hope it was not ominous Admiral Hood made his appearance with *eighteen* sail of the line last Wednesday week,[4] the Count De Grass with *twenty two* sail of the line immediately weighed anchor fourteen of which engaged *Hood,* the other eight could not get up in time as the British Admiral fled too soon for anything but an act of choice, may he not wish to draw *De Grasse* towards New York and expose him to the effects of the Equinoctial storm, whilst the British lay snug in harbor. The Count *De Estaing* was taken in by Lord Howe this time three years by a manœuvre of the same kind.[5] But it cannot, it must not be the case now—the Count has left six sail of the line to block up the entrance of the Chesapeake during his absence—he also has another object—i.e. the junction of the Rhode Island fleet in a given latitude which may account for his long absence.[6]

Unless Fortune is uncommonly unkind Lord Cornwallis and his army must submit to our combined force, his numbers are more than generally given out, we shall find at least six thousand combatants, officers included, exclusive of negroes &c &c So that during the absence of the Count de Grasse who has a large body of marines on board destined to act with us we could not conveniently complete the investiture of York and Glocester. However the arrival of his Excellency General Washington with the troops under his immediate command will enable us to commence our operations immediately. I must acknowledge that I could wish to bring his Lordship to an action previous to the investiture, as it would certainly very much accelerate his reduction.

The Marquis Lafayette one of the best of Officers and first of men has for some days been laid up with a fever which added to my own misfortune tended not a little to retard this essential business; he is now much recovered and my wound is in so fair a way that I can mount my horse and lead the troops in case of emergency. From Lord Cornwallis's character it may yet be possible to tempt him to a field day, and his Excellency being now arrived I am in hopes matters will be put in a proper train for the purpose, otherwise you may depend upon it that the siege will be very tedious—for the enemy have improved every moment in fortifying and procuring a supply of provisions &c &c.

Their principal works are at Yorktown, which is nearly surrounded by the river and a morass, except a narrow isthmus, upon which is erected a strong independent redoubt with a ditch, frize and abbatis.[7] They also occupy Glocester on the opposite side the river where they have one or two little works to preserve a communication with the Country, but they will certainly evacuate that side as soon as the investiture is complete.

You know that I am of a desponding disposition and was I to *adopt* that character at this crisis, I ought to be d——d, but these are a train of eventual circumstances that I cant help revolving in my mind, all of which makes me most anxiously wish his Lordship to play this *duet* out of the lines, in which case, I would risk my soul and body on figuring into York with him, and bringing the affair to a speedy issue from a full conviction that a victorious army meets no difficulties, and that we possibly may be pressed for *time*—(between you and me) I have some reason to wish for the power of *Joshua*. I certainly would give the good old gentleman a holiday until the American colours were displayed upon the British lines. Until when, and ever believe me Yours most Sincerely,

Anty. Wayne

I found a *leasure* hour to write this scrawl—I hope you may find one to decipher it in, for I realy can scarcely read it myself however it contains some ideas warm from the heart—I therefore send it uncorrected—in which state I commit it to the hands of a friend.

☞ Before sealing I recd the Inclosed note [8]—my Doubts are removed—success is certain—if the fleet can *wait*—time, time, time—is all.

PRINTED: "Letters to Robert Morris, 1775–1782," N.-Y. Hist. Soc., *Colls.*, XI (New York, 1879), 467–470. MSS: ADft, incomplete, Wayne Papers, PHi; Bancroft transcript, incomplete, NN.

1. Brigadier General Wayne had joined Lafayette's forces in June 1781 with three battalions of the Pennsylvania line. At Yorktown he commanded one of two brigades under Major General von Steuben. Ward, *War of the Revolution*, II, 873–877, 886.

2. The editors have reprinted verbatim (except for a partial expansion of the dateline) a text of this letter which internal evidence suggests probably derived either from Wayne's final draft or a copy which may have been received by RM, although no acknowledgment has been found. The extant manuscript texts of this letter are in different stages of completion. The ADft, part of which has been lost, is more complete than Bancroft's transcript (of what probably is a still earlier draft) and has a variant arrangement of the text than that printed here, with some passages omitted and others altered.

3. On the arrival of de Grasse, see notes to Washington to RM, August 27. For RM's receipt of this intelligence, see Diary, September 1–5.

4. Rear Admiral Sir Samuel Hood and Admiral Sir Thomas Graves (ca. 1725–1802) appeared with their fleets off the Chesapeake and, as noted by Wayne, on September 5 were engaged by de Grasse, who gained the upper hand. The British forces returned to New York and subsequent relief to Cornwallis was closed. Ward, *War of the Revolution*, II, 885; *DNB*; notes to Timothy Matlack to RM, September 11.

5. Possibly a reference to an engagement between French and British naval forces off Newport, Rhode Island, in August 1778. Following his arrival from France in July 1778 and the frustration of his plan to attack the British at New York, Jean Baptiste Charles Henri Hector Théodat, Comte d'Estaing (1729–1794) agreed to undertake an operation against the British garrison at Newport jointly with American land forces. On August 10 d'Estaing sailed from Newport to meet the fleet of Admiral Lord Richard Howe (1726–1799), British commander-in-chief of the American station, 1776–1778, who was bent on reinforcing the garrison, but a severe storm cast both fleets into disarray. Inconclusive fighting followed, and d'Estaing, after putting into Boston for repairs, sailed for the West Indies, leaving Newport still in British hands. William C. Stinchcombe, *The American Revolution and the French Alliance* (Syracuse, N. Y., 1969), 49–57; Ward, *War of the Revolution*, II, 587–591; on Howe, see *DNB*; on d'Estaing, *La grande encyclopédie: inventaire raisonné des sciences, des lettres et des arts* (Paris, [1886–1902]), XVI, 398.

6. While de Grasse diverted Hood and Graves, the fleet from Newport, Rhode Island, under Admiral de Barras slipped unnoticed into Chesapeake Bay. Ward, *War of the Revolution*, II, 885.

7. Respectively, *chevaux de frise*, a defensive obstacle of timber tipped with iron spikes; and abatis, an obstruction of felled trees with sharp protruding branches.

8. Enclosure not found.

Diary: September 15, 1781

Applications at 6 OClock this Morning for Money.

In my Letter of yesterdays date to The Honorable Major Genl. Greene I remitted enclosed a Draft of Jno. Matthews Esqr. on Chas. Drayton for 173 hard dollars for which Doctor Witherspoon is to be paid when Genl. Greene obtains payment there.

Sundry applications for Money this day. Vizt. Mr. Lowrey,[1] The Paymaster General,[2] Mr. Witherspoon the younger,[3] Express that came with Colo Laurens, And the Cloathier Genl. who wants to purchase Goods for the Indians, &Ca.[4]

Wrote Letters, To Matthew Ridley Esqr. of Baltimore respecting Flour.

To His Excellency The Governour of Massachusetts Bay.

To Tench Francis Esqr. advising of Order on him in favour of Thos Lowrey Esqr. for £8000 Pensylvania Currency; drew Order.

Issued a Warrant in favour of Wm Scott of York Town for Supplies there Amounting to £635.3.10.[5]

Issued a Warrant in favour of Thos. Lowrey On Account of Flour £1000.

Issued a Warrant in favour of Colo Laurens Express £7.10.

---

1. On Thomas Lowrey's applications, see this Diary below, Diary, September 12, 13, and 14, and RM to Tench Francis, September 15 (two letters).

2. John Pierce.

3. Probably David Witherspoon (1760–1801), a son of Doctor John Witherspoon, member of Congress from New Jersey. On January 20, 1781, the Board of Treasury had awarded Witherspoon a warrant for $450 new emission on the United States Treasury in discharge of his salary, probably as secretary to former President of Congress Samuel Huntington. Since there was no new emission money in the treasury, on February 21 Witherspoon asked Congress for a warrant on the Continental loan officer of Pennsylvania, but although Congress the next day referred the matter to a committee, no action appears to have been taken on his request. David Witherspoon to the President of Congress, February 21, 1781, PCC, no. 78, XXIV, 179; *JCC*, XIX, 185–186; Varnum Lansing Collins, *President Witherspoon: A Biography* (Princeton, 1925), I, 7, 25, 193.

4. The application of Clothier General John Moylan possibly may be related to the problem of supplying the Oneidas and Tuscaroras in New York. See Philip Schuyler to RM, August 31, Diary, September 12 and 14, and RM to Schuyler, September 14.

5. See RM to William Scott, August 25.

To Tench Francis

Office of Finance 15th. Sepr. 1781.

Sir

Finding myself indebted to Mr Lowrey about eight thousand Pounds Pennsylvania Money on Account of the United States I have agreed with him to pay it in Boston;[1] for which Purpose I will give an Order on you,[2] with Directions to apply to Mr. Russell,[3] in Case you should have left that Place. You will therefore (if you come away before the Draft arrives) leave the Money to Answer it in Mr. Russell's Hands. I am Sir very respectfully, &Ca.

RM.

MS: Ofcl LbC, DLC.
    1. See Diary, September 12, 13, 14, and 15.
    2. See RM to Tench Francis, September 15 (second letter).
    3. Thomas Russell, agent for raising subscriptions to the Bank of North America in Boston.

To Tench Francis

Office of Finance 15th. Septr. 1781.

Sir

On Sight of this my sole Bill, be pleased to pay unto Thomas Lowrey Esqr. the Sum of Eight thousand Pounds Pensylvania Currency in Spanish Dollars at seven Shillings and sixpence each or french Crowns at Eight Shillings and four pence each being in Payment for flour by him delivered to the Use of the Army in Consequence of my Engagements with him on that Behalf.[1] I am Sir your obedient Servant

RM

MS: Ofcl LbC, DLC.
    1. See RM to Tench Francis, September 15 (first letter).

To Horatio Gates

Philada. Septr. 15th 1781

Dear Sir

My visit to Camp was rendered agreable by many Circumstances;[1] how far it will prove usefull time must show; hitherto our affairs seem to mend without the assistance of paper Money the loss of which seems to be regretted by very few.

I am sorry you did not get the Answers you expected from Congress and the Commander in Chief,[2] but it does not appear to me that either one or the other are inimical to you. My opinion is that you shou'd turn out a Volunteer in *your Own service,* and now that Genl Washington and so large a part of the Army is in Virginia, call for a Court of Enquiry or a Court Martial or whatever it is, or ought, to be; be assured by staying at home complaining and dissatisfied, you are playing a game against yourself and laying a foundation from which others will pluck your Laurels. I know that you have doubts or suspicions that fair play is not meant for you. I differ very much in this respect and have not the least reason to suppose that any Man in high Authority wishes or means you an injury; discard therefore at once, all such Jealousies, and never let them plague you more; they are the greatest Enemies you have. Repair to the busy Scenes of the World, call loudly for the Justice You think your due, insist on being heard, and appear again a champion for fresh Laurels and renewed Glory. The present Moments are Critical, Fate is busy and important Events on the eve of breaking Forth. I shall be sorry indeed, if with a Supineness unworthy of your Active Mind, you are contented to be a meer Spectator at the Close of a War in parts of which you have made so Capital a Figure. You see I write to you with the same Freedom that I speak and with the zeal that a Warm Heart indicates. You will determine for yourself, but you have my real Sentiments. The Capture of the Trumbull Frigate was a great loss to the Public and a disapointment to a most promising plan I had laid for turning, as you desired I shou'd, our paper into Silver.[3] However we have learnt to bear losses and endure disapointments and what is still better we have courage always to try again, which is what I advise you to do. My Sons are still here.[4] Doctr Booth [5] invites them down again to his School, but the great Numbers he took there last year, put it out of his power to attend to them sufficiently and it seems to be a general opinion here that the Boys lost their time. I am sorry he injured himself in this way as I respect both his Abilities and Character. Mrs Morris joins me in Compliments to Mrs. Gates. She must not blame me for urging you to depart and I am sure on reflection she will not, because she has your Peace of Mind, and Fame, as much at Heart, as she ought.

I am very Sincerely Dear General Your most Obedient and very humble Servant

Robt Morris

The Honble Major General Horatio Gates
Berkley County
Virginia

ENDORSED: From R: Morris/Phila: 15th: Sept: 1781
MS: ALS, Gates Papers, NHi.
    1. See Diary, August 21, for RM's account of his visit to Washington's headquarters.
    2. See Gates to RM, September 4, and notes, to which RM here replies.
    3. On the *Trumbull*, see RM to the Governor of Cuba, to James Nicholson (two letters), and to Robert Smith, all July 17, and Diary, August 15, 1781, and notes.
    4. RM's plans for educating his two eldest sons in Europe are discussed in letters to Matthew Ridley and Benjamin Franklin, both October 14, 1781.

5. Reverend Bartholomew Booth (d. 1785), an Episcopal clergyman whose school at Needlewood Forest in Frederick County, Maryland, had been attended by RM's two eldest sons. Nelson W. Rightmyer, *Maryland's Established Church* (Baltimore, 1956), 162; Ethan Allen, *Clergy in Maryland of the Protestant Episcopal Church since the Independence of 1783* (Baltimore, 1860), 10; RM to Booth, March 18, 1778, Booth Papers, MdAA; RM to Booth, July 26, 1782, Robert Morris Papers, NN.

To the Governor of Massachusetts (John Hancock)

Office of Finance September 15th. 1781.

Sir

I was honored with your Excellency's Favour of the 23rd. August,[1] by the last Post. I should sooner have answer'd it but a multiplicity of Business would not permit me. I am very sorry to learn, that the Impost recommended by Congress will go heavily thro your Legislature.[2] I thank you for your Promise that you will candidly lay the Matter before the Assembly. To reiterate Arguments will be unnecessary. It is a plain Matter, parallell to the Observation of every Man, and must be determined on the simple question; Shall the Faith of the United States be supported? You Sir who know the Value of Credit, and the Duty of supporting it; you who feel the Force of those Moral Obligations on which that Duty is founded, you I hope will enforce my Applications, or rather the Applications of our Sovereign, by that Energy which accompanies the Voice of the supreme Executive, when standing on the Ground of Information, and speaking the Language of Reason and Truth.

In my Letter of the twenty fifth of July last, [3] I gave you Assurances that I would press forward the Settlement of Accounts, and these Assurances I now repeat. On the 27th. of August last, I prepared and delivered to a Committee of Congress a plan for arranging the Treasury Board, and on the 11th Instant the United States in Congress assembled passed an Ordinance, nearly Conformable to that Plan, for regulating the Treasury and adjusting the Public Accounts, of which I now do myself the Honor of enclosing a Copy.[4]

On the twenty third of August last, a Letter from the honorable Nathaniel Gorham, J. Lowell and Henry Higginson,[5] to the Delegates of the Massachusetts, dated the 24th of May last, and a Letter from your Excellency of the 18th. of June last, to the President of Congress, were referred to me by the United States in Congress assembled; [6] and on the tenth Instant, the Resolutions of the House of Representatives of Massachusetts of the thirtieth of June last, were also referred to me.[7] The Subject of those Letters and Reports is so connected with other Matters, that it is necessary the whole should be taken up together. The Injuries which some States may have sustained, by the Neglect of others in complying with Requisitions of Congress, must be redressed by those who are in Default. I shall constantly press the Measures necessary to procure that Redress, which Justice may dictate, and I hope the public Business will soon be so Methodized that the United States on the one Hand will have full Leizure to attend to the important Objects of Administration, without being interupted by that small detailed attention which a Regard to their own Dignity must render very disagreeable, and which is equally troublesome and pernicious; and that on the other Hand, the Individual States will by cheerful confidential Compliances with the Demands of the Union, give to our Government that Vigor, Energy and Vivacity which can alone secure our Freedom and Happiness.

My general Arrangements will include the Matters referred to me from your State.[8] I can safely promise you that they shall be founded in Justice, as far as lies in my Power, and that no delay shall intervene, except what may be unavoidable. With the greatest Respect I have the Honor to be Sir, Your Excellencys Most Obedient and humble Servant [9]

Robt Morris

His Excelly. The Governor
of the State of Massachusetts

ENDORSED: Robert Morris/Septemr 15 1781
MSS: LS, Robert Morris Collection, PHarH (photostat); Ofcl LbC, DLC; copy, Bache Collection, PPAmP.
   1. Letter not found.
   2. On the impost, see the headnote to RM's Circular to the Governors of Massachusetts, Rhode Island, New York, Delaware, Maryland, and North Carolina, July 27, 1781.
   3. RM's Circular to the Governors of the States.
   4. See RM's Plan for Arranging the Treasury Department, August 27, and notes.
   5. All members of a committee of the Massachusetts House of Representatives.
   Nathaniel Gorham (1738–1796), a merchant and politician of Charlestown, Massachusetts, was a member of the state house of representatives, 1781–1783, a delegate to the Continental Congress, 1782, 1783, and 1785–1787, serving as president, June 6, 1786–February 2, 1787, and a member of the Philadelphia Convention of 1787. DAB.
   John Lowell (1743–1802), a Boston lawyer, legislator, and jurist, was a member of the Massachusetts House of Representatives, 1778, 1780–1782, of the Continental Congress, 1782 and 1783, and of the state senate, 1784 and 1785. Biog. Dir. Cong.
   Henry Higginson (1747–1790) of Salem, a privateer captain and son of the distinguished merchant Stephen Higginson (1716–1761), was elected to the Massachusetts House of Representatives in 1780 and 1781. Thomas Wentworth Higginson, Descendants of the Reverend Francis Higginson . . . ([Cambridge, Mass.?], 1910), 16, 17; Joseph B. Felt, The Annals of Salem, from Its First Settlement (Salem, 1827), 507, 509, 510, 512.

6. *JCC*, XXI, 897. These two letters have not been found.

7. *JCC*, XXI, 947. On these resolutions, see notes to RM to the President of Congress, August 28.

8. For these "general Arrangements," see RM to the President of Congress, August 28, November 5, and December 10, 1781.

9. A copy of this letter was enclosed in RM to Benjamin Franklin, November 27, 1781 (first letter).

To Matthew Ridley

Office of Finance Sepr. 15. 1781.

Sir,

In Answer to your Letters of the tenth Instant [1] I can tell you that the sole Cause of my anxiety to have the three thousand Barrels of Flour ready in your Hands is because I promised that it should be so; that flour is for the Use of Count de Grass's fleet and must be delivered whenever he sends for it. There is the same Quantity or more ready for him here, consequently they do not want [to] buy. The french Army will want some but it is so cheap in Virginia where their hard Money is also most Welcome that if your People think of rising Prices I foretel they will loose their Custom. The specific Supplies which Virginia, Maryland and Delaware are to render to our Army will be more than their Wants, consequently there cannot be any unless small occasional Calls to purchase on that Account. I have desired William Smith Esqr.[2] to deliver you for the Use of Mr Holker or to be held at his Order six hundred and ten Barrels of Superfine flour to replace so much that he lent me.[3] This Mr Smith gives me reason to expect he shall soon be able to do, from Effects of mine in his Hands. I have some Plans in Agitations for a general System of supplying both Armies [4] and thank you for your hints on that Subject, And am Sir your obedient and humble Servant

RM

MS: Ofcl LbC, DLC.

1. Letters not found.

2. Smith was a Baltimore merchant.

3. On these flour transactions, see RM to John Holker, August 7, and notes.

4. On RM's idea of supplying both the French and American armies by contract, see RM to La Luzerne, August 2, La Luzerne to RM, August 3, and Diary, August 21, and notes.

From the Commissary General of Purchases (Ephraim Blaine)

[*September 15, 1781.* On September 18 RM wrote to Commissary Blaine: "I was yesterday favored with your Letter dated Saturday Morning the fifteenth of September 1781 [from which] you have omitted the Place where it was written." This letter undoubtedly concerned the procurement and delivery of salt to the Head of Elk; see RM to the Commissary General of Purchases, October 4, 1781. *Letter not found.*]

From William Heath

Head Quarters Continental Village [New York] Sept. 15th. 1781
Sir

I was this Day honored with yours of the 11th. per Tench Francis Esqr with an order from the Board of War.[1] You may rely on every attention in my Power to render his Commission safe and expeditious. I have the honor to be with great regard Sir your most Obedient Servant

W Heath
M[ajor] General

Hon Robert Morris Esqr

ENDORSED: To Robert Morris esqr./respecting Tench Francis/esqr. &c./Sept. 15. 1781.
MS: ADftS, Heath Papers, MHi.
1. See Diary, and RM to the Board of War, both September 10, and RM to Tench Francis, September 11 (first letter), and notes.

From Hector Daure[1]

[Baltimore, September 16, 1781]
The American Commissaries have doubtless informed you that the Gentlemen employed to superintend the victualling Department have delivered to them all the Flour and Biscuit which was deposited at Albany, Rhinebeck, Fishkill landing, Peeks Kills and Kings Ferry.[2] This Affair being therefore compleated on the Part of the french Administration will you be so good as to give Orders to have replaced as soon as possible by a Delivery to Monsr.

Dumas [3] charged with the victualling Service at Baltimore twelve
hundred Barrels of Flour.[4] This first Payment is so much the more
necessary as that Article begins to grow Scarce.

ENDORSED: Extract of a Letter from Monsr. Daure,/dated Baltimore the 16th. January
[i.e. September] 1781, to the Superintendt. of Finance
MS: Ofcl LbC (extract), DLC.
    1. Comte Hector Daure, described by RM as "Regisseur general des vivres" (stew-
ard of provisions) of the French army in America, was later active in French service
in Santo Domingo, in Bonaparte's Egyptian expedition, as a government minister
in the Kingdom of Naples, and in the French ministry of war after the revolution
of 1830. Balch, French in America, II, 94.
    2. Daure refers to an agreement reached in August at Washington's headquarters
in Dobbs Ferry, New York, between RM and the French, calling for the latter to
deliver whatever flour they had on the Hudson River to Washington's order and for
RM to furnish them with an equal quantity in Maryland. See Diary, August 21, and
notes.
    3. Guillaume Mathieu Dumas (1753–1837), who joined the French army in 1773,
was appointed captain and assigned to the American campaign in 1780 as an aide
to Rochambeau, serving with the engineers, grenadiers, and chasseurs, and as deputy
quartermaster general. Following his departure from the United States in 1782,
Dumas established a notable military and political record in the French service under
the Bourbons, the First Empire, the Restoration, and the July Monarchy. Hoefer,
ed., Nouvelle biographie générale, XV, 155–163; Balch, French in America, II, 108–109;
for an autobiographical account of his part in the American campaign, see Dumas's
Memoirs of his Own Time, including the Revolution, the Empire, and the Restoration (Philadelphia, 1839), I, 19–63.
    4. For RM's compliance with this request, see RM to William Heath, September
17, to Daure, September 19, and to the Commissary General of Purchases, and to
Matthew Ridley, both September 20.

Diary: September 17, 1781

Mr Brown called on me and I directed him to prepare for a
Journey to Boston and informed him that I wished to know many
things of him with respect to the Navy. He promises to write to me
on the subject.[1]

At The request of a Committee of the Assembly of Pennsylvania
met that Committee and the Council and Conferred with them on
the State of their Treasury and Finances; urged to them strongly
a Continuance of Taxation. This Conference lasted till 2 OClock.[2]

Honble. Mr Jenifer called with his Nephew Mr Stone to be placed
with me as a Clerk; desired the latter to come hither tomorrow
Morning.[3]

During the Absence of the Superintendant,[4] Mr Pierce [5] called
and mentioned that the Honble Mr Matthews [6] had recommended
the issuing Warrants in Favor of the Officers of South Carolina for
Specie as they were in great Want. Told Mr Pierce that all the

Officers were in Want. That the Warrants ought all to be for Specie. But that we had no Money to discharge them; their Applications must be to the States to supply Money.

Mr Mercier [7] called with a Warrant, is much distressed &Ca. Will accept of only a Part; told him we had no Money. Mr Gibson with Capt Ysnardy called in Consequence of an Act of the United States of the 21st June; [8] requested them to Call tomorrow.

A Conference with the Board of War respecting Saddles, Boots, Caps and Breeches for 100 Lighthorsemen for S[outhern] Army, and agreed to pay for them.

Wrote a Letter to His Excellency The Governour of New Jersey.

Wrote a Letter to John Nelson [Neilson] Esqr. D[eputy] Q[uarter] M[aster] G[eneral] Trenton.

Wrote a Letter to His Excellency Thos. Nelson Esqr. Govr. Virginia. [9]

Wrote a Letter to The Honorable Genl. Heath.

Issued a Warrant on Mr Swanwick in favour of Colo Miles, for £56.17.6.

Issued a Warrant on Mr Swanwick in favour of D Clayepoole for printing Advertisements. £3.7.6. [10]

Issued a Warrant on Mr Swanwick in favour of Singer and Vrimmell [11] for Flour £119.7.6.

1. No record of this communication has been found. On the background of John Brown's mission, see notes to Diary, September 7, and for his journey to Boston, RM to Brown, September 19.

2. This conference followed President Joseph Reed's transmittal on September 14 of unspecified letters which he had received from RM concerning state finances. The following day the assembly appointed a committee consisting of Samuel Morris, Jr., Sharp Delany, James Smith, Thomas Mifflin, and John Harris to request a conference with the Supreme Executive Council and RM. On September 17 the parties met in the council chambers where, according to the council's minutes, "a free conference on the subject of the treasury was had, in which there appeared the greatest harmony and good understanding between the Assembly and the Council, and a mutual good disposition to enforce the speedy and effectual collection of the public taxes, as a measure absolutely necessary, and probably effectual, in the present critical and important crisis, was evinced." No report of the committee of assembly has been found. *Journals of the House of Representatives of Pennsylvania, 1776–1781,* 684; *Colonial Records of Pennsylvania,* XIII, 60; see also Diary, September 18.

3. See Diary, September 7, and notes, and 18.

4. Gouverneur Morris is the author of this, and possibly the following, paragraph.

5. Paymaster General John Pierce.

6. John Mathews, delegate to Congress from South Carolina.

7. John Dyer Mercier, a Quebec merchant and officeholder, was imprisoned in 1775 following the interception of a letter from Benedict Arnold urging him to assist the invading American forces. After his release and the loss of much of his property, Mercier joined the American army laying siege to the city and later resettled in the United States. It may have been owing to the patronage of Arnold, Philip Schuyler, and William Duer that Congress on July 29, 1779, elected Mercier a commissioner

of claims in the Treasury Department and, in a departmental reorganization on November 9, a commissioner in the chambers of accounts. With the reconstitution of the Treasury under RM on September 11, 1781, Mercier lost his office. His interview with RM concerned a warrant for $1309 specie granted him by the Board of Treasury in February 1781 for back pay which, despite a previous application to Congress, he had not received. RM's negative response no doubt induced Mercier to ask Congress on September 21 for $500 of the warrant in specie and the remainder in bills of exchange on France, where he desired to go to recoup his business affairs. Although Congress did not act on his request, it elected him one of two auditors in the Treasury Department on January 28, 1782. He was still seeking congressional benevolence in 1783. Mercier to the President of Congress, April 9 and September 21, 1781, the latter enclosing Benedict Arnold to Philip Schuyler, June 12, 1778, and petition of Mercier *et al.* to Congress, April 18, 1783, PCC, no. 78, XVI, 167, 235–237, 239–240, no. 41, II, 134–135; see also notes to RM's Plan for Arranging the Treasury Department, August 27.

8. On Ysnardy's purpose in calling, see Diary, September 10, and notes, and 18.

9. This letter is dated September 18.

10. David Claypoole, printer of the *Pennsylvania Packet,* published Office of Finance advertisements soliciting contract proposals for supplying Continental posts in Pennsylvania.

11. Not further identified.

To William Heath

Office of Finance
Septbr. 17th. 1781

Sir

I pray you will accept my thanks for your Favor of the twelfth Instant, and beg Leave to assure you how much I am obliged by your attention to my Requests.

With respect to what you mention about Flour, I am to observe That before I left Camp I agreed with Genl. Rochambeau that whatever Flour he should not have Occasion for, should be delivered to the Use of your Army; and I would supply a like Quantity to the Southward.[1] I do not yet know how much has been furnished under this Agreement, but suppose it to be about 1200 Barrells. Mr Lowrey was to send forward 2000 Barrells, a Part of which was stopped for the use of the Troops on their March thro Jersey, the rest has been I suppose duly delivered. In addition to this, Colo Udney Hay, the Agent for the State of New York, was to have furnished 3000 Barrells begining on the tenth Instant, and to continue in Proportion to the demand on him, and to facilitate his Compliance with his Promise, I procured him an Order for all the empty Casks at the Posts on Hudson's River.[2] I cannot, in this Situation of things, imagine that you can have any Danger of Want; but I shall nevertheless be much Obliged if you will enquire into the different Supplies Obtained from the several quarters I have mentioned, and send me a State of them, in order that I may be able thereby to govern my future Operations.[3] I am Sir Very respectfully Your most Obedient and humble Servant

Robt Morris

The Honble Major Genl. Heath
Commanding the Army
Continental Village
State of New York

ENDORSED: [Robert Morris Esqr.?]/respecting a Supply of/Flour Sept. 17th./1781
MSS: LS, Heath Papers, MHi; Ofcl LbC, DLC.
    1. On this transaction, see Diary, August 21, and notes.
    2. For RM's arrangements with Thomas Lowrey, see Diary, August 21; for those with Udny Hay, see Hay to RM, RM to Hay, to the Commissary General of Issues, and to the Governor of New York, all August 15, and Diary, August 21.
    3. See RM to Heath, September 24, in which a duplicate of this letter was enclosed, and Heath to RM, September 20 and October 4, 1781.

To John Neilson

Office of Finance 17. Septemr. 1781.

Sir,

I am to acknowlege the Receipt of your Letter of the eighth Instant [1] and to express my Sense of your Activity and Zeal in the Public Service which have been great and meritorious. I wish it were in my Power to meet it with a Return equal to your Wishes in which Case I would readily charge myself with the Performance of your Engagements. But while the several States continue to Neglect those pecuniary Supplies which it is both their Duty and Interest to furnish I dare not involve myself in Promises which the Inattention of others may prevent me from performing.

I enclose you a Letter to the Governor of your State [2] which you will be pleased to Seal and send to him. I hope it may produce you the Money and I expect you will urge the Payment; if it cannot be obtained I will endeavor to procure you Releif from some other Quarter. I am Sir your most obedient and humble Servant.

RM

MS: Ofcl LbC, DLC.
    1. Letter not found. Neilson was deputy quartermaster general for New Jersey.
    2. RM to the Governor of New Jersey, September 17.

To the Governor of New Jersey (William Livingston)

Office of Finance 17th. Sepr. 1781.

Sir

John Neilson Esqr. has transmitted to me in a Letter of the eighth Instant [1] his Estimate of the Expence of sundry Teams procured in New Jersey for the Service of the United States amounting to four thousand four hundred and fifty five Dollars of which Sum he requests the Payment. You must be Sensible Sir that the States having neglected to comply with the Requisitions of Congress have not put it in my Power to support the Expence of the War. Until that is done I cannot undertake to defray it. And therefore I have directed Mr Neilson to apply to your Excellency and I hope and expect that his Demand will be paid from the Treasury of your State. In which Case the Money which may be paid will be carried to the Credit of your Account with the United States.[2] With great Respect I have the Honor to be Sir your Excellency's most obedient and humble Servant

RM.

MS: Ofcl LbC, DLC.
1. Letter not found.
2. See RM to John Neilson, September 17 and October 22, and to the Governor of New Jersey, October 22, 1781, and notes.

From Nathanael Greene

[*High Hills of Santee, South Carolina, September 17, 1781.* On November 2, 1781, RM wrote to Greene: "Your Favor of the seventeenth of September last has been delivered to me by your Aid Capt. Pierce." *Letter not found.*]

Diary: September 18, 1781

Mr. Gibson applied with the Resolutions of Congress and of the Board of Treasury respecting Capt Dn. Miguel Lorenzo Ysnardy and I agree to pay his Warrant for $1967^{83}/_{90}$ dollars immediately in Consideration of his Services and Necessities and further as he Offers to relinquish his Claim for $2237^{1}/_{2}$ dollars allowed him by Congress provided the first is immediately satisfied.[1]

A Gentlemen in distress for Want of Money due to him from [the] Qr [Quarter] Masters department applied very pressingly for Money and it hurt my feelings much not to be able to relieve him.

Mr. Stone came this Morning as a Writer in this Office.[2]

Mr. Anspach Attended for Money.[3]

Wrote a Letter to Colo. Ephraim Blaine C[ommissary] G[eneral] of] Purchs. to S[outhern] Army.

Wrote a Letter to John Hotham [Hathorn] and Isaac Nicholls [Nicoll] Esqrs. Orange County State of New York.

Wrote a Letter to His Excellency The Governour of Massachusetts.

Wrote a Letter to His Excellency The Governour of Delaware.

Wrote a Letter to John Loyd [Lloyd] Esqr. at Danbury.

The Pay Master General [4] applied for Money for two Officers; desired him to make such applications in Writing.

Waited On the Minister of France [5] to confer on sundry Matters but found him engaged.

Held a Conference with the Speaker and some Members of this State on its Finances.[6]

Applied to Dd. Rittenhouse Esqr.[7] for information as to the Sums of Paper Money of the several sorts now in Circulation &Ca. which he promises to send me.[8]

Sent for Thos. Paine Esqr.[9] Author of the Pamphlet called Common Sense and several other performances, and proposed that for the Service of the Country he should write and publish such Pieces respecting the propriety, Necessity and Utility of Taxation as might be likely to promote the Public Service of America, as the Support of the War does and must Ultimately rest on the Taxes to be raised in the United States.

Several Members of Congress and others called on me last Evening desirous to know the reasons for my writing to Mr Jay a letter of the 15th August last which being intercepted Mr. Rivington has published and graced with his remarks, wherein I direct Mr Jay to Protest certain Bills of Exchange drawn by Authority of Congress. This explanation is easily given as the Ship On board which I had remitted these Bills was taken. The moment I knew her Fate I judged it proper to stop payment of the Bills least the Enemy with their usual Cunning might Attempt to receive the Money for them, but I am now of Opinion that the Captain Sunk them when Captured.[10]

1. See Diary, September 10, and notes, and 17.
2. See Diary, September 7, and notes, and 17.

3. On the application of Peter Anspach, paymaster of the Quartermaster Department, see Diary, September 11, and notes.

4. John Pierce.

5. Chevalier de La Luzerne.

6. See Diary, September 17, and notes. RM addressed Speaker Frederick A. Muhlenberg of the Pennsylvania Assembly on September 28.

7. Treasurer of Pennsylvania.

8. See RM to the Speaker of the Pennsylvania Assembly, September 28.

9. Thomas Paine (1737–1809), the English-born pamphleteer who came to America in 1774, adopted the American cause, and promoted it with resounding success in the widely disseminated *Common Sense* and *Crisis* papers. In the years that followed, RM's connection with Paine shifted with the ebb and flow of politics. After Paine was elected secretary of the Committee for Foreign Affairs by Congress on April 17, 1777, he plunged into the Deane-Lee controversy, inveighing at length in the press against Silas Deane and RM's connections with him. A complaint by Gérard, the French minister at Philadelphia, that Paine's use of the committee papers had disclosed secret French aid before the Franco-American alliance resulted in his resignation on January 8, 1779.

Meanwhile, Paine had been drawn into opposition to RM in yet another way: he was an active constitutionalist in Pennsylvania politics. After his resignation as secretary of the Committee for Foreign Affairs, Paine appealed to the Supreme Executive Council of Pennsylvania for employment, and in November 1779 was appointed clerk of the assembly. This position he gave up a year later, having conceived the idea of going secretly to England to write newspaper articles urging the acknowledgment of American independence. He soon abandoned this hazardous project in favor of accompanying John Laurens to France as his unpaid companion.

Though Paine was in the opposite political camp from that of RM, he was not far distant from the Financier in some of his views. A democrat in political philosophy, he nevertheless had only a tenuous commitment to the anti-statist, agrarian traditions prevalent in the United States. He regarded commerce as the progenitor of higher civilization, replacing war as the principal occupation of mankind. He was later an ardent champion of the Bank of North America and defender of the sanctity of its charter against abrogation by the Pennsylvania legislature. Above all, however, Paine was concerned with the prosecution of the war and the establishment of American independence. When news arrived of the surrender of Charleston on May 12, 1780, he initiated, according to his own account, a subscription in aid of the Continental army which, upon being taken up by the merchants of Philadelphia, led to the establishment of the Bank of Pennsylvania.

Soon afterward, his public writings and correspondence registered the idea that the support of the wealthier part of the community was essential to victory in the war. "The valor of a country may be learned by the bravery of its soldiery, and the general cast of its inhabitants, but confidence of success is best discovered by the active measures pursued by men of property," he wrote in the ninth *Crisis*. "Unless the wealthier part throw in their aid," Paine observed to his friend Joseph Reed, "public measures must go heavily on." He also began espousing the policies and powers of Congress. In two pamphlets written late in 1780 he strongly urged compliance with Congress's act of March 18, 1780, intended to restore the value of Continental currency. Finally, he called on Virginia to cede her western claims and suggested a national convention to redefine the powers of Congress.

Less than a month after Paine's return from France with John Laurens, he was summoned to the Office of Finance, as this Diary entry discloses. The Financier's recognition of Paine's skill with the pen, once wielded against him so effectively, together with the disclosure of Deane's apostasy in November led to a reconciliation between them. It must have given Paine considerable satisfaction to receive RM's personal assurances "that he had been totally deceived in Deane; but that he now looked upon him to be a bad man, and his reputation totally ruined," and to watch while the volatile Gouverneur Morris, RM's official assistant in the Office of Finance, "hopped round upon one leg, [and] swore they had all been duped, himself among the rest."

During the winter Paine solicited the aid of Washington, who was then residing in Philadelphia. Apparently at Washington's suggestion, an agreement was made among RM, Secretary for Foreign Affairs Robert R. Livingston, and Washington to pay Paine an annual salary of $800 for writing publications in the interest of the United States. The sum was to be paid by Livingston from secret service funds supplied by RM. From this agreement, among other publications, came Paine's six letters to Rhode Island advocating the 5 percent impost. Paine also received money during this period from the French minister at Philadelphia, Chevalier de La Luzerne, whose confidence was elicited by the apparent shift in Paine's political views. *DAB;* Alfred Owen Aldridge, *Man of Reason: The Life of Thomas Paine* (Philadelphia and New York, 1959), 64–100; Stinchcombe, *American Revolution and the French Alliance,* 127–128; The American Crisis IX, June 9, 1780, Crisis Extraordinary, October 4, 1780, Letter to the Abbé Raynal, [1782], Public Good, [December 30, 1780], and Paine to Joseph Reed, June 4, 1780, to Jonathan Williams, November 26, 1781, and to a Committee of Congress, [October 1783], Philip S. Foner, ed., *The Complete Writings of Thomas Paine* (New York, 1945), I, 169, 171–188, II, 241–242, 303–333, 1186, 1200, 1230–1231; Paine to RM, September 20 and November 26, 1781, Diary, January 26, 1782, and RM's Agreement with Robert R. Livingston and George Washington, February 10, 1782.

10. See RM to John Jay, August 15, and notes, Diary, August 15, and notes, and RM to the President of Congress, October 1, 1781.

To the Commissary General of Purchases (Ephraim Blaine)

Office of Finance 18th. Septemr. 1781.

Sir,

I was yesterday favored with your Letter dated Saturday Morning the fifteenth of September 1781. As you have omitted the Place where it was written and given no other Mark by which to discover where you want the Salt that Matter must wait your farther Explanation.[1] No Person has yet called on your Part to obtain Money for the Purchase of this Salt. I suppose you have given the necessary Instructions to your Agent on that Subject and he will probably be able to determine whereabouts you wish it to be deposited.

You will recollect that the State of Delaware is indebted five hundred Bushels of Salt and therefore altho is may not be proper entirely to rely on them you will not cease to press them on the Subject and to complain of a non Performance. I am Sir respectfully, your most obedient and humble Servant

RM

MS: Ofcl LbC, DLC.

1. The salt was needed at Head of Elk, where Blaine probably had addressed his September 15 letter to RM, which has not been found. See RM to the Governor of Delaware, September 18, and to the Commissary General of Purchases, October 4, 1781.

To the President of Delaware
(Caesar Rodney)

Office of Finance
September 18th. 1781.

Sir

The Commissary General of Purchases, in a Letter of the 15th Instant, mentions to me that he shall want a considerable quantity of Salt at the Head of Elk.[1] As this is very convenient for the State of Delaware, and there is now an existing Demand by the Requisitions of Congress for five hundred Bushels of Salt,[2] I have directed applications to you which I hope will be complied with. I have the Honor to be very respectfully Sir Your most Obedient and humble Servant

Robt Morris

His Excelly.
The Governor of Delaware.

ENDORSED: Sept. 18. 1781./Letter from the Financier on/the Subject of Supplies.
MSS: LS, Executive Papers, De-Ar; Ofcl LbC, DLC.
1. Letter from Commissary General of Purchases Ephraim Blaine not found. See RM to the Commissary General of Purchases, September 18 and October 4, 1781.
2. As part of its requisition of November 4, 1780, Congress called on Delaware for 500 bushels of salt payable on or before July 15, 1781.

To John Hathorn and Isaac Nicoll[1]

Office of Finance 18th. Septr. 1781.

Gentlemen

I have received the Letter you was so kind as to write to me on the twenty ninth of August last [2] and am much obliged as well by the favorable Sentiments you have expressed of me as by the Offer of your Services. It will always give me Pleasure to employ Men of fair Character; such Men shew Government in its proper point of Dignity, by others it is abused.

I expect that such Purchases as I shall have Occasion to make will be by Contract, that being the most œconomical Mode and I had hopes that the States would e'er this have put into my Hands such Revenues as would have enabled me to contract for all our Supplies. The Neglect of the several Legislatures in this Capital Object must give Pain to every true Friend of America.

I have the Honor to be Gentlemen your most obedient and humble Servant

RM

MS: Ofcl LbC, DLC.

1. John Hathorn (1749–1825), surveyor, school teacher, and merchant of Orange County, New York, was a colonel in the county militia during the Revolution, served in the state assembly, 1778, 1780, 1782–1785 (as speaker, 1783–1784), and later, in the state senate, and in Congress after the adoption of the Constitution. *Biog. Dir. Cong.*

Issac Nicoll of Orange County, New York, also a colonel in the county militia, had been county sheriff, September 1777–March 1781. He resettled in New Jersey in 1783 or 1784 and served seven terms in the state assembly. William L. Nicoll, *The Nicoll Family of Orange County, New York* (New York, 1886), 28, 29, 35, 36.

2. Letter not found.

To John Lloyd, Jr.[1]

Office of Finance
Septbr. 18. 1781.

Sir

I have been favored with your Letter of the fifth Instant, enclosing one from the honorable Mr. Elsworth of the third.[2] I have the Pleasure to inform you, that on the eleventh Instant an Ordinance was passed, by the United States In Congress Assembled, for regulating the Treasury and adjusting the public Accounts.[3] The Officers are not yet appointed, but I hope that will soon be done; and then you may depend that I shall endeavor to obtain the most speedy Settlement of Accounts which I can. You must be very sensible that I can with no Propriety shew any Preferences, and that it is impossible for me to attend to the Liquidation of Accounts; you will not therefore expect any immediate Interference on my Part, that your Claim against the United States should be admitted or advanced. But, on the other Hand, I will readily promise that in common with all others it shall receive every Facility in my Power, and that you shall have Justice to the full Extent of those Means which the States may put in my Power. I will never deceive, and therefore I must candidly declare to every public Creditor, that while the Wealth of the People is in the Hands of the several Legislatures, Redress must come from them and from them only. I hope that a Sense of Justice and Honour, with a patriotic Regard for those Rights which we have long laboured to establish, will prompt every State in the Union to make those liberal Efforts which are necessary to produce public Confidence, and secure public Freedom.

I pray you Sir to make my Respects acceptable to the honorable

Mr. Elsworth, and to assure him that it will always give me a very particular Pleasure to attend to his Recommendations and forward his Views, as far as may lay in my Power. I have the honor to be very respectfully Sir your Most obedient and humble Servant

Robt Morris

John Lloyd Junr. Esqr.
at Danbury

ADDRESSED: John Lloyd Junior ENDORSED: The Honble. Robt Morris/18. Septr. 1781
MSS: LS, Lloyd Family Papers, NHi; Ofcl LbC, DLC.
1. When the British occupied Long Island in August 1776, John Lloyd, Jr. (1744/ 45–1792), of Queens County, New York, fled to Connecticut, where he undertook to furnish supplies to Commissary General Joseph Trumbull, agreeing to accept payment in Continental loan office certificates. These he never received, and because of Trumbull's death in 1778, it was not until February 22, 1780, that he settled his accounts with Jonathan Trumbull, finding a balance in his favor of £2,010 in lawful money of New England. To save himself from "Utter ruin," Lloyd petitioned Congress on March 11 for payment in loan office certificates backdated to 1776. Congress referred his application to the Board of Treasury, which took no action. On November 10 Lloyd proposed to accept the interest on his claim in a bill of exchange on France and the principal in a certificate or new emission money equivalent, but in January 1781 the Board of Treasury recommended delay because the accounts of the department of commissary general had not yet been settled. Following another appeal by Lloyd, the board proposed in April that Lloyd accept only an acknowledgment of the settlement and balance due with annual interest, but Congress took no further action. This course doubtlessly prompted Lloyd's appeal to RM, which apparently was seconded by Congressman Oliver Ellsworth of Connecticut, and to which RM replied in the letter printed here. Lloyd to Joseph Trumbull, December 6, 1776, and Agreement, March 8, 1777, *Papers of the Lloyd Family of the Manor of Queens Village, Lloyd's Neck, Long Island, New York, 1654–1826* (N.-Y. Hist. Soc., *Colls.*, LIX–LX [New York, 1927]), II, 757, 758–759, 886, 889; Lloyd's memorial to Congress, March 11, 1780, and Lloyd to [the President of Congress], November 10, 1780, PCC, no. 78, XIV, 393–400; *JCC*, XVI, 275, XVIII, 1116, XIX, 36, 321–323, 323n., 401, XX, 453–454.
2. Lloyd's letter of September 5 and Oliver Ellsworth's of September 3 have not been found.
3. On this ordinance, see notes to RM's Plan for Arranging the Treasury Department, August 27.

To the Governor of Massachusetts (John Hancock)

Office of Finance 18th. Sepr. 1781.

Sir

Yesterday the United States in Congress Assembled referred to me your Letter of the sixth Instant.[1] Before this can possibly reach Boston you will have been informed of the Measures I had taken with Respect to the Money;[2] as I am sure you will give them every

Facility in your Power I have nothing to add on that Subject more than to express my Thanks for your Care and Attention. With the greatest respect I have the Honor to be Sir your Excellency's most obedient and humble Servant.

RM

MS: Ofcl LbC, DLC.
1. Letter from Governor John Hancock to the President of Congress, September 6, 1781, not found.
2. An allusion to the French specie which had arrived at Boston on August 25 with John Laurens aboard the *Résolue*. See Diary, September 10, and RM to the Governor of Massachusetts, September 11, and to Tench Francis, September 11 (first letter), and notes.

To the Governor of Virginia
(Thomas Nelson)

Office of Finance 18th. Septemr. 1781[1]

Sir

I have receiv'd your Excellency's Favour of the fifth Instant, from Richmond, and thank you for your attention to my several Letters of the 16th. and 25th. July and 23rd. August. Accept also Sir my Thanks for the good Wishes you have expressed, that I may be enabled effectually to execute the Duties of my Office. Your Goodness and your Patriotism both assure me of your Sincerity in those Wishes. To produce their Completion, nothing more is necessary than that the States should exert themselves to furnish solid effectual Revennue; with that every Thing is possible, and without it nothing. I am Sir, very respectfully Your Excellency's Most Obedient and humble Servant

Robt Morris

His Excelly. Thomas Nelson Esqr.
Governor of Virginia

ENDORSED: Sept 18th 1781/Letter of/Ro. Morris/to/Govr Nelson
MSS: LS, Continental Congress Papers, Vi; Ofcl LbC, DLC.
1. The Ofcl LbC is dated September 17, the date RM registered it in his Diary.

To George Washington

[*Philadelphia, September 18, 1781.* Washington wrote to RM on October 1 (second letter): "Your Note of the 18th. I have received, with your Letter directed to Major Genl Greene." RM's letter to Nathanael Greene was undoubtedly that dated September 14. *Letter not found.*]

Diary: September 19, 1781

Gave Mr Brown an Order on Colo. Miles for a Horse.[1]

Many Applications for Money, and none to give them.

This Morning I waited on His Excellency The President of Congress [2] to know if it was His Opinion or in the Expectation of Congress that I should take the Oath prescribed to be taken by the intended Agent of the Marine in the Act of the 29th August, before I entred on the execution of the duties devolved on me by the Act of the 7th.[3] And His Excellency giving it as his Opinion that these Duties and Authorities being Committed to me in my Official Character in which I had already taken the Oaths it was not necessary to take any Other, in which Opinion several Members of Congress and the Secrety.[4] then present Concurring, I shall therefore proceed to give the needfull Orders respecting the Navy without taking any other Oaths. And as Mr John Brown Secretary of the Board of Admiralty stands in the same point of View I shall continue to employ him in the Management of Naval Affairs as he must now have the best knowledge of them from his long continuance in that department. Before I left the State House I was informed by The President and many Members of Congress that all the Intelligence from New York and New Jersey imparted a design of Sir Henry Clinton to make an Attempt on this City with 5000 or 6000 Men that are embarked on board Transports now at the narrows near Statens Island. For my part I cannot beleive that they are destined hither because such an Expedition cannot be supported by good reasons; [5] however that may be I have been teazed and harrassed the Whole day for Money, Aid, Assistance &Ca. in Consequence of the said Alarm. Mr Peters of the Board of War called to know if I could supply Money to remove Stores, Prisoners &Ca. from this City Which I answered in the Negative, as no Money is in the Treasury, and my personal Credit already pledged for Considerable Sums borrowed to forward the Public Service, in several Branches which must be repaid and my other Engagements fulfilled before I strike out anew. Otherwise I shall soon lose that Credit which has hitherto been so Usefull. Colo Miles applied for money to enable him to send off Expresses but I had none for him.

Wrote a Letter to John Brown Esqr. respecting Marine affairs.

1. On John Brown, who is mentioned again in the Diary of this date, see notes to Diary, September 7.

2. Thomas McKean.

3. On these acts of Congress, see the headnote to RM to the President of Congress, September 8.

4. Charles Thomson, secretary of Congress.

5. For a discussion of this threat, see notes to Timothy Matlack to RM, September 11.

To John Brown

Office of Finance
Philada. Septbr. 19th. 1781

Sir

The Office you have so long filled must have afforded you the best information on the affairs of our unfortunate Navy,[1] and Having the greatest Confidence in your Zeal, Attachment, and Abilities, I am now to employ you, in consequence of three several Acts of Congress which are inclosed,[2] in a Business of very considerable Trust and Importance.

I want to have the most precise and accurate State of the Marine Department; wherefore I in general instruct you, during the Course of the Business, more particularly committed to you, to obtain that state as far as may be in your Power.

You must proceed from hence to Boston, with all convenient Speed; and when there appoint a Deputy Agent of the Marine, whose Duties, Powers and Emoluments will appear from the several Enclosures on that Subject. Among these is an Appointment signed by me, with a blank direction, which you will be pleased to fill up,[3] and the better to fix on a proper Person for that purpose you will apply to his Excellency the Governour of the State of Massachusetts, for his Advice and Assistance. It may be well also to consult the Gentlemen of the Navy Board, respecting the properest person for this Agency unless some objection to such Consultation should occur there. When you have fixed on the Agent he must give Bond with good and sufficient Security, for the due and faithfull performance of his Office, in the Sum of £10,000 Lawfull Money in Specie to the Superintendant of Finance and his Successors in Office. I have in a Letter enclosed requested His Excellency the Governour to give you Aid on all Occasions, where it may be necessary;[4] you will therefore apply to him on every such occasion. In the same letter is also contained a Request that he will furnish Money for fitting out the Frigates Alliance and Deane;[5] you will therefore make as pressing Solicitations on that Subject as decency will permit, and you will cause Solicitations to be made by the Navy Board, and others who may be concerned. Lest you should not obtain the necessary Funds from this quarter, you have enclosed a Letter to Tench Francis Esqr.[6] which will give you further Resourse; but get as much as you possibly can from the State, taking from Mr Francis only so much as may be absolutely and Indispensibly necessary to send the Ships to Sea, after applying all other Funds assigned you towards that Service.[7] Enclosed you have two Letters, the one to the Navy Board, and the other to the Continental Agent; [8] these you will read before you deliver them, and you will receive by your self, or the Agent whom you shall appoint, all the Books, Papers, Accounts, Public Property &ca &ca. which are therein respectively mentioned. And as these must eventually go into the Hands of the Agent, which you may appoint, you will take duplicates of the Receipts which he shall give, and bring them with you on your Return. In Conjunction with the Navy Board you will take the Necessary Measures for sending the Alliance and Deane to sea, immediately, and I expect that those Gentlemen will give you all the Aid in their Power. But if they should decline, let it immediately be undertaken by the Person whom you shall Appoint the Deputy as aforesaid. You will find enclosed, a letter to Capt. Barry and one to Capt. Samuel Nicholson; [9] these you will deliver and communicate the Instructions for manning the Navy as mentioned in my said Letters to them.[10] I have been told that Captn. Samuel Nicholson will decline going in the Deane. I should be sorry it were so, because I consider him as a Valuable Officer and it would give me pain that he should forfeit his Station in the American Service, by a Breach of Order. But if Capt. Saml. Nicholson should decline going in the Deane,[11] you will make your Report thereof to me very particularly, and lest in such case any Delay should happen, you will deliver to Captn John Nicholson [12] a Copy of my Letter to his Brother, and desire him on my Part in all Things to obey it, as if directed particularly to him, and give him for his further Satisfaction a Copy of this Part of my Letter to you.

Should the Measures I have proposed for Manning the Navy be insufficient, you will concert with His Excelly. The Governour, [and] such others as time and Circumstances may render necessary, observing always not to exceed the allowances of Congress; but on the Contrary as payments are now made in Hard Money, those Bounties are far too high. You must Moderate them as much as you shall find practicable. The Crews must be engaged for a Year, as the Alliance in particular being now Coppered, will only need occasionally to run in for Provisions and Stores, and may be kept constantly cruizing. Besides this, the Men enlisted for a year may be better disciplined, than when only entered for a Cruize. Whatever Monies you may receive for the fitting out these Vessells, you will superintend the Expenditure of, and bring with you any balance that may remain, as well as the Accounts compleated, and also exact Inventories of every Article on Board the Frigates at the time of their Sailing.[13]

I recommend to you Attention, Dispatch, and Oeconomy, and with the best Wishes that you may have an useful and agreable Journey, very respectfully I am Sir your most Obedient and humble Servant

Robt Morris

To John Brown Esqr.
Philadelphia

ENDORSED: Honbl Robt. Morris/Philada. Septr. 19th 1781/Instructions
MSS: LS, Ferdinand J. Dreer Collection, PHi; Ofcl LbC, DLC.

1. On Brown and his mission, see notes to Diary, September 7.
2. Probably the acts of August 29, and September 7 and 12. See the headnote to RM to the President of Congress, September 8.
3. See RM's Letter of Appointment to a Deputy Agent of Marine for Massachusetts, September 21; also RM to John Paul Jones, September 25. The appointment went to Thomas Russell.
4. See RM to the Governor of Massachusetts, September 21.
5. On this subject, see RM to the Governor of Massachusetts, and to the Navy Board of the Eastern Department, both August 4, and the Navy Board of the Eastern Department to RM, August 29 and September 5.
6. Dated September 22. Brown also had instructions to draw on Thomas Russell. See RM to Russell, September 21.
7. Ultimately, Brown had to draw on Francis. See RM to Brown, October 26, 1781.
8. RM to the Navy Board of the Eastern Department, and to John Bradford, both September 21. See also RM to Bradford, September 22.
9. Both dated September 21.
10. These instructions, which Brown was to "shew" to Barry (see RM to Barry, September 21), have not been found. As the text of the letter printed here subsequently indicates, they related to the offer of enlistment bounties. In a letter to Barry of November 27, 1781, after changing his sailing instructions, RM suggested a resort to other measures, including the impressment of seamen.
11. In a letter to RM of October 17, 1781, not found, Nicholson accepted the command of the Deane. See RM to Nicholson, November 2, 1781.
12. John Nicholson (1756–1844) of Maryland, the brother of Captains James and Samuel Nicholson of the Continental navy, was probably the one who on April 5, 1776, was appointed first lieutenant of the Defence, a ship in the Maryland navy, by the state council of safety, and who on August 22 was commissioned by Congress second lieutenant of the Continental frigate Washington. In October he was promoted to lieutenant and in November appointed captain in command of the Continental sloop Hornet, which he lost to the British in the summer of 1777 off the coast of South Carolina. In late 1780 Nicholson took temporary command of the frigate Deane while his brother Samuel was on leave, but in 1783, when he was a member of a marine court of inquiry, he still lacked a command. Journal of the Maryland Council of Safety, April 5, 1776, Clark and Morgan, eds., Naval Documents, IV, 671; Marine

Committee to William Bingham, December 14, 1776, Paullin, ed., *Out-Letters*, I, 57–58; *Dict. Amer. Naval Ships*, III, 367, V, 88; Gardner Weld Allen, *A Naval History of the American Revolution* (Boston, 1913), II, 511; *JCC*, XI, 687; James Read to Joseph Pennell, May 29, 1783, AM LbC, MdAN.

13. Additional instructions to Brown are contained in letters of September 21, 22 (three letters), 25, and 26.

To Hector Daure

Office of Finance 19th. Septemr. 1781.[1]

Sir,

I received your Letter of the sixteenth from Baltimore last Evening. In consequence of the Agreement between the Commander in Chief and Count de Rochambeau I have made various Applications to discover what quantity of Flour had been delivered to the Use of the American Army: [2] but I have not yet obtained the Returns or I should have before this taken Measures to replace it.

Having every Disposition to forward your Views I have now given the necessary Orders to the American Commissary for the Delivery of the twelve hundred Barrels of Flour mentioned in your Letter.[3] I shall be glad to be favored as speedily as possible with the Account of what has been delivered in the State of New York to the American Army that I may Cause the whole to be repaid. It may probably be more convenient both to you and to us that the twelve hundred Barrels should be delivered at a different Place from that which you mention for if it be on the navigable waters you can easily transport it to your Army which is now very distant from Baltimore. It may perhaps be obtained much nearer to the Place where it is to be consumed. Colo. Blaine the american Commissary has Orders to enter into the necessary Engagements on this Subject and to give it every Facility. With the greatest Respect I have the Honor to be Sir &c &ca.

RM

MS: Ofcl LbC, DLC.

1. This letter is registered in the Diary, September 21, where it is assigned the date of September 20.

2. See RM to William Heath, September 17, and for the origin of this agreement, Diary, August 21, and notes.

3. See RM to the Commissary General of Purchases, and to Matthew Ridley, both September 20.

From the Commissary General
of Military Stores (Samuel Hodgdon)

Philadelphia 19th. Sepr. 1781

Sir,

In consequence of a Letter from Capt Nathl. Irish, Commissary of Military Stores, at the post establish'd by order of Congress in Virginia, setting forth, the Necessity of his being immediatly supplied with a sum of money, to enable him to procure materials, and perfect stores expected from him, for the support of the Army, in the southern department and prevent the dissolution of the Post,[1] I applied to the honble Bd of War for the approval of an estimate, for that purpose. The importance of the Case, induced them to report to Congress, that a Warrant be drawn, on the state of Virginia, for ten thousand dollars new emission, which was accepted, and ordered to be carried into immediate execution; in compliance with this resolve, the inclosed bill was drawn, and by me forwarded, for the purposes mention'd in the requisition.[2] The unexceptionable mode of drawing adopted, and the importance of the stores being procured for the immediate preservation of the state, on which it was drawn then actually invaded, and menaced, with total subjugation, left me no reason to doubt it would have been duly honoured and consequently prevented my making any other disposition to obtain the supplies. The inclosed document No. 2 will shew the cause assigned, why this was not the case,[3] which whether sufficient, to justify the protest, is not for me to determine, however duty oblidges me to submit the Matter to you, that if possible, some other mode may be pointed out, for the obtaining the money, without which I am fearfull, the post will be broken up, the consequences of which at this time, I will not anticipate, but leave to those, who are better informed, of the designs of the enemy in that quarter, and the propriety of keeping up the post. With due respect I am Sir your most obedient Humble Servant

Saml Hodgdon
CG MS.

Robt Morris Esqr.

MS: LbC, WDC, DNA.
1. Letter not found.
2. On Captain Nathaniel Irish and the warrant for $10,000 new emission, see Diary, July 10, 1781, and notes.
3. Enclosure not found. The reason for Virginia's refusal to honor the warrant, according to Governor Benjamin Harrison, who succeeded Thomas Nelson, was that

the draft, although for new emission money, was drawn against the state treasury and not against the Continental loan officer, in whose hands was deposited Congress's four-tenths share of new emission money issued under its act of March 18, 1780. The draft was expected to be paid out of the state's contribution under the requisition of May 22, 1781 (an implementation of resolutions of August 26, 1780), which the state had already expended for Continental purposes. Harrison to the Virginia Delegates in Congress, February 2 and 9, 1782, Hutchinson and Rutland, eds., *Madison Papers*, IV, 53, 59; for RM's further endeavors to supply Irish with funds and persuade Virginia to pay the warrant, see Diary, October 16, November 10, 12, and 16, and RM to the Governor of Virginia, November 16, 1781.

From the Commissary General of Purchases (Ephraim Blaine)

[*Alexandria, Virginia, September 19, 1781.* On October 4 RM wrote to Commissary Blaine: "I have received your Letters dated at Alexandria the nineteenth and Williamsburgh the twenty third of September last." *Letter of September 19 not found.*]

From James Nicholson

[*New York, September 19, 1781.* On September 24 RM wrote to the president of Congress enclosing "a Letter received on Saturday last from Captn. James Nicholson of the Trumbull Frigate." According to the endorsement on RM's communication, Nicholson's letter was dated September 19. Another endorsement was written on RM's letter at a later date by Secretary of Congress Charles Thomson: "NB The letter of J[ames] N[icholson] missing." *Letter not found.*]

Diary: September 20, 1781

This morning begins as usual with applications for Money.

Mr. John Moylan the Cloathier General called respecting the Cloathing at Boston but being Engaged I will send for him again this Morning.

Wrote a Letter to His Excellency The Minister of France.

Wrote a Letter to The President of Pennsylvania.

Wrote a Letter to Peter Thomson and Isaac Howell Esqs Inspectors of the Press.

Wrote a Letter to Thomas Russell Esqr. Boston.

Wrote a Letter to His Excellency The Governor of Massachusetts.[1]

Wrote a Letter to His Excellency the Governour of Connecticut.

Wrote a Letter to John Moylan Esqr. Cloathier Genl.

Wrote a Letter to John Townes Esqr. a distressed Officer.

Issued a Warrant in favour of Hazlewood and Blackiston, Contractors for Philada. £500.

Went With Mr. Moylan to the Board of War and after a long Conference it was agreed that Mr Moylan shoud proceed to Boston in Order to land the Cloathing, Medicine &Ca from the Transports [2] and bring the same to this place by Land transportation which we all wished to avoid if possible but the uncertainty we are in respecting the Operations of Count de Grasse makes it very difficult to determine on the propriety of Waiting for Water Carriage and as it is absolutely necessary to determine now if Land Carriage is to take place because if longer delayed it will become impossible to make use of it on Account of bad Weather and Roads which will come on soon after these Goods can be ready for moving; therefore came to a resolution that Mr Moylan should go forward. I required an Estimate of Monies necessary to be supplied to Mr. Moylan for this purpose which the Board sent in their Letter of this date,[3] whereupon I have Written several Letters relative to this Subject.[4] From the Board of War I went to the Hotel of His Excellency the Minister of France and told him that being engaged to repay on the first day of next October to The Treasurer of the French Army the Money advanced me by Count de Rochambeau, I find it will be very inconvenient to accomplish that payment at the time and will impede necessary Services for our Army at the same time that I apprehend the Money is not essentially necessary to their Service. His Excellency agreed with me in this point and therefore desired me to write him on the Subject [5] and he Would forward my Letter with his Opinion to the Count and engaged they should wait Contentedly for the Money untill Ours Arrive from Boston.

Received a Letter from the President of the State respecting Assistance to the Militia, Which I wrote An Answer to.

1. This and the following letter were circulars.

2. See Diary, September 12, and notes.

3. Letter not found.

4. See RM's Circular to the Governors of Massachusetts and Connecticut, and RM to the Clothier General, and to Thomas Russell, all September 20. For further references to this subject, see Diary, October 29 and November 2, and RM to William Heath, November 2, 1781.

5. See RM to La Luzerne, September 20.

Circular to the Governors
of Massachusetts and Connecticut[1]

Office of Finance
September 20th. 1781.

Sir

John Moylan Esquire the Cloathier General is ordered by the Honble. The Board of War to bring on from Boston some Cloathing and Stores indispensibly necessary.[2] I have directed him to apply to your Excellency for assistance to get these Things forward to Fish Kill, and I am perswaded you will exert yourself for so important a Service.[3] It is probable that Aid can be more conveniently afforded to the United States in this way, than by the payment of considerable Sums of Money, which is an additional Inducement to me in making the present request.

You will be pleased to inform me of the Amount of your Expenditures in this Business as soon as may be convenient and it shall immediately be passed to the Credit of your State in the Public accounts.

I have the Honor to be very respectfully your Excellency's Most Obedient and humble Servant

Robt Morris

His Excellency
The Governor of the State
of Connecticutt

ENDORSED: Septr 20th 1781/Robt Morris Esqr. Financier
MSS: LS, to the Governor of Connecticut, Jonathan Trumbull Papers, Ct; Ofcl LbC, DLC.

1. The Ofcl LbC, which is undated, is identified as a circular.
2. See Diary, September 20; and RM to the Clothier General, September 20, in which this circular was enclosed.
3. Transmitting RM's request to the legislature on October 18, Governor John Hancock of Massachusetts recommended compliance, pointing out that "the Cloathing is now ready for Transportation, and the Season of the year is fast advancing when it will be absolutely necessary for the Comfort and Security of our Troops." After "a good deal of trouble and difficulty"—during which, Moylan subsequently reported, Hancock was "from the first moment earnestly disposed to contribute, as much as in his power, to the dispatch of my business"—the legislature responded on October 23 by granting Jabez Hatch, deputy quartermaster general for New Hampshire, Massachusetts, and Rhode Island, £2,500 in state certificates for the transportation of the clothing. On November 2 Moylan informed Major General William Heath that part of the clothing shipment was already on its way, with the remainder to follow in a few days, but added: "The clothing I came here in quest of will not, I apprehend, be adequate to the wants of the rest of the troops. I have,

however, good hopes to be able to make up any deficiency in a short time after my return to Phila; what gives me pain is that it will not be in my power to make as early a distribution of this clothing as I coud wish." Bacon, ed., *Supplement to the Acts and Resolves of Massachusetts, 1780–1784,* 90–91; *Acts and Laws of Massachusetts,* 1780–1781, p. 762; Moylan to Heath, November 2, 1781, *Heath Papers,* III, 297–298; the response of Governor Jonathan Trumbull of Connecticut has not been ascertained.

To the Clothier General (John Moylan)

Office of Finance 20 Sepr. 1781.

Sir,

Enclosed you have three Letters which you will Deliver.[1] The Letter to Mr Russell will procure you four thousand Dollars or more if necessary which I expect you will use with the utmost Oeconomy and endeavor to get by Means of the other two Letters the whole of the Transportation accomplished. I hope this may be the Case but at any Rate get as much as you can and be assured that you will receive my Warmest Thanks if you should be able to bring with you to Philadelphia all the Money you may receive of Mr. Russell. I am Sir very respectfully your most obedient and humble Servant

RM

MS: Ofcl LbC, DLC.
1. RM to Thomas Russell, and Circular to the Governors of Massachusetts and Connecticut, all September 20. See also Diary, September 12, and notes, and 20; and RM to Thomas Russell, September 21.

To the Commissary General of Purchases (Ephraim Blaine)

Office of Finance 20 Sepr. 1781.[1]

Sir,

I enclose you the Copy of a Letter from Monsr. Daure with my Answer to him.[2] The latter you will peruse, Seal and Deliver. I desire you will deliver twelve hundred Barrels of Flour at such Place as you and he may agree from the specific Supplies of Maryland and Virginia. But if that should not be in your Power then send the enclosed Letter to Mr. Ridley of Baltimore [3] having previously according to the Tenor of my letter to Monsr. Daure agreed on that Place for the Delivery. And let my Letter to Mr. Ridley be enclosed in one from you to him mentioning the quantity necessary to be procured by him and the Person to whom it is to be delivered.[4] The State of our Finances will not permit of Expence, you will therefore exert yourself to supply this Flour from the Quota of Maryland or Virginia. I am very respectfully Sir, your most obedient and humble Servant

RM.

MS: Ofcl LbC, DLC.
1. RM registered this letter in his Diary, September 21.
2. Dated September 16 and 19 respectively. On RM's transactions with the French, see Diary, August 21, and notes.
3. Dated September 20.
4. Letter not found.

From Isaac Howell and Peter Thomson

[*Philadelphia, September 20, 1781.* RM acknowledged their "Note of this Day" in his reply of September 20. *Letter not found.*]

To Isaac Howell and Peter Thomson[1]

Office of Finance 20 Sepr. 1781.

Gentlemen,

I received your Letter of the twelfth to which no reply was made; as I conceive the most agreeable Answers in these Cases are a Compliance with the Request but in Circumstances like ours such compliances cannot be made as fast as Necessities on one side and Inclination on the other would require. I find by your Note of this Day that your Patience is exhausted while my Means still continue deficient; I must therefore refer you to the Persons to whom your Warrants are directed, with this Assurance however that every exertion of mine shall take place for the Releif of the Civil List. I am Gentlemen your obedient Servant

RM

MS: Ofcl LbC, DLC.
1. Both Isaac Howell (1722–1797), businessman, promoter of American manufactures, state and municipal officeholder, and a signer of Pennsylvania's bills of credit in 1775 and 1776, and Peter Thomson, otherwise unidentified, were Philadelphia Quakers who were disowned by the Society of Friends because of their active participation in the war. With others they founded in February 1781 a group known as the "Free Quakers."
RM addressed Howell and Thomson in their capacities as inspectors of the Continental presses for striking bills of credit and exchange and loan office certificates, appointments they had received from Congress on July 27, 1778; they were among five who held this position until Congress on December 4, 1780, reduced the number of inspectors to three: Howell, Thomson, and Nathaniel Falconer. The letters of

Howell and Thomson to RM, which have not been found, probably concerned a warrant for $1,402 new emission which Congress on February 9, 1781, ordered on Thomas Smith, Continental loan officer of Pennsylvania, in favor of Howell, Thomson, Falconer, and the two former inspectors of the press in partial payment of their account settled up to December 4, 1780. Henry D. Biddle, "Owen Biddle," *PMHB*, XVI (1892), 315; Frank W. Leach, "Old Philadelphia Families" (mounted newspaper articles from the Philadelphia *North American*, November 24, 1907–June 29, 1913, New York Public Library, 1907–1913), II, article of January 14, 1912; *JCC*, XIX, 132.

To Chevalier de La Luzerne

Office of Finance 20th. Septembr. 1781.

Sir

His Excellency the Count De Rochambeau, having generously made me a very considerable Advance of Money, I was thereby enabled to give the Detachment of our Army under General Lincoln, one Months pay, which was earnestly prest upon me by the Commander in Chief. I promised Monsr. de Rochambeau that I would replace the Sum borrowed on the first of next Month, wherever the Army should then be.[1]

The Movement which lately took Place, to the Southward, has been attended with a Variety of Expences which have been very heavy, and have absorbed all the Money I could command; notwithstanding which many Demands still remain unsatisfied, so that I cannot obtain the Sums necessary for the Service, from any ordinary Means.

As it is probable that the Monies which the Count de Grasse has brought will prevent any immediate Want, by the Fleets or Armies of his Most Christian Majesty, in the States of Maryland and Virginia, I am induced to believe that no Inconvenience would arise from delaying the Payment, untill the Money in Boston shall be brought forward, which will be speedily; as a very active Person is gone for it, who will loose no Time in the Business committed to him.[2] Should your Excellency be of this Opinion, I should be glad that you would signify it to me, and if that be in your Power, extend the Time when payment is to be made. But if you think the Money is to be forwarded to Virginia immediately, You may depend that I will instantly endeavour to procure it; and altho that cannot be done, but with great difficulty and much loss, yet nothing shall deter me from complying with my Engagements.

I have the Honor to be with great Respect Your Excellency's Most Obedient and humble Servant

Robt Morris

His Excy The Minister of France

MSS: LS, Correspondance politique, supplément, Etats-Unis, AMAE; Ofcl LbC, DLC.
1. See Diary, September 1–5, and notes. This letter was written in consequence of RM's interview with La Luzerne on September 20. See Diary of that date.
2. See Diary, September 10, and RM to Tench Francis, September 11 (first letter), and notes.

From the President of Pennsylvania
(Joseph Reed)

[Philadelphia, September 20, 1781]

Sir

The Advices received, and the general Opinion of the Intentions of the Enemy with the Sense of Congress on this Subject have induced us to permit the Militia to assemble according to original Orders: [1] We should therefore be obliged to you for Information what Assistance you can give us in providing for them. The Demands on us which are proper to the State on this Occasion will be so numerous and heavy and our Treasury so low that we fear our Difficulties will be insurmountable if we cannot receive some Aid in this particular. Some of the Militia are already on the March to Newtown so that we beg to be favoured with an Answer as soon as possible.[2] I am Sir, with much Esteem and Consideration Your Obedient Humble Servant

JR.

MS: ADftS, Records of the Supreme Executive Council, RG 27, PHarH.
1. For the threat of a diversionary attack on Philadelphia by the British, see notes to Timothy Matlack to RM, September 11, and documents cited there.
2. For RM's reply, see the following letter.

To the President of Pennsylvania
(Joseph Reed)

Office of Finance
Septbr. 20th. 1781

Sir

I am honoured with your Excellency's Letter of this date, and most sincerely wish my situation was such as to justify a promise of Aid, equal to the present Necessities, I mean the Necessities that will be created by the Call of Militia at this time, but unluckily the late Movements of the Army have so entirely drained me of Money, that I have been Obliged to pledge my personal Credit very deeply, in a variety of instances, besides borrowing Money from my Friends; and advancing, to promote the public Service, every Shilling of my own: In this situation, I was preparing an application to the honourbl. Council and Assembly for relief from my advances for the State of Pensylvania, and this will be the more necessary, as this Alarm whilst it lasts will cut of[f] all possibility of recruiting the Treasury. Those who possess hard Money will keep it, and those who have Demands will become more eager for payment, therefore all I can promise is the use of my Credit, and an exertion of any influence I may have in favour of such measures as may be deemed necessary. At the same time I do not recede from my first Opinion, that the Enemy do not Meditate An Attack on this City. I have the honor to be Your Excellencys Most Obedient humble Servant.

Robt Morris

His Excellency The President of the State of Pensylvania

ENDORSED: 1781 September 10th [i.e. 20]/From Honble Robert Morris/Esqr. Superintendant of Finance
MSS: LS, Society Miscellaneous Collection, PHi; Ofcl LbC, DLC; transcript, Robert Morris Collection, CSmH.

To Matthew Ridley

Office of Finance 20 Septr. 1781[1]

Sir,

In Consequence of a Letter of the sixteenth from Mons. Daure Regisseur general des vivres I am to request that you will purchase twelve hundred Barrels of good Merchantable Flour and deliver them on my Account as Superintendant to Mr. Dumas [2] charged with the Care of that Business on the Part of France in your City or such lesser quantity and to such other Person as the American Commissary General shall by Letter accompanying this direct.[3] I [request you to] transmit the Accounts as soon as may be and take duplicate Receipts of your Deliveries of which one must be forwarded to me. I am Sir very respectfully your most obedient and humble Servant

RM

MS: Ofcl LbC, DLC.
1. RM registered this letter in the Diary of September 21.
2. Guillaume Mathieu Dumas was deputy quartermaster general of the French army in America.
3. On the exchange of flour supplies with the French forces, see Diary, August 21, and notes, and the documents cited there.

To Thomas Russell

Office of Finance 20 Sepr. 1781.

Sir,

Under Date of the fourteenth Instant I advised of my Draft in favor of General Schuyler for three thousand five hundred Dollars [1] and having further Occasion for Money in Boston to promote the public Service I deliver this Letter to Jno. Moylan, Esqr. Cloathier General of the American Army to whom I pray you to supply any Sum he may want to the extent of four thousand Mexican Dollars, or even as far as five or six thousand if he finds it absolutely necessary to take up so much, in Order to accomplish the Business that leads him to your Place; [2] be pleased to take his Drafts on Michael Hilligas Esqr. Treasurer of the United States for the Sum you supply and remit those Drafts to Messrs. Clymer and Nixon on Account of the national Bank and I will see them paid.[3] I shall be cautious of drawing more on you for account of the Bank without your future Advices encourage it; but the thirty Subscriptions you had obtained will exceed the Sums yet required.[4] I am Sir your most obedient and humble Servant

RM

MS: Ofcl LbC, DLC.
1. See RM to Philip Schuyler, and to Thomas Russell, both September 14.
2. See Diary, September 20, and notes, and documents cited there.
3. Russell was soliciting subscriptions in Boston for the Bank of North America on behalf of George Clymer and John Nixon. See RM's Plan for Establishing a National Bank, with Observations, May 17, 1781, and notes.
4. At $400 per share, subscriptions collected by Russell amounted to $12,000. RM addressed him again on September 21, requesting money for John Brown.

To John Townes[1]

Office of Finance 20th Sepr. 1781.

Sir,

No Man laments more than I do the Situation of military Gentlemen in want of the Pay that is due to them and it is one Part of my Study to provide a Remedy; this however must be done by general System and not by partial Dispensations, and you will be Sensible that if I act the Paymaster I shall of Necessity neglect what is of much more Importance my proper Duties; whilst it was in my Power I was happy to Administer to the Releif of Gentlemen who like you were involved in Distress by Misfortune, but the late Movements of the

Army have drained me of the Means and I am obliged to refer you to the Paymaster General [2] where your Application should in Propriety be made.

I have the Honor to be Sir your most obedient and humble Servant

RM

PS. Being unacquainted with your Rank I am obliged to direct to John Townes Esquire.

MS: Ofcl LbC, DLC.
1. John Townes of Virginia rose in the ranks of the Virginia line of the Continental army from ensign in November 1776 to first lieutenant in July 1779. Captured at Charleston in May 1780, he was exchanged and arrived in Philadelphia under a flag of truce in April 1781. While still a captive, Townes had been court-martialed by order of Brigadier General William Moultrie, himself a prisoner, for disobedient conduct while in Charleston and sentenced to be cashiered. Although Moultrie did not sanction the result and Major General Nathanael Greene questioned the legality of court-martial proceedings ordered by a captured officer and refused to approve or disapprove them, Washington declined Townes's requests to call a new trial or reverse the decision of the court. Meanwhile, Townes sought to recover back pay, and on the recommendation of the Board of War, Congress on June 2 rejected his appeal, ordering instead an advance of $380 in new emission currency in the form of a warrant drawn on the paymaster general. On August 13, still in Philadelphia and short of cash sufficient even for lodgings, Townes reminded Congress that it owed him over two years' back pay and requested money to enable him to return to Virginia to join the army. Congress the same day ordered the Board of War to draw warrants on the paymaster general for six months "nominal pay" in new emission money for those Continental officers who had arrived in Philadelphia from Charleston and St. Augustine. Townes's unsuccessful application to RM no doubt concerned the first, and probably the second, of these warrants. RM again declined to assist Townes in December, although he referred to his case sympathetically in February 1782. Congress on May 2, 1782, however, tabled his petition for $410 back pay from December 1, 1779, to March 12, 1782. Although Heitman says Townes retired from Continental service on January 1, 1783, his petition of May 1, 1782, indicates that he had already resigned. Heitman, *Register;* Townes to Washington, April 25, May 10, and July 2 and 10, 1781, Nathanael Greene to the Board of War, and to Townes, both May 24, 1781, and Townes's defense before the court-martial, January 15, 1781, all in the Washington Papers, DLC; Washington to Townes, May 2, and July 10 and 16, 1781, Fitzpatrick, ed., *Writings of Washington*, XXII, 25, 356n., 389; Townes to the President of Congress, August 13, 1781, and his memorial to Congress, May 1, 1782, with enclosure, PCC, no. 78, XXII, 467–468, no. 41, X, 151–152, 155; RM to Townes, December 12, 1781, and Diary, February 20, 1782.
2. John Pierce.

From William Heath

Head Quarters Continental Village [New York] Sept 20th 1781
Sir

This army is at present threatned with a Scarcity of Flour. Since the armies parted, we have been principally Supplied with Flour from what was turned over by the French.[1] The whole of that will be soon exhausted, very little has as yet been received from the agent of the State of New York [2] and I very much doubt of a Supply through that Channel. What other resources we are to depend on I know not. I request that Seasonable and ample Supplies may be afforded, and that the D[eputy] C[ommissary] [3] may be informed through what Channel they are to be expected.[4]

We are also in great want of Forage; there is n[e]ither requisition on the State, or money in the hands of the Quarter Master, to obtain it. We have hitherto drawn our Supplies from below the Lines, but the Forage there is nearly exhausted and some new resource must be opened.[5]

I have the honor to be with much respect Sir your most obedient Servant

W Heath
M[ajor] Genl

Hon Robert Morris Esqr

ENDORSED: To Rob. Morris Esqr./respecting flour and forage/Sept. 20. 1781.
MS: ADftS, Heath Papers, MHi.

1. See Diary, August 21, and notes, RM to Heath, September 17 and 24, and Heath to RM, October 4, 1781.

2. Udny Hay. See Diary, August 21, and notes, and Hay to RM, RM to Hay, to the Commissary General of Issues, and to the Governor of New York, all August 15.

3. Nathaniel Stevens (1753–1832) of Canaan, Connecticut, formerly assistant commissary of issues at Fishkill, New York, was appointed deputy commissary general of issues in 1780. At the date of the letter printed here, he was also assistant commissary general of purchases for the main Continental army. Plowdon Stevens, *Stephens-Stevens Genealogy* (New York, 1909), 56; Bread and Flour in the Several [New York] State Stores, March 8, 1779, Charles Stewart to Robert Howe, April 4, 1780, and Stevens to Washington, December 9, 1780, Hastings and Holden, eds., *Clinton Papers*, IV, 596, V, 587–588, VI, 485–486; Roster of the Commissariat of Purchases, July 1, 1781, enclosed in the Commissary General of Purchases to RM, July 2, and Heath to RM, November 20, 1781.

4. For an account of the flour Heath received from all sources, see Heath to RM, October 4, 1781.

5. On September 18 Heath informed Governor George Clinton of New York that Westchester County was virtually destitute of forage and appealed for his aid in gathering a supply. Replying on September 22, Clinton declared himself unauthorized to grant relief and declined to order the impressment of forage, which he believed only an emergency would justify; however, he promised to take up the subject with the state legislature the following month. The correspondence is in Hastings and Holden, eds., *Clinton Papers*, VII, 337–338, 347–348.

From Thomas Paine[1]

[Philadelphia] Second Street, Sept. 20th, [1781.]

Sir,

As your acquaintance with the finances, your being a member of the House,[2] and an inhabitant of the City give you a united knowledge and interest, I therefore trouble you with a hint which occurred to me on the reports of yesterday.[3]

I conjecture that one fourth or one third part of the rental of Philadelphia will defray the expense of a body of Men sufficient to prevent the Enemy from destroying it. I estimate at a guess the yearly rental to be £300,000.

As I need not mention to you to [4] great difference between giving up a quarters rent and losing the whole rental together with the Capital, I shall therefore make no remarks thereon, the hint I mean to convey is, to bring in a provisionary bill for the supply of the City at all times, where the destruction of it appears to be the object of the Enemy by empowering the tenant to pay immediately into the Treasury one quarters rent to be applied as above, and in case it should not be necessary to use the money when collected, the same so paid to be considered as part of the customary taxes—this all our circumstances considered appears to me the readiest and most eligible mode of procuring an immediate supply.[5] Your obt Hble Servt

Thomas Paine.

The Honble Robt Morris, Esq., Front Street.

PRINTED: "Letters to Robert Morris," N.-Y. Hist. Soc., *Colls.*, XI, 470.

1. Several careful searches at the New-York Historical Society have failed to locate the manuscript on which the text reprinted here by the editors (verbatim except for a partial expansion of the dateline) and that in Foner, ed., *Writings of Paine*, II, 1197–1198, were based.

2. An error RM corrected in his reply to Paine, September 21.

3. Whatever the form of these reports, they no doubt referred to the threat of a diversionary attack on Philadelphia by Sir Henry Clinton. A September 21 postscript to the Philadelphia *Freeman's Journal* and a September 19 dispatch in the *Pennsylvania Journal* of September 22 disclosed the embarkation of 5,000 troops at New York, reportedly for an attack on Pennsylvania. See notes to Timothy Matlack to RM, September 11.

4. Thus in text.

5. RM relayed Paine's suggestion to President Joseph Reed and other authorities at a conference concerning the British threat held the following day. See Diary, and RM to Paine, both September 21.

Thomas Paine. Portrait by A. Millière after George Romney.

From the Board of War

[*Philadelphia, September 20, 1781.* In this day's Diary RM recorded the receipt of an estimate of money to be furnished Clothier General John Moylan for his journey to Boston "which the Board sent in their Letter of this date." *Letter not found.*]

Diary: September 21, 1781

Genl. St Clair attended for Money, none to give him; referred him to the Contractors at this Post for Supplies of Rations to his Troops expected down here.[1]

The Cloathier General, for Money. I could not assist him with any, but agreed to accept his draft for 30 Guineas at 6 Weeks, as he alledged the impossibility of proceeding without it to Boston; gave him his dispatches.[2]

The Honorable Mr Boudinot[3] paid me a Visit and mentioned that it had been asserted, I had sufficient knowledge of Mr Halls[4] Abilities to pronounce him a proper person for Comptroller of the Treasury. I assure him that no such Sentiment has ever escaped me as I had determined not to interfere in that appointment nor to recommend anyone. Mr Hall had my good Opinion as far as I knew of his Character and Abilities but this knowledge does not extend to that degree, that would be necessary to Authorize such an Opinion as above mentioned. He informed me of certain Medical Appointments taking place in Congress, wherefore I send to Congress this Morning the Plan approved by Doctrs. Jones, Clarkson and Hutchinson.[5]

Issued a Warrant on Mr Swanwick in favor of E Bartholemew[6] for Flour, £16.16.6¼. Ordered payment to Mr Marbois[7] of half Amount of his Bill of Exchange &Ca. £   .[8]

Wrote a Letter to His Excellency The President of Congress.

Wrote a Letter to Capt John Barry of the Frigate Alliance.

Wrote a Letter to Capt Samuel Nicholson of the Frigate Deane.

Wrote a Letter to Messrs. Wm. Vernon and J. Warren Commsr[s]. of the Navy Board, Boston.

Wrote a Letter to John Bradford Esqr. Agent of the United States at Boston.

Wrote a Letter to Thos. Russell Esqr. Merchant at Boston.

Wrote a Letter to His Excellency The Governour of Massachusetts.

Wrote a Letter to Benjamin Bourne Esqr. A[ssistant] Q[uarter] Masr. [Master] State of Rhode Island.

Wrote a Letter to Nicholas and John Brown Esqrs. Rhode Island.

Wrote a Letter to John Brown Esqr.

Wrote a Letter to Ephraim Blaine Esqr. Commsy. G[eneral] of Pe. [Purchases] dated 20th instant Omitted in yesterdays Minutes.

Wrote a letter to Monsr Duare [Daure], Regisseur General des Vivres do.[9]

Wrote a Letter to Matthew Ridley Esqr. do.[10]

Doctr. Oliphant applied respecting the Estimates for Stores and Medicine for the Southern Army and I am sorry it is not in my power to give him encouragement to Expect Money &Ca. wherewith to procure those Supplies.[11]

Applications from Mr Hilligass [12] and Mr Gibson,[13] the former for Money to pay sundry Warrants &ca but I have none, and the latter respecting Rent of The Treasury Office due to Mrs. Keppele [14] Which must be paid.

Received a Letter from His Excellency The President of the State inviting me to a Conference for providing the Means of defending this City in Case of Attack &ca.[15]

At One OClock I waited on His Excellency The President of the State at his House in Markett Street and met there Mr Peters and Mr Cornell of the Board of War, Genl St Clair, Genl. Irvine [16] and General Irwin of the Militia.[17] This Conference lasted a considerable time and in its Consequence took up the rest of the day. I gave it as my Opinion that Sir Henry Clinton did not intend for this City, Nevertheless as the Inhabitants are alarmed and uneasy I agreed to the propriety of being prepared altho I lamented the expence such preparations would put us to. I advised the placing a Garrison at Mud Island [18] and putting that place in a Posture of Defence and mentioned the Plan proposed to me by Mr Paine of Collecting immediately one quarters Rent from all the Houses in Philada. in order to have an immediate supply of Money to defray the Expences &Ca.[19]

1. Major General Arthur St. Clair, who was recruiting troops of the Pennsylvania line for service in the southern campaign, had petitioned Congress earlier in September for an allowance prior to his pending departure. Although St. Clair was ordered on September 19 to bring his troops to Philadelphia for the protection of the city, Congress on September 21 referred to RM his memorial and a committee report recommending that the Board of War draw a warrant on the paymaster general for $500 specie "on account of his pay that he may be enabled to proceed on the duties of his command," doubtless the subject of his call on RM. The Financier apparently caviled at giving him specie, but recorded in his Diary of September 24 that he offered him paper. Nevertheless, although St. Clair's troops were reassigned to

Washington, Congress ordered RM on September 29 to proceed with the payment to St. Clair. St. Clair's memorial to Congress [ca. September 12, 1781], PCC, no. 43, p. 247; *JCC*, XXI, 954, 970, 1018; notes to Diary, August 28; Diary, September 24 and October 6, 1781; on the provisioning of St. Clair's troops and the military alarm that resulted in their assignment to the defense of Philadelphia, see Timothy Matlack to RM, September 11, and notes.

2. See Diary, September 12, and notes. John Moylan was clothier general.

3. Elias Boudinot (1740–1821), New Jersey lawyer and former commissary general of prisoners by a commission of Congress granted June 6, 1777, and backdated to April 15. He remained in this post until July 1778 when, pursuant to his election the preceding year, he entered Congress. Elected to Congress again in July 1781, he served until the end of 1783, presiding over that body for a year beginning November 4, 1782, besides performing the duties of Secretary for Foreign Affairs after June 16, 1783. *DAB*.

4. George Abbott Hall.

5. See RM to the President of Congress, September 21, and notes.

6. Possibly Edward Bartholomew (1751–1802) of Philadelphia, member of the state constitutional convention of 1776, commander of a battalion of associators in New Jersey in 1778, and holder of city and county offices. William H. Egle, "The Constitutional Convention of 1776: Biographical Sketches of Its Members," *PMHB*, III (1879), 101.

7. François, Marquis de Barbé-Marbois, secretary to the French legation in Philadelphia.

8. Space left blank in manuscript.

9. This letter is dated September 19.

10. This letter is dated September 20.

11. On this subject, see RM to Nathanael Greene, September 14, and Diary, September 14, 24, 26, and 27.

12. Michael Hillegas, Treasurer of the United States.

13. John Gibson, a member of the Board of Treasury prior to the reconstitution of the Treasury Department by Congress on September 11.

14. Not further identified, but possibly Catherine Keppele (d. 1793), who may have been the wife of George Keppele, a merchant of 98 High (Market) Street; or Catherine Gross Keppele, the wife of Henry Keppele, Jr. (1745–1782), of Philadelphia. Butterfield, ed., *Rush Letters*, II, 707n.; Charles I. Landis, "The Juliana Library in Lancaster," *PMHB*, XLIII (1919), 245; see also Diary, October 3, 1781.

15. This letter is dated September 21. On this subject, see notes to Timothy Matlack to RM, September 11.

16. William Irvine (1741–1804), an Irishman who emigrated to Carlisle, Pennsylvania, in 1763, received a commission as colonel in the Pennsylvania line of the Continental army on January 9, 1776, and was promoted to brigadier general on May 12, 1779. Congress on September 24, 1781, directed him to assume command of Fort Pitt, where severe discontent existed among the officers and men of the garrison as to rations and pay. Irvine took command of the post after receiving Washington's orders in March 1782 and held it until October 1, 1783, resigning from the army shortly thereafter. In the summer of 1781, prior to his assignment to Fort Pitt, Irvine had been extremely apprehensive of a possible British attack upon York and Lancaster to free the Convention prisoners held there and was bitterly critical of RM's failure to provide supplies for the forces he was trying to organize. *DAB; Biog. Dir. Cong.;* Boatner, *Encyclopedia of the American Revolution*, 545–546; Washington's Instructions to Irvine, March 8, 1782, Fitzpatrick, ed., *Writings of Washington*, XXIV, 48–49; Irvine to President Joseph Reed of Pennsylvania, August 9, 1781, *Pennsylvania Archives*, 1st ser., IX, 345–346; Diary, July 6, 1781, and notes.

17. Probably James Irvine (1735–1819) of Philadelphia, who joined the Continental army as a lieutenant colonel in November 1775, rose to the rank of colonel in October 1776, and resigned June 1, 1777. Appointed brigadier general of the Pennsylvania militia the following August, Irvine was captured in December but not

exchanged until June 1, 1781. He advanced to the rank of major general on May 27, 1782, serving to the end of the war, and was a member of the Supreme Executive Council, 1782–1785. Heitman, *Register;* Butterfield, ed., *Rush Letters,* I, 117n.

18. A small island located in the Delaware River at the convergence of the Schuylkill River about seven miles below Philadelphia. See the map in Marion Balderston, "Lord Howe Clears the Delaware," *PMHB,* XCVI (1972), 335.

19. See Thomas Paine to RM, September 20, and RM to Paine, September 21.

To John Barry

Office of Finance 21. Septemr 1781.

Sir,

John Brown Esqr. who is the Bearer of this Letter is charged by me in Consequence of three several Acts of Congress of which Copies are enclosed with the Care of sending to Sea the Frigates Alliance and Deane.[1] You will therefore exert yourself to assist him to the utmost of your Power. When those Ships are ready you will proceed to Sea. The Ships are both under your Command, the Captain of the Deane being instructed to obey your Orders [2] wherefore you had best to furnish him with a Copy of these Instructions giving such in Addition as you shall judge necessary for keeping Company respecting Signals, Places of rendevous in Case of seperation and all other Things that tend to promote Success and Glory or secure Safety against superior Force. It is my Intention that you should go upon a Cruize and therefore you will when ready sail from the Harbor of Boston and use your best Efforts to distress the Enemy. Such Prizes as you may make you will send into the Port which you may think most proper and you will find enclosed a List of Persons in several Ports to whom to apply in Case you go yourselves or send your Prizes thither.[3] Mr Brown will shew you the Instructions I have given him as to the manner of manning the Ship[s] [4] which I hope you will approve and endeavor to execute but if exact compliance is not likely to succeed you will deviate no more than absolute necessity requires. I do not fix your cruizing Ground nor limit the length of your Cruize because I expect you will know the most likely Course and will be anxious to meet such Events as will do honor to the American flagg, and promote the general Interest. When you want Provisions I think it will be best that you should enter the Delaware and send up as far as New Castle to which Place they can be sent in Shallops.

The Latitude I have given precludes both the Necessity and Propriety of more particular Instructions.[5] Let me hear from you by every convenient Opportunity and dont fail to transmit to His Excellency the Commander in Chief of our Army as well as to me any

Intelligence that you obtain which you think may in any wise affect his Operations. Beleive me to be, With great Respect Sir your most obedient and humble Servant

RM

mss: Ofcl LbC, DLC; LbC, John Barry Letterbook, Naval History Society Collection, NHi; copy, Naval History Manuscript Collection of Franklin D. Roosevelt, NHpR.

1. See RM to John Brown, September 19, and notes. On Barry and the *Alliance,* see notes to RM to the President of Congress, June 22, 1781 (second letter).

2. See RM to Samuel Nicholson, September 21.

3. Enclosure not found. RM sent another list in a letter to Barry of July 12, 1782.

4. Instructions not found. See RM to John Brown, September 19, and notes.

5. For changes in these instructions, see RM to Barry, October 17 and November 27, 1781.

To Benjamin Bourne[1]

Office of Finance Sepr. 21. 1781.

Sir,

The Honble. Board of War inform me that they have given you Instructions in pursuance of an Act of Congress of the twenty eighth of August last to make Sale of certain Cannon and Stores continental Property in the State of Rhode Island and to Pay the Produce thereof in hard Money to my Order.[2] I am therefore to request you will pay the same to John Brown Esqr. late Secretary of the Admiralty or to his Order and his Receipt or Draft shall be your Discharge.[3] I am Sir your obedient humble Servant

RM

ms: Ofcl LbC, DLC.

1. Benjamin Bourne (1755–1808) of Rhode Island, Harvard graduate, lawyer, revolutionary war soldier, and clerk of the state assembly from 1780 to 1786, was also at this time assistant deputy quartermaster general for Rhode Island at Providence, in which capacity he appears to have remained until 1782. *DAB;* "Return of all Persons employ'd in the Quarter Master General's Department in the States of Massachusetts, Rhode Island and New Hampshire," August 31, 1781, Manuscript Large, MHi; Timothy Pickering to Bourne, September 30, 1782, WDC, no. 84, p. 166.

2. See notes to RM to Nicholas and John Brown, September 21.

3. See RM to John Brown, September 21.

To John Bradford[1]

Office of Finance 21. Septemr. 1781.

Sir,

I do myself the Honor to enclose to you Copies of two Acts of Congress of the twenty ninth August and seventh Instant.[2] By these

Acts it becomes my Duty to attend to the Business of the Marine and by the latter all the several civil Offices of the Admiralty are determined. I must therefore request that you will with all convenient Speed complete the Accounts of your Department so that they may be finally settled.

I have deputed John Brown Esqr. late Secy. of the Admiralty Board the Bearer of this Letter to act for me at Boston on the present Occasion and I must intreat you to deliver to him or his Order agreeably to the Acts above referred to all the Registers, Books and Papers in your Custody belonging to the Marine Service and also all Public Stores and Property of every Kind which may be in your Possession.

With great Respect I have the Honor to be Sir your most obedient and humble Servant

RM

MS: Ofcl LbC, DLC.
1. This letter to Bradford, Continental prize agent at Boston, was enclosed in RM to John Brown, September 19, and was accompanied by RM's September 22 letter to Bradford.
2. See the headnote to RM to the President of Congress, September 8.

To John Brown

Office of Finance
Sept 21st. 1781.

Sir

You will find herein an Act of Congress of the 28th. of August last, by which the Board of War are directed to make Sale of certain Cannon and Stores in the State of Rhode Island, and the Money arising therefrom is ordered into my hands. The Board of War inform me that they have given orders to Benjn. Bourne Esqr. to make the said Sales, and pay the Money to my order, and you will find herein my order on him in your favor, for the Amount of the Net Proceeds, which be pleased to receive and apply the same to the fitting the Alliance and Deane Frigates to Sea.[1]

This Sale was ordered by Congress with a view to enable my discharging a draft of Messrs. Panet da Costa & Co,[2] on Messrs. Nichs. and Jno. Brown, to whom be pleased to deliver the enclosed letter on that Subject.[3] I am Sir your obedient Servant

Robt Morris

Mr. John Brown.

ENDORSED: Honble Robert Morris Esqr./September 25th. [i.e. 21] 1781/Receiving Money for Cannon/at Providence
MSS: LS, Andre deCoppet Collection, NjP; Ofcl LbC, DLC.
1. See RM to Benjamin Bourne, and to Nicholas and John Brown, both September 21.
2. J. Pierre Penet, formerly a "journeyman gunsmith" at Strasbourg and a ship's surgeon in the West Indies, where he had formed mercantile connections, arrived at Providence, Rhode Island, from Santo Domingo in December 1775 with his partner, Emmanuel de Pliarne, seeking a supply contract with the Continental army. Following conversations with Washington in Cambridge, Massachusetts, Penet and Pliarne concluded a contract with the Secret Committee of Trade for supplying munitions to the United States. Sailing for France early in 1776, Penet settled at Nantes, where he sought to establish the political and commercial connections needed to fulfill the contract, and entered into business arrangements with the ill-fated Thomas Morris, RM's half brother. With a number of associates, under the names of Penet, Pliarne and Company and, following Pliarne's death in 1778, Penet, d'Acosta Frères and Company, Penet, Wendel and Company, and Penet and Coulaux (with J. Coulaux da Vigne, the firm's agent in the United States as late as April 1781), Penet carried on his American commerce, some of it—as the letter printed here indicates—with Nicholas and John Brown of Providence. Penet and Wendel, following the authorization by Congress on January 2, 1779, contracted with the Board of War to manufacture firearms in the United States with French craftsmen under the direction of the firm, but the board terminated the contract in March 1781 when the company failed to carry out the terms, in part, no doubt, because France prohibited the emigration of munitions workers. Penet also concluded a similar contract with Virginia in July 1779 and was also named state agent for securing a loan and procuring supplies in France. These efforts as well as his attempt in October 1781 to solicit additional American business failed, and in 1782 Penet went bankrupt and absconded. James B. Hedges, *The Browns of Providence Plantation: Colonial Years* (Cambridge, Mass., 1952), 229–233, 235, 236, 244–245, 248; Price, *France and the Chesapeake*, II, 702, 705, 716, 1074n.; Hutchinson and Rutland, eds., *Madison Papers*, I, 294n.–295n.; Silas Deane to the Secret Committee, August 18, 1776, and Deane's Reply to the Slanders of Joseph Reed, 1784, *Deane Papers*, I, 196–197, V, 413; Ferguson, *Power of the Purse*, 91–92; memorial of Penet and J. Coulaux to Congress, [ca. October 24, 1778], and Penet to the Board of War, May 20, 1780, PCC, no. 41, VIII, 60–63, no. 147, VI, 231–234; *JCC*, XII, 1059, 1167, 1185n., XIII, 134, 303–305, XIX, 241; the documents in Boyd, ed., *Jefferson Papers*, III, 36, 49–50, 70, 90–93, 131–146, 147n., 299–301, 315, 358, 382–385, 551, IV, 144–147, 147n.; Penet to George Clinton, October 7, 1781, Hastings and Holden, eds., *Clinton Papers*, VII, 382–383; see also Diary, November 10, 1781, and January 24, 1782, and RM to César Louis de Baulny, January 22, 1782, for RM and the settlement of Penet's accounts.
3. Dated September 21.

To Nicholas and John Brown[1]

Office of Finance 21. Sept. 1781.

Gentlemen

Your Letter of the thirtieth of July last to Messrs. Varnum and Mowrey respecting certain Bills drawn upon you by Messrs. Penet & Co. for a balance due them on certain Transactions you had with that House on behalf of the Secret Committee of Congress, has been referred to me by the Honble. Congress.[2] And I write this to releive you from any Anxiety on that Account. There are several

Accounts depending between that House and the United States. I shall take the needful steps to have the whole settled and the Balance they require of you shall be comprehended in the Settlement.[3] I have the Honor to be Gentlemen Your obedient Servant

RM

MS: Ofcl LbC, DLC.
1. Nicholas (1729–1791) and John (1736–1803) Brown were two of four brothers, including Joseph and Moses, who in late colonial times composed a dynamic commercial and manufacturing firm in Providence, Rhode Island. Although by the outbreak of the Revolution the general partnership had dissolved, John and Nicholas conducted joint enterprises. During the Revolution they employed their wide mercantile connections in the West Indies and Europe to import munitions and clothing on contract for the Secret Committee of Trade, but they drew RM's criticism for work done on behalf of the Marine Committee. *DAB;* Hedges, *The Browns: Colonial Years,* 11–21, 218–239, 270–271, 279–280; East, *Business Enterprise,* 71–72.
2. The balance due Penet, d'Acosta Frères and Company was in the form of a bill of exchange dated March 10, 1781, for some 3,738 livres which the French firm had drawn on Nicholas and John Brown for a debt the Browns had contracted as agents of the Secret Committee of Trade. On July 3 Congress ordered the Board of Treasury to issue the Browns a warrant for this sum in new emission on Joseph Clark, Continental loan officer of Rhode Island. But in a July 30, 1781, letter to James Mitchell Varnum and Daniel Mowry, Jr., Rhode Island delegates to Congress, the Browns returned the draft on Clark. Penet's agent would not accept payment stated in new emission currency, and Clark could apparently neither pay the draft out of funds in his hands nor could he sell it for specie. The Browns proposed instead that Continental cannon and stores in Rhode Island formerly belonging to the sloop *Argo* be sold to raise the cash. Following Varnum's motion to this effect on August 27, Congress the following day directed the Board of War to sell the cannon and stores for specie, which was to be placed in RM's hands, and referred the Browns' letter and the order on Clark to RM "to take order." As indicated by this letter and those of the same date to John Brown and Benjamin Bourne, RM ignored Congress's intentions. A draft of the Browns' letter to Varnum and Mowry is in the Brown Papers, RPJCB; on Mowry (1729–1806) of Smithfield, Rhode Island, a cooper by trade, assemblyman, 1766–1776, judge of the court of common pleas, 1776–1781, and delegate to the Continental Congress, 1780–1782, see *Biog. Dir. Cong.*
3. This letter was enclosed in RM to John Brown, September 21.

To the President of Congress
(Thomas McKean)

Office of Finance September 21st. 1781.

Sir

In the Month of July last, I think on the fifteenth, I was favored with certain Observations, from Doctor Tilton, on military Hospitals.[1] I thought them worthy of Attention, as well from the Reasonableness of them, as from the Probity and Abilities of the Gentleman by whom they were written. These Observations are enclosed in No. 1 the Copy of a Letter which I wrote on the 17th. July, to Doctors Jones, Hutchinson and Clarkson.

On the 30th. of July, I received a Letter from the Director General with two Returns; [2] all which are enclosed in No. 2, the Copy of my Letter of that Date to the same Gentlemen.[3]

No. 3 is a Letter from Doctor Tilton dated the ninth of August which was also sent to the Gentlemen above named. On the fifteenth Instant I received the Letter of the 30th. of August with the Observations it refers to, contained in the Enclosure No. 4.[4]

It becomes my Duty to lay these Things before the United States in Congress assembled. They must be forcibly impressed with the Necessity of curtailing their Expences as much as possible. The People may perhaps be induced to bear those Burthens which the War shall render indispensible; but they will very reluctantly contribute to the Support of Idleness, Waste or Extravagance.[5]

With all possible Respect I have the Honor to be Sir, Your Excellency's Most Obedient and humble Servant

Robt Morris

His Excellency The President of Congress.

ENDORSED: 20/Letter./Superintendant of/Finance. Sept 21. 1781/Hospital department/Read. Sept. 21./Referred to Mr Sherman/Mr Montgomery/Mr Boudinot/[*At a later date:*] NB Doct Tilton's plan is missing
MSS: LS, PCC, DNA; Ofcl LbC, DLC.

1. James Tilton's Observations on Military Hospitals and Plan of Arrangement, dated January 1, 1781, is printed as the enclosure to RM to Gerardus Clarkson, James Hutchinson, and John Jones, July 17, 1781.

2. The letter from the Director General of Military Hospitals is dated July 26, 1781.

3. RM to Gerardus Clarkson, James Hutchinson, and John Jones, July 30, 1781.

4. Gerardus Clarkson, James Hutchinson, and John Jones to RM, August 30, enclosing their Remarks on Tilton's Observations on Military Hospitals and Plan of Arrangement.

5. This letter was prompted by information from Congressman Elias Boudinot of New Jersey that "certain Medical Appointments [were] taking place in Congress" (Diary, September 21). These appointments of September 20 were based on resolutions adopted that day and explained in notes to the Director General of Military Hospitals to RM, July 26, 1781. Congress committed RM's letter on September 21 and, in a roll call vote requested by James Duane, rejected a motion of Duane, seconded by James Mitchell Varnum, which would have suspended the resolutions and appointments of the preceding day until the committee had reported. Except for the South Carolina delegates, Congress was nearly unanimous in favoring the suspension, but insufficient representation of several states prevented approval by the necessary majority. It was not until November 3 that the committee submitted its lengthy report, and not until December 24 that an ordinance respecting the Hospital Department received its first reading. However, on January 3, 1782, Congress discarded the idea of a complete reorganization and approved instead amendments to the existing establishment of September 30, 1780. See notes to RM to Gerardus Clarkson, James Hutchinson, and John Jones, July 17, 1781.

Letter of Appointment to a Deputy Agent of Marine for Massachusetts

Office of Finance [ca. September 21, 1781] [1]

Sir

You are hereby appointed Deputy Agent of Marine of the United States for the State of Massachusetts. You will therefore immediately take upon you the Duties of that Office previous to which you shall take the following Oath before a Magistrate legally authorized to administer the same, to Wit:

I _____ Deputy Agent of the Marine of the United States of America do solemnly swear upon the holy Evangelists of Almighty God that I will well and faithfully execute the Trust reposed in me according to the best of my Skill and Judgment. With full trust and Confidence in your Zeal, Fidelity and Integrity, I am respectfully your most obedient and humble Servant

RM

MS: Ofcl LbC, DLC.

1. This letter, enclosed in RM to John Brown, September 19, is found among letters dated September 21 in RM's Official Letterbooks. Brown was directed to make the appointment with the advice of Governor John Hancock of Massachusetts. Thomas Russell received the appointment. See RM to the Governor of Massachusetts, September 21.

To the Governor of Massachusetts (John Hancock)

Office of Finance 21. Septemr. 1781.

Sir

This Letter will be delivered to you by John Brown Esqr. late Secretary of the Admiralty who is employed by me in Consequence of two Acts of Congress of the twenty ninth of August and the seventh Instant, of which he will shew you Copies.[1] Mr Brown is directed to employ a proper Person to act as Deputy in Boston under the Agent of the Marine in which as well as the other Matters submitted to his Care and Attention I pray that he may be favored with your Excellency's Advice and Assistance for which Purpose I have directed him to apply to you as Occasion may require.[2] And should the Alliance and Deane meet Difficulty in getting manned I hope the Powers of Government may be exerted to accomplish that Object on this as on other Occasions; but this I would not Wish unless it becomes absolutely necessary.

On the fourth of August last I did myself the Honor to request that you would furnish Money for fitting out the Alliance and Dean Frigates which request I now beg to reiterate in the most pressing Manner.

With all possible respect I have the Honor to be Sir your Excellency's most obedient and humble Servant.

RM

MS: Ofcl LbC, DLC.
1. On the acts of Congress, see the headnote to RM to the President of Congress, September 8.
2. See RM to John Brown, September 19, in which this letter was enclosed.

To the Navy Board of the Eastern Department

Office of Finance 21. Septemr. 1781.

Gentlemen[1]

By the enclosed Acts of Congress of the twenty ninth of August and seventh Instant you will perceive that the United States have devolved upon me the Care of their Marine until the future Appointment of an Agent for that Purpose.[2] I could have wished that this Task had fallen to the Lot of some other Person. I could have wished to bestow on this Object an Attention undissipated by other Cares. But it is now some time since I have learnt to Sacrifice to the public Service my Ease, my Wishes, and my Inclinations.

You will perceive Gentlemen that it now becomes my Duty to request that you will compleat the Accounts of your Department as speedily as possible, to the End that they may be settled and all the Books and Papers relating to the Business of the Admiralty delivered over as well as the several Articles of Public Property which may be in your Possession agreeably to the Acts above referred to.

John Brown Esqr. late Secretary of the Admiralty is deputed by me on this Occasion to take the necessary Measures in the Business committed to me wherefore I pray you to deliver to him or his Order all the Register Books and Papers belonging to the Admiralty and Navy Boards in your Custody and also all public stores and Property of every Kind which may be in your Possession or subjected to your Order.[3]

I have however to observe that as the Frigates Alliance and Deane will probably be almost if not altogether ready for Sea by the Time this Letter shall have arrived in Boston, It is my Wish and Desire that those Frigates may be compleated and fitted under your Inspection as heretofore so that your Accounts may conclude with them and no Part of the Expenditure be carried to the new Accounts. Mr Brown is instructed to take the necessary Measures and Arrangements with you for that Purpose and I shall be very thankful for your Advice and Assistance to him in whatever he may find necessary.[4] With the greatest Respect I have the Honor to be Gentlemen your most obedient and humble Servant

RM

MS: Ofcl LbC, DLC.
    1. The commissioners of the Navy Board were William Vernon and James Warren.
    2. On these acts of Congress, see the headnote to RM to the President of Congress, September 8.
    3. See RM to John Brown, September 19, in which this letter was enclosed.
    4. See RM to the Governor of Massachusetts, September 21.

To Samuel Nicholson

Office of Finance 21. Septemr. 1781.

Sir

John Brown Esqr. who is the Bearer of this Letter is charged by me, in Consequence of three several Acts of Congress of which Copies are enclosed,[1] with the Care of sending to Sea the Frigates Alliance and Deane.[2] You will be pleased to take the Command of the Deane immediately and give Mr. Brown all the Aid in your Power in fitting her immediately for Sea and getting her manned according to the Instructions given to him which he is directed to communicate.[3] When the Dean is ready you are to proceed to Sea in Company with the Alliance; you are to receive the Orders of Capt Barry and in all Things to obey them.[4] If while you are in Company together Capt. Barry should loose his Life which I pray God to prevent, the Senior Lieut. will take Command of the Ship you assign him until a Captain is appointed and he is to obey your Instructions which will be conformable to those I have given to Capt. Barry and these will in such Case regulate your Conduct likewise. I wish you Success, and am Sir your most obedient and humble Servant

RM

MS: Ofcl LbC, DLC.
    1. Probably the acts of August 29 and September 7 and 12. See the headnote to RM to the President of Congress, September 8.

2. See RM to John Brown, September 19, in which this letter was enclosed.

3. On these instructions, which have not been found, see RM to John Brown, September 19, and notes.

4. See RM to John Barry, September 21.

To Thomas Paine

Office of Finance
Septr. 21st. 1781

Sir

I received your note [1] last evening by which I perceive you are not informed that my Acceptance of an Office under the United States has Vacated my Seat in the assembly. Consequently that I cannot introduce any matter into that House upon a different footing from other Citizens. Your Idea I think a very good one, well deserving the attention of Government and as such very proper to be proposed to them by its author.[2] For my own part I cannot find sufficient reasons whereon to ground apprehensions of an Attack on this City by Clinton. Nevertheless if Government are of a different opinion and take Measures accordingly, I am determined to give them every Aid and Support in my power.

Accept my thanks for this communication and be assured of my disposition to pay the utmost attention to every proposal that has the Public Good for its object. I am Sir your very humble Servant

RM

Thos Paine Esqr
Second Street

ENDORSED: draft of a letter the/21st Septr 1781/to Thos Paine Esqr.

MS: ADftS, Robert Morris Papers, NN.

1. Dated September 20 and proposing a means of financing the defense of Philadelphia from a threatened diversionary attack by the British. See notes to Timothy Matlack to RM, September 11.

2. RM mentioned Paine's plan at a meeting he attended with President Joseph Reed of Pennsylvania and other officials to prepare for the defense of the city. See Diary, September 21.

To Thomas Russell

Office of Finance 21. Sepr. 1781.

Sir,

I have written you by Mr Moylan Requesting you to pay him to the Amount of four, five or six thousand Dollars, this Payment with the Amount of my Draft on you in favor of Genl. Schuyler already advised being for three thousand five hundred Dollars.[1] I desired these two Sums might be paid out of the Subscription you advised to have been made to the Bank; [2] and that I would see the Amount paid to Messrs. Clymer and Nixon here upon your Drafts and those of Mr Moylan. Having hopes that the Subscriptions to the Bank will be much encreased when you receive the Letters adviseing how soon that Plan is to be compleated, I desire the Bearer hereof John Brown Esqr. late Secretary of the Admiralty now employed by me on the Service of the Navy to wait on you for Information on this Point.[3] He will probably want Money for the public Service; should that be the Case and you can from an encrease of Subscriptions supply what he wants I beg you will do it and his Drafts on me for the Amount shall be paid to Messrs. Clymer or Nixon. If you cannot Supply him from this Bank fund, but can do it from private Property I will punctually Discharge Mr. Browns Drafts. I beg to introduce him as a Worthy young Gentleman to your Notice, and remain Sir your obedient humble Servant.

RM

MS: Ofcl LbC, DLC.
1. See RM to the Clothier General, September 20, and to Russell, September 14 and 20.
2. Russell had advised RM of 30 subscriptions of $400 each raised in Boston. See RM to Russell, September 14.
3. For Brown's business in Boston, see RM's letter to him, September 19.

From the President of Pennsylvania
(Joseph Reed)

[Philadelphia, September 21, 1781]

Sir

In the present Situation of Affairs I should be happy in being assisted with your good Judgment and Advice in forming such Arrangements as may be most effectual for drawing forth the Strength and Resources of the State in the most effectual Manner and concerting a previous general Plan for this Purpose and defending this City.[1]

I shall therefore beg the Favour of your Company in Market Street at 1 oClock, to meet a few other Gentlemen proper to be consulted on such an Occasion.[2]

I am Sir, with much Esteem Your Obedient and very Humble
Servant

Gen St. Clair
Gen. Irvine
Genl. Irwin
Hon. Board of War
Hon. Mr. Morris

ENDORSED: 1781 September 21st. To/Honble Robt Morris/Honble Board of War/
and others
MS: ADft, Records of the Supreme Executive Council, RG 27, PHarH.
    1. This letter was occasioned by reports that Sir Henry Clinton threatened an
attack on Philadelphia. See notes to Timothy Matlack to RM, September 11.
    2. See Diary, September 21, for RM's account of this meeting and fuller identifica-
tion of the other participants named as addressees to this letter.

Diary: September 22, 1781

Colol. Miles applied respecting Forage and I agreed to his purchasing a few Tons of Hay for the Horses in Mr. Hiltzheimers
Stable.[1]
    This day the Quarters Rent is due for the Office which I mean
to give up and sent Word to the Landlord accordingly, which Occasions several People coming to look at it to rent the same.[2]
    Met a Committee of Congress on the Papers respecting Colo
Armands demand on Congress for performance of Promises &Ca.
on Which I am to confer with the Board of War.[3]
    Received a Letter from the President of the State of Pensylvania
relative to Supplies of Provision for the Militia &Ca.[4]
    Much employed in preparing Dispatches for Mr Browns Journey
to Boston.
    Issued a Warrant on Swanwick in favor of A Doz [5] for 1 Quarter
House Rent. £35.
    Wrote 2 Letters to John Brown Esqr.[6]
    Wrote a Letter to Tench Francis Esqr.
    Wrote a Letter to John Bradford Esqr. Boston.
    Issued a Warrant in favour of Philips, Steward to the Presidt of
Congress. For £37.10.

    1. Colonel Samuel Miles was deputy quartermaster general for Pennsylvania;
Jacob Hiltzheimer was the stabler of government-owned horses in Philadelphia.
    2. See Diary, September 24.
    3. Following congressional orders to raise money for the recruitment of men for

his badly depleted legion of dragoons, Colonel Charles Armand had gone to France in February to purchase equipment on his own credit with the approval of Congress, which had agreed on January 23, 1781, to repay his advances within four years at 5 percent interest. At the request of the Board of War, RM had provided money for equipping the corps during Armand's absence. Armand arrived in Boston from France on August 16 with the necessary equipment and, after reaching Philadelphia, addressed Congress on September 19, requesting that a committee be appointed to examine his purchases and assure repayment. The Board of War, to whom Congress committed the letter, recommended in a report dated September 20 but presented the following day that Congress comply with its agreement with Armand and that RM, in consultation with the board, be directed to take steps to complete the recruitment of men and the supply of horses for Armand's corps. It appears from the Diary entry under discussion here that this report was given to a committee of Congress to which had been referred another letter from Armand of September 21 requesting money to repay advances to him from Governor John Hancock of Massachusetts for travel expenses to Philadelphia. On September 26 and 27 RM conferred respectively with the Board of War and the committee of Congress. Following the committee's report, Congress on September 28 directed RM to pay Armand the money he had requested for expenses and ordered the Board of War, with RM's assistance, to recruit and mount Armand's legion to its full complement. Armand to Washington, August 17, 1781, "Letters of Col. Armand (Marquis de la Rouerie), 1777–1791," N.-Y. Hist. Soc., *Colls.*, XI, 321; Armand to the President of Congress, September 19 and 21, 1781, PCC, no. 164, fols. 454–457, 466–469; *JCC*, XXI, 976, 984; Diary, June 23, and notes, July 20, September 24, 26, 27, and 29, October 11, 12, 16, and 26, Armand to RM, September 24, and RM to Armand, and to John Brown, both October 11, and the enclosure to RM to the President of Congress, October 18, 1781.

4. Dated September 22.

5. Andrew Doz (1727–1788), a Philadelphia merchant, was elected by Congress on April 12, 1779, a commissioner for destroying Continental paper money removed from circulation, an office he still held in January 1781. Doz subscribed £1,000 to the Bank of Pennsylvania in 1780. "Notes and Queries," *PMHB*, V (1881), 235–236; Lewis, *Bank of North America*, 20n.; *JCC*, XIX, 6, 94.

6. RM addressed three letters to Brown on September 22.

To John Bradford

Philadelphia Septr. 22. 1781

Dear Sir

You will see by the Official Letter which I have written you [1] by Mr. Brown that Congress tired of the heavy Expences attending the Boards formerly established for the Purpose of managing the Affairs of our Infant and unfortunate Navy, have entirely dismissed those Arrangements in which I find your Office is also comprehended. The small Number of Ships which now remain to the Continent certainly justifies this measure at present as the Business of those may with ease be conducted by an Agent, and it was in Contemplation of Congress to appoint one, but not being able to agree on the Person at the Day of Election they thought proper to devolve the Duties of that Station pro tempore on the Superintendant of Finance,[2] Who God knows, had already more to do than either his Time or Abilities permitted him to execute equal to his Wishes. You

will therefore very readily beleive me when I tell you that this Task
is burthensome and disagreeable under present Circumstances.
However the same Reasons that inducd me to enter at all into Public
Employment, prevail with me to render all the Services in my Power
in whatever Line they may be called for and desirous of introducing
Oeconomy into every Department I shall do what is in my Power
to complete the Views of Congress. It seems to be their strong
Desire that all the Accounts of the Navy up to the present Arrangement should be settled with all possible Expedition; and I shall
accordingly Allot this Duty to some one of the most Capable and
industrious Auditors of the public Accounts who with a sufficient
Number of Clerks and close Application may be able to go through
it within a reasonable time; as your Accounts must be lengthy and
of great import I give you this Notice that you may get them ready
and as I am certain you will have been regular in keeping them so
I am sure it will give you Pleasure to have such an Opportunity of
evincing your inflexible Integrity to these Republic's already
become susceptible of Jealousies even with Respect to all their most
faithfull Servants. In Order that the Navy Accounts under this new
Direction may [be] kept separate from the former Mr Brown who
is best acquainted with our marine Affairs, goes to Boston to receive
the Books, Papers, Property &Ca. and to fix the Terms with the
Deputy Agent at your Port on which he is to Conduct the Business
in future.[3] As this Business will probably be of no great Amount
it is with the less reluctance that I see it pass into other Hands than
yours, which you will observe by what I have already said is become.
Judging it would be agreable to you to have this Information from
me I have taken the Opportunity to assure you that I am dear Sir
your most obedient and very humble Servant

RM

MS: Ofcl LbC, DLC.
  1. Dated September 21.
  2. See the headnote to RM to the President of Congress, September 8.
  3. See RM to John Brown, September 19.

To John Brown

Office of Finance
September 22d, 1781

Sir

You will find herein a Copy of a representation made to me by
the Board of Treasury of the United States,[1] respecting Freight due
to Mr. Josiah Batchelor [2] of Boston for Goods imported in a Vessel

of his I believe from Spain on Public Account. This Freight is said to amount to £62.10/ Stg. and in order to pay it I deliver you herewith two Bills of Exchange as Noted hereunder equal to £50 Stg each. One of these Bills you will deliver to Mr. Batchelor and if the Exchange be unfavourable to the Seller of Bills pay the remainder in Money, but if Exchange be favorable then deliver both Bills and receive the Balance from him or if he prefers it sell the Bills and pay the whole Freight at the same rate of Exchange at which the Bills sell. Mr. Batchelor must make out his Account of this Freight, mentioning the Goods imported, the manner in which the Freight is ascertained, the Ship by which they came, the Amount and give you a discharge thereon, all which you will bring with you.

You will also observe what is said by the Board respecting the Freight for which they drew on Mr. Gardner the Treasurer of the Massachusetts.[3] I beg you will enquire what was done thereon and if that Freight has not been satisfied desire the Claimant to state his demand to me. I am Sir Your Obedient Servant

Robt Morris

The Bills enclosed are

No. 30. one Sett at six months sight dated 6th. July 1780 in favor of Jos. Charleton [Carleton] Paymaster of the Board of War or order for five hundred and fifty Guilders signed by F. Hopkinson Treasurer of Loans on Henry Laurens Esqr. Commissioner of the United States of America, Amsterdam.

No. 31 One Sett the same as above.

John Brown Esqr.

ENDORSED: Honble Rob. Morris/Sept. 22d 1781/respecting payment/of Freight to Batchelor.
MSS: LS, Andre deCoppet Collection, NjP; Ofcl LbC, DLC.

1. Enclosure not found.

2. Not so identified, but possibly Josiah Batchelder (1736–1797) of Beverly, Massachusetts, who was active in the opposition to Britain, served six terms in the General Court, and engaged in extensive mercantile business. The Josiah "Batchelor" mentioned in this letter probably was one of the owners of the *Lively* to whom the Committee of Commerce owed £62 sterling (cf. RM's figure) for freight from Bilbao. At the request of the Board of Treasury, Congress on January 30, 1781, ordered a credit for that amount entered in favor of the owners on the treasury books at 6 percent annual interest. On Batchelder, see Frederick Clifton Pierce, *Batchelder, Batcheller Genealogy* (Chicago, 1898), 415–416.

3. Henry Gardner (1731–1782) of Massachusetts served in the colony's House of Representatives from 1757 to the Revolution and from July 1775, when he was elected by the General Court, until his death was state treasurer and receiver general. On the recommendation of the Board of Treasury, Congress on January 30, 1781, ordered a warrant issued on Gardner for $32,553 old emission from funds raised by Massachusetts for the use of the United States; the warrant was to be issued in favor of the Committee of Commerce for payment to James Warren, one of the commissioners of the Navy Board of the Eastern Department. Sibley-Shipton, *Harvard Graduates*, XII, 558–560; *JCC*, XVIII, 1100.

John Brown. Portrait by an unknown artist.

To John Brown

Office of Finance 22d Sept. 1781

Sir

The enclosed resolution with the Indorsement thereon impowers you to settle the Account therein mentioned with the Board of War of the State of Massachusetts.[1] For your further Information I am to mention that an Arbitration took Place between the Captain of the Portugueze Vessel and the Owners of the Privateer by which she was taken. Mr. Bradford,[2] Mr. James Bowdin[3] and Mr. John Rowe[4] will be able to give you the Particulars from which you can determine the just Value mentioned in the Resolution. The Monies you shall receive you will be pleased to apply to fitting out the Deane and Alliance. I am Sir your most humble servant

Robt Morris

To John Brown Esqr.

MSS: LS, Andre deCoppet Collection, NjP; Ofcl LbC, DLC.

1. RM thus closed an episode which had troubled his earlier career in Congress: the case of the Portuguese snow (a small vessel resembling a brig). In 1777 an American privateer, the *Phoenix,*, commanded by Captain Joseph Cunningham, was cruising in the West Indies under a Continental commission. Besides RM, who had a one-twenty fourth share in the voyage, the only visible partners among the numerous and widely dispersed shareholders were Carter Braxton, the *Phoenix*'s owner of record, and Matthew Phripp, both of Virginia. In dispatching the ship, Braxton had instructed Cunningham to capture British shipping and to seize Portuguese vessels in the event he should "hear that the Portuguizi are actually taking our Vessels." Acting on reports that American vessels had been seized by the Portuguese, Cunningham on August 28, 1777, captured a Portuguese snow, *Nostra Senhora de Carmo è Santo Antonio,* which was bound from Rio de Janeiro to the Portuguese island of Fayal in the Azores with a rich cargo of sugar, leather, cotton, oil, farina, hair powder, some specie and precious metals, and other goods. The vessel with most of its crew was taken to Boston, but the captain, João Garcia Duarte, and a few crew members were put aboard a Newfoundland fishing brig subsequently captured by the *Phoenix* and carried into St. John's, where they obtained passage to Lisbon.

Hearing of the incident in October, RM immediately grasped the seriousness of the matter, for the seizure was illegal under international law and threatened to embarrass American relations with Portugal. The incident more immediately affected the owners of the *Phoenix,* who would be liable to the owners of the Portuguese snow for damages in the likely event of its acquittal by the Massachusetts admiralty court. Captain Duarte's return to Portugal further complicated the affair because the ship and its cargo could not now easily be restored to their owners. If the vessel were sent to Portugal under an American captain and captured en route by the British, the owners of the *Phoenix* would be liable for the entire value of ship and cargo.

Confidently wielding his influence in Congress, RM requested its intervention in behalf of the owners of the *Phoenix.* In March 1778, after consulting with Braxton and John Rowe, the owners' agent in Boston (see note 4 below), he submitted a memorial recounting the circumstances and suggesting a course of action which would render justice to the Portuguese owners, deliver the owners of the *Phoenix* from their predicament, and preserve "inviolate" the "National Faith and Credit of these Infant States." One of his enemies in the Deane-Lee controversy, Henry Laurens, then president of Congress, described the plan with some sarcasm as "an attempt to dupe Congress into a participation of the Crimes or follies of those good Owners." Nonetheless, RM's scheme was well conceived and practical. He proposed that Congress appoint someone to sell the Portuguese snow and its cargo and invest the money in Continental loan office certificates, which were less subject to depreciation than paper money and could be held over a period of time with less loss. By communicating with the American commissioners in France and through them with the Portuguese minister in that country, Congress was to notify the owners of the snow that compensation was awaiting them. On May 11, 1778, after a roll call vote in which all of the New England delegates but one voted in the negative, Congress adopted RM's suggestions. Gouverneur Morris, a delegate to Congress from New York who had voted affirmatively on the question, passed word to RM, who was then living at Manheim, Pennsylvania, that his "Portugueze Affair is settled much against the wishes of his Eastern Friends."

The affair, however, was by no means settled. RM's arrangement was fatally ruptured at the beginning by the refusal of the Massachusetts Board of War (to whom the sale of the snow was entrusted) to invest the proceeds in loan office certificates. The board claimed that Congress's resolution merely directed investment in "public funds of [the] United States" rather than in loan office certificates specifically, and it retained the money, whose value, as time passed, depreciated to the vanishing point.

Early in 1779 Captain Duarte arrived in Boston with a power of attorney from the owners of the Portuguese snow and a letter of safe conduct from the Queen of Portugal. Duarte at first asked Congress to order the Massachusetts Board of War to give him the proceeds of the sale and authorize him to bring suit for damages against the owners of the *Phoenix*. Congress complied, but Duarte soon saw the futility of this procedure, for the paper money received in the sale of the vessel was now of little value and would be reduced still further by the commissions charged by the board. Legal suit against the owners of the *Phoenix* would be protracted, impractical, and of dubious result, and Captain Cunningham was liable only to the amount of the $5,000 bond he had posted upon receiving his privateer commission. Duarte therefore insisted that Congress pay him the value of the ship and cargo in specie or bills of exchange on Europe, with additional allowances for a reasonable profit on the snow's voyage as well as the expense of supporting its crew in Boston.

Congress received Duarte's petition at the height of the Deane-Lee controversy, when RM was under attack for his connections with Silas Deane and for failing to settle the accounts of the Secret Committee of Trade. Nevertheless, a committee headed by James Lovell merely declared that Congress had done all it could; if after receiving the money and unsold cargo from the Massachusetts Board of War Duarte was still unsatisfied, he could bring suit against the owners of the *Phoenix*. Meanwhile, Duarte, who could not communicate in English, hired John Codman, Jr., of Boston as his representative, and they both went to Philadelphia to besiege Congress at close range. They interviewed RM, who told them that he would not be personally responsible for damages beyond his share in the *Phoenix* and that he was not authorized to represent the owners of the vessel in negotiations. Duarte then addressed further memorials to Congress, and on July 5, 1779, his remonstrance was assigned to a committee which included James Searle and Henry Laurens, political antagonists of RM. At a conference which the committee demanded, RM reiterated his refusal to stand liable beyond his share in the *Phoenix*, and in response to questioning said that except for Braxton and Phripp, he did not know who the owners were. The committee reported its disbelief of this statement to Congress and, having consulted Duarte, proposed that the Massachusetts Board of War restore to him the specie and precious metals originally aboard his vessel and that Congress assume the debt of £6,235 sterling to Duarte arising from the sale of ship and cargo, pay him in loan office certificates, and recover the same from the owners of the *Phoenix*. The committee also suggested that each owner of the privateer be declared liable for the entire amount of damages and that the governor of Virginia be requested to sue Braxton for the debt assumed by Congress.

Congress backed away from this proposal, partly, no doubt, from reluctance to give up bills of exchange. The measure it adopted on July 21 was to order the Massachusetts Board of War to restore to Duarte the coin and unsold property together with the previously requested money arising from the sale of the ship and cargo. Congress also directed that the documents in the case be sent to the governor of Virginia, the president of Pennsylvania, and the council of Massachusetts with a recommendation that they obtain full satisfaction for Duarte and take steps to inflict "condign punishment" upon Braxton and Cunningham.

The vote on this resolution was nearly unanimous, but it accomplished nothing because Duarte, regarding legal action as impossible, refused this disposition of his case. In response to his further memorials, Congress on July 19, 1780, directed the Massachusetts Board of War, which retained all the money in its hands, to remit £18,461 in paper money received from the sale of the snow to John Bradford, Continental prize agent at Boston, who was instructed to buy bills of exchange to whatever amount the paper money would bring and deliver them to Duarte. Bradford was also instructed to bring suit against Captain Cunningham for the amount of his bond as master of the *Phoenix* and to pay this sum to Duarte. Beyond this, Congress could only advise Duarte to seek further redress by suing the owners of the privateer. Even these arrangements shortly proved abortive because the board, disagreeing with Bradford as to commissions and its liability for the depreciation of the money received in the sale of the snow, refused payment. Reviewing the case once more, Congress finally capitulated to Duarte's demands and on August 30 granted him $29,105 specie in bills of exchange on Franklin, which were sent to Bradford in Boston, who delivered them to Duarte in full payment of the amount due him. Ultimately, only $18,000 of these bills was necessary.

The residue of the affair was the problem of determining what proportion of the money arising from the sale of the snow still held by the Massachusetts Board of War was properly due to Congress. On September 5, 1781, Congress entrusted the settlement of these accounts to RM, who was to receive from the board the net proceeds of the sale of the ship and cargo (according to their value at the time of the sale with 6 percent interest) or the equivalent in loan office certificates if the proceeds had been deposited in the loan office as previously directed. RM enclosed the resolution in a communication to John Brown, September 22 (third letter), and committed the task to him in the letter printed here. How Congress settled accounts with the owners of the *Phoenix* is not evident. This account is based on the documents relating to the case of the Portuguese snow in PCC, no. 44, fols. 1–175; RM to James Searle, [ca. July 7, 1779], PCC, no. 137, Appendix, 53; John Bradford to the President of Congress, July 6, 12, and 31, August 10 and 28, and September 28, 1780, and January 10, 1781, PCC, no. 78, III, 493–500, 517–520, IV, 7–10, 15–20, 73; Joseph Cunningham to Willing and Morris, October 13 and December 24, 1777, Naval History Manuscript Collection of Franklin D. Roosevelt, NHpR; and Henry Laurens to Samuel Adams, March 7, 1778, and Gouverneur Morris to RM, [May 11, 1778], Burnett, ed., *Letters*, III, 113–114, 230; on Congress's actions, see *JCC*, XIII, 78, 115–116, 137, 158, XIV, 749, 777, 788, 793–794, 838–842, 883, XVII, 498, 505, 681, 692–694, XIX, 75, 108–109, XXI, 908.

2. John Bradford, Continental prize agent for Massachusetts. See the preceding note.

3. James Bowdoin (1726–1790), prominent merchant and politician of Boston, headed the Massachusetts executive council, 1775–1777, was president of the convention which drafted the state constitution in 1779 and 1780, and later was governor, 1785–1787, and a delegate to the convention called to ratify the federal Constitution. *DAB*.

4. John Rowe (1715–1787), Boston merchant, lukewarm whig, and purveyor for the British fleet until the beginning of the war, had been agent for RM and the other

owners of the privateer *Phoenix* (see note 1 above) and at the time of this letter was a member of the Massachusetts House of Representatives, where he served, 1780–1784. Anne Rowe Cunningham, ed., *Letters and Diary of John Rowe, Boston Merchant, 1759–1762, 1764–1779* (Boston, 1903), 1–60; Butterfield, ed., *Adams Diary and Autobiography*, I, 267n.

To John Brown

Office of Finance, September 22, 1781. "I do hereby authorize and direct you to settle the Accounts mentioned in the written Resolution, To receive the Amount and give a Discharge therefor." [1]

MSS: LS, Naval History Manuscript Collection of Franklin D. Roosevelt, NHpR; Ofcl LbC, DLC.
1. This letter, the text of which is in the writing of Gouverneur Morris, was subjoined to a copy of a congressional resolution of September 5, 1781, signed by Secretary of Congress Charles Thomson. See RM to Brown, September 22 (second letter), and notes, in which this letter and resolution were enclosed.

To Tench Francis

Office of Finance 22 Septr. 1786 [i.e. 1781]

Sir,

I have employed John Brown Esqr. to send the Alliance and Dean to Sea.[1] There are several Sources from which he is to obtain the Money but he is directed if he should be disappointed to make Application to you with an Estimate of the Expence. I am therefore to request that you will advance the Amount of such Estimate and take his Duplicate Receipt therefor on Account.

Mr. Brown has before his Departure paid me the Sum of £2077.-18.7. Pennsylvania Currency for which I have agreed to give him Bills of Exchange at a certain Rate on his Return but if he can get them on Terms more agreable to him in the Eastern States he is to receive the above Sum of you.[2] In which Case you will take his duplicate Receipt as for so much paid him by me thro your Hands.

I am respectfully Sir your most obedient and humble Servant

RM

MS: Ofcl LbC, DLC.
1. See RM to John Brown, September 19.
2. See Diary, September 12.

From the President of Pennsylvania
(Joseph Reed)

[Philadelphia, September 22, 1781]

Sir

After deliberating upon the best Mode of supplying the Militia with Provisions [1] we are of Opinion that the Revival of Commissioners of Purchase will be attended with many Inconveniences, enhance Prices, and affect your Plan of Supply by Contract [2] which is certainly most beneficial to the publick and certain to the Troops. We would therefore refer it to your Consideration whether it will not be best for you to assume the Direction of it in this Case and we on our Parts will engage to furnish you with Money from Time to Time to perform any Engagements you may enter into on [their?] Account. This we think we can now perform from the Taxes collecting. There will also be a farther Advantage that should it be proper to dismiss the Militia at an early Day as we hope will be the Case the Expence will cease immediately, whereas the necessary Arrangements in the other Mode and Supplies on Hand as well as the contingent Charges allways create and continue Expence.

ENDORSED: 1781 September 22nd. To/Honble Robert Morris/Esquire/Superintendant of/Finance
MS: ADft, Records of the Supreme Executive Council, RG 27, PHarH.
    1. For the call-up of the Pennsylvania militia, see Timothy Matlack to RM, September 11, and notes, and RM's correspondence with the president of Pennsylvania under dates of September 12, 20, and 21.
    2. On RM's financial arrangements with Pennsylvania, see the headnote to RM to the Speaker of the Pennsylvania Assembly, June 26, 1781. RM contemplated entrusting the supply of the militia to the existing contractors for the post at Philadelphia. See RM to the President of Pennsylvania, September 23 and 24.

To the President of Pennsylvania
(Joseph Reed)

Sunday morning. [Philadelphia, September 23, 1781] [1]

Mr. Morris presents his Compliments to His Excellency, the President of the State. He rec'd his Excy's letter of yesterday just as he was going out of Town, & this morning he has not been able to see some persons he thinks it necessary to converse with relative to the supplies before he gives a positive answer, but at same time he has little doubt of being able to comply with the wishes of Council in that respect. [2]

PRINTED: *Pennsylvania Archives,* 1st ser., IX, 418.

1. According to the *Pennsylvania Archives,* from which this text is reprinted verbatim except for the expanded dateline, the letter is addressed to "His Excellency, the President of Pensylvania" and endorsed "Sept. 23, 1781."

2. For a fuller communication, see RM to the President of Pennsylvania, September 24.

From the Commissary General of Purchases (Ephraim Blaine)

[*Williamsburg, Virginia, September 23, 1781.* On October 4 RM wrote to Commissary Blaine: "I have received your Letters dated at Alexandria the nineteenth and Williamsburgh the twenty third of September last." *Letter of September 23 not found.*]

Diary: September 24, 1781

This day gave up the Office next to my House and moved Books and Papers over to the Marine Office which being rented for a Year on Public Account and little used by any other Department, I now shall employ it as the Office of Finance, by that means saving £140 per annum rent that was paid for the Other Office.[1]

Employed Mr Wilcocks[2] the Paper maker to make paper for the Bank and Mr Sellers[3] to make the Molds &Ca.

This day Colo. Armand called respecting his Horse and Men which by Agreement of Congress were to be raised for him.[4]

Mr. Pierce,[5] respecting payments of Money to Officers. I desired him to pay Major De Brahm[6] One Months pay as he is going on the Southern Service.

Doctr. Oliphant called. I desired him to get Medicines from Doctr Bond and I would try to procure him a Pipe of Wine.[7]

Genel. St Clair applied for Money. I offered him paper.[8]

The Honorable Mr. Livermore[9] applied respecting a Sum of hard Money to be sent to the State of New Hampshire for the purpose of paying the Expence of driving Cattle thence to the Army. I gave him my Opinion against the Measure and promised to Write to the President of that State on the Subject.[10]

This day agreed with Jacob Smith[11] that He is to Continue in the Office I now Occupy. His Wife is to keep the House Clean by Washing, Scrubbing, Sweeping, &Ca. He is to make Fires and put them out, attend at all Hours, run of[f] all Errands and perform all Services required of him. He is to live in the Kitchen, have firing and Candle and be paid One hard dollar per day.

This day entered Mr James Rees [12] as a Copier and for carrying Messages, going of errands &Ca for Which I agree to allow him   [13] dollars per Annum.

Had a Conferrence this Evening with the Honorable Mr Duane who on behalf of a Committee of Congress Communicated the Sundry Papers, letters &Ca. laid before said Committee by His Exy. The Chevr De la Luzerne.[14]

Wrote a Letter to The Honble Major General Heath.

Wrote a Letter to His Excellency The President of Congress.

Wrote a Letter to His Excellency The President of N Hampshire.

Wrote a Letter to The Commissioners of the Navy Board Boston.[15]

Wrote a Letter to The President of Pennsylvania, that the Contractors for supplying Rations at this Post are willing to furnish the Militia called into Service.

Issued a Warrant in favour of John Brown to defray his Expences to Boston £73.10.

1. See Diary, September 22.

2. In 1767 Mark Willcox (ca. 1744/1745–1815) became proprietor of a paper mill founded in 1726 by his father Thomas (d. 1779) on the west branch of Chester Creek in Chester (now Delaware) County, twenty miles from Philadelphia. Willcox was employed by Congress to make paper for loan office certificates and bills of exchange, and in consequence of employment by RM, described in the Diary printed here, manufactured the first bank note paper in the United States for the Bank of North America. Thereafter, Willcox continued to make bank paper, including United States bank notes, and his sons continued the business after his death. Isaiah Thomas, *The History of Printing in America, with a Biography of Printers, and an Account of Newspapers,* 2d ed. (Albany, 1874), I, 23–24; Clarence S. Brigham, ed., "William McCulloch's Additions to Thomas's History of Printing," American Antiquarian Society, *Proceedings,* n.s., XXXI (1921), 92, 122–127; *JCC,* VII, 302, XIII, 157; see also Diary, and RM to Joseph Pennell, both October 16, 1781.

3. Nathan Sellers (1751–1830), a Philadelphia Quaker, wireworker, and manufacturer of paper molds. Upon the petition of a number of paper makers, Congress on August 26, 1776, requested Sellers, who had marched to New Jersey as an associator, to return and make molds and other equipment for the manufacture of paper. Sellers established a factory for making paper molds in Upper Darby, Chester County, Pennsylvania, in June 1778 and was employed by Pennsylvania and Congress during the Revolution. He purchased one share of stock in the Bank of North America. Leach, "Old Philadelphia Families," III, article of October 27, 1912; Brown and Brown, "Directory of the Book-Arts in Philadelphia to 1820," *Bull. N. Y. Pub. Lib.,* LIV (1950), 124; *JCC,* IV, 194, XI, 415, XIII, 96, 141; Lewis, *Bank of North America,* 142.

4. See Diary, September 22, and notes, and Charles Armand to RM, September 24.

5. Paymaster General John Pierce.

6. On furlough from a military commission held under the Elector of Treves in Germany, where he made his home, Ferdinand Joseph Sebastien de Brahm entered the South Carolina service as an engineer on February 19, 1776, and was appointed by Congress as an engineer in the Continental army with the rank of major on February 11, 1778. Taken prisoner at Charleston on May 12, 1780, he was exchanged

on April 22, 1781, and, following his arrival in Philadelphia, asked Congress for $400 specie and two horses against his account of pay and subsistence to enable him to rejoin the army. His request was passed successively to the Board of Treasury, the paymaster general, the office of the auditor of the main army and, after a second request by de Brahm, to the Board of War, which on August 8 was ordered by Congress to draw a warrant on the paymaster general in de Brahm's favor for $1,500 new emission on account of his pay. In accordance with a policy of promoting foreign officers at the end of the war, Congress raised de Brahm to the rank of brevet lieutenant colonel and retired him from service on February 6, 1784. Heitman, *Register;* de Brahm to the President of Congress, [ca. June 22] and July 16, 1781, and December 29, 1783, PCC, no. 78, IV, 179, 237, no. 19, II, 23; *JCC,* XX, 690, 751, 759–760, XXI, 818, 835; Diary, September 28.

　7. On this application, see Diary, September 14, and notes, 21, 26, and 27, and RM to Nathanael Greene, September 14.

　8. For Major General Arthur St. Clair's business with RM, see notes to Diary, September 21.

　9. Samuel Livermore (1732–1803), a New Hampshire lawyer, legislator, and jurist, was a delegate to Congress from 1780 until his resignation on June 21, 1782. Chief justice of the state supreme court, 1782–1789, Livermore served again in the Continental Congress in 1785 and in the United States Congress, 1789–1801. *Biog. Dir. Cong.*

　10. See RM to the President of New Hampshire, September 24.

　11. Not further identified.

　12. James Rees (1763–1850?) entered the employ of Willing and Morris in 1776 and probably remained there until joining the Office of Finance. After October 13, 1783, he was employed in RM's personal affairs for at least a year and had minor business dealings with him during the next two decades. In 1798 Rees settled in Geneva, New York, where he was active in local affairs. Orasmus Turner, *History of the Pioneer Settlement of Phelps and Gorham's Purchase, and Morris' Reserve* (Rochester, 1852), 237–240; RM's account with Rees, [ca. November 16, 1784], Robert Morris Papers, NN; RM to Rees, December 31, 1798, CSmH; [Robert Morris], *In the Account of Property* ([Philadelphia], n.d.), 43; Sumner, *Financier,* II, 259.

　13. Space left blank in manuscript.

　14. At the request of Chevalier de La Luzerne, French minister at Philadelphia, Congress on September 19 instructed a committee headed by James Duane to confer with him concerning official dispatches relative to the proposed mediation of peace by European powers and the financial assistance rendered to the United States by France in 1781. The burden of the dispatches on the latter subject was that France had made its supreme effort, and the United States could expect no more money in the future. The committee's lengthy report was delivered in two installments on September 21 and 24 and recommitted. On October 8 RM held a conference with the committee, and the members agreed to advise Congress to submit the papers to him so he might "state proper Representations thereon to the several States as well as to the Ministry of France." Upon the committee's report of October 15, Congress referred what pertained to finance in the French and other related documents to RM for transmittal to the states "in such manner as he shall think proper." Following a further conference with the committee on October 18, RM the following day addressed the governors of the states on the subject. La Luzerne to the President of Congress, September 18, 1781, Wharton, ed., *Rev. Dipl. Corr.,* IV, 715; *JCC,* XXI, 928; Diary, September 25, and October 8 and 18, RM to La Luzerne, September 25, RM's Circular to the Governors of the States, October 19, and RM to Benjamin Franklin, November 27, 1781 (first letter).

　15. This letter is dated September 25.

To the President of Congress (Thomas McKean)

Office of Finance
September 24th. 1781.

Sir

I do myself the Honor to enclose for the perusal of Congress a Letter received on Saturday last from Captn. James Nicholson of the Trumbull Frigate.[1] In Addition to what is contained in that Letter I learn by private Information that his Conduct since he has been a Prisoner is such as to merit the favourable Notice of the United States in obtaining his Exchange or liberating him on Parole.[2]

I have the Honor to be with the greatest Respect Your Excellency's most obedient and humble Servant

Robt Morris

His Excellency
The President of Congress.

ENDORSED: Letter Septr. 24. 1781/Superint: Finance/with a letter of 19 Sept from/ Capt James Nicholson/Read/[*At a later date:*] NB The letter of J[ames] N[icholson] missing
MSS: LS, PCC, DNA; Ofcl LbC, DLC.
1. Nicholson's letter, dated September 19 and undoubtedly addressed to RM, has not been found. On the capture of the *Trumbull,* see notes to Diary, August 15.
2. Congress took no action on this letter (*JCC,* XXI, 996). On Nicholson's exchange, see notes to the Navy Board of the Eastern Department to RM, September 5, and RM to the Navy Board of the Eastern Department, September 25, and notes, and to the Board of War, September 25 and 29.

To William Heath

Office of Finance 24th September 1781.

Sir

I was honored with yours of the 20th. this Morning, and for Answer beg Leave to refer to mine of the 17th. of which I enclose a Duplicate. I must wait the State of Supplies mention'd in that Letter, before I can proceed to take any farther Steps in the Business. I cannot but flatter myself that you will have Flour enough, as the quantity turn'd over by the French was, I suppose, not less than 1200 Barrels, that delivered by Mr. Lowrey about 1800, and that due by Col. Hay 3000.[1] There are in 5000 Barrels at least one Million Rations which is one hundred Days for 10.000 Men. As for

Forage the State of New York on the 25th. Feby. 1780 was required to Supply five hundred Tons of Hay and thirty thousand Bushels of Corn. If that has been done Col. Hay agreed with me to furnish more on my promising that it should be deducted according to the Mode chalked out in the Resolutions of Congress from the other Supplies called for.[2] I have no doubt therefore that he will take upon him the supplying of your army if called upon for that purpose, which I wish you would do and let me know the Result.

I have the Honor to be Sir Your most Obedient and humble Servant.

Robt Morris

PS I received also your letter of the 15th and return thanks for your attention to Mr Francis.[3]

The Hon Major General Heath.

MSS: LS, with autograph postscript, Heath Papers, MHi; Ofcl LbC, DLC.
1. Respectively, Thomas Lowrey of New Jersey and Udny Hay, New York State supply agent. On these supplies, see Diary, August 21, and notes, RM to Heath, September 17, and Heath to RM, September 20 and October 4, 1781.
2. The congressional requisition of February 25, 1780, provided that the states which furnished more supplies than were required would be paid the value of the surplus at specified rates in specie with an annual interest of 6 percent from the time the surplus was deposited.
3. The postscript is in RM's writing.

To the President of New Hampshire (Meshech Weare)

Office of Finance 24th. Sept. 1781.

Sir

A Resolution of the House of Representatives of the State of New Hampshire the 31st. of August last to which the Council concurred on the same Day, was referred to me by the United States in Congress assembled, and two Days ago the honble Mr Levermore enclosed to me your Letter of the 4th. Instant to him on the same Subject with the Resolution.[1]

The Various pressing and urgent Calls for Money require much more to answer them than can be obtained. We must therefore prefer Those which are indispensible and these I am sorry to say, exceed the Means in our Power. It is to be lamented that the Droviers of Cattle should be obliged to sell a Part to defray the Expence of the Rest. This is certainly the Source of Waste and Extravigance. It is still more to be lamented that any of the States should call on

Congress for Money, when it must be well known that Congress cannot obtain it honourably but from the States themselves. Where a Variety of Difficulties present themselves it is Wisdom to chuse the least. With that View I am to recommend that honest Droviers be chosen and the Cattle sold as heretofore to pay the Cost of bringing them forward. I wish the Funds of the State may enable your Excellency to have this Business transacted on more eligible Terms.

With the greatest respect I have the Honor to be Sir Your Excellency's Most obedient and Humble Servant

Robt Morris

His Excellency The President of
The State of New Hampshire.

ENDORSED: Financier 24 Sepr 1781/Beef-Cattle to be sold to defray/Expences &c
MSS: LS, Weare Papers, Nh-Ar; Ofcl LbC, DLC; Force transcript, DLC.

1. In a letter of September 4 to Congressman Samuel Livermore, Weare reported that both the old and new emissions of Continental currency in the state recently had become utterly depreciated and unacceptable, that the state had no hard money in its treasury, and that a new tax would not call forth any specie, a situation which required the drivers of cattle sent to the Continental army to sell some of the animals in order to forward the remainder. "I cannot see Any way that we can Answer the Expectations of Congress in furnishing Supplies &c:," Weare wrote, "without their Assistance in Supplying some Specie for this purpose." He enclosed a vote of the general assembly, which was probably dated September 1, requesting Livermore to represent to Congress "the difficult Situation we are in Respecting a medium And in the most urgent terms to Sollicit some Assistance." On September 17 Livermore presented the resolution to Congress, which referred it to RM, and on September 24 interviewed the Financier, to no avail. "Every argument in my power was used to inforce the measure," Livermore reported to Weare. "I suppose the result will be for the quarter master to receive the Cattle from you within the state. Hard money is hard to part with. However if they take the Cattle at the borders of the state, that will answer your purpose." Weare to Livermore, September 4, 1781, Weare Papers, MHi; Livermore to Weare, September 18 and 25, 1781, Burnett, ed., *Letters*, VI, 221, 226; *New Hampshire State Papers*, VIII, 913; Diary, September 24.

To the President of Pennsylvania
(Joseph Reed)

Office of Finance
Septbr. 24th, 1781

Sir

In consequence of the Letter which your Excellency did me the honor to Write the 22d. instant in Council I have had a Conference with the Contractors for supplying this Post with Rations [1] and have the pleasure to inform you that they are ready to undertake the supplies of Provision to the Militia now called into service and to attend them for that purpose to whatever part they March or Move, therefore I will send them to receive your Orders whenever you think it necessary, and I suppose it will be proper that they should be informed of the Number of Rations that will be required, and the place of Rendevouz.[2] I have assured them of Punctual payment depending on your assurances on that head.

At the same time that I determine to give every aid in my power to the measures of Goverment, I cannot help expressing my hopes that the present Circumstances and intelligence will admit of the Militia being with propriety dismissed, as I think it very evident the Enemy do not mean any attack on this State, and I dread to have its Funds unnecessarily exhausted.[3] With great Respect I have the honour to be Your Excellencys Most Obedient Servant

Robt Morris

His Excellency Jos. Reed Esqr.
Presidt of the State of Pensylva.

ENDORSED: From Robt. Morris Esqr/Sept: 24. 1781
MSS: LS, Simon Gratz Collection, PHi; Ofcl LbC, DLC.

1. See the President of Pennsylvania to RM, September 22, and notes. The contractors for Philadelphia were John Hazelwood and Presley Blackistone.

2. For the call-up of the state militia, see Timothy Matlack to RM, September 11, and notes.

3. For a fuller expression of this opinion, see RM to the President of Pennsylvania, October 1, 1781.

From Charles Armand

Philadelphia 24th Sept. 1781

Dear Sir

I wish not to divert you from your affairs which no doubt are of importance, but in the mean time my present uncertain condition and my stay at this place are so much a heavyer burden on me that my post at this time should be in the army, and that non[e] is to be lost in taking the necessary steps towards the remounting and recruiting of the Corps.[1]

I am assured that spe[e]dy decission and expedition on the subject depend much on you, and when I remember the friend ship you shewed me and your past valuable services to me I can not help of hoping [2] that on this occasion you will give some moments of your time to promote my wishes while they are bound within Justice and the [promises?] of Congress.

I am with respect Sir your most humble obedient servant

C Armand

ENDORSED: The honorable/Robert Morris Esq:
MS: ALS, PCC, DNA.
  1. On this subject, see Diary, September 22, and notes, and documents cited there.
  2. MS: "hopping."

From Chevalier de La Luzerne

[*Philadelphia*], *September 24,* [*1781*]. "The Minister of France presents his Compliments to Mr. Morris and desires to know what is the Sum in Bills drawn on Messrs. Le Couteux, above the 500,000 livres agreed in May last. The Chevalier desires to know exactly the Sum."[1]

ENDORSED: No. 23.
MS: Copy, probably of a translation, Bache Collection, PPAmP.
  1. RM replied on September 25. La Luzerne's note was enclosed in RM to Benjamin Franklin, November 27, 1781 (first letter).

From the Governor of Massachusetts (John Hancock)

[*Boston, September 24, 1781.* On October 4 RM wrote to Governor Hancock: "Your Favor of the twenty fourth Ultimo by express reached me Yesterday." *Letter not found.*]

Diary: September 25, 1781

Mr. Telfair applied respecting settlement of some accounts and Assistance to a Friend of his.[1]

Mr. Boudinot respecting Communications from The Minister of France &ca.[2]

Several applications made to me for Money.

Mr. John Ross informed me he has a quantity of Flour in Baltimore. I have agreed that if he delivers it to Monsieur Dumas, the French Agent for Victualling at that Place, I will pay him the Current Price there for the same. This Flour if delivered is to replace in part the flour Our Army received from the French on the North River.[3]

Employed in reading and Considering the communications of His Excellency The Minister of France to Congress [4] and in writing several Letters by Mr Brown and Post.

Wrote a Letter to His Excellency The Minister of France relative to Bills of Exchange he Authorized me to draw &Ca.

Wrote a Letter to Capt John Paul Jones.

Wrote a Letter to John Brown Esquire.

Wrote a Letter to The Honorable Board of War.

Wrote a Letter to John Langdon Esqr. Portsmo. Nw. Hampshire.[5]

Issued a Warrant in favour of Wm Parr,[6] for £250 State and £100 Specie, being in part payment of Henry Dering's Supplies at the Post of Lancaster.

1. Georgia Congressman Edward Telfair's "Friend" was probably John Skey Eustace, whose letter to RM of August 29 was committed to Telfair's care.

2. Congressman Elias Boudinot of New Jersey was a member of a committee appointed to confer with Chevalier de La Luzerne. See Diary, September 24, and notes.

3. See Hector Daure to RM, September 16, and notes, and the documents cited there.

4. See the document cited in note 2 above.

5. This letter is dated September 28. RM registered his September 25 letter to the Navy Board of the Eastern Department in the Diary of September 24.

6. William Parr, an English-born lawyer and judge of Philadelphia and Lancaster who was admitted to the bar in 1751 and held several judicial and civic offices in Philadelphia during the 1760s and 1770s, including a seat on the common council and the office of recorder of deeds, was a partner of Henry Dering in the contract for Lancaster. Although once suspected of loyalist sympathies, he was elected to the state assembly in 1783 as an anticonstitutionalist. John Hill Martin, *Martin's Bench and Bar of Philadelphia* (Philadelphia, 1883), 34, 46, 69, 106, 112, 299; Brunhouse, *Counter-Revolution in Pennsylvania*, 145–146; Diary, November 10, 1781, and January 19 and 22, 1782.

To John Brown

Office of Finance 25. Sepr. 1781.

Sir,

The Active Packet having arrived at Boston it becomes necessary to take Measures for employing her immediately.[1] I am therefore to request that upon your Arrival at Boston you will appoint a proper Master for this Packet and have her prepared for Sea. Put on Board as much of the Public Copper which is at present in Mr. Bradford's Care [2] as will ballast her and then take in any Goods which the Board of War or other Public Officers may think proper to Ship: [3] and in Case that few or none are put on Board on Account of the United States let her receive such as may offer on Freight for Philadelphia so as not to lade her to[o] deep for Sailing well. Let her come round to this Place as speedily as possible that I may send her with Flour or Iron to Portsmouth for the Use of the Ship America.[4] I am Sir your most obedient and humble Servant

RM

PS. The usual Freight given to other armed Vessells from Boston hither will regulate you in fixing the freight of Goods by the Active.

MS: Ofcl LbC, DLC.

1. On the *Active,* see the Navy Board of the Eastern Department to RM, September 12, and notes.

2. The copper held by John Bradford is discussed in the notes to Diary, July 16, 1781.

3. See RM to the Board of War, September 25.

4. See RM to John Langdon, September 28.

To John Paul Jones

Office of Finance 25th. Sepr. 1781.

Sir,

On my Return from Camp to this City I found your Letter of the eighth of August with its Enclosures [1] and the Contents of both one and the other will have that Share of my Attention they Merit at the proper Seasons of Execution. This goes by John Brown Esqr. late Secretary to the Admiralty who amongst other Things that he has to do at Boston is to fix on a Deputy Agent for the Naval Affairs of the Continent. I have mentioned Capt. Mc Niel [2] but we must consult the Government in the Choice as it is necessary to have their Approbation in Order to secure their Assistance when necessary.[3]

Your Letter of the ninth Instant came to Hand by Yesterdays Post as also one from Mr. Langdon on the same Subject.[4] It gives me Pleasure to find this Ship so far as the Work is done meets with your entire Approbation and that such Pains has been taken to make the Timbers lasting; this Circumstance is particularly agreable as I had the greatest Apprehensions that she would Cost much Money and reign but a short Time.

Upon full Consideration on the State of this Ship and of our Finances I conclude that the most eligible Mode of proceeding will be to employ as Mr Langdon and you propose a few Hands on her this Fall and Winter to do such Work as may be necessary to shut in her upper Works and preserve her from the Weather, and next Spring it will depend on the then Circumstances of Things whether to push her on vigorously or to finish her at our Leisure. I agree in your Opinion that it is best to complete the Hull on the Stocks and to have her Coppered; we shall however have full Time for Consideration and all I can now request is your Attention to get as much Work done for a[s] little Money as is practicable; for our Affairs require the most rigid Oeconomy.

I hope Mr Brown will be able to supply some Money from the Sources pointed out to him to keep you in Motion and you will constantly keep me advised of such Things as you judge necessary for me to know. I am Sir your most obedient and humble Servant.

RM

MS: Ofcl LbC, DLC.

1. Letter and enclosures not found. For RM's visit to Washington's headquarters at Dobbs Ferry, New York, see Diary, August 21.

2. Almost certainly Hector McNeill (1728–1785) of Boston, Irish-born veteran ship captain of the French and Indian War and Jones's friend, who was appointed by Congress commander of the Continental frigate *Boston* on June 15, 1776, and became the third highest ranking officer in the American navy. He was court-martialed and suspended in June 1778 for failing to come to the aid of Captain John Manley, his squadron commander, during a British attack. Despite McNeill's appeals and the Marine Committee's recommendation that his sentence not be executed, Congress let the decision stand. McNeill then turned to privateering and, after the war, to merchant service. *DAB;* Gardner Weld Allen, "Captain Hector McNeill, Continental Navy," Massachusetts Historical Society, *Proceedings,* LV (1921–1922), 46–71, 134–135, 143–145; Morison, *John Paul Jones,* 89, 90, 91; *JCC,* XIII, 69–70.

3. See RM to John Brown, September 19. Thomas Russell received the appointment.

4. These letters, concerning the construction of the *America* at Portsmouth, New Hampshire, have not been found. For a reply to John Langdon's letter, which was dated September 10, see RM to Langdon, September 28.

To Chevalier de La Luzerne

Office of Finance September 25th. 1781.

Sir

I received, last Night, your Excellencys Billet [1] requesting to be inform'd the Amount of the Bills drawn by me, as Superintendant of Finances, on Messrs. Le Couteulx & Co. of Paris, under the Sanction of your engagements. This Communication I intended making to your Excellency, in Consequence of the Conversation that passed between us a few days since,[2] but it was only yesterday that I compleated the delivery of such Bills as had been Sold previous to that Conversation, which amounted to Lrs. 57.780. And now on Summing up the whole, I find that I have drawn One hundred and eighty one Setts of Bills, all at Sixty days Sight, in favour of various Persons to whom they have been sold, amounting to Nine hundred and One thousand and Eighteen Livres 4S. 8D. Tournois; of these Bills Lrs. 376,122.10 have been Sold at 5/6 for five Livres, and Lrs. 524895.14.8 at 6/ per five Livres [3] by which it appears the Discount does not exceed $16^5/_8$ per Cent on the Value in Europe; and was this Money to be imported, I suppose the Freight and Insurance might amount to nearly the Value of that Discount: if so, this Mode of bringing it into use is not a bad one. Beside[s] I must again observe that by an Union of Management in the Sale of Bills, drawn for the Service of His Most Christian Majesty's Fleets and Armies and those drawn for account of the United States, still better Prices might be obtain'd, nay I should not despair of bringing the price of Exchange to par, by means of partial Importations of

Money, and passing Bills before the Expenditure thereof, so that
Necessity might not have any Influence in fixing the Price.[4]

❖ What your Excellency has said to me respecting the advances
made, this Year, by His Majesty to the United States, has left on my
Mind those impressions you intended to make. You may depend Sir,
that it is my Wish, and shall be a part of my Study, to render these
States as little troublesome to His Majesty as possible, and I shall
probably have many Opportunities to convince you, that it is a fixed
point with me That the United States, to become truly Independant,
must trust more to their own exertions, and lean but lightly on their
Allies. But Sir you must remember the Situation in which I found
their affairs. You are not ignorant, that altho I have cut of[f] entirely
many Sources of Expence, and Curtailed others, yet that I have not
been able to obtain either Supplies of Money, or permanent Revennue from the States, which however I attribute chiefly to the recess
of the several Legislatures, during the greatest part of the time that
I have been in Office, for I hope and expect that they will severally
attend to the calls upon them, when they shall come to know their
real Situation. But in the mean while, what am I to do if the means
of supplying indispensible wants are cut off? The Important Operations now Carrying on, by His Excellency General Washington,[5]
depend so materially on the performance of my engagements, that
the most fatal Consequences may ensue from any breach of them.
Your Excellency well remembers, that you thought yourself Justifi-
able in giving me assurance, that Messrs. Le Couteulx & Co. should
be supplied with Livrs. 1.500.000 Tournois,[6] to answer my drafts
to that extent, the produce whereof to be employed in the Service
of the present Campaign. You will also recollect that previous to
my Journey in August, to Camp, I judged it necessary to know
whether that Sum was the whole on which I could place dependance, because as the Generals operations would in a great Measure
depend on the Aids I could afford him, it was absolutely incumbent
on me to be informed of their extent, in every Channell through
which I expected them to flow. Your Excellency, convinced of the
propriety of my observations and of the actual Necessities of our
Situation, ventured the assurance of another Million of Livres.
Therefore, whilst I was at Camp, during the Consultations on the
measures to be pursued, I gave His Excellency reason to believe that
the Amount of 2.500.000 Livres of Bills on France, in conjunction
with the resources provided by Congress, should be brought to the
Support of his operations.[7] Counting on this as certain, General
Washington has taken his measures accordingly; it has been my
Study to make the Bills as productive as Circumstances would per-

mit, and to apply the Money to the purposes for which it was granted under the most Scrupulous and assiduous attention to the principles of Oeconomy, and I may hazard the Opinion that no Money has been more frugally or usefully expended by the United States during the War without the least danger of being put in the Wrong. You are Sensible that the Money which arrived with Col. Laurens, altho landed on the Continent, cannot be brought into use untill its arrival here, and altho I have sent for it, yet it is but now on the Road, and the General cannot stop his operations, nor can I refuse or defer complyance with my engagements, untill its arrival.[8] The ruinous consequences that will follow must appear too strong and clear to a Gentleman of your reflection and information, to need any other demonstration than the bare mention of the Facts. Consequently Your Excellency will be well Convinced of the absolute Necessity of permitting me to draw to the extent agreed upon, and I hope His Majestys Ministers will be too strongly impressed with apprehensions of the fatal Consequences that would follow any neglect of my Bills, to suffer the least inattention to them, and as the Sum in total will not be of such Magnitude as to occasion great inconvenience, I hope His Majesty will find cause to applaud Your Zeal and attention upon the occasion.[9]

A Committee of Congress have laid before me the Communications your Excellency has lately made to Congress, which will claim my utmost attention; [10] and your Excellency will do me the Justice to believe, that my most strenuous endeavours shall be used to promote what is so strongly urged by His Majesty's Ministers, The most Spirited exertions of these States to drive the Enemy from our Country; and that my affection for and gratitude to France are unalterably fixed, as is also my respect and esteem for Your Excellency's Person and Character, being Sir Your most Obedient and very humble Servant

Robt Morris

P.S.[11] Upon a more exact Calculation of the Sale of Bills a few of which were sold a little higher than the rest I find that Lrs. 901,018.4.8 produced £52,211.10.9 Pennsylvania Currency which is equal to 125.307 french Crowns and $7/_{10}$ths of a Crown at 8/4d Pennsylva. Currency for a Crown, and the same Number of Livres reduced into Crowns at 6 Livrs. each Crown is 150.169[4]/$_6$ [12] Crowns. Consequently the discount is little more then $16^1/_2$ per Cent.[13]

His Excellency
The Minister of France

mss: LS, Correspondance politique, supplément, Etats-Unis, AMAE; Ofcl LbC, DLC; copy, Bache Collection, PPAmP; French translation, Correspondance politique, supplément, Etats-Unis, AMAE; French translation, Correspondance politique, Etats-Unis, AMAE.

1. Dated September 24.

2. Perhaps on September 20 when the two conversed on a related money matter. See Diary of that date.

3. On these rates of exchange, which were favorable to RM's negotiation of bills, see notes to Gouverneur Morris to RM, August 8, 1781.

4. For previous discussion of the management of the sale of bills of exchange, see RM to Barbé-Marbois, July 4, and to La Luzerne, August 2 and 4, La Luzerne to RM, August 3, Gouverneur Morris to RM, August 8, and Diary, August 21, 1781.

5. RM refers to the Yorktown campaign.

6. La Luzerne had advised Congress on May 25, 1781, that he would authorize drafts of 1.5 million livres against unexpended funds remaining of the French subsidy of 6 million livres granted for 1781. RM, who was put in charge of the money, had been allowed two deposits of 500,000 livres each to his account with Le Couteulx and Company of Paris for the payment of his drafts. See notes to RM to the Secretary of Congress, May 28; RM to Le Couteulx and Company, August 26, and notes, Diary, June 4, 8, and 20, and notes, and RM to La Luzerne, November 22, 1781.

7. For an account of RM's visit to Washington's headquarters, see Diary, August 21.

8. On the money brought by Laurens, see the headnote to RM's Plan for Establishing a National Bank, with Observations, May 17, RM to Benjamin Franklin, July 19, and notes, Diary, September 10, and notes, and RM to Tench Francis, September 11, 1781 (first letter), and notes. La Luzerne had already agreed to support RM's request that he be permitted to delay repayment of money borrowed from Rochambeau to pay Washington's troops on their march to Yorktown until arrival of the funds from Boston. See Diary, and RM to La Luzerne, both September 20.

9. In spite of RM's importunities, La Luzerne would consent only to further drafts up to a total of 1.2 million livres. See La Luzerne to RM, September 26, and RM to Benjamin Franklin, November 27, 1781 (first letter).

10. See Diary, September 24, and notes, and 25.

11. The postscript is omitted from the two French translations.

12. MS: "9/8." The correct figure has been supplied from the Official Letterbook and PPAmP copies.

13. A copy of this letter was enclosed in RM to Benjamin Franklin, November 27, 1781 (first letter).

To the Navy Board of the Eastern Department

Office of Finance 25 Sepr. 1781.[1]

Gentlemen

I have been honored with your several Favors of the fifth and twelfth Instant which are now before me. I am very sorry to learn that your Prospect of obtaining Money is so indifferent but I hope you may be agreably disappointed for I cannot suppose that the Legislature will be inattentive to a Matter of this Nature the urgency of which cannot but strike their notice.[2]

With respect to Capt. Edward's Exchange I have no Objection to his being liberated on Parole with the Alternative of obtaining either Capt. Harding or Capt. Nicholson which ever shall be called for by us.[3] Congress before they devolved the Affairs of their Marine upon me had directed the Board of War to attend to the Business of naval Prisoners.[4] I have no Desire to draw it out of their Hands having already but too much to think of. I shall therefore lay the Matter before them and desire they will send you their Answer.[5]

I approve of sending the Letters which the Packett brought by the Post.[6] Every thing which prevents Expence must be agreable to me while our Means are so slender and our Wants so numerous and great. With great Respect I have the Honor to be Gentlemen your most obedient and humble Servant

RM

MS: Ofcl LbC, DLC.
1. This letter was registered in the Diary of September 24. The commissioners of the Navy Board were William Vernon and James Warren.
2. RM refers to the Navy Board's application to Massachusetts for money to outfit the *Alliance* and *Deane* for sea.
3. On this subject, see the Navy Board of the Eastern Department to RM, September 5, and notes, and RM to the President of Congress, September 24.
4. On July 18, 1781, Congress transferred the care of marine prisoners from the defunct Board of Admiralty to the commissary of prisoners under the Board of War.
5. See RM to the Board of War, September 25.
6. On the letters brought by the packet *Active*, see the Navy Board of the Eastern Department to RM, September 12.

To the Board of War

Office of Finance 25th. Septemr. 1781.

Gentlemen

I do myself the Honor to enclose a Letter from the Navy Board at Boston of the fifth Instant in which is a Recommendation of the Governor and Council for the Exchange of Capt. Edwards. This Matter being in your Department I have referred them to such Answer as you may send approving in the mean Time of liberating him on Parole to return either Capt. Nicholson or Harding as you may direct.[1]

I have the Pleasure also to inform you of the Arrival of the Packet Active at Boston on Board of Which are some Articles within your Department. I have ordered that Vessel to be speedily fitted out and sent round to this Port wherefore if there are any Stores which you may think it proper to send with her you will be pleased to transmit the necessary Orders. I have already directed them to be received on Board.² I have the Honor to be Gentlemen your most obedient and humble Servant

RM

PS. Capt. Nicholson has behaved in a Manner to deserve the favorable Attention of the United States, and the sooner he is liberated the better.

MS: Ofcl LbC, DLC.
    1. On this subject, see notes to the Navy Board of the Eastern Department to RM, September 5, and notes, and RM to the President of Congress, September 24, and notes.
    2. See the Navy Board of the Eastern Department to RM, September 12, and RM to John Brown, September 25.

From James Smith

[*Philadelphia, September 25, 1781.* On September 26 RM wrote to Smith: "I received your Letter of Yesterday." *Letter not found.*]

From the Board of War

[*Philadelphia, September 25, 1781.* In a communication to the Board of War on September 27, RM acknowledged its "Letter of the twenty fifth Instant" concerning the procurement of "Setts of Horse furniture." *Letter not found.*]

Diary: September 26, 1781

This day delivered to Mr Anspach, Paymaster to the Qr Mr. [Quartermaster] Generals department, Mr Thoms. Pleasant junr. his draft on David Ross & Co. Petersburg Virginia for 1213 Silver dollars in my favour at ten days Sight endorsed to Colo Pickering who is to return the same if not paid or to be charged therewith if he receives the Money.¹

Had a Conference with the Board of War respecting Colo Armand and his Claims, for a Legionary Corps agreable to the Act of Congress of the 23d. January last and as it appears that Congress are bound by that Resolution to comply with their part of the engagement now that Colo Armand has made a Voyage to Europe and performed his part, it seems agreed that Colo Armand is to attempt raising the Men and if he succeeds therein then the Horses are to be purchased &Ca.² The Board also delivered me their Letters,

Estimate and the proposals for supplying Saddles and Accoutrements for 300 Grenadiers necessary to the Southern Army; these I wish to Supply but having no Money and little expectation of a speedy Supply I fear to consent, altho I sincerely Wish to do it.[3]

Doctr. Oliphant applied respecting Wine for the Hospital of the Southern Department. I agreed that he might purchase a Pipe at New Burn in No. Carolina and draw on me for the Cost of it.[4]

Mr Hilligass called, respecting the Warrants to be given in Exchange for General Lincolns bills drawn at Charles Town on President of Congress &Ca.[5]

Many applications for Money this day.

Had a Conference with Colo. Miles respecting an Application from the President and Council of Pennsylvania for payment of sundry Persons for Waggon Hire &Ca [6] but cannot find any particular grounds whereby to justify a payment to these in particular, whilst other Creditors equally or more distressed remain unpaid.

Went to Mr Rittenhouse [7] this Evening to know what hard Money was brought into the Treasury, and found very little encouragement from him.

Received a Letter from the Minister of France, in Answer to mine relative to Bills of Exchange &Ca.

Wrote a Letter to John Brown Esquire.

Wrote a Letter to James Smith Esqr.

Wrote a Letter to The Paymaster Genel.

1. Above RM's signature on the verso of Pleasants' draft on Ross, dated September 13, 1781, is his autograph endorsement: "Pay the Contents to Colo. Timothy Pickering or Order on public Account." Beneath RM's signature is the following note by an unidentified writer: "Memo. the 1st bill paid by D Ross Esqr. Octr. 81." The draft is in the Manuscript File, no. 28487, WDC; see Diary, September 11, and notes.

2. On Armand and his claims, see Diary, September 22, and notes.

3. See RM to the Board of War, September 27, and notes.

4. On David Olyphant's application, see Diary, September 14, and notes, 21, 24, and 27, and RM to Nathanael Greene, September 14.

5. See Diary, July 25, 1781, and notes.

6. On July 16, 1781, President Joseph Reed of Pennsylvania informed RM that the state wagon law had expired and that the state lacked specie to pay wagoners for the transportation of military stores. The following month Reed reminded Colonel Samuel Miles, deputy quartermaster general for Pennsylvania, that the Quartermaster Department previously had assumed such payments. Although the Supreme Executive Council authorized an advance to Miles provided he could obtain a warrant on Congress to reimburse the state government, Reed insisted that the Quartermaster Department rather than the state was liable. Miles did not deny that the payments were ultimately a federal responsibility, but cited an action of the Supreme Executive Council authorizing state payment of such charges on order of Congress. RM's interview with Miles appears to have concerned this matter. Pennsylvania revived its wagon law on September 28, 1781. See the President of Pennsylvania to RM, July 16, 1781; Miles to Reed, May 8, and Reed to Miles, May 19 and August 17, 1781, *Pennsylvania Archives*, 1st ser., IX, 127, 153, 357.

7. David Rittenhouse, treasurer of Pennsylvania.

To John Brown

Office of Finance
September 26th. 1781

Sir

Before your departure you intimated that probably Captn Corban Barnes who Commands the Brigantine Active would decline the service and in that Case you will have to settle Accounts with him.[1] I have thought proper to send you Copies of that Brigantines Disbursements and the several Accounts and Receipts in Nantes that respect him and her in order that you may be able to do Justice between him and the United States. I am Sir Your Obedient Servant

Robt Morris

John Brown Esqr.
at the Navy Board
Boston

ENDORSED: Honble Robt. Morris/September 26th 1781/relating to the Active
MSS: LS, Ferdinand J. Dreer Collection, PHi; Ofcl LbC, DLC.
1. See the Navy Board of the Eastern Department to RM, September 12, and notes.

To the Paymaster General
(John Pierce)

Office of Finance 26 Sepr. 1781.

Sir

A Resolution of Congress of the twenty fifth Instant having directed me to ascertain the Value of a Ration and certify the same to you,[1] I do hereby determine that previous to the first of August last a Ration be estimated at ten Pence and subsequent to that Period at nine Pence half Penny Pensilvania Currency Whereof you will be pleased to take Notice from Your most obedient and humble Servant [2]

Robt Morris
S. I. of Finance

To John Pierce Esqr.
Pay Master Genl.

ENDORSED: Sept. 26. 1781 from Mr/Morris ascertaining the/value of a ration/Copied
MSS: LS, Manuscript File, WDC, DNA; Ofcl LbC, DLC; copy, Jonathan Trumbull Papers, Ct; copy, Lawrence and Smith Papers, NHi.
1. Congress had declared on August 24, 1780, that if the subsistence money

allowed to officers of the Continental army in lieu of withheld rations did not equal the "cost" of the rations, they were to receive the deficiency. On the motion of Roger Sherman, a Connecticut delegate, Congress on September 25, 1781, directed RM "to ascertain the value of a ration, from time to time, and certify the same to the paymaster general, who shall govern himself accordingly in settling with the officers." The value of a ration as fixed by RM was very close to what he paid contractors for supplying Lancaster and Philadelphia. See Diary, July 16, and RM to Washington, July 23, 1781.

2. Except for RM's signature and title, the text of this letter is in the writing of Gouverneur Morris.

To James Smith

Office of Finance 26. Sepr. 1781.

Sir,

I received your Letter of Yesterday [1] and attempted an immediate reply; but the numerous Calls on me and the constant Interruptions I meet with do not permit the Accomplishment of that exactitude I desire. Be assured that Nothing would gratify me so much as to alleviate the Distresses of Gentlemen in your Situation; but as yet it is impossible. The Public Creditors are numerous and the Sufferings of many are great; equitable Taxes on the Inhabitants of these States at large will afford the solid sources of releif; and these are the only Sources that can be applied to that Purpose with Justice, for if your Property and that of many others has been applied to the Service and Benefit of the whole, that whole ought to reimburse the Individuals and I hope our Legislatures will soon be so strongly impressed with this Idea as to afford me the Means of doing that Justice between Individuals and the United States which ought to take Place, and in the mean while I shall endeavor to get all the Commissaries Accounts examined and settled as they ought to be. I am Sir your obedient humble servant

RM

MS: Ofcl LbC, DLC.

1. Letter not found. James Smith of Carlisle, in Cumberland County, Pennsylvania, was an assistant commissary of purchases for a Susquehanna River district from June 1777 until May 1778, during which time he made purchases on credit totalling £478,000 on behalf of the United States, in addition to borrowing on his own credit and expending part of his private funds. In March 1781, pressed by creditors, Smith petitioned Congress to settle his accounts and reimburse his advances. His petition was referred to Commissary General of Purchases Ephraim Blaine, who pronounced his accounts satisfactory, but no action was forthcoming from Congress, Blaine, or the Board of Treasury, to which a subsequent application of April 24 was referred by Congress. Consequently Smith appealed to RM in a letter of September 25, only to receive this polite but firm refusal to intercede in his case.

It was not until after additional petitions by Smith that Congress, on June 3, 1784, directed RM to order the commissioner for settling the accounts of the Commissary

Department, Jonathan Burrall, to effect a "speedy settlement" of Smith's account and to pay whatever was due him, the finances of the United States permitting, "without giving him any undue preference to other creditors." Congress on March 21, 1785, paid Smith some $2,500 for cattle purchases made during the war (perhaps on the same account), and on October 25, 1787, authorized certification of the interest due him. Smith to the President of Congress, April 24, 1781, and February 10, 1784, and petition to Congress, October 5, 1786, PCC, no. 78, XXI, 61, 345–348, no. 42, VII, 263–264; *JCC*, XIX, 264, XX, 458n., XXIII, 470 and n., XXVI, 82n., XXVIII, 130n., 148n., 186–187, XXXI, 753n., 769–770, 886n., 889 and n., XXXIII, 703 and n.; see also Diary, December 15, 1781, and February 16 and 19, 1782. According to an "Estimate of Money due to the several Deputy and Assistant Commissaries of Purchases employed under the direction of Ephraim Blaine C[ommissary] G[eneral] of Purchases," April 6, 1780, PCC, no. 165, fol. 412, £375,000 was due to Smith in connection with his purchases.

Account of John Brown

[*Philadelphia, September 26, 1781*]. An account to RM of "Expences in a journey to the Eastern States on the business of the Navy Department." The first entry is for September 26, 1781, the last for May 24, 1782.[1]

MS: AD, collection of Harry Ackerman, Burbank, California.

1. It was probably this account which Brown presented to RM on May 29, 1782 (see Diary of that date). For RM's instructions to Brown concerning his mission, see RM to Brown, September 19, 21, 22 (three letters), 25, and 26.

From Chevalier de La Luzerne

A Philadelphie le 26 7bre. 1781.[1]

Monsieur

J'ai reçu la lettre que vous m'avez fait l'honneur de m'écrire le 26. de ce mois.[2] C'est avec bien du plaisir que je joins ma voix à celle du public pour applaudir à toutes les operations par lesquelles vous avez ramené l'ordre et l'économie dans le département dont vous êtes chargé. L'usage avantageux que vous faites des resources publiques redouble la satisfaction que nous avons à assister les Etats unis: Mais comme administrateur de leurs finances vous êtes plus en état que tout autre de juger qu'il est indispensable que les instructions donnés par les Ministres dirigeans soient exécutées à la lettre et qu'on ne cause aucun embarras au département des Finances par des traites, non autorisées, pour des Sommes considerables, et dont par conséquent les Fonds ne peuvent avoir été faits. Il m'est donc impossible, Monsieur, de m'écarter des instructions précises que j'ai reçues à cet égard et de vous autoriser à tirer jusqu'à la concurrence de 2,500,000 livres. L'arrivée tardive du

Colonel Laurens et le retard qu'eprouvera ici l'arrivée des fonds qu'il a aportés me paroissent néanmoins meriter attention,[3] et comme vous êtes d'opinion que les opérations du General en chef pourroient en souffrir, je prends sur moi de vous autoriser, Monsieur, à joindre une Somme de 298,981 livres 15S. 4d. à cette de 901,018 livres [4]S. [8]d.[4] que vous avez tiré jusqu'à ce moment. Cette augmentation portera à 1,200,000 livres la totalité des sommes tirées sur Mr. le Couteux [5] et il me paroit qu'avant que les traites soient entierement négociées, une grande partie des fonds arrivés à Boston sera entre vos mains. Quant aux vues que vous avez pour le retablissement du Change je desire bien qu'elles puissent se réaliser, et personne n'est plus en Etat que vous Monsieur, d'operer un changement aussi utile. J'ai l'honneur d'être avec le plus sincere attachement, Monsieur Votre tres humble et tres obeissant Serviteur.[6]

(signe) Le Chevl. de la Luzerne

ENDORSED: No. 25
MSS: Copy, Bache Collection, PPAmP; copy, Correspondance politique, supplément, Etats-Unis, AMAE; copy, Correspondance politique, Etats-Unis, AMAE.

1. The following translation of this letter was prepared by the late Professor Beatrice Hyslop of Hunter College of the City University of New York and Mary A. Gallagher. It has been reviewed by Professor Robert W. Hartle of the Department of Romance Languages, Queens College of the City University of New York.

"I have received the letter which you have done me the honor of writing the 26th of this month. It is with much pleasure that I add my voice to that of the public to applaud all the operations by which you have restored order and economy in the department of which you have charge. The advantageous use which you make of the public resources redoubles the satisfaction that we have in assisting the United States: but as administrator of their finances you are in a better position than any other to realize that it is absolutely necessary that the instructions given by the directing ministers should be carried out to the letter and that there should be no cause for problems in the department of finance by bills of exchange, without authorization, for considerable sums, and for which consequently the funding can not have been made. It is therefore impossible, Sir, for me to deviate from the precise instructions which I have received in this respect and to authorize you to draw to the amount of 2,500,000 livres. The delayed arrival of Colonel Laurens and the delay which will be felt here of the funds which he has brought seem to me nonetheless to merit attention, and as you are of the opinion that the operations of the commander in chief will suffer from it, I take it upon myself to authorize you, Sir, to add a sum of 298,981 livres 15S. 4d. to that of 901,018 livres [4]S. [8]d. that you have drawn up to this time. This increase will bring the total sum drawn on Mr. Le Couteulx up to 1,200,000 livres and it seems to me that before the bills are entirely negotiated a great part of the funds arrived at Boston will be in your hands. As for the views you have for the reestablishment of the price of exchange I very much desire that they may be realized, and no person is in a better position than you, Sir, to effect such a useful change."

2. RM's letter is dated September 25 and is given as such in the copy, Correspondance politique, Etats-Unis, AMAE.

3. On the French specie landed at Boston with Colonel John Laurens and RM's plans for shipping it overland to Philadelphia, see Diary, September 10, and notes, and RM to Tench Francis, September 11 (first letter), and notes.

4. MS: "15S. 4d." The correct figures have been supplied from the AMAE texts.

5. AMAE texts: the foregoing words in this sentence are omitted.

6. This letter was enclosed in RM to Benjamin Franklin, November 27, 1781 (first letter), in which RM alludes to his disagreement with La Luzerne as to the financial obligations of France to the United States.

From Donaldson Yeates

[*Head of Elk, Maryland, September 26, 1781.* On October 6 RM wrote to Yeates: "It is some Days since I received your Letter dated the twenty sixth of September last at the Head of Elk. *Letter not found.*]

Diary: September 27, 1781

Mr. Govr. Morris is Seized with the Fever and Ague, and cannot attend this day.

Monsr. Du La Vallette applied for Money, but he not speaking my Language nor I his appointed him to call tomorrow Morning.[1]

Mr. Hodgdon applied for Money and I ordered him £1000 State Paper at $2^{1}/_{2}$ for 1 hard.[2]

Mr. Jonatn. Penrose,[3] for Money, being for Hay which I had engaged to Pay, and I desired him to send the D[eputy] Quarr Master Generl.[4] who should receive it.

Had a Conference with the Committee of Congress respecting Colo. Armands Claims and agreed that they should report that an advance of Money should be made to him to pay what he borrowed of His Excellency John Hancock Esqr. and for the Horses he bought there, and for the recruiting his Legionary Corps.[5]

Doctr. Oliphant, and Mr Stanley of No. Carolina,[6] applied and I agreed to pay the formers Bills for such Wine and Stores as he might Purchase for the use of the Hospitals in Conformity with the Lists, at Newburn from Mr Stanleys House there.

Monsr. Lomagne applied respecting his Pay &Ca. but as he had prepared a Petition to Congress for further allowance, I declined doing anything with him untill they decided thereon.[7]

Honble. Mr Sharpe applied for Money. I told him he must have an Order of Congress for such Advances as he Wants.[8]

Sent for Mr Sharpe Delaney [9] and had a Conferrence with him and with Mr Hill [10] respecting the Old and new Continental Money &Ca.

Issued a Warrant On Mr Swanwick in favour of Colo Miles for £80 Specie.

Issued a Warrant On Mr Swanwick in favour of Hazlewood and Blackiston [for] £50 Specie.[11]

Issued a Warrant On Mr Swanwick in favour of S. Hodgdon for £1000 State Paper.

Wrote a Letter to the Board of War.

1. Louis de La Valette was one of a guard of French marines assigned to the *Ariel*, a British sloop of war captured by the French in September 1779, loaned the following year to the Continental navy, and refitted in France to carry a cargo of arms and ammunition to America under the command of Captain John Paul Jones. For this assignment La Valette apparently was appointed a lieutenant of marines in the Continental navy. Following its safe arrival at Philadelphia on February 18, 1781, the *Ariel* was returned to the French during the summer, and the marines apparently rejoined the French fleet at Newport. According to the payroll of the *Ariel* submitted by Jones to Congress, $289 was due La Valette for his services. La Valette's petition for payment was referred to RM by Congress on September 18, but it was not until October 19 that the Financier issued him a warrant for £108.10.6 specie. *Dict. Amer. Naval Ships*, I, 59; Morison, *John Paul Jones*, 291, 301–314; Paullin, *Navy of the American Revolution*, 513; *JCC*, XXI, 942–943; Diary, October 19, 1781, and Diary, Minutes of Sundry Transactions for 1781.

2. Samuel Hodgdon was commissary general of military stores. See below in the Diary of this date.

3. Probably Jonathan Penrose (1752–1801) of Philadelphia, who served in the first troop Philadelphia city cavalry at the battles of Trenton and Princeton. In September 1781 Penrose directed the transportation of cannon by wagon to the Head of Elk for the Yorktown campaign. He was later elected justice of the peace for Philadelphia County, and from 1798 until his death was county sheriff. Josiah Granville Leach, *History of the Penrose Family of Philadelphia* (Philadelphia, 1903), 52–53.

4. Probably Colonel Samuel Miles, deputy quartermaster general for Pennsylvania.

5. On Colonel Charles Armand's claims and the result of this conference, see notes to Diary, September 22.

6. On the application of Dr. David Olyphant, see Diary, September 14, and notes, 21, 24, and 26, and RM to Nathanael Greene, September 14. John Wright Stanly (1742–1789), born in Virginia, had failed in business in Honduras and was imprisoned for debt in Philadelphia before removing ca. 1773 to New Bern, North Carolina, where he became a successful merchant and participant in the revolutionary movement. Having invested heavily in privateers and furnished supplies to the Continental army, Stanly emerged from the war as a substantial property holder—an owner of a wharf, a distillery, and a plantation—but his promising career was cut short by early death. Alonzo T. Dill, Jr., "Eighteenth Century New Bern: A History of the Town and Craven County, 1700–1800, Part VII: New Bern During the Revolution," *North Carolina Historical Review*, XXIII (1946), 347–349.

7. Etienne, Vicomte de Lomagne (b. 1733), an officer in the French army, 1747–1786, came to the United States in 1778 as captain of a company of grenadiers and served as a major in the cavalry corps commanded by Colonel Charles Armand. Beset by serious illness, Lomagne in May 1781 initiated a series of applications to Congress for financial assistance. In response to his first request, for a year's back pay and leave of absence for six months, Congress on May 28 granted him $225 new emission, a sum equal to three months' pay and subsistence. Disappointed with this response, Lomagne in subsequent applications not only requested $500 new emission and permission to retire from the American army in order that he might return to France and receive proper medical care, but asked that his accounts be settled and the balance paid him in bills of exchange on Europe, and that he be awarded half pay for life and compensation for his losses in the American service. Citing Lomagne's

"personal bravery," Congress on September 24 permitted him to retire because of his poor health and referred the settlement of his accounts to RM, but granted no further compensation. On September 26, the day before his interview with RM (recorded in the Diary entry under discussion), Lomagne again wrote a letter to Congress requesting money to defray the costs of his return to France. After referring his application to a committee, a member of which conferred with RM on September 28, Congress that day directed RM to furnish Lomagne with a gratuity of $140 in bills of exchange for that purpose in addition to his pay. Lasseray, *Les Français sous les treize étoiles,* I, 268–269; Lomagne to the President of Congress, May 23, August 10, and September 21 and 26, 1781, PCC, no. 78, XIV, 437, 449, 491, 495; *JCC,* XX, 532, XXI, 851, 984, 1016; see also Diary, September 28, 29, October 2, and November 27, 1781.

8. Acting on RM's advice, William Sharpe, a delegate to Congress from North Carolina, addressed Congress on October 1 requesting a warrant on RM for $350 to enable him to return to North Carolina. In a postscript to his letter Sharpe wrote: "I have spoke with Mr: Morris who will make out to pay the warrant with paper money and some specie." Congress authorized the warrant on the same day, charging it to the account of North Carolina. Congress had already resolved on July 30, 1781, to give a monthly allotment to southern delegates who were cut off from state support as a result of enemy invasion, but rejected a blanket commitment to discharge debts they had already contracted. This obliged the delegates to apply individually to Congress for relief; however, their appeals received prompt approval. Sharpe to the President of Congress, October 1, 1781, PCC, no. 78, XXI, 133, 136; for RM's disbursement of the funds, see Diary, July 11, and notes, and October 1 and 2, 1781.

9. An Irish-born Philadelphia druggist of means, Sharp Delany (ca. 1739–1799) had served in the Continental army, attaining the rank of colonel. Active in Pennsylvania politics before, during, and after the Revolution, Delany served in the state assembly, and was a prominent anticonstitutionalist and political ally of RM, to whom, apparently, in November 1780 he addressed a series of "Hints" on state finances. Delany subscribed £1,000 to the Bank of Pennsylvania in 1780, was one of the managers of the United States lottery (in which capacity he corresponded with RM), and from 1784 until his death was collector of the port of Philadelphia. Sketches of Delany may be found in Campbell, *Sons of St. Patrick,* 108; and Jackson Turner Main, *Political Parties before the Constitution* (Chapel Hill, N. C., 1973), 432–433; see Lewis, *Bank of North America,* 20, for the amount of Delany's subscription to the Bank of Pennsylvania; also Brunhouse, *Counter-Revolution in Pennsylvania,* 29, 30, 72, 89; Delany to [RM?], November 27, 1780, and enclosed "Hints," Robert Morris Collection, CSmH; and RM to the Managers of the United States Lottery, January 10, 1782.

10. Henry Hill (1732–1798), a Philadelphia merchant and importer of choice Madeira wine, a member of the Pennsylvania constitutional convention of 1776, and leader of a battalion of associators during the New Jersey campaign. Hill subscribed £5,000 to the Bank of Pennsylvania in 1780 and was a stockholder in the Bank of North America, serving as a director from November 1, 1781, until January 9, 1792. An anticonstitutionalist in Pennsylvania politics, Hill was a member of the state assembly, 1780–1784, and of the Supreme Executive Council, 1785–1788. Egle, "Constitutional Convention of 1776: Biographical Sketches," *PMHB,* III (1879), 441–442; Lewis, *Bank of North America,* 20n., 120, 133; Brunhouse, *Counter-Revolution in Pennsylvania,* 86; East, *Business Enterprise,* 127n.; Diary, November 1, 1781.

11. John Hazelwood and Presley Blackistone, contractors for the Continental post at Philadelphia.

To the Board of War

Office of Finance 27. Sepr. 1781.

Gentlemen

Indispensible Necessity admits of very little reasoning and as this is the Argument you make use of in favor of procuring the Setts of Horse furniture mentioned in your Letter of the twenty fifth Instant,[1] I now return you the Papers that relate thereto with the Assurance that I will do every Thing in my Power to enable you to fulfill the Contracts you shall make and I am satisfied that you will obtain them at the lowest Prices and longest Credit that is practicable. I am with great Respect Gentlemen your most obedient and humble Servant

RM

MSS: Ofcl LbC, DLC; copy, Nathanael Greene Papers, MiU-C.

1. This letter, not found, was one of several documents delivered by the board to RM on September 26 (see Diary of that date) concerning the procurement of saddles and accoutrements requested for the southern army by Major General Nathanael Greene. Enclosing a copy of RM's reply, the board observed in a letter to Greene that "our prospects are mending, but our present situation is really distressing, and tho' the Financier has the best inclinations, his funds are extremely inadequate. This will be the leading reason why your supplies are scanty, but you may be satisfied of our unremitting endeavours to render them complete." Richard Peters for the Board of War to Nathanael Greene, September 29, 1781, Greene Papers, MiU-C.

From the Board of War

[*Philadelphia, September 27, 1781.* According to the Diary of September 28, RM "Wrote an Answer to a Note received last Night from the Board of War" concerning the sale of public stores. *Letter not found.*]

From George Washington

Head Quarters Williamsburg [Virginia]
Septr. 27th. 1781

Dear Sir

It is of such essential consequence, in my opinion, that the Army should be regularly supplied with rum during the present operation, that I cannot forbear interesting myself on the subject. When we take into consideration how precious the lives of our Men are, how much their Health depends upon a liberal use of Spirits in the judgment of the most Skilful Physicians, who are best acquainted with the Climate, how meritorious their Services have been, and what severe and incessant duties and fatigues are expected from them, we cannot hesitate to determine that the Public ought to incur a small expence to answer the most valuable purposes, and preserve the lives of a great number of Men who have merited extremely well of their Country; I consider it therefore a duty to them as well as to My Country to request, that the 50 Ho[gsheads] of Rum Mentioned in the enclosed Letter from the Commissys Genl of Purchases and Issues may be procured and forwarded as soon as it is practicable.[1] I am Dear Sir

The Honble R Morris Esqr
S. G. Finances

ENDORSED: Williamsburgh Septr. 27th. 1781/to/The Honble. Robt. Morris Esqr.
MSS: Dft in the writing of David Humphreys, Washington Papers, DLC; Varick transcript, Washington Papers, DLC.
    1. On September 27 Commissary General of Purchases Ephraim Blaine and Commissary General of Issues Charles Stewart informed Washington of an impending shortage of rum. "The Rum on hand and on the Way from Elk, with twenty five Hhds. to be sent by Mr. Morris, and fifty Hhds. to be received from the State of Maryland," they wrote, "will last twenty two days, allowing ten per Ct. for wastage in Boating, Carting &c. Therefore suppose the whole to arrive, which is by no means certain, the Troops will want about the 18th. of October. But it appears to us that during the Seige double allowance will be wanted for the Troops, especially those in Trenches, and as so many are daily falling sick, if Mr. Morris can send fifty Hhds. more, it may be of most singular service" (copy, Washington Papers, DLC). RM, who unaccountably did not receive Washington's letter until October 16, the following day ordered the rum purchased and forwarded. Diary, and RM to Washington, both October 17, 1781.

Diary: September 28, 1781

Wrote an Answer to a Note received last Night from the Board of War relating to the Sale of 70 bbls of Flour, 12 bbls of Bread, 27 bbls Clams and 1 bbl Whiskey said to be in the public Stores and spoiling as represented by the Depty. Qr Master Genl.[1] I therefore agreed they shall be sold at Vendue and the Nett Proceeds be laid out by Colo. Miles in Wood for the Barracks here and at Lancaster.

Mr. Nourse[2] called with the Amount of Bills drawn on France, Spain and Holland &Ca. I desired him to give me a state of those drawn on France for interest also.

Honorable Mr Walton, a delegate from the State of Georgia, applied for his monthly allowance Agreable to the Resolution of Congress 30th of July last, but as he is now left out of that Delegation I desired him to write me stating the time of his attendance in Congress.[3]

Honorable Mr Patridge [4] called respecting the papers and Letters referred to me, relating to Massachusetts Bay and their Complaints on the subject of Continental Money &Ca. I shewd him my Letter to Governour Hancock on that subject, and explained to him my plan [5] which he approved as did also the Honorable Mr Sherman, who called on behalf of a Committee of Congress respecting Major Lomagne's Accounts and allowances which I requested the Committee to settle.[6]

Major De Brahm applied respecting his Warrants &Ca.[7]

Wrote a Letter to His Excellency The President of Congress.

Wrote a Letter to The Honorable Speaker of Assembly.

Issued a Warrant On Swanwick in favour of the Honorable Geo: Walton for £67.10 Specie.

1. Neither the board's letter nor RM's reply has been found. Colonel Samuel Miles was deputy quartermaster general for Pennsylvania.

2. Joseph Nourse (1754–1841) was born in London, emigrated to Virginia in 1769, joined the Continental army as Major General Charles Lee's secretary in 1776, and was employed as a clerk to the Board of War by January 1777, thereby beginning his long career as a civil servant in the Continental and federal governments. In February 1778 Congress elected him secretary of ordnance and paymaster to the Board of War and Ordnance, but he retired from this post the following September and entered the Treasury Department in May 1779 upon his election as assistant auditor general. Although nominated for several other positions, he held this office until September 19, 1781, when he was elected Register of the Treasury under a departmental reorganization initiated by RM. (His duties as Register are described in RM's Plan for Arranging the Treasury Department, August 27.) Nourse continued in this capacity until the end of the Confederation, was reappointed by Washington in 1789, and continued in office until his retirement in 1829. James Grant Wilson and John Fiske, eds., *Appleton's Cyclopædia of American Biography* (New York, 1886–1900), IV, 541, which contains erroneous data on Nourse's service on the Board of War; *JCC*, VII, 48, 361, VIII, 473–474, X, 154, XII, 879, 916, XIV, 666, 955, XV, 1165, 1241, 1251, XVI, 388.

3. George Walton apparently withdrew from Congress following the accreditation of Noble Wimberly Jones as a delegate from Georgia on September 27. As recorded below in the Diary printed here, RM issued a warrant to Walton for his monthly allowances as provided by the resolution of Congress of July 30, 1781 (see notes to Diary, July 11, 1781). On October 10 Walton asked Congress for additional money to enable him to return to Georgia and to discharge debts he had accumulated on official business. RM supported Walton's request, and Congress granted him $500 on October 13. Walton to the President of Congress, October 10, 1781, Burnett, ed., *Letters*, VI, 236; *ibid.*, xlv; *JCC*, XXI, 1044; notes to Diary, July 23; and Diary, October 13 and 23, 1781; on congressional advances to southern delegates, see notes to Diary, September 27.

4. George Partridge (1740–1828) of Duxbury, Massachusetts, a delegate to the Continental Congress, 1779–1782 and 1783–1785. He was sheriff of Plymouth County for 35 years beginning in 1777 and was a member of the state house of representatives, 1775–1779 and 1788, of the Massachusetts convention called to ratify the Constitution, for which he voted, and the United States Congress until his

resignation in 1790. *Biog. Dir. Cong.;* Sibley-Shipton, *Harvard Graduates,* XV, 282–285.

5. See RM to the Governor of Massachusetts, September 15. The "plan" to which RM refers is undoubtedly that contained in his letter to the President of Congress, August 28, which he did not submit to Congress until November 5, 1781.

6. Roger Sherman was a member of Congress from Connecticut. On the accounts of Vicomte de Lomagne, see notes to Diary, September 27.

7. On de Brahm's business, see Diary, September 24, and notes.

To the President of Congress
(Thomas McKean)

Office of Finance 28th. Sept. 1781.

Sir

I do myself the Honor to enclose to your Excellency a Bill of Exchange drawn by Genl. Lincoln [1] in favor of John Owen [2] or Order for fifty three thousand four hundred and seventy two Dollars and one third for Articles supplied the continental Army in South Carolina, in January, February and March 1780.

This Bill is dated the 3d. and accepted the 5th. Instant, but by the Account enclosed it appears, that the Articles for which it is drawn were delivered on the fourth of January, eighth of February and seventh and tenth of March 1780. It seems that the Party not being able to obtain Access to Genrl. Lincoln untill lately, could not sooner get the Bills. The Late Auditor Genl. by the Resolution of the twenty third of July last has fixed the Value at $1190^{33}/_{90}$ Dollars, but Mr. Owen thinks that the Certificate in his Favor should be dated at an earlier Period than the Date or Acceptance of the Bill, which indeed seems to be reasonable.

As I am now about adjusting the Form of the Certificates in question, I must pray the Attention of Congress to their Resolution above mentioned of the twenty third of July. Altho I cannot suppose it to have been the Intention of Congress, yet from the Face of the Resolution it would seem as if the Interest was payable from the respective Dates of the Bills, at least the Holders might contend for this Interpretation, wherefore the decided Sense of Congress becomes necessary. Most of the Bills, if not all of them, except that to Mr. Owen, were drawn at ten Days Sight, and if the Money, had been regularly paid according to the Tenor of the Bill, there could have been no Claim of Interest whatever. Nor even for the intermediate Depreciation, the Party having voluntarily assumed that Risque upon himself. If therefore a reasonable Time were allowed, after the Date, for Presentation &c. including the Usance; [3] Equity might dictate that the Interest should commence from that Period. As to the Time when the Depreciation is to be settled, that is perfectly just as it is.[4] The not having received the Money being in itself a sufficient Injury to the Party, without the additional one of a Loss by Depreciation.

I have also to observe, that it would be of a great public Convenience that these Certificates should all be dated on the same Day, for Instance the first of October next, and the Interest on the several Sums calculated untill that Day, and made a Part of the Principal.

If these Ideas meet the Approbation of Congress, I shall be happy that they would pass such Resolutions relative to the Subjects above mentioned, as may be proper for my Direction.[5] I have the Honor to be with great Respect, your Excellency's most Obedient and Humble Servant

Robt Morris

ENDORSED: 28./Letter 28 Sept 1781/Superintendant of Fin./Read 1 Octr./Referred to Mr Clymer/Mr Osgood/Mr Hanson
MSS: LS, PCC, DNA; Ofcl LbC, DLC.

1. On Major General Benjamin Lincoln's drafts and the act of Congress of July 23 mentioned by RM below, see notes to Diary, July 25, and RM to the President of Congress, July 25, 1781.

2. Following the fall of Charleston to the British in May 1780, John Owen (d. 1815), a merchant and attorney of that city and business associate of Henry Laurens, had been imprisoned at St. Augustine. Upon his release, Owen probably went with other refugees from the southern states to Philadelphia where, on August 6, 1781, he requested Congress to settle an account of articles he had furnished to the Continental army at Charleston prior to its capitulation. Congress the same day referred the account to the Board of Treasury, which returned it on August 8 and directed Owen to apply for settlement in the Southern Department. Subsequently, Owen received from Lincoln the September 3 bill drawn in his favor, which was accepted by the Board of Treasury on September 5. He then returned to South Carolina, where he had been elected to the House of Representatives. Richard Walsh, ed., *The Writings of Christopher Gadsden, 1746–1805* (Columbia, S. C., 1966), 198; Owen to the President of Congress, August 6, 1781, PCC, no. 78, XVII, 333, 336; Owen's account, the bill drawn in his favor, and the calculations of former Auditor General James Milligan, all of which are referred to by RM in this letter, are in PCC, no. 137, I, 177, 179, 181.

3. The customary period of time allowed for the payment of a bill of exchange. *OED.*

4. The resolution of July 23, 1781, provided that the bills were to be adjusted to their specie value at the time of issue.

5. RM's letter was read in Congress on October 1 and referred to a committee headed by George Clymer, who on October 6 received from RM and Gouverneur Morris a report drafted for the committee in the latter's writing. Read in Congress on October 8, the report recommended that the certificates issued by RM for Lincoln's bills according to the resolution of July 23, 1781, be dated October 1, 1781, and bear 6 percent interest calculated on the "real Value" of the bills from the period due (which was to be fixed at forty days from the original date of the bill) until October 1. This interest was to be added to and included in the principal sum in the certificates. The report also proposed that Owen's bill was to be considered due on April 19, 1781, or forty days from the last charge in his account. Congress did not adopt the report and apparently took no further action in the matter. See Diary, October 6, and Report of a Committee of Congress, October 8, 1781.

To John Langdon

Office of Finance 28th. Sepr. 1781.

Sir,

Your Letter of the fourth of August has been here some time and that of the tenth September arrived by Yesterdays Post as did one from Capt. Jones on the same Subject.[1] He seems much pleased with the America so far as the Work is done and what above all the rest gives me Satisfaction is the Pains that has been taken to Season the Timber &ca. so as to make her a lasting Ship. Your Letters and his respecting this Ship convince me clearly that in our present Circumstances it will be most consistent to proceed slow and sure. Money is very scarce and much wanted for every Department, too much has been expended on the America to suffer it to be lost and yet it will require too much to bring forward that Ship with the Celerity I could wish, therefore on a review of all Circumstances I am of Opinion that it is best, to set only the Carpenters to Work and but so many of them as may be necessary to shut in the Ship fast enough to preserve her from Destruction by the Weather. You will therefore proceed in the Manner most conformable to these Ideas and most consistent with the true Principles of Oeconomy. With respect to Masts and Spars necessary for this Ship and for her Cargo I will write you particularly at a future Period. And if I can meet good Conveyances I will try to send you some Iron and flour for the Service of the America.[2] John Brown Esqr. who goes to Boston on the Business of our unfortunate Navy will forward this from thence; and I hope before he leaves that Place he may be able to Supply you with some Money to Pay Workmen &ca.[3] I am very sorry to find your Citizens so backward in promoting the Measures adopted for the Service of the United States. You are in a State of Peace in New Hampshire and therefore Individuals want the Spirit of Exertion. But to find your Government without Money or the Means of rendering those Aids they ought to afford is very discourageing. For if the States which are not molested by the Enemy will not do the Part which is incumbent on them what is to become of us? As I see you are Speaker to the Assembly, I hope you will endeavor to inspire them with proper Sentiments and impress them with a just Sense of the absolute Necessity there is for complying with the Requisitions of Congress if they really wish to establish the Freedom and Independence of the Country.

I observe your Desire to subscribe to the Bank and will put your Name down for five Shares equal to two thousand hard Dollars; [4]

so much therefore you will Credit to the United States as a remittance towards the Ship America and I shall pay the Money for you into the Bank.

With much esteem I am Sir your very humble Servant

RM

MS: Ofcl LbC, DLC.

1. Neither of Langdon's letters nor that of John Paul Jones of September 9 concerning the construction of the *America* at Portsmouth, New Hampshire, has been found. RM replied to Jones on September 25.

2. See RM to John Brown, September 25.

3. For Brown's mission to Boston, see (in addition to the letter cited in the preceding note) RM to Brown, September 19, 21, 22 (three letters), and 26.

4. In 1784 Langdon subscribed an additional five shares. Lewis, *Bank of North America*, 134, 143.

To the Speaker of the Pennsylvania Assembly (Frederick A. Muhlenberg)

Office of Finance 28th. Septemr. 1781

Sir,

As the Honorable House of Assembly are now sitting and have before them the several Letters which I had the Honor to write during their recess to His Excellency the President in Council [1] I shall now Endeavor to State in a short Manner the Situation of Accounts depending between Pennsylvania and the United States and propose such Measures as I think will lead to a speedy and satisfactory Settlement of them.

In the Treasury Books of the United States there is an Account Current open for Transactions commencing with the Revolution and continuing to the eighteenth March 1780 wherein the State of Pennsylvania stands charged with Advances made at different Periods during that Time to the Amount of four Million four hundred and forty four thousand seven hundred Dollars and has Credit to the Amount of one hundred and thirty Six thousand and ninety eight Dollars. Most of these Advances were made whilst Money was valuable; but I expect that the Expenditures of the State on behalf of the United States kept Pace with the Advances made and that probably when this Account comes to be settled there may be no great Balance either Way,[2] but in this Respect I do not pretend to Speak with certainty; however I must here observe that every State in the Union has an Account of the same sort depending; wherefore I propose that Congress should fix such general Principles as will tend to Justice in the Settlement of the whole and appoint immediately Auditors to go through the whole so that when the Balances of cash shall be justly ascertained, they may be paid or received according as the same shall happen to be due to or from the United States and this will put every State on a footing so far.[3]

You will find that by the Resolution of Congress of the twenty second of November 1777, Pennsylvania is called on to Pay in four quarterly Payments commencing on the first Day of January 1778 the Sum of six hundred and twenty thousand Dollars. By the Resolutions of the third [4] and fifth of January 1779 Pennsylvania is called on to Pay during that Year the Sum of one Million nine hundred thousand Dollars. By the Resolution of the twenty first of May 1779 Pennsylvania was called on to Pay by the first of January 1780 [5] the Sum of five Millions seven hundred thousand Dollars. By the Resolutions of the sixth and seventh of October 1779 A monthly Tax of fifteen Millions is called for of which the Proportion of Pennsylvania is two Million three hundred thousand Dollars making for the two Months payable the first of February and first of March four Million six hundred thousand. Thus the whole of these Requisitions appear to have amounted to twelve Million eight hundred and twenty thousand Dollars of which there appears to have been paid on different Drafts to the Amount of six Million four hundred and fifty four thousand one hundred and fourteen Dollars and two thirds leaving a Balance still due of six Million three hundred and sixty five thousand eight hundred and eighty five Dollars and one third of the old Emissions.

By the Resolution of the [18th] [6] of March 1780 the fifteen Million of Monthly Taxes is continued so as to include thirteen Months making for the Proportion of Pennsylvania twenty nine Million nine hundred thousand Dollars of which Sum ten Million six hundred thousand Dollars has been paid into the Loan Office. Of Consequence there remains due nineteen Million three hundred thousand.

By the Resolutions last mentioned new Money was to be issued at the Rate of one for every twenty of the Old of which new Money Congress had reserved four tenths to their Disposal; and the Treasury Board have already issued Warrants to the Amount thereof. The State Paper being of equal value with the new Emission and the former not bearing Interest I have thought it most for the Benefit of this State and of the United States to draw from the Treasurer a Sum of the new State Paper equal to the Balance of those four tenths and have accordingly done so.[7]

By the Resolution of the twenty sixth of August 1780 The States are called on to pay into the Treasury by the last Day of December these next three Million of Dollars of which the Quota of Pennsylvania is four hundred and sixty thousand Dollars. By the Resolution of the fourth of November 1780 Pennsylvania is called upon to pay two hundred and seventy three thousand eight hundred and thirty two Dollars and two thirds in quarterly Payments commencing the first Day of May last and by the Resolution of the sixteenth of March 1781 Pennsylvania is called upon to Pay one Million and fifty nine thousand eight hundred and sixty three Dollars in quarterly Payments commencing the first Day of June last. All these are Payable in the new Emission or Specie. Thus the whole of these Requisitions will on the first Day of March next Amount to one Million seven hundred and ninety three thousand six hundred and ninety five Dollars and two thirds. Of this Sum, there appears to have been paid seventeen [8] thousand seven hundred and forty Dollars wherefore there will still remain a Balance of one Million seven hundred and seventy five thousand nine hundred and fifty five Dollars and two thirds.

By a Note from David Rittenhouse Esquire [9] I find that he has in his Hands one hundred and thirty eight thousand nine hundred Dollars of the new Emission and fourteen Million one hundred and forty five thousand six hundred Dollars of the Old in which latter Sum nevertheless is included some State Money received at seventy five for one, The Amount of which cannot be determined until it is sorted and counted, wherefore the old Emission may be estimated at about fourteen Millions.

On this State of Things I take the Liberty of proposing to the honorable House that all the Old Money be immediately paid in and the new taken out which will be about seven hundred thousand Dollars and that with what is now in the Treasurers Hands will make eight hundred and thirty eight thousand nine hundred Dollars. I further propose that this be paid to me as Superintendant of Finance on Account of the above Balance of one Million seven hundred and seventy five thousand nine hundred and fifty five Dollars and two thirds [10] which will then be reduced to nine hundred and thirty seven thousand and fifty five Dollars and two Thirds. I further Propose that the remaining Sums of Old continental due from the State be collected and paid as soon as possible, which besides discharging that Demand will also enable the State to receive the further Sum of two hundred and sixty thousand Dollars of the new Emission [11] and that being paid in as before will still further reduce the Balance against the State to six hundred and seventy two thousand and fifty five Dollars and two thirds. There are at present in Circulation of the new Emissions three hundred and ninety one thousand one hundred Dollars which ought certainly to be brought in as soon as possible and applied to the same Purposes already specified [12] by which means the eventual Balance payable in Specie would be two hundred and eighty thousand nine hundred and fifty five Dollars and two thirds to which must be added thirteen thousand three hundred and thirty four Dollars required by Congress on the eighth Day of January last to be paid in Specie being together one hundred and ten thousand three hundred and fifty eight Pounds twelve Shillings and six Pence. To explain all which more fully I enclose the Accounts Number one, two, and three [13] to which I pray Leave to have Reference.

The Specifick Supplies [14] will still remain to be provided for in Order that all the Demands of Congress may be fully answered but I hope the Specie Tax now collecting [15] will go a great Way towards the Accomplishment of this necessary Object and at any Rate as the State of Paper notwithstanding every Effort has not yet appreciated to Par [16] I would propose that no more of it be issued from the Treasury except as equal to Gold and Silver and then the Collection of the present Taxes will at least prevent any Depreciation and in the mean Time the Fund on which it was emitted becoming more productive, The next Assembly will be able to take such additional Measures as may be necessary further to raise the Value of it. This can only be done by holding it up from Circulation on the one Hand and on the other by raising Taxes in which the Public receive it as equivalent to the precious Metals.

It is my Determination as Superintendant to deposit all the Money of the new Emissions which shall be received from the several States in the continental Treasury and not to issue one shilling of it unless compelled by absolute Necessity which I hope will not be the Case if the States take Measures to Pay in the eventual Balances.

Whether the House will find it consistent with the Situation of their Constituents to lay an additional Tax this Session is for them to determine; But it is my Duty to mention it which I do from a Conviction that it is necessary. They will perceive that very great Arrearages are due and they must be Sensible that Taxation alone can support the Public Credit or enable Government to carry on the War.[17]

With the greatest Respect I have the Honor to be Sir your most obedient and humble Servant.

RM

MSS: Ofcl LbC, DLC; copy, Bache Collection, PPAmP; [LS?], incomplete, Records of the Supreme Executive Council, RG 27, PHarH.

1. RM's letters (including circulars) to the President of Pennsylvania during the assembly's recess between June 27 and September 3 were dated July 4, 6, 9, 14, 16 (two letters), 17, 25, and 30, and August 23 and 31. Subsequent letters were dated September 4, 12, 20, 23, and 24.

2. For a general discussion of state accounts with the Union, see volume I of this series, xx–xxi, and notes to RM's Circular to the Governors of the States, July 25, 1781.

3. RM presented his proposals concerning the settlement of state accounts with the Union in a letter to the President of Congress, August 28.

4. That is, January 2. Congress did not meet on Sunday, January 3, 1779.

5. PPAmP text: "1781."

6. Correction supplied from PPAmP text. Ofcl LbC: "tenth." On the requisition of March 18, 1780, see notes to John Morin Scott to RM, May 30, 1781.

7. See RM to the Treasurer of Pennsylvania, July 16, 1781, and notes. On RM's management of Pennsylvania's revenues, see the headnote to RM to the Speaker of the Pennsylvania Assembly, June 26, 1781.

8. PHarH text: "seven."

9. Letter not found. See Diary, September 18. Rittenhouse was treasurer of Pennsylvania.

10. PPAmP text: the remainder of this sentence omitted.

11. This figure is also found in the PPAmP text, but in the enclosed account no. 2 (see note 13 below) it is given as $265,000, a sum which makes correct the total for "the eventual Balance payable in Specie" mentioned by RM in the following sentence.

12. Since RM, as he declares at the end of this letter, was committed to not issuing the new emission money, these suggested payments of the state to Congress, as well as those proposed in old Continental currency, were not intended to furnish revenues to Congress but to reduce the state's balance on requisitions.

13. MSS: Official Letterbook copies, DLC; copies, Bache Collection, PPAmP. Enclosure no. 1 is an account of Pennsylvania with the United States with respect to requisitions of Congress payable in old Continental currency. Account no. 2 is a statement of Pennsylvania's accounts relative to the act of Congress of March 18, 1780, and several other requisitions in 1780 and 1781 payable in specie or new Continental emission bills. It includes a partial exposition of the effect of Pennsylvania's compliance with the procedure advised in this letter. Account no. 3 concludes this exposition, incorporating the balance due from the state on specific supply requisitions.

14. On specific supplies, see volume I of this series, xix–xx, and notes to John Morin Scott to RM, May 30, 1781.

15. See the headnote to RM to the Speaker of the Pennsylvania Assembly, June 26, 1781.

16. For RM's efforts to appreciate Pennsylvania currency, see Diary, July 19, and RM to Benjamin Franklin, July 21, 1781.

17. This letter was read in the assembly on October 2, the last day of its sessions, and "recommended to the serious attention and consideration of the succeeding house of assembly" (*Journals of the House of Representatives of Pennsylvania, 1776–1781*, 697–698). Copies of this letter and of the accounts described in note 13 above were enclosed in RM to Benjamin Franklin, November 27, 1781 (first letter).

Diary: September 29, 1781

Lieutt. Flemming [1] called respecting Capt Nicholsons Letter to me in which there is an implied Charge on his Conduct.[2] I shewed him the letter and told him Capt Nicholson would soon be exchanged and therefore he determined to Wait his Arrival.

Major Lomagne called and I Wrote to the Paymaster Genl. requesting him to pay the balance of Eight hundred and odd paper dollars of the new Emission due to this Gentleman for Pay as appeared by a Certificate from the Paymasters Office, he having received Certificates before for his depreciation.[3]

Colo. Armand Called respecting his Affairs. I agreed to pay Mr Hancock the Money he advanced and for the Horses he bought in Boston and to meet the Board of War on his recruiting Services &Ca.[4]

Issued a Warrant on Swanwick in favor of J. Pierce Paymaster Genl. for £468.15.} £306.11.3} State Paper.

Issued a Warrant on Swanwick in favour of Alexr Mitchell for Supplies at Wyoming £78.19.10 Specie.[5]

Wrote a Letter to The honorable Board of War.

Wrote a Letter to Saml Patterson Esqr. Loan Officer of Delaware State.

1. Not further identified.
2. Probably an allusion to the letter RM received on the evening of September 28 from Captain James Nicholson, who was imprisoned in New York following his capture by the British aboard the frigate *Trumbull* en route to Havana. See RM to the Board of War, September 29.
3. Letter to Paymaster General John Pierce not found. On Major Lomagne's applications to Congress for back pay and financial assistance, see Diary, September 27, and notes.
4. On Colonel Charles Armand's affairs, see notes to Diary, September 22.
5. See George Washington to RM, August 9.

To Samuel Patterson

Office of Finance 29. Septem: 1781.

Sir,

Your Letter of the twenty fifth Instant to His Excellency the President of Congress was yesterday referred to me to take Order [1] in Consequence of which I request that you will immediately forward all the old Continental Money in your Custody to Michael Hillegas Esquire Treasurer of the United States who will give the necessary Receipts. I shall be well Content that this Money be sent by Water as I conceive that Mode to be sufficiently Safe and most Oeconomical. With great Respect I have the Honor to be Sir your most obedient and humble Servant

RM

MS: Ofcl LbC, DLC.
1. Patterson was Continental loan officer of Delaware. His letter, read in Congress and referred to RM on September 28, has not been found.

To the Paymaster General
(John Pierce)

[*Philadelphia, September 29, 1781.* In the Diary of this date RM wrote: "Major Lomagne called and I Wrote to the Paymaster Genl. requesting him to pay the balance of Eight hundred and odd paper dollars of the new Emission due to this Gentleman for Pay as appeared by a Certificate from the Paymasters Office, he having received Certificates before for his depreciation." *Letter not found.*]

To the Board of War

Office of Finance 29th. Septr. 1781.

Sir,

I received late last Night the enclosed Letter from Capt. James Nicholson late Commander of the Trumbull Frigate [1] with a Letter from Mr. David Sproat british Commissary of Naval Prisoners at New York to him [2] proposing an Exchange between Capt Nicholson, his Officers &ca. which appears to me so favorable to our Side, Capt. Nicholson being of superior Rank to Capt. Stirling,[3] that I presume your Board will Order a Compliance therewith immediately. I think myself bound in Justice to mention to you that Capt. Nicholsons Conduct since taken Merits our Attention, having spurned at Offers that would have tempted a Man of less Virtue and Patriotism.[4] I have the Honor to be Gentlemen your most obedient and humble Servant

RM

MSS: Ofcl LbC, DLC; Bancroft transcript, NN.
1. Letter not found. On the capture of Nicholson and the frigate *Trumbull,* see Diary, August 15, and notes.
2. Letter not found. David Sproat (ca. 1734–1799), a Philadelphia merchant who had emigrated from Scotland in 1760, remained loyal to the crown at the outbreak of hostilities, moved to New York in June 1777, and joined the forces of Sir William Howe as a volunteer. At the battle of Brandywine the following September he received the title of commissary general of prisoners and on October 13, 1779, was appointed commissary general of naval prisoners, an office he held until the end of the war. Sproat returned to England in December 1783 and thereafter held several local offices in Scotland. James Lenox Banks, *David Sproat and Naval Prisoners in the War of the Revolution* ([New York], 1909), 3–4, 26, 116–118; a sketch also appears in Lorenzo Sabine, *Biographical Sketches of Loyalists of the American Revolution with an Historical Essay* (Boston, 1864), II, 324–325.
3. Captain Charles Stirling (1760–1833), commanding the British 16-gun sloop of war *Savage,* surrendered to the American privateer *Congress* under the command of Captain George Geddes of Philadelphia after a bloody battle on September 6,

1781. Stirling, who received the commendation of Lord Richard Howe for his bravery during this engagement, eventually attained the rank of vice-admiral in 1810, but ended his career under a cloud of corruption. *DNB;* Allen, *Naval History of the American Revolution,* II, 565–567.

4. On Nicholson's exchange, see RM to the Navy Board of the Eastern Department, and to the Board of War, both September 25. RM enclosed Nicholson's earlier communication of September 19 in his letter to the President of Congress, September 24.

From the Navy Board of the Eastern Department

Navy Board Eastern Department
Boston Septemr. 29. 1781

Honble: Robert Morris Esqr.

Sir

Our last of the 12th. instant has Informed you what little Expectation we had of a Supply of money from this State. We see at this time no reason to Alter the Judgment we then formed of that matter and as it gives us pain to see the Ships laying in the manner they do not only usless but expensive to the public we have thought it best to dispatch Capt Barry to Philadelphia that he may be able to give you a true and Compleat State of the Situation of the Ships and the sums of money necessary to fit them for Sea.[1] We cant estimate the sums Necessary for that purpose and for paying off the last rolls at less than Twelve thousand pounds Specie exclusive of many debts already Incurred and which must be discharged and will require a Considerable sum besides. You may rely upon it we shall expend whatever sums you Supply us with in the most frugal manner and are with respect Your Most obedient humble Servants

Wm Vernon
J Warren

P. S. Inclosed is a paragraph of a letter from Mr Bondfield Agent at Bourdeaux to Mr Vernon proposing a plan from which it Appears to us great Advantages may be derived to America.[2]

MS: LbC, Letterbook of the Navy Board of the Eastern Department, DLC.

1. RM previously had placed Captain John Barry in command of both the *Alliance* and the *Deane,* which were being refitted in Boston. See RM to Barry, September 21.

2. The letter in question probably is John Bondfield to William Vernon, July 10, 1781, Vernon Papers, RNHi, which contains the following paragraph: "We are just advised of the Active Packet Capt Barns pulling into this River to go under Convoy of the Fleet under Sailing orders for the Cape. We could wish to see establishd packets to Sail the first of every Month from each Side. Eight proper Vessels well equipt and constructed for Sailing would supply the purpose by which regular ad-

vices would get to hand and by them could be transported Cloathing and Military Stores for the States without Injury to their quick Sailing and would secure the supplys or at least carry a greater probability of getting Safe than shiping the Annual Supply on board in [*one word illegible*] Old heavy Sailing french East India Men where at one Blow all is lost. I have offerd to Build four and take the reimbursment by the returns to be shipt by the States to be navigated on their Account and Risk; the same Number Built by America would admit each to sail the same Day and so in rotation continue. The Channel in which affairs have been conducted on this side have had difficulties to surmount of a private Nature which have Clogd the publick concerns." No response to this proposal by RM has been found. On the packet *Active*, see notes to the Navy Board of the Eastern Department to RM, September 12.

From Thomas Jefferson

Monticello Sep. 30. 1781

Dear Sir

The bearer Mr William Short purposing to Philadelphia for the prosecution of his studies I take the liberty of introducing him to your notice.[1] To this I am induced not more by my friendship for him, than by a desire of availing myself of the opportunity of assuring you that I cherish as a valuable acquisition the acquaintance with which you were pleased to honour me in Philadelphia, and of adding to the number of your well wishers a gentleman of very uncommon genius, learning and merit.

I have the honor to be with great respect and esteem Dear Sir your most obedient and most humble servant

Th: Jefferson

ADDRESSED: The honourable/Robert Morris/Philadelphia/favored by/Mr Short
MS: ALS, Jefferson Papers, DLC.

1. This letter was never delivered to RM. William Short (1759–1849) of Virginia, who graduated from William and Mary College in 1779, received similar letters of introduction to James Madison, a Virginia delegate to Congress, Thomas McKean, president of Congress, and Richard Peters, a member of the Board of War. Short apparently returned them to Jefferson when, after Cornwallis's surrender, he decided to pursue his studies in Williamsburg. Later, Short accompanied Jefferson to France as his private secretary, entering upon a diplomatic career that included assignments in Paris, the Netherlands, and Spain, where he participated in the negotiation of Pinckney's treaty. *DAB;* Boyd, ed., *Jefferson Papers,* VI, 123nn.; Hutchinson and Rutland, eds., *Madison Papers,* III, 270n.

From the President of Pennsylvania (Joseph Reed)

[*Philadelphia, September 30, 1781.* On October 1 RM wrote to President Reed: "I had the Honor to receive your Excellency's Letter of the thirtieth of September late last Night." *Letter not found.*]

From James Nicholson

[*New York, September 1781*. On September 29 RM wrote to the Board of War: "I received late last Night the enclosed Letter from Capt. James Nicholson late Commander of the Trumbull Frigate with a Letter from Mr. David Sproat british Commissary of Naval Prisoners at New York to him proposing an Exchange between Capt Nicholson, his Officers &ca." See also Diary, September 29. *Letter not found.*]

From the Treasurer of Pennsylvania (David Rittenhouse)

[*Philadelphia, September 1781*. In his September 28 letter to the Speaker of the Pennsylvania Assembly RM acknowledged the receipt of "a Note from David Rittenhouse Esquire" concerning the amounts of old and new emissions of Continental currency in the state treasury. RM had requested this information on September 18 (see Diary of that date). *Letter not found.*]

INDEX

Page references to the notes identifying persons are italicized and immediately follow the names of the persons identified.

THE PAPERS OF ROBERT MORRIS
has been set in the Linofilm version of Baskerville type, a transitional face first cut in the eighteenth century and in use during Morris's lifetime.

The book was composed, printed by offset lithography, and bound in Holliston cloth by the Kingsport Press, Inc., Kingsport, Tennessee. The designer was Margot Barbour.